AF832426

Palgrave Studies in Indian Management

Series Editors

Pawan Budhwar, Aston Business School, Aston University, Birmingham, UK
Arup Varma, Quinlan School of Business, Loyola University Chicago, Chicago, IL, USA

Palgrave Studies in Indian Management

In Association with the Indian Academy of Management

The Palgrave Studies in Indian Management series, in association with the Indian Academy of Management, publishes books which are designed to inform and inspire academics, practitioners, and anyone else with an interest in understanding the issues involved in management of organizations in India.

Since the economic reforms began in the early 1990's, the Indian economy has been growing at a steady pace, and the country has rightfully assumed its place among the leading economies of the world. Indian organizations are increasingly going global and setting up operations and/or acquiring organizations in different parts of the world. At the same time, multinationals from around the world have made a beeline to India to capitalize on the huge market, as well as to draw upon the highly qualified workforce.

Of course, the world's largest and most diverse democracy faces numerous challenges—from infrastructure needs, to dismantling bureaucracy, and creating systems and processes that are more investor-friendly. In 2014, the Indian electorate picked a new government with overwhelming majority, and charged it with helping the Indian economy grow faster, so that the benefits may reach a wider section of the population. The new government has been busy creating policies that are designed to foster innovation, entrepreneurship, and business leadership. Indeed, in the first year since the government assumed office, the inward flow of FDI has increased substantially, and several multinational corporations have announced setting up operations in India, in response to the Prime Minister's "Make in India" campaign.

These are very exciting and volatile times for the Indian economy, and the expectations from the corporate world—both public and private are immense. The focus of this series is on the continuous evolution and growth of the Indian economy and related management issues.

All submissions to this series are double blind peer reviewed. For further information on Palgrave Macmillan's peer review policy please visit this website: https://www.palgrave.com/gp/book-authors/your-career/early-career-researcher-hub/peer-review-process

For information on how to submit a book proposal for inclusion in this series please contact Liz Barlow: liz.barlow@palgrave.com. For general information on the book proposal process please visit this website: https://www.palgrave.com/gp/book-authors/publishing-guidelines/submit-a-proposal

More information about this series at
https://link.springer.com/bookseries/14620

Ashish Pandey · Pawan Budhwar ·
Dharm P. S. Bhawuk
Editors

Indigenous Indian Management

Conceptualization, Practical Applications and Pedagogical Initiatives

palgrave
macmillan

Editors
Ashish Pandey
Shailesh J. Mehta School of Management
Indian Institute of Technology Bombay
Mumbai, India

Pawan Budhwar
Aston Business School
Aston University
Birmingham, UK

Dharm P. S. Bhawuk
Shidler College of Business
University of Hawai'i at Mānoa
Honolulu, HI, USA

ISSN 2662-1126 ISSN 2662-1134 (electronic)
Palgrave Studies in Indian Management
ISBN 978-3-030-87905-1 ISBN 978-3-030-87906-8 (eBook)
https://doi.org/10.1007/978-3-030-87906-8

© The Editor(s) (if applicable) and The Author(s), under exclusive license to Springer Nature Switzerland AG 2022
This work is subject to copyright. All rights are solely and exclusively licensed by the Publisher, whether the whole or part of the material is concerned, specifically the rights of translation, reprinting, reuse of illustrations, recitation, broadcasting, reproduction on microfilms or in any other physical way, and transmission or information storage and retrieval, electronic adaptation, computer software, or by similar or dissimilar methodology now known or hereafter developed.
The use of general descriptive names, registered names, trademarks, service marks, etc. in this publication does not imply, even in the absence of a specific statement, that such names are exempt from the relevant protective laws and regulations and therefore free for general use.
The publisher, the authors and the editors are safe to assume that the advice and information in this book are believed to be true and accurate at the date of publication. Neither the publisher nor the authors or the editors give a warranty, expressed or implied, with respect to the material contained herein or for any errors or omissions that may have been made. The publisher remains neutral with regard to jurisdictional claims in published maps and institutional affiliations.

This Palgrave Macmillan imprint is published by the registered company Springer Nature Switzerland AG
The registered company address is: Gewerbestrasse 11, 6330 Cham, Switzerland

Ashish dedicates this book to his mentor
—Professor Rajen K. Gupta

Pawan dedicates this book to his sister-in-law
—Deepa Budhwar

Bhawuk dedicates this book to his wife
—Poonam Bhawuk

Preface

The community of management scholars and practicing managers are recognizing the limitations of management concepts and theories assumed to have generalization and universal application. While international membership of Academy of Management (AOM) surpassed the members of USA many years ago, most of the constructs and models are still developed in the USA, and they are implicitly accepted, a priori, as universal. This book challenges the universality of management constructs and theories by bringing together the conceptual and empirical work on several aspects of management from the Indian context. The chapters in the volume discuss the concepts arising out of the Indian culture and traditions and how they shape management of organizations. The book presents an overview of grounded and empirical work predominantly carried out with the emic perspective in the Indian context. It discusses frameworks that are useful in conducting indigenous studies in Indian management and also presents innovations in management education in India. The chapters in the book present research in indigenous Indian management from the psychological, social, economic, and cultural and historical perspectives. Authors provide insights derived from empirical research and relevant examples for the readers to connect with different topics covered in the book. The major focus of the book is to extend the theoretical and philosophical critique of the dominant Western management concepts. We present research conducted in the Indian context and also show its implications for the broad discipline and practice of management. In this way, the volume is written for management academics, practitioners, and students who have interest in understanding management theories and practices in the Indian context.

In this preface, we express our gratitude to many senior scholars and colleagues who inspired and helped us in this enterprise. We acknowledge the writings of S. K. Chakraborty, Pulin Garg, Udai Pareek, J. B. P. Sinha, Pradeep Khandwalla, Rajen K. Gupta, Preetam Singh, S. K. Kalra, and Subhash Sharma, to name a few, who started to write on indigenous Indian management, which created the foundation for it to reach the level of acceptance it has today among management academics. We were also inspired by the writings of K Ramakrishna Rao, Anand Paranjpe, Matthijs Cornelissen, Sudhir Kakkar, Ashish Nandy, and others involved in the Indian Psychology movement to pursue our own research in this area and to take on a project like this.

The Indian Academy of Management (an affiliate of the AOM), of which Pawan Budhwar is the co-founder and first President (2009–2012), has provided the much needed platform for scholars pursuing India related research to meet, exchange ideas, and to pursue projects like this. We thank Vishal Gupta and Naresh Khatri, the organizers of a Professional Development Workshop during the 2018 Academy of Management Meetings where the idea for this book was formed. We owe our deepest gratitude to the contributing authors of this volume. Most of them have been working in different areas of indigenous Indian management for many years. In spite of their busy schedule and multiple academic commitments, they not only agreed and wrote the chapters but also revised them several times on our request to make this volume insightful and useful to the management scholars and practitioners. Liz Barlow from Palgrave has been very supportive of the project and accommodative of our requests about the structure, design and the length of this volume. We are also thankful to editing team of Palgrave for copy editing and design of the book.

While working on this volume, we realized that there is a lot which add to the unique aspects of management in the Indian context not discussed in this volume. For example, management approaches adopted by small and medium size enterprises in India, consumer behavior in Indian retail market, financial and non-financial reward systems in Indian organizations, loosely coupled designs of many Indian organizations based on unique socio-cultural norms and spiritual principles, which could be unique to the Indian context. There may be many such issues which are not even mentioned in this volume. Many of those topics could be outside of academic discourse at present. We hope that this volume will stimulate discussion on various aspects of Indian management which will eventually go through rigorous multiple-method and multi-paradigmatic inquiry, leading to theoretical and practical insights.

Mumbai, India — Ashish Pandey
Birmingham, UK — Pawan Budhwar
Honolulu, USA — Dharm P. S. Bhawuk

Contents

Notes on Contributors

Upasna A. Agrawal is an Associate Professor of Organization Behavior and Human Resource Management at NITIE. An M.B.A. and Masters in Labor Law from Symbiosis, Pune, she is a Ph.D. from Indian Institute of Technology Bombay, Mumbai. Her research is in the areas of strategic human resource management, psychological contract, leadership, diversity and inclusion, workplace bullying. She has authored more than sixty research papers in reputed journals and periodicals like *Personnel Review, International Journal of Human Resource Management, International Journal of Productivity* among others. She is a recipient of the 2010 Award for Excellence in thesis work from IIT Bombay. She has also received the Outstanding Paper Award from Emerald Literati Network.

Kumar Alok is an Assistant Professor of Organizational Behaviour at XLRI Xavier School of Management, Jamshedpur. He has completed his fellowship from XLRI - Xavier School of Management in Management and Organizational Development. His work has appeared in leading journals such as *Human Resource Management Review, Journal of Business Ethics, Management and Labour Studies, International Journal of Education Reform and Leadership and Organization Development Journal.* Apart from teaching and research, he has offered management training on leadership, motivation, team building, stress management, and change management. He is curious about leveraging Sāṁkhya philosophy for developing theories and measures of personality, leadership, and organization.

Richa Awasthy is an Associate Professor at the School of Business, Public Policy and Social Entrepreneurship, Ambedkar University, Delhi. She is a university rank holder in Applied Psychology (Graduate) and Post-Graduate in Psychology (Specialization Organizational Behaviour) from Delhi University. Her Ph.D. is on 'the Indian employees' perception of transplanted organizational practices of MNCs operating in India. Her current interests are cross-cultural studies, intercultural relations, organizational culture, organizational diagnosis, learning organizations. She has published several papers in national and international journals, such as *Learning Organization, The International Journal of Indian Culture and Business Management*, and *Asian Case Research Journal*.

Juili Ballal is a Doctoral Student at Shailesh J. Mehta School of Management in IIT Bombay, Mumbai, India, researching in the discipline of Family Business. She has published her work in reputed journals like *Indian Journal of Industrial Relations, Asian Journal of Innovation and Policy* and presented at national and international conferences. She has a Master's degree in Commerce and Post-Graduate degree in Business Management. Prior to academics, she worked with a financial data and software multi-national company as a Consultant.

Varadraj Bapat is a Chartered Accountant. Dr. C. A. Varadraj Bapat has consulting and teaching experience of 15 years in Accounting, Audit, and Finance. He has obtained professional qualifications in Chartered Accountancy, Cost Accountancy, and Information System Audit before obtaining Ph.D. from IIT Bombay. He has been a faculty at Somaiya and NITIE. He has published a book titled *Investment Analysis and Portfolio Management*. His work has also appeared in leading journals, such as *International Journal of Bank Marketing, International Journal of Social Economics*, and *Accounting and Finance Research*. His areas of research are Accounting Standards, Managerial Finance, Portfolio Management,

Developmental Finance, and Taxation. His teaching interest includes Managerial Accounting, Financial Accounting, and Cost Accounting.

Dharm P. S. Bhawuk is a Professor of Management and Culture and Community Psychology at the University of Hawai'i at Manoa, USA. His research interests include indigenous psychology and management (focus on India and Nepal) and cross-cultural training. Bhawuk is a citizen of the USA and was born and raised in Nepal. He has completed his B Tech (Hons.) in Mechanical Engineering from IIT Kharagpur (1979), MBA from the University of Hawai'i at Manoa (1989), and Ph.D. from the University of Illinois at Urbana-Champaign (1995). He is the author of the book, *Indian Psychology: Lessons from the Bhagavad-Gita* (2011), and co-editor of the books, *Cambridge Handbook of Intercultural Training* (with Dan Landis, 2020), *Barriers and opportunities at the base of the pyramid, (*2014, published by UNDP: Istanbul International Center for Private Sector in Development), and *Asian Contributions to Cross-Cultural Psychology* (with Janak Pandey & Durganand Sinha, 1996). He has published more than 100 papers and book chapters and made over 250 presentations internationally. He is a Founding Fellow of the International Academy of Intercultural Research (IAIR), Fellow of Indian Academy of Management (INDAM), Foreign Fellow of National Academy of Psychology (NAoP), India, and was H Smith Richardson, Jr. Visiting Fellow, Center for Creative Leadership, Greensboro, North Carolina (2009–2010), and recipients of many awards. He has regularly presented at the National Academy of Psychology (NAoP) in India and organized symposia on Indian Psychology at NAoP and other universities. He is involved with other Indian academics in the Indian Psychology movement and also in the Indian Management movement. He has taught in China (2015–2019), New Zealand (2002), and Nepal (2002) as a Visiting Professor.

Som Sekhar Bhattacharyya is a faculty and researcher in the area of Strategy and Organization at the Indian Institute of Management Nagpur. He completed his Fellowship program in Strategic Management from the Management Development Institute and has an MBA from the Indian Institute of Forest Management. His work appears in leading journals such as *European Business Review, Social Responsibility Journal,*

Information Processing & Management, Journal of Management Development and *International Journal of Business Innovation & Research.* He was awarded the Emerald Literati Awards for Excellence for his papers that were published in *Asia-Pacific Journal of Business Administration* and *European Business Review.*

Pawan Budhwar is the 50th Anniversary Professor of International HRM, Head of Aston Business School, and an Associate Pro-Vice Chancellor International (India) at Aston University, UK. He is the Co-Editor-in-Chief of *Human Resource Management Journal* and is globally known for his research in the fields of strategic and international HRM and emerging markets with a specific focus on India. He has published over 140 articles in leading journals and has also written and/or co-edited 25 books. Pawan is the co-founder and first President of the Indian Academy of Management, an affiliate of the Academy of Management. He has served as an advisor to the Commonwealth Commission for six years, co-editor-in-chief of the *British Journal of Management* from 2014 to 2020 and is a Fellow of the Higher Education Academy, British Academy of Management, the Academy of Social Sciences, and the Indian Academy of Management. He has won numerous awards for his research.

Rajesh Chandwani is a faculty of Human Resource Management and the Chairperson of the Centre for Management of Health Services at the Indian Institute of Management Ahmedabad. He was trained as a Medical Practitioner and Researcher at Baroda Medical College and IIM Bangalore. His work has appeared in leading journals such as *The International Journal of Human Resource Management, Business Ethics: A European Review, Information Systems Frontier, Journal of Knowledge Management,* and *International Journal of Information Management.* His research interests lie at the intersection of healthcare management, human resource management, and information technology.

Chirag Dagar is a Ph.D. scholar at Shailesh J. Mehta School of Management in IIT Bombay, Mumbai. He holds an MBA from Great Lakes Institute of Management, Chennai, and was awarded the National Research Fellowship. He has published a research article in the *Journal of*

Business Ethics and presented papers during the Academy of Management Meetings. His research areas are Positive Organizational Scholarship and spirituality in management.

Rajen K. Gupta is a Professor of Organization Behaviour. He is a Fellow (equivalent to Ph.D.) from the Indian Institute of Management Ahmedabad. He also holds a B.Tech. (Electrical Engineering) from the Indian Institute of Technology, Kanpur. Academically, he has a special interest in the linkage between Indian culture and management. A collection of his papers on this theme has already been published. He has published over 100 articles in leading journals and supervised fifteen doctoral thesis. He has authored books titled, *Towards the Optimal Organisation: Indian Culture and Management, Organisational Behaviour,* and *Designing and Developing Organizations for Tomorrow.* He is also on the International Editorial Boards of a number of journals such as *International Journal of Cross-Cultural Management* (Sage, London), *Journal of Research Practice* (Online journal), and *International Journal of Indian Culture and Business Management* (Inderscience, Switzerland).

R. M. Harindranath has a mix of industry and academic experience. He worked as a business manager in German Remedies Ltd. and then moved to academics. He completed his Ph.D. from the College of Engineering, Anna University. He has an experience of teaching at business school and Anna University MBA students. His research studies are published in the journal like *Journal of Business & Industrial Marketing, Management Research Review, International Journal of Pharmaceutical and Healthcare Marketing.* He has conducted over 25 faculty development programs (FDPs) and corporate consultancies.

Mala Kapadia has a rich and varied background in Psychology, Literature, and Human Resources. She is the Director of Centre for Wellbeing & Wellness, Professor and Resident Mentor at Rashtram School of Public Leadership. She was Adjunct Faculty with S.P. Jain Global School of Management for Singapore, Dubai, and Australia campuses from 2005 to 2020. She is MBTI Qualified (Step 1 & 2) and also a licensed practitioner of NLP. She has a Diploma in Ayurveda & Yoga, giving her an edge in the Behavioral Sciences. Her research work is on emotional and integral intelligence in Indian wisdom literature. Her book *Heart Skills Emotional Intelligence for work and life* has been awarded ISTD Award 2008–2009.

Venkat R. Krishnan is the Director of the Center of Oneness and Transforming Leadership. He is a member of the editorial board of *Leadership & Organization Development Journal, Electronic Journal of Business Ethics and Organization Studies,* and *Journal of Managerial Psychology.* He has received his Ph.D. in Business Administration from the Fox School of Business and Management, Temple University with a specialization in Organizational Behaviour. He is credited with instituting the Leadership Experiential Project (Karma-Yoga) at both XLRI and Great Lakes Institute of Management Chennai. He is currently doing research in the areas of transformational leadership, value systems of individuals in organizations, and Indian philosophy.

Sushant Kumar Mishra is a Professor in the Department of Organizational Behaviour and Human Resource Management at IIM Bangalore, India. He holds a Ph.D. in Organizational Development Consulting from IIM, Ahmedabad. His work appears in leading journals such as *International Journal of Education Management, Journal of Organizational Behaviour, International Journal of Human Resources Management, Personnel Review,* and *Journal of World Business.* One of his papers has been awarded as the Best Accepted Paper in the Academy of Management Meeting held in Chicago. He is the recipient of the Emerging Diversity Scholar Award from NCID, University of Michigan. He has received the IFCI Award at IIM Ahmedabad. Currently he is in the Editorial Board of Academy of Management Learning and Education and in the review panel of many international journals of repute.

Gopal Prasad Mahapatra is a Professor of Practice, OB & HRM at IIM, Bangalore. He is a Fellow in Management (Doctoral Programme) from IIM, Bangalore & Post-Graduate in Personnel Management & IR from Xavier Institute of Social Service, Ranchi. He has thirty plus years of corporate, consulting, and academic experience in leading: Organisational Transformation, Talent and Leadership Development, Executive Coaching, Career Management, Assessment and Development Center and, Strategic HR and at RPG Group, Oracle, Gujrat Gas, TV Rao Learning Systems, BPL, INDAL, XIMB, and BEL. He is the editor of *South Asian Journal of Human Resource Management* and author of about thirty research articles in the journals and book chapters.

Zubin R. Mulla is a Professor at the School of Management and Labour Studies at the Tata Institute of Social Sciences. He has a degree in mechanical engineering from Pune University, a post-graduate diploma in business management, and a doctorate in management from XLRI Jamshedpur. He has seven years of experience in engineering and management consulting prior to moving to academics in 2005. His work has appeared in leading journals such as *Journal of Human Values, Psychology and Developing Societies, Psychological Studies, International Journal of Police Science & Management,* and *The Journal of Entrepreneurship.* His areas of research interest include ethics, leadership, executive compensation, and evidence-based HRM.

Abinash Panda is an Associate Professor of Organizational Development at Management Development Institute, Gurgaon. Prior to joining MDI, he was with the Indian Institute of Management Kashipur as an Associate Professor in the area of Organizational Behaviour and Human Resource Management. He is a graduate from International University of Japan (IUJ) and is a Fellow of Management Development Institute. He also has a Master's degree in Computer Applications from Regional Engineering College (currently National Institute of Technology), Rourkela. He has published more than 45 research papers in various international and national journals such as *International Journal of Indian Culture and Business Management, Global Business Review, Psychology and Developing Societies,* and *Management and Labour Studies.*

Ashish Pandey is an Associate Professor and teaches Organization Behaviour (OB), Organization Development (OD), Human Resource Management (HRM) related subjects at Shailesh J. Mehta School of Management, IIT Bombay. He has completed his doctoral fellowship from Management Development Institute, Gurgaon, India. His research is in areas of Positive Psychological outcomes of Yoga and mindfulness, interface of business and society, spirituality at workplace. Recognition to his research comes from the awards conferred to his work in the forums held at I.I.Sc. Banglore, I.I.M. Indore and Infosys Leadership Institute, Case Western Reserve University, Cleveland, Academy of Management, and Indian Academy of Management. His research papers have appeared in several leading international journals and periodicals like *Journal of Management, Journal of Business Ethics, Business Ethics: European Review, Personnel Review,* etc.

Nisha Pandey is an Associate Professor and Associate Dean (Research) with VESIM Business School, Mumbai. She is also the Chairperson of the Yunus Centre of Social Business at VESIM, Mumbai. She completed her Ph.D. from Harcourt Butler Technological Institute, Kanpur in the area of Environmental Economics. She has co-authored a book titled *Building a Model of change: Achieving Sustainability Through Social Entrepreneurship* and about twenty research-based articles in the journals like *International Journal of Environment and Sustainable Development, Asian Case Research Journal,* and so forth.

Arunaditya Sahay is the Dean (Research) and Professor of Strategic Management at Birla Institute of Management Technology. He is a member of the Governing Council of International Sustainable Development Research Society. He holds a Ph.D. from the Technical University Brno, Czechoslovakia. His work appears in leading journals such as *International Entrepreneurship and Management Journal, Social Enterprise Journal, Journal of Global Entrepreneurship Research,* and *Journal of Education and Practice.* Dr. Sahay's teaching and research interests are in the area of Strategic Management, M&A, Strategic Alliance & JV, Innovation, Entrepreneurship, Sustainability, and CSR.

Bharadhwaj Sivakumaran is currently the Director (Research) and Chair Professor of Marketing at Great Lakes Institute of Management. Prior to this, he worked at the Department of Management Studies, IIT Madras and Nanyang Business School, Singapore. He holds a Ph.D. in Marketing from the Robert Smith School of Business, University of Maryland, College Park, USA. He has an MBA from BIM, Trichy and a B.Sc. in Chemistry from Vivekananda College, Chennai. His work appears in leading journals such as the *Journal of Academy of*

Marketing Science, Journal of Business Research, Journal of Advertising, European Journal of Marketing, Journal of Marketing Management, Journal of Retailing and Consumer Services, and *Marketing Intelligence and Planning.* His main research interests are in the areas of Variety Seeking Behavior, Impulse Buying Behavior and the effect of other marketing variables and phenomena on these behaviors.

List of Figures

List of Tables

1

In Search of Indian Management

Ashish Pandey, Pawan Budhwar,
and Dharm P. S. Bhawuk

In Search of Indian Management

India is the fifth largest economy in the world (third largest by Purchasing Power Parity or PPP criterion). Its GDP was $2.87 trillion in

A. Pandey (✉)
Shailesh J. Mehta School of Management, Indian Institute of Technology Bombay, Mumbai, India
e-mail: ashish.pandey@iitb.ac.in

P. Budhwar
Aston Business School, Aston University, Birmingham, UK
e-mail: p.s.budhwar@aston.ac.uk

D. P. S. Bhawuk
Shidler College of Business, University of Hawai'i at Mānoa, Honolulu, HI, USA
e-mail: bhawuk@hawaii.edu

© The Author(s), under exclusive license to Springer Nature Switzerland AG 2022

A. Pandey et al. (eds.), *Indigenous Indian Management*,
Palgrave Studies in Indian Management,
https://doi.org/10.1007/978-3-030-87906-8_1

2019. India's GDP grew more than 4% from 2018 to 2019. However, India's per capita GDP is US$2,100, which is the lowest of the top ten economies, and poverty is a major economic and social problem facing India. India exports technology services and is a hub for business outsourcing. Indian economy is characterized by a contrasting mixture of low end farming and handicraft and high end industry and mechanized agriculture. India's service sector contributes a large portion of its economic output. Often India's business regulation is criticized as being inflexible. India is also notorious for corruption.[1] The social and cultural setting of India is unique because of its diversity, large population and social and economic stratification. From world trade to climate change to democratization, India matters now. Therefore, an understanding of Indian management principles arising from its culture has the potential of enriching the extant management literature.

In spite of these facts the representation of Indian thoughts and reality are rarely mentioned in the globally recognized journals of management. Bruton and Lau (2008) reviewed a total of 306 articles that addressed Asian management during the ten years from 1996 to 2005 in the ten leading management journals. Most of the articles that focused on China and India's representation were sparse on the list. We compared Indian focused research in the nine journals[2] from the list of Bruton and Lau (2008) to better represent the different branches of management. A review of articles mentioning India (in the title or in the abstract) in this list of journals from the years 1996 to 2005 and 2010 to 2020 was carried out. A count of these articles showed that between 1996 and 2005 there were 654 articles that mentioned India in the body and 43 had India mentioned in the title or the abstract. A similar count on the same set of journals between 2010 and 2020 showed that 1,937 articles mentioned India in the body and 115 had India mentioned in the title or the abstract. An in-depth analysis would be required to uncover

---

1 CIA World Factbook. 'INDIA'. Accessed April 13, 2021.

2 The nine journals are, *Academy of Management Journal*, *Academy of Management Review*, *Administrative Science Quarterly*, *Journal of Applied Psychology*, *Journal of Business Venturing*, *Journal of International Business Studies*, *Journal of Management*, *Journal of Management Studies*, and *Strategic Management Journal*. To expand the scope further, to this list we added six other journals, namely, *Human Relations*, *MIS Quarterly*, *Strategic Management Journal*, *Journal of Marketing*, *International Journal of Human Resource Management* and *Journal of Finance*.

what aspect of Indian management these articles are capturing, but it is clear that representation of India is increasing in the globally recognized journals, though it is still marginal (see table in Appendix).

Scholarship and practice of management is context sensitive in nature and has to be informed by the social realities. There is a growing concern for producing useful and credible knowledge that addresses problems important to business and society. An initiative for 'Responsible Research' led by past ten presidents of Academy of Management (AOM) called for both basic and applied research contributions valuing plurality and multidisciplinary collaboration with stakeholder involvement for service to society and impact on stakeholders.

India matters not only for the economic and the political reasons of current times. It is a living culture of more than three thousand years. It matters for its wisdom traditions. The world views and ideals of human life expounded in its traditions enrich global pluralism, since its cultural diversity is second to the continent of Africa (Bhawuk, 2012). India also showcases its propensity to simultaneously embrace traditional and contemporary beliefs and practices as it offers unique solutions to numerous challenges it faces. However, the voice of indigenous Indian scholarship has been stifled by the dominant western ideas and theories, making it difficult for pluralism to flourish in management literature. This volume is an attempt to addresses that lacuna in the management literature. Many authors have argued that indigenous research is essential for understanding local phenomena as well as context-sensitive theoretical development (Gupta, 1994; Sinha, 2000; Tsui, 2004). This volume attempts to synthesize management scholarship in the Indian context.

Toward the Definition of Indigenous Indian Management

The debate about indigenous research is deepened with many questions. Does any research that cover indigenous phenomenon qualify as indigenous research? Does indigenous research require contextual factors where dominant theoretical framework can be borrowed from the West? Is indigenous research aimed at verification of the western theories and models or development of new theoretical insights? In agreement with Sinha (2000) we define Indian management as an approach to management based on the Indian worldview, ethos and the characteristics of the Indian society. We consider Indian management research as broad-based management research including etic and emic perspectives capturing Indian settings, whereas Indigenous Indian management research focuses on local phenomena from emic or culture specific perspective. In this way contextualization is necessary but not a sufficient condition to call any study to be indigenous. Therefore, context-sensitive research following the etic approach is also valuable for comparative studies. Recognizing the fact that almost any phenomenon can be studied from the outside (etic) as well as from the inside (emic) we hold that both the kind of studies are important and useful to understand the phenomenon from local, transnational and global perspectives.

We define Indigenous Indian management research as the study of local phenomenon, adopting indigenous constructs, concepts and approach which aim at creating locally relevant knowledge which may substitute or substantiate the knowledge developed in the western part of the world. Scientific studies of local phenomena employing Indian languages, subjects, and constructs to build or test management theories (see Van de Ven et al., 2018) can be called indigenous Indian management. Historical perspective is naturally another important aspect of indigenous research. Indian management is not necessarily about people living in the Indian sub-continent or of Indian origin. It can make valuable contributions to the management practices in general and global theories by modifying, enriching, or supplementing management concepts or theories predominantly developed in the Western world and also by offering novel concepts and theories.

Indigenous research is aimed at what, why and how questions on management in India. Emic research on Indian management answer these questions to different degrees. Some studies primarily build on 'what' questions and are aimed at presenting different constructs and concepts in the Indian context like the Rajshri approach of leadership (Chakraborty, 1995), or śraddhā (Bhawuk, 2020). Other studies move beyond what, and aim at 'why' questions about explaining managerial behaviors in Indian organizations like Indian mindset and Nurturant task leadership (Sinha, 1984, 2007; Sinha et al. 2010), or present holistic theories like spiritual theory of creativity in India (Bhawuk, 2003, 2019a). Yet another group of studies focus more on how questions like how mindfulness influences moral reasoning (Pandey et al., 2018), how societal culture influences Indian economic and business systems in India (Vijayabaskar & Kalaiyarasan, 2014), or how social entrepreneurship has evolved in India (Shukla, 2019).

Forms and Types of Indian Management Research

The search for a pluralistic framework to understand research on Indian management ideas and theories has led us to propose a novel typology. We posit that the distinction between an 'emic' and 'etic' perspective (Pike, 1954) and 'atomistic' and 'holistic' constructs (Savory & Butterfield, 1998; Waddock & Lozano, 2013) provides such a typology. Evered and Louis (1981) have termed inquiry from the inside as emic and that from the outside as etic. Atomistic concepts and constructs result from breaking a phenomenon into constituent subcomponents and studying them individually. Also, independent studies are carried out with each subcomponent or variable, or their interactions, keeping all else constant, with the hope and assumption that these studies can be aggregated into the understanding of the phenomenon as a whole. In contrast, the holistic approach examines the overall likelihood of the event in the context of multiple variables that influence the phenomenon. The holistic perspective does not typically examine the interactions of individual variables but, instead, views the event and circumstances as irreducible whole.

Four types of research studies can be found in the Indian context at the intersection of the emic-etic and atomistic-holistic continuums depicted in Fig. 1.1. Chapter numbers of this volume that discuss the specific types of research studies are also mentioned in the table. The first category of this typology is based on the individual or micro-level constructs and concepts drawn from the Indian culture from various Indian sources (e.g., texts) and languages. The importance of these constructs is that

	Atomistic Constructs /Concept	Holistic Constructs/ concepts
Emic research	Ex.: Nurturant task Leadership, Lajja, Karm Yoga, zraddhA (Chapters 2 to 8)	Ex.: Indian economic System, Indian Business System (Chapters 9 to 13 and 15)
Etic research	Most researches studies Using transnational / Western Construct	Ex. GLOBE study on Indian Culture, Understanding advertisement in India using Hofstede's typology (Chapter 14)

Fig. 1.1 Four types of research studies in the Indian management

they capture the reality that is left unattended in the Western literature. This work is based on the argument that western value systems persuaded Indian employees to internalize western styles of working and interaction but they were also socialized to Indian values that contradicted many such values. Studies in this category help understand the worldview and behavior of Indians, which in turn has implications for management. Chapters 2–6 which are based on Indian Psychology (*manas, buddhi, Atman* and so forth), notion of *Karma-Yoga, Ayurveda* and personality studies of Indian system primarily represent the studies under this category. Many individual and group level ideas like *adhy-Atma, lajjA, zraddhA, tapas, prema, lokasaMgraha, Karm Yoga,* spiritual climate, *puruSArtha,* and *RNas,* fit this category. Chapter 7 and 8 also report the studies in this category wherein the constructs of Indian mindset and nurturant task leadership are derived from the social reality grounded in the Indian context. Despite our collective sincere efforts some constructs and theories are not included in the volume, and we hope that this book will be a part of many future volumes that will help create a comprehensive knowledge base for Indian management.

The second category of studies in this typology captures macro-level phenomena like the Indian economic system, social entrepreneurship, health care industry and so forth. Emic research in Indian management of this kind arises from the recognition that culture and economic factors affect the practices of management and organizational behaviors. Holistic constructs examined from emic perspective aim at capturing the social reality from the cultural and institutional perspectives. Cultural perspective refers to differences in the shared norms across societies that generate distinctive forms of successful business organizations and practices, which are specific to their context. Institutional perspective directs attention to the institutions in society such as state, market, religion, family, corporation and profession. Community is another factor that influences organizations and their members (Fang, 2010; Scott, 2007, Thornton et al., 2012). Institutional perspective offers theoretical lens through which holistic constructs or concepts are understood, developed and examined. Chapters 9–13 of this volume elaborate the macro aspects by covering Indian culture and economic system, organizations and business ecosystems in India using Business Systems Framework, social entrepreneurship, Indian business models for affordable healthcare, and societal culture and management practices.

The third category of research is at the macro level and captures the Indian socio-economic milieu using etic categories. The cross-cultural etic research like Global Leadership and Organizational Behavior Effectiveness Project (GLOBE) study may come under this category, which examines the Indian society and organizations based on the pre-existing categories about the culture. Chapter 15 of this volume fits this category wherein an etic categorization of the culture provided by Hofstede (1980) is used to explain the impact of Indian culture on advertising in India. Indian management according to Cappelli et al. (2010, p. 5), comprises a mix of organizational capabilities, managerial practices and distinctive aspects of company cultures that set Indian enterprises apart from firms in other countries. Research studies in this category examine these aspects within the larger socio-economic and cultural context of India using etic categories. One of the key findings of their work (Cappelli et al., 2015) is that the two guiding principles of the Indian business leaders are broad mission and purpose, i.e. servicing the needs of stockholders but also focusing on family prosperity, regional advancement, national growth, and devising new products and services to meet the needs of large numbers of low-income consumers with extreme efficiency. Some of these broad missions would fit the construct of *lokasaMgraha* (Bhawuk, 2019b), which is reviewed in this volume.

Related to the socio-economic and cultural features of India are unique practices of finding fixes, workarounds, and shortcuts that constitute a way of life in India, which is colloquially referred to as *jugaad*, loosely translated as 'making do' or 'improvisation'. Kumar and Puranam, (2012). identified four types of innovations emerging from India from its socio-economic context. First, there are innovations led primarily by multinational corporations that have set up captive innovation and R&D centers in India. Second, R&D services are provided on contract to Indian businesses (outsourced to India by multinational corporations) to support new product development for consumers in the developed world. Third, type of innovation results in process innovation by Indian firms based on their own experience. And finally, management innovation that serves global delivery through scaling and cost efficiencies. Thus, the entire range of organizational innovation patterns can be found in India where many of the ideas are shaped by its cultural worldview.

The fourth category of research examines the etic constructs, also referred to as pseudo-etic or imposed etic, where the concepts originate in the west, and they are tested on Indian data at the individual or group level of analysis. This is useful for testing the validity of western theories in India. It is also useful for comparative studies in which data is collected in two or more countries. Most of the research studies in management in India fall into this category. Following the classification of "high-context" versus "low-context"[3] theorizing of Hall (1976), with the former stressing national differences and the latter emphasizing universal applicability in models and constructs, most of the studies in this category aim at low context theorizing. A large number of studies have aimed at creating knowledge that is context-free, which can be applicable across national boundaries. For example, Biswas et al. (2013) highlighted the

[3] Hall (1976) provided the framework that some cultures are high context and others are low context. Western countries are generally found to have low context culture.

antecedents of employee engagement with the social exchange perspective. They found that distributive and procedural justices are primary determinants of perceived organizational support, whereas procedural justice is a key antecedent of a psychological contract in organizations. However, in addition to procedural justice, Indian managers and executives place a strong emphasis on distributive justice perceptions when evaluating support from their employers, which finds support in other countries in Asia.

Another type of contextual research in this category is using national level attributes (e.g., individualism) as moderators rather than as main effects. This involves a higher level of contextualization by theorizing how the relationship between an independent and dependent variable may vary depending on the national level attribute being considered. For example, Ardichvili et al. (2012) compared ethical cultures in large business organizations in BRIC (Brazil, Russia, India and China) and USA. They found that individualism in the US and collectivism in India accounted for managers in India emphasizing corporate social responsibility, focusing on stake-holders rather than on shareholder, and placing more importance on environmental sustainability.

We submit that all four types of research studies can influence each other. Eventually, all these types of research can help in understanding Indian people and Indian organizations and their development. All four types of studies can also contribute to a global knowledge base of management. However, research in management seems to have a bias toward context-free knowledge (Tsui, 2004) and most of the studies on Indian data published in the leading journals fit this mold. This approach is not conducive to the development of Indian management theories, and the relevant parts of the literature are synthesized in the literature review sections of the chapters in this volume.

Objectives of the Volume

The objectives of this volume are twofold. The first objective is to identify and recognize insights in traditional wisdom and culture that can contribute to the field of management and organizational psychology in terms of theoretical models and practical applications, and also pave the way for future research. This objective arises from the recognition that theory and practice in social domains tend to be self-fulfilling (Gergen, 1973). For example, Ghoshal (2005) explained that a theory in natural sciences does not influence the natural processes. For example, the theory about subatomic particles does not influence the behaviors of those particles. If a theory holds wrong assumptions it does not change the phenomenon as such. On the contrary, if a management theory is subscribed to and adopted by the practitioners in the field, that changes their behaviors and they start behaving in accordance with the theory. The chapters aimed to address this objective in this edited volume are conceived based on the concepts and constructs and perspective of the Indian wisdom and traditions. The chapters in this part aim at understanding different aspects of management through the Indian way of seeing reality.

The second objective of the volume is to present research that is grounded in the Indian context, and examine its implications for management. This objective emanates from recognizing the uniqueness of local phenomena and to unravel their implications for local and global levels. The chapters addressing this objective focus on how Indians think, feel and behave. They examine societal culture of India and its implication for management including culture in Indian organizations, the nature and functioning of the institutions in India, Indian economic and financial systems, unique practices in Indian organizations or the Indian subsidiaries of MNCs, and novel features of certain institutions in India. Deliberation of this kind is important because it can provide practical insights for addressing pressing problems confronting the Indian society, organizations and employees.

Structure of the Book

This volume contains principles, concepts and ethos widely shared in Indian culture that is relevant for management. Chapters 2–6 of this volume present the ontological notions given in major philosophies and wisdom tradition of India like *Vedanta*, *Sankhya* and *Ayurveda.*

Authors present the concepts about nature and ideals of human life, nature and human connections, role and approach of work, ways of attaining well-being individually and socially found in the major schools of thought of Indian culture and their potential implications on management theory and practices. Chapters 7–15 of the book present the findings of empirical studies, which have implications for management theory and practices. These chapters are arranged from micro to macro perspectives. Each chapter presents historical developments that are relevant to a given topic, the underlying theories, the current state of the topic, and the unique aspects that are valid in present day India. Each chapter also points out directions for future research. We hope that the insights are useful for stimulating future research in the field of Indian management. We also hope that managers will find the ideas useful for practice.

Chapter 2 by Pandey initiates the discussion on Indian management by unraveling the Indian worldview. It aims to decipher the Indian worldview by elaborating the nature of human self, goals of human life and the role of work in human life subscribed in the Indian traditional wisdom and their theoretical implications for management theories and practices at the individual, group and organizational levels. The author provides examples of how Indian view is incorporated in organizational practices in two case studies of organizations. The chapter also elaborates concepts and framework in Indian worldview for future research in management.

Chapter 3 by Bhawuk is based on the premise that the principles and practices of psychology are applied in almost every major branch of management, and a discussion on Indian management will be significantly inadequate without discussion about the core tenets of Indian psychology. The field of Indian psychology unravels many positive aspects of human nature and its manifestations in the workplace. In the wake of technological advancement and globalization of businesses, performance is coming at the cost of stress, environmental degradation and meaninglessness. The field of positive psychology is offering a wealth of solutions to our modern challenges related to organizations and their management. Indian psychology can offer a distinct and a fresh perspective and a wide range of interventions to positive psychology for the benefit of organizations and its members. The chapter reviews indigenous constructs like the Indian concept of self, *adhyAtma* or spirituality, *zraddhA*, *tapas*, *prema* or love, and *lokasaMgraha* that are unique to India, but contribute to global psychology and management by challenging some of the western constructs and theories. Then it reviews a theory of creativity that synthesizes spirituality and creativity. The chapter also presents some methodological innovations in developing constructs from texts, which can serve indigenous psychology in general and Indian management in particular.

In Chapter 4, Alok reviews the current state of *triguṇa*-based personality research. Study of personality has a long history in the field of management and influences the sub fields like motivation, leadership, conflict handling and so forth. *Sāṁkhya*-based model of personality has attracted the attention of psychology and management scholars since the early twentieth century. It is one of the oldest known system of Indian philosophy with a pervasive influence on Indian culture and thought and even recognized as the cultural code for the Indian intellectual milieu. Sāṁkhya holds that two fundamentally distinct real principles exist: '*prakṛti*', the principle that generates the categories of known, and '*puruṣa*', the knowing principle. The generic principle of *prakṛti* manifests in three specific manners or *Gunas* known as '*sattva*', '*rajas*' and '*tamas*'. Indian scholars have primarily leveraged the idea of '*triguṇa*' (three *gunas*) to develop their accounts of personality. In this chapter, the author enumerates the challenges of imposed etic biases in the form of epistemological and ontological biases. He enumerates the common pitfalls in the conceptualization of *triguna* in contemporary literature due to inadequate understanding of the original text. He also offers future directions regarding leveraging the Sāṁkhya system of thought for personality research.

In Chapter 5, Krishnan and Mulla elaborate the concept of Karm Yoga, which offers a way to be in unison with the supreme self by engaging in the otherwise ordinary vocation of life. Authors describe the philosophy of *karma-yoga*, the beliefs which sustain and explain karma-yoga, detail the operationalization of *karma-yoga*; and locate this variable in relationship with other work-related correlates and outcomes. They also highlight the practical implication of *karma-yoga* for present day individuals and organizations.

Chapter 6 by Kapadia and Dagar explain how wellness, well-being and happiness, the three major concerns of contemporary management, can be attained with the help of Ayurveda. Pursuits of happiness and well-being are identified as a 'self-evident truth' in life as well as in the workplace. Further, there has been a focus on well-being in the workplace at the level of not only HR policy but also in general managerial perspective. Naturally, this leads to the inclination of scholars to attain a nuanced understanding of factors influencing well-being in the workplace. Ayurveda is an important component of Indian culture and heritage, which continues to be practiced by experts and used in day-to-day life by the vast population of India. It is not confined to being merely a system of medicine to prevent and treat diseases; it is a way of leading a healthy and fulfilling life.

Chapters 7–15 of the volume are focused on Indian economic, financial and business systems. They also focus on the cognitive, affective and behavioral systems shaped by the Indian culture and how they shape organizational and management practices. In Chapter 7 Agrawal and Pandey review the literature on Indian mindset and how it acts as enabling or disabling conditions in day-to-day life in general, and in work settings in particular. The mindset is conceptualized as a configuration of collectively held beliefs, preferences and action orientations that let Indians to respond to their environment in particular ways (Sinha, 2009, 2014; Sinha et al., 2010). Naturally the Indian mindset has a major impact on culture and behaviors of Indian organizations. The authors synthesize the research on Indian mindset, reflect on the changing values of Indians and delineate the implications for future managerial practices and research.

In Chapter 8, Panda first explains the three groups of leadership studies in India. Leadership studies make critical contribution to the management literature and leadership development is considered as an integral aspect of management development at individual and collective level. The first group of descriptive studies is about the evolutionary account of business families. The second group of studies focuses on examining the efficacy of participative/democratic leadership in the

Indian context. The third group of studies includes indigenous leadership studies like *nurturant task leadership* (NTL), paternalistic leadership, consultative managerial leadership, *Sannyasin* and *Karmayogin* leaders, and *lokasamgraha* approach to leadership. This chapter presents a synthesis of these studies and their implications for the present day organizations in India. Reviewing the major studies Panda explains the challenges, useful norms and best practices for developing leaders in Indian organizations and sets a research agenda on leadership development in India.

Chapter 9 by Bapat and Ballal presents the core features of Indian economy and how culture and economic factors play complementary roles as it is increasingly recognized in the contemporary literature (e.g. Granato et al., 1996; Kapás, 2017). Economic, political and social institutions are known to significantly influence management practices of a given country. First the authors present about India's contribution toward the world GDP in the last two millennia. This historical account is important to underscore the importance of economic activities embedded in the Indian culture and society since the ancient times. Second, they elaborate the unique features of Indian society like family and community orientation, prevalence of a large informal sector (and self-employment), and importance of spirituality. They also discuss the impact of these factors on economic activities. Finally, they briefly present the key ideas of thinkers like Kautilya, Gandhi, Ambedkar and Upadhyaya as the representative leaders of ancient and modern India who have influenced the economic and financial thinking in this country.

Chapter 10 by Panda and Gupta applies the institutional perspective to understand Indian business organizations. Organization theorists from various academic disciplines have attempted to explore and understand the form, characteristics and economic behavior of organizations from different perspectives (for details, see Scott, 2014). Presenting business system framework as a unit of organizational analysis, they argue for a holistic perspective to understand and analyze organizations from a cross-disciplinary and evolutionary perspective. They also present Indian business system (IBS) for understanding Indian business ecosystem and organizations. They point out that not many studies in India have examined the influence of institutions on organizational patterns and management systems. Even in international comparative studies which have included India, researchers have adopted a cultural frame of reference, ignoring institutional differences across societies and nations. This chapter has also attempted to bridge these knowledge gaps and present the IBS as a starting point for further research.

In Chapter 11 Pandey and Sahay examine Social Entrepreneurship (SE) as a field of knowledge. They discuss how social entrepreneurs work to address the unmet needs of society. They present the history of development of SE in India and a typology of social entrepreneurs in the Indian context. SE has emerged as a strong force to bridge the gap between the demand and supply for fulfillment of socio-economic and environmental needs of India, which are not met by the market system, especially for the Bottom of Pyramid (BoP). SE has been rapidly growing in all sectors: private, public and non-profit and focuses on social impact and innovative approach to achieve its purpose with the combination of social mission, entrepreneurship and creativity. It is of particular importance to India because the developmental needs of India cannot be solely addressed by government efforts or by the private sector.

Chapter 12 by Bhattacharya and Chandwani discusses innovations in healthcare management in India that provides affordable, accessible and quality healthcare to underprivileged section of the population. Indian civilization has had a long and rich history of giving and caring. The Hindu, Buddhist and Jain religious scriptures celebrated the notion of the wealthy and healthy taking care of the poor and the sick. In the current times, provision of healthcare has been a principal theme of social engagement by Indian firms. This has been pursued by firms as a part of both core business activities as well as a part of the Corporate Social Responsibility (CSR) initiative. India has been the home to a substantial section of BoP customers. Healthcare for BoP customers has thus become a dominant theme in the conversations about Indian healthcare system. The vision for healthcare engagements for such customers has been to provide quality healthcare at affordable price points. This is carried out by many Indian organizations both through technological as well as business model innovation in healthcare. Authors present a historical overview of the healthcare industry in India, and discuss the current infrastructure, capabilities, innovation and business models. They also synthesize research findings about innovations in healthcare industry in India.

Chapter 13 by Awasthi deciphers the special features of the interface between business and socio-cultural system of India and how it has evolved in the last two millennia. India had for centuries been the center of trade and has had long history of intercultural exchanges starting from ancient period of silk route to the liberalization of the economy in early 1990s. After independence, many government owned organizations were started, and many multinational companies also set up operations in India. This chapter maps the socio-cultural changes during the different economic phases of India through the Vedic period, post Vedic period, Mughal period, British colonial period to the modern times. The chapter also reviews the research on organizational culture of MNCs operating in India. The chapter ends by providing guidance for management research at the interface of societal culture and management practices in India in the future.

Chapter 14 by Bharadhwaj and Harindranath deals with the effect of culture on advertising. We know that culture affects the way individuals behave with others, it affects their saving and spending habits; it affects the way they dress and so on. If the effect of culture is so pervasive, it ought to affect the way consumers are influenced by advertising. Evidence suggests that in India, the effect of culture is stronger than in many other countries. It is not a surprise, therefore, that advertising in India has extensively used tenets of Indian culture. This chapter describes extant research in this area, and presents examples from the world of marketing. Through a series of propositions, the authors delineate avenues for future research in the field of Indian culture and advertising.

Chapter 15 by Mishra, Mohapatra and Dagar provides an overview of management education in India and discusses how Indian management institutions employ innovative pedagogies. Management is an applied field of knowledge and management research findings need to be imparted to management students. There have been some interesting experiments conducted in several management schools in India for making the students familiar with peculiar features of Indian society, Indian business or financial system or to impart insights of Indian wisdom traditions relevant in management. For example, students of

S. P. Jain Institute of Management Research, Mumbai, are required to work with non-profit organizations in the development sector as a part of the regular MBA program. Karma Yoga project in Great Lakes Institute engages management students in village service projects that sensitizes them to rural India and the needs of people in the BOP. In the School of Management at IIT Bombay, Yoga based practices are used effectively to enhance moral reasoning, engagement and psychological capital of the students.

In Chapter 16 the editors present the major themes, patterns and insights emerging from all the chapters of this volume. The key insights from each of the chapters are noted. They propose how to develop the field of Indian management. They also reflect on challenges and opportunities in the development of Indian management as a discipline of research. The indigenous research discussed in the volume highlight that most of the management theories developed in the West are inadequate to create context-sensitive management theories and practices. We propose that indigenous research in diverse socio-cultural contexts like India should be encouraged and the primary goal of the indigenous research should be to help develop local context relevant theories and management practices. Indigenous theories derived from the Indian context should be utilized to effectively understand and manage organizations. Global relevance of these ideas also needs to be tested. Conceptual, philosophical and grounded research and empirical research studies are equally relevant and useful for indigenous research. We hope this volume will initiate and strengthen the dialogue among management scholars and lead them to develop meaningful indigenous Indian management principles and theories. We also hope that this volume will persuade practitioners not to mindlessly borrow concepts from the West, and apply some of the models and practices presented in this volume in managing organizations and people in India.

Appendix: Number of Articles Mentioning India in Few Leading Management Journals

Name of journal	1995–2005		2010–2020	
	Anywhere	Title/abstract	Anywhere	Title/abstract
Academy of Management Journal	24	0	83	3
Academy of Management Review	27	1	29	1
Administrative Science Quarterly	18	0	53	4
Journal of Applied Psychology	4	2	22	4
Journal of Business Venturing	22	5	28	5
Journal of International Business Studies	130	4	341	8
Journal of Management	14	0	61	1
Journal of Management Studies	20	0	88	0
Organization Science	0	0	0	0
Strategic Management Journal	33	2	84	4
International Journal of Human Resource Management	74	12	305	33
Journal of Marketing	29	1	41	6
MIS Quarterly	1	1	10	4
Journal of Business Ethics	177	11	619	32
Journal of Finance	51	0	67	0
Journal of Organizational Behavior	15	0	40	1
Journal of Human Relations	15	4	66	9

References

Ardichvili, A., Jondle, D., Kowske, B., Cornachione, E., Li, J., & Thakadipuram, T. (2012). Ethical cultures in large business organizations in Brazil, Russia, India, and China. *Journal of Business Ethics, 105*(4), 415–428.

Bhawuk, D. P. S. (2003). Culture's influence on creativity: The case of Indian spirituality. *International Journal of Intercultural Relations, 27*(1), 1–22.

Bhawuk, D. P. S. (2012). India and the culture of peace: Beyond ethnic, religious, and other conflicts. In D. Landis & R. Albert (Eds.), *Handbook of ethnic conflict* (pp.137–174). Springer. https://doi.org/10.1007/978-1-4614-0448-4_7.

Bhawuk, D. P. S. (2019a). Toward a spirituality-based theory of creativity: Indigenous perspectives from India. In K.-H. Yeh (Ed.), *Asian indigenous psychologies in the global context* (pp. 139–168). Palgrave Macmillan. https://doi.org/10.1007/978-3-319-96232-0_7.

Bhawuk, D. P. S. (2019b). *lokasaMgraha*: An indigenous construct of leadership and its measure. In S. Dhiman & A. D. Amar (Eds.), *Managing by the Bhagavad Gita: Timeless lessons for today's managers* (pp. 273–297). Springer. https://doi.org/10.1007/978-3-319-99611-0_14.

Bhawuk, D. P. S. (2020). *Śraddhā*: Construct Definition from the Bhagavad-Gītā. *Psychology and Developing Societies, 32*(1), 1–16. https://doi.org/10.1177/0971333620906758

Biswas, S. A., Varma, A., & Ramaswami, A. (2013). Linking distributive and procedural justice to employee engagement through social exchange: A field study in India. *The International Journal of Human Resource Management, 24*(8), 1570–1587. https://doi.org/10.1080/09585192.2012.725072

Bruton, G. D., & Lau, C.-M. (2008). Asian management research: Status today and future outlook. *Journal of Management Studies, 45*, 636–659. https://doi.org/10.1111/j.1467-6486.2007.00758.x

Cappelli, P., Singh, H., Singh, J., & Useem, M. (2010). *The India way: How India's top business leaders are revolutionizing management*. Harvard Business Press.

Cappelli, P., Singh, H., Singh, J., & Useem, M. (2015). Indian business leadership: Broad mission and creative value. *The Leadership Quarterly, 26*(1), 7–12.

Chakraborty, S. K. (1995). Wisdom leadership: Leading self by the SELF. *Journal of Human Values, 1*(2), 205–220.

Evered, R., & Louis, M. R. (1981). Alternative perspectives in the organizational sciences: "Inquiry from the inside" and "inquiry from the outside." *Academy of Management Review, 6*(3), 385–395. https://doi.org/10.5465/amr.1981.4285776

Fang, T. (2010). Asian management research needs more self-confidence: Reflection on Hofstede (2007) and beyond. *Asia Pacific Journal of Management, 27*(1), 155–170.

Gergen, K. J. (1973). Social psychology as history. *Journal of Personality and Social Psychology., 26*(2), 309–320.

Ghoshal, S. (2005). Bad management theories are destroying good management practices. *Academy of Management Learning & Education, 4*(1), 75–91. Chicago.

Granato, J., Inglehart, R., & Leblang, D. (1996). The effect of cultural values on economic development: Theory, hypotheses, and some empirical tests. *American Journal of Political Science, 40*(3), 607–631.

Gupta, R. K. (1994). Challenges in developing indigenous theories of organisation and management: An Indian perspective. *Indian Journal of Social Work, 55*, 220–220.

Hall, E. T. (1976). *Beyond culture*. New York, NY: Doubleday. ISBN: 9780385124744.

Hofstede, G. (1980). Culture and organizations. *International Studies of Management & Organization, 10*(4), 15–41.

Kapás, J. (2017). How cultural values affect economic growth: A critical assessment of the literature. *Ekonomska misao i praksa, 1*, 265–285.

Kumar, N., & Puranam, P. (2012). *India inside: The emerging innovation challenge to the West*. Harvard Business Press.

Pandey, A., Chandwani, R., & Navare, A. (2018). How can mindfulness enhance moral reasoning? An examination using business school students. *Business Ethics: A European Review, 27*(1), 56–71.

Pike, K. L. (1954). Emic and etic standpoints for the description of behavior. In K. L. Pike (Ed.), *Language in relation to a unified theory of the structure of human behavior* (pp. 8–28). Summer Institute of Linguistics.

Savory, A., & Butterfield, J. (1998). *Holistic management: A new framework for decision making*. Island Press.

Scott, W. R. (2014). *Institutions and organizations: Ideas and interests* (4th ed.). Sage.

Shukla, M. (2019). *Social entrepreneurship in India: Quarter idealism and a pound of pragmatism*. Sage Publications Pvt. Limited.
Sinha, J. B. (1984). A model of effective leadership styles in India. *International Studies of Management & Organization, 14*(2–3), 86–98.
Sinha, J. B. (2000). Integrative indigenous management in India: practices and prospects. *Indian Journal of Industrial Relations, 35*(4), 439–460.
Sinha, J. B. (2009). The shifting mindset of Indians. In *Discipline of psychology in the series "The history of indian science, philosophy and culture"*.
Sinha, J. B. (2014). *Psycho-social analysis of the Indian mindset*. Springer India.
Sinha, J. B. P., & Pandey, A. (2007). Indian mindset and condition that provoke them. *Psychological Studies, 52*(1), 1–13.
Sinha, J. B., Singh, S., Gupta, P., Srivastava, K. B., Sinha, R. B. N., Srivastava, S., ... & Pandey, A. (2010). An exploration of the Indian mindset. *Psychological Studies, 55*(1), 3–17.
Thornton, P. H., Ocasio, W., & Lounsbury, M. (2012). *The institutional logics perspective: A new approach to culture, structure, and process*. Oxford University Press on Demand.
Tsui, A. S. (2004). Contributing to global management knowledge: A case for high quality indigenous research. *Asia Pacific Journal of Management, 21*(4), 491–513.
Van de Ven, A. H., Meyer, A. D., & Jing, R. (2018). Opportunities and challenges of engaged indigenous scholarship. *Management and Organization Review, 14*(3), 449–462. https://doi.org/10.1017/mor.2018.28
Vijayabaskar, M., & Kalaiyarasan, A. (2014). Caste as social capital: The Tiruppur Story. *Economic and Political Weekly, 49*(10), 34–38.
Waddock, S., & Lozano, J. M. (2013). Developing more holistic management education: Lessons learned from two programs. *Academy of Management Learning & Education, 12*(2), 265–284. https://doi.org/10.5465/amle.2012.0002

2

Human Self, Work and of Human Being: Indian Worldview and Implications for Management Practices and Scholarship

Ashish Pandey

Introduction

Social science theories have the potential to influence the human behaviour and shape the social reality (Callon, 1998; Marti & Gond, 2018). For example, a theory that assumes that people can behave opportunistically and draws its conclusions for managing people based on that assumption can induce managerial actions that are likely to enhance opportunistic behavior (Ghoshal & Moran, 1996). Ghoshal (2005) observed that 'management theory - if gains sufficient currency' has a potential to change the behaviors of managers in accordance with the theory. Theories in social sciences are also context sensitive and the theoretical premises are based primarily on acquired dispositions. In a

A. Pandey (✉)
Shailesh J. Mehta School of Management, Indian Institute of Technology Bombay, Mumbai, India
e-mail: ashish.pandey@iitb.ac.in

© The Author(s), under exclusive license to Springer Nature Switzerland AG 2022

A. Pandey et al. (eds.), *Indigenous Indian Management*, Palgrave Studies in Indian Management,
https://doi.org/10.1007/978-3-030-87906-8_2

different culture, such dispositions can also be different and the premises may be invalidated from different point of view of reality (Gergen, 1973). The self-fulfilling and the context-sensitive nature of theories and scholarship is increasingly recognized in the current discourse in the field of management (e.g. Bosse & Phillips, 2016; Ketokivi et al., 2017; Mckiernan & Tsui, 2019).

India is a unique social and cultural setting; a living culture of more than three thousand years besides with immense diversity in languages and subcultures, having youngest population in the world besides being the third largest economy in terms of Purchasing Power Parity and one of the fastest growing large economies in the world. India's actions are bound to affect the whole world. Hence, it may be interesting as well as useful to examine the management theories from the Indian perspective. Examining the management thoughts in Indian worldview may be useful in Indian culture and the organizations emerging from there or MNCs operating in India and may even contribute toward the global repository of management knowledge.

The notion of 'worldview' is especially relevant to venture into this pursuit. The worldview is defined as a way of describing the universe and life within it, both in terms of what is and what it ought to be. In addition to defining what goals can be sought in life, it also defines what goals should be pursued (Koltko-Rivera, 2006). The remainder of the chapter is divided into five sections. The next section elaborates the notion of the 'worldview' and its relevance for management practice and scholarship. The second section provides details on Indian worldview drawn from the deliberations of Indian philosophy and culture. The implications of Indian world view on management at individual, interpersonal and collective levels in organizations are discussed in third section. The fourth section presents the two cases, let as exemplars of the business organizations which have made deliberate efforts to embrace the Indian worldview in their functioning and finding it highly beneficial. The last section presents a discussion on key observations, conclusion and proposes an agenda for future research.

What Is Worldview? What Constitutes It and Why That Matters?

First, mentioned prominently in the writings of Kant as Weltanschauung, worldview means a view used to describe one's overall conception of reality and human existence rooted in the existential experiences of life (Wolter in Cobern, 1991). It is a framework of meaning and meaning making that informs our understanding and enactment of reality (Hedlund-de Witt, 2012). This is almost synonymously used with the terms like "philosophy of life" Jung (1942/54) in Koltko-Rivera (2004), "self-and-world construct system", "cultural orientation" and "core culture" (Kluckhohn & Strodtbeck, 1961). A worldview is a way of describing the universe and life within it. It is a set of beliefs about good and bad about life goals, relationships and behaviors. Worldview includes 'beliefs and assumptions which may or may not be provable but provide epistemic and ontological foundations for other beliefs and belief system' (Koltko-Rivera, 2000, p. 2). Worldviews are overarching systems of meaning and meaning-making that substantially informs how humans interpret, enact, and co-create reality (Hedlund-de Witt et al., 2014).

Worldview is a philosophical as well as psychological construct with wide research implications across the fields of social sciences. A review of the major approaches to worldview during the twentieth century emphasizes dimensional rather categorical approaches to worldview that differentiate individuals with respect to degree or level of the target construct (Koltko-Rivera, 2004). The grouped dimensions and options referred in the different models of world view are human nature, will, knowledge and consciousness, behavior, interpersonal engagements, work and life and the nature truth. Anthropologist Florence Rockwood Kluckhohn (Kluckhohn & Strodtbeck, 1961/1973), discussing about worldviews, provided an intricate model of the values orientation. It expresses the values common across societies and which shape the attitudes, cognition, emotions which eventually determine behaviors. The worldview of an individual or of a culture according to Kluckhohn and Strodtbeck (1961) can be defined by the answers to questions in five areas or "orientations" of human thought—human nature orientation and possibility of its change, relation of man and nature, relational orientation, activity orientation and temporal focus of human life.

Kluckhohn's model has been widely used, especially in multicultural counseling and assessment (Dana, 1993; Ibrahim et al., 2001; Sue & Sue, 1999; Treviño, 1996 in Koltko-Rivera, 2004). Kluckhohn's approach is perhaps the most articulated of various theories and models in the discussion about worldview (Koltko-Rivera, 2004). Though this model lacks some important dimensions like epistemology, ontology, and meaning of life, the dimensions explicated in Kluckhohn's model are important in other models as well. This fact underscores the choice of this model of values orientation as the basis of explicating the worldview.

The importance of worldview is recognized in the fields of developmental psychology, sport psychology, general counseling and psychotherapy. The importance of philosophical understating of the management concepts and examining the worldviews influencing the management theories is increasingly recognized over the last few decades (Joullié, 2016; Laurie & Cherry, 2001). Emphasizing the importance of worldview in field of management, Ghoshal (2005) observed that by propagating amoral theories, business schools have actively unfettered their students from any sense of moral responsibility. The statement of Giacalone and Thompson (2006) that 'existing organization focused worldview needs to be changed to society centric worldview to make the learning effective in the field of ethics and social responsibility', highlights the importance of the worldview in management research and education.

Indian Worldview: An Overview

In order to present the Indian worldview, I primarily draw from the writings of three renowned scholars, who explored the Indian culture with three distinct approaches. These are S. Radhakrishnan, S. Abid Husain, and Hajim Nakamura. Radhakrishnan (1888–1975) is universally recognized as modern India's greatest philosopher who philosophized in the true Indian tradition. Husain (2018) studied the emergence of national culture of India in last two and a half millennia as the common temperament and outlook which constitutes the Indian mind. He explained that the intellectual influences of the various movements and cultures have been incorporated harmoniously with national mind and examined the emergence of Indian culture and Indian mind through the wider ecological, socio-political and philosophical undercurrents. Nakamura (1964) examined the Indian culture in his classical book titled 'Ways of Thinking of Eastern People'. This book explicates the process of thinking of Indians as well as Chinese, Japanese and Tibetan civilizations based on the interpretation of their language and logic.

Before explicating the matter further, three caveats will be befitting at this stage. First, about drawing 'a Indian worldview' out of many schools of '*Darshanas*' or philosophies evolved and prevalent in India. Though the nine major schools of thoughts are found and still pursued in the Indian philosophy and knowledge system there is inherent commonality in their approach to life except that of '*Charvaks*'.[1] The work of above-mentioned three scholars acknowledges all the schools and is aimed at revealing the integral vision cutting across all the major schools of thoughts on Indian culture. The second caveat is about using the term 'men' in this chapter. It is warranted to clarify that the term 'men' is not used in exclusivist term and encompasses men and women and all in between. The third caveat is about ideals of Indian worldview and socio-economic cultural reality of current Indian society. Though, Indian worldview considers that each human being is inherently divine, truth and righteousness are the highest values, nature and earth is mother to all, man and women are complimentary and human beings behold equal spiritual potential irrespective of caste, gender and aptitude, this chapter does not claim about to what extent these values are followed in the day-to-day life of Indians in current times.

[1] Charvaka, also called Lokayata (Sanskrit: Worldly Ones), a quasi-philosophical school of materialists who rejected the notion of an karma, liberation (*moksha*), the authority of the Vedas, and the immortality of the self. Of the recognized means of knowledge (*pramana*), the Charvaka recognized only direct perception (*anubhava*). Sources critical of the school depict its followers as hedonists.

In the upcoming sub sections, I present the different aspects of Indian worldview like nature of man and possibility of its change, relation of man and nature, temporal focus of human life, relational orientation, and work orientation based on the writing of Radhakrishnan, Husain and Nakamura.

Human Nature Orientation and Possibility of Its Change in Indian Worldview

In the model of the worldview elaborated by Kluckhohn and Strodtbeck (1961/1973), the first area or the set of questions is related to the character of innate human nature and the possibility of changing. In the Indian worldview, the human is not altogether separate and peculiar being. He is part of universal nature, 'a whole carved out of nature's continuum' (Radhakrishnan, 1948/2009, p. 269). Radhakrishnan pointed out the inadequacy of conditioned response and solely stimulus response view of human behavior in light of the values and higher purpose that inspire the human dispositions and behavior, mind–body as a whole and self as the emergent unity which is more than a sum of its subordinate parts. In Indian traditional wisdom, the notion of '*Brahman*', the ultimate reality is not different than '*Ātman*'—'the true self'. Brahman is considered true 'self' and the realization of that is considered to be the highest goal of human life. *Śvetāśvetaropaniṣada*, one of the nine principal *Upaniṣadas*, addresses human beings as *Amrutasya putrah*, the children of the immortal being.[2] The core nature of human self is *sat*, *chit* and *anand*, i.e., the truth, the eternal and blissful, but it is veiled under ignorance. The veil of ignorance can be removed by '*Sadhana*'—the spiritual pursuits identified and developed in multiple pathways of Yoga like *Jnan Yoga*, the path of knowledge, *Bhakti yoga*, the path of devotion to ones chosen deity, *karm Yoga*, the path of action or *Raj Yoga*, the path of *Ashtang Yoga*.

---

[2] Amrutasya putrah

May all the sons of the Immortal listen, even those who have reached their heavenly abodes (Radhakrishnan, 1953/2016, p. 720).

Husain (2018) writes that the capacity for contemplation dominates all other mental powers and the capacity to see and apprehend unity in diversity is the two main characteristics of Indian mind. As a result of that the Indian mind held 'thought' very high, and on the scale of values it is not purely abstract or speculative in nature and direct intuitive form of comprehension is valued the most. Love and reverence, as Husain (2018) proposes are the natural expression of the mind of this nature. Husain (2018) also points out that Indian culture has evolved on a land which consists of plains, are well irrigated, and has ample sunshine for the greater part of year which are the most suitable condition for agriculture. Though different parts of country produced different products, these can easily be transported by means of natural ways or roads and that resulted in extensive internal trade. The mental capacity for contemplation and the physical conditions that facilitated the reaching out to the length and breadth of the subcontinent prepared or set free the Indian mind to embrace the subjective experience of unity to the objective world.

Nakamura (1964) points out that unlike Western philosophy where the focus of inquiry is on the "I", the Indian philosophy discusses so much about "the Self". The essence or '*karan*' of human self is *Atman* that is regarded as identical with the ultimate being.[3] Nakamura points out that for all the schools of thought of Indian philosophy, except *Charvaka*, the relation of the individual self and the Higher Self is one of the major quest. He concludes that the idea of *Avatara* or incarnation of the Supreme Being is also based on the notion of non-duality between the individual self and the Higher Self. Buddhism and Jainism also deny the concept of "mine" and "my possession". For most religions in India, the ultimate goal of freedom is the realization of one's true self. From this approach emerges the view that beyond the plane of appearances there is no "other self".[4] The *Maitri* (friendship) and *Karuna* or *Daya* (compassion) are the natural expressions of this worldview.

---

[3] The latter is called Paramatman and former is called Jivatman.

[4] yastu sarvANi bhUtAni AtmanyEva anupashyati |
sarva bhUtEShu cha AtmAnaM tatO na vijugupsatE
One who perceives in the Atman everything, and in the same way Atman in everything, does not hate.

Then Indian worldview then does not uphold the individualist perspective of self in the sense it is upheld in Greek and Latin philosophical traditions. *Upanishads* and *Vivek Chudamani* and traditions of Yoga conceive human existence in the form of sheaths or Kosha. The outermost sheath, or Kosha is called the *annamaya kosha* (anna meaning food grain), the physical body or *sthūla-śarīra*, the gross body. The next three layers are called sheath of vitality (*prāṇamaya kośha*), the sheath of emotions and thoughts and behavioral intentions (*manomaya kosha*), and the sheath of ratiocination (*vijnānamaya kosha*). These three bodies together constitute what is called the "subtle body" (*sūkṣma-śarīra*).

The sheath of vitality roughly corresponds to the subjective vitality. Spiritual and traditional health systems originated in India have linked vitality to mental, physical and spiritual health. *Pranayam* or breathing exercises are the major ways to nourish and strengthen the sheath of vitality. The sheath of emotions and rationality or intellect corresponds to the innate and acquired affective and cognitive faculties. The innermost layer, the sheath of bliss (*ānandamayakosha*), comprises the "causal body" (*karana sharīra*). It is experienced by everyone in the state of deep, dreamless sleep (*suṣuptī*), as well as during certain forms of meditation. Dualities and distinctions are not completely destroyed at this level, but they are harmonized so completely that this state is experienced as the one of profound relaxation and bliss (*Ānanda*). Referring the five sheath or *Pancha Kosha* aspect of self, Radhakrishnan points out that, "the realm of the spirit is not cut off from the realm of life and the two orders of reality, the transcendent and the empirical are closely related". In fact, there is no parallel or exact translation of the word 'individual' in Sanskrit. For a person the term used is *Vyakti*, meaning 'the expressed' one, expression of the supreme. The common greeting Namaste for the singular and Namo Namaha for the larger gathering in Indian system that means 'obeisance', 'reverential salutation' or 'adoration' and that means 'bowing to you'.

A large number of the mantras in the Vedas are not addressed to the power external to the reciter of the mantra like deity or God. These mantras are addressed to the inner self of reciter only aimed at the self-invocation of certain attitude or qualities. This nature of Mantra indicates the power and significance assumed in human self[5] and faith to evolve itself.

The Relation of Human Being and Nature in Indian Worldview

This aspect of worldview is related to the relation of human beings to nature, i.e., people live in subjugation to nature, or should they attempt to live in harmony with it or in mastery over it (Kluckhohn & Strodtbeck, 1961/1973). In the Indian worldview, the connection is regarded as 'integral' between human self and the nature at large. We quote three widely acknowledged viewpoint in the Indian culture to explicate the ideas of relation between man and nature. First is the notion of five basic elements and the three characteristics as the constituents of all the manifestations of nature. Second, we quote a reference about the characteristic of the person of the real knowledge given in Bhagwad Gita (holy book) that indicates the place of human being in the nature. The third exemplar quote is about the Hymn or Kanto about the earth given in *Atharvaveda* (holy book).

According to Indian perspective, the basic constituents of the human body are same as all other manifestations of nature which are ether, fire, air, water and earth arranged from subtle to gross in nature.[6] Fundamentally all the plants, animals and anything part of nature is made of few or all of these elements. Similarly, the three fundamental characteristics *Sattva*, *Rajas*, *Tamas* are the bases of all substance of nature whether it is human body and mind, plants or animate objects. *Sattva* is translated

[5] *uddhared atmanatmanam natmanam avasadayet*
atmaiva hy atmano bandhur atmaiva ripur atmanah

Let a man lift himself by himself; let him not degrade himself; for the Self alone is the friend of the self and the Self alone in the enemy of the self (p. 189).

[6] Akasha has sound as its characteristic property. Touch combines with Sound to form characteristic property of Vayu (Air). Rupa (Form) combines with Touch + Sound to form characteristic property of Agni (Fire) Rasa (Taste) combines with Rupa + Touch + Sound to form characteristic property of Apah (Water) Gandha (Odour) combines with Rasa + Rupa + Touch + Sound to form characteristic property of Prithvi (Earth).

—From Sankhya Karika. Karika 22 (Author: Shri Ishwara Krishna)

as radiance and goodness, *Rajas* as passion and attachment and *Tamas* is inertia (Radhakrishnan, 2014, p. 374).

The second noticeable reference is about the truly knowledgeable or learned man. The eighteenth verse of fifth Kanto of Bhagwad Gita says that with knowledge comes humility and the learned one sees with an equal eye a Brahmin, a cow, an elephant or even a dog or an outcaste. Radhakrishnan explains that (2014, p. 181) nature is the world of objectivization and distinction is there among minerals, plants, animals and men but they all have an inner non-objective existence. Realizing this truth is the sign of knowledge and learned person in Indian worldview.

The third example is drawn from a recitation mantra of Atharvaveda, a Eulogy called Prathvi Sukta.

> *Satyam Brhad-Rtam-Ugram Diikssaa Tapo Brahma Yajnyah Prthiviim Dhaarayanti.*
> *Saa No Bhuutasya Bhavayasya Patny[i]-Urum Lokam Prthivii Nah Krnnotu.*

Meaning of the hymn is as follows:

> (Salutations to Mother Earth) The Truth (*Satyam*), the Cosmic Divine Law (*Ritam*), the Spiritual Passion manifested in Mighty Initiations, Penances and self-dedications to the search of Brahman (by the sages); these have sustained the Mother Earth for ages (Who in turn have supported these in Her Bosom).

The earth is revered as the mother in many hymns of Vedas. The mountains, caves, rocks, forests, trees, plants, healing herbs, rivers, streams, lakes were revered as expression of love of mother earth and the gratitude toward earth as beholder and nurturing power of life.[7]

---

[7] 1.2: *Asambaadham Badhyato Maanavaanaam Yasyaa Udvatah Pravatah Samam Bahu. Naanaa-Viiryaa Ossadhiiryaa Bibharti Prthivii Nah Prathataam Raadhyataam Nah.*
Meaning:
She, Who is to us the Consort of the Past and the Future (being its witness), May She expand our inner life in this World towards the Cosmic Life (through Her Purity and Vastness).
2.1: (Salutations to Mother Earth) Who extends Unimpeded Freedom (both outer and inner) to Human Beings through Her Mountains, Slopes and Plains.

The entire existence is governed by cosmic principle. This is known as *Rta* or *Ritam* in Vedic literature and constitute a very important feature of Indian worldview. The word ṛta is derived from the root word ṛ which means 'dynamism,' 'vibrancy,' 'seasoning,' and 'belongingness'. Rta has a threefold aspect as referred in the Rigveda, the nature's course of things or the regular and general order in the cosmos, the correct and ordered way of the *devatas* (with respect to yajnas) and the moral conduct of man. The whole of creation is called *sat*, which has an inbuilt cosmic law, *ṛta*. If *sat* (existence) is a fact, then the value which we realize out of it is *ṛta* (cosmic law). When we realize *ṛta* and thus the value of the whole of creation, we are humbled and naturally become more caring toward the universe. The realization that what appears an individual life is possible only with the support of the universe infuses immense gratitude in our hearts. This indebtedness that arises in a sensitive mind is called *ṛṇa*. The notion of Ṛṇa suggests that all human beings must discharge certain obligations toward parents and forefathers (*Pitṛ-ṛṇa*), toward sages and knowledgeable people from the society (Ṛṣi-ṛṇa), toward super-natural powers (*Deva-ṛṇa*) and toward all other plants and animals beings (Bhūta-ṛṇa). The notion of panch-yajna explained in the next section arose from the notion rna.

Relational Orientation in Indian Worldview

This aspect of the worldview is related to the preferred modality of interpersonal relationship. I provide two examples of relational orientation in Indian worldview. First example is the notion of the 'world as a family' '*vasudhaiva kuṭumbakam*' (world as a family). One of the most cited verse from *Mahopaniṣada* (verse 4.71[8]) presents the notion of '*Vasudhaiva kuṭumbakam*' i.e. this whole world is a family. Similar verse with slightly different wordings appears in *Hitopadeśa*, which is a book on

2.2: She bears many Plants and Medicinal Herbs of various Potencies; May She extend Her Riches to us (and make us healthy).

[8] *ayaṃ nijaḥ paro veti gaṇanā laghucetasām* | *udāracaritānāṃ tu vasudhaiva kuṭumbakam* ||
Meaning: Narrow-minded people make distinction like 'this person is mine and this is not'; but people with noble conduct and character consider the whole world as one family.

social and political skills. *Vasudhaiva kuṭumbakam* depicts the worldview of considering the whole world as a family. Family holds a very important place in the Indian worldview and other dispositions. Idea of family doesn't restrict only to the immediate relatives, but extends to the other members of the society. For example, the ruler and the head of the educational institution (*kulagurū*) are considered as father figure to her subjects and students. The wife of *kulagurū* is revered as the mother. Common people in India use words like *baṃdhū* (in Sanskrit, Bengali), *bhaiyā* (in Hindi), *bhāū* (in Marathi), *āṇṇā* (in Tamil) meaning 'brother' to address even strangers. Idea of being the member of family entails the sense of belongingness, compassion and care toward the other family members. It further embraces the sense of responsibility toward wellbeing of all the members. This idea is also reflected through one of the well-known *Śāṃtipāṭha*[9] of *Upaniṣada*—"*sarve bhavantu sukhinaḥ*" (let all be happy). In summary, the notion of *Vasudhaiva kuṭumbakam* characterizes the expression of the worldview of inherent oneness behind varied expressions and manifestation of human beings and other forms of the nature, and the sense of compassion, care and responsibility toward them.

The second example is the notion of 'yajña'. The notion of *yajña* reflects the interaction of man with the social and the natural environment. Literally speaking, *yajña* means—selfless sacrifice for noble purposes. The basic philosophy of *yajña* is about offering the sacrifice first to the nature, then to the parents, sages and fellow human beings, and then finally consuming for oneself. The importance of *yajña* and sacrifice is also elaborated in *Bhagavadgītā* (verse 3.13[10]). This verse has interpretation at two levels. At metaphysical level, sacrifice or *yajña* is understood as an interchange between the gods and men. At another level, it talks about the action of humans in the context of the interdependence of beings in the nature. *Yajña* is based on the realization of

---

[9] A prayer that is chanted before and after the recital of Upaniṣada. Wordly meaning of Śāṃtipāṭha is recitation for peace.

[10] *yajñaśiṣṭāśinaḥ santo mucyante sarvakilbiṣaiḥ* | *bhuñjate te tvaghaṃ pāpā ye pacantyātmakāraṇāt* ||

Meaning: The good people who eat what is left from the sacrifice are released from all sins but those wicked people who prepare food for their own sake-verily eat sin. (Translated by Radhakrishnan, p. 136).

constant inevitable interchange between human life and the social and natural environment. The notion of *pañca-yajña* or five sacrifices explicates the idea of *yajña* into daily life. *Pañca-yajña* are very important for the householders. *Pañca-yajña* include *deva yajña* (to the Lord or *īśvara*), *pitṛ yajña* (to the family and ancestors), *brahma yajña* (to knowledge creators and disseminators), *manuṣya yajña* (to the fellow human beings), and *bhūta yajña* (to the natural environment). Human existence marked by its footprints on various resources. Thus, Bhave (1946) noted that *yajña* is a sacrifice made with the purpose of refreshing, restoring and recreating the resources essential for coexistence.

Nature of Activity in the Form of Work and Wealth Creation in Indian Worldview

This aspect of the worldview is about person's beliefs regarding the preferred mode of human self-expression in activity. In order to untangle the nature and role of work with special reference to economic activities or wealth creation in the Indian worldview we take four examples from the Indian traditional wisdom. First example is about four broader aims of life (*puruṣārtha*), second example is about the notion of *Svadharma* and *Lokasaṃgraha* as explained in *Bhagavadgītā*, the third example is about the eight forms of the deity *Lakṣmī* the Goddess of wealth, and the fourth is about a common ritual followed at the place of business and homes particularly during the festival of Diwali, a festival dedicated to *Lakṣmī* (also called as festival of light). The first two concepts are about the work and latter two concepts are about the wealth and wealth creation.

Four *Puruṣārtha* or aims of life are widely subscribed in the Hindu view of life. These are *dharma*, *kāma*, *artha*, *mokṣa*. Dharma is righteousness, virtue, or duty. *Kāma* refers to the fulfillment of our biological needs or sensual pleasures. *Artha* refers to fulfillment of our social needs including material gains, acquisition of wealth, and social recognition. *Mokṣa* means liberation from worldly bondage and union with the ultimate reality (Radhakrishnan, 1927/2009, p. 54). These four aims highlight harmony of different dimensions in life. Dharma has pivotal role around which life rotates. When *kāma* and *artha* are regulated by dharma, and lead to liberation or *mokṣa*. It is evident from the notion of four *Puruṣārtha* that spiritual and material aspects of life seen as constituting an integral whole in the Indian worldview.

The appropriate work of a human being is considered to be according stage of life (*āśrama*) and the *Dharmic* expression of temperament and attitude (*varṇa*). There is a lot of emphasis on finding individual dharma or work that is according to one's temperament, and the role in family and society. It is termed as *Svadharma* in *Bhagavadgītā*. *Lokasaṃgraha* is another construct associated with work. *Svadharma* and *Lokasaṃgraha* are realized together. *Lokasaṃgraha* is translated as working for the world maintenance. *Lokasaṃgraha* stands for the unity of the world, the interconnectedness of the society. *Svadharma* and *Lokasaṃgraha* are the notion of ideals of action in the world; *Svadharma* signifies the nature of work according to one's aptitude and situation in life and *Lokasaṃgraha* is performing action in harmony with social and natural environment (Pandey et al., 2009).

Śrīsūkta of *Ṛgveda* is dedicated to *Lakṣmī*—the Goddess of wealth. In the hymn—the Vedic seer prays to the Goddess to remove poverty from both within and without and seek blessings with (inner) wisdom and outer independence and abundance. The prayer in this hymn is for boundless wealth in the form of cows, servants, horses, family and good children, that bring joy and peace. In later period, the form of *Aṣṭa-Lakṣmī* (Eight *Lakṣmī*) a group of eight manifestations of the Goddess of wealth became popular. Different forms of *Lakṣmī* presides over eight sources of wealth such as prosperity, fertility, good fortune or good luck, good health, knowledge, strength, progeny and power.

The practice of writing '*Śubha*' and '*Lābha*' on both sides of entrances is very common in northern India. The same can be observed with little variations in Gujarat, Maharashtra and entire south. This is a beautiful example of the espoused values for traders and businesspeople. '*Lābha*' means profit and '*Śubha*' means virtuous. Aim of any productive work, may it be farming, mining, manufacturing, trading or banking, all these are to be carried out with noble aim of earning virtuous profit. We find evidence in the economic history of the world edited by Angus Madison for world's richest organization OECD, India was leading economy till eighteenth-century AD (Maddison, 2003, 2007). This phenomenal consistency of productivity and wealth creation shows the relevance of ancient wisdom in business policies and practices.

At this point, it is befitting to quote Chanakya or Kautilya. Chanakya was a mastermind behind the magnum opus of the post-vedic period of India called 'Arthashastra'. Chanakya has the recognition of being the most influential political philosopher and guide for Chandragupta Maurya during the 326 B.C., Mauryan era. The Chanakya's sutra[11] beautifully summarizes the Indian wisdom about material wealth and Dharma. It says, the basis of '*sukha*' (all true pleasantness) is '*dharma*' (the righteous conduct). The basis of all '*dharma*' is '*artha*' (wealth). The basis of all '*artha*' is '*rājya*' (the State) and the basis for the stability of the State lies in control over '*indriya*' (sense faculties providing pleasures).These examples indicate that spirituality is an integral part of human life in the Indian worldview. The Indian concept of self is closely related to spirituality or adhyAtma, and balancing the spiritual and the material aspirations is one of the most important aspirations for living the ideal life of a householder in Indian worldview.

Management Theories: Possibilities of Alternative Theoretical and Pedagogical Perspective in Indian Worldview

The Indian worldview and wisdom traditions can contribute to present day management education, practice and research in the form of offering an alternate perspective, new knowledge and interventions. In this section we elaborate on key ideas arising out of Indian worldview having potential to present alternate theoretical perspectives on management at micro, group and macro levels.

---

[11] *sukhasya mūlaṃ dharmaḥ, dharmasya mūlaṃ arthaḥ* | *arthasya mūlaṃ rājyaṃ, rājyasya mūlaṃ indriya jayaḥ* ||

Theoretical, Practical and Pedagogical Implications at Individual Levels

Many individual level constructs are examined and developed with Indian worldview and drawn from the Indian tradition wisdom literature. The work of Chakraborty (1995) and Chakraborty and Chakraborty (2004) on wisdom leadership is based on the notion of *Rajarshi*, (*Raja* meaning king and *Rishi* being sage) the sage king who embodies *satya* (truth) and *Rita* (the universal order). Krishnan and colleagues have developed the idea of *karm Yoga* (Mulla & Krishnan, 2008, 2014), the path of action in the world for spiritual awakening. They have demonstrated its impact and association with transformational leadership, moral development and duty orientation (Mulla & Krishnan, 2009, 2012). Bhawuk (2011) has developed many concepts and the constructs drawn from Indian worldview like *manas* the notion of self in Indian worldview, *Lajja*—the positive side of shame (2017), *Loksangrah*—the Indian approach to leadership (2019) and creativity (2003) from Indian cultural perspective. Kumar's work on *triGuna* (2015), which is the most commonly referred in the Indian worldview is valuable in terms of conceptualization and measurement of aptitude and attitude of human beings. Kumar's work on *Satvik* leadership (2017) is drawn from the notion of *triGuna* and demonstrates its implication on leadership, moral concerns and impact on psychological capital, empowerment and engagement. Similarly, Sinha's work on nurturant task leadership and Indian Mindset (Sinha et al. 2010) is groundbreaking in nature which has strong implication on management theories and practices particularly in Indian context. The work of Sinha is summarized in Chapter 13 of this handbook on psycho-social analysis of Indian mindset summarizes.

I provide three examples where Indian worldview and wisdom tradition which can be further useful and insightful for management teaching, practice and research. First example is holistic view of personality and its development, the second example is about the levels of consciousness described in Indian worldview and knowledge system. Both these concepts can have theoretical and practical implication in management.

The third example contains of several constructs found in Indian traditional text and wisdom. These constructs reflect the Indian worldview of reality and may also prove to be insightful to understand, enhance and interpret the current reality of management.

The five layered model of the 'self' explained above is similar to the contemporary understanding of 'self' in terms of cognitive, affective and conative aspects similar to contemporary psychology but also includes *Pranamaya Kosh*—the sheath of vitality and *Anand Maya Kosh*—the sheath of blissfulness. The indigenous approach to 'self' as the five layers can bring a useful perspective to management practice, teaching and research. First, it is an integral approach and acknowledges that interdependence and impact of physical body, emotions and thoughts on each other. *Pranamaya Kosh* may not be directly observable but it can be experienced with simple breathing exercises known as *Pranayam* in the Yoga. There are constructs in the contemporary literature like subjective vitality, chi, energy which describe the subjective experience comparable to *Pranamaya Kosha*. The impact of *Pranayam* are studied on many psychological and physiological aspects (see Sengupta, 2012; Büssing et al., 2012 for latest developments in this area). There is then abundant research potential in the field of *Yoga* and *Paranayam* as the interventions for personality development and wellbeing.

Ayurveda is another Indian tradition knowledge system build on uniquely Indian worldview and useful to understand the wellbeing in general and at workplace (Dagar & Pandey, 2020). Ayurveda is one of the oldest systems of traditional medicine in the world and has been practiced in the Indian subcontinent since 5000 BC (Dasgupta, 1992; Mukherjee & Wahile, 2006). Please see Chapter 6 of this book on understanding self and wellbeing based on Ayurveda written by Kapadia & Dagar.

At the individual level, perception, attribution, decision making and problem solving are based on certain worldview and assumptions about human consciousness, personality and identity. For example, wakefulness is considered as the base level of human consciousness, 'self' is considered individualized in most of personality theories, ego is understood to be inevitable that needs to be strengthened and identity is considered personal in nature. However, if we look at these notions from the perspective of Indian Psychology, we may reach a very different understanding of these notions and concepts.

Human consciousness on which most of the management related concepts are based on the recognition of three states—wakeful, dream and deep sleep as the levels of consciousness. The perspective on Indian Psychology recognizes the fourth stage of consciousness called *Turiya*. This state is trans-cognitive in nature where the distinction between the subject and object, knower and known, disappears. After this state is attained the practical reality of ordinary experience changes (Paranjpe, 1998, p. 161). Generally, it is said to be experienced in the meditation practices in Ashtang Yoga. This level of consciousness underlies particular awareness and functions in gaps between experiences, connecting individual perceptions into a continuous stream (Travis & Pearson, 2000). Many new insights can be found about perception, attribution, decision making and problem solving, learning and related constructs if research is carried out considering research questions about the change in emotional and cognitive faculties after experiencing *Turiya* state of consciousness.

The third example of plausible research studies in management referring Indian traditional wisdom can be in form of developing concepts, constructs and models elaborated in the literature of Indian languages. Many Indian constructs like five *Yamas* (Ahimsa-non-violence, *Sathya*-truthfulness, *Asteya*-non-stealing, *Aparigraha*-non-hoarding, *Brahmcharya*-penance and self-control and *Niyamas Santosh*-Contentment, *Saucha*-inner and outer cleansing, *Swadhyay*-self-study as well as study of self, *Tapa*-penance and austerity and *Ishwar Pranidhan*-surrender to grand order or superpower in Yoga tradition. Similarly, Bhagwad Gita mentions some of the positive qualities as *Daivi Sampada* or divine treasure like *abhayam*-fearlessness; *sattva-samsuddhih* the cleansing, *jnana*-knowledge; yoga-of linking up; *danam*-charity; *dama*-the controlling the mind; *yajnah* ca-selfless sacrifice, i.e. sacrificing ego, selfishness and material attachments for noble purposes; *arjavam*-simplicity, akrodhah-freedom from anger fearlessness purification of one's existence *apaisunam*-aversion to fault-finding; *daya bhutesu*-compassion toward all living entities; *aloluptvam*-freedom from greed; *mardavam*-gentleness; *hrih*-modesty; *acapalam*-determination; *tejah*-vigor; *ksama*-forgiveness; *dhrtih*-fortitude and so on. These constructs are imperfectly translated here and systematic studies can unravel the not yet examined aspects of human self and its impact on the range of outcomes related to personal and professional life. Bhawuk (2010) explains the method of developing constructs and psychological models drawn from the traditional wisdom.

The scholarly work on Indian Psychology is then a fruitful area for drawing insights that have strong theoretical and practical implications for present day management. Self and identity from Indian perspective (Paranjpe, 2006), convergence of Indian psychology and positive psychology (Salagame, 2014), Indian mindset (Sinha et al. 2010) are few examples of the areas of research in Indian psychology which have strong potential impact on management. Walsh (2001) noted that Buddhism and yoga contain insights for exceptional psychological health and post-conventional transpersonal development.

Theoretical, Practical and Pedagogical Implications at Interpersonal and Group Level

Interpersonal relationship is an important aspect in Indian worldview. In fact, sometimes relationship is valued more than the content of the relationship. Nuances in roles and expectations are attached to varied relations within larger family hence there are specific words to specific relationship like *Chacha* (father's brother), *Tai* (wife of fathers elder brother), *mama* (mother's brother), *bua* (sister of father), *fufa* (husband of father's sister), *Bhabhi* (brother's wife), *sarhaj* (wife of wife's brother) and so on. The place of mother, father, teacher and the guest is considered with reverence in the Indian system.[12]

Three constructs at interpersonal and group level developed in Indian context or drawn from the Indian traditional wisdom. Nurturant task leadership, individualized familial self and spiritual climate are presented here. A nurturant leader "cares for his subordinates, shows

[12] mātr̥devo bhava | pitr̥devo bhava | ācāryadevo bhava | atithidevo bhava |

May your mother be to you a worshiped; may your father be a worshiped to you; may your teacher be a worshiped to you, and so also may a guest be a worshiped to you (Taittiriya Upanishad, Shikshavalli, Anuvaka 11.2).

affection, takes personal interest in their well-being, and above all is committed to their growth" (Sinha, 1984, p. 87). Relationship of understanding, paternal symbol, warmth and interdependence, leading to higher productivity and better growth of both subordinate and the leader are the hallmarks of nurturant task leader and subordinate relationship. Chapter 12 in this handbook on effective organizational leadership in the Indian context elaborates this construct in greater details.

The idea of individualized familial self has emerged in the study of Panda & Gupta (2004) with qualified technocrats in India. The qualified technocrats in India seem to be concerned about their professional growth, while preferring an emotionally intimate hierarchical mode of interactions. The concern for professional growth is the expression of individualized self, whereas preference for 'emotionally intimate hierarchical mode of interactions' are the manifestations of the familial self (1988). The construct of individualized familial self has the potential to explain the 'Indian Self' beyond the categories of individualist and collectivist binary. This construct is elaborated in the Chapter 7 of this book about organizations and business ecosystems in India using business systems framework.

Perceptions of the work environment constitute organizational climate (Rousseau, 1988). The construct of spiritual climate was developed by Pandey et al. (2009) based on the integration of Indian traditional wisdom and contemporary literature on spirituality at workplace. Like most of the other climate research this is also grounded in the Gestalt psychology of Kurt Lewin. Organizational climate is a gestalt—'whole'—that is based on perceived patterns in the specific experiences and behaviors of people in organization. In line with the other works on climate (e.g., innovation climate and climate for inclusion), the concepts of shared perceptions were applied to understand the spiritual climate of work groups. Variables like *Swadharma* and *Lokasangraha* along with authenticity and sense of community form the construct of spiritual climate. The word '*swadharm*' is the combination of two terms: swa and dharma ('swa' means self and 'dharma' derives from the root $\sqrt{}$dhṛ, which means to bear, to support and to uphold). *Swadharma* is the action in accordance with one's nature. It is acting in accordance with one's skills and talents, one's own nature (swabhava) and that which one is responsible for (karma). In the contemporary literature, two constructs capture the essence of *Swadharma*; meaningful work and meditative work. LoksaMgraha in Indian philosophy depicts the self-transcendence aspect in a work climate. Radhakrishnan (1948/2009, p. 141), defines this term as "working for world maintenance". It is conceptualized as the concern for social and natural environment in the spiritual climate construct. Sense of community refers to interconnectedness and interdependence among employees, signified by and operationally defined as collaborative problem solving. Authenticity is a socially situated phenomenon, characterized by genuineness and openness among employees. It is integral to inner life, which is nourished through self-reflection and meditation (Gardner et al., 2005). Pandey and colleagues have found the impact of spiritual climate on learning (Pandey et al., 2016) and innovative work behavior (Pandey et al., 2019). Garg (2017) expanded this construct by adding Karma theory, i.e. putting one's 100 percentage without expecting any fruits for the action and studied its impact on organization citizenship behavior, job satisfaction, etc.

I present three references to convey the ideals of Indian worldview about the interactions with óthers' which can be further developed with conceptual and theoretical elaboration and empirical examination. First example is of '*Samanyadharma*', the general guidelines of interaction with the others. The second example is of '*çhittaprasad*' drawn from the Yoga Sutra of Patanjali and specific kind of response suggested for the person with specific situation. The third example is of notion of óther' in the Indian worldview.

The ideals about interpersonal interactions are the part of general guidelines called Samanyadharma. *Manusmṛti* (10.63) gives a list of five tenets—as *ahiṃsā* (non-injury), *satya* (truth), *asteya* (non-stealing), *indriya-nigraha* (Sense-restraint) and *śauca* (Cleanliness) as the general guidelines for day-to-day interaction. These ideals are common in Ashtang Yoga Sutra in the form of Yama and in Mahabharat.[13] Five

---

[13] Truthfulness, to be free from anger, sharing wealth with others, (samvibhaga) forgiveness, procreation of children from one's wife alone, purity, absence of enmity, straightforwardness and maintaining persons dependent on oneself are the nine rules of the Dharma for persons belonging to all the yarnas (Mahabharata Shantiparva—6–7–8).

Yamas stand for *Ahimsa* (non-violence), *Satya* (truthfulness), *Asteya* (non-stealing), *Aparigraha* (non-hoarding) and *Brahmacharya* (continence in emotional desire including sexual desires). *Yama* are social codes or principles of self-control within social situations. *Yamas* provide a background for a theoretical framework linking experiential practice of Yoga to spirituality and ethics at workplace by harmonizing and deepening social connections according to Corner (2009). She advocates for employing Yoga based practices including Yama and Niyama to provide experiential foundation for building knowledge alongside more positivist ways of knowing. Such an approach is likely to yield novel insights about the relationships between spirituality and ethical behavior at workplace and beyond.

The second example is of Chittaprasad which is drawn from Yoga Sutra. In "The Yoga *Sutras* of *Patanjali*" cultivating '*citta prasadanam*' is considered a task of great importance. *Citta* may be translated as "that which is conscious", "ordinary consciousness" or "the act of mental apprehension"; and *prasadanam* may be translated as "happiness" "filled with grace," "joyfulness". *Yoga Sutra* (Aphorism on Yoga) teach that *Chittaprasadm* is cultivated by practicing *Maitri*—universal friendship, *Karun*-compassion, *Mudita*-happiness for others and *Upeksha*-indifference. For the interpersonal interaction matri, karun, mudita and upeksha are considered as the ideal. The Yoga Sutra of Patanjali says that *Maitri – Karuna – Mudita – Upeksanam – Sukha – Dukha – Punya – Apunya – Visayanam – Bhavanatah – Chitta – Prasadanam* (1.33). For attaining Chittaprasad, the Yoga Sutra prescribe Maitri or cultivation of feelings of amity for happy people, karuna or compassion for miserable, goodwill for virtuous and indifference toward sinful creatures (Saraswati, 2013). Buddhist teaching also describes these four qualities in the same order as metta, karuna, mudita, and upeksha. Brahmavihara ('Brahmn' means the highest, the supreme. 'Vihara' means dwelling, abode) is the term used in for the technique in which one meditates and dwells on these four states of mind (Cullen, 2011). Brahmavihara also referred to as the four cardinal virtues of Buddhism (Pace, 2013). Emphasis on Brahmavihara is on the self as well as others. They are a result of cultivating unconditional love toward both self and others (Jayawardena-Willis et al., 2019). The notion of Karuna is captured to a great extent in the contemporary literature on compassion in organization and management (e.g. George, 2014; Rynes et al., 2012) the other three constructs of *Maitri*, *Mudita* and *Upeksha* can be examined as individual constructs and in combination in terms of their manifestation and implications for management.

The third example most clearly demonstrates the tenet of one supreme reality underling various manifestations. The ideal of Indian worldview recognizes 'no other' and all is the expression of the same underlying consciousness. *yo māṁ paśhyati sarvatra sarvaṁ cha mayi paśhyati tasyāhaṁ na praṇaśhyāmi sa cha me na praṇaśhyati.* For those who see me everywhere and see all things in me, I am never lost, nor are they ever lost to me. (Trans. Radhakrishnan, 2014, p. 204). Similarly Ishopnishad says that *yastu sarvANi bhUtAni AtmanyEvAnupashyati* |*sarva bhUtES cAtmAnaM tato na vijugupsate.* One who perceives in the Atman everything, and in the same way Atman in everything, does not hate.

The relationship with others is *vyavharik* (worldly) truth that is based on the adhyatmik (spiritual) truth of oneness in the Indian worldview. It is noticeable that these thoughts indicate the ontological assumptions different from materialist and dualist perspective and are not logically deducible and cannot be without experiential learning. Studies in these aspects of Indian worldview like these need to present epistemic and ontological assumptions as well, from Indian perspective before examining and presenting these ideas to the wider and global community of management scholars.

Theoretical, Practical and Pedagogical Implications at the Macro Level

The emergence of large business organizations is a modern phenomenon. Though, the earlier human collective systems were in the forms of large empires, universities and spiritual and religious sects and canons of Indian worldview about maintaining harmony in the large human collective system are the likely reflections in reference to these systems.

In the contemporary literature we come across the work of Khandwalla on organization design, public sector management (1973) and corporate turnaround (1992). Organizational Designs for Excellence discussed six different kinds of organizational excellence, namely competitive excellence, institutionalized excellence, rejuvenatory excellence, missionary excellence, versatile excellence, and creative excellence. Chapter 7 by Panda and Gupta in this book on organizations and business ecosystems in India using business systems framework further elaborates the work of Khandwalla on different aspects of organizational excellence and design in India.

In this section we elaborate two examples from Indian worldview having implication at collective or societal level. First example is of the *Sangathan Mantra* of Rig Veda. *Sangathan* means collective system. This example is about collective mind and collective self and its ideals. The second reference is of integral humanism based on the notion and the symbol of *Akhandmandal* the traditional depiction of the relation and place of individual within family, society and larger social and natural environment.

Sangathan mantra is from RigVeda is as follows:

> *san gacchadhvam sam vadadhvam sam vo manamsi janatam/ deva bhagam yatha purve sanjanana upasate// samano mantra: samiti: samani samanam mana: saha cittamesam/ samanam mantramabhi mantraye va: samanena vo havisa juhomi// samani va akuti: samana hrdayani vah/ samanamastu vo mano yatha va: susahasati//*

Meaning, come together! Speak together! Let our minds be all of one accord as the gods of old sat together in harmony to worship. Let our speech be one; united our voices! May our minds be in union with the thoughts of the Wise. Sharing a common purpose; we worship as one. Let our aim be one and single! Let our hearts be joined as one. United be our thoughts. At peace with all, may we be together in harmony.

Unity of mind is emphasized for the collective success at many places in Vedas. The hymn mentioned above is an example. Like '*vyakti*' or individual a collectivity like family, team organization also assumed to have a physical body, emotional aspect called Mann, intellect called Buddhi and Soul. Upadhyay (2016) explained this with the metaphor of a club of forty members. The people constituting is the body. A shared collective will or desire to be together or *Ichha* is its *Man.* The policy, systems and processes to fulfill the resolve is the intellect or *Buddhi* of the club. The mission, purpose or ideal of the group is reflection of the spiritual aspect of the group. A collective system according to Indian worldview will have all these components.

The hymn of the Rigveda mentioned above is a self-invocation to attain the harmony among the members of the collectivity in their man; the emotional aspect, thoughts and speech and that of the purpose. Family like environment helps in building emotional bonds among the members of the collective. Intellect and logic are applied in building the systems and processes of any collective. In the organizational context it is systems and processes and in the context of the nation it is constitution. The mission and purpose of the collective is *Atma* or spiritual aspect of the collective.

The second example is the integral humanism given in the context of the larger society. Upadhyay (2016) invokes the notion of *karma, Yjna, Sanskar* and *Shiksha, Yogakshem* in the interaction of *vyakti* and *samashti.* The *samshti* is the collective form and can be a family, an organization the *sanstha, samaj,* the society; *rastra,* the nation or the *vasudha,* the world. First I will explain the core idea of integral humanism and later I explain its relevance for management in business organizations.

Akhand Mandal the depiction of integral humanism is the representation of the universe. The expanding spiral of the depiction represents the continuous extensions of oneness in existence. The individual expands into a family which further grows into society. Societies integrate themselves with larger entity called nation. The whole humanity is considered as family of nations. This expansion of oneness continues beyond humanity into the whole nature and then ultimately transcends in the *Parameshti*—the universal intelligence. '*Akhand Mandalakar*' represents the interconnected, interrelated and interdependent nature of the universe.

Integral humanism recognizes the spiritual aspect of human self to be as essential as physical, emotional and rational aspects and importance of nurturing all the aspects of self for *vyakti* and samshti, the individual and societal wellbeing. *Vyakti, parivar* and *samshti* are not considered in struggle but conceived as being integral in their existence Dharma being the governing principle of their interaction. Aiming to think beyond class struggle the essence of communism and competition among the individual, the essence of capitalism, the integral humanism sees the relation between *vyakti* and *samshti* and interaction within them to be of interdependence, cooperation and concord. Integral humanism is characterized by the recognition of diversity as the most natural process and the expression of life and the gaze towards the oneness underneath all kinds of diversity. Unity and not equality is considered to be the ideal for the social life where in *Yjna* and *Yogakshem* are the mutual offerings of *vyakti* and *samshti* to each other for achieving the objective of wellbeing and harmony. Not merely achieving equality in the economic and social sense but experience of the oneness is considered to be the highest goal of human life. Its perspective is all comprehensive and it aims at the wellbeing for all and not maximum good for maximum number of people or survival of the fittest (Upadhyay, 2016).

A member learns and does *Karma* in a collective. The first manifestation of collective in *vyakti* life or the interaction of *vyakti* and *samshti* is *Shiksha*, i.e. education and socialization. The *karma* of *vyakti* is according to the *Shiksha*. In return of *Vyakti's* karma the collective system takes care of his or her needs called *Yoga Kshem*. Indian worldview says that we can never pay back for anyone's *karma* in monetary form. For example, it is impossible to pay back in the monetary terms for the education one receives from teachers, or to the coach who teaches sports and the recipient becomes a champion or the doctor who saves one's life with a right treatment. In the ancient Indian culture, education or medicine were offered as Sewa and charging money in return of these was considered inauspicious. They are priceless and hence performed in the form of *Sewa* i.e. duty toward the society. Man cannot live without karma. In response to *karma*, the samashti—the collective system needs to offer the *YogaKshema*. The Sanskrit word "*Yogakshema*", means wellbeing of the lives on earth and taking care of in all ways. The term *Yogakshem* was used by Chanakya to elaborate the disposition of state toward its subject. His explanation is very similar to the idea of the welfare state. According to Kautilya, attainment of good governance entails that the objectives of the state are fulfilled and realized. The three important internal issues for the ruler to attend to are: *Raksha*, or protection of life and liberty within the state; *Palana*, or law and justice; and *Yogakshema*, or welfare of the people. Yoga (addition to or furtherance of, and not the depletion of, all resources) and *Kshema* (proper utilization of resources) in all human pursuits. Material prosperity and spiritual merit both were considered as the goal of the state toward its subject. Upadhyay (2016) also used this term in the same way and mentioned that *Yogakshem* is the ideal disposition of any collective human system; *samshti* toward the *vyasti*. Collective gives for consumption and for *Yogakshem* and that is not supposed to be consumed fully. *Vyakti* has to perform *Yajna*, consume after offering to other saying *Edam Na Mamah*, it is not mine and the cycle of interactions between man and nature and society continues. For a healthy society, *Shikha*, *Yogakshem*, *Yjna* and *Karma* all four need to be intense and practiced. The larger system or social system suffers if anyone of the four is weakened.

Figure 2.1 depicts the major notions of Indian wisdom and its implications at individual, interactional and organizational level of management.

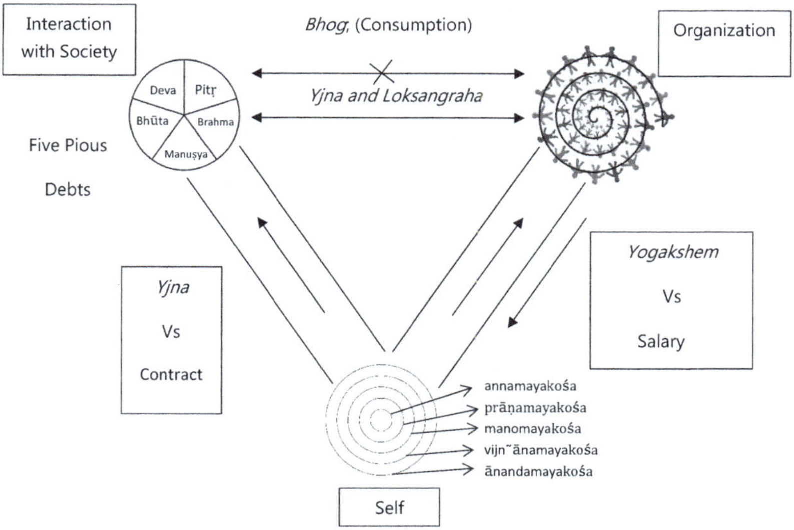

Fig. 2.1 Indian wisdom and its implications at individual, interactional and organizational level of management

Exemple Case Studies

In the concluding section, I present examples of two successful Indian organizations of different size operating in diverse fields which explicitly embrace the Indian worldview above analyzed and is reflected in their values and practices. These organizations are Piramal Group and Excel industries.

The Piramal Group founded in 1871 and currently valued at US$ 10bn, is a global business conglomerate with diverse interests in Pharma, Financial Services, Healthcare Information Management, Real Estate and Glass Packaging. The Group has offices in over 30 countries and a global brand presence in more than 100 markets. The leaders of this group, Mr. Ajay Piramal and Anand Piramal are conferred with many awards and recognition by professional bodies and forums like Indo American Chamber of Commerce, Great Place to Work Institute, All India Management Association and so on. In 2008, the group was conferred with the Spirit at Work award by Tyson Centre of Faith and Religion at Work. A social entrepreneurial initiative Piramal Sarvajal is also recognized and awarded as an impactful social innovation by the professional bodies like World Intellectual Property Organization, Nominate Trust and at the forums like Fast Company, USA and so on.

The Piramal brand is represented by the *Gyan Mudra*, the posture of hand representing the knowledge and wisdom in Yogic tradition and in *Natya Shastra* of sage Bharat. Yoga tradition we know is about three thousand years old and *Natya Shastra* or treatise on drama was composed sometime in third century AD. It is explained on the group website that each finger represents one of the five elements (Air, Water, Earth, Fire and Sky). The logo symbolizes the harmony of these elements with each other and the mudra or posture reflects the aspiration to form a circle of perfection, peace and happiness.

The purpose of the group i.e. 'Doing well by doing good' is based on the tenets that economic wealth creation and the spiritual pursuits like service and care for all can be integrated in business. During the field visit and interview with the author, Anand Piramal, the son of the Chairman of the Board and the member of the board and management team explained that the core values of knowledge, action, care and impact of the group are drawn from the major paths of spiritual awakening explained in BhagwadGita, i.e. *Jnan Yoga*—the path of knowledge, *Karma Yoga*—the path of action and *Bhakti Yoga*—the path of devotion.

This worldview and values are perpetuated and inculcated throughout the organization in the Piramal Group. In order to sensitize and perpetuate the values of knowledge, action, care and impact the vice chairman of the group Dr Swati Piramal traveled length and breadth of the country, visited dozen of factories and office sites of the group. She conducted workshops and asked the employees to collect and share the stories related to these values. The best stories were compiled in the form of a book and shared with a large number of internal and external customers. The performance management system was modified and assessment on these values in the 360 degree format was included in the appraisal system.

The management and the owner family picked up 18 verses of Bhagwad Gita which have direct implication on management. These include setting up the highest standard, having compassion for all, dealing with duality (pleasure and pain, joy and sorrow), rising above the shackles of sin, having faith, action without worrying about the fruits of action, fighting against injustice etc. The corporate office published a book entitled "The Light has come to me" about these ideas. The book lists real life anecdotes which illustrate how the company dealt with issues using these 18 edicts. To convey the message of this philosophy the organization used sound, light and dance in a performance for the whole company. Piramal Enterprises Limited is one of the highest CSR spender in India driven by their desire to uplift the impoverished and unlock India's socio-economic potential. The Piramal Foundation was singled out as the Best Corporate Foundation of 2017 on the World CSR Day (Bhatnagar et al., 2019). These and many other evidences suggest that ideal of the Indian worldview about integrating spirituality in day-to-day action and taking care of people as ones' family are the ideal of this organization and illustrated by the people at the top.

The second caselet is of Excel Industries Limited (EIL) is one of the first agricultural chemical company in India started in 1941 and currently valued at \$114mn. Excel Industries is India's leading company in agro chemical intermediates and phosphorous derivatives. It is a premier manufacturer of specialty Polymer Additives and high quality Veterinary APIs and an emerging company in pharmaceutical intermediates industry. Excel Industries is a pioneer in indigenous chemical technology and sustainable waste management (Vaidyanathan et al., 1983; Shroff, 1993). Recognition to the Chairman of the Excel comes with awards by the professional bodies like Indian Chamber of Commerce (ICC), Indian Environmental Association (IEA), and Indian Chemical Council. EIL identifies with innovation, in-house research and development, cost-efficiency, quality, environmental-friendliness ethos and ethics as its core competencies. Dynamics, compassion, expertise, tradition and employees' loyalty are the core values of EIL. The founder and his family have been active members of Ramkrishna Mission. Ramkrishna Mission was established by Swami Vivekanand on the ideals of Raj Yoga[14] and service to the needy people in society. The industry recognizes EIL as an organization which has achieved value based growth.

Over the past seven decades, innovation and sustainable business practices have formed the cornerstone of growth at EIL. Going beyond the call of mandatory requirement about Corporate Social Responsibility, EIL has generously invested toward environment compliant practices such as installing state-of-the-art effluent treatment plant and developing innovative solutions in the areas of waste management. In the last decade, this group has been instrumental in rejuvenation of a river in arid area of Kuchh in western part of India and set up skill development center for the local community. It is named after Swami Vivekanand and known as Sri Vivekanand Research and Training Institute[15] http://www.vrti.org/history.

This all has its roots in the strong values, heritage and ideals of the leaders. The purpose of business at Excel is to add value and happiness. The leaders lead by example and bear all the values, thus promoting responsible behavior throughout their organization (Suriyaprakash, 2016). Chairman (Emeritus) and promotor K. C. Shroff

[14] Raj Yoga as explained by Vivekananda is an expression of Ashtang Yoga of Patanjali's Yoga Sutras. Raja Yoga mainly consists of components of Hath Yoga, Pranayam and Dhyan.

[15] http://www.vrti.org.

posits that at the company, service is the motivation and profit a by-product of the services provided. His successors continue to apply and utilize his philosophy and practices with as much sincerity, passion and devotion. At EIL, we see the example of deeply committed leaders who believe in spirituality, thus tapping into a profound and sustainable source of commitment.

The *Loksangraha* is the guiding principles of business decisions at EIL. According to the ideal of *Loksangraha*, the most important question that EIL asks itself is: what will be the impact of my action or inaction on the society? *Loksangraha* requires transcendence of egocentric motives to existential motive by seeing the self as part of everything. *Loksangraha* is proving to be the catalytic process in EIL to achieve sustainability goals.

Conclusion

The predominant management narrative somehow conveys to management students that wellbeing depends on wealth which equals to monetary wealth (Kipka & Painter-Morland, 2014). Organization centric worldview dominates the human-centered worldview (Giacalone & Thompson, 2006). The self-centered careerism is implicitly supported by most contemporary management education (Schoemaker, 2008). Whereas Indian worldview holds a philosophical system and popularly held concepts to convey alternative ideas in management that *arth*—the material possession and *kama* the consumption are to be governed by *Dharma*, the dynamic ethico-moral perspective. The *integral humanistic* view of organization can help in embracing more humanistic and society centric view of business. *Swadharm* and *Lokasangrah* and approaching the work as a *Karm Yoga* can be practical alternative to the self-centered careerism.

Democracy and capitalism are the defining features of the Indian society and a large number of nations across the world. But both market economy and democracy can be morphed by greed for money and power. Democracy and capitalism can result in wellbeing and welfare for all only if restrained by nobler concerns and effective regulatory institutions (Khandwalla, 2019). Indian worldview inspired by the vision of integral humanism if translated into institutional structures can result into more responsible management in the current times. For example, corporate and society interface can be conceived in more holistic and integrative terms based on the notion of *Akhandmandalakar*. Notion of *Yjna, Sewa* and *Yogakshem* can help in holistically redefining the relation between employee, organization and their role in larger social and natural environment. Notions like these can help in redefining the business and society interface, objective of business beyond monetary wealth creation, employee employer relationship beyond the transaction and contract.

Worldview is an important yet less examined aspect of management theories and practices. Indian worldview is about recognizing oneness underlying varied manifestations of nature and integral perspective of spiritual, family and materialist pursuits of life. This perspective is different from the heroism, positivism, rationalism which are the predominant philosophical paradigm in management which emphasize on the individualism and economic performance. Moving beyond cognition and the emphasis on the experiential knowledge is held by the traditional wisdom traditions of Yoga, mindfulness and Ayurveda which are the hallmarks of the Indian worldview.

I hope that existing management philosophy, theories and approaches are critiqued in light of the Indian worldview and their utility, potential and limitations are compared and discussed in Indian and western cultures and organizations. I also hope that scholars attempt to develop new concepts and theories arising out of Indian worldview and experiential and contemplative practices of Indian tradition. Case studies are fertile grounds for developing new concepts and constructs. Majority of business organizations in India are family owned. Cultural values, social norms, religious practices, spiritual quest and nurturance are generally the binding forces of a family in India. Hence, the family business research and deciphering the Indian worldview in the functioning of family business can have significant theoretical and practical implications for management. Conceptual and theoretical research, empirical research, comparative research and grounded research all are required to unravel the 'Indian management' from the Indian worldview.

References

Bhatnagar, N., Sharma, P., & Ramachandran, K. (2019). Spirituality and corporate philanthropy in Indian family firms: An exploratory study. *Journal of Business Ethics, 163*(4), 715–728.

Bhave, V. (1946). Sthitaprajña Darśana (12th ed.). Vardha: Parmdham Publications.

Bhawuk, D. P. (2010). Methodology for building psychological models from scriptures: Contributions of Indian psychology to indigenous and universal psychologies. *Psychology and Developing Societies, 22*(1), 49–93.

Bhawuk, D. P. (2011). *Spirituality and Indian psychology: Lessons from the Bhagavad-Gita*. Springer Science & Business Media.

Bosse, D. A., & Phillips, R. A. (2016). Agency theory and bounded self-interest. *Academy of Management Review, 41*(2), 276–297.

Büssing, A., Michalsen, A., Khalsa, S. B. S., Telles, S., & Sherman, K. J. (2012). Effects of yoga on mental and physical health: A short summary of reviews. *Evidence-Based Complementary and Alternative Medicine*, *2012*, 1–7.

Callon, M. (1998). Introduction: The embeddedness of economic markets in economics. In M. Callon (Ed.), *The laws of the markets* (pp. 1–57). Blackwell.

Chakraborty, S. K. (1995). Wisdom leadership: Leading self by the SELF. *Journal of Human Values, 1*(2), 205–220.

Chakraborty, S. K., & Chakraborty, D. (2004). The transformed leader and spiritual psychology: A few insights. *Journal of Organizational Change Management, 17*(2), 194–210.

Cobern, W. W. (1991). *World view theory and science education research* (p. 14).

Corner, P. D. (2009). Workplace spirituality and business ethics: Insights from an eastern spiritual tradition. *Journal of Business Ethics, 85*(3), 377–389.

Cullen, M. (2011). Mindfulness-based interventions: An emerging phenomenon. *Mindfulness, 2*(3), 186–193.

Dagar, C. & Pandey, A. (2020). Well-being at workplace: A perspective from traditions of yoga and Ayurveda. In *The Palgrave handbook of workplace well-being* (pp. 1–28). Springer.

Dasgupta, S. (1992). *A history of Indian philosophy*. Motilal Banarsidass Publishers Private Limited.

Gardner, W. L., Avolio, B. J., Luthans, F., May, D. R., & Walumbwa, F. (2005). "Can you see the real me?" A selfbased model of authentic leader and follower development. *The leadership quarterly, 16*(3), 343–372.

Garg, N. (2017). Workplace spirituality and employee well-being: An empirical exploration. *Journal of Human Values, 23*(2), 129–147.

George, J. M. (2014). Compassion and capitalism: Implications for organizational studies. *Journal of Management, 40*(1), 5–15.

Gergen, K. J. (1973). Social psychology as history. *Journal of Personality and Social Psychology, 26*(2), 309.

Ghoshal, S. (2005). Bad management theories are destroying good management practices. *Academy of Management Learning & Education, 4*(1), 75–91.

Ghoshal, S., & Moran, P. (1996). Bad for practice: A critique of the transaction cost theory. *A Cademy of Management Review, 21*(1), 13–47.

Giacalone, R. A., & Thompson, K. R. (2006). Business ethics and social responsibility education: Shifting the worldview. *Academy of Management Learning & Education, 5*(3), 266–277.

Hedlund-de Witt, A. (2012). Exploring worldviews and their relationships to sustainable lifestyles: Towards a new conceptual and methodological approach. *Ecological Economics, 84*, 74–83.

Hedlund-de Witt, A., De Boer, J., & Boersema, J. J. (2014). Exploring inner and outer worlds: A quantitative study of worldviews, environmental attitudes, and sustainable lifestyles. *Journal of Environmental Psychology, 37*, 40–54.

Husain, S. A. (2018). *The national culture of India*. National Book Trust.

Jayawardena-Willis, T. S., Pio, E., & McGhee, P. (2019). The divine states (brahmaviharas) in managerial ethical decision-making in organisations in Sri Lanka: An interpretative phenomenological analysis. *Journal of Business Ethics, 168*(1), 151–171.

Joullié, J. E. (2016). The philosophical foundations of management thought. *Academy of Management Learning & Education, 15*(1), 157–179.

Ketokivi, M., Mantere, S., & Cornelissen, J. (2017). Reasoning by analogy and the progress of theory. *Academy of Management Review, 42*(4), 637–658.

Khandwalla, P. N. (1973). Viable and effective organizational designs of firms. *Academy of Management Journal, 16*(3), 481–495.

Khandwalla, P. (1992). *Organizational designs for excellence*. Tata McGraw-Hill.

Khandwalla, P. (2019). *Fast forward toward civilizational greatness: Agenda for India*. Academy of Human Resources Development.

Kipka, C., & Painter-Morland, M. (2014). The experience of learning: Approaches to sustainability and ethics education. *Journal of Management Development, 33*(6), https://doi.org/10.1108/JMD-05-2014-0043.

Kluckhohn, F. R., & Strodtbeck, F. L. (1961/1973). Variations in value orientations. Row, Peterson.

Koltko-Rivera, M. E. (2000). *The Worldview Assessment Instrument (WAI): The development and preliminary validation of an instrument to assess world view components relevant to counseling and psychotherapy*. New York University.

Koltko-Rivera, M. E. (2004). The psychology of worldviews. *Review of General Psychology, 8*(1), 3–58.

Koltko-Rivera, M. E. (2006). Rediscovering the later version of Maslow's hierarchy of needs: Self-transcendence and opportunities for theory, research, and unification. *Review of General Psychology, 10*(4), 302–317.

Laurie, N., & Cherry, C. (2001). Wanted: Philosophy of management. *Philosophy of Management, 1*(1), 3–12.

Maddison, A. (2003). *Development centre studies the world economy historical statistics: Historical statistics*. OECD Publishing.

Maddison, A. (2007). *The world economy volume 1: A millennial perspective volume 2: Historical statistics*. Academic Foundation.

Marti, E., & Gond, J. P. (2018). When do theories become self-fulfilling? Exploring the boundary conditions of performativity. *Academy of Management Review, 43*(3), 487–508.

Mckiernan, P., & Tsui, A. S. (2019). Responsible management research: A senior scholar legacy in doctoral education. *Academy of Management Learning & Education, 18*(2), 310–313.

Mukherjee, P. K., & Wahile, A. (2006). Integrated approaches towards drug development from Ayurveda and other Indian system of medicines. *Journal of Ethanopharmacol, 103*, 25–35.

Mulla, Z. R., & Krishnan, V. R. (2008). Karma-Yoga, the Indian work ideal, and its relationship with empathy. *Psychology and Developing Societies, 20*(1), 27–49.

Mulla, Z. R., & Krishnan, V. R. (2009). Do Karma-Yogis make better leaders? Exploring the relationship between the leader's Karma-Yoga and transformational leadership. *Journal of Human Values, 15*(2), 167–183.

Mulla, Z. R., & Krishnan, V. R. (2012). Transformational leadership and Karma-Yoga: Enhancing followers' duty-orientation and indifference to rewards. *Psychology and Developing Societies, 24*(1), 85–117.

Mulla, Z. R., & Krishnan, V. R. (2014). Karma-yoga: The Indian model of moral development. *Journal of Business Ethics, 123*(2), 339–351.

Nakamura, H. (1964). *Ways of thinking of eastern peoples: India-China-Tibet-Japan* (pp. 407–530). East-West Center Press, Honolulu and The University Press of Hawaii.

Pace, S. (2013). Does religion affect the materialism of consumers? An empirical investigation of Buddhist ethics and the resistance of the self. *Journal of Business Ethics, 112*(1), 25–46.
Panda, A., & Gupta, R. K. (2004). Mapping cultural diversity within India: A meta-analysis of some recent studies. *Global Business Review, 5*(1), 27–49.
Pandey, A., Gupta, R. K., & Arora, A. P. (2009). Spiritual climate of business organizations and its impact on customers' experience. *Journal of Business Ethics, 88*, 313–332.
Pandey, A., Gupta, R. K., & Gupta, V. (2019). Spirituality and innovative behavior in teams: Examining the mediating role of team learning. *IIMB Management Review, 31*(2), 116–126.
Pandey, A., Gupta, R. K., & Kumar, P. (2016). Spiritual climate and its impact on learning in teams in business organizations. *Global Business Review, 17*(3 Suppl.), 159S–172S.
Paranjpe, A. C. (1998). *Self and identity in modern psychology and Indian thought*. Plenum.
Paranjpe, A. C. (2006). *Self and identity in modern psychology and Indian thought*. Springer Science & Business Media.
Radhakrishnan, S. (1927/2009). *The Hindu view of life*. Noida: HarperCollins Publishers.
Radhakrishnan, S. (1948/2009). *The Bhagavadgita: With an introductory essay, Sanskrit text [transliterated] English translation, and notes*. HarperCollins.
Radhakrishnan, S. (1953/2016). *The principal Upaniṣadas*. Noida: HarperCollins Publishers.
Rousseau, D. M. (1988). *The construction of climate in organizational research.*
Rynes, S. L., Bartunek, J. M., Dutton, J. E., & Margolis, J. D. (2012). Care and compassion through an organizational lens: Opening up new possibilities. *Academy of Management Review, 37*(4), 503–523.
Salagame, K. K. (2014). Positive psychology and Indian psychology: Birds of the same feather. *Psychological Studies, 59*(2), 116–118.
Saraswati, S. (2013). *Four chapters on freedom: Commentary on the yoga sutras of Patanjali* (2nd ed.). Yoga Publications Trust.
Schoemaker, P. J. (2008). The future challenges of business: Rethinking management education. *California Management Review, 50*(3), 119–139.
Sengupta, P. (2012). Health impacts of yoga and pranayama: A state-of-the-art review. *International Journal of Preventive Medicine, 3*(7), 444.
Shroff, K. C. (1993). *Experiences in regenerative industrial development*. Excel Industries, Bombay.

Sinha, J. B. (1984). A model of effective leadership styles in India. *International Studies of Management & Organization, 14*(2–3), 86–98.

Sinha, J. B., Singh, S., Gupta, P., Srivastava, K. B., Sinha, R. B. N., Srivastava, S., ... & Pandey, A. (2010). An exploration of the Indian mindset. *Psychological Studies, 55*(1), 3–17.

Suriyaprakash, C. (2016). Spiritual-based leadership from the perspective of the Bhagavad Gita. In M. Chatterji & L. Zsolnai (Eds.), *Ethical leadership.* Palgrave Macmillan.

Travis, F., & Pearson, C. (2000). Pure consciousness: Distinct phenomenological and physiological correlates of "consciousness itself." *International Journal of Neuroscience, 100*(1–4), 77–89.

Upadhyay, D. (2016). *Integral humanism: An analysis of some basic elements.* Prabhat Prakashan.

Vaidyanathan, S., Kavadia, K. M., Rao, M. G., Basu, S., & Mahajan, S. P. (1983). Removal of phenol using water hyacinth in a continuous unit. *International Journal of Environmental Studies, 21*(2), 183–191.

Walsh, R. (2001). Shamanic experiences: A developmental analysis. *Journal of Humanistic Psychology, 41*(3), 31–52.

3

Indian Management: Constructs, Models, and Theories

Dharm P. S. Bhawuk

We often start with the western literature when we think of any idea not only in psychology and management but also in other areas of social sciences. There is some merit to this approach, considering that these

Harvard-Kyoto protocol for transliteration for *devanagarI* is used for all *saMskRit* and *hindI* words and names, and the first letters of names are not capitalized. All non-English words are italicized.

अ a आ A इ i ई I उ u ऊ U ए e ऐ ai ओ o औ au ऋ R ॠ RR ऌ lR ॡ lRR अं M अः H क ka ख kha ग ga घ kha ङ Ga च ca छ cha ज ja झ jha ञ Ja ट Ta ठ Tha ड Da ढ Dha ण Na त ta थ tha द da ध dha न na प pa फ pha ब ba भ bha म ma य ya र ra ल la व va श za ष Sa स sa ह ha क्ष kSa त्र tra ज्ञ jJa श्र

D. P. S. Bhawuk (✉)
Shidler College of Business,
University of Hawai'i at Mānoa, Honolulu, HI, USA
e-mail: bhawuk@hawaii.edu

© The Author(s), under exclusive license to Springer Nature Switzerland AG 2022

A. Pandey et al. (eds.), *Indigenous Indian Management*, Palgrave Studies in Indian Management,
https://doi.org/10.1007/978-3-030-87906-8_3

areas of research have been dominated by western researchers. However, this approach does not allow the indigenous ideas to surface, and often leads to epistemic violence (Spivak, 1998; Held, 2020), which is perpetuated by either well-meaning uninformed researchers or those who believe in the cultural superiority of the West (Bhawuk, 2020a). To encourage a dialogue between cultures we need to develop indigenous ideas, models, and theories (Bhawuk, 2011, 2020a). Ignoring indigenous ideas or over emphasizing western knowledge systems often leads to a disconnect between the scientific world or the world of research, and the life-world or the phenomenon world where culture shapes human endeavor. In this chapter, an effort is made to review indigenous Indian constructs that could enrich organizational research and management literature.

An advantage of starting with Indian constructs is that often we have positive constructs like *adhyAtma* (Bhawuk, 2019a, b), *lajjA* (Bhawuk, 2017, 2019c, 2021, in press a), *lokasaMgraha* (Bhawuk, 2019d), *zraddhA* (Bhawuk, 2020b), *tapas* (Bhawuk, 2021, in press a), and so forth rather than the negative constructs like anxiety, depression, shame, guilt, aggression, absenteeism that come from the deficit theories era and crowd the western psychological literature.[1] When we

[1] Industrial and organizational psychology and organizational behavior are the two disciplines that address issues pertaining to individuals, which is referred to as management of people. An analysis of the *APA Handbook of Industrial and Organizational Psychology* (Zedec, 2010) shows that of the 64 chapters in the three volumes, only eight chapters have a positive focus: Creativity, Flexible Work Schedules, Organizational Citizenship Behavior, Training and Employee Development for Improved Performance, Mentoring, Executive Coaching, and Proactive Work Behavior: Forward-Thinking and Change-Oriented Action in Organizations. There are five chapters that pertain to negative topics: Conflict at Work, Managerial Derailment, Workplace Aggression and Violence, Sexual Harassment, and Organizational Downsizing. The negative topic of stress is combined with the positive construct of well-being to downplay stress in organizations. Similarly, other potential negative issues are presented as neutral topics: Work Matters: Job Design in Classic and Contemporary Perspectives (dehumanizing of work in the factory is glossed over), Workplace Safety and Accidents: An Industrial and Organizational Psychology Perspective (accidents are downplayed under safety, see Business Week that covered flagrant disregard to worker safety in the USA). Similarly, six negative topics are presented as neutral topics: Disability and Employment: New Directions for Industrial and Organizational Psychology (disability is often created by organizations through repetitive works), Nonstandard Workers: Work Arrangements and Outcomes (labels like nonstandard workers hides how organizations treat people who are on the fringes of the society), Work Team Diversity (often neglects the issues of diverse workforces and paints a positive picture of how organizations celebrate diversity), Organizational Exit (how employees are terminated unfairly is glossed over). Also, topics like leadership, motivation, and team building are presented as positive constructs and the negative issues like autocratic

start with the western literature, it is not only difficult to discover positive constructs like *hrI* or *lajjA*, but also harder to see them as positive constructs. Therefore, it is important to start with Indian constructs. To illustrate this, some Indian constructs, models, and theories are reviewed in this paper. It is hoped that the paper will show the need for developing indigenous constructs that are useful in the cultural milieu of India.

Indian constructs and practices are primarily positive ideas. They allow us to bypass the negative literature completely, leaving behind western deficit-theories. Thus, the second theme of the chapter is to review Indian concepts that contribute to positive psychological research. In what follows, the Indian concept of self, and constructs like *adhyAtma* or Spirituality, *zraddhA*, *tapas lajjA*, *prema*, and *lokasaMgraha* are reviewed. An Indian theory of creativity is also reviewed to illustrate how indigenous Indian theories could contribute to global knowledge systems. The chapter is concluded with a discussion of future research directions and implications for global psychology and management.

Indian Concept of Self

What is interesting is that in the Indian worldview on the concept of self itself is a positive construct, which allows us to see the self in the universe and the universe in the self (*IzopaniSad*, verses 6 and 7[2]). Such a perspective is not only missing in the Western literature, but is also unthinkable because of differences in the two worldviews. Indian concept

managers, managers who use cane rather than carrot, and negative aspects of working in teams that are cliques are glossed over. Of the 64 chapters, 43 chapters are couched as neutral topics that refer to management functions like performance appraisal, compensation, selection, and so forth. The handbook chapters support the observation that researchers and practitioners in the fields of management, industrial organizational psychology, and human resource management are known to have adopted a pro-management approach, which is reflected in the aggressive deunionization (Lawler, 1990, 1994) of the workplace globally sacrificing workplace democracy and dehumanization of work in not only manufacturing but service industry also (see Hochschild's work on emotional labor, 1983).

[2] Verse 6: *yastu sarvANi bhUtAnyAtmanyevAnupazyati, sarvabhUteSu cAtmAnaM tato na vbjugupsate*. But that person who sees all the beings in the self and the self in all the beings, does not abhor anybody. Verse 7: *Yasmin sarvANi bhUtAnyAtmaivAbhUd vijAnataH, tatra ko mohar kaH zoka ekatvamanupazyataH*. In the state in which all beings become the self itself, seeing union of all, what attachment or sorrow would the knowing person experience?

of self allows us to sidestep the deficit approach that western psychology has adopted, which has also been criticized in the literature on positive psychology. The Indian concept of self is multilayered and captures the physical, psychological, metaphysical, and social elements. In the Indian worldview, one is perfect to begin with, and there is no need to acquire anything. This eliminates the deficit theory of self that has dominated Western psychology and management. This should not be interpreted as denial of the material world since Indians are guided to pursue *dharma* (duty), *artha* (wealth), *kAma* (desire), and *mokSa* (emancipation) (see also Pandey, 2021). The Indian concept of self and four-fold pursuits of life are briefly presented below to facilitate understanding how the Indian concept of self is positive, and therefore, conducive to positive psychological and organizational research.

The Indian concept of self consists of gross and subtle elements, which can be further categorized as social, physical, psychological, and metaphysical selves (Bhawuk, 2011). More specifically, in the Indian worldview there is social self that is ever expanding by additions of various social roles and attributes. Though it is subtle, it has concrete attributes and also has psychological characteristics. Physical self and sense organs are the grossest. The internal self that consists of *ahaGkAra*, *manas*, and *buddhi*, is also called *antaHkaraNa*[3] or the internal organ or agent. Beyond the physical and psychological constructs is *Atman*, which is the subtlest (Bhawuk, 2011). This conceptualization of self is captured schematically in Fig. 3.1.

There is general agreement that the metaphysical self, *Atman,* is the real self. This metaphysical self is embodied in a biological or physical self, and situated, right at birth, in a social structure as a result of past *karma.* The importance of the metaphysical self is reflected in the belief

[3] See Bhawuk (2011), Chapter 4, for a definition and discussion of *manas*, *buddhi*, *ahaGkAra*, and *antaHkaraNa*. The closest translation of *ahaGkAra* would be ego, which comes at the cost of much loss of meaning. People often use mind for *manas*, which is simply wrong, since *manas* is the locus of cognition, affect and behavior, whereas mind is only cognitive. And *buddhi* is closest to the super-ego in Freudian parlance, but without ego, which makes the similarity rather superficial. And *antaHkaraNa* is the composite internal organ or agent combining *manas*, *buddhi*, and *ahaGkAra* according to *sAGkhya darzana*. However, *Adizankara* also includes *citta* in the definition of *antaHkaraNa* (see Bhawuk, 2014 for a discussion of *citta*).

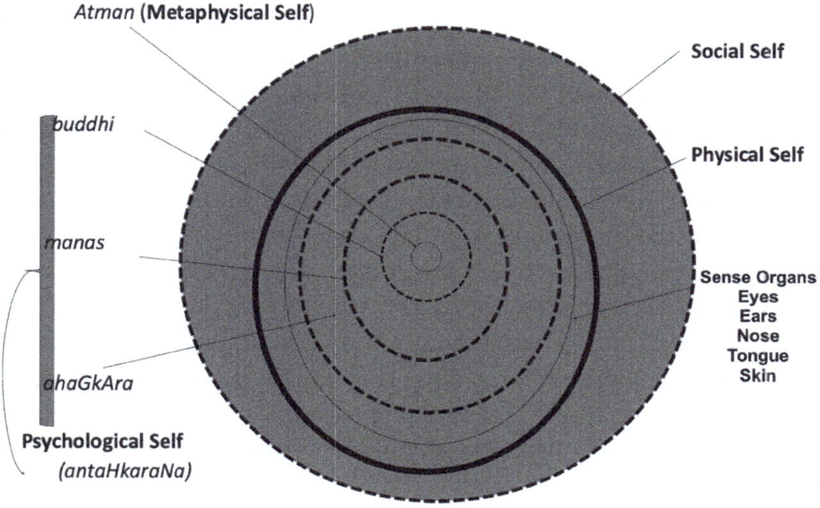

Fig. 3.1 Indian Concept of Self

that of all the living beings, human beings are the only ones that can pursue *mokSa* (or liberation), enlightenment, *jJAna* (or knowledge), or self-realization, which is presented as the highest pursuit of human life. Most Indians, including Hindus, Buddhists, Jains, Sikhs and people of many other religious groups believe that they go through many life forms on their way to ultimatum liberation, and the pursuit of self-realization is a common part of Indian identity (see Paranjpe, 1975, 1984, 1998; Rao et al., 2008).

In the traditional Indian worldview, people were assigned social roles according to their phase of life. The first phase was called the *bramhacarya Azrama* in which people got education and learned life skills. In this phase, the primary focus was on achievement of skills, and traditionally one lived with a *guru* in his *Azrama* and led a frugal life. The five characteristics of students according to *nitizlokas* that are often cited in daily conversations are as follows: students should be persistent like a crow and make effort to achieve their learning goals, be single-minded like a heron focused on catching a fish, sleep lightly like a dog, eat lightly, and live away from home. *cANakya,* an ancient Indian scholar of the third-century BCE, also had some guidelines for students. He suggested that happiness and comfort do not go hand in hand with learning, and so those who want to learn should be willing to forego comfort and happiness. He also stated that one who is attached to home (i.e., cannot leave home) cannot learn, so students have to be ready to go away from home to find a teacher. He also listed the following eight "don'ts" for students: desire, anger, greed, taste, finery or paying attention to how one looks, pleasure or entertainment (e.g., song, dance, show, spectacle, and so forth), too much sleep, and enjoying anything excessively or immoderately. Indian boarding schools emulate the British system, however, they are contemporary versions of *gurukula*, and culturally, people are comfortable sending their children away from home for education starting as early as elementary school. In 1901, Rabindranath Tagore started a Brahmacharyaashrama in Shantiniketan following the spirit of *gurukula*, which grew to become Visva Bharati, a college, in 1921, and a university in 1951.

Upon completion of education at the age of twenty-five, traditionally people entered the *gRhastha Azrama* or the second phase of life in which they became householders and led a married life raising children. In this phase of life the focus was on family and community responsibilities. One lived to find meaning in life by pursuing *dharma* (duty), *artha* (money), *kAma* (pleasure), and *mokSa* (liberation), noted above. In this stage of life money and pleasure were allowed,[4] though in moderation, and were to be guided by *dharma* or duty. This stage of life was clearly a preparation for the next stage, rather than a phase of unbridled excesses of "do what you like." *dharma* was always to be used to

[4] *bhagavadgItA* Verse 7.11: *balaM balavatAM cAhaM kAmarAgavivarjitaM, dharmAviruddho bhUteSu kAmo'smi bharatarSabha.* I am also the strength of the strong who are without desire and attachment. I am the desire in all beings, which is not against the *dharma*. In this verse, first *kRSNa* tells *arjuna* that he (*kRSNa* himself) is strength of those who are devoid of desire and attachment, which speaks against having desires or attachment to anything. Strength lies in being without desire and attachment alludes to *niSkAma karma*, or performing actions without desiring the outcomes of the actions, which is the basic tenet of the *bhagavadgItA*. *niSkAma karma* is always for *lokasaMgraha* or common good, and, therefore, without craving for any outcome. Then he further explains that he is *kAma* or desire that is consistent with *dharma*. This indicates that desire or pleasure is to be guided by *dharma*. Thus, the guiding principle for leading one's life as a *gRhastha* or householder is to practice *niSkAma karma* and to follow the *dharma*.

guide behavior, and one was never to lose sight of *mokSa* or liberation. In *gRhastha Azrama* while pursuing the four *puruSArthas*, people are socialized to strive to pay three debts (*Rgveda*, 8.32.16; 6.61.1; *taittiriya saMhitA*, 6.3.10.5), *deva-RNa*, *pitR-RNa*, and R*Si-RNa*. To repay *deva-RNa*, a householder engages in various activities of prayers (*yajJas* or Vedic sacrifices) and through them makes progress toward *mokSa*. To repay the debts to the *RS*i, the householder studies texts like the *Bhagavad-Gita*, the *upaniSads*, *viSNUsahasranAma*, and so forth, which is called *svAdhyAya*, and is a practice that directs one toward *mokSa*. RSi-RNa is also paid by performing *tapas* or austerities, which again directs one to *mokSa*. To pay the debt to the *pitR*, the householder engages in procreation and also makes offerings as *zrAddha* (for a discussion of *RNa* see Pandey, 2021; see also Pandey & Navare, 2018). Also, enjoying anything excessively or immoderately, as noted in *cANakya*'s teachings, is not an Indian cultural value. The first two stages of life are still accepted by Indians, and people refer to themselves as *gRhasthas* or householders and remind their children that they need to live a life of moderation as students for they are in the *bramhacArI* phase of life. Traditional *gurukula* or *saMskRta pAThazAlA* students unequivocally refer to themselves as *bramhacArins*.

At age fifty, one entered the third phase of life or *vAnaprastha Azrama* and became a forest-dweller, and focused on his or her spiritual life. In this phase of life, people led an austere life and stopped the pursuit of *artha* and *kAma* and only pursued *mokSa*. This phase of life included the practice of *tapas* or penance gradually increasing in severity, and one would reduce the food intake gradually to live on fruits only. People would often live near or in an *Azrama* to get guidance from a *guru* to pursue a spiritual practice. Finally, at the age of seventy-five one entered *sannyAsa Azrama* or the fourth phase of life, and became a *sannyAsin* or a monk, and renounced all pleasures of life to pursue *jJAna* (or knowledge) or self-realization. The third and fourth phases of life are not adopted by most Indians today, who remain *gRhasthas* all their lives. However, many do cultivate spiritual practices after retirement, which is the pursuit of *mokSa*.

Depending on which phase of life one is in, the self is viewed differently. Life style completely changes from phase to phase. For example, as a student one ate less (*alpAhAri*), but as a householder there were fewer restrictions on what to eat and when to eat. As a forest-dweller one ate fruits and roots, and as a monk one begged three houses, washed whatever food one received from them, and then ate the "taste-free" food. Thus, stage of life clearly defined one's occupation and role in the society, and, therefore, the Indian concept of self was socially constructed and varied with stage or phase of life.

Foster (1924) noted his surprise in the book, *A Passage to India*, about meeting the Prime Minister of the Kingdom of Mysore in his ministerial capacity first and then the very next year as a mendicant. He found it amazing that someone could go from being a minister in a palace and having a luxurious life to voluntarily becoming homeless. There is little adherence to the stage of life in India today on a mass scale, but the idea still persists. A few people from all professions still gravitate toward *vAnaprashtha* and *sannyAsa* providing cultural continuity for *varNAzrama dharma* or the normative stage of life principle.

It is not unusual for people to start slowing down on their worldly commitments. It is more pronounced in the villages among farmers and traders among whom the elders pass on the baton to the next generation. With the retirement age of 58 for people who work in the organized sectors, the *vAnaprastha* stage only starts after retirement, and it is not unusual for people to commit to social service organizations or to spend some time in traveling to holy places or relocating in such places for the part of the year. There are also some *vAnaprastha Azramas* available for people to move into, and the earliest one was started by *Arya samAj* in *hardwar* in the early twentieth century. Many other organizations have sprung up for retirees following the *Arya samAj* model, and are run on six principles of devotion, contemplation, humanity, all are one, serve all, and love all (Cohen, 1998). Thus, the concept of stages of life though not popular, is still a relevant concept in India, and, thus, important for understanding the psychology of Indian people.

We can see that spirituality, which emerges as the highest desideratum of human living and pursuit in Indian culture, is captured in the concept of self, in the normative prescription about how to lead one's life in phases where the last two phases are clearly dedicated to the pursuit of spiritual practice. Both *dharma* and *mokSa* are related to spirituality, and are positive constructs. India claims to have one of the longest historical traditions of innovation in spirituality (Bhawuk, 2003, 2011, 2018, 2019a). However, as noted above, the focus on spirituality in the Indian culture should not be construed as the neglect of material world.

The Indian concept of self offers valuable insights into existing western psychological theories. Leung and Bond (2010) presented social axiom theory, which posits that human behavior is a function of generalizable beliefs about the world (people, groups, institutions, environment, spirituality), which are cognized as causal relationship between any two concepts of interest (A causes B format). They identified five factors—social cynicism, social complexity, reward for application, religiosity, and fate control—that influence how we act. Social cynicism is a negative worldview, whereas reward for application and social complexity are positive ways of looking at the world around us. Religiosity refers to the influence of religion on human behavior, whereas fate control parallels external locus of control (Rotter, 1966). The Indian concept of self, if employed to inform this theory, would posit that human behavior is guided by *varNAzrama dharma*, and so it depends on one's stage of life. Guidance for behavior would be drawn from *zAstras* or texts and teachers and elders. One should use *buddhi* and *viveka* in resolving issues. As *Atman* is the reflection of *brahman*, a person can achieve anything through *saMkalpa* or intention and effort. Also, the Indian concept of self would not allow for cynicism, and the word itself is not translatable in Indian languages. Indian proverbs provide insight into how people are practical rather than cynical (*TenDhI ungali se ghI nikAlana* or being crooked if necessary, *kAnTe se kAnTA nikAlana* or employing negative means in a negative situation, *pAnI me rah ke magar se vair* or it is not wise to fight powerful people, *nAchane na Aye Angan TeDhA* or blaming the context for one's own failure, and so forth). Such perspectives are not readily available from the social axiom theory since it does not synthesize the concept of self at multiple levels. The study of the Indian concept of self also provides a research methodology in which researchers wade through a text and combine various verses to create a complex model (see Bhawuk, 2010, 2011). This strategy can be employed for other constructs like *adhyAtma* or spirituality, *zraddhA*, *tapas*, *prema*, *lokasaM-graha*, which are reviewed in what follows (see Bhawuk, 2011, Chapter 7 for a discussion of *zAntiH* or peace).

The Indian concept of self allows us to go beyond the social self (e.g., independent and interdependent concepts of self; see Markus & Kitayama, 1991; Triandis, 1989, 1995; Sinha & Tripathi, 1994), and examine self in a much nuanced way by classifying issues that are related to physical, psychological, and metaphysical self. There is an entire business industry associated with each of the five senses (taste-food-2018 totaled about USD 8.7 trillion, smell-fragrance-USD 70.70 billion in 2018, sound-music-USD 21.6 billion in 2020, touch-apparel-USD 1.5 trillion in 2020, and sight-film-USD 136 billion in 2018 and tourism-USD 2.9 trillion in 2019; the film industry captures both sight and sound, and perhaps that is why video games are so addictive-USD 115 billion in 2018). A construct like transcendence can be captured with much clarity employing the Indian concept of self; transcendence refers to going beyond the physical, psychological, and social self. Transcendence pertains to the *Atman*, and is, therefore, about *adhyAtma* or spirituality, which is discussed next.

adhyAtma or Spirituality

Management has emerged as a profession in the last one hundred years in the West, but the basic principles have existed for centuries in most cultures around the world. Although the role of meditation in reducing stress has been studied since the 1950s, spirituality has emerged in management literature only since the 1990s (Dale, 1991; Dehler & Welsh, 1994; Holland, 1989; Lee, 1991; Mitroff & Denton, 1999). However, not much research is devoted to the development of indigenous constructs of spirituality. Bhawuk (2019b) presented a systematic definition of the construct of *adhyAtma* or spirituality from the Indian perspective, and showed that Indians balance material consumption with spirituality.

Management is about planning, organizing, commanding, coordinating, and controlling resources toward an objective (Fayol, 1949), which is necessarily about effecting some change in the environment by employing the resources procured. Managing, therefore, is about an outward process for the self, which is encompassed by others, organizations, nations, earth, and the universe (see Fig. 3.2). We interact with others and live in the organizational context. All our needs, from birth to death, from food to education, from social to spiritual, and so forth are processed by interacting with others and organizations. Organizations operate in the socio-political and legal framework provided by a nation, and other nations in the globalized world. The contributions of the world's ecosystem to human economy was estimated to be US$33 trillion in 1997 when the global gross national product was about US$18 trillion (Costanza et al., 1997). So, we must include earth, and the universe beyond it, into our socio-economic deliberations. Thus, management is an outward looking process. In contrast, spirituality is an inward looking process, without neglecting the impact of the outside world on the person as shown in Fig. 3.2. The internal and external difference is captured in the dictum of *ramaNa maharSi,* "It is only rarely that a man becomes introverted. The intellect delights in investigating the past and the future but does not look to the present." The

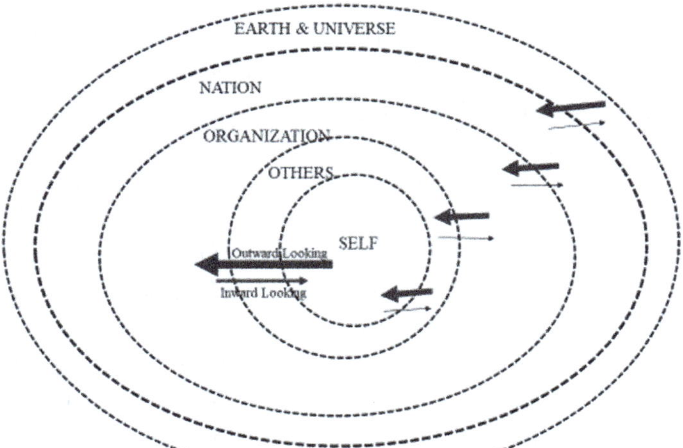

Fig. 3.2 Spirituality and Management: Inward and Outward Looking Processes

focus on other versus self is also captured succinctly into *Daodejing*, Chapter 33 in the following words: "To know others is wisdom; to know oneself is acuity (*ming*). To conquer others is power; to conquer oneself is strength. To know contentment is to have wealth; to act resolutely is to have purpose. To stay one's ground is to be enduring; to die and yet not be forgotten is to be long-lived" (Ames & Hall, 2010, p. 132). Swami Chinmayanand captured the difference between the outward and inward processes succinctly—"When I slip outside, I fall; when I slip inside, I rise."

India has a long tradition of spirituality (Bhawuk, 2003, 2011, 2012, 2019a, b). Moore (1967) distilled seventeen themes from a thorough study and analyses of Indian philosophical thoughts. The most important theme, he concluded, was spirituality—"a universal and primary concern for, and almost a preoccupation with, matters of spiritual significance (p. 12)." In stating how closely Indian philosophy is related to life, the general agreement seems to be that truth should be realized, rather than simply known intellectually. This further emphasizes and clarifies spirituality as the way of living, to not merely know the truth but to become one with the truth (Sheldon, 1951).

Though most Indian bilinguals translate spirituality as *adhyAtma* and spiritual as *AdhyAtmika* or *dhArmika* in common parlance, the *saMskRtam* to English dictionary by Monier-Williams (1899) defines *adhyAtma* as "the Supreme Spirit, own, belonging to self, concerning self or individual personality," and the one by Apte (1890) defines *adhyAtma* as ("*Atmana saMbaddhaM, Atmani adhikRtaM vA*") "belonging to self or person, or concerning an individual." Clearly, *adhyAtma* is related to self, the Supreme Spirit or *brahma,* and the individual being or person that we are. In the Indian worldview, *brahman* permeates everything in the world (*IzAvasyamidam sarvam yatkiJca jagatyAm jagat*, verse 1, *IzopaniSad*), and so the universe itself is a positive construct.

In the *bhagavadgItA*, *adhyAtma* appears eight times (see Gambhirananda, 1998) in verses 3.30, 8.3, 8.3, 10.32, 11.1, 13.11, and 15.5, and presents a thick description of the construct. *adhyAtma* is about centering the mind on the Self or *Atman*, and it is related to *brahma*, *karma*, *adhibhUta* (the entity existing in the physical plane), *adhidaiva* (the entity existing in the divine plane), and *adhiyajJa* (the entity existing in the sacrifices or all actions). *adhyAtma* is the pious knowledge (*jJAna* or *vidyA*) of self, and knowledge related to *adhyAtma* is superior to all types of knowledge. *adhyAtma* is one of the criteria of *mokSa* or freedom along with having no pride, delusion, attachment, or desire, and being free of all duality like happiness and sorrow. It is to act without agency or as the servant of God in pursuit of *mokSa* or liberation. *adhyAtma* is the inward looking process that leads to find pleasure, contentment, and satisfaction in *Atman* such that the person interacts energetically with the outside world without neglecting it or getting snared in it (*bhagavadgItA* 3.17; see also 18.26). Thus, *adhyAtma* or spirituality is a positive construct, and it permeates everyday living (see Bhawuk, 2019b for an illustration of how *adhyAtma* shapes daily behavior of business people).

Being *adhyAtmika* or having an orientation for spirituality invariably means cultivating the 26 virtues presented as *daivika sampadA* in the *bhagavadgItA* in Canto 16 (the first three verses). They are: *abhayam* or fearlessness, *sattvasaMzuddhi* or purification of the *antaHkaraNa* or internal agent, *jJanayogavyavasthiti* or constantly being aware of the spiritual self, *dAnaM* or charity, *damaH* or restraint of senses, *yajJaH* or self-purifying activities, *svAdhyAyaH* or regular study of scriptures, *tapaH* or austerity, *ArjavaM* or straightforwardness, *ahiMsA* or non-violence of thought, speech, and deed, *satyaM* or truth, *akrodhaH* or non-anger, *tyAgaH* or non-attachment, *zAntiH* or peace, *apaizunaM* or non-calumny, *dayAbhuteSu* or compassion for all beings, *aloluptvaM* or non-covetedness, *mArdavaM* or gentleness, *hrIH* or sense of propriety, and *acApalaM* or absence of unsteadiness, *tejaH* or moral power, *kSamA* or forgiveness, *dhrItiH* or steadfastness, *zaucaM* or external and internal self-purification, *adrohaH* or absence of resentment, and *nAtimAnita* or absence of seeking any attention or importance.

These 26 virtues not only capture most of the popular positive psychological constructs like compassion, resilience, forgiveness, and so forth that are presented in the western literature, but also offer constructs like *abhaya*, *svAdhyAya*, *Arjavam*, *ahimsA*, *nAtimAnitA*, *adrohaH*, *tejaH*, and so forth that continue to be absent from the literature (Lopez et al., 2019; Snyder et al., 2021, the following 20 constructs are covered in these two publications: resilience, subjective well-being, happiness, creativity, spirituality, mindfulness, meditation, optimism, hope, courage, compassion, forgiveness, altruism, love, humility, toughness, self-efficacy, self-esteem, self-verification, emotional intelligence). It is particularly intriguing that *ahimsA* should be missing from the literature considering its acceptance in political science and Gandhiji's popularity even in the USA through the work of Martin Luther King, Jr.

zraddhA

Bhawuk (2020b) derived nine themes from the verses of the *bhagavadgItA* that presented a thick description of the intricate relations among the various ideas related to the construct of *zraddhA*. Etimologically, *zraddhA* (*zrat* or *zrad*, which means *satya* or truth is compounded with the root *dhA*, which means holding or placing; so *zraddhA* means staying truthful. The nine themes presented a meaning space that went far beyond either the dictionary meaning or the commonly held ideas of the word.

zraddhA can be of several types. According to the *bhagavadgItA*, the *zraddhA* of a devotee following the path of devotion is of the highest type. It is clear that *zraddhA* occupies a central place in whatever path of spirituality is followed. Also, *zraddhA* is the antecedent of *jJAna*, and the relationship between *zraddhA* and *jJAna* is moderated by *tatparaḥ* (or eager engagement in a practice) and *saMyatendriyaH* (or practicing self-restraint). The value of an individual's effort who is on the path of spirituality is not lost either. Further, as jJAna acts as a mediator between *zraddhA* and *mokSa* (or liberation), *zraddhA* becomes an instrument of *mokSa*, the highest life pursuit of humans in the Indian worldview, the other three being *dharma* or duty, *artha* or wealth, and *kāma* or pleasure. Such a complex understanding cannot be captured by single word translations of the construct of *zraddhA* in English or other languages; though it may be available to those who are immersed in Indian culture.

According to the *bhagavadgItA*, one must always perform *yajJa, dAna, tapas*, and *karma*. When one gives away something (dAna), one may suffer some loss but that may be considered *tyāga* or sacrifice, which is considered a kind of *tapas.* Considering the complex relationship between *dAna* and *tapas,* I would like to propose that *dAna* and *tapas* are interrelated constructs and can be visualized as occupying a common semantic space. In a similar fashion, all activities (*karma*) done for *lokasaMgraha* or for the good of people too may be considered sacrifice or *tapas.* All *karma, dAna,* and *tapas* done with *niSkAmabhAva* or without attachment to the rewards from the expected outcomes are considered *sāttvika* acts. They are part of a *sAttvika yajJa,* and constitute components of a spiritual practice. Thus, *dAna* and *tapas, karma* and *tapas, karma* and *yajJa, dAna* and *yajJa, tapas* and *yajJa,* are pairs of constructs that not only intercorrelate but also share common semantic spaces. What is central to all the activities is that if *yajJa, dAna, tapas,* and *karma are* performed with *zraddhA,* it makes these four activities part of *sat* or truth. Its absence makes them go futile as they lose their relationships. Thus, *zraddhA* occupies a central position in the nomological network of *yajJa, dAna, tapas,* and *karma*

zraddhA reflects the basic nature of people and a person may be seen more or less as personification of *zraddhA.* It expresses itself in very different kinds of behaviors that people engage in. For example, many people in India go to temples like the one at *guruvAyura,* but depending on their *zraddhA,* each acts differently. Some go around the temple by walking at normal pace; others walk slowly, foot-to-foot, much like a mindful walk; and yet others roll over sideways in going around the temple. Similarly, in Lhasa, people prostrate in front of temples hundreds of time or go around the temple by prostrating, depending upon their *zraddhA.* This perhaps illustrates how *zraddhA* captures the basic nature of people.

In the West, optimists are those who have a positive attitude and find the proverbial glass as half full. They are known to find opportunities even in difficult and dire situations. Contrary to them, pessimists see the glass as half empty, and are often cynical and unwilling to work through challenges to bring about changes in their own personal lives, organizations, or societies. It may be considered that such basic nature of the optimists or pessimists reflects *zraddhA* of the person in self, others, society, and the Divine. Thus, *zraddhA* may be used as a foundational construct for understanding both positive and negative psychologies, and has implications for personal growth as well as social change.

From interpersonal perspective it was found that *zraddhA* is an emotion that one has for another person (Bhawuk, 2020b). For example, a '*zraddhAvAn*' student, much like *arjuna* did to *kRSNa*, follows the instructions of a teacher by surrendering to him or her. The teacher fulfills the student's wish for knowledge and provides necessary instructions to guide him or her to perform his or her duty. The characteristics of *zraddhA* is based on exchange between a teacher and a student will also apply to all superior-subordinate dyads like parent–child, older-brother-younger-brother, and so forth. The same dynamics is likely to be at play between a person and his or her deity or God. Since *zAstras* or scriptural texts, which provide instructions in guiding human behavior, they too are treated in the same manner by a *zraddhAvAn* individual.

It was noted that though individual effort moderates the relation between *zraddhA* and liberation, *zraddhA* is also considered a gift of God or divine grace. Such grace of God that appears as *zraddhA* can be seen reflected in the daily interactions of spiritual practitioners. For example, a spiritual practitioner's harmonizing behavior is likely to emerge from his or her neutrality toward all, and not viewing people (or contexts) in terms of dichotomies like friend or enemy, good or bad, favorable or antagonistic, and so forth. Thus, the construct of *zraddhA* can be employed to examine how social entrepreneurs can possibly effect social change.

Thus, *zraddhA* is a unique Indian indigenous construct that also helps us understand other Indian constructs. It should also help us understand interpersonal relationships, since *zraddhA* is the foundation of many relationships, which hitherto has been neglected by researchers. Also, analyses of all the verses that refer to a construct in a text can be employed as a research methodology as was carried out by Bhawuk (2020b).

tapas

Bhawuk (in press a) derived nine themes from the verses of the *bhagavadgItA* that describe *tapas* beyond what is obtained from the dictionary meaning of the word. The comparison of the 26 *daivika sampadas* and the typology of *tapas* based on *manasA* (practices of the *manas* or mind), *vAcA* (practices of speech), and *karmaNA* (actions or practices of the body), shows that 14 of the 26 virtues fall in the category of *tapas* (Bhawuk, in press a). Of these six (*svAdhyAya tapa Arjavam ahiMsA satya* and *zauca*) appear on both networks. Eight others are quite similar in meaning. For example, *akordha* is captured by *anudveg-akaram vAkya, dayAbhUteSu* is captured by *hitam vAkya,* and *mArdava* is captured by *priya vAkya* and *hitam vAkya,* which are all *tapas* of speech. Similarly, *adroha* and *nAtimAnitA* are captured by *saumyatvam, sattvasaMzuddhi* by *mauna* and *Atmavinigraha,* and *jJAnayogavyavasthiti* by *manaHprasAdah,* which are all *tapas* of *manas.* Finally, *yajJa* is captured by *tapayajJa.* The overlap of these 14 *daivika sampadas* with tapas indicates that *tapas* is a fundamental *daivika sampada.*

As noted above, the process of cultivation of virtues itself is *tapas,* and so cultivating the other 11 virtues, namely, *abhaya, dAna, dama, tyAga, zAnti, apaizuna, aloluptva, acApalam, teja, kSamA,* and *dhRti* will amount to doing *tapas. hrI* is the only one that is fundamental enough to stand by *tapas* as a partner, if not an independent construct, since cultivating any virtue requires having a sense of what one ought to do and what one ought not to do. This sense is *lajjA* or *hrI*. However, with the consistent cultivation of a virtue, *lajjA* also become crystallized and stronger. An advanced *sAdhaka* or practitioner engaged in cultivating these virtues is likely to catch the thought itself as it arises in the *manas,* and thus prevents any lapse at the speech and action level.

Similarly, the comparison of the *daivika sampadas* and the nine natural duties of a *brAhmaNa* shows that four of them appear on both lists, namely, *dama, tapas, zauca,* and *Arjavam* (Bhawuk, in press a). Two of them are different simply in formation of the words, e.g., *jJAna* or *jJAnayogavyavasthiti* and *ksAnti* or *kSamA.* The seventh one, *zama,* means quietening of the *antaHkaraNa.* If the *antaHkaraNa* is not calm, one gets angry whenever a desire is not fulfilled (*gItA* 2.62). Thus, cultivating *zama* is similar to cultivating *akrodha*. The only two duties of a *brAhmaNa* that are not on the list of *daivika sampadas* are *vijJAna* & *Astikya*. Therefore, *brAhmaNas* are supposed to be *tapasvis* and lead an austere life. As the exemplars of *daivika sampadas*, they are supposed to lead others in the society by example. Therefore, in the Indian worldview, those who want to lead people should live an austere life, which is consistent with Plato's Philosopher King (Republic V.473d) who was supposed to pursue wisdom (*jJAna* and *vijJAna*) more than power.

The importance of *zraddhA* is clear in the typology of *tapas* based on the three *guNas* of *sattva*, *rajas*, and *tamas*, since it only appears in the category of *sattvika tapas* (Bhawuk, in press a). Since *zraddhA* also defines *sattvika yajJa*, and absence of *zraddhA* makes all actions, *yajJa*, *dAna*, and *tapas* futile, it is clear that *zraddhA* is necessary for performing anything worthwhile. *tapas* can become mechanical, and the practitioner can lose perspective and become what is called *zuSka* (or vain) *tapasvi*, someone who revels in the austerities and forgets that the purpose of *tapas* is to not get attached to anything, not even *sattvaguNa* or positivity. Thus, *tapas* is necessary but not sufficient, and cultivating *zraddhA* keeps the *sAdhaka* or spiritual aspirant focused on self-realization.

In *pAtaJjal-yogasUtra* 1.20 *zraddhA* is presented as the first *upAya* or method for the practitioner. The *vyAs-bhASya* explains the *sUtra* as follows: From *zraddhA* (*manas* filled with delight) follows *vIrya* (or enthusiasm for *sAdhanA* or spiritual practice), *smRti* (or recollection of *Izvara* and his attributes), *samAdhi* (or concentration or one pointed *manas*), and *prajJA* (or insight). With *prajJa* the practitioner gains direct experience, and with the practice of *viveka* (discrimination) and *vairAgya* (detachment) he or she achieves *asamprajJAt-samAdhi* or self-realization. Thus, *zraddhA* is emphasized in yoga *darzana* also. However, it is quite clear that there is no other way but to cultivate *tapas*, since it is the source of all virtues.

lajjA as behavioral guide

Bhawuk (2017, 2019c) developed the concept of *lajjA* by examining dictionary meanings, synonyms, and antonyms of the word in *saMskRtam* and *hindI,* analyzing its usage in two popular scriptural texts, the *bhagavadgItA* and *drugA saptazatI,* analyzing its usage in literature, in *kAmAyanI*, a modern *hindI mahAkAvya* or epic, and mapping its usage in daily communication and proverbs. This multi-method approach resulted in a thick-description of the construct, showing that *lajjA* is one of the 26 virtues enumerated in the *bhagavadgItA* that guides human behavior, and has both internal and external aspects, or guilt and shame elements, and it synthesizes them. Such a structure is at odds with the Western literature that views guilt and shame as distinct and independent constructs (Creighton, 1990; Lewis, 1971; Tracy & Robins, 2006). There is evidence that *lajjA* is an important virtue that guides human behavior in Asia (for example, Fung, 1999; Lebra, 1983) in general, and India in particular (Bhawuk, 2017; Menon & Shweder, 1994, 2003; Sinha & Chauhan, 2013). These studies challenge the belief that there are guilt-cultures and shame-cultures.

Menon and Shweder (1994, 2003) concluded that *lajjA* is associated with being shy, having modesty, and showing deference to elders; having *lajjA is* akin to being a civilized person who knows his or her place in the society and acts properly as demanded by one's duties and responsibilities; it prevents people from any transgressions. Sinha and Chauhan (2013) captured the behavioral representations of *lajjA* by employing films, advertisements, conversations, and written narratives. They found that *lajjA* is used by women in constructing their identity in India—it makes them feel like a woman; it makes their mannerism graceful; having it does not make them less determined, less ambitious, or less strong as a human being. They noted that *lajjA* not only seems to be the core of womanhood in India, but also can be used as a manipulative tool against women in certain situations.

Bhawuk (2017) identified 32 attributes of *lajjA* from the literature. Some of them are gender free, whereas some apply to women only. When a person experiences *lajjA,* (1) the person feels as if she or he is shrinking within; (2) keeps the head down; (3) eyelids are down covering the eyes while looking; (4) responds in murmurs or the voice is barely audible, (5) there is redness in the cheeks, (6) thoughts freeze on the lips, (7) ears turn red, and (8) body stoops like a branch of tree laden with fruits. When a woman experiences *lajjA*, (9) she feels like an adornment or the mascara in her eyes; (10) she puts her finger on her lips; (11) her body becomes soft and supple like melting wax; (12) there is a fluid smile on her face; (13) her eyes shine with playfulness; (14) she hesitates to touch anything, These 14 attributes are psycho-somatic expressions of the emotion of *lajjA*, and would be useful to discuss in management education programs using video clips from Bollywood films and other internet sources.

Further, *lajjA* (15) protects the fickle and the youthful; (16) is a restraint that says, "Stop, think about the action you are contemplating to perform;" (17) is the flash of prudence that soothes the *manas;* (18) teaches the value of dignity; (19) softly reminds one of the impending stumble; *and* (20) teaches the value of honor. These definitions of *lajjA* are consistent with the definitions presented in the *bhagavadgItA* and *durgAsaptazatI*, and are cultural expressions of how *lajjA* guides one through appropriate and inappropriate behaviors.

Also, *lajjA* is (21) tender, like a bud hiding in its delicate new petals or a lamp just lit at dusk and seen through the veil of dust raised by the hooves of the cows returning home at the end of the day; (22) about *zRGgAra* or adornment, and can be both external or internal—like a garland worn in the *manas*, (23) an experience of being controlled by someone else, (24) one that plucks away the flowers of independence blooming in life, (25) comparable to the redness of dusk, (26) characterized by innocence, (27) a yearning to do something, (28) the bearer of the youth's spontaneity, (29) personification of *ratI* (the Hindu Goddess of love similar to Venus), (30) helpless without her own arrows (only *kAmddeva*, the God of love has bows and arrows) (31) not content with her past experience, and (32) like an anklet in a young woman's feet, for the sound of the anklet forewarns that somebody is coming. These 12 attributes are literary expressions of *lajjA*, and are likely to be useful in the analysis of shame in literatures across cultures. Understanding the nuances of *lajjA* can also help understand behavior in informal settings at a deeper level.

The meaning of *lajjA* gets quite saturated with these 32 attributes. These 32 usage not only converge on the basic meaning of *lajjA* as a forewarning about non-performance of appropriate behavior and performance of inappropriate behaviors, but also present many other physical and psychological attributes of *lajjA,* thus providing a thick description of the construct. Looking at other texts, for example, *tulsi's mAnas* (or *rAmAyana*) did not add any new meaning of the construct (Bhawuk, 2017).

Bhawuk (2017) showed that *lajjA* is aroused in both situations, when one is tempted not to do what should be done (or quit a task because it is difficult or challenging), and to do what should not to be done. Therefore, *lajjA* is the inner impediment guided by scripture or cultural norm of appropriateness that leads one to act appropriately. It is a mental process that restrains a behavior or another mental process, i.e., a thought or desire. One of the many names of devI provides insight in the meaning of *lajjA,* and that is, *om icchAzakti-jJAnazakti-kriyAzakti-svarUpiNyai namaH!* (I bow to one who is the power of will (or desire), power of wisdom, and power of action! #658). The sequencing of the three names, will (or desire), wisdom, and action, provides insight in understanding *lajjA*. When we have a desire, it propels us into action, and since both of these are powered by the same source, *devI*, they would be instantaneous. But she also provides the power of wisdom, which comes between desire and action, and *lajjA* is that wisdom as it guides us to choose desires that are appropriate and reject those that are not. Thus, *lajjA* mediates between desire and action, according to this name of *devI*, which provides a model of how desire, *lajjA*, and action are related. A deeper understanding of *lajjA* may also help use *lajjA* effectively as a way to motivate Indian employees for doing prosocial behavior and prevent them from using undesirable behaviors in organizations.

The studies on *lajjA* employed multiple research strategies that are illustrative. First, the construct of interest can be studied by examining dictionary meanings, synonyms, and antonyms of the construct of interest in *saMskRtam* and an Indian language, say, Hindī. Second, the construct of interest can be examined in multiple texts. For example, the usage of *lajjA* was examined employing two popular texts in *saMskRtam*, the *bhagavadgItA* and *drugA saptazatI*, as well as in literature, in *kAmAyanI*, a modern *hindI mahAkAvya* or epic (Bhawuk, 2017). Third, the use of the construct can be examined in daily communication and proverbs as was done in the study of *lajjA* (Bhawuk, 2017). Fourth, researchers can employ autoethnography to tease out a processual understanding of a construct. For example, this procedure allowed to develop an understanding of how *lajjA* is learned, unlearned, and can be relearned (Bhawuk, 2019d). Thus, for the development and elaboration of Indian constructs multiple methods and texts can be employed. Such a multi-method approach not only provides a thick description of the construct but also presents its validity in the contemporary times. For example, it was found that lajjā has both internal and external aspects and it synthesizes guilt and shame, which have been viewed as distinct and non-overlapping constructs in the western literature. Further, *lajjA* emerged as an important virtue that guides human behavior (Bhawuk, in press a).

prema or Love

Bhawuk (2021) analyzed how saint *kabIr* (1398–1448) uses *prem* in his *sAkhI* or teachings by employing the collection of *kabIr sAhab*'s teachings published by the center in *dAmAkheDA*, *rAypur*, *chattisgaDha*, India. Seven themes emerged that provide a thick description of *prem* or love. Love is non-transient (or *aghaT prem piMjar base).* Love cannot be hidden (*prem chipAyA nA chipe).* Love is difficult (*kaThin galI hai prem kI or zISa kATa Age dhare*). Love for God is superior to material love (*prem hai doya prakAra kA*). Love without understanding is useless (*prem akelA kyA kare*). Compassion causes humbleness, which in turn generates love (*jahAM dInatA tahAM prem*). Love, detachment and *sadguru* are interdependent ideas (*prem binA dhIraja nahIM*).

kabIr sAhab also uses the simile of a drink for love (*kabIr pyAlA prem kA*) that emerges as the eighth theme. It is a drink that quenches thirst. One who drinks from the goblet of love, does not drink water anymore, for only love can quench one's thirst. One who has love is content and has no desire left for any drink. Love is also compared to an alcoholic drink, and said to be the most addictive, once one drinks from the goblet of love, the user has no need for other substance. The drink is love is said to be not for ordinary people; only when one relinquishes the self based in the body (this body is me!) is one able to drink from the goblet of love. Love is compared to nectar, and only a select few like *kabIr sAhab* himself gets to drink it. Finally, love is said to be the essence of essences, the rasa that makes one forget all others; and all rules are broken. Drinking has social rules, but love is a drink that breaks all such social rules. One who drinks from the goblet of love proceeds to the *satyaloka*, the abode of truth and God. Thus, love is a drink that transports one to the spiritual world.

The eight themes that emerged present a thick description of what *prem* or love is in the Indian cultural context. We see a synthesis of what is love in the wisdom tradition of India in the words of *kabIr sAhab*, *nisargadatta mahArAja* (Nisargadatta, 1973), and *jiddu kRSNAmurtiji* (Krishnamurti, 1979). Love is not about pleasure or desire, it is not about seeking, wanting, pursuing, and requires a total abandonment of self. Love is a different dimension, a vastness characterized by I am the world and the world is myself, and because it is different from the pursuance of material things, different from grasping and holding, without a center of selfishness, it is about spirituality. It is no surprise that in one of the famous verses of *kabIr sAhab* that is quoted in daily interactions by most people who speak *hindI states-- pothI paDh paDh jag muA panDit bhayA na koi, DhAi Akhar prem kA paDhe so panDit hoye* (one does not become learned by studying scriptural texts but by understanding the two and one half letters that make the word *prem)*. By analyzing *kabIr sAhab*'s teachings on love, Bhawuk (2021) also provides a new approach for developing constructs by employing cultural texts of the *bhakti* movement. The work of other saints can be employed to develop other constructs in the future.

lokasaMgraha: The Sociology of Positive Psychology

Bhawuk (2019a) analyzed the construct of *lokasaMgraha* as it appears in the *bhagavadgItA* (verses 3.20 and 3.25) in the context of *karmayoga*. Grammatically, *lokasaṁgraha* is *ṣaṣṭhī tatpuruSa samAsa* of *lokAnAm* (of the world) and *saMgrahaH* (holding properly). In his commentary on the *bhagavadgItA*, *Adi zaMkara* interprets *lokasaMgraham* as *lokasya unmArgapravRttinivAraNaM lokasaMgrahaḥ tam eva api prayojanam* or correcting people's propensity to pursue the opposite path is called *lokasaMgraha*. Ramanuja interprets *lokasaMgraha as lokarakSaNArtham* or protection of people. In *zrIjJAneswarI, saint jJAnadeva* elaborates it further that one should protect the social systems in all possible ways by acting according to the *zAstras*, directing others on the noble path, and not becoming disconnected from the society. The message of the *bhagavadgItA* is unequivocal, one has to be engaged in action, and pursue enlightenment through serving the society. The concept of *lokasaMgraha* is briefly reviewed here (see Bhawuk, 2019a for a full discussion).

lokasaMgraha is about leadership. The common tendency of people to deviate from the normative course is to be corrected by the leader through his or her own example. Unlike traditional leadership, which focuses on the leader as a person, *lokasaMgraha* shifts the focus to the well-being of the society. As a spiritual practice *lokasaMgraha* entails cultivating one's outer senses to see the benefit of others in everything, all the time. This reduces selfishness or self-centeredness. A person pursuing *lokasaMgraha* is not reclusive but passionate about the welfare of all beings or is *sarvabhUtahite ratāḥ* (*Gītā* verse 12.4). When one works for the benefit of others following the credo of *lokasaMgraha*, a path or practice to break the bondage of *karma* or actions becomes available, which leads to the highest goal of life, the pursuit of *mokSa* or *brahman.*

The material way of life, in which we constantly chase the fruits of our ventures, is inherently pitiable as it distracts from the higher goals of life. *lokasaMgraha*, by comparison, is the only outward focused approach that leads to higher goals, and therefore, is comparable to the inward focused spiritual practice. Thus, though *buddhiyoga* refers to inner directed *buddhi* (intellect), it applies equally to the practice of *lokasaMgraha* when one focuses on the outside world, but for the well-being of others. *Adi zaṁkara* suggested that excellence is achieved when one performs his or her prescribed duties or work by surrendering the consciousness to *brahman* (see his commentary on *bhagavadgItA* verses 2.48, 2.50, and 3.30), which leads to having a balance in success and failure. The same excellence is achieved when all actions performed are for *lokasaMgraha* or the common good.

The philosophy of *karma* is often viewed as the doctrine of *niSkAma karma*, which can be stated in the following four statements: (i) work is to be done, and never to be avoided; (ii) work is to be done without seeking its outcomes; (iii) work is to be done without paying attention to success or failure; and (iv) when work is performed with a balanced mind, one achieves excellence in his or her performance, work does not cause bondage to life and death cycle, and one achieves the purpose of life—union with *brahman*. These four fundamentals are equally applicable to *lokasaMgraha*.

Employing in-depth interview, Wilson (2010) studied 100 senior Indian managers and discovered *lokasaMgraha* to be the overarching theme that integrated the seven core experiences that provided learning experiences to managers pertaining to learning from superiors, working on a turnaround project, launching a new initiative, job rotation or horizontal move, crossing cultures, increases in scope of job, and adjusting to the world of work. These core or essential experiences provided opportunity to develop eleven skills, namely, managing and motivating subordinates, developing subordinates (boss related), confidence, effective execution (turnaround related), self-awareness, innovation and entrepreneurship, navigating politics and gaining influence (initiative related), engaging multiple stakeholders (related to the horizontal move), cross-cultural skills (from crossing cultures), functional and technical expertise (from increase in scope of work), and personal leadership insights (from early direct workplace experience). The Indian managers emphasized that all these managerial skills acquired through life experiences are ultimately valuable in serving the organization to contribute to the service of the society and nation building, or *lokasaMgraha*. This finding is consistent with the work of other researchers (Agarwal, 1995; Chakraborty, 1995) *lokasaMgraha* captures the activities of people that could be called *karma-yogi* leaders (Bhawuk, 2008) that span spiritual leaders (e.g., work done by *Azramas*), social entrepreneurs (*bhUdAna yajJa* of Vinoba Bhave), and the variety of causes served by people leading NGOs (see Pandey & Sahay, 2021, Chapter 11 in this volume). Many of the recipients of Right Livelihood Award like Ela Bhatt of SEWA—Self-Employed Women's Association, Vandana Shiva of Navdanya (conservation of biodiversity), Dr H. Sudarshan of Vivekananda Girijana Kalyana Kendra, Medha Patkar and Baba Amte of the Narmada Bachao Andolan or Save Narmada Movement, Sunderlal Bahuguna, Chandi Prasad Bhatt, Dhoom Singh Negi, Bachni Devi, Ghanshyam Raturi, and Indu Tikekar of the Chipko Movement (save the forests of Himalaya), and Helena Norberg-Hodge of Ladakh Ecological Development Group are living examples of people who have dedicated their lives to *lokasaMgraha*.

India has a tradition of creating institutions like *dharmazAlAs* (shelters for travelers to *tirths* or holy places in India), *anAthAlayas* (orphanages), *gurukuls* or *pAThazAlAs* (schools), which serve people and are guided by the spirit of *lokasaMgraha*. Therefore, *lokasaMgraha* can also provide a pathway to study altruism in India. It is no surprise that Agarwal (1995) considered *lokasaMgraha* the social message of *Gita*. However, Chakraborty (1995) elevated *lokasaMgraha* to cosmic centered consciousness,[5] which is above the socio-centric consciousness that guides social ethics. Also, *lokasaMgraha* is a construct that appears not only in scholarly discourses but also in daily communication showing its relevance not only in the scientific-world but also in the life-world. It is a construct that could replace the discourse on the sociology of positive psychology in India beyond leadership research and practice for private, public, and non-government organizations.

It should be noted that the Indian culture emphasizes *karma* or actions, and shows how pursuing desires is binding but acting with *niSkAma-bhAva* or not pursuing the outcomes of actions allows one to break the bondage of actions. The Indian worldview considers actions to be binding, but also provides a way out of this bondage through

---

[5] In the Indian worldview, there are seven *lokas* or universes, namely, *bhUH, bhuvaH, svaH, mahaH, janaH, tapaH, and* satyam. Therefore, Chakraborty's observation that *lokasaMgraha* pertains to the cosmic consciousness is quite consistent with the Indian knowledge systems.

many paths (see Bhawuk, 2011, Chapter 7), and one of them is through actions themselves by performing them with *niSkAma-bhAva,* which is also referred to as *karmayoga.* It is not surprising that all Indian leaders in every domain of life have championed *niSkAma-karma* or *karmayoga,* and it is not merely a buzz word in India, but a way of life. *lokasaMgraha* is closely associated with *niSkAma-karma,* and these constructs enrich both the literatures on leadership and social entrepreneurship.

Spirituality-based Theory of Creativity

Bhawuk (2019e) presented a spirituality-based theory of creativity and demonstrated how it is supported in the Indian philosophical tradition. According to the Indian worldview, creativity is bidirectional; the outward creativity is ever growing and transient, while the inward creativity is implosive. The inward journey also meets the two criteria of creativity—newness and discovery. The iterative process of *neti-neti* (the process of distancing oneself from the physical-social-psychological self by saying "I am not this-I am not this" to experience the *Atman*) leads to dropping elements of social selves. The process of dropping our social and other selves one by one means change and the creation of a new perspective of oneself, which meets the newness criterion, and the indescribable experience of the self or reality meets the criterion of discovery. The synthesis of internal and external journey not only supports the holistic view but also provides a synthesis of material and spiritual worldviews.

Spirituality is also shown to add value to the material product oriented creativity by improving the capacity of individuals through the practice of meditation. There is much research finding to support this, especially using Transcendental Meditation (TM), which is a particular type of meditation. TM practitioners of all ages have also shown improved scores on tests of both cognitive and affective functioning, including variables like "fluid intelligence" and "field Independence," which are found to become stable after the age of seventeen (Roth, 2011).

Bhawuk (2019e) showed that the spirituality-based theory of creativity is compatible with other extant theories of creativity, and enriches them by extending their boundaries rather than taking anything away from them. Though western researchers have argued that the early association of creativity with mysticism and spirituality might have hindered the growth of the field since spirituality and the scientific approach are not viewed as compatible (Isaksen & Murdock, 1993). In view of the long history of creativity in the domain of spirituality in India (Bhawuk, 2003, 2011), it seems it is necessary to relinquish the mindset that spirituality and creativity cannot go hand in hand.

In the Indian perspective, the spiritual and material journeys are not exclusive but complementary in nature—"When you desire and fear, and identify yourself with your feelings, you create sorrow and bondage. When you create with love and wisdom, and remain unattached to your creations, the result is harmony and peace (nisargadatta, 1973, p. 496)." This holistic perspective is consistent with what characterizes other eastern cultures (see Nisbett et al., 2001).

Discussion

Thousands of years of history of India provides a rich backdrop for all types of cultural studies, indigenous or comparative, in all domains of management. Scholars have called India a wonder all through history (Basham, 1954; Rizvi & Basham, 1987), and Bhawuk (2012, 2020c) argued that it continues to be a wonder as diversity in geography, culture, language, religion, and spirituality continues to collide and create new models of living in harmony. India is not only a wonder in cultural diversity but also in maintaining harmony among stark contradictions, giving its people a unique mindset (Sinha, 2014; Khandwalla, 2018) that is open to cultural differences. The constructs derived from Indian culture discussed above illustrate the possibility of developing meaningful indigenous constructs that would contribute to the literatures on not only indigenous but also global psychology and management. They show how indigenous constructs can enrich the global knowledge system beyond western ideas and theories. For example, the studies on *lajjA* (Bhawuk, 2017, 2019a, b, c, d, e, 2020a, b, c, d) challenged the belief that there are guilt-cultures and shame-cultures, thus making significant contribution to global psychology (Marsella, 1998).

It is better to start with an Indian construct like *lokasaMgraha*, but not doing so is not necessarily a disadvantage. For example, in the west, self-oriented leaders are found to be authoritarian and exploitative, whereas other-oriented leaders are found to be participative, but not as effective with objectives or outcomes. Starting with the western model of leadership, Sinha (1980, 1995) found that effective leaders in India are not autocratic or participative as proposed in the west, but *Nurturant-Task Leaders*. These leaders are found to be more effective for the subordinates who are dependence prone, status conscious, and leisure seeking (i.e., not overly work oriented). A nurturant task leader is not only able to engage the subordinates in participation, but also retain a moral superiority that is recognized by the subordinates rather than being imposed by the leader. People who demonstrate a high dependence on the leader are found to take greater risk if the supervisor expects them to do so. Though it is a counter-intuitive finding, it makes the theory insightful.

This model is inspired by the traditional wisdom that parents should shower love on the children up to the age of five, discipline them for the next 10 years, and treat them like friends when they turn 16. The nurturant task leader cares for his or her subordinates and their success, and also connects with them socially, acting like a mentor not only at work but also in other areas of life. The model fits with the social mores of India where every decision is discussed informally in the community in an Indian village, be it selection of seed for a crop or a bridegroom for one's daughter (Sinha, 2010). The theory is grounded in the observation that unconditional support, or nurturance alone without task focus, turns the subordinates into unproductive sycophants, which is not good for them, the leader, or the organization. The model also taps into the idea of *lokasaMgraha* (Bhawuk, 2019a) or general good of the organization and the society as the *Nurturant-Task-Leader* derives the moral superiority from acting for *lokasaMgraha*, and not merely maximizing his or her personal gain.

Chakraborty (1987, 1993) proposed that a leader so acts in the service of others that his or her individual self-expands to encompass the subordinates creating a larger collective self (see Bhawuk, 2011, Chapter 4, for the concept of expansion of self in the Indian worldview). Leaders and subordinates sacrifice for each other unconditionally, and such interactions transform the leader, the subordinates, and the organization (Bhawuk, Mrazek, & Munusamy, 2009). The spirit of *lokasaMgraha* diminishes the self-other dichotomy, allowing both the leader and the subordinates to realize limitless transformation. Success, achievement, and possession for the individual are replaced by those for the group. When this is practiced in the organizational context *Nurturant Task Leadership* emerges. When the scope is expanded to the socio-political and religio-spiritual contexts, *karmayogin* and *sannyasin* leaders emerge (Bhawuk, 2008). Thus, *sannyasin* and *karmayogin* leaders constitute two spiritually oriented indigenous models of leadership, whereas nurturant-task leader is a socially-oriented model from India that also taps into the spiritual idea of *lokasaMgraha*.

The construct of *adhyAtma* or spirituality is emphasized so much that it has been an integral part of the concept of self as well as the four pursuits of life (*dharma*, *artha*, *kAma*, and *mokSa*) emphasized in the Indian culture. This construct also permeates the other constructs discussed above. When we look at creativity from the Indian perspective, spirituality and creativity get synthesized, and the elaborate practices of yoga, *prANAyAma*, and *dhyAna* (meditation) become relevant. *adhyAtma* or spirituality also goes hand in hand with two other constructs, *yama* (or self-restraint: *ahimsA* or nonviolence, *satya* or truth, *asteya* or non-stealing, *brahmacarya* or celibacy, *aparigraha* or non-possession) and *niyama* (or restraint of the *manas: zauca* or purity of thought, speech, and action, *santoSa* or contentment, *tapas* or austerity, *svAdhyAya* or regular textual study, *IzvarpraNidhAna* or surrender to God) (Bhawuk, 2019a), which form the foundation of all spiritual practices, and therefore, are necessarily positive constructs.

Indian positive approach does not neglect the negative, and includes it in the discussion of positive psychology, which can be seen in the *Bhagavad-Gita* not only in the discussion of actions (*karma, akarma, vikarma*), meditation (how hard it is to control the mind and how to control it), but also virtues (both *daivika* and *AsurI sampadas*). In the Indian worldview, all actions including *yajJa*, *dAna*, and *tapas* are futile if not done with *zraddhA*, thus the general orientation to all actions is supposed to be positive. *zraddhA* is relevant in understanding interpersonal relationships in the workplace in India. When a subordinate has *zraddhA* for the superior, their relationship is likely to develop into high-LMX (Leader-Member Exchange) (Graen & Uhl-Bien, 1995). *zraddhA* can also be a candidate for being the defining characteristic of followership (Uhl-Bien et al., 2014), a fast growing area of research. Similarly, *lajjA* can enrich research in decision making by bringing Indian perspective. Cultivation of *lajjA* as an organizational culture can lead people to take personal responsibility, and also eliminate organizational bullying since individuals would be self-censoring and not need shaming from the superiors. Finally, love is an aspect of spirituality as presented by *kabIr sAhab*, and organizations that are spiritually inclined can cultivate unconditional love for work (work is worship) and people. Matsushita was inspired by the dedication of people at a monastery, and strove to create the same environment in his organization (Kotter, 1997) making his organization more rather than less competitive, against the common perception that competitiveness comes from business analytics rather than soft values like love. More research as well as cultivation of Indian constructs like these are needed if we are going to develop culturally appropriate management principles beyond the current western principles and practices.

The discussion of the constructs also presented some research strategies. First, the construct of interest can be studied by examining dictionary meanings, synonyms, and antonyms of the construct of interest in *samskRtam* and an Indian language, say, *hindi*. Second, the construct of interest can be examined in multiple texts. Third, the use of the construct can be examined in daily communication and proverbs. Fourth, researchers can employ autoethnography to tease out a processual understanding of a construct. Fifth, models can be drawn from texts and polished to fit with the extant literature. Sixth, the text of all the verses that refer to a construct in a text could be analyzed to decipher the meaning of the construct. Seventh, researchers can wade through a text and combine various verses to create a complex model. Thus, for the development and elaboration of Indian constructs multiple methods and texts can be employed (see Bhawuk, 2020d for elaboration of the methodologies).

There are some methodological advantages of employing cultural texts for developing indigenous constructs. First, the material employed is cultural, since it is passed on from generation to generation. Second, it is likely to have been safeguarded from distortions resulting from colonization. Finally, texts are not random juxtapositions of clauses. They have texture (Halliday & Hasan, 1976), which is a semantic property. A text is a semantic unit that has a unity of meaning (Lemke, 1991). When one studies verses from a text like the *bhagavadgItA*, the reader experiences the texture at multiple levels, in words, in feelings, and in some unnamable spiritual depth. She or he does this simultaneously or in an indeterminable sequence. As the examination of the verses on a theme progresses, the texture becomes a web of meaning, an indigenous thick description, which often is an improvement on those presented by non-native researchers (see discussion of thick descriptions by non-native researchers in Ryle, 1949, 1971; and Geertz, 1973).

In this chapter, indigenous constructs were reviewed to show how Indian culture is intrinsically positive, facilitating the development of positive psychological and management research. It is hoped that the thick-description of the construct of *adhyAtma*, *zraddhA*, *tapas*, *lajjA*, *prema*, *lokasaMgraha* and their nomological networks will contribute to both Indian and global psychologies, and stimulate both basic and applied research in the future. It is also hoped that the chapter will not only stimulate research by academics but also guide practitioners to build on the positive Indian concepts in managing people in organizations, and will be useful for international scholars venturing into doing cultural or cross-cultural research in India or on Indian management.

Reference

Agarwal, S. P. (1995). *The social message of the Gita symbolized as lokasaMgraha*. MLBD.

Ames, R., & Hall, D. (2010). *Dao De Jing: A philosophical translation*. Ballantine Books.

Apte, V. S. (1890). The practical *saMskRta*-English dictionary. Shiralkar & Co.

Basham, A. L. (1954). *The wonder that was India*. Grove.
Bhawuk, D. P. S. (2003). Culture's influence on creativity: The case of Indian spirituality. *International Journal of Intercultural Relations, 27*(1), 1–22.
Bhawuk, D. P. S. (2008). Toward an Indian organizational psychology. In K. R. Rao, A. C. Paranjpe, & A. K. Dalal (Eds.), *Handbook of Indian psychology* (pp. 471–491). Cambridge University Press.
Bhawuk, D. P. S. (2010). Methodology for building psychological models from scriptures: Contributions of Indian psychology to indigenous and global psychologies. *Psychology and Developing Societies, 22*(1), 49–93.
Bhawuk, D. P. S. (2011). *Spirituality and Indian psychology: Lessons from the Bhagavad-Gita*. Springer.
Bhawuk, D. P. S. (2012). India and the culture of peace: Beyond ethnic, religious, and other conflicts. In D. Landis & R. Albert (Eds.), *Handbook of ethnic conflict* (pp. 137–174). Springer.
Bhawuk, D. P. S. (2014). *citta* or consciousness: Some perspectives from Indian psychology. *Journal of Indian Psychology, 28*(1 & 2), 37–43.
Bhawuk, D. P. S. (2017). *lajjA* in Indian psychology: Spiritual, social, and literary perspectives. In E. Vanderheiden & C.-H. Mayer (Eds.), *The value of shame—Exploring a health resource across cultures* (pp. 109–134). Springer.
Bhawuk, D. P. S. (2018). Cultivating meditation for leading a peaceful life. *3D...IBA Journal of Management and Leadership, 9*(2), 24–27.
Bhawuk, D. P. S. (2019a). *adhyātma* or spirituality: Construct definition and elaboration using multiple methods. In Sushanta K. Mishra & Arup Varma (Eds.), *Spirituality in management: Insights from India* (pp. 19–41). Palgrave-Macmillan.
Bhawuk, D. P. S. (2019b). *adhyātma* or spirituality: Indian perspectives on management. In Pawan S. Budhwar, Rajesh Kumar, & Arup Varma (Eds.), *Indian business: Understanding a rapidly emerging economy* (pp. 256–266) . Routledge.
Bhawuk, D. P. S. (2019c). *lajjA*: Learning, unlearning, and relearning. In Elisabeth Vanderheiden & Claude-Hélène Mayer (Eds.), *The bright side of shame: Transforming and growing through practical applications in cultural contexts* (pp. 35–49). Springer.
Bhawuk, D. P. S. (2019d). *lokasaMgraha*: An indigenous construct of leadership and its measure. In S. Dhiman & A. D. Amar (Eds.), *Managing by the Bhagavad Gita: Timeless lessons for today's managers* (pp. 273–297).
Bhawuk, D. P. S. (2019e). Toward a spirituality-based theory of creativity: Indigenous perspectives from India. In Kuang-Hui Yeh (Ed.), *Asian indigenous psychologies in the global context* (pp. 139–168). Palgrave MacMillan.

Bhawuk, D. P. S. (2020a). *vAde vAde jAyate tattvabodhaH*: Toward epistemic harmony through dialogue. *Theory and Psychology, 30*(3), 472–478. https://doi.org/10.1177/0959354320922613

Bhawuk, D. P. S. (2020b). *śraddhā*: Construct definition from the Bhagavad-Gītā. *Psychology and Developing Societies, 32*(1), 1–16. https://doi.org/10.1177/0971333620906758

Bhawuk, D. P. S. (2020c). Indian psychology and intercultural training. In Dan Landis & Dharm P. S. Bhawuk (Eds.), *The handbook of intercultural training* (4th ed., pp. 540–563) Cambridge University Press.

Bhawuk, D. P. S. (2020d). Research on *zAstras* in contemporary times: Methodological strategies for indigenous research. *Journal of Psychosocial Research, 15*(2), 325–338. https://doi.org/10.32381/JPR.2020.15.02.30

Bhawuk, D. P. S. (2021). prem in Kabīrsāhab'ssākhī: Indigenous perspectives on love. In Elisabeth Vanderheiden & Claude-Hélène Mayer (Eds.), *Love in cultural and transcultural contexts*. Springer.

Bhawuk, D. P. S. (in press a). Developing an indigenous thick-description: Tapas in the Bhagavadgītā. In Sanjeev P. Sahni, Pankaj Gupta, & Tithi Bhatnagar (Eds.), *Spirituality and management: From models to applications*. Springer.

Bhawuk, D. P. S. (in press b). lajjA and the Fourth Industrial Revolution (4IR): The need for pause. In Claude-Hélène Mayer, Elisabeth Vanderheiden, & Paul Wong (Eds.), *Shame 4.0: Investigating an emotion in digital worlds and the fourth industrial revolution*. Springer.

Bhawuk, D. P. S., Mrazek, S., & munusAmy, V. P. (2009). From social engineering to community transformation: Amul, Grameen Bank, and Mondragon as exemplar organizations. *Peace & Policy: Ethical Transformations for a Sustainable Future, 14*, 36–63.

Chakraborty, S. K. (1987). *Managerial effectiveness and quality of work life: Indian insights*. Tata McGraw Hill.

Chakraborty, S. K. (1993). *Managerial transformation by values: A corporate pilgrimage*. Sage.

Chakraborty, S. K. (1995). *Ethics in management: Vedantic perspectives*. Oxford University Press.

Cohen, L. (1998). *No ageing in India: Alzheimer's, the bad family, and other modern things*. University of California Press.

Costanza, R., d'Arge, R., de Groot, R., Farber, S., Grasso, M., Hannon, B., Naeem, S., Limburg, K., Paruelo, J., O'Neill, R. V., Raskin, R., Sutton, P., & van den Belt, M. (1997). The value of the world's ecosystem services and natural capital. *Nature, 387*, 253–260.

Creighton, M. R. (1990). Revisiting shame and guilt cultures: A forty-year pilgrimage. *Ethos, 18*(3), 279–307.
Dale, E. S. (1991). *Bringing heaven down to earth: A practical spirituality of work*. Peter Lang Pub Inc.
Dehler, G. E., & Welsh, M. A. (1994). Spirituality and organizational transformation: Implications for the new management paradigm. *Journal of Managerial Psychology, 9*(6), 17–26.
Fayol, H. (1949). General and industrial management (Constance Storrs. Trans,). Sir Isaac Pitman and Sons. (Original work published 1916).
Forster, E. M. (1924). *A passage to India*. Harcourt, Brace and Company.
Fung, H. (1999). Becoming a moral child: The socialization of shame among Young Chinese Children. *Ethos, 27*(2), 180–209.
Gambhirananda, S. (1998). bhagavadgItA with the annotation guDhArthadIpikA madhusudana saraswati. zrI rAmakRSNa tapovanam.
Geertz, C. (1973). *The interpretation of cultures: Selected essays*. New York: Basic Books.
Graen, G. B., & Uhl-Bien, M. (1995). Relationship-based approach to leadership: Development of leader-member exchange (LMX) theory of leadership over 25 years: Applying a multi-level multi-domain perspective. *The Leadership Quarterly, 6*(2), 219–247.
Halliday, M. A. K., & Hasan, R. (1976). *Cohesion in English*. Longman.
Held, B. S. (2020). Epistemic violence in psychological science: Can knowledge of, from, and for the (othered) people solve the problem? *Theory & Psychology, 30*(3), 349–370.
Hochschild, A. R. (1983). The managed heart: Commercialization of human feeling. University of California Press. ISBN 0520054547
Holland, J. (1989). *Creative communion: Toward a spirituality of work*. Paulist Press.
Isaksen, S. G., & Murdock, M. C. (1993). The emergence of a discipline: Issues and approaches to the study of creativity. In S. G. Isaksen, M. C. Murdock, R. L. Firestien, & D. J. Treffinger (Eds.), *Understanding and recognizing creativity: The emergence of a discipline* (pp. 13–47). Norwood, NJ: Ablex.
Khandwalla, P. (2018). *Fast forward towards civilizational greatness: Agenda for India*. Vikas Publishing.
Krishnamurti, J. (1979). What love is not. Talk given in Saanen 1979, Discussion 2.
Kotter, J. P. (1997). *Matsushita leadership: Lessons from the 20th century's most remarkable entrepreneur*. The Free Press.

Lawler, J. J. (1990). *Unionization and deunionization: Strategy, tactics, and outcomes*. University of South Carolina Press.

Lawler, J. J. (1994). Testimony of John J. Lawler before the commission on the future of worker- management relations. Retrieved April 19, 2021 from Cornell University, School of Industrial and Labor Relations site: http://digitalcommons.ilr.cornell.edu/key_workplace/354/

Lebra, T. S. (1983). Shame and guilt: A psychocultural view of the Japanese self. *Ethos, 11*(3), 192–209.

Lee, M. (1991). Spirituality in organisations: Empowerment and purpose. *Management Education and Development, 22*(3), 221–226.

Lemke, J. L. (1991). Text production and dynamic text semantics. In E. Ventola (Ed.), *Functional and systemic linguistics: Approaches and uses* (pp. 23–38). Mouton/deGruyter (Trends in Linguistics: Studies and Monographs 55).

Leung, K., & Bond, M. H. (Eds.). (2010). *Psychological aspects of social axioms*. Springer.

Lewis, H. B. (1971). Shame and guilt in neurosis. *Psychoanalytic Review, 58*(3), 419.

Lopez, S. J., Pedrotti, J. T., & Snyder, C. R. (2019). *Positive psychology: The scientific and practical explorations of human strengths* (4th ed.). SAGE Publications.

Markus, H. R., & Kitayama, S. (1991). Culture and the self: Implications for cognition, emotion, and motivation. *Psychological Review, 98*(2), 224–253.

Marsella, A. J. (1998). Toward a" global-community psychology": Meeting the needs of a changing world. *American Psychologist, 53*(12), 1282–1291.

Menon, U. & Shweder, R. (1994). Kali's tongue: Cultural psychology and the power of "Shame" in Orissa, India. In S. Kitayama & H. Markus (Eds.), Emotion and culture: Empirical studies of mutual influence. American Psychological Association.

Menon, U. & Shweder, R. (2003). Dominating Kali: Hindu family values and tantric power. In R. McDermott & J. Kripal (Eds.), *Encountering Kali: In the margins, at the center, in the west*. University of California Press.

Mitroff, I. I., & Denton, E. A. (1999). *A spiritual audit of corporate America: A hard look at spirituality, religion, and values in the workplace*. Jossey-Bass.

Monier-Williams, M. (1899). A saMskRta-English Dictionary. Oxford University Press. Reprinted in 1960.

Moore, C. A. (1967). Introduction: The comprehensive Indian mind. In C. A. Moore (Ed.), *The Indian mind: Essentials of Indian philosophy and culture* (pp. 1–18). University of Hawai'i Press.

Nisargadatta, M. (1973). I am that: Talks with nisargadatta mahArAja. Chetana.

Nisbett, R. E., Peng, K., Choi, I., & Norenzayan, A. (2001). Culture and systems of thought: Holistic versus analytic cognition. *Psychological Review, 108*(2), 291.

Pandey, A., & Navare, A. V. (2018). Paths of yoga: Perspective for workplace spirituality. In S. Dhiman, G. Roberts, & J. Crossman (Eds.), *The Palgrave handbook of workplace spirituality and fulfillment* (pp. 101–126). Palgrave Macmillan.

Pandey, A. (2021). Human self, work and of human being: Indian worldview and implications for management practices and scholarship. This volume, Chapter 2.

Pandey, N. & Sahay, A. (2021). Social entrepreneurship in India. This volume, Chapter 11.

Paranjpe, A. C. (1975). *In search of identity*. Halsted Press.

Paranjpe, A. C. (1984). *Theoretical psychology: The meeting of East and West*. Plenum Press.

Paranjpe, A. C. (1998). *Self and identity in modern psychology and Indian thought*. Plenum Press.

Rao, K. R., Paranjpe, A. C., & Dalal, A. K. (Eds.). (2008). *Handbook of Indian Psychology*. Cambridge University Press.

Rizvi, S. A. A., & Basham, A. L. (1987). *The wonder that was India* (Vol. 2). Sidgwick & Jackson.

Roth, R. (2011). *Transcendental meditation.* Fairfield, IA: Maharishi University of Management Press.

Rotter, J. (1966). Generalized expectancies for internal versus external control of reinforcements. Psychological monographs, 80, Whole No. 609.

Ryle, G. (1949). *Concept of the mind*. Hutchinson and Company.

Ryle, G. (1971). *Collected papers. Volume II collected essays, 1929–1968.* Hutchinson.

Sheldon, W. H. (1951). Main contrasts between Eastern and Western philosophy. In C. A. Moore (Ed.), *Essays in East-West philosophy* (pp. 288–297). University of Hawaii Press.

Sinha, D., & Tripathi, R. C. (1994). Individualism in a collectivist culture: A case of coexistence of opposites. In U. Kim, H. C. Triandis, Ç. Kâğitçibaşi, S.-C. Choi, & G. Yoon (Eds.), *Individualism and collectivism: Theory, method, and applications* (pp. 123–136). Sage Publications Inc.

Sinha, J. B. P. (1980). *The nurturant task leader*. Concept Publishing House.

Sinha, J. B. P. (1995). *The cultural context of leadership and power*. Sage.

Sinha, J. B. P. (2010). Living and doing psychology. *Psychology and Developing Societies, 22*(1), 95–120.

Sinha, J. B. P. (2014). *Psycho-social analysis of the Indian mind-set*. Springer.

Sinha, M., & Chauhan, V. (2013). Deconstructing LajjA as a marker of Indian womanhood. *Psychology and Developing Societies, 25*(1), 133–163.

Spivak, G. (1998). Can the subaltern speak? In Cary Nelson & Lawrence Grossberg (Eds.), *Marxism and the interpretation of culture*. University of Illinois Press.

Snyder, C. R., Lopez, S. J., Edwards, L. M., & Marques, S. C. (Eds.). (2021). *The Oxford handbook of positive psychology* (3rd ed.). University of Oxford Press.

Tracy, J. L., & Robins, R. W. (2006). Appraisal antecedents of shame and guilt: Support for a theoretical model. *Personality and Social Psychology Bulletin, 32*(10), 1339–1351.

Triandis, H. C. (1995). *Individualism & collectivism*. Westview Press.

Wilson, M. S. (2010). *Developing tomorrow's leader today: Insights from Corporate India*. Wiley.

Triandis, H. C. (1989). The self and social behavior in differing cultural contexts. *Psychological Review, 96*, 506–520.

Uhl-Bien, M., Riggio, R. E., Lowe, K. B., & Carsten, M. K. (2014). Followership theory: A review and research agenda. *The Leadership Quarterly, 25*(1), 83–104.

Zedec, S. (Ed.). (2010). *APA handbook of industrial and organizational psychology*. American Psychological Association. ISBN 978-1-4338-0727-5

4

Indian Psychology for Personality Studies: Need, Challenges, and Future Directions

Kumar Alok

Introduction

Humans need to interact with other humans on a day-to-day basis. Interactions may be more meaningful and more manageable when people can anticipate others' behaviors. Behaviors typically depend on both personal and situational factors. Nevertheless, individuals generally have some preferred ways of dealing with situations that others may associate with them. Anticipating others' behaviors is possible when people may know their characteristic attributes. The set of attributes that differentiate people from one another regarding what they experience and what they do is called personality. Personality refers to "the complexity of psychological systems that contribute to unity and continuity in the individual's

K. Alok (✉)
XLRI Xavier School of Management, Jamshedpur, Jharkhand, India
e-mail: kumar.alok@xlri.ac.in

© The Author(s), under exclusive license to Springer Nature Switzerland AG 2022
A. Pandey et al. (eds.), *Indigenous Indian Management*, Palgrave Studies in Indian Management,
https://doi.org/10.1007/978-3-030-87906-8_4

conduct and experience, both as it is expressed and as it is perceived by that individual" (Caprara & Cervone, 2000, p.10).

Characterizing others is so central to human knowledge that all human languages likely contain numerous one-word descriptors of human attributes (Leary & Hoyle, 2009). However, conceiving attributes and their favorable or unfavorable evaluations may vary across cultures and languages (Cheung et al., 2011; De Raad et al., 2010). A case in point is extraversion as a fundamental personality dimension reported across divers languages and cultures (McCrae & Costa, 2008).

Western scholarship conceives extraversion (e.g., talkative, assertive, active, and energetic)—introversion (e.g., quiet, reserved, shy, and silent) as a dimensional continuum. According to that, where extraversion traits are absent, introversion naturally exists and vice versa. On the other hand, most systems of Indian thought or Darshanas hold that absence is not a form of existence by itself (Radhakrishnan, 1996). Descriptions of the simultaneous presence of opposite attributes are commonplace in Sanskrit literature (Brockington, 1998; Burrow, 2001). The Bhagavadgītā (10.33) describes dvandva as the most excellent among the compounds (Shastri, 1936). Dvandva refers to a coordinate or copulative compound having two or more words all of equal importance.[1] Such words may as well be pairs of opposites such as pleasure and pain. From this perspective, it makes more sense to think of extraversion–introversion as two functionally opposite, yet existentially independent dimensions rather than a dimensional continuum.

Western cultures tend to value extraversion, whereas Eastern cultures tend to value a degree of introversion (McCrae & Terracciano, 2005). The undesirability of introversion for the Western mind was evident when it was proposed to be one of the six personality disorder dimensions for inclusion into the Diagnostic and Statistical Manual of Mental Disorders (DSM-5) (Esbec & Echeburúa, 2011). It is another thing that was not included in the final version of DSM-5. Thus, implicit ontological and normative assumptions of Western personality models may not resonate with Indian thought and culture.

[1] Sa ubhayapadārthapradhānatvenotkṛṣṭaḥ (Ramanuja commentary on the Bhagavad-Gita, X.33) (G. S. S. Shastri, 1936). Traditional commentaries are in agreement on this reason of superiority of dvandva samāsa: its emphasis on equal importance of the words in a compound.

Indian psychology is an emergent discipline that seeks to provide native ontological and normative assumptions to the study of Indian realities. It "utilizes and incorporates concepts, categories, and models derived from thought native to the Indian subcontinent and practices that have been developed and preserved for centuries" (Rao & Paranjpe, 2015, p.1). This chapter presents how Indian psychology may enrich personality studies. It outlines the need for and significance of Indian psychology as a discipline. It focuses on how Indian Psychological studies of personality have leveraged Sāṁkhya for their purposes. It also outlines the underlying issues and challenges for leveraging Sāṁkhya constructs while providing some future directions.

Indian Psychology: An Emerging Theoretical Lens on Indian Realities

A cherished goal of science is the generalization of its findings (Kaplan, 2009). Mainstream psychology assumes that there are psychological universals that can be determined rationally and empirically in a similar manner as physical universals are determined in physics (Leahey, 2001). Cross-cultural psychology seeks to achieve generalizability by testing rather than assuming the universal validity of theories and models in different cultural settings (Berry et al., 2002). Indigenous psychology is a bottom-up approach to achieve generalizability by building on studies of native realities and contributing to native concerns (Kim et al., 2006).

Indian psychology is similar in some and different in other ways to the three approaches. Like the mainstream and cross-cultural approaches, Indian psychology traces its roots to antiquity—not ancient Greece but ancient India (Rao & Paranjpe, 2015). Like the mainstream approach, it assumes the universal validity of its theories and constructs; however, like the cross-cultural approach, it may empirically examine that assumption within and outside India (Rao & Paranjpe, 2015). Like the three approaches, it emphasizes robust empirical research to justify its place in the world of science (Salagame, 2011). Like indigenous psychology, it incorporates context and first-person, second-person, and third-person perspectives in studying psychological phenomena (Dalal & Misra, 2010).

Unlike the cross-cultural approach (Berry et al., 2002), Indian psychology is not primarily identified by its methods. Also, unlike indigenous psychology, it does not make a sharp distinction between psychology, spirituality, and philosophy (Bhawuk, 2010). It considers all three as different aspects of human fulfillment. It draws from ancient scriptures to develop theories and models for understanding psychological phenomena (Bhawuk, 2010). Unlike indigenous psychology, its point of departure is the commonality of ultimate human concerns rather than the diversity of immediate concerns (Rao & Paranjpe, 2015). It holds that human beings are essentially spiritual, and in that sense, they share similar concerns for a fulfilled life. With that backdrop, it studies psychological phenomena relevant to their immediate concerns (Dalal & Misra, 2010). A diverse society like India has many culturally distinct groups, and in that sense, it offers scope for several versions of indigenous psychology rather than India's indigenous psychology. However, such diversity does not hinder the path of Indian psychology, given its primary focus on a universally shared human concern for a fulfilled life. It can accommodate diverse spiritual, religious, and philosophic traditions such as Vedic systems of thought, Buddhism, and Jainism (Dalal & Misra, 2010).

Indian psychology's emphasis on classical Indian thought reflects neither national pride nor any revivalist ideology. It reflects an appreciation of certain well-considered characteristics of Indian philosophies. Systems of Indian philosophies are generally denoted by a Sanskrit term darśana that comes from the root dṛśir prekṣaṇe—to observe intensely. Epistemologies of every major darśana accord primacy to sense-mediated knowledge, followed by inferential knowledge (Radhakrishnan, 1996). Moreover, systems of darśana generally accept transcendent as a valid area of inquiry. Inquiry into transcendent is an essential aspect of human fulfillment in the view of Indian psychology (Bhawuk, 2011). Therefore, systems of darśana are better suited for Indian psychology compared to a philosophy of science that would deny any inquiry into transcendent.

Western philosophy has maintained a distinction between the philosopher and the philosophy such that philosophers' character and conduct need not reflect on the worth of their philosophies. This position may have unintended consequences. Bandura (1999) lamented that psychologists display agency in thinking, arguing, and acting, whereas their theories deny people of such capabilities. Darśana, on the other hand, have a practical bent in the sense that they emphasize living espoused philosophical truths rather than just thinking about them (Vivekananda, 1915). It is not considered acceptable if the character and conduct of scholars are uninformed by their darśana. This intimate connection with life makes darśana particularly relevant for Indian psychology to understand and transform the human condition (Dalal & Misra, 2010). Methodologically, it means that first-person approaches to study a phenomenon can be as meaningful as second- or third-person approaches (Rao & Paranjpe, 2015). Moreover, it offers an avenue for scholars who seek personal inner growth as one of the outcomes of their scholarly work (e.g., Bhawuk, 2011; Paranjpe, 2011; Varma, 2011).

Indian Psychology for Personality Studies: An Overview

There are two essential terms related to personhood: self and personality. Self is about the sense of "I." Both self and personality bestow unity and continuity in conduct and experience. Their conceptual difference is not entirely clear in mainstream psychology. Nevertheless, the self is generally researched in social psychology, whereas personality is generally researched in personality psychology. Accordingly, the self is a relatively malleable conception of personhood, whereas personality is a relatively enduring conception of personhood. The conceptualization of self-external world interactions is in motivational terms such as self-knowledge and self-enhancement (Banaji & Prentice, 1994). The conceptualization of personality-external world interactions is generally in dispositional terms such as extraversion and neuroticism (McCrae & Costa, 2008).

Indian psychology has a better opportunity for differentiating self from personality. Self in Indian thought is of three distinct kinds: transcendental, conditioned, and reflexive. The transcendental self is commonly called ātmā or puruṣa in Vedic systems of thought (Rao & Paranjpe, 2015). Personhood is not meaningful at the level of the metaphysical transcendental self. The conditioned self is called the jīva that is ātmā or puruṣa metaphorically associated with anātma or non-self. At this level, any discussion of personhood becomes meaningful (Rao & Paranjpe, 2015). The reflexive self is called ahaṁkāra in Sāṁkhya, Yoga, and Vedānta (Salagame et al., 2005). The reflexive self manifests as reflexive self-awareness or a sense of "Me." It has its core function as abhimāna that makes any non-self as self ("Mine") through the process of identification. The social self of mainstream psychology (Banaji & Prentice, 1994) comes closer to the reflexive self in Indian psychology.

Personality in Indian thought is indicated by the terms svabhāva or prakṛti (Rao & Paranjpe, 2015). The Advaita Vedānta commentaries on the Bhagavadgītā define the term svabhāva in three different ways: pratyagātma, māyā, and vāsanā (Shastri, 1936). Pratyagātma is the conditioned self or jīva.[2] Māyā is the potency of Īśvara.[3] Vāsanā refers to the saṁskāra acquired through previous births manifesting in the present birth as tendencies to engage in corresponding actions.[4] The third definition of svabhāva is relevant for personality studies. This definition is consistent with the conception of svabhāva in Sāṁkhya (Shastri, 2010) and Yoga (Agashe, 1904).

The acquisition of vāsanā takes place by experiencing the results of one's actions (Āraṇya, 1983). Therefore, vāsanā or any saṁskāra falls in the domain of non-self. The Sāṁkhya Sūtra (II.42) considers buddhi as the receptacle of all saṁskāra[5] (Garbe, 1888). Buddhi is an instrument of self and, therefore, a non-self. Sāṁkhya considers all external (bahiṣkaraṇa) and internal (antaḥkaraṇa) instruments as adhyātma rather than ātma (Dvivedin, 1918). This principle generally holds good for

---

[2] ātmānaṁ dehaṁ adhikṛtya pratyagātmatayā pravṛttaṁ paramārthabrahmāvasānaṁ vastu svabhāvaḥ (Śāṅkara Bhāṣya, Bhagavadgītā, VIII.3): ātmā controls the body as indweller self and in reality, is Brahma, that is svabhāva.

[3] svabhāvaḥ Īśvarasya prkṛtiḥ triguṇātmikā māyā (Śāṅkara Bhāṣya, Bhagavadgītā, XVIII.41): svabhāva is the potency of Īśvara that is māyā of the form of triguṇa.

[4] janmāntarakṛtasaṁskāraḥ prāṇināṁ vartamānajanmani svakāryābhimukhatvena abhivyaktaḥ svabhāvaḥ (Śāṅkara Bhāṣya, Bhagavadgītā, XVIII.41): as translated above.

[5] tatrādhārāsarvasaṁskāratvāt: Moreover, it (buddhi) is the receptacle of all saṁskāra (Garbe, 1892).

Yoga (Āraṇya, 1983) and Vedānta as well. For example, Rāmānuja, a Vedānta scholar par excellence, considered adhyātma as non-self associated with self[6] (Shastri, 1936).

Indian philosophies generally accept the principle of rebirth, which postulates that jīva does not become different by taking up different physical bodies (Radhakrishnan, 1996). If svabhāva were to refer to jīva as such, it would have no bearing on explaining observed differences in various organisms' behavioral tendencies. Therefore, svabhāva is meaningful for only the jīva that has become associated with a physical body. The tendencies of adhyātma as conditioned by the physical body qualify as svabhāva. Svabhāva does not refer to the tendencies of jīva as such. It underlines the need to make a clear distinction between self (jīva) and personality (svabhāva) in Indian psychology.

Based on this explicit distinction, current Indian psychological conceptions of personality (Jha, 2008; Rao & Paranjpe, 2015; Srivastava, 2012; Varma, 2011) drawn from Vedānta, Nyāya-Vaiśeṣika, Jaina darśana, and Integral Yoga of Sri Aurobindo would qualify as the models of self rather than personality. For example, Paranjpe (1988) advanced the model of the embodied jīva as the five-sheathed entity, which he considered an Advaita Vedānta-based model of personality. Each of the five sheaths is non-self; however, jīva identifies itself with the sheaths; thereby, making them identical to self. These sheaths include the elements that Vedānta does not consider as adhyātma—physical body, prāṇa or vital energies, and ajñāna or fundamental ignorance. Therefore, the five sheath model can qualify as a model of jīva rather than svabhāva due to two reasons: (a) the five sheaths become integral to self by identification, and (b) the five sheaths include non- adhyātma elements. Reviewing the literature on self is beyond this chapter's scope (for excellent reviews, see Jha, 2008; Paranjpe, 2002; Rao & Paranjpe, 2015).

Āyurveda is considered as an important source of personality models in Indian psychology (Rao & Paranjpe, 2015; Srivastava, 2012). Sāṁkhya is foundational to the personality conceptions in Āyurveda;

---

[6] The Bhagavadgītā (VIII.3) says svabhāvo 'dhyātmaṁ ucyate. Its Ramanuja commentary defines adhyātma as anātmabhūtaṁ ātmani saṁbhdhyamānaṁ - non-self associated with self (Shastri, 1936).

however, it also leverages Vedānta and Vaiśeṣika (Suśruta, 1954). The self in Āyurveda is karmapuruṣa that is amenable to medical treatment[7] (Suśruta, 1954). Karmapuruṣa is the inherence of jīva in the five great elements that constitute the physical body.[8] The postulation of the relationship of inherence allows Āyurveda to conceptualize svabhāva in terms of dehaprakṛti or the body's innate nature.

Dehaprakṛti comprises various combinations of tridoṣa: kapha, vāta, and pitta.[9] The Śārīra Sthānam (IV. 80–96) of the Suśruta Saṁhitā enumerates 16 types of dehaprakṛti (Suśruta, 1954). For example, Brāmakāya dehaprakṛti manifests as tendencies for cleanliness, faith in scriptures, engagement with scriptural studies, respect for elders and preceptors, hospitality, and worship of God, or performance of sacrifices. The concept of dehaprakṛti includes enduring physiological, psychological, and spiritual tendencies. In this sense, it is a much broader concept than either svabhāva or personality. It is a highly promising avenue for personality research in Indian psychology. Āyurveda also gives separate consideration to sattvaprakṛti or the mind's innate nature (Dwivedi, 2002). Sattvaprakṛti comprises various combinations of triguṇa: sattva, rajas, and tamas. Research on sattvaprakṛti follows Sāṁkhya conceptions of triguṇa.

Buddhism is a system that does not postulate a self (Rao & Paranjpe, 2015). The Puggalapannatti text of the Abhidhamma Pitaka presents a complex personality typology using character descriptors such as the hypocrite and the charlatan (Rao & Paranjpe, 2015). It seeks to classify individual characteristics concerning their stages of spiritual development on the Buddhist path. It represents an early school of Buddhism called Pudgalavāda that postulated a conception of personality without self; however, it gradually lost its acceptance within the Mahāyāna Buddhism (Werner, 1996). Indian psychology scholars have taken note of it;

[7] sa eva karmapuruṣascikitsā 'dhikṛtaḥ (Suśruta Saṁhitā, śārīra Sthānam, I.21): as translated above.

[8] pañcamahābhūtaśarīrisamavāyaḥ puruṣa (Suśruta Saṁhitā, śārīra Sthānam, I.21): as translated above.

[9] sapta prakṛtayo bhavanti - doṣaiḥ pṛthag dviśaiḥ samastaisca (Suśruta Saṁhitā, śārīra Sthānam, IV.61): there are seven kinds of prakṛti: doṣa taken separately, (three combinations of) two doṣa together, and all three doṣa together.

however, it is yet to gain significant research attention. Its complexity and deep connections with the spiritual development on the Buddhist path may restrict its general applications.

Sāṁkhya: A Mainstay of Personality Studies in Indian Psychology

Sāṁkhya is the system of Indian thought that has anchored a majority of empirical research concerning personality (Salagame, 2011). Sāṁkhya has been used to develop personality measures (Biswas, 2010) as well as to study how personality influences important outcomes such as workplace ethics (Bhal & Debnath, 2006), leadership (Alok, 2017), and managerial effectiveness (Chakraborty, 1987). The Bhagavadgītā presents a Sāṁkhya-based model of personality that attracted the attention of psychology and management scholars since the early twentieth century (Misra & Paranjpe, 2012).

Indian psychology's preoccupation with Sāṁkhya is not without reason. It is the oldest known system of Indian philosophy with a pervasive influence on Indian culture and thought (Larson & Bhattacharya, 2012). Larson and Bhattacharya (2012) described Sāṁkhya ideas as cultural codes for the Indian intellectual milieu. Such influence of Sāṁkhya is evident in a psycho-lexical study of Hindi—a major Indian language (Singh et al., 2013).

Recognizing the need to study the personality trait descriptors in non-Western languages spoken by a vast majority of humanity, Singh et al. (2013) conducted a psycho-lexical analysis of Hindi. They followed a systematic protocol for identifying trait-relevant adjectives such as jujhārū (one who never gives up). They eliminated ambiguous words describing roles, physical features, ideological epithets, health, power and status, politics, and religion. Thus, an initial set of 3,300 adjectives was reduced to 295 trait-relevant adjectives. Both self and peer ratings obtained from 511 student respondents were subjected to principle component analytical procedures. The resultant components supported a robust three-dimensional structure resembling Sāṁkhya ideas rather than Western trait taxonomies. Evidently, Sāṁkhya ideas are significant for Indian psychological studies of personality.

Sāṁkhya ideas are found in many ancient texts such as the Nāsadīya Sūkta of the Ṛgveda, Chāndogya upaniṣada, Kaṭha upaniṣada, Śvetāśvatara upaniṣada, Maitrī upaniṣada, Māhābhāratā, and the Bhagavadgītā (Larson & Bhattacharya, 2012). However, its systematic presentation is available in three primary texts that have managed to survive the ravages of time: Sāṁkhya Sūtra, Tattva Samāsa, and Sāṁkhya Kārikā. The first two are written in the form of aphorisms, and even the Sāṁkhya Kārikā, an apparently poetic text, is held to be aphoristic by its Yuktidīpika commentary (Wezler & Motegi, 1998). Evidently, these texts require the help of commentarial tradition for reasonable comprehension.

Western scholars continue to hold that the Sāṁkhya Sūtra is the most recent of the three, and it may be dated circa fourteenth century CE (Larson & Bhattacharya, 2012). However, Shastri (1950) convincingly argued that it is the oldest of the three such that it is the Ṣaṣṭitantra itself—the original Sāṁkhya text authored by its founder, Kapil and elaborated by his grand disciple, Pañcaśikha. He refuted each of the three key arguments advanced to establish recency of the Sāṁkhya Sūtra. First, recency of the Sāṁkhya Sūtra is supposed because some aphorisms adopt the substance and the style of the Sāṁkhya Kārikā. Shastri (1950) showed that there are only three such aphorisms, and they, too, had a proper aphorism-style older version, as found cited in other ancient texts. Sāṁkhya Kārikā itself is shown to be a summary of the first three chapters of the Sāṁkhya Sūtra (Shastri, 1950). Second, recency of the Sāṁkhya Sūtra is supposed because the scholarly tradition in India has cited the Sāṁkhya Kārikā rather than the aphorisms. Shastri (1950) showed that many aphorisms are found cited in the Indian scholarly tradition. Some such citations are in texts that are believed to be older than the Sāṁkhya Kārikā (Shastri, 1950). Third, recency of the Sāṁkhya Sūtra is supposed because several aphorisms appear to refute views of later darśana such as Buddhism and Jainism. Shastri (1950) showed that it is more meaningful to consider such aphorisms as a case of later interpolation rather than considering the whole text itself as of recent origin. Perhaps, his elaborate and painstakingly evidenced work has remained rather unnoticed by the Western scholarship. A possible reason could be that he chose to publish his work in Hindi rather than Sanskrit or English that Western Sāṁkhya scholars generally cultivate.

Tattva Samāsa is a small text of 25 aphorisms that looks more like an index and less like an independent text (Larson & Bhattacharya, 2012). Shastri (1950) argued that it is an index of the Sāṁkhya Sūtra. It is comprehensible with the help of its ancient commentary called Tattvasamāsasūtravṛtti or Kramadīpikā (Dvivedin, 1918).

Nevertheless, the most popular primary Sāṁkhya text, both in the Indian scholarly tradition and abroad, has been the Sāṁkhya Kārikā (Larson & Bhattacharya, 2012). It is a 72-verse pithy and systematic summary of the Ṣaṣṭitantra such that only the fundamental principles of Sāṁkhya are covered while leaving out expository narratives as well as refutations of other darśana (Larson & Bhattacharya, 2012). It was written by Iśvarakṛṣṇa, the Sāṁkhya teacher who came in the spiritual lineage of Pañcaśikha. Such was the influence of this work that it authoritatively represented Sāṁkhya for scholars in India and abroad (Larson & Bhattacharya, 2012). In Western scholarship, the version of Sāṁkhya present in the Sāṁkhya Kārikā is generally considered as the "classical" Sāṁkhya such that it becomes a reference point for studying other texts and schools of Sāṁkhya (Larson & Bhattacharya, 2012).

Sāṁkhya holds that two fundamentally distinct real principles exist: prakṛti, the principle that generates the categories of known and puruṣa, the knowing principle (Larson, 1998). The generic principle prakṛti manifests in three specific manners—sattva, rajas, and tamas[10] (Rao, 1963). These are ever-transforming real principles and, as such, non-different from prakṛti. These principles are known as guṇa. The Sanskrit word guṇa refers to a strand in a rope as well as a tendency to diminish. One typically needs three strands of fibers to make a rope. The three

[10] pravartate triguṇataḥ samudayācca (Sāṁkhya Kārikā, 16): prakṛti operates through the combination of three guṇa (Virupakshananda, 1995). Its Gauḍapāda commentary explains triguṇa as sattvarajastamoguṇāḥ yasmiṁstat triguṇam - triguṇa refers to sattva, rajas, and tamas (J. Shastri, 2010).

guṇa or triguṇa must be together to make any form of manifestation possible.[11] Further, the three guṇa tend to diminish. Thus, triguṇa take turns in dominating each other (Larson, 1998; Pulingandla, 1994). Consideration of guṇa is so central to Sāṁkhya that the Bhagavadgītā[12] (XVIII.19) refers to Sāṁkhya as Guṇa-Saṁkhyāna (Bolle, 1979).

Indian psychology scholars have primarily leveraged the idea of triguṇa to develop their accounts of personality (Salagame, 2011). They commonly refer to the idea of triguṇa and its human manifestations mentioned in the Bhagavadgītā. This research tradition has emphasized conceptual models as well as measures of personality. Nevertheless, scholars share considerable disagreement regarding what triguṇa are and how to conceptualize them (Murthy & Salagame, 2007).

Sattva-rajas-tamas are variously conceptualized as illumination-passion-dullness (Bhal & Debnath, 2006; Biswas, 2010), stability-activation-inertia (Mathew, 2001), and spiritual-mundane-degrading (Wolf, 1999). Also, researchers have generally treated them as purely positive-moderately positive–negative qualities, respectively (Salagame, 2011). Indian psychology scholars have conceptualized the triguṇa construct in at least six different ways: (a) personality dimensions, (b) personality types, (c) behavioral tendencies, (d) components of mind, (e) levels of consciousness, and (f) fundamental characters (Salagame, 2011).

Murthy and Salagame (2007) conducted a conceptual analysis of triguṇa construct using etymological meanings of these terms as well as meanings based on primary texts such as Sāṁkhya Kārikā, its traditional commentaries, the Bhagavadgītā, and Māhābhāratā. They concluded that the terms: triguṇa, sattva, rajas, and tamas have complex meanings in the source texts that might lead to their diverse conceptualizations in Indian psychology. The etymological method and the conclusion needs further reflection. The etymological meaning is relevant for terms that are general rather than definitional. The terms, triguṇa, sattva, rajas, and

[11] anyo'nyābhibhavāśrayajananamithunavṛttayaśca guṇāḥ (Sāṁkhya Kārikā, 12): triguṇa are mutually dominating, supporting, productive, and cooperative (Virupakshananda, 1995).

[12] jñānaṁ karma ca kartā ca tridhaiva guṇabhedataḥ procyate guṇasaṁkhyāne yathāvacchṛṇu tānyapi (Bhagavadgītā, XVIII.19): Knowledge, work, and actor are verily of three kinds based on different guṇa. Listen to that as well how they are described in Sāṁkhya.

tamas are Sāṁkhya jargon. Therefore, their diverse etymological meanings need not be a source of confusion as long as the terms are precisely defined in Sāṁkhya texts. Given the strong polemic argumentations developed within Sāṁkhya tradition (Larson & Bhattacharya, 2012), it is legitimate to expect that at least one traditional commentator would consider definitions of the triguṇa terms as imprecise. However, none of the traditional Sāṁkhya commentators have considered triguṇa definitions as imprecise. Therefore, it may be pertinent to look elsewhere for the possible reasons for such disagreements and confusion.

What follows is an investigation of the two key challenges plaguing triguṇa research in Indian psychology. The challenges are discussed in the context of triguṇa as personality types since that has been the dominant stream of research in Indian psychology (Rao & Paranjpe, 2015). In typological conceptions, the terms sāttvika, rājasika, and tāmasika and their possible combinations are considered qualitatively distinct such that people can be sorted into one of the possible categories or types.

Challenge 1: Imposed Etic Biases

Imposed etic bias is an anthropological concept that refers to interpreting native realities using alien frameworks. Such interpretations may distort the meaning of the ideas and practices studied. Indian psychology seeks to remedy imposed etic biases that creep in due to reliance on Western theories and models for interpreting Indian realities (Bhawuk, 2010, 2011). It is indeed an irony that Indian psychological studies of personality demonstrate evidence of imposed etic biases.

Epistemological Bias

Modern science recognizes efficient cause as the only form of causation (Clatterbaugh, 1999; Kaplan, 2009). An efficient cause (nimitta kāraṇa) is that which influences rather than constitutes its effects. Science would explain the conversion of soil into an earthen pot in terms of its specific properties that influence whether it can take and hold specific shapes in the presence of enabling conditions. However, the idea of triguṇa in Sāṁkhya is rooted in material causation (upādāna kāraṇa) that is critical for its systemic framework (Larson & Bhattacharya, 2012). The Yuktidīpikā (Sāṁkhya Kārikā, 9) states that an effect is only a particular arrangement of its material cause[13] (Wezler & Motegi, 1998). For example, it is soil that takes the form of an earthen pot when arranged in a particular manner.

Sāṁkhya seeks to attain the state of absolute cessation of all kinds of sufferings (Dvivedin, 1918). The Sāṁkhya Sūtra (I.1) describes this state as the absolute purpose of puruṣa[14] (Pandeya, 1989). In other words, Sāṁkhya sets out to explicate its system from the perspective of this absolute purpose of puruṣa. This point is of fundamental importance for understanding the Sāṁkhya view of material causation. Sāṁkhya holds that puruṣa and prakṛti are fundamentally distinct such that material causation in its entirety is attributable to only prakṛti[15] (Shastri, 2010). Nevertheless, discussing material causation in terms of the knower's experiences is meaningful due to the Sāṁkhya focus on the perspective of puruṣa.

There are three ultimate categories of experiences that knowledge of anything may produce for a knower: contentment, discontent, and indifference (Saraswati, 2008). Given that Sāṁkhya considers an effect as a particular arrangement of its material cause, three ultimate material causes are posited, respectively, for the three distinct experiences: sattva, rajas, and tamas (Shastri, 2010). It is to be noted that this view of material causation holds cause and effect as same in essence. That is why the Sāṁkhya Kārikā (12) characterizes the three in terms of contentment, discontent, and indifference[16] (Shastri, 2010). The generic name for the three ultimate material causes is guṇa or triguṇa. Triguṇa or the three strands form the rope that symbolizes the metaphorical bondage

[13] sanniveśa viśeṣa mātra abhyupagamāt: (effect) is agreed to be mere particular arrangements (of its cause).

[14] atha trividhaduḥkhātyantanivṛttiratyantapuruṣārthaḥ: Let the eligible equire into the ultimate purpose of puruṣa viz. complete cessation of three forms of suffering.

[15] kāraṇamastyavyaktaṁ (Sāṁkhya Kārikā, 16): The Unmanifest (prakṛti) is the cause.

[16] prītyaprītiviṣādātmakāḥ: as translated above.

of puruṣa, whose metaphorical release is the stated purpose of Sāṁkhya (Wezler & Motegi, 1998).

The 12th verse of the Sāṁkhya Kārikā mentions the characteristics of triguṇa[17] (Shastri, 2010). Sattva, rajas, and tamas are of the form of pleasurable contentment, discontent and pain, and indifference, respectively. It refers to the material causation of triguṇa from an experiential perspective. Sattva, rajas, and tamas serve the purposes of knowledge, actuation, and restraint, respectively. It refers to the efficient causation of triguṇa. Triguṇa exist and manifest their effects in an interdependent rather than independent manner.

Sāṁkhya holds that general and particular cannot be mutually exclusive[18] (Wezler & Motegi, 1998). Therefore, a general can manifest as subservient to a particular. In other words, a particular manifestation of a guṇa can allow general manifestations of the other two guṇa. Since the effect is continuous with its material cause, it is the particular manifestation of a guṇa that primarily determines the effect's nature[19] (Wezler & Motegi, 1998). Therefore, particular manifestations of sattva and subservient manifestations of rajas and tamas denote a sāttvika effect. Rājasika and tāmasika effects refer to particular manifestations of rajas and tamas, respectively, along with general manifestations of the other two guṇa. For example, the Bhagavadgītā (XVIII.38) calls a pleasure as rājasika, even though sattva is the material cause of pleasure (Bolle, 1979). In this case, particular manifestations of discontent would accompany subservient manifestation of general pleasure. Therefore, rājasika pleasures fuel the desire for more rather than causing contentment.

Imposing an efficient causation framework on triguṇa has a significant epistemological consequence. In the efficient causation framework, any aspect of a cause relevant to the effect must be treated as an attribute that influences the effect rather than a substance that constitutes the effect. This consequence is already apparent in the adaptation of triguṇa

---

[17] prītyaprītiviṣādātmakāḥ prakāśapravṛttiniyamārthāḥ.
anyo'nyābhibhavāśrayajananamithunavṛttayaśca guṇāḥ: as explained above.

[18] sāmānyāni tvatiśayaiḥ saha vartante (Yuktidīpikā on Sāṁkhya Kārikā, 13): general can co-exist with particular.

[19] kiṁtarhi mahatī svabhāvātivṛttiḥ prakṛtitaḥ (Yuktidīpikā on Sāṁkhya Kārikā, 43): as traslated above.

for personality studies in Indian psychology. The 17th and 18th chapters of the Bhagavadgītā offer 12 illustrations of what sāttvika, rājasika, and tāmasika things are like (Alok, 2014). Indian psychology scholars have generally used these illustrations to develop their sattva, rajas, and tamas conceptualizations. Due to the imposition of an efficient causation framework, they could only treat the terms sāttvika, rājasika, and tāmasika as adjectives rather than effects of sattva, rajas, and tamas. Modern philosophers had to devise their causal logic system when they discarded the metaphysical bases of causation (Clatterbaugh, 1999). However, Indian psychology scholars have continued to leverage the causal efficacy of triguṇa without accepting material causation. Sāttvika, as the adjective of sattva, needs an exact causal theory to account for any influence that it is expected to have on any issue of human concern. Without such a causal account, sāttvika as an adjective can refer to only the observer's attributions rather than any internal dispositions of a person.

Ontological Bias

Doing indigenous scholarship in English has its own perils. The Sanskrit word guṇa has quality as one of its meanings. The definitional Sāṁkhya term guṇa is frequently translated in English as quality (e.g., Radhakrishnan, 1996). In the modern Sāṁkhya scholarship, they are frequently considered as psychological states (Larson & Bhattacharya, 2012; Radhakrishnan, 1996). Together, the English translations and modern Sāṁkhya scholarship in English give the impression that triguṇa are psychological qualities or attributes that characterize people in a relatively stable manner. Indian psychology scholars generally draw from modern Sāṁkhya scholarship in English. Thus, it appears to have influenced their view that triguṇa must be a personality construct; however, it reflects an imposed etic bias regarding the ontology of triguṇa.

The Bhagavadgītā (XVIII.40)[20] says that triguṇa constitutes the entire manifest world (Bolle, 1979). Therefore, it is a mistake to consider them as mere psychological entities. The Bhagavadgītā (III.27)[21] asserts that all human actions are effects of triguṇa. Therefore, triguṇa cannot be a personality construct since personality is supposed to influence rather than constitute human actions. Triguṇa are ontological real substances rather than attributes or qualities of some kind (Rao, 1963). It is evident that the imposed etic bias changes the entire ontology of triguṇa.

Indian psychology scholars consider triguṇa as a personality construct after converting their effects to adjectives. Adjectives can only refer to attributes rather than substances that Sāṁkhya posits them to be. Radical ontological transformation, coupled with epistemological impositions, has contributed to the present situation where the fundamental questions are unsettled: what triguṇa are and what they do (Salagame, 2011).

Challenge 2: Evading Traditional Scholarship

Classical texts of darśana are generally available in Sanskrit. Students of psychology in India are hardly required to cultivate familiarity with Sanskrit. Therefore, scholars with an interest in Indian psychology may typically resort to available translations of the texts. Translations may not be substitutes for original texts since the translators may not have the perspective that may be critical for the research in Indian psychology. Translations such as "quality" for "guṇa" may change the ontological and epistemological nature of the idea altogether. Therefore, translations may not be valid substitutes for the original texts for scientific purposes.

Considering the modern scholarship of Indian philosophy as a sufficient base for Indian psychological research is prone to imposed etic influences. The modern philosophical scholarship is yet to ascertain why there may be only three guṇa, and why pleasure should not be a

---

20 na tadasti pṛthivyāṁ vā divi deveṣu vā punaḥ sattvaṁ prakṛtijair muktaṁ yadebhiḥ syāt tribhirguṇaiḥ: There exists nothing on earth or in heaven among the gods that is free from triguṇa.

21 prakṛtaiḥ kriyamāṇāni guṇaiḥ karmāṇi sarvaśaḥ: all actions in their entirety are performed by the guṇa of prakṛti.

passion (rajas) like sorrow or grieving (Wezler, 1999). It is important to note that the commentarial tradition on Sāṁkhya Kārikā has no confusion regarding the two questions (Virupakshananda, 1995). Vācaspati (Sāṁkhya Kārikā, 12) argued that pleasure and pain could not be treated as mere mutually opposite experiences since in that case, pleasure must be the absence of pain and pain must be the absence of pleasure[22] (Virupakshananda, 1995). It would present the undesirable contingency where the absence of one must lead to the absence of both (Virupakshananda, 1995). Therefore, pleasure and pain must be ontologically real and must be causally different (Virupakshananda, 1995). Evidently, modern Sāṁkhya scholarship may not always be a valid substitute for a traditional scholarship.

Some scholars may unduly rely on their own reading of the classical texts, which may be at variance with existing translations, modern philosophical scholarship, and traditional scholarship. For example, Datar and Murthy (2012) considered triguṇa as composed of pañca mahābhūta or five great elements; thereby, reducing them to derivative effects rather than fundamental causes. The Ayurvedic concept of tridoṣa: kapha, vāta, and pitta are also derivatives of pañca mahābhūta (Agniveśa, 1948). Datar and Murthy (2012) considered triguṇa and tridoṣa as of common origin, and therefore, they studied their correlations in human personality (Shilpa & Murthy, 2012). It reflects a fundamental misunderstanding of triguṇa and tridoṣa in Āyurveda.

[22] netaretarābhāvāḥ sukhādayaḥ, api tu bhāvāḥ, ātmaśabdasya bhāvavacanattvāt: "Pleasure and pain are not merely mutual negations, but they are positive entities and the term ātma connotes this positive reality." (Virupakshananda, 1995, p. 43).

Āyurveda accepts triguṇa as the fundamental material causes[23] and postulates tridoṣa as their effects in the physical body.[24] Tridoṣa constitute dehaprakṛti, and triguṇa constitute sattvaprakṛti or psychological constitution[25] (Dwivedi, 2002). It is meaningful to study how dehaprakṛti and sattvaprakṛti are correlated since they may influence but not constitute each other. However, it is not meaningful to study how tridoṣa and triguṇa correlate because triguṇa constitute tridoṣa.

Reliance on translations, misreading in the name of self-study, or modern philosophical interpretations of Sāṁkhya may be significant reasons for the confused state of triguṇa scholarship in Indian psychology. It is rather uncommon in Ayurved-based personality scholarship to cite the exact verses from the primary texts for developing personality models. It indicates almost total reliance on translations or secondary sources. There may not be any real alternative to a traditional scholarship if the aim is to use valid adaptations of triguṇa for personality studies.

Future Directions

Whether Indian psychology must adhere to the causal conceptions of science remains an open question. There may be three different approaches, each with a successively reduced scope. First, attempts may be made to develop an epistemology of material causation that may be suitable for the scientific enterprise. The explanatory framework is an essential feature of modern science such that a fundamental departure

[23] sarvabhūtānāṁ kāraṇamakāraṇaṁ sattvarajastamolakṣaṇamaṣṭarūpamakhilasya jagataḥsambhavaheturavyaktaṁ nāma (Suśruta Saṁhitā, Śārīra Sthāna, I.3): The uncaused cause of all created things, connotes sattva, rajas, and tamas, expresses eight forms, the material cause of the entire world is called Avyakta or the Unmanifest.

[24] tatra sattvabahulāmākāśaṁ, rajobahulo vāyuḥ, sattvarajobahulo agniḥ, sattvatamobahulā āpa, tamobahulā pṛthvīti (Suśruta Saṁhitā, Śārīra Sthāna, I.27): The ākāṣa (space) mahābhūta comprises predominant sattva, the vāyu (air) mahābhūta comprises predominant rajas, the agni (fire) mahābhūta comprises predominant sattva and rajas, the āpa (water) mahābhūta comprises predominant sattva and tamas, and the pṛthvī (earth) mahābhūta comprises predominant tamas.

[25] vāyuḥ pittaṁ kaphaścoktaḥ śārīro doṣasaṁgrahaḥ mānasaḥ punuruddiṣṭo rajaśca tama eva ca (Charaka Saṁhitā, Sūtra Sthāna, I.57): Vāta, pitta, and kapha are called causes of all physical diseases in brief. Rajas and tamas are causes of mental diseases.

from the prevalent scheme would be akin to redefining science in some significant ways. A paradigm shift attempt often faces issues of legitimacy (Kuhn, 1962). Indian psychology, as an emerging movement, has already faced considerable reluctance from mainstream psychologists working in India (Dalal & Misra, 2010). Therefore, the path to redefining science for it may be daunting. Second, attempts may be made to develop an epistemology of efficient causation for triguṇa as found adapted in Indian psychology. This version of triguṇa would be fundamentally different from that in Sāṁkhya, and in that sense, might undermine the motivation of Indian psychology to remain rooted in classical thought. Third, attempts may be made to leverage such Sāṁkhya ideas that reflect on personality through efficient causation logic. This approach would maintain the integrity of the source darśana while contributing to the scientific character of Indian psychology.

Efficient causation is well-accepted in Sāṁkhya (Larson & Bhattacharya, 2012). It comes into the picture once the idea of buddhi is introduced as the first effect of triguṇa. Buddhi represents the most subtle manifestation of individuality in Sāṁkhya (Larson, 1998). The 23rd verse of the Sāṁkhya Kārikā defines buddhi as ascertainment[26] (Wezler & Motegi, 1998). Further, the verse defines eight kinds of predispositions that mark such ascertainment (Alok, 2014). These basic predispositions are called as bhāva. Bhāva relate to perceptions and actions of people as efficient causes (Larson, 1998). Therefore, some Sāṁkhya scholars have suggested that the bhāva doctrine may be suitable for personality studies (Bhattacharya, 2010; Larson, 1998; Larson & Bhattacharya, 2012). It is about time that svabhāva research considers bhāva rather than triguṇa as its fundamental construct.

Organizational Implications

Western personality models are rooted in dehātmavāda—the view that the physical body itself is the basis of self. Dehātmavāda has two fundamental implications for the human condition: (a) humans are not

[26] adhyavasāyo buddhiḥ: buddhi is ascertainment (Wezler & Motegi, 1998).

qualitatively different from other living beings, and (b) satisfying the body is the summum bonum of life. Semitic religions prevalent in the West consider non-human living beings as resources for people to use, whereas they consider humans qualitatively different in having souls (Linzey, 2003). Dehātmavāda does not accept the idea of the soul. Therefore, humans also become similar to other living beings in being valuable for instrumental purposes. It translates into the idea of human resources or human capital in organizations.

Satisfying the body as the highest good in life affords primacy to consumption. It translates into organizational policies and practices that control human behavior by controlling their incentives. Since psychological needs are insatiable, humans must face the ineluctable condition of continuously chasing the elusive satisfaction. It motivates people to find shortcuts for need satisfaction and to engage in ethically questionable behaviors. Western personality models do not provide a basis for morality in human personality since they seek to be descriptive rather than normative. These assumptions and their implications need attention since social sciences' theories and models can be self-fulfilling by influencing institutional designs, social norms, and language (Ferraro et al., 2005).

Indian Psychological models of personality consider the body and the self as distinct entities such that the self takes primacy over the body. This view upholds that people are intrinsically valuable and promotes their dignity in every walk of life, including organizations. Therefore, this view has the potential to anchor an organizational discourse that does not reduce humans to mere resources or capital. Further, the philosophical assumptions underlying these models do not emphasize consumption as the highest good. Therefore, they do not promote the quest for satisfying the insatiable needs. These models also provide a basis for morality in human svabhāva. Sāttvika personality seeks to do good rather than consume more. Organizations that promote these social discourses are likely to have more satisfied and ethical people working for them. Indian Psychological models of personality are the need for the hour for modern organizations marred by corruption, burn out, and extended workhour cultures. These models can initiate an organizational discourse that can heal the ills of dehātmavāda.

Conclusion

To the extent indigenous ideas and tools represent the meaning system of a population, developing indigenous theories and measures is a matter of validity. Western models and measures may have a degree of predictive power; however, their explanations need not be valid for Indian people with a distinctive way of making sense of their world. The argument for indigenous need not be an excuse for doing poor science. Simultaneously, the argument for indigenous need not be an excuse to take liberty with classical ideas. Therefore, indigenous sources' ideas should be taken with utmost care and rigor to maintain their underlying assumptions.

It may be a worthwhile endeavor to cultivate familiarity with Sanskrit and invest in formal training in traditional Sāṁkhya scholarship. The traditional scholarship would genuinely represent the indigenous element in Indian psychology. It would help develop a proper understanding of Sāṁkhya without fear of imposed etic biases that often creep in with Western scholarship of Indian thought.

Indian psychology is an exciting area of research that can significantly enrich modern psychology. Triguṇa has been one of its most popular constructs for personality studies. The unquestioned belief regarding triguṇa as a personality construct impeded its coherent conceptualization. It may be worthwhile to explore alternative concepts such as bhāva for personality purposes. Bhāva may be amenable for efficient causation in the frameworks of both Sāṁkhya and science. Like triguṇa, bhāva has also been a part of Indian ethos for millennia. Its scientific study can significantly enrich our understanding of what humans are and what they do.

References

Agashe, K. S. (Ed.). (1904). *Pātañjalayogasūtrāṇi* (Vol. 47). Anandashrama Mudranalaya.

Agniveśa. (1948). Caraka Saṁhitā (A. Gupta, Trans.). In (2 ed., Vol. 1). Bhargava Pustakalaya.

Alok, K. (2014). The rāga bhāva in the Sāṁkhya Kārikā: Rectifying an age-old mistake. *Asian Philosophy: An International Journal of the Philosophical Traditions of the East, 24*(2), 133–146. https://doi.org/10.1080/09552367.2014.917831

Alok, K. (2017). Sāttvika leadership: An Indian model of positive leadership. *Journal of Business Ethics, 142*(1), 117–138. https://doi.org/10.1007/s10551-015-2790-2

Āraṇya, S. H. (1983). *Yoga philosophy of Patañjali* (P. N. Mukerji, Trans.). State University of New York Press.

Banaji, M. R., & Prentice, D. A. (1994). The self in social contexts. *Annual Review of Psychology, 45*(1), 297–332. https://doi.org/10.1146/annurev.ps.45.020194.001501

Bandura, A. (1999). Social cognitive theory: An agentic perspective. *Asian Journal of Social Psychology, 2*(1), 21–41.

Berry, J. W., Poortinga, Y. H., Segall, M. H., & Dasen, P. R. (2002). *Cross-cultural psychology: Research and applications* (2nd ed.). Cambridge University Press.

Bhal, K. T., & Debnath, N. (2006). Conceptualising and measuring Gunas: Predictor of workplace ethics of Indian professionals. *International Journal of Cross Cultural Management, 6*(2), 169–188.

Bhattacharya, R. S. (2010). *Sāṃkhya Tattva Kaumudī.* Motilal Banarsidass.

Bhawuk, D. P. S. (2010). Methodology for building psychological models from scriptures: Contributions of Indian psychology to indigenous and universal Psychologies. *Psychology & Developing Societies, 22*(1), 49–93. https://doi.org/10.1177/097133360902200103

Bhawuk, D. P. S. (2011). *Spirituality and Indian psychology: Lessons from the Bhagavad-Gita.* Springer.

Biswas, M. (2010). In search of personality inventory for Indian managers: An application of structured equation modelling. *Journal of Services Research, 10*(1), 101–123.

Bolle, K. W. (1979). *The Bhagavadgītā: A new translation.* University of California Press.

Brockington, J. (1998). *The Sanskrit epics.* Brill.

Burrow, T. (2001). *The Sanskrit language.* Motilal Banarsidass.

Caprara, G. V., & Cervone, D. (2000). *Personality: Determinants, dynamics, and potentials.* Cambridge University Press.

Chakraborty, S. K. (1987). *Managerial effectiveness and quality of work life: Indian insights.* McGraw-Hill.

Cheung, F. M., van de Vijver, F. J. R., & Leong, F. T. L. (2011). Toward a new approach to the study of personality in culture. *American Psychologist, 66*(7), 593–603.

Clatterbaugh, K. C. (1999). *The causation debate in modern philosophy, 1637–1739*. Routledge.

Dalal, A. K., & Misra, G. (2010). The core and context of Indian psychology. *Psychology & Developing Societies, 22*(1), 121–155. https://doi.org/10.1177/097133360902200105

Datar, S., & Murthy, C. G. V. (2012). Development and standardization of Mysore Triguna scale. *Sage Open*, 1–10. https://doi.org/10.1177/2158244012436564

De Raad, B., Barelds, D. P. H., Levert, E., Ostendorf, F., Mlačić, B., Di Blas, L., . . . Perugini, M. (2010). Only three factors of personality description are fully replicable across languages: A comparison of 14 trait taxonomies. *Journal of Personality and Social Psychology, 98*(1), 160–173.

Dvivedin, V. P. (Ed.). (1918). *Sāṁkhya Saṅgrahaḥ* (Vol. 246). Chowkhambā sanskrit series office.

Dwivedi, C. B. (2002). Ayurvedic concepts of the purusha, dehaprakriti and sattvaprakriti. In G. Misra & A. K. Mohanty (Eds.), *Perspectives on indegenous psychology* (pp. 305–325). Concept Publishing.

Esbec, E., & Echeburúa, E. (2011). New criteria for personality disorders in DSM-V. *Actas Españolas De Psiquiatría, 39*(1), 1–11.

Ferraro, F., Pfeffer, J., & Sutton, R. I. (2005). Economics language and assumptions: How theories can become self-fulfilling. *Academy of Management Review, 30*(1), 8–24. https://doi.org/10.5465/amr.2005.15281412

Garbe, R. (Ed.). (1888). *The Sāṁkhya Sūtra Vṛtti: Or Aniruddha's commentary and the original parts of Vedantin Mahadeva's commentary to the Sāṁkhya Sūtras (1888)*. Kessinger Publishing.

Garbe, R. (Ed.). (1892). *Anirudhha's commentary and the original parts of Vedāntin Mahādeva's commentary on the Sāṁkhya Sūtras*. Baptist Mission Press.

Jha, A. K. (2008). Personality in Indian psychology. In K. R. Rao, A. C. Paranjpe, & A. K. Dalal (Eds.), *Handbook of Indian psychology* (pp. 348–360). Cambridge University Press/Foundation Books.

Kaplan, A. (2009). *The conduct of inquiry: Methodology for behavioral science*. Transaction Publishers.

Kim, U., Yang, K.-S., & Hwang, K.-K. (Eds.). (2006). *Indigenous and cultural psychology: Understanding people in context*. Springer.

Kuhn, T. S. (1962). *The structure of scientific revolution*. University of Chicago Press.
Larson, G. J. (1998). *Classical Saṁkhya: An interpretation of its history and meaning* (2nd ed.). Motilal Banarsidass.
Larson, G. J., & Bhattacharya, R. S. (Eds.). (2012). *Sāṁkhya: A dualist tradition of Indian philosophy* (Vol. 4). Motilal Banarsidass.
Leahey, T. H. (2001). *A history of modern psychology* (3rd ed.). Prentice-Hall.
Leary, M. R., & Hoyle, R. H. (Eds.). (2009). *Handbook of individual differences in social behavior*. Guilford Press.
Linzey, A. (2003). Animal rights. In J. W. V. V. Huyssteen (Ed.), *Encyclopedia of science and religion* (pp. 10–12). Macmillan Reference.
Mathew, V. G. (2001). Models of consciousness and its transformation. In M. Cornelissen (Ed.), *Consciousness and its transformation*. SAICE.
McCrae, R. R., & Costa, P. T. (2008). The five-factor theory of personality. In O. P. John, R. W. Robins, & L. A. Pervin (Eds.), *Handbook of personality: Theory and research* (3rd ed., pp. 159–181). Guilford Press.
McCrae, R. R., & Terracciano, A. (2005). Personality profiles of cultures: Aggregate personality traits. *Journal of Personality and Social Psychology, 89*(3), 407–425.
Misra, G., & Paranjpe, A. C. (2012). Psychology in modern India. In R. W. Rieber (Ed.), *Encyclopedia of the history of psychological theories* (pp. 881–892). Springer.
Murthy, P. K., & Salagame, K. K. (2007). Concept triguna: A critical analysis and synthesis. *Psychological Studies, 52*(2), 103–113.
Pandeya, J. S. (Ed.). (1989). *Maharṣi Kapilapraṇītaṁ Sāṁkhyadarśanaṁ: Vyākhyācatuṣṭayopetaṁ*. Motilal Banarsidass.
Paranjpe, A. C. (1988). A personality theory according to Vedānta. In A. C. Paranjpe, D. Y. F. Ho, & R. W. Rieber (Eds.), *Asian contributions to psychology* (pp. 185–214). Praeger.
Paranjpe, A. C. (2002). *Self and identity in modern psychology and Indian thought*. Kluwer Academic Publishers.
Paranjpe, A. C. (2011). Indian psychology and the international context. *Psychology and Developing Societies, 23*(1), 1–26.
Pulingandla, R. (1994). *Fundamentals of Indian philosophy*. D. K. Printworld.
Radhakrishnan, S. (1996). *Indian philosophy* (Vol. 2). Oxford University Press.
Rao, K. B. R. (1963). The Gunas of Prakrti according to the Samkhya philosophy. *Philosophy East and West, 13*(1), 61–71.
Rao, K. R., & Paranjpe, A. C. (2015). *Psychology in the Indian tradition*. Springer.

Salagame, K. K. (2011). Indian indigenous concepts and perspectives: Developments and future possibilities. In G. Mishra (Ed.), *Psychology in India: Theoretical and methodological developments* (Vol. 4, pp. 93–172). Dorling Kindersley.

Salagame, K. K., Archana, R., Murthy, P. K., Parimala, Rekha, & Gaur, S. (2005). Concept ahamkara: Theoretical and empirical analysis. In K. R. Rao & S. B. Marwaha (Eds.), *Towards a spiritual psychology: Essays in Indian psychology* (pp. 97–122). Samvad India Foundation.

Saraswati, S. N. (2008). *Samkhya Darshan: Yogic perspective on theories of realism*. Yoga Publications Trust.

Shastri, G. S. S. (Ed.). (1936). *The Bhagavadgītā with eleven commentaries: First collection* (2nd ed., Vol. 2). Gujarati Printing Press.

Shastri, J. (2010). *Sāṁkhya Kārikāḥ* (J. Shashtri, Trans.). Motilal Banarsidass.

Shastri, U. (1950). *Samkhya darshan ka itihas*. Virajanand Vaidika Sansthan.

Shilpa, S., & Murthy, C. G. V. (2012). Interrelatedness of Tridoshas and Trigunas in personality: An empirical investigation. *Indian Social and Psychological Studies, 5*(1), 32–40.

Singh, J. K., Misra, G., & De Raad, B. (2013). Personality structure in the trait lexicon of Hindi, a major language spoken in India. *European Journal of Personality, 27*(6), 605–620.

Srivastava, K. (2012). Concept of personality: Indian perspective. *Industrial Psychiatry Journal, 21*(2), 89–93.

Suśruta. (1954). Suśruta Saṁhitā (A. Shastri, Trans.). In *Kashi Sanskrita Granthamala* (1st ed.). Chowkhamba.

Varma, S. (2011). Integral psychology: A new science of self, personality, and psychology. In R. M. M. Cornelissen, G. Misra, & S. Varma (Eds.), *Foundations of Indian psychology: Concepts and theories* (Vol. 1, pp. 170–197). Pearson.

Virupakshananda, S. (1995). *Sāṁkhya Kārikā of Īśvarakṛṣṇa* (1st ed.). Ramkrishna Math.

Vivekananda, S. (1915). *The science and philosophy of religion: A comparative study of Sankhya, Vedanta and other systems of thought* (2nd ed.). Ramkrishna Math.

Werner, K. (1996). Indian conceptions of human personality. *Asian Philosophy: An International Journal of the Philosophical Traditions of the East, 6*(2), 93–107. https://doi.org/10.1080/09552369608575432

Wezler, A. (1999). On the origin(s) of the Guna-theory: Struggling for a new approach (I): Wrestling with Frauwallner. *Asiatische Studien: Études Asiatiques, 53*(3), 537–551.

Wezler, A., & Motegi, S. (Eds.). (1998). *Yuktidīpikā: The most significant commentary on the Sāṁkhya Kārikā* (Critical ed. Vol. 1). Steiner.

Wolf, D. (1999). A psychometric analysis of the three Gunas. *Psychological Reports, 84*, 1379–1390.

5

Karma-Yoga: Philosophy of Moral Development and Work Motivation

Venkat R. Krishnan and Zubin R. Mulla

Introduction

Upanishadic worldview on which karma-yoga is based has always been distinct from that of other worldviews, and has influenced Indian psychology and ethics. One of the distinguishing features of Upanisadic thought is its holistic understanding of a person consisting of the physical body (sthūla śarīra), subtle body (sūkshma śarīra) that includes manas (sensory processing faculty) and buddhi (discriminative faculty), and ātman or the real self (Rao & Paranjpe, 2016, p. 5). Corresponding to

V. R. Krishnan
Center for Oneness and Transforming Leadership, Chennai, India

Z. R. Mulla (✉)
School of Management and Labor Studies, Tata Institute of Social Sciences, Mumbai, India
e-mail: zubin@tiss.edu

© The Author(s), under exclusive license to Springer Nature Switzerland AG 2022

A. Pandey et al. (eds.), *Indigenous Indian Management*, Palgrave Studies in Indian Management,
https://doi.org/10.1007/978-3-030-87906-8_5

these three levels of personhood are three corresponding ways of being aware—the physical body through the five senses observes the external world, the subtle body feels and understands the world of objects, and the ātman is capable of realization (Rao & Paranjpe, 2016, p. 6). Each of these three levels of personhood also imposes various limitations on the individual. While the physical body being made up of gross matter is restricted in time and space, the subtle body being more subtle, though relatively unrestricted in time and space, is limited by various identities—individual and social. The ātman being completely unconstrained by time and space is infinite and hence unitary across all beings. It is the realization of this ātman, the one universal consciousness, that is the goal of human life. Various methods have been advocated to achieve this realization. Karma-Yoga is one such method.

This chapter comprises five sections. The first section on the philosophy of karma-yoga summarizes the beliefs that form its foundations. It defines karma-yoga as the technique of intelligent action or the way of performing actions without being tainted. It also outlines the four categories of actions that may be performed without being tainted. The second section on operationalizing karma-yoga describes how karma-yoga can be measured and how its relationship with other variables can be studied. The third section on antecedents and consequents of karma-yoga summarizes the various studies that have looked at the relationship between karma-yoga and other variables. The last two sections provide an overview of the implications for global management theory and practice.

Philosophy of Karma-Yoga

Karma-Yoga may be seen as a system of ethics, morality, and work (Vivekananda, 1972, Vol. 1, p. 109), which is described in the Bhagavad-Gītā. The Bhagavad-Gītā is the most popular work among the śāstras or texts of India, and it has influenced Indian life through the generations (Prabhavananda, 1960). The philosophy of karma-yoga is based on some fundamental beliefs.

The foundation of karma-yoga is characterized by three fundamental beliefs (Dasgupta, [1922] 1991; Prabhavananda, 1960). The first belief is in the existence of a permanent reality, the ātman, which is our true nature, pure and untouched by the impurities of our ordinary life. The second belief is the law of karma that requires every action to have its consequence, which suggests that the world is a just place and that justice may be served over several lifetimes of birth and death. The third is that of mukti or liberation from the cycle of birth and death (and the law of karma) is possible through multiple ways.

Ātman

There are two types of knowledge—physical science and non-physical science. Physical science is the study of the world of objects. Physical or positivistic science, also known as materialism or behaviorism, provides an understanding of "things" including nature and our physical bodies. It treats only what the senses reveal to be valid. It ignores that the knowledge of sensory data is only a part and not the whole of knowledge. Non-physical science is the study of the subject, the one who studies the world of objects. It is an investigation into a realm that sense organs cannot reveal. It is an inquiry into the inner world, the subject, the real self, the ātman (Ranganathananda, 2005, pp. 11–20).

In the Rg-Veda, the word ātman is used to describe breath or vital essence (Radhakrishnan, 1940), and gradually it has been used to mean the real self of every being (Ghanananda, 1958). The ātman is the eternal subject, which is free from all impurities like sin, old age, death, grief, hunger, and thirst. The ātman is not born, and it does not die when the physical body dies. The real self or ātman is complete and hence, it is free from all forms of desires (Radhakrishnan, 1940).

The indestructible element in us has gotten mixed with the condition of change which permeates everything that is finite. We are imbued with the world of finites, of the bodily individuality of ours, and even the psychic isolation of ours is a character of our finitude. The finite struggles to align itself with the Infinite, to which it really belongs, and this struggle of the finite to move toward the Infinite is the whole story of evolution (Krishnananda, 1991, p. 42).

When we go beyond and penetrate the root of our ahankara (sense of I), when we enquire who we really are, we reach the infinite self, the ātman. The ātman in us is one with all. The attitude that this is *my* work, and everything belongs to *me* is based on ignorance. Realizing the ātman requires detachment from the ahankara, the little self that is centered in our genetic system. Until this little "I" is overcome and a larger "I" manifests in us, we remain stunted individuals. When this little "I" expands, it becomes the ripe expanded self, which alone can experience its oneness with everyone else. The self that is contained in the organic system is only a convenient provisional delusion. When that is set aside, our concept of self begins to expand, and we feel oneness with others. Therefore, whatever work we do, the fruits of it are not for us alone; they belong to everyone. This losing ourselves in the universal is the goal of existence (Ranganathananda, 2001, Vol. 1, pp. 177–186).

Law of Karma

The second of the three beliefs that comprise the foundation of karma-yoga is the belief in the law of karma, i.e., all actions that are done have the power to ordain for their doers joy or sorrow in the future depending on whether the action is good or bad. Often, individuals may be required to take birth in another body to experience fully the joy or suffering that is due to them because of their past actions.

The law of *karma* is perhaps one of the most widely known and misunderstood beliefs (Mahadevan, 1958). It is equivalent to the belief in a just world (Connors & Heaven, 1990; Hafer & Begue, 2005) plus transmigration. It states that individuals get what they deserve (Connors & Heaven, 1990). Law of karma extends the concept of justice to other worlds and other births, thereby implying that all good and bad deeds of all of one's previous lives are accounted for cumulatively. Accordingly, in every life one reaps what one has sown in one's previous lives (Radhakrishnan, 1926). The law of karma provides a parsimonious explanation of the inequality that exists in the world. Belief in law of karma reaffirms one's faith in natural justice and makes every person responsible for his or her own well-being and suffering. Thus, positive deeds are believed to lead to good outcomes, while tragic happenings are explained as an outcome of negative deeds done in the past (Agrawal & Dalal, 1993; Dalal & Pande, 1988). The law of karma is not a blind mechanical framework in which a human being is trapped for eternity, but provides a mechanism for explaining the circumstances that one finds oneself in, until one is completely free of the cycle of birth and death.

Mukti or Moksha (Freedom or Liberation)

The third of the three beliefs that comprise the foundation of karma-yoga is about mukti or moksha (freedom or liberation). While the pursuit of artha (wealth) and kāma (pleasure) is a legitimate human aspiration, they should be gained in ways of dharma (righteousness), if they are to lead ultimately to moksha (Radhakrishnan, 1926, p. 80). These four comprise the purusharthas (life goals). Freedom of the individual from the cycle of births and deaths is possible and is the ultimate goal and destiny of every being (Mahadevan, 1958). This freedom from the cycle of birth and death is termed as moksha. It is not selfish individual salvation as it is sometimes wrongly understood, but it is the expansion of one's self toward the universal Self, resulting in oneness with all beings. Moksha is the state of oneness with all. It results when the bonds of ignorance have been broken and is a state which is free from all imperfections and limitations (Prabhavananda, 1960). Since actions lead us through the endless cycle of birth and death, if we could be free of all such emotions or desires that lead us to action, there would be no fuel (in the form of joys or sorrows to be experienced) to propel us into another birth and we would be free of this cycle.

Karma-Yoga: The Technique of Intelligent Action

Derived from the root, *yuj* (to bind together, or to join), yoga means binding one's potential, balancing, and enhancing it. By yoking together and harnessing our energies, we force the passage from the limited individual self (jīvātman) to the supreme unlimited self (paramātman). The way the finite moves toward the Infinite is called yoga. The limited individual self tears itself away from its prison house, stands out of it, and reaches its own innermost being. Yoga is a method or discipline that leads to the liberation of the individual and a new understanding of the unity of all beings (Radhakrishnan, 1971, p. 50). When one is convinced of the law of universal cause and effect, the existence of an eternal ātman, and the objective of life as liberation of the individual from the cycle of birth and death, one seeks opportunities for moksha (realizing one's oneness with all beings). The yoga (path or technique) to be selected for moksha must be suited to the temperament and disposition of the seeker.

According to Swami Vivekananda (2009, pp. 102–103), until we give up the strong attachment to this our transient conditioned existence, we have no hope of catching even a glimpse of that infinite freedom beyond. There are two ways to give up our attachment to this little universe of the senses or of the mind, and to get out of this complex world. One is called the "*neti, neti*" (not this, not this), the other is called "*iti*" (this); the former is the negative, and the latter is the positive way. Bhagavad-Gītā (śloka 3.3) says, "In the beginning (of creation), O sinless one, the two-fold path was given by Me to this world—jñāna-yoga (the path of knowledge) for the people of contemplation, and karma-yoga (the path of action) for the active people."

The negative way—jñāna-yoga—is to give up all concerns with the world, to let it go and stand aside, to give up our desires. It constitutes the denial of all attributes of the self (Rao & Paranjpe, 2016). It comprises the three steps of *shravana* (listening), *manana*, (reflecting), and *nididhyāsana* (contemplating). It involves the pursuit of knowledge and truth through the process of reflection and examination of the nature of the self through mental effort (Rao & Paranjpe, 2016). It is only possible to people with gigantic wills who simply stand up and say, "No, I will not have this," and the mind and body obey their will, and they come out successful. However, such people are very rare (Vivekananda, 2009: 102–103).

The other way is to plunge into the world and learn the secret of work, and that is the way of karma-yoga. It requires not giving up the world, but living in the world and learning the secret of work. Most people choose this positive way, the way through the world, making use of all the bondages themselves to break those very bondages. However, really speaking, this is also a kind of giving up; only it is done slowly and gradually, by knowing things, enjoying things and thus obtaining experience, and knowing the nature of things until the mind lets them all go at last and becomes unattached. In karma-yoga, there is no cessation from work. Karma-Yoga is the means for active people to realize their true nature. Through working in the world, with the proper attitude, it is possible to go beyond this world (Vivekananda, 2009, p. 128).

Karma-Yoga provides a path for freedom from the cycle of birth and death, which is suited for people with an active temperament who have chosen to remain in the world and aspire for liberation. In other words, the process of discovering one's true self through work is karma-yoga. That is the development of thought in the Bhagavad-Gītā, that, by a certain spiritual technique, you can convert action into inaction: you get the fruit of inaction through action itself (Ranganathananda, 2001, p. 259).

The word karma comes from the Sanskrit root *kri*, which means doing, affairs, or activity and includes all actions that a person performs whether they are of body, speech, manas, or buddhi. In other words, karma consists of all deliberate human actions. In the Bhagavad-Gītā, the word yoga is used in three ways: as a special skill, device, intelligent method, or graceful way of performing actions (Chapter 2, Verse 50); as equability of mind toward success and failure (Chapter 2, Verse 48); and as the device for eliminating the natural tendency of law of karma to create bondage (Chapter 2, Verse 50). Since these meanings of yoga speak of the relationship of yoga with action, the terms "yoga" and "karma-yoga" are used interchangeably at various instances in the Bhagavad-Gītā (Tilak, [1915] 2000). Tilak defines the word "yoga" to mean "device" or "intelligent method" and hence the term "karma-yoga" means "a technique for intelligently performing actions."

Here the world "intelligent" is used by Tilak in a specific sense to denote an action which is conducive to one's end goals and since the ultimate goal of all beings is to free the individual from the cycle of birth and death, any method that enables release from this perpetual cycle is preferable to any other method that is likely to bind the human being to the cycle. Hence, whether karma-yoga is defined as "a technique for intelligently performing actions" or as "a technique for performing actions in a manner that the individual is not bound by the effects of the action," it means the same thing (Tilak, [1915] 2000).

Karma-yoga may be simply defined as a path toward moksha through performing actions without being tainted (Īśa Upanishad, Śloka 2). Ranganathananda (2000, p. 93), commenting on Īśa Upanishad Śloka 2, says that all our life, we are engaged in so many activities, but we find that, instead of releasing us from bondage, they have merely increased our bondage. The way to come to grips with life, therefore, is to use every action as a means for freeing ourselves from that bondage.

Another explanation for karma-yoga being the technique of intelligent action deals with the nature of action and its outcomes. According to the Bhagavad-Gītā (Chapter 18, Verse 14), there are five factors which together determine the accomplishment of actions—the body, the agent of action, the sense organs, the specific activities involved in the action, and the divinity. The first factor, "body" can also be explained as the "historical, geographical, ecological, and social context in which the action takes place" (Rao & Paranjpe, 2016, p. 199). Hence, it is quite clear that the agent of action is only one of the many factors that determine the outcome of an action. Given this reasoning, a subsequent verse in the Bhagavad-Gītā (Chapter 18, Verse 16) suggests that perceiving oneself as the sole cause of one's actions is being unintelligent.

Karma-yoga should not be confused with mere work. To work like a bullock, or to work in any way one likes, is not karma-yoga. The work that most people do is nothing but a semi-conscious, passion-driven, aimless rat race for name, fame, and sense enjoyment, and to call it karma-yoga is an insult to the great teachers of karma-yoga (Bhajanananda, 2006, pp. 8–9). The goal of karma-yoga is not worldly success. Karma-yoga is a spiritual discipline that aims at liberation—mukti. The aim of karma-yoga is not to change the world, but to change oneself by transcending the material part (Bhajanananda, 2006, pp. 8–9).

Karma-Yoga is a path toward moksha, through performing actions without being tainted. Four categories of actions may be performed without being tainted—unselfish actions, actions without attachment, actions originated by svadharma, and actions permeated by sattva guna

(Vivekananda, 2009). According to karma-yoga, unselfishness is considered as the highest virtue. An individual practicing karma-yoga performs actions without a sense of attachment to the individual outcomes that he or she expects to receive from the action. Performing actions without being tainted is easily achieved when an individual pursues his or her natural duty or svadharma. Finally, gunas are the three building blocks of all elements in the universe, which can explain how to perform actions intelligently.

Nishkama Karma (Unselfishness or Self-Abnegation)

"Karma-yoga is the attaining through unselfish work of that freedom which is the goal of all human nature" (Vivekananda, 2009, p. 120). Selfish actions reinforce our identification with the body and the mind, which limits us and retards our realizing our goal i.e., the one universal consciousness. On the other hand, unselfish actions help us to go closer to our goal of realizing the underlying unity in all beings. Hence, the only definition that can be given of morality is this: "That which is selfish is immoral, and that which is unselfish is moral" (Vivekananda, 2009, p. 120). Karma-Yoga, therefore, is a system of ethics intended to attain freedom through unselfishness, and by good work. Karma-Yoga does not require belief in a personal god (Vivekananda, 2009, p. 121), though it requires a belief in the ātman, moksha, and the law of karma.

According to Bhawuk (2011, pp. 153–155), the doctrine of nishkama karma also focuses on self-interest, but proposes that in one's own interest one should not chase the fruits of his or her endeavor. It is not only possible but also preferable to live for the well-being of others in the society. Those who work hard to serve others pursue a path of spiritual self-development through their work itself.

Bhagavad-Gītā (śloka 5.7) says: "With the mind purified by devotion to karma-yoga, and the body conquered, and sense organs subdued, one who realizes one's self, as the Self in all beings, though acting, is not tainted" (Swarupananda, 1909). With the development of spirituality, one feels one's oneness with others, and feels the desire to serve others. The sufferings and joys of all others become one's own sufferings and joys. There is only one infinite ātman; one realizes that truth. Even though he or she is constantly performing actions, he or she will never be tainted. Such a person is not subject to the law of karma. Performing actions like this, without being tainted, is called karma-yoga (Ranganathananda, 2001, Vol. 2, pp. 32–33).

Ranganathananda (2001, Vol.1, p. 285) wrote: "Suppose you have no desires of your own. You don't need to work at all. Still you must work, because there are others who are in need; you are there to help. That is called lokasangraha or ensuring the stability of the human society." Bhagavad-Gītā (śloka 3.20–3.21) says: "Verily, through action alone, Janaka and others attained perfection; even with the view to ensure lokasangraha, the stability of human society, you should perform action. Whatsoever the superior person does, that is followed by others. What he demonstrates by action, that people follow."

The most important question is: "How is it possible to do work without *expecting any result*? How can teachers teach without expecting their students to pass examinations creditably? How can doctors treat patients without expecting them to be cured?" The answer is, what one is asked to give up is not the result, but the selfish expectations about it. Teachers should strive their utmost to teach their students well, but they should do it for their students' own welfare, and not to earn money, or name and fame. Doctors should strive their best to treat their patients, but they should do it for the patients' welfare only, and not to get money or name and fame. Working without selfish desires is what is known as nishkāma karma or unselfish work or *work for work's sake*. This is karma-yoga (Bhajanananda, 2006, pp. 30–31).

Anāsakti (Non-Attachment)

Giving up all attachment to work, while working incessantly, is a way to perform actions without being tainted. Attachment means expecting returns for oneself. It requires not identifying oneself with anything. It requires that we recognize that all our pains and miseries exist at the level of the physical body and the subtle body and not at the level of the ātman which is our true self. Vivekananda (2009) explains how ahankara and mamatva (sense of I and mine) are the causes of attachment, with the help of an example:

> If a beautiful picture belonging to another is burnt, a man does not generally become miserable; but when his own picture is burnt, how miserable he feels! Both were beautiful pictures, perhaps copies of the same original; but in one case very much more misery is felt than in the other. It is because in one case he identifies himself with the picture, and not in the other. (pp. 105–112)

According to Bhawuk (2011, pp. 150–151), if work is done without attachment, then it frees one of all bondage. Thus, work is couched in a spiritual worldview as a path leading to self-realization if done properly without pursuing their outcomes. Whatever actions an unattached person performs is for the sake of yajña (sacrifice), and the karma, its fruits, and the accompanying bondage are destroyed. When one so performs his or her work without attachment, it becomes yajña and frees the person of kārmic bondage.

Gandhi (1980) considered the central teaching of the Bhagavad-Gītā to be detachment—abandonment of the fruit of action. He used the phrase "anāsakti yoga" (yoga of non-attachment) to refer to karma-yoga, and considered Bhagavad-Gītā to be a text on anāsakti yoga. He exhorted that non-attachment should be a part of all our actions. Gandhi was emphatic that we should do no work with attachment. Even attachment to good work is wrong. Gandhi gave the example that if we are attached to our goal of winning liberty, we shall not hesitate to adopt bad means. Hence, we should not be attached even to a good cause. Only then will our means remain pure and our actions, too.

There are two ways of giving up all attachments. The one is for those who do not believe in a personal god, or in any outside help. They are left to their own devices; they have simply to work with their own will, with the powers of their mind and discrimination, saying, "I must be non-attached." For those who believe in a personal god, there is another way, which is much less difficult. They give up the fruits of work unto the Lord; they work and are never attached to the results (Vivekananda, 2009, pp. 108–109).

Svadharma (Natural Duty)

Svadharma means one's own dharma, or an individual's innate nature, way of life, natural duty, the purpose of living. Svadharma is that activity which fits one the best. The test of svadharma is to see if while doing one's svadharma, the sense of time vanishes. Svadharma changes from person to person and for the same person, it changes from time to time. As one's mind grows and develops through reflection and experience, one's old svadharma drops off and a new svadharma comes in its place (Bhave, 2005, pp. 22–23). Hence, different rules of conduct are applicable to different types of beings depending on their state of growth (Prabhavananda, 1960, p. 105).

Individuals will not be tainted by the actions they perform, when work is done by considering it as svadharma. For individuals pursuing karma-yoga, the work indeed helps them earn a means of livelihood, but their purpose for working is not just to earn livelihood but to earn enough and keep their body healthy to be able to perform their svadharma. Hence, the end is svadharma and earning is a means for that. For individuals who are not pursuing karma-yoga, the work is a means for earning. These are two opposite attitudes to work. Karma-Yogis performing svadharma link their work to the welfare of the society (Bhave, 2005, pp. 48–50).

Svadharma is an individual's duty in a context and as a member of a group (e.g., family, community, or nation; Rao & Paranjpe, 2016). This is the duty that arises most naturally to an individual based on the time and context in which he or she is located. Since svadharma arises as a natural consequence of one's position in life and society, one does not need to put in extra efforts in order to plan or contemplate this and hence it is easiest to cultivate an attitude of service to the collective and to give up the expectation of a personal reward (Bhave, 2005).

It is necessary in the study of karma-yoga to know what duty is. Since environments change the nature of our duties, doing the duty, which is ours at any particular time, is the best thing to do. It is work through the sense of duty that leads us gradually to work being done for its own sake. The objective of fulfilling duties is the attenuating of the lower self, so that the real higher Self may shine forth—the lessening of the frittering away of energies on the lower plane of existence, so that the self may manifest itself on the higher ones. Hence, the only way to rise is by doing the duty next to us, and thus gathering strength to go on until we reach the highest state (Vivekananda, 2009, pp. 52–60).

Gunas (Ultimate Entities)

Knowledge-complexes that exist in living beings are different from those that exist in external inanimate objects in that they are far subtler and have a preponderance of a special quality of plasticity and translucence (sattva). The fundamental characteristic of external gross matter or an inanimate object is its mass (tamas). Energy (rajas) is common to both gross matter and the subtle thought-stuff that is unique to living beings. However, mass is at its lowest minimum in thought-stuff, whereas the capacity of translucence or intelligence-stuff is at its highest in thought-stuff (Dasgupta, 1991, p. 241).

Thus, both thought and gross matter are made up of three elements—a plasticity of intelligence-stuff (sattva), energy-stuff (rajas), and mass-stuff (tamas) or the factor of obstruction. Of these, the last two are predominant in gross matter and the first two in thought (Dasgupta, 1991, p. 242).

These three types of ultimate subtle entities are called gunas. These subtle guna substances are united in different proportions, and because of this, different substances with different qualities come into being. For example, a larger number of sattva substances may unite with a lesser number of rajas or tamas substances, or a larger number of tamas substances may unite with a smaller number of rajas and sattva substances, and so on in varying proportions. (Dasgupta, 1991, pp. 243–244).

Another way to look at gunas is to view them as three forces that are manifested in the physical world as inertness or inactivity (tamas), activity, expressed as attraction or repulsion (rajas), and the equilibrium between activity and inactivity (sattva). When tamas is predominant, we become lazy and dull, when rajas dominates us, we engage in feverish activity, and when sattva dominates, we engage in calm activity. Karma-Yoga has specially to deal with these three factors (Vivekananda, 2009, p. 13).

For those who are predominantly tamasic (highest on tamas and comparatively low on rajas and sattva), performing any action is difficult, leave alone unattached action or karma-yoga. Once they increase their levels of rajas, they will start doing some action. However, karma-yoga is possible only if they reduce their levels of rajas and increase sattva. Changing oneself from being tamasic to being rajasic to being sattvic is a simple way to start performing actions without being tainted. Sāttvic performers will not be tainted by their actions.

According to our mental constitution or the different planes of existence in which we are, duty and morality may vary. For individuals who are passive, dull, and dormant, performing at least some action (even violence) is prescribed as svadharma. On the other hand, for someone who has courage and ability to fight, svadharma may involve resisting violence or fighting only for the welfare of the world. The important thing is to know that there are gradations of duty and of morality—that the duty of one state of life, in one set of circumstances, will not and cannot be that of another (Vivekananda, 2009, pp. 15–18).

Absence of Doership

The four categories of action listed above, that can be performed without tainting oneself, all have one thing in common: they all lead to an absence of a sense of doership. It is the sense of doership that results in bondage and accumulation of further karma. In unselfishness, the sense of self does not exist at all. In non-attachment, not expecting outcomes for oneself is equivalent to not performing the action itself. When people are discharging their svadharma, they are so involved in the action that they are not even aware that they are doing anything. And finally, the sāttvic performer of action sees every action as a result of only gunas acting on gunas, and does not identify with them.

Operationalizing Karma-Yoga

Karma-Yoga may be operationalized in organizations as detached involvement. It means gradual detachment from exclusive or dominating personal interests, and progressive attachment to concerns and causes more and more transcending oneself, like the family, the organization, the country, and the world at large. Attachment to higher order concerns demands detachment from lower order concerns. Increasing concern for results for the organization or the nation is dependent on lessening concern for results for one's own sake (Chakraborty, 1998, p. 94).

The essence of karma-yoga is given in the Bhagavad-Gītā (Radhakrishnan, 1948/1993) Chapter 2, Verse 47, which says, "To action alone hast thou a right and never at all to its fruits; let not the fruits of action be thy motive; neither let there be in thee any attachment to inaction." This verse of the Bhagavad-Gītā is also mentioned by Tilak (1915/2000 p. 895) as giving the entire import of karma-yoga in a short and beautiful form. Later in the Bhagavad-Gītā (Radhakrishnan, 1971, Chapter 3, Verses 12, 13, and 16), Arjuna is told that persons who survive on this earth and use its resources without working are living in sin, and hence human beings are obliged to work selflessly in order to fulfill their duty toward the world. Hence, based on the results of Mulla and Krishnan's (2006) content analysis and the interpretation of the Bhagavad-Gītā verses, karma-yoga could be operationalized as made up of three dimensions: duty-orientation, indifference to rewards, and equanimity.

The metaphysical explanation of karma-yoga is presented in Fig. 5.1. The eternal cycle of birth and death driven by reincarnation and the law of karma is defined in the form of a three-step procedure (Tilak, 1915/2000). The first step is the interaction of the five senses with external objects; this in turn leads to a perception of pain or happiness in the mind of the agent of the action (Bhagavad-Gītā Chapter 2, Verse 14). Perceiving pleasure or pain further leads to a desire to experience again what has been experienced (in the case of happiness) or a desire to avoid what has been experienced (in the case of pain). The presence of an unfulfilled desire to experience or avoid a certain experience is the essential fuel, which drives individuals to being reborn again in a body

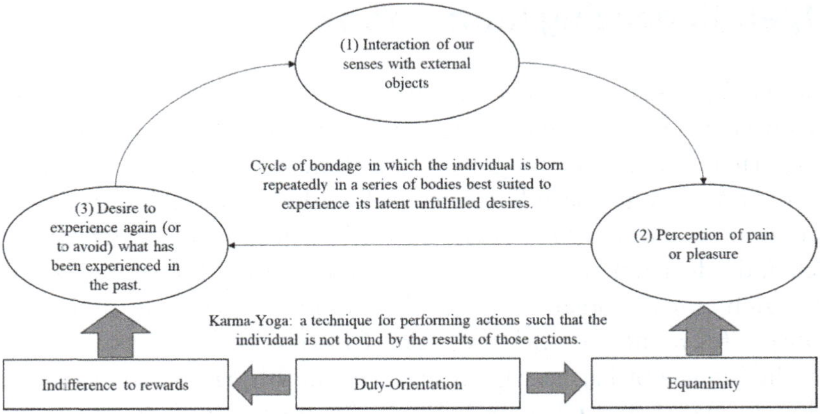

Fig. 5.1 Metaphysical Explanation of Karma-Yoga

most suited to their experiencing their latent unfulfilled desires. In this manner, the cycle of birth and death is repeated to eternity. The cycle can be broken in three ways. First, an individual may choose to avoid all interaction of his or her senses with external objects. However, in the case of an active person, this path is not suitable. Hence, the only two ways of breaking the cycle of birth and death are to be endure pleasure and pain with equanimity and to be indifferent to the rewards (and punishments) of one's actions (Tilak, [1915] 2000).

Breaking the Cycle of Birth and Death through Equanimity and Indifference to Rewards

One way out of this perpetual cycle of desire is to be able to control in one's mind the experience of pain and happiness i.e., being neutral to the experiences of our senses (Tilak, 1915/2000). When one does what one has to do, with perfect mental control and after giving up the desire for the result, and with a frame of mind that is equal toward pain and happiness, there remains no fear or possibility of experiencing the unhappiness of actions. If one can perform actions with such a spirit, it does not become necessary to give up actions. Hence, karma-yoga requires that we keep our organs under control and allow them to perform the various activities, not for a selfish purpose, but for the welfare of others (Tilak, [1915] 2000).

In addition, since the outcomes of one's actions are dependent on an elaborate chain of cause and effect, all that is in the individual's control is performance of that action. Hence, one ceases to have a feeling of ownership toward one's actions and believes that the actions happen naturally, and the bodily organs are just an instrument for their execution. This lack of ownership for actions coupled with the sense of obligation to others creates a complete disinterest in the mind of the seeker for any form of material or social rewards (Tilak, [1915] 2000).

Duty-Orientation as a Precursor to Developing Equanimity and Indifference to Rewards

A question that is often asked is: how is it possible for an individual to maintain equanimity to pleasure and pain, and be indifferent to rewards? By developing duty-orientation, it is possible to develop equanimity and indifference to rewards.

The belief in the law of karma makes us realize that we are placed in a situation because of unfulfilled past obligations on our part and we develop a sense of connectedness with all beings. In other words, irrespective of the situation that we are placed in, we can look upon those around us as our creditors in our past lives to whom we are obliged to discharge certain obligations (which were unfulfilled earlier). The belief in the law of karma coupled with the belief in moksha (realization of oneness with all beings) as goal, makes us strive to discharge our obligations to those around us. In this manner, all actions become a repayment of a debt and the actor is free of any motive for the actions.

Alternative Conceptualizations

There have been several alternative conceptualizations of karma-yoga. An early conceptualization by an eminent social worker described karma-yoga as "attainment of God through work" (p. 230) and acting with evenness of mind and performing duties as an instrument of God

(Banerjee, 1964). Other similar definitions of karma-yoga were transcending nature and doing one's duty in a dedicated manner (Menon & Krishnan, 2004), treating work as worship (Madhu & Krishnan, 2005), and "doing one's duty and not being attached to outcomes" (Narayanan & Krishnan, 2003, p. 3).

Rastogi and Pati (2015) employed a qualitative method to identify the distinct dimensions of the karma-yoga construct, and offer an alternative conceptualization of the construct. Accordingly, they defined karma-yoga as a persistent positive state of mind that is characterized by absorption and service consciousness. They also identified sense control and equanimity as the necessary prerequisites for individuals to practice karma-yoga.

Navare (2019) proposed a five-factor model of karma-yoga. The five factors were: *manonigraha* (controlling the mind and refraining oneself from the over-indulgence in the sensual desires); *samabuddhi* (keeping the intellect steadfast in extreme life situations and preserving rational decision-making ability); *phalāśā tyāga* (renunciation of attachment to external reward and remaining anchored in duty-bound actions); *svadharma* (performing actions in accordance with one's innate nature); and *lokasamgraha* (developing the sense of belonging and responsibility toward larger social and natural system). Navare (2019) found that karma-yoga had positive impact on mindfulness, self-transcendence, thriving, flourishing and psychological capital, and negative impact on job burnout.

Antecedents and Consequents of Karma-Yoga

Studies have been done to understand the profile of karma-yogis or persons high on karma-yoga. Mulla and Krishnan (2006) studied the impact of karma-yoga on two facets of the personality trait of conscientiousness, viz. dutifulness and achievement striving. Karma-Yoga was operationalized in terms of two dimensions—sense of duty and absence of desire for rewards. Belief in Indian philosophy was significantly related to sense of duty. There was moderate support for their hypothesis that dutifulness was more strongly related to karma-yoga when achievement striving was low than when it was high.

People who scored high on karma-yoga showed a distinct value system from those who were low on karma-yoga scale. Those high on karma-yoga gave significant preference to other-oriented values in case of terminal values and greater preference to moral values as far as instrumental values are concerned. Individuals' scores on karma-yoga were also found to be highly correlated with emotional intelligence (Mulla & Krishnan, 2007).

People who scored high on karma-yoga also showed a distinct value system with respect to the two values of being "ambitious" and being "hardworking." The word "ambitious" refers to having a desire to achieve a goal. Clearly, the focus is on the motives of a person's actions. On the other hand, the word "hardworking" implies being industrious or diligent. It focuses on the visible behaviors and not the motives. Individuals who were high on karma-yoga gave higher importance to being "hardworking" as compared to being "ambitious," whereas individuals who were low on karma-yoga gave higher importance to being "ambitious" as compared to being "hardworking" (Mulla & Krishnan, 2011). Similarly, rajas guna (characterized by ambition driven feverish activity) was negatively related to karma-yoga (Narayanan & Krishnan, 2003).

Moreover, karma-yoga was stronger for individuals who were high on empathic concern and this relationship was strengthened when personal distress was low (Mulla & Krishnan, 2008). In other words, this meant that those who scored high on karma-yoga were more likely to help others due to their genuine concern for others' well-being rather than to relieve their own distress.

Individuals who scored high on karma-yoga had more social identities in their self-concept (Mulla, Krishnan, & Kumar, 2018). Karma-Yoga is a means for achieving self-expansion or oneness with others, and self-expansion can be seen as increasing the proportion of social part of self-concept.

Another important area of study has been to see if karma-yogis will be transformational leaders. Mulla and Krishnan (2009) studied whether the karma-yoga of a leader and the follower's belief in Indian philosophy enhanced transformational leadership. Karma-Yoga was conceptualized as made up of three dimensions: duty orientation, indifference to rewards and equanimity. Only the duty-orientation aspect of karma-yoga was found to affect three dimensions of transformational leadership, viz. charisma (attributed), charisma (behavior) and inspirational motivation. They also found that a leader's karma-yoga was more strongly related to charisma, when a follower's belief in Indian philosophy was high as compared to when the follower's belief was low. They concluded that the relationship of belief in Indian philosophy is strongest with duty-orientation because sense of duty constitutes the core of the philosophy of karma-yoga. The other two dimensions are perhaps the consequences of duty-orientation, which manifest over time.

Efforts have also been made to understand whether transformational leadership can enhance the duty orientation and spirituality of followers and help to increase their commitment toward the organization. Krishnan (2007) found that transformational leadership enhances duty-orientation and spirituality (oneness with all beings) of followers. Krishnan (2008) studied the relationship of transformational leadership with followers' karma-yoga, spirituality, organizational identification, and normative organizational commitment. The karma-yoga of followers was significantly enhanced by the transformational leadership exhibited by their superiors. This study thus showed that transformational leaders, by enhancing the karma-yoga and oneness of followers, increase their organizational identification and normative commitment and help to address the goals of the organization. However, Menon and Krishnan (2004) showed that follower's karma-yoga was positively related to leader's transformational leadership for male followers but not for female followers.

Mulla and Krishnan (2012) found that transformational leadership was positively related to two of the three dimensions of karma-yoga (viz., duty-orientation and indifference to rewards). Analysis of split samples of high/low duration of leader–follower relationship and high/low frequency of leader–follower interaction showed that the duration of leader–follower relationship and frequency of leader–follower interaction moderated the relationship between transformational leadership and follower's karma-yoga such that high duration of leader–follower relationship and high frequency of leader–follower interaction enhanced the impact of transformational leadership on follower's karma-yoga.

The Bhagavd-Gītā (Radhakrishnan, 1971) predicts several positive states which arise as a result of karma-yoga such as—the end of sorrow (Chapter 2, Verse 65), peace (Chapter 2, Verses 66, 70, & 71); happiness (Chapter 2, Verse 66), bliss (Chapter 2, Verse 72), and satisfaction (Chapter 3, Verse 17). A karma-yogi is described as one who is completely satisfied with his or her current state and is not hankering after any other state of existence (Mulla & Krishnan, 2006).

Several studies have identified the beneficial outcomes of karma-yoga in the organizational context. Karma-Yoga was found to be positively related to spirituality, normative commitment (Krishnan, 2008), life satisfaction (Mulla & Krishnan, 2006; Rastogi et al., 2015), happiness (Pati et al., 2017; Rastogi et al., 2015), conscientiousness, self-efficacy (Rastogi et al., 2015), mindfulness, self-transcendence, thriving, flourishing, and psychological capital (Navare, 2019).

When faced with circumstances that are unfavorable to us, our interpretation of those events trigger emotions and distress. A "commitment to some higher goal in life enables people to meaningfully reconstruct difficult experiences" (Pande & Naidu, 1992, p. 92). It was found that those high on non-attachment experienced less distress and exhibited fewer symptoms of strain when faced with stressful life events (Pande & Naidu, 1992). Also, individuals who scored high on the "absence of desire for rewards" dimension of karma-yoga had enhanced life satisfaction (Mulla & Krishnan, 2006). Karma-Yoga was also found to be negatively related to depression (Rastogi et al., 2015) and burnout (Navare, 2019; Pati et al., 2017).

Karma-Yoga can also enhance the positive effect of transformational leadership. Madhu and Krishnan (2005) showed that karma-yoga and transformational leadership had an enhanced effect on altruism, conscientiousness, and courtesy. Courtesy was enhanced only when there was an interplay between transformational leadership and karma-yoga. This study thus showed that the transformational leadership of a manager will lead to higher display of organizational citizenship behavior, if it is combined with karma-yoga.

Joshi and Krishnan (2015) showed that leader's svadharma-orientation mediated the positive relationship that leaders' need for power and activity inhibition had with each of the five factors of transformational leadership. Mehra and Krishnan (2005) found that svadharma-orientation was positively related to transformational leadership.

Agarwalla et al. (2015) used an experimental study to examine whether transformational leadership would be affected by the predominance of a particular guna (sattva, rajas, & tamas) in a leader and his or her karma-yoga. They found that leader's karma-yoga enhanced his or her transformational leadership when the leader was high on sattva, but did not enhance transformational leadership when the leader was high on rajas.

Mulla and Krishnan (2014) showed that karma-yoga constitutes a holistic model for moral development. Karma-Yoga or the technique of intelligent action was described in the form of three interrelated constructs viz. duty-orientation, indifference to rewards, and equanimity. Each of these dimensions of karma-yoga was related to moral sensitivity, moral motivation, and moral character. Even though constructs like conscientiousness have some commonality with one of three crucial dimensions of karma-yoga (duty-orientation, indifference to rewards, and equanimity), none of those constructs is like the composite construct of karma-yoga. Karma-Yoga's uniqueness is about merging those three dimensions into a composite whole.

Implications for Global Management Theory

The traditional models of motivation have a bias toward assuming that all individuals are self-interested and take up activities only based on self-interested, hedonistic, and cost–benefit calculations (Shamir, 1991). These traditional models of motivation fail to explain actions of individuals when there are no tangible rewards for action, such as when actions are inspired by charismatic leaders or when individuals act due to their values or moral obligations (Shamir, 1991; Shamir et al., 1993). In Indian context, studies have shown that self-sacrifice and altruistic behaviors are extremely effective leadership behaviors (Singh &

Krishnan, 2005). The philosophy of karma-yoga if properly understood provides fortitude in times of difficulty and lays the foundation for self-determination—a firm understanding that one's actions today form the basis on one's outcomes tomorrow (Banerjee, 1964). Karma-Yoga constitutes the Indian work ideal and can be harnessed by leaders to motivate their team (Mulla & Krishnan, 2007) to be sensitive to their obligations and thereby serve customers with devotion.

Implications for Global Management Practice

Indian culture is made up of traditionally idealized values as well as operative values (Sinha, 1997). Some of the operative values, formed because of historical and social factors may be contrary to the values of a contemporary organization. Several of India's traditionally idealized values are highly relevant to the needs of contemporary organizations. The philosophy of karma-yoga is one of these idealized values which provides a strong framework for developing efficient and humane organizations as well as a professional and fulfilled workforce (Banerjee, 1964; Mulla & Krishnan, 2006).

Over the years, several prominent Indians such as Bal Gangadhar Tilak, Mahatma Gandhi, and Vinoba Bhave have practiced and propagated the philosophy of karma-yoga. Even in the business world, there have been several successful business professionals such as—Gurcharan Das (1993), Indra Nooyi, (*Indian Express*, 2007), and Satya Nadella (Stampler, 2014) who attribute their success to practicing karma-yoga. Karma-Yoga has several applications to issues faced by organizations today.

Refining Leadership Behavior

Moral development of the leader is an essential element of transformational leadership which inspires and motivates teams to perform far beyond expectations (Burns, 1978). In fact, merely executing the behaviors of transformational leadership does not have any positive follower outcomes unless followers perceive that leaders also have self-transcendent (other-oriented) values (Fu et al., 2011). Visualizing the leader's role as that of a servant who seeks to meet the needs of his or her team (Hunter, 1998) automatically incorporates other-oriented values. The need for leadership to be rooted in values is essential not only to inspire followers (Burns, 1978), but also to prevent the abuse of power by those in high office (Keltner, 2016). Leaders who practice karma-yoga consider themselves as debtors to their team. They recognize that they find themselves in a position of responsibility with respect to others due to some past debt which they are obligated to repay. This development of a collective identity in the place of an individual identity is an important predictor of positive leadership behavior (Johnson et al., 2012). Hence, instead of exploiting others for their own benefit, karma-yogi leaders are more likely to serve their team members selflessly and thereby enhance team outcomes.

Dealing with Crucible Experiences

One of the biggest sources of development of leadership ability is when managers go through intense, often traumatic, and unplanned experiences (called crucibles), which help them to discover their best capabilities (Bennis & Thomas, 2002). The personal strengths that help an individual to make sense of and deal with these crucibles include taking responsibility for one's life and the ability to find meaning in negative events (Thomas, 2008). The ability to find meaning in negative events is an important predictor of psychological well-being (Tavernier & Willoughby, 2012). The belief in the law of cause and effect (karma) helps individuals to make sense of negative events, stop blaming others, and take charge of their life; and thereby overcome personal crises (Agrawal & Dalal, 1993; Dalal & Pande, 1988). Moreover, karma-yoga was negatively related to depression (Rastogi et al., 2015) and burnout (Navare, 2019; Pati et al., 2017).

Model of Moral Development

Karma-Yoga constitutes a holistic model of moral development (Mulla & Krishnan, 2014). It emphasizes taking into account an individual's unique circumstances and context while making a decision regarding the appropriate ethical action. This is especially true for managers making decisions in a real-world context where abstract and lofty principles such as utilitarianism and deontology are often useless and what really matters is a nuanced understanding of the details of each situation and one's personal circumstances (Badaracco, 1997). Karma-Yoga provides a framework for moral decision-making by taking into account the needs of others and following the principles of unselfishness, non-attachment, and svadharma (Vivekananda, 2009).

Conclusion

According to Sumantra Ghoshal (2005, p. 76) "By propagating ideologically inspired amoral theories, business schools have actively freed their students from any sense of moral responsibility." Hence, management educators must develop theories which would help build moral/ethical organizations (Ghoshal, 2005). Another requirement for management theories is that they must be culturally relevant and rooted in indigenous insights (Gupta, 1992, 2011). Karma-yoga is a response to Ghoshal (2005) and Gupta (1992, 2011). It is an excellent solution to address the problem of increasing greed and selfishness in modern society by making people focus on their duties toward others.

When individuals focus on their duties toward others, they will not be hankering after the personal outcomes of their actions; thereby enhancing the quality of the process and outcomes. Being duty-oriented and not hankering after personal outcomes will make the individuals calmer, resulting in a higher quality of life. Empirical studies (e.g., Pati et al., 2017; Navare, 2019) have shown the positive effects of karma-yoga in the work context. As organizations strive to enhance workplace happiness and reduce stress and burnout, karma-yoga provides a way out.

Individuals are likely to benefit by learning this philosophy of karma-yoga. Swami Vivekananda's (2009) book "*Karma-Yoga: The Yoga of action*" is an edited version of eight lectures he delivered during December 1895 to January 1896 and is an excellent summary. For a more technical understanding of karma-yoga, Tilak's (2000) *Gita Rahasya* is an excellent source. Mahatma Gandhi and Vinoba Bhave were two foremost teachers of karma-yoga in modern times (Bhajanananda, 2006, p. 8). Studying their lives and writings would help in getting a deeper understanding of karma-yoga.

References

Agarwalla, S., Seshadri, B., & Krishnan, V. R. (2015). Impact of Gunas and Karma Yoga on transformational leadership. *Journal of Human Values, 21*(1), 11–22.

Agrawal, M., & Dalal, A. K. (1993). Beliefs about the world and recovery from myocardial infarction. *The Journal of Social Psychology, 133*, 385–394.

Badaracco, Jr., J. L. (1997). *Defining moments: When managers must choose between right and right*. Harvard Business Press.

Banerjee, G. R. (1964). Karma Yoga and social case work practice in India. *The Indian Journal of Social Work, XXIV*(4), 229–234.

Bennis, W. G., & Thomas, R. J. (2002, September). Crucibles of leadership. *Harvard Business Review*, 39–45.

Bhajanananda, S. (2006). *Selfless work: Its basis, methods, and fulfilment*. Ramakrishna Mission Vivekananda University Press.

Bhave, V. (2005). *Talks on the Gita* (16th ed.). Paramdham Prakashan Paunar.

Bhawuk, D. P. S. (2011). *Spirituality and Indian psychology: Lessons from the Bhagavad-Gita*. Springer.

Burns, J. M. (1978). *Leadership*. Harper.

Chakraborty, S. K. (1998). *Foundations of managerial work: Contributions from Indian thought*. Himalaya Publishing House.

Connors, J., & Heaven, P. C. L. (1990). Belief in a just world and attitudes toward AIDS sufferers. *The Journal of Social Psychology, 130*, 559–560.

Dalal, A. K., & Pande, N. (1988). Psychological recovery of accident victims with temporary and permanent disability. *International Journal of Psychology, 23*(1–6), 25–40.

Das, G. (1993, March–April). Local memoirs of a global manager. *Harvard Business Review*, 38–47.

Dasgupta, S. (1991). *A history of Indian philosophy* (Vol. 1). Motilal Banarasidas (Original work published 1922.).

Fu, P. P., Tsui, A. S., Jun, L., & Lan, L. (2011). Pursuit of whose happiness? Executive leaders' transformational behaviors and personal values. *Administrative Science Quarterly, 55*(2), 222–254.

Gandhi, M. K. (1980). *The Bhagvadgita.* Orient Paperbacks.

Gandhi, M. K. (2001). *The gospel of selfless action* (M. Desai, Trans.). Navajivan Publishing House (Original work published 1946).

Ghanananda, S. (1958). The dawn of Indian philosophy. In S. Radhakrishnan, H. Bhattacharyya, R. C. Majumdar, S. K. Chatterji, H. Kabir, S. K. De et al. (Series Eds.) & S. K. Chatterji, N. Dutt, A. D. Pusalker, & N. K. Bose (Vol. Eds.), *The cultural heritage of India: Vol. 1. The early phases* (2nd ed., pp. 333–344). Ramakrishna Mission Institute of Culture.

Ghoshal, S. (2005). Bad management theories are destroying good management practices. *Academy of Management Learning & Education, 4*(1), 75–91.

Gupta, R. (1992). Crisis of Management Research in India. *Economic and Political Weekly, 27*(34), 1785–1786.

Gupta, R. K. (2011). The process of developing new concepts and theories, and its implications for doctoral education and research. *Keynote address presented at the National Association of Psychologists*, IRMA, Anand on December 12, 2011.

Hafer, C. L., & Begue, L. (2005). Experimental research on just-world theory: Problems, developments, and future challenges. *Psychological Bulletin, 131*, 128–167.

Hunter, J. C. (1998). *The Servant: A simple story about the true essence of leadership* (2012th ed.). Crown Business.

Indian Express (2007, December 24). Nooyi in Chennai, enjoying curd rice and katcheri. *The Indian Express.* Accessed from http://archive.indianexpress.com/news/nooyi-in-chennai-enjoying-curd-rice-and-katcheri/253599/ on August 21, 2019 at 0939 hours.

Johnson, R. E., Venus, M., Lanaj, K., Mao, C., & Chang, C.-H. (2012). Leader identity as an antecedent of the frequency and consistency of transformational, consideration, and abusive leadership behaviors. *Journal of Applied Psychology, 97*(6), 1262–1272. https://doi.org/10.1037/a0029043

Joshi, N., & Krishnan, V. R. (2015). Impact of leader's motives and Svadharma-orientation on transformational leadership. *Great Lakes Herald, 9*(1), 1–18.

Keltner, D. (2016). *The power paradox: How we gain and lose influence.* Penguin.

Krishnan, V. R. (2007). Effect of transformational leadership and leader's power on follower's duty-orientation and spirituality. *Great Lakes Herald, 1*(2), 48–70.

Krishnan, V. R. (2008). The impact of transformational leadership on followers' duty orientation and spirituality. *Journal of Human Values, 14*(1), 11–22.

Krishnananda, S. (1991). *The philosophy of the Bhagavadgita.* Divine Life Society.

Madhu, B., & Krishnan, V. R. (2005). Impact of transformational leadership and Karma-Yoga on organizational citizenship behaviour. *Prestige Journal of Management and Research, 9*(1), 1–20.

Mahadevan, T. M. P. (1958). The religio-philosophic culture of India. In S. Radhakrishnan, H. Bhattacharyya, R. C. Majumdar, S. K. Chatterji, H. Kabir, S. K. De, et al. (Series Eds.) & S. K. Chatterji, N. Dutt, A. D. Pusalker, & N. K. Bose (Vol. Eds.), *The cultural heritage of India: Vol. 1. The early phases* (2nd ed., pp. 163–181). Ramakrishna Mission Institute of Culture.

Mehra, P., & Krishnan, V. R. (2005). Impact of Svadharma-orientation on transformational leadership and followers' trust in leader. *Journal of Indian Psychology, 23*(1), 1–11.

Menon, A., & Krishnan, V. R. (2004). Transformational leadership and follower's Karma-Yoga: Role of follower's gender. *Journal of Indian Psychology, 22*(2), 50–62.

Mulla, Z. R., & Krishnan, V. R. (2006). Karma Yoga: A conceptualization and validation of the Indian philosophy of work. *Journal of Indian Psychology, 24*(1/2), 26–43.

Mulla, Z. R., & Krishnan, V. R. (2007). Karma-Yoga: Construct validation using value systems and emotional intelligence. *South Asian Journal of Management, 14*(4), 116–136.

Mulla, Z. R., & Krishnan, V. R. (2008). Karma-Yoga, the Indian work ideal and its relationship with empathy. *Psychology and Developing Societies, 20*(1), 27–49.

Mulla, Z. R., & Krishnan, V. R. (2009). Do Karma-Yogis make better leaders? Exploring the relationship between the leader's Karma-Yoga and transformational leadership. *Journal of Human Values, 15*(2), 167–183.

Mulla, Z. R., & Krishnan, V. R. (2011). Is Karma-Yoga possible? Can we be hardworking without being ambitious? *Great Lakes Herald, 5*(2), 46–55.

Mulla, Z. R., & Krishnan, V. R. (2012). Transformational leadership and Karma-Yoga: Enhancing followers' duty-orientation and indifference to rewards. *Psychology & Developing Societies, 24*(1), 85–117.

Mulla, Z. R., & Krishnan, V. R. (2014). Karma-Yoga: The Indian model of moral development. *Journal of Business Ethics, 123*(2), 339–351.

Mulla, Z. R., Krishnan, V. R., & Kumar, N. P. (2018). Self-Concept of a Karma-Yogi. *LBS Journal of Management and Research, 16*(1 & 2), 4–10.

Narayanan, J., & Krishnan, V. R. (2003). Impact of Sattva and Rajas Gunas on transformational leadership and Karma-Yoga. *Journal of Indian Psychology, 21*(2), 1–11.

Navare, A. (2019). *Karma Yoga: Conceptualization, scale development, and the implications on spirituality and positive psychology outcomes at the workplace* (Unpublished Doctoral thesis). IIT Bombay.

Pande, N., & Naidu, R. (1992). Anasakti and health: A study of non-attachment. *Psychology & Developing Societies, 4*(1), 89–104.

Pati, S. P., Rastogi, A., & Kumar, P. (2017). *Arresting burnout: The role of Karma yoga* (Indian Institute of Management Kozhikode Working Paper, IIMK/WPS/221/OB&HR/2017/05).

Prabhavananda, S. (1960). *The spiritual heritage of India.* Vedanta Society of Southern California.

Radhakrishnan, S. (1926). *The Hindu view of life*. HarperCollins.

Radhakrishnan, S. (1940). *Indian Philosophy* (Vol. 1). George Allen & Unwin.

Radhakrishnan, S. (1971). *The Bhagavadgita.* George Allen & Unwin.

Ranganathananda, S. (2000). *The message of the Upanishads: An exposition of the Upanishads in the light of modern thought and modern needs* (8th ed.). Bharatiya Vidya Bhavan.

Ranganathananda, S. (2001). *Universal message of the Bhagavad Gita: An exposition of the Gita in the light of modern thought and modern needs (3 volumes).* Advaita Ashrama.

Ranganathananda, S. (2005). *The message of the Brhadaranyaka Upanisad: An exposition of the Brhadaranyaka Upanisad in the light of modern thought and modern needs* (8th ed.). Advaita Ashrama.

Rao, R. K., & Paranjpe, A. C. (2016). *Psychology in the Indian tradition.* Springer.

Rastogi, A., & Pati, S. P. (2015). Towards a conceptualization of Karma Yoga. *Journal of Human Values, 21*(1), 51–63.

Rastogi, A., Pati, S. P., & Kumar, P. (2015). *Measurement of Karma Yoga: Development and validation of Karma Yoga Instrument (KYI-6).* Academy of Management Proceedings, 15941. https://doi.org/10.5465/ambpp.2015.15941

Shamir, B. (1991). Meaning, self, and motivation in organization. *Organization Studies, 12*(3), 405–424.

Shamir, B., House, R. J., & Arthur, M. B. (1993). The motivational effects of charismatic leadership: A self-concept based theory. *Organization Science, 4*(4), 577–594.

Singh, N., & Krishnan, V. R. (2005). Towards understanding transformational leadership in India: A grounded theory approach. *Vision: The Journal of Business Perspective, 9(2),* 5–17.

Sinha, J. B. P. (1997). A cultural perspective on organizational behavior in India. In P. C. Earley & M. Erez (Eds.), *New perspectives on international industrial/ organizational psychology* (pp. 53–74). The New Lexington Press and Jossey-Bass Publishers.

Stampler, L. (2014, October 9). Microsoft's CEO tells women it's bad karma to ask for a raise. *Time.* Accessed from https://time.com/3486673/microsofts-ceo-satya-nadella-women-work-gender-pay-gap/ on August 21, 2019.

Swarupananda, S. (1909). *Srimad Bhagavad Gita.* Advaita Ashrama.

Tavernier, R., & Willoughby, T. (2012). Adolescent turning points: The association between meaning-making and psychological well-being. *Developmental Psychology, 48*(4), 1058–1068.

Thomas, R. J. (2008). *Crucibles of leadership: How to learn from experience to become a great leader.* Harvard Business Press.

Tilak, B. G. (2000). *Srimad Bhagavadgita-Rahasya* (B. S. Sukhantar, Trans.). Kesari Press. (Original work published 1915).

Vivekananda, S. (1972). *The complete works of Swami Vivekananda (eight volumes).* Advaita Ashrama.

Vivekananda, S. (2009). *Karma-Yoga: The Yoga of action.* Advaita Ashrama.

6

Understanding Self and Well-Being Based on Ayurveda: Implications for Indian Management

Mala Kapadia and Chirag Dagar

Introduction

Ayurveda is commonly known as the Indian traditional medical system. Etymologically, there are two words *Ayus* and *Veda* that combine to make the word Ayurveda. *Ayu* has been understood simply as 'life' and *Veda* as 'knowledge'. *Ayus* also means longevity, meaningfulness in life,

M. Kapadia
Rashtram School of Public Leadership, Rishihood University, Sonipat, Haryana, India
e-mail: mala@rashtram.org

C. Dagar (✉)
Shailesh J. Mehta School of Management, Indian Institute of Technology Bombay, Mumbai, India
e-mail: chirag.dagar@som.iitb.ac.in

© The Author(s), under exclusive license to Springer Nature Switzerland AG 2022
A. Pandey et al. (eds.), *Indigenous Indian Management*, Palgrave Studies in Indian Management,
https://doi.org/10.1007/978-3-030-87906-8_6

well-being, and health (Vasudevan, 2000).[1] Ayurveda is the knowledge that helps one lead such a life by discriminating what is good and what is unwholesome, what will create happiness and what will create pain and disease (Shukla & Tripathy, 2002).[2] Life or *Ayus* itself is a much larger concept in Sanskrit. *Ayus* means the conjunction of the body, sense organs, mind and Self. The synonyms for *Ayus* in Ayurveda are *dhaari*—one that sustains life, *jeevitam*—one that is alive and vibrant, *nityaga*—constantly changing, and *anubandha*—one that is creating continuity (Shukla & Tripathy, 2002).[3] Life is described in an inclusive way where the body, mind, spirit, their processes and functions, purpose and meaning, well-being and health are all integrated into one word, *Ayus*. Hence, being more than the narrowly defined medical science, Ayurveda is a holistic system of knowledge rendering on what is life-promoting and what is not, for the physical body, mind, heart, senses, and spirit. This encompasses guidelines on the kind of diet, lifestyle, and behavior, which is optimal for well-being (Frawley, 1999).

Ayurveda follows the same path as the earlier *Vedic* literature has followed, i.e., an inquiry into the meaning and purpose of life, evolving principles of well-being for all. This is a stream of knowledge of well-being focusing on experiencing life that goes beyond momentary happiness. The four main purposes or *Purusharthas* of human life *artha*, *dharma*, *kaama*, and *moksha* in Indian culture described in Chapter 2 form the basis of Ayurveda as well. As described in Ayurveda, pursuit

---

[1] Ayursmin vidhyate anen va ayurvindatityaurved, *Sushrut Sutrasthan 1.13.*

Ayurveda is that which deals with life or which helps a man to enjoy a longer duration of life.

[2] Hitahitam sukham dukhamayustsya Hitahitam.

Manam ch tachch yatroktamayurvedah sa uchyate, *Charak Samhita 1.41.*

The *Shastra* in which four kinds of *Ayus* or life are described, *hita, ahita, sukha,* and *dukha*, and the science to identify them, or measure them is described, what is life and how to live life well is described, that *Shastra* is called Ayurveda.

[3] Shareerendriyasatvaatmasamyogo dhaari jiveetam.

Nityagashchanubandhshch paryayairayuruchyate, *Charak Samhita 1.42.*

Body or sharer, senses or *indriyas*, mind or manas, and soul or *atma* their combination creates life. They hold life—*dhaari,* continuity and movement—*jeevit* and *nityaga,* of life, interconnection—*anubandha* of life are synonyms to their existence.

of happiness or *Sukha*, needs to be guided by *Dharma* to be a sustainable one (Sreekumar, 2013).[4] Happiness cannot be experienced without health; hence the health-promoting way of life is essential. Good health is the foundation to achieve the four purposes of human life (Shukla & Tripathy, 2002).[5]

The primary aim of Ayurveda is to help attain health by advising a way of life and living, and the secondary aim is to treat the diseases (Shukla & Tripathy, 2002).[6] Individual happiness and well-being is interconnected with well-being at all levels. The inclusiveness of happiness and health of all is the Indian philosophical foundation shared by Ayurveda as well and described in the ancient *shloka* as follows:

> *Om Sarve Bhavantu Sukhinah, Sarve Santu Nir-Aamayaah* I
> *Sarve Bhadraanni Pashyantu, Maa Kashcid-Duhkha-Bhaag-Bhavet* I
> *Om Shaantih Shaantih Shaantih* II
> *May everyone be happy, May everyone be free from all diseases,*
> *May everyone see goodness and auspiciousness in everything, May none be unhappy or distressed,*
> *Om peace, peace, peace!*

The aim of this chapter is to share insights from Ayurveda that can help establish well-being at individual, organizational, societal, and national levels. The flow of the chapter is as follows: the next section delineates the philosophy and the fundamental concepts of health and well-being as per Ayurveda. The third section overviews the challenges to

---

4 Sukhartha sarvabhootanam mataha sarvaha pravruttaya.

Sukham cha na vina dharmattsmatdharmaparo bhavet, *Astanga Hrdaya Vagbhata Sutrasthana 2.20.*

All impulses of all beings are directed toward happiness. Happiness comes from following *dharma*. Hence, in order to achieve happiness, we must follow *Dharma*.

5 Dharmarthakaammokshanamargyaam moolamuttamam, *Charak Samhita 1.15.*

To achieve the four *prusharthas* or aims of life—*dharma*, *artha*, *kaama*, and *moksha*, one's health should be in optimal state.

6 Prayojanam chaasya swasthsya swasthyakshanmatursya vikarprashamanam cha, *Charak Samhita 30.26.*

The aim of Ayurveda is to protect the health of healthy people, and cure the ones who are diseased.

Human Resource (HR) in present times, concern areas of well-being, and how Ayurveda can help in addressing those. The final section discusses future research areas for Indian Management integrating Ayurveda.

Traditional Indian Worldview: Putting Ayurveda in Context

Worldview refers to the way of interpreting things and forms an intrinsic part or reality of a culture, wherein the beliefs, values, and behaviors of a culture originate from its worldview (Hill, 2007). To understand Ayurveda, it is essential to put *Vedic* world-view into perspective as Ayurveda is the extension of the *Vedas* and started as an oral tradition (Singh, 1977). Original *Vedas* (four) comprise of- *Rig, Yajur, Sama*, and *Atharva*. Ayurveda is regarded as *Upveda* or extension of *Atharva Veda* (Vasudevan, 2000).[7] *Atharva Veda* is also known as *Brahma Veda, Atma Veda*, or *Amrit Veda* (Singh, 1977). Max Muller says, "*Brahma* meant originally force, will, wish and the propulsive power of creation. *Atma* means breath or spirit or self, *Brahma* itself is but Self" (Singh, 1977). Hence, the subject matter of *Atharva Veda* is to understand and attain the self as *Brahma* or *Atma*. In this journey of self-discovery, *manas* or mind as psychic energy is explored, and practical application of psychic energy over matter is established. *Atharva Veda* can be seen as one of the oldest texts on nature and functions of the human mind that is rooted in the knowledge of the connection between the universe and psychic energy. The psychic harmony and unity of universe consider *Brahma* as all-inclusive and powerful (Singh, 1977). The titles and initial *sutras* of the first chapters of three classical texts of Ayurveda, namely *Charak Samhita, Sushruta Samhita*, and *Ashtang Hrdaya* are reflecting this foundation.

Charak Samhita's first chapter is titled *Deerghjeevitatiyam*—the science of longevity and guidance on how to achieve this (Shukla & Tripathy,

---

[7] Iha khalvaayurvedo naam yadupangamatharvavedasya, *Sushrut Sutrasthan 1.6.*

Ayurveda is regarded as *Upang* or *Upaveda* of *Atharva Veda*—Ayurveda is derived from *Atharva Veda.*

2002).[8] *Sushruta Samhita's* first chapter starts with the *sutra* on physical and metaphysical aspects of all living beings (Sharma, 2009).[9] Understanding the physical and metaphysical are basis for understanding one's own self. *Ashtang Hrdaya*, written by *Vagbhat*, begins with the chapter titled *Ayushkameeyam*, quest for longevity, and the first *sutra* itself begins with integrating body and mind (Sreekumar, 2013). These texts establish Ayurveda as a holistic science for life and understanding self; however, they begin with the philosophy of interconnectedness of not just body and mind, but the entire Universe. This is the reflection of the world-view of Ayurveda.

The metaphysical notion of *Vedas*, which holds Macrocosm as within the Microcosm (Vasishtha, 2009), is shared in Ayurveda as well. As per this notion, the self (individual) evolves from Self (the universal) as a result of involution of Universe from unmanifest energy to the manifest. Life is interconnected, and so compassion for everyone around is essentially a life process.

Four Ways of Life in Ayurveda

A classic definition of Ayurveda is found in the chapter called *Sutrasthana* in the *Charaka Samhita (1, 42–43).*

ayurhitahitamvyadhe nidaanamshamanam thathaa.
vidyate yatra vidhwadhihi tatra ayurveda uchyate.

Meaning is that Ayurveda is the science of health and disease, which deals with good, bad, happy, and unhappy life, its promoters and non-promoters, measurement, and nature.

Ayu or life is also described in depth, describing four ways of life. *Hitayu, Ahitayu, Sukhayu,* and *Dukhayu.*

---

[8] Athato deerghajeevitiyamadhyayam vyakhyasyamah, *Charak Samhita 1.*
Now the chapter titled long life is being described.

[9] Iha khalvaayurvedo naam yadupangamatharvavedasya, *Sushrut Samhita 1.6.*
It is the truth that Ayurveda is derived from *Atharva Veda* and hence an *Upanga.*

Hita hitam sukham dukham ayus tasya hitahitam |
Mana ch tachha yatrokatam ayurveda sa uchyate || *Charaka Samhita, Sutrasthana, 1, 41.*

Four ways of life described in Ayurveda are explained in this sub section:

Hitayu comprises of two words: *Hita* and *Ayu* wherein *'Hita'* is in alignment with others and Universe and *Ayu* meaning life. A person is living *Hitayu* when s/he does not harm others in thought, speech, and action; lives, moves, and acts in kindness, humility, goodness; seek harmony in a family and society, is self-disciplined, controls her/his negative traits like anger, agitation, excitement, etc. Such a life always enjoys good health, harmony, and happiness.

Ahitayu comprises of *Ahit* and *Ayu* wherein *Ahit* means non-aligned or concerned for others. *Ahitayu* refers to a life guided by her/his self-interest, prejudices, manifests negative traits of anger, agitation in personal, professional and social lives, distracted, and harming others for own benefits in life. A person leading *Ahitayu* is destructive and suffers from many disorders and may be very competitive, unmindful, selfish, greedy, and myopic.

Sukhayu means a life of joy wherein—*Su* means auspicious, and *Kha* is space. *Sukha* is to be in a state of happiness and wellness. *Sukhayu* represents a lifestyle where a person enjoys material and spiritual aspects of life as he or she is physically and mentally fit, having strength and vitality. S/he is having intellect and is knowledgeable, and her/his senses are under control and is able to do their work.

Dukhayu, or life of sorrow (as *Dukh* means sorrow), refers to a life of ignorance and falsehood. *Dukhayu* means living life which contradicts the ways of living, as mentioned in the core, falls into this category of living. S/he suffers and lives a stressful life, is not able to enjoy relationships and worldly pleasures, going through motions of life reacting with aggression or depression.

Hitayu and *Sukhayu* create sustainable life, well-being, and world peace. *Dukhayu* and *Ahitayu* are commonly seen in the volatile, uncertain, complex, and ambiguities world suffering. *Hitayu* and *Sukhayu* also relate closely to positive psychology in terms of aspirations and characteristics of a good life.

Core Principles of Ayurveda

As discussed above, Ayurveda is considered as the continuation of *Rig Veda* and *Atharva Veda*. Passages linked to Ayurveda from the various *Vedas* were synthesized into separate books dealing specifically with Ayurveda. Among the 10,572 hymns of *Rig Veda*, there are discussions on the three constitutions (*Doshas*): air (*Vayu*), fire (*Pitta*), and water (*Kapha*). Further, deliberations on topics comprise of organ transplants, artificial limbs, and the use of herbs to heal (mind and body) diseases and to promote longevity. Within *Atharva Veda's* 5,977 hymns are discussions on anatomy, physiology, and surgery (Tirtha, 2005).

The origin is ancient, and it's difficult to create exact timelines of how Ayurveda spread to the larger healthcare field and holders. However, compassion for humanity and concern for the state of the planet where people were suffering at many levels could be seen as the origin of Ayurveda. The story goes that in order to alleviate the suffering, the *Rishis* and *Maharishis*, i.e., the seers sent a representative, *Rishi Bhardwaj*, to *Indra*, a celestial God who possessed the knowledge of Ayurveda. Indra accepted *Rishi Bhardwaj* as his disciple and shared the knowledge of Ayurveda with him. Hence, *Rishi Bhardwaj* is believed to have created the tradition of knowledge sharing which resulted in many schools of Ayurveda that exist today (Shukla & Tripathy, 2002). Compassion to heal humanity, i.e., the origin of Ayurveda, is imperative and the need of the hour today again.

The metaphysical tenet of *Upanishads* is *Yat Pinde Tat Brahmande*; self, is a reflection of the Self. As the Universe is ever-expanding, manifesting, and full of possibilities, the same is with the self. The epistemology of Ayurveda is founded on the relationship between microcosm and macrocosm constituted of five basic elements (*mahabhoota*), three principles similar to humors (*dosha*), seven types of tissues (*dhatus*), and several other unique concepts (Patwardhan, 2014). Ayurveda as a therapeutic approach focuses on *prakriti* and *tridoshas*. These principles delineate that every individual has one's unique constitution called *prakriti*. *Prakriti* ascertains the characteristic response of an individual to factors such as medication, environmental condition, and diet. 'Ayurgenomics' an emerging research field, aims to bridge the gap between genomics and Ayurveda to aid in understanding inter-individual differences with respect to therapies for various diseases (Gupta, 2015). These concepts are shared in detail in the later sections of the article. The following section briefly describes the history of Ayurvedic knowledge, education, and practice.

History of Ayurveda

In older India, Ayurveda enjoyed an integrated part in education, practice, and everyday life. *Agnivesha* compiled the knowledge from the *Vedas*, which was edited by *Charaka* and some other scholars and is currently known as "*Charaka Samhita*". While *Charaka Samhita* describes various aspects of Ayurvedic medicine, *Sushruta Samhita* explains the practices and notions of surgery (Sharma, 1979). The third classical text which has made an impact is *Ashtang Hrdaya* and *Ashtang Samgraha*, written by *Vagbhat*. These ancient texts have been translated into various languages, including Tibetan, Greek, Chinese, Arabic, and Persian (Ray & Gupta, 1965). Also, there exist several allied minor compilations such as *Nighantu Granthas*, *Madhava Nidana,* and *Bhava Prakasha* emerging from the contributions of various scholars; however, *Charaka Samhita* remains the most revered of all the records (Leaman, 1999).

The *Atreya Samhita* is probably the oldest medical book in the world and has survived from the Takshila University that was operating as early as 800 BC. There is evidence suggesting that around 600 A.D., Chinese scholars were studying medicine in India at Nalanda University including the well-known Tang Dynasty Chinese monk I-Ching, who authored his eponymous poetic philosophical work. The Indian thought, as well as Chinese spirituality and philosophy of Buddhism, influenced Chinese medicine and herbology through Ayurveda. Evidence suggests that scholars from present-day China, Tibet, Greece, Rome, Egypt, Afghanistan, Persia, or Iran and others traveled to India and took back the knowledge of Ayurveda to their native countries. A key role was played by India's Silk Road, an established trade route between Asia (China, Tibet, etc.), the Middle East (Afghanistan, Persia, etc.), and

Europe (Rome, Greece, etc.), serving as a link between cultures. Travelers first discovered Ayurveda on this route (Tirtha, 2005). Further, Arabic translation of Ayurvedic works took place in 800 A.D.. Ayurveda strongly influenced the two Islamic physicians: Avicenna and Razi Serapion, who helped establish the European tradition of medicine.[10]

The arrival of Moghuls, who brought the Unani medicine to India, led to Ayurveda becoming a secondary mode of medicine. Further, in February 1835, Thomas Macaulay drafted a powerful minute recommending the government to withhold further grants to institutions, "conferring instruction in the native languages".[11] In 1835, the Native Medical Institution was abolished along with the discontinuation of the classes held at the *madrasa* and the Sanskrit *Pathshalaa,* which were very small schools and seminaries of modern times. While Western medicine was granted the status of official medicine, with the increasing power of colonization, the state turned discriminatory and exhibited hostility toward the other systems and even labeled them as unscientific or irrational (Anshu, 2016). Vaidya Prabhuram Jeevanram founded the first Ayurvedic Institute in Mumbai. The first Ayurvedic College in India, named as the Prabhuram Ayurvedic College, was established in 1896 with the intention to provide better education to the practitioners or inspiring practitioners of Ayurveda. Ayurveda continued to be in practice after independence independently and in combination with naturopathy, Yoga and spa, and commercial activities conducted with the promise of providing wholesome well-being to the clients. In recent decades, Ayurveda has witnessed a significant shift in its paradigm. The shift is from Ayurveda as a non-scientific herbal folk medicine to a well-documented ancient healthcare system. There has been a change in the outlook of researchers toward its applications as well. Additionally, with global interest and awareness in Ayurveda, many institutes in the United States and Europe are teaching Ayurveda to create practitioners. Ayurved Sadhana, Colorado—Bharat Vaidya; Council for Ayurveda Research,

[10] Scott Gerson, M.D., Ph.D. (Ayurveda) www.gersonayurveda.com

[11] Minute by Hon'ble T. B. Macaulay. 1835. February 2, Available from:http://www.columbia.edu/itc/mealac/pritchett/00generallinks/macaulay/txt_minute_education_1835.html.

Danvers—Dr. Pratibha Shah; The Ayurvedic Institute, New Mexico—Dr. Vasant Lad; National Ayurvedic Medical Association (NAMA) in Los Angeles, and Europe Ayurveda Academy in France are the few notable examples of the international centers of Ayurveda.

Definition of Health in Ayurveda

As per Ayurveda, the ideal model of health is called *swastha*. *'sva'* means self, *'stha'* means situated, located, or grounded. An individual who is grounded within her or his pure being is called *swastha*, which is the root of perfect health. That person is balanced in the physical body (*sharira*), the mind (*sattva*), and the conscious principle or self (*atma*). This tripod represents the foundation of health (Lad, 2006).

> *Samadosha, samagnischa samadhatumala kriyaha prasanna atmenindriya manaha swasthya ityabhidheeyate. (Sushruta Samhita, 15.38)*

"A person, whose all three humors or *Doshas*: *Vata* (air), *Pitta* (fire), and *Kapha* (water) are in balance, whose metabolism-appetite and digestion are in balance; whose seven body tissues (Seven *dhatus*: *rasa, rakta, mamsa, med, majja, asthi,* and *shukra*) are functioning normally; whose *malas* (urine, faeces, and sweat) are eliminated properly and whose spirit, senses, and mind (*sattva, rajas, tamas*), remain in joyful state is considered healthy". Figure 6.1 represents the balanced scorecard of health and happiness.

Health, according to Ayurveda, is achieved by understanding and integrating rituals and practices in one's life to stabilize one's energy, balance processes in body and mind, senses, and spirit. Well-being thus becomes a personal responsibility and even empowers one to be healthy. *Swasthavrutta* in Ayurveda is comparable to the balanced scorecard approach. The balance pertains to *Dosha, Agni, Dhatu, Malkriya, Atman* or spirit, senses and mind. When these seven factors are balanced, happiness or bliss is experienced. Such a person is a healthy person. Ayurveda takes the whole person into consideration. Hence, biology is understood from a very different perspective in Ayurveda. As discussed before, sama

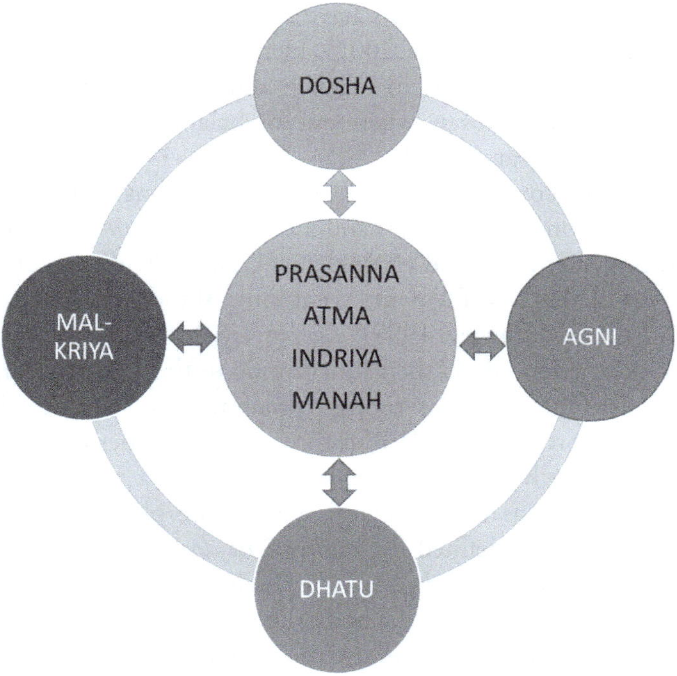

Fig. 6.1 Balanced scorecard of Health and Happiness (© Mala Kapadia)

or balance is the key to health and well-being. How to create this balance is given in *DinCharya, RatriCharya, RituCharya, Sadvrutta*, and *Achaar Rasayan.* The seven factors of physio-psychology and biological processes are discussed below:

Pancha Mahabhoota to Tridosha

Metaphysics in the *Vedas* upholds the evolution of the Universe as a progression from the unmanifest state of Consciousness to manifest consciousness. First appeared the Ether or Space Element, the subtlest form existing, the all-pervading home for all objects in the Universe. From the space resulted air, fire, water, and earth in this order, space being the subtlest. Air includes space, fire also includes space and air, water includes the previous three, and earth includes all other 4 elements. All these Elements are agents of the Consciousness. Out of the five Elements all the matter is born, and thus, the body is also made up of these Elements. These Elements have specific qualities that create the mind–body continuum. (Lad, 2002). Hence, they also give the Psycho-physiological profile. When in balance and harmony, these Elements create well-being, however, when out of balance, there is stress and dis-ease in the body and mind.

The Elements combine to give form and functions within the body–mind constitution. *Vata* is space and air element, *Pitta* is fire and water element, *Kapha* is water and earth element. An individual's constitution is made up of the Five Elements combining the three *Doshas* of *Vata, Pitta,* and *Kapha* (Frawley, 1999). *Doshas* are the life force that are not visible, but experienced via their functioning in the constitution. *Doshas* can be seen as bio-programs trying to maintain and balance the body harmoniously (Sreekumar, 2013) or three functionalities that regulate all physiological, psychological, and spiritual facets of a person. *Dosha* can also be referred to as the biological type or the physical constitution. In Sanskrit, *dosha* is defined as *"dushyati iti doshah"*. This means "that which contaminates is called *"doshah"*. The imbalance of *vata, pitta,* and *kapha doshas* cause disease in the body. Therefore, the imbalance of these elemental combinations denotes the cause of an illness. The *Vata* or the air element governs inhalation, exhalation, movements, impulses, and the human senses. The *Pitta* or the fire element deals with hunger, thirst, digestion, excretion, body warmth, and circulation. It also relates to body strength, energy, youth intelligence, and executive abilities. The *Kapha* or the water element controls the stability, lubrication, movements, body luster, digestive tract, glands, and fluids of the body.

This Constitution, combination of *Pancha Mahabhoota* into *Tridosha*, is the Ayurvedic Profile called *'Prakriti'* in Sanskrit. Profile is more than temperament, traits, or type. All three Ts have their limitations. Profile is based on Universal Principles and gives an understanding of who an individual is, based on these principles. The Elements and *Doshas* are the blueprint of who one is. It is natural to have the qualities associated with the Elements to manifest in the body and personality.[12] A lot of research

[12] Kapadia, M. (2020). *Deep Psychology and Ayurveda: Creating Engaging Classrooms with Ayurvedic Profile*. In print.

is now available on how *doshas* and sub *doshas* make up the constitution (Govindaraj et al., 2015; Rhoda, 2014).

Every human being has her or his own nature (*prakriti*) and temperament (*svabhava*). Thus, while everyone is constituted of the three primordial or basic attributes called the *TriGunas*, i.e., *sattva*, *rajas*, and *tamas*, they differ in terms of the pattern of their relative salience. The unique pattern of behavior exhibited by a person depends on the combination of these attributes. The lifestyle and (ill) health-related behaviors and practices also function in relation to these attributes. The difficulties arise when there is a deviation from the balanced state, and therefore restoration of health and well-being requires steps to compensate for the imbalance. The remedies prescribed include (re)organization of diet, thought, and action (*ahaar*, *vichaar*, and *vyavahaar*) (Dalal & Mishra, 2011).

The factor that can help this reorganization is the fire that creates metabolism. This fire in Ayurveda is called *Agni*. Ayurveda suggests practices for keeping the digestive fire strong, vis a vis, proper eating habits, a diet based on the six tastes, daily routine (*dinacharya*), and leading life aligned with nature's rhythms. *Agni* is responsible for transformation, digestion, and metabolism.

Agni

From an ayurvedic perspective, the digestive fire, *Agni*, is the power through which one digests and assimilates everything one takes in—using what is useful and releasing the rest. This digestion happens not only on the level of food, but also in mind, on the level of sensory impressions and experiences.

The Latin word *"ignis"*, from which the English word *"ignite"* is derived, has a common root with the Sanskrit word *"agni"*. *Agni* means that which ignites, which is fire.

A. Awareness: Each cell is a center of awareness. That awareness is governed by *agni*.
G. Governor: of digestion, assimilation, and transformation of matter into energy. *Agni* also governs the structural and functional activities of all cells and tissues.

N. Nutrition: of all bodily tissues; also, neutralization of toxins (*ama*) in the tissues.
I. Intelligence: cellular intelligence and cellular selectivity and choice (Lad, 2002).

Lad identifies 40 types of *Agni* in the system: body and mind together (Lad, 2002).

Two examples of how *Agni* works will explain how Ayurveda creates well-being differently. Osteoporosis is seen as the weakening of bones due to calcium deficiency in modern medicine, however, it is seen as an impaired *agni* in the bones and *asthi dhatu* in Ayurveda. Hence, contrary to taking calcium supplements, rekindling the fire that turns nutrition into nourishment for the bones is the approach adopted in Ayurveda. The *Agni* works differently in different constitutions or *Prakriti* dominated by *Vata, Pitta,* and *Kapha*. *Agni* also works differently in seasons, stages in lifespan, day-night cycles, and during phases of digestion of food (Sreekumar, 2013). Second example relates to understanding the working of *Agni* holistically to create well-being through right lifestyle. Not to drink water during eating food or immediately after food, drink only warm water throughout the day and not cold water that dilutes the *Agni*, etc.

Dhatu

Dhatu provides firmness and nourishment to the body. The word *Dhatu* is derived from the root *du—dhatru* meaning to support and nourish. *Dhatu* is which supports body, mind, and *prana* (Sreekumar, 2013). The seven *dhatus* work like the supply chain principles, each one nourishing the next level. Each *dhatu* is responsible for the metabolic conditions which are conducive for the next in line. The nourishing and nurturing cycle can also become depleting cycle if there is a lack of health at an earlier level. All *dhatus* are made up of minute *paramanu* (cells or atoms or tiny particles) of varied structure and function, constituting the different organs of the body. Each cell is linked with another cell with *suksma srota* (minute channels), through which cells distribute nutrients and (metabolic) wastes. This description of cellular communication, although written 1200 years ago, aligns with the contemporary understanding of inter-cellular exchange (Mishra et al., 2001).

Dhatus work at physiological levels and psychological/emotional levels and comprise of *rasa* (essence, engagement), *rakta* (blood), *mamsa* (muscle tissue), *med* (lipid), *asthi* (bones), *majja* (marrow), *shukra* (reproductive tissue) (Lad, 2002). *Shukra* gives rise to *ojas* (pure essence of all bodily tissues) (for details, see notes). In the organization context, *rasa* represents engagement and *ojas* denotes vitality, wherein *rasa* nurtures *ojas* and a lack of *rasa* depletes *ojas*. Figure 6.2 denotes the nurturing cycle of *dhatu*.

Mal Kriya

Understanding *'ama'* or toxins is essential to explore *Mal Kriya*. Balance of *doshas* and digestion of anything consumed by the senses are the basic principles of health and well-being in Ayurveda. Undigested toxic particles create *ama* that clogs the channels in the body. In Sanskrit, a healthy person is also called *'Niramaya'*, *'ni'* is without and *'ama'* is toxins. *'Mal'*

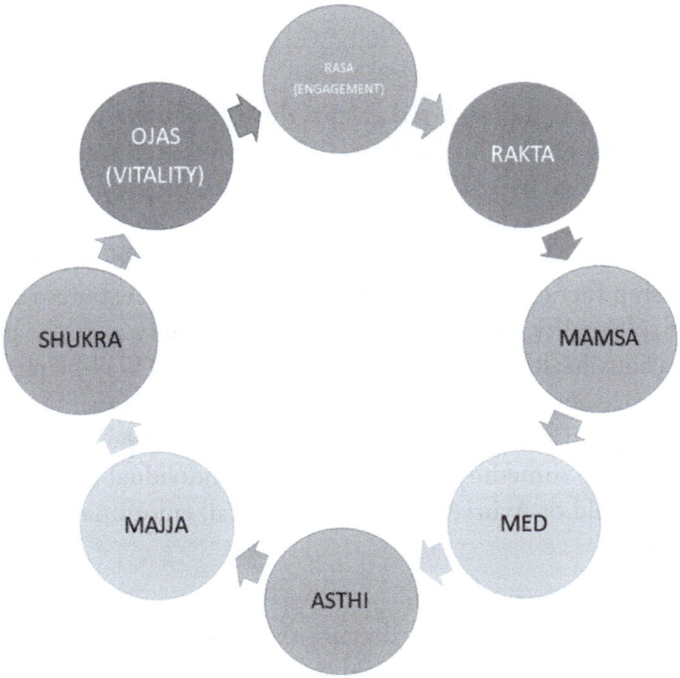

Fig. 6.2 Engagement and vitality: Nurturing cycle of *Dhatu* (© Mala Kapadia)

is waste products and *'kriya'* is the action of throwing out these waste products from the body (Monier-Williams, 1872). Eliminating waste is crucial to good health, but *ama* in the channels and imbalance of *doshas* can stifle the flow of *mal*. This creates further *ama* in the body.

One of the key aspects of *mal kriya* is gut health. *Harvard Heart Letter* (Harvard Medical School, 2018) reports that there exists a complex interplay between the microbes in the intestines and the body systems, including the vascular, nervous, endocrine, and immune systems. These inter-relationships are highly relevant to cardiovascular health. Further, emerging evidence suggests that dietary habits that are crucial for heart disease prevention have a desirable impact on gut health as well. Not just heart, poor gut health has now been found to be the cause of many other health issues like blood pressure, lungs, and kidney problems, etc. Interestingly, modern medicine is finally opening up to the idea that a powerful immune system, optimal physical health, and even mental and emotional well-being—all starts in the gut and *Mal Kriya* is much more than just intestinal or gut health.

Atman

Ayurveda, with its root in *Veda*, accepts the role of consciousness or spirit as *Atman* that resides in the body. The Universe is seen as a play of consciousness, Self as *atman*, and individual self as *jivatma*. The Higher Self is where the individual self ultimately returns. Emotional intelligence and spiritual intelligence are becoming accepted fields in the domain of leadership literature. While existing research demonstrates the importance of spirituality on overall well-being, spirituality is rarely addressed in the various health and wellness courses. Spiritual well-being entails a sense of peace and contentment arising from an individual's relationship with the spiritual aspects of life, namely meaning and purpose of life, and a connection to something bigger than one's individual self (Patel et al., 2019). The field of Ayurveda connects physical, emotional, and spiritual well-being.

Indriyas and Manas

Indriya is a sense and action organ—there are five each that connect an individual with the outer world and allow one the field of activity.

The body is *Pancha Mahabhautic*, made of Five Elements that are characterized by the three *Gunas* or Energy of *Sattva, Rajas*, and *Tamas*. The *indriyas* represent the bridge between the inner and the outer, between the mind and the physical body and environment. The five senses take in information from the outer world and relay them to the mind in the form of sound; touch, pressure, and temperature; light, color and form; taste and smell. Senses and their capability to discriminate between life-promoting and harmful sensations are crucial as desirable sensations will lead to growth and evolution, while harmful sensations toward pain, disintegration, and disease.

Manas is loosely translated as mind. It is also considered the 11th *indriya*. Nonetheless, it is closely connected with the senses, guiding the senses, or getting hijacked by them. The excessive, lack, or wrong indulgence of senses and mind causes a lack of well-being; using the power of discrimination and keeping senses and mind focused in the right direction is crucial for well-being. The quality of the mind determines the caliber of sensory function and discrimination. A *rajasic* mind seeks out sensory input that overly-stimulates the senses, such as loud music, action-oriented movies, and spicy foods. A *tamasic* mind dampens and damages the receptive capacity of the senses, which distorts the transmission of information about the body and environment. However, a *sattvic* mind chooses sensory nourishment, which supports and strengthens life, promotes health and happiness, and a strong vital body. All Five Elements have the Energy of *Gunas* in their template. *Vata, Pitta, Kapha* become the template and can only be kept in balance; they can't be reversed or changed unless through some major influence. However, the template of *Sattva, Rajas*, and *Tamas* is the evolutionary profile and does change with lifestyle and Yogic practices. In the context of well-being and self, being more in the *Sattva* and having a minimal impact of *Rajas* and *Tamas* on the mind is adequate.

Similar to the food consumed via mouth, there are foods or diets for all other senses and the mind. Right nutrition, along with digesting what is injected, is critical to avoid the formation of toxins. *Charaka Samhita* gives utmost importance to the sense of touch. The sense of touch alone pervades all the senses and is associated with the mind (Shreevathsa &

Dwivedi, 2011). Interestingly, modern medicine and psychology have also started to recognize the importance of touch for healing and well-being (Benoit et al., 2018; Harmon, 2010).

Prana, Tejas, and Ojas

Right nourishment to the senses and *manas* creates vital energy. *Prana, Tejas,* and *Ojas* are the vital essences of *Vata, Pitta,* and *Kapha*. These three forces are pivotal to the vitality, clarity, and endurance of an individual and necessary for one to feel healthy, fearless, and confident. On a gross level, they derive from the essence of nutrients absorbed in the form of food, heat, and air. On a subtle level, they are fed by the impressions imbibed through the senses (Frawley, 1998). *Prana* is responsible for enthusiasm and expression; a lack of *Prana* creates depression and mental stagnation. *Tejas* governs mental digestion and absorption; its absence results in a lack of clarity and determination. *Ojas* provides psychological stability and endurance, without which one experiences anxiety and mental fatigue (Frawley, 1998).

Individual and organizational Health Index can be created with the balanced scorecard of Ayurvedic definition of a healthy person. *Prana, Tejas,* and *Ojas* are the results of the right balance in lives. Another by-product of this balanced living is *Prasannata*: Wellness, well-being, and happiness; all three are integrated in this term.[13]

Prasanna

> "Well-being" and "wellness" are often used interchangeably, but technically; they have different meanings. They do, however, influence each other. Well-being is the experience of feeling satisfied with one's life-when one's mind, body, and spirit feel healthy and fulfilled. In order to achieve well-being, one must engage in wellness practices. Wellness is physical health. Wellness and well-being together create happiness. Susie Ellis, Chairman, and CEO, the Global Wellness Institute, states, "When you think wellness, think prevention and health. When you think about well-being, think happiness".

[13] From the forthcoming book by the Author of the paper, Mala Kapadia.

In the West, the era of positive psychology is a recent advent. The science of psychology started with a desire to understand the pathology of the mind. Brain, mind, and heart are all used interchangeably in contemporary literature largely developed in the western world (Gilbert, 2009). Ayurveda, on the other hand, has a very elaborated understanding of the body–mind–spirit continuum. Brain is the part of the body, while mind is the subtle aspect of the matter-energy continuum. Heart, as the organ that pumps blood, is one organ that is closely connected to mind, as most of the nervous system—*manovahini nadis*—originates from the heart (Lad, 2002). Heart as a seat of consciousness, as Yogic biology reveals, is another Heart, which exists at *Chakra* level in the subtle body. Well-being is the result of the happiness of both these hearts functioning without any toxins or blocks. Faith, optimism, gratitude, all the constructs of positive psychology are connected with the hearts. In the field of Psychoneuroimmunology (PNI), Pert has done revealing work of connecting heart, mind, and body. She recommends that there is a need to go beyond the brain, heart, and mind and to "refer to the whole system as a psychosomatic information network, linking 'psyche,' which comprises all that is of an ostensibly nonmaterial nature, such as mind, emotion, and soul, to 'soma,' which is the material world of molecules, cells, and organs. Mind and body, psyche, and soma".[14] These thoughts of the contemporary knowledge echo the age-old wisdom of Ayurveda. She has also coined a new term of Psychosomatic Wellness, as opposed to psychosomatic illness. HeartMath is a psychophysiological approach aimed at helping people establish heart-based living and global coherence through heart rate variability (HRV) training, especially through heart rhythm coherence feedback (Institute of HeartMath, 2013). The HeartMath Institute has also been doing interesting research on this integrated view of self and global connectedness (Edwards, 2014, 2015).

[14] www.candacepert.com

Causes of Disease According to Ayurveda

Ayurveda entails balance as the key to health and well-being. Hence, lifestyle and diet become major reasons for or lack of well-being. Diet is not limited to the food consumed, according to Ayurveda, but all that is absorbed through the five senses- eyes, ears, touch, smell, and tongue. The right diet to all senses creates well-being. Excess, lack, or wrong diet will create dis-ease or stress and lifestyle-related disorders. In the Ayurvedic language, the union or connection with diet of the senses is known as Yoga. Excess is called *Atiyoga*, while a lack is called *Ayoga*. And, the wrong diet is called *Mithya Yoga*, where *mithya* denotes counterproductive. When these are connected with the five senses, the cause is called *Asatmyeindriyaartha samyoga*: Yoga or union with senses that is not good for the body. This can be termed as lifestyle created disorders and are easy to correct at individual levels and organizational levels. However, when they are connected with outer environmental causes, it is called *Parinaam* in Ayurveda, which in today's modern term is known as climate change (Shukla & Tripathy, 2002). Research discusses the impact of ecology on mental well-being, whereby climate change affect people as they experience ecological grief due to loss of species, landscapes, and ecosystems (Cunsolo & Ellis, 2018), and expose them to trauma, impacting their physical health and social environments (Berry et al., 2010).

Jeffry Pfeiffer had proposed the construct of Knowing-Doing (K-D) Gap Principles to explain what creates best organizational practices. However, only 1/8th of organizations do something sustainable about implementing them (Luthans, 2005). Knowing-Doing Gap is known as *Pragna Aparaadh* in Ayurveda. *Pragna* is wisdom, *Aparaadh* is sin or acting against it (Monier-Williams, 1872). This is also a cause of lack of well-being in individual and collective lives.

Asatmyeindriyaartha Samyoga: Indulgences of the Senses

Excess or *Atiyoga*: Too much use of electronics-computers, TV, phones, artificial lights at workplaces, too much indoors or outdoors in harsh Sun. Continuous noise or smell of chemicals at factories. Sitting or standing for too long. Offices lack eco-friendly design with ergonomic furniture.

Lack or *Ayoga*: sunlight during the day, darkness while sleeping, lack of sky, or lack of open space coming into offices, lack of touch, lack of appreciation are the common forms of *Ayoga*. Sunlight via eyes stimulates the pineal gland, which secrets serotonin. Serotonin is the key to calmness, happiness, and enduring motivation. Sunlight makes serotonin, and darkness trigger melatonin in the pineal gland, a hormone that regulates biological rhythms such as sleep and wake cycles (Church, 2002).

Counter-productive or *Mithya Yoga—Virrudh Ahaar*: Ayurveda has scientific research on what combination of foods is good or toxic for the body. The toxic combinations are called *Virrudh* or contrary *Ahaar* or diet (Monier-Williams, 1872). Indulging in negative talks while eating is also considered bad for digestion. Any canteen visit during lunch break will reveal how often this simple norm of well-being is broken. Ayurveda also considers the cycle of seasons where the physical and mental strengths are high, medium, or low.

Pragna Aparaadh: Knowing-Doing Gap

Ayurveda identifies specific functions of intelligence and mind. They are known differently, *Dhi* or *Buddhi* is intelligence, *Dhriti* is the ability to sustain the intelligence, and *Smriti* is the memory of knowledge in mind (Monier-Williams, 1872). When *Dhi*, *Dhriti*, and *Smriti* are not functioning well, a lack of well-being happens due to incorrect decisions. This also connects to what was described earlier as *Hitayu*—a life guided by social and individual well-being. For example, not suppressing natural urges of thirst, hunger, and excretion; excessive negative emotions of anger, sadness, or grief; and knowing that some habits like smoking could be injurious to health, yet not able to leave the habit.

Ways to Inculcate Well-Being at the Individual and Organizational Level with Ayurveda Insights

Swasthavrutta or Balanced Scorecard of health prescribed in Ayurveda can be a useful way to bring back well-being at individual and organizational levels. *Swasthavrutta* comprises of (a) definition of a healthy person, (b) *Dinacharya* and *Ratricharya*; i.e., comparable to Circadian rhythms, (c) *Rutucharya*: optimal routine according to seasonal changes during the year, and (d) *Sadvrutta* plus *Achaar Rasayana*: behavior in general (Singh, 2012). These are practices to create balance and well-being. Each of the components is discussed in this section.

Dinacharya and Ratricharya

A daily routine is necessary to balance the *Vata, Pitta*, and *Kapha*, the *Doshas* in the human body. Routine facilitates establishing balance in one's constitution. It also helps regulate an individual's biological clock, assists in digestion, absorption, and assimilation, and generates self-esteem, discipline, peace, happiness, and longevity.[15] Alignment with nature and the circadian rhythm is very important for Ayurveda. Hence, waking up early in the morning, creating positive vibrations through prayers, cleaning the body, exercises, breathing rituals, breakfast, lunch, and dinner schedules, rituals before retiring at night are all given their due importance. In the evening, a whole set of rituals is delineated by Ayurveda, known as *Ratricharya*, or a wise nightly routine (Bhattacharya, 2015).

Following *Dinacharya* and *Ratricharya* as daily practices and personal development goals ensure that secretion of serotonin and melatonin occurs in the natural cycle of the body's rhythm. Melatonin rules the night as the precursor of serotonin, the mood-lifting brain chemical. Serotonin is at its highest level in the body early in the morning (Bhattacharya, 2015).

[15] Vasant Lad, ayurveda.com https://www.ayurveda.com/resources/articles/the-daily-routine.

The lifestyle prevailing in recent times is far away from what is necessary to be healthy. The biggest individual and organizational challenge faced by HR is managing the energy of the people in relation to time. Tiredness, fatigue, stress, lethargy, and overload of sensory stimuli are resulting in procrastination, impaired decision-making, and strained relationship. This is also creating a lack of trust and enthusiasm. Creating routines aligned with nature's rhythm will certainly help in enhancing the engagement at work and alleviate the above maladies.

Rutucharya: Seasonal Changes-Aligning the Microcosm with Macrocosm

In Ayurveda, the knowledge of *Rutucharya* is a first-hand guide to the concept that explicates the modes and stages of the development of diseases concerning the state of *Doshas- Vata, Pitta*, and *Kapha* according to the changes in *Rutu* (or season). A good understanding of *Rutucharya* is essential for early diagnosis and prognosis of any disease and for adopting preventive and curative measures (Aphale Vaibhavi & Gokhale, 2016). The preventive aspect comes from guidelines of changes in diet and lifestyle according to the seasons.

A good example of this is the time correction in many countries according to the changes in seasons. In the same way, an internal correction of the bio-clock is required. A detailed account is available for making these changes gradually to make the transition to the next season without any health-related crisis (Singh, 2012).

Sadvrutta Plus Achaar Rasayan

Principles of self-control and correct action aligned with conscience are known in Ayurveda as *Sadvrutta*. The Sanskrit term *sad* or *sat* means truthful, pure, or good, depending on the context. The Sanskrit term *vrutta* refers to a systematic collection of information translated into behavior. Ayurveda describes three sets of specific guidelines for behavior in society: those for improving physical and mental health, those for proper function in society, and those rightful actions that will align us to achieve *moksha* or ultimate liberation of the soul (Bhattacharya, 2015).

The concept of *Achaar Rasayana* (behavioral regenerative therapy) is a unique concept in Ayurveda that implies moral, ethical, and benevolent conduct: truth, non-violence, personal and public cleanliness, mental and personal hygiene, devotion, compassion, and a yogic lifestyle. These behaviors bring about rejuvenation in the body–mind system.

The above guidelines have pertinent implications for employees at the workplace, including the intra- and inter-personal levels and the organizational levels. For instance, imbibing self-control, truthfulness, steady orientation, compassion, and non-violence would be crucial for internal communication, a central process through which employees share information, form relationships, make meanings, and construct organizational culture and values (Berger, 2008). These manifest into higher productivity, improved performance, organizational learning (Berger, 2008), and better external relations (Kim & Rhee, 2011). Further, the guidelines are likely to engender trust that has been linked to organizational commitment, as well as job performance and organizational citizenship behavior (Aryee et al., 2002; Watson & Papamarcos, 2002). A spiritual orientation has also been posited to be associated with connectedness, loyalty, and employee engagement (Pawar, 2008; Poole, 2009; Quatro, 2004).

Discussion

This section renders a brief overview of well-being in the contemporary literature, mostly developed in the euro-centric western world and its state in the current times, discusses challenges to the HR function, and the bridging role of the principles and practices of Ayurveda in HRM policy. The linkages of Ayurveda with Maslow's ideas of self-actualization and self-transcendence, and Depth Psychology have also been discussed.

Overview of Well-Being in Contemporary Literature

Based on a state of harmony, Hippocrates created the concept of "positive health", which depended on the primary human constitution (known as genetics today), diet, and exercise. He posited that proper diet and exercise were essential for health and that seasons' changes had a profound effect on the mind and body, resulting in different types of predominant diseases during the winter (respiratory tract diseases) and summer (digestive tract diseases) (Larson, 1999). This aligns with the history of well-being in India.

However, the path taken changed to that of fixing illnesses rather than creating health in modern times. The body was seen as made up of parts and processes, where specialization was developed to treat them. It is noteworthy that the shift from Hippocrates' to the modern view came along at the same time as the Industrial Revolution. What followed was a rise in infectious diseases that became more prevalent as the way people were living and working changed dramatically (Medical News Today, 2018). The Germ theory proposed by Louise Pasteur became more popular than the Cellular theory of Bechamp, who proposed that the seed is not important, the terrain is (Marone Family Wellness, n.d.). The terrain is the individual whose immunity (*ojas*) protects the health from germs. Yet, the healthcare industry remained focused on germ theory and exploited the business opportunities in the pharma industry.

As health and healthcare became a business in earlier times, wellness and well-being have become a business today, rather than a proactive, preventive lifestyle and living in accordance with our inner and natural rhythms. Serotonin and Melatonin, the natural hormones for happiness and sound sleep, are now available as outside medication, rather than as a correction of lifestyle, which Ayurveda prescribes. This takes away the self-responsibility for good health-promoting habits for wellness and continue with the pill-popping culture. In response to the health crisis due to lifestyle, the digital well-being market is exploding. Over the last two years, more than $2 billion in venture capital has been invested in this area, creating a flood of online videos, apps, and tools to help assess, monitor, and improve all aspects of health. Driven by these innovations, the corporate wellness market, including healthcare programs, screening, assessment, education, and applications, has reached nearly $8 billion in the United States alone, and is expected to touch $11.3 billion by 2021 (Deloitte Global Human Capital Trends, 2018).

Collectively as a society, a stage has reached where happiness courses are having great participation from students as they seek solace in the VUCA world. Governments of developed countries like the UK and UAE are establishing Happiness Ministries to take care of people (Barron, 2018; Chew, 2016).

Challenges to Human Resource Function Today

In the Industrial Era, work got done with process adherence and efficiency playing the most important role. Today, organizations are not confined by fixed workplaces, nine-to-five working hours, or by a set of homogenous employees. Owing to technological advancements, on the one hand, organizations have become boundary-less; on the other hand, it has left people digitally overwhelmed (Boswell & Olson-Buchanan, 2007).

The issue of highly stressed workers is not new; however, the relentless pace of business today has worsened the problem. Due to the always-on nature of digital business and 24/7 working styles, research shows that more than 40% of all workers face high stress in their jobs, negatively affecting their productivity, health, and family stability (Deloitte Global Human Capital Trends, 2018). While the hourly workers complain of inflexible schedules, the white-collar workers complain of endless emails that disallow them to disconnect from their jobs. In some countries, people are working for more hours and taking fewer vacations than ever. And, according to Deloitte's millennial survey 2017,[16] a majority of the millennials surveyed in 19 out of 30 countries do not expect to be "happier" than their parents (Deloitte Global Human Capital Trends, 2018).

Additionally, in a research with LinkedIn it was found that 27% of employees believe they waste an entire day each week on distracting,

[16] Deloitte, *The 2017 Deloitte millennial survey: Apprehensive millennials: Seeking stability and opportunities in an uncertain world*, 2017.

trivial emails and messages (Bersin, 2018). Also, with people working for more hours, work-life balance has become a huge challenge. People are sleep deprived and anxious. Despite the upsides, i.e., the innovations, the same progress has led to 24/7 availability at work and the rise of artificial intelligence as a threat to jobs. Put differently, technological progress has not created healthier and happier individuals and societies.

From the industrial era until now, the era of knowledge and service, the mechanistic model has been dominant (Ghosal & Bartlett, 2000). However, the economic value can't be the only measure to value life. In *the Compassionate Mind*, Paul Gilbert (2009) describes the current state in society as:

> It's really quite strange because many of us live in a world of unprecedented wealth and comfort. Yet despite our apparently insatiable drive for efficiency, the competitive edge and the "business model" influencing all the aspects of our lives, there is no evidence that this is making us any happier than we were 50 years ago. Actually, there is evidence that we are becoming more unhappy and irritable as levels of stress increase our hurry-hurry society. Despite our wealth and comforts, half of us will have some kind of mental health problem at some point, with depression, anxiety, alcoholism and eating disorders topping the list. The world health organization has worked out that depression will be the second-most burdensome disorder on earth by 2020 and other mental health problems will be in the top ten. We are also becoming less trusting and feeling more threatened. (p. 9)

This business model has given us materialistic wealth, but taken away our physical health, and created mental health issues. Relatedly, "affluenza", a mode of psychological discomfort, has been characterized by distress and anxiety arising from a pursuit of more. Also, an excessive emphasis on uncontrolled economic growth has been linked to detrimental consequences of overconsumption, stress, and impaired relationships (De Graaf, 2002). For many years HR professionals looked at monetary benefits as a competitive edge to attract and retain people. And, subsequently, challenging roles and growth opportunities took precedence. However, the business model caught up in a culture driven by the need for profit and efficiency missed the point of human welfare

(Gilbert, 2009). It is vital to note that being Human is more than money, roles, and status. Deep within the psyche, in the heart, there is a deeper yearning that veils the human psyche.

Benefits of Wellness and Well-Being to Organization

In light of the above, well-being has become a fundamental responsibility of good corporate citizenship and a critical performance strategy to propel employee engagement, organizational energy, and productivity. Indian Management, inclusive of Ayurvedic wisdom, can create wellness, well-being, and happiness in the organizations. The benefits to organizations are manifold. With well-being as a consideration, sustainable human resource management practices proffer a holistic view to positive social relationships at work, which enhances performance (Cooperider & Fry, 2012), including greater cooperation among people, commitment to the common goal, resilience, knowledge sharing, and collaborative orientation, which have enduring results for the organization as well. Enhanced employee performance, reduced expenditure on medical costs, employee retention, and becoming Employer of the Choice are some of the benefits to organizations for introducing wellness and well-being initiatives (Macdonald, 2005).

The Bridge to HR

Kapadia (2013) proposed a holistic, integrative, and sustainable model of well-being that connects individual, organization, and society's well-being at physical, emotional, economic, environmental, and spiritual levels based on the insights of Ayurveda and Yoga. Well-being as per the model is not just an absence of disease; it is holistic health and growth conducive for well-being at the societal level. It aims to integrate insights from Biology, Energy Sciences, medical research, Yoga, neurological research, other sciences like Physics and Positive Psychology.

The well-being model requires taking a pause, reflecting, and re-focusing to ask: Is this sustainable? Is this decision holistic? Are the strengths and talents of people being utilized at the workplace? Will it create organizational effectiveness? Will it be in the interest of societal well-being? The sustainability of humans and the environment both are unique to the Well-being model of Indian Management.

In 'Managing Human Assets,' Beer and colleagues (1984) proposed a model for 'causal mapping of the determinants and consequences of HRM policies' that includes individual and societal well-being along with organizational effectiveness. The model maps HRM territory as Internal HRM Policy choice in four areas: Employee Influence, Human Resource Flow, Reward Systems and Work Systems; Resulting in HR outcomes of Commitment (Employee Engagement), Competence, Cost Effectiveness and Congruence (Culture Fit); Creating long-term consequences for individuals, organizations and society—Individual Well-being, Organizational Effectiveness, and Societal Well-being. What precedes the HRM policy choice are Stakeholders Interests and Situational Factors. Within situational factors, workforce characteristics and management philosophy are the foundation on which HRM policy and practices are built. The Harvard Human Resource Management (HRM) Map can be revisited, and Indian Management wisdom inclusive of Ayurveda can be integrated. Incorporating the practices and principles of Ayurveda, i.e., *hitayu* and *sukhayu* worldviews, *sadvrutta*, *prakriti* (psycho-physiological profile), and *Sarve pi Sukhinah Santu* from *Vedas*, can help in building a management culture characterized by positive energy, trust, self-reflection, self-discipline, and responsibility in the employees. As a result, this will be instrumental in effective internalizing and implementation of the HRM policies and the long-term positive consequences (Kapadia, 2013).

Revisiting Maslow and Depth Psychology

In 'Towards A Psychology of Being', Maslow (1968) mentions, "I consider Humanistic, Third Force Psychology to be transitional, a preparation for a still "higher" Fourth Force Psychology, transpersonal, transhuman, centered in the cosmos rather than in human needs and interest, going beyond humanness, identity, self-actualization, and the like" (p. iii–iv). Humanistic Psychology posits a view of the human being as irreducible to parts, needing connection, meaning, and creativity

(Resnik, Warmoth, & Serlin, 2001). With Rogers, Maslow, and May as its intellectual leaders (Smith, 1990), it aims to present a holistic view of human life with a focus on capabilities such as love, self, growth, need-gratification, self-actualization, higher values, being, becoming, autonomy, transcendental experience, psychological health to name a few (Sutich, 1962).

Ayurveda also posits a positive view of health that includes thoughts, feelings, and an overall state of being. It is a holistic system that aims to achieve a balance of an individual's whole bio-psycho-spiritual dimensions (Morandi et al., 2011). Therefore, psychology centered in the cosmos, forms a part of the principles of Ayurveda.

Maslow has described self-actualization and self-transcendence as higher human needs. He explains self-actualization as a 'being' need (biologically ingrained in human beings) that represents 'full humanness'. Maslow (1968) describes other basic needs as deficiency needs, "born out of being deprived of certain satisfactions, ungratified wishes for safety, for belongingness and identification, for close love relationships and for respect and prestige" (p. 21). He explains further that healthy people who have satisfied their basic needs are motivated by the self-actualization needs comprising of meeting their full potential, fulfilling their call, destiny, gaining an understanding of and accepting one's self leading to integration within a person. Self-actualization connects with the construct of flourishing. Flourishing as a concept is associated with happiness (Haidt, 2006) and high levels of well-being (Hone et al., 2014) and is defined as a state of complete or maximal well-being coupled with optimal functioning (Keyes, 2002). It is a holistic and broader representation of well-being comprising of intra-personal and inter-personal dimensions (Keyes, 2002; Seligman, 2011). Both are a result of holistic health and *hitayu* and *sukhayu* as described in Ayurveda. Ayurveda describes 'self-rooted in cosmos' as Maslow has expressed. When one understands the role of 5 Elements, *Doshas*, *Dhatu*, *Agni* in one's body and mind, one not only creates well-being; one also connects with the gifts of Elements, which are the talents and full potential within one's personality.

Depth Psychology

Depth Psychology entails that in addition to the general conscious experience, there exists the unconscious aspect of the human psyche (Schroeder, 1992; Stewart, 2014). As a mode of therapy, the depth approach comprises traditions that explore the unconscious by studying dreams, complexes, and archetypes. Further depth psychology is non-pathologizing and strength affirming.[17] Spirituality holds a crucial place in depth psychology, wherein the unconscious plays the medium through which spiritual experiences manifest (Schroeder, 1992). This implies that the choice of being a spiritual person or not does not exist; however, the key question is whether it is lived consciously or unknowingly invested in unspiritual aspirations (perfectionism, addictions, greed, fame) that eventually possess individuals by virtue of their ignored, but frightfully potent, intrinsic spiritual power.[18]

Indian Management, integrating Ayurvedic principles, comes very close to Depth Psychology in understanding self and human behavior. As per Ayurveda, evolution starts with consciousness creating five elements; space, air, fire, water, and earth. These five elements in different combinations subsequently create the three *Doshas*. These *Doshas* are the physiological governing principle of the body. Each person is born with a unique combination of the three *Doshas* called *Garbhaj Prakriti*, which remains fixed for life. The effect of factors such as environment, food, and lifestyle alteration, and stress can lead to disequilibrium of *Dosha* (*Jataj Prakriti*). Too much alteration of *Dosha* results in pathology or *Vikruti* causing diseases, if not checked. Parallels to this concept are being drawn in basic science laboratories. Epigenetic alterations can impact certain genes in response to the environment, diet, and lifestyle-with consequences of aging and diseases (Gibbs, 2003). Hence, *prakriti* becomes the blueprint that contains the unconscious, subconscious, as well as potential for well-being and path to self-actualization and spiritual development.

---

[17] cgjungcentre.org.

[18] www.Newworldencyclopedia.org

Future Research Scope

Ayurvedic wisdom can be integrated into Indian Management as philosophy and practice as a future area of research. Ayurvedic philosophy explores human beings or the construct of self as Macrocosm created as Microcosm and hence an expanded understanding of what Self is. This understanding helps a person choose a life based on wellness, well-being, and happiness described as *Hita* and *Sukha ayus* in Ayurveda, integrating principles of sustainability of Universe and self. These principles of Ayurveda with an underlying positive outlook hold the potential to contribute toward the emerging fields of research and practice pertaining to positive psychology and positive organizational scholarship (POS). For instance, positive citizenship represents the reciprocal relationship between the individual and civil society, whereby the society encourages each citizen to pursue their highest purpose and calling for the greater good, thus enabling citizens to experience existential well-being (Rifkin, 2016).

At the practice level, future research can explore applying Ayurveda knowledge of constitution or *Prakriti* at many levels of HR functions: for achieving person-job fit, team building, management, and leadership development. Correlation between constitution (*Prakriti*) and various personality instrument such as Myers & Briggs Type Indicator, BELBIN Team Roles, DISC Personality Profile can be a useful area of inquiry. These instruments are useful in identifying the mental dispositions, whereas Ayurvedic profiling can provide a holistic understanding of mental and physical constitution and interventions.

Similar to the concept of *Prakriti*, when the biology and psychology, or body and mind are revisited from Yoga perspective, interesting research areas of *Pancha Kosha* theory of Self emerges. Yoga is very popular world over; however, only the physical practices or meditation and mindfulness have become part of larger populaces.

Ayurgenomics is an emerging field of research already. Genomics has ushered in an era of predictive, preventive, and personalized medicine wherein it is hoped that not too far in the future, there would be a shift in the practice of medicine from a generalized symptomatic approach to an individualized approach based on her or his genetic makeup. Management can help preventive healthcare planning through Ayurgenomics and save on post-medical care expenses and loss of productive workdays.

The future course of research can focus on implementing the concept of balance to be integrated into the organizational culture to increase *Prana, Tejas,* and *Ojas* through its vision, goals, policies, and practices. Health is a result of balanced *doshas, dhatus,* the right food to all senses, and an individual is empowered to make the right decisions to keep the health balanced through Ayurvedic wellness coaching. Energy management, personal and team effectiveness with Ayurveda can be mapped.

As the world comes to a standstill due to Pandemic Covid-19, humanity is facing two profound truths in their life. One, all the healthcare systems, surveys on wellness and well-being, and pharmaceutical research have proved to be limiting. Secondly, the traditional and indigenous medicine sciences that were called complementary or alternate are now proving to be the strong complementary factor to the mainstream healthcare system as they are more holistic, life-affirming, economical, and affordable by the populace. A major area of research at this moment is understating and applying Ayurveda principles for coping with COVID-19. AYUSH Ministry, comprising of traditional medical wisdom of the land of India, has come out with treatment protocols and prophylaxis. Ayurvedic Hospitals are chosen with great care to treat COVID-19 patients and create awareness of the holistic healthcare possible through Ayurveda. One such case is written by the author of this paper on the success story of Ayurveda for the treatment of 3000 + COVID-19 patients with no fatalities (Kapadia, 2020).

An important area of inquiry includes taking the Ayurvedic path to wellness, well-being, and happiness (WWH) to create healthy individuals and healthy organizations in the form of wellness programs and initiatives proposed by HR. The 3 Ps that emerge as vital are Pathway, Participate, and Practices. *Swasthavrutta* in Ayurveda denotes WWH. Physical wellness, emotional well-being, and spiritual happiness that is sustainable when combined together can create transformation at individual, organizational, and universal levels. Well-being represents an ongoing personal journey toward wholeness and connection. It is a journey of inner work that encompasses healing, personal development, and integration of self. HR can invite individuals to take part in inner development work while providing the freedom and flexibility to choose how to engage, establish specific time and space for inner development work, and generate opportunities for the discovery and integration of capacity-building practices and experiences that reinforce enhanced self-care.

WWH can be implemented through the following steps: (a) Perceived Health Deficiency (lack of optimism, creativity, engagement, conflicts, knowledge hoarding, aggressive behaviors), (b) Need Analysis (physical and/or emotional at individual levels, wrong roles, extended working hours, inappropriate team formation, not enough exercise, sunlight and sleep), (c) Design Rituals (lifestyle corrections, ergonomically designed workplaces, rejuvenation breaks), (d) Implement Rituals at individual and organizational levels (offer WWH coaching, encourage and incentivize health-enhancing behaviors, encourage positive emotions of gratitude, compassion, and contentment, manage negative emotions through constructive expression), and (e) Health Evaluation.

In recent years, Indian concepts have attained a new prominence at the global level. Yoga and its varied forms have become very popular (Sharma, 2005). Integration of Ayurveda for a holistic understanding of being human, and the well-being of humanity at large, is still an emerging field with immense scope for further research. Ayurveda, the science of living a healthy and happy life, is emerging as critical science as the world is learning to live beyond the pandemic and create New Normal. World-view and Self-view based on the wisdom of ancient wisdom of Ayurveda can be the foundation for this New Normal if researched well and communicated well among the researchers, managers, and people at large.

Notes

The seven *dhatus* are:

Rasa: *Rasa* has at least ten meanings in Sanskrit—water, taste, juice, essence, or interest in anything, plasma, lymph, and emotion.[19] *Rasa Dhatu* is the nutrient, the precursor for all other *dhatus*. *Rasa* is the nutrition or essence of food injected, and the juice of life experienced. In the organizational context, *rasa* denotes the engagement levels, or juice of life employees experience at the workplace. Engagement at the workplace then nourishes all other *dhatus* and results in vitality at optimal functioning at the individual and organizational level.
Rakta: Translated as blood, *rakta* is the erythropoietin element of blood.[20] In Ayurveda blood means the red blood cells. *Rasa* and *Rakta Dhatus* work together to reach nutrition and heat to all body parts. While *Rasa dhatu* provides nutrition (*prirana*), *rakta dhatu* provides life function (*jivana*) and gives oxygen to every cell, a function of *prana* (Lad, 2002).
Mamsa: Muscle tissue or flesh that plasters the body provides protection and gives shape to the body.[21] During an emergency, muscles become rigid, contracted, and produce resistance against movement, where the flow of awareness is blocked. Emotions such as fear, anxiety, grief, sadness, and anger, in the form of neurotransmitters, become stuck in that muscle and create a neuromuscular block (Lad, 2002). On the other hand, the psychological manifestation of healthy *mamsa dhatu* are ambition, competition, courage, and determination (Lad, 2002).
Med: Adipose tissue, lipid stores in the body. Lubrication, or *snehana* is the function of fat in the body. The Sanskrit meaning of *snehana* is love and protection.[22] Lubrication provides the freedom of movement and insulation to hold heat in the body. *Med Dhatu* also offers groundedness. Obesity, a major health issue in today's times, is a result of excess *med dhatu*, where the reasons could include lifestyle and food, also a lack of love, protection, and groundedness.

[19] Monier-Williams, M. (1872). *A Sanskrit-English Dictionary (digitized by Google)*. Clarendon Press.

[20] Monier-Williams, M. (1872). *A Sanskrit-English Dictionary (digitized by Google)*. Clarendon Press.

[21] Ibid.

[22] Ibid.

Asthi: Bones provide internal support and structure of the body.[23] Healthy bones are a result of nourishment from earlier *dhatus*. Bones are composed of a solid structure organized as a matrix (visualized as the letter X). The lines forming the letter (X) are solid and made up of earth. The space in between the lines is filled with air. Thereby, bones create solid but light structure, enabling the body to move easily.
Majja: Anything inside a bone: red and yellow bone marrow,[24] and the brain and spinal cord. It is present from the brain to the surface of the skin. The autonomic nervous system, which is one part of *Majja Dhatu*, is closely connected to the subconscious mind. A major function of this *dhatu* is to fill the spaces of the innermost tissues of the body, the bones.
Shukra: Structural elements of reproductive tissue.[25] Marrow nourishes the *Shukra* in men and *Artava* in women. This is the reproductive capacity. *Shukra* being the last *dhatu* in the supply chain, *Shukra's* health creates *Ojas*, i.e., the aura, the pure essence of all bodily tissues. *Ojas* provides vitality and immunity and is the media through which mind and body are related (Shreevathsa & Dwivedi, 2011). Lack of health at any level in the *dhatu* cycle will deplete the *Ojas*.

References

Anshu, A. S. (2016). Evolution of medical education in India: The impact of colonialism. *Journal of Postgraduate Medicine, 62*(4), 255.

Aphale Vaibhavi, M., & Gokhale, V. (2016). Lifestyle management by Sadvrittacharana. *International Ayurvedic Medical Journal, 4*(4), 758–761.

Aryee, S., Budhwar, P. S., & Chen, Z. X. (2002). Organizational justice, trust foci, and work outcomes: Test of a mediated social exchange model. *Journal of Organizational Behavior, 23*(3), 267–285.

---

[23] Ibid.

[24] Monier-Williams, M. (1872). *A Sanskrit-English Dictionary (digitized by Google)*. Clarendon Press.

[25] Ibid.

Barron, L. (2018, January 17). British people are so lonely that they now have a Minister for Loneliness. *Time*. https://time.com/5107252/minister-for-loneliness-uk/

Beer, M., Spector, B. A., Lawrence, P. R., Mills, D. Q., & Walton, R. E. (1984). *Managing human assets*. Free Press.

Benoit, B., Boerner, K., Campbell-Yeo, M., & Chambers, C. (2018). *The power of human touch for babies*. Canadian Association of Paediatric Health Centres.

Berger, B. (2008). *Employee = organizational communications*. Institute for Public Relations. http://www.instituteforpr.org/topics/employee-organizational-communications/

Berry, H. L., Bowen, K., & Kjellstrom, T. (2010). Climate change and mental health: A causal pathways framework. *International Journal of Public Health, 55*(2), 123–132.

Bersin, J. (2018, December 31). *The economy and wages In 2019: What HR can do to help*. Linkedin. https://www.linkedin.com/pulse/uncertain-economy-2019-what-hr-can-do-help-josh-bersin/

Bhattacharya, B. (2015). *Everyday Ayurveda: Daily habits that can change your life*. Penguin Random House.

Boswell, W. R., & Olson-Buchanan, J. B. (2007). The use of communication technologies after hours: The role of work attitudes and work-life conflict. *Journal of Management, 33*(4), 592–610.

Chew, J. (2016, February 11). *This country just appointed a Minister of happiness*. Fortune. https://fortune.com/2016/02/10/uae-minister-happiness/

Church, M. (2002). *High life 24/7 balance your body chemistry & feel uplifted*. Thought Leaders.

Cooperider, D., & Fry, R. (2012). Minor flourishing and the positive psychology of sustainability. *Journal of Corporate Citizenship, 46*, 3–12.

Cunsolo, A., & Ellis, N. R. (2018). Ecological grief as a mental health response to climate change-related loss. *Nature Climate Change, 8*(4), 275.

Dalal, A. K., & Mishra, G. (Eds.). (2011). *New directions in health psychology*. Sage.

De Graaf, J. (2002). Affluenza: The all-consuming epidemic. *Environmental Management and Health, 13*(2), 224–224.

Deloitte Global Human Capital (D.G.H.C.) Trends. (2018). *The rise of the social enterprise*. Deloitte Development LLC.

Edwards, S. D. (2014). Evaluation of a heartmath workshop for physiological and psychological variables. *African Journal for Physical Health Education, Recreation and Dance, 20*(1), 236–245.

Edwards, S. D. (2015). HeartMath: A positive psychology paradigm for promoting psychophysiological and global coherence. *Journal of Psychology in Africa, 25*(4), 367–374.

Frawley, D. (1998). *Ayurveda and the mind: The healing of consciousness* (1st ed.). Motilal Banarsidass.

Frawley, D. (1999). *Yoga and Ayurveda.* Lotus Press.

Ghosal, S., & Bartlett, C. A. (2000). *The individualized corporation.* Random House Business Books.

Gibbs, W. W. (2003). The unseen genome: Beyond DNA. *Scientific American, 289*(6), 106–113.

Gilbert, P. (2009). *The compassionate mind*. Constable & Robinson.

Govindaraj, P., Nizamuddin, S., Sharath, A., Jyothi, V., Rotti, H., Raval, R., & Sule, M. (2015). Genome-wide analysis correlates Ayurveda Prakriti. *Scientific Reports, 5*, 15786.

Gupta, P. D. (2015). Pharmacogenetics, pharmacogenomics and ayurgenomics for personalized medicine: A paradigm shift. *Indian Journal of Pharmaceutical Sciences, 77*(2), 135.

Haidt, J. (2006). *The happiness hypothesis: Finding modern truth in ancient wisdom.* Basic Books.

Harmon, K. (2010, May 6). *How important is physical contact with your infant?* Scientific American. https://www.scientificamerican.com/article/infant-touch/

Harvard Medical School. (2018, June). *Healthy gut, healthy heart? How the trillions of bacteria in your intestinal tract play a role in your cardiovascular health.* https://www.health.harvard.edu/heart-health/healthy-gut-healthy-heart

Hill, C. A. (2007). A third alternative to concordism and divine accommodation: The worldview approach. *Perspectives on Science and Christian Faith, 59*(2), 129–134.

Hone, L. C., Jarden, A., Schofield, G. M., & Duncan, S. (2014). Measuring flourishing: The impact of operational definitions on the prevalence of high levels of wellbeing. *International Journal of Wellbeing*, 4(1).

Jung, C. G. (1971). *The collected works of C.G. Jung, Vol. 6: Psychological types* (H. G. Baynes, Trans., revised by R. F Hull.). Princeton University Press (originally published 1921).

Kapadia, M. (2013). Human Re-sourcing. *IBA Journal of Management & Leadership, 5*(1), 79.

Kapadia, M. (2020, September 25–27). *A success story from India- CBPCACS* [Case Presentation]. Covid-19: Lessons and Emerging Strategies in Ayurveda. Council for Ayurveda Research, USA.

Keyes, C. L. (2002). The Mental Health Continuum: From languishing to flourishing in life. *Journal of Health and Social Behavior, 43*(2), 207–222.

Kim, J., & Rhee, Y. (2011). Strategic thinking about employee communication behavior (ECB) in public relations: Testing the models of megaphoning and scouting effects in Korea. *Journal of Public Relations Research, 23*, 243–268.

Lad, V. (2002). *Textbook of Ayurveda: Fundamental principles of Ayurveda* (Vol. 1). Ayurvedic Press.

Lad, V. (2006). *The role of devotion in life*. Ayurveda Today.

Larson, J. S. (1999). The conceptualization of health. *Medical Care Research and Review, 56*(2), 123–136.

Leaman, O. (1999). *Key concepts in Eastern philosophy*. Routledge.

Luthans, F. (2005). *Organizational behavior* (10th ed.). McGraw- Hill.

Macdonald, L. A. (2005). *Wellness at work: Protecting and promoting employee health and wellbeing*. CIPD.

Marone Family Wellness. (n.d.). *Pasteur vs. Bechamp: An alternative view of infectious disease*. http://maronewellness.com/pasteur-vs-bechamp-an-alternative-view-of-infectious-disease/

Maslow, A. H. (1968). *Toward a psychology of being*. D. Van Nostrand Company.

Medical News Today. (2018, November 2). *What is modern medicine?* https://www.medicalnewstoday.com/articles/323538.php

Mishra, L. C., Singh, B. B., & Dagenais, S. (2001). Ayurveda: A historical perspective and principles of the traditional healthcare system in India. *Alternative Therapies in Health and Medicine, 7*(2), 36–43.

Monier-Williams, M. (1872). *A Sanskrit-English dictionary (digitized by Google)*. Clarendon Press.

Morandi, A., Tosto, C., Di Sarsina, P. R., & Dalla Libera, D. (2011). Salutogenesis and Ayurveda: Indications for public health management. *EPMA Journal, 2*(4), 459–465.

Patel, S., Klagholz, S., Peterson, C. T., Weiss, L., Chopra, D., & Mills, P. J. (2019). Psychosocial effects of a Holistic Ayurvedic approach to well-being in health and wellness courses. *Global Advances in Health and Medicine, 8*, 2164956119843814.

Patwardhan, B. (2014). Bridging Ayurveda with evidence-based scientific approaches in medicine. *EPMA Journal, 5*(1), 19.

Pawar, B. S. (2008). Two approaches to workplace spirituality facilitation: A comparison and implications. *Leadership & Organization Development Journal, 29*(6), 544–567.

Poole, E. (2009). Organisational spirituality: A literature review. *Journal of Business Ethics, 84*, 577–588.

Quatro, S. A. (2004). New age or age old: Classical management theory and traditional organized religion as underpinnings of the contemporary organizational spirituality movement. *Human Resource Development Review, 3*(3), 228–249.

Ray, P., & Gupta, H. N. (1965). *Caraka Saṃhitā: A Scientific Synopsis*. Sree Saraswati Press.

Resnick, S., Warmoth, A., & Serlin, I. A. (2001). The humanistic psychology and positive psychology connection: Implications for psychotherapy. *Journal of Humanistic Psychology, 41*(1), 73–101.

Rhoda, D. (2014). Ayurvedic psychology: Ancient wisdom meets modern science. *International Journal of Transpersonal Studies, 33*(1), 14.

Rifkin, L. V. (2016). *Defining a positive citizenship: Wellbeing for emancipation.* (Master's thesis). University of Pennsylvania, Philadelphia. Retrieved from https://repository.upenn.edu/mapp_capstone/104/

Seligman, M. E. (2011). *Flourish: A visionary new understanding of happiness and well-being* (1st Free Press hardcover ed.). Free Press.

Severns Guntzel, J. & Murphy Johnson, N. (2020). *Wellbeing inspires welldoing: How changemakers' inner wellbeing influences their work* (Report). The Wellbeing Project. http://wellbeing-project.org/wp-content/uploads/2020/03/research_report.pdf

Sharma, S. (2005, April 14–16). *Indian ethos, Indian culture and Indian management: Towards new frontiers in management thinking*. In 'Indian Culture and Management' Conference Proceedings of the ICSSR and COSMODE Workshop, Hyderabad.

Sharma, A. (2009). *Sushrut Samhita Chaukhamba*. Surbharati Prakashan.

Sharma, S. (Ed.). (1979). *Realms of Ayurveda*. Arnold-Heinemann.

Shreevathsa, & Dwivedi, R. (2011). *Manas Prakriti*. Chaukhambha Visvabharati.

Shriwas, H. K., & Chandrakar, R. (2018). Conceptual study of achara rasayana in ayurvedic science. *European Journal of Pharmaceutical and Medical Research, 5*(7), 146–149.

Schroeder, H. W. (1992). *The spiritual aspect of nature: A perspective from depth psychology*. In Proceedings of Northeastern Recreation Research Symposium (p. 25–30), April 7–9, 1991, Saratoga Springs, NY.

Shukla, A. V., & Tripathi, P. R. D. (2002). *Charak Samhita* (2nd ed., Vol. 1). Chaukhamba Sanskrit Pratishthan.

Singh, H. G. (1977). *Psychotherapy in India: From Vedic to modern times*. National Psychological Corporation.
Singh, R. H. (2012). *SwasthVrutta Vignyan*. Chowkhamba Sanskrut Pratishthan.
Smith, M. B. (1990). Humanistic psychology. *Journal of Humanistic Psychology, 30*(4), 6–21.
Sreekumar, T. (2013). *Astanga Hrdaya Vagbhata Sutrasthana*. Harisree Hospital Publication Department.
Stewart, D. J. (2014). The emergence of consciousness in Genesis 1–3: Jung's depth psychology and theological anthropology. *Zygon, 49*(2), 509–529.
Sutich, A. J. (1962). American association of humanistic psychology: Progress Report. *Palo Alto, CA: AAHP, 1*.
Tirtha, S. S. S. (2005). *The Ayurvedic encyclopedia*. Ayurveda Holistic Center Press.
Vasishtha, S. (2009). *Nadi Tattva Darshanam*. Ramlal Kapoor Trust.
Vasudevan, V. (2000). *Sushrut Sutrasthan*. Ayurvedatatvaprakashini AVP.
Watson, G. W., & Papamarcos, S. D. (2002). Social capital and organizational commitment. *Journal of Business and Psychology, 16*(4), 537–552.

7

Indian Mindset and Its Implications on Management Practices and Scholarship

Upasna A. Agarwal and Ashish Pandey

Introduction

Mindsets are defined as the constellations of beliefs, preferences, and practices that the people possess for maintaining continuity in the ways they react and adapt to the changing environment. While the process of evolution in mindsets is universal, the extent to which the people of a given society shift the frames of their mind depends on, among other factors, how open is the culture to incoming influences and the potency of the incoming influences in confronting and prevailing upon

U. A. Agarwal (✉)
National Institute of Industrial Engineering, Mumbai, India

A. Pandey
Shailesh J. Mehta School of Management, Indian Institute of Technology Bombay, Mumbai, India
e-mail: ashish.pandey@iitb.ac.in

© The Author(s), under exclusive license to Springer Nature Switzerland AG 2022
A. Pandey et al. (eds.), *Indigenous Indian Management*, Palgrave Studies in Indian Management,
https://doi.org/10.1007/978-3-030-87906-8_7

the existing beliefs, preferences, and practices (Sinha & Pandey, 2007). In this chapter, we present the existing research on Indian mindset which is most extensively comprehended and developed in the writings of J.B.P. Sinha (e.g. Sinha, 2014; Sinha et al., 2010). We review and summarize the work of Sinha and colleagues and also present the work of other scholars which corroborate or contradict the propositions and findings of them. The chapter is organized into five sections. In the next section, we present the predominant features of Indian mindset. Then we discuss how the Indian mindset and cultural context act as enabling or disabling conditions in day-to-day living in general and in work settings in particular. In the last two sections, we synthesize the research and delineate the implications for managerial practices and research respectively.

Predominant Indian Mindsets

Power Distance, Collectivism, Adaptability, and Spirituality constitute as key aspects of the Indian mindset. These aspects have overwhelming influence on Indians because of the milieu in which they live and function and have significant impact on their behaviour (Sinha & Pandey, 2007). In this section, we describe each of these in light of the extant research.

Power Distance *Mindset*

Individuals everywhere in the world are arranged into hierarchies on some bases or others. A large part of Indian society still lives in a system of social stratification based on castes under four categories, known as varnas viz. Brahmins, Kshatriyas, Vaishyas, and Shudras (Pio, 2007). There are thousands of other sub-castes vying for superiority over each other. Within a caste, superiority depends on gender, age, and seniority in relationships. The hierarchy of the caste gets diluted though in case of exceptionally powerful and talented people like spiritual authority (e.g. Acharya Sriram Sharma), social reformer and leaders committed for social development (e.g. Anna Hazare), and renowned scholars (e.g.

Babasaheb Ambedkar). Partly, for the genuine concern for the people from the castes which were historically suppressed and partly for the political befits a large number of initiatives[1] taken by various governments in India for the castes historically classified as Sudras and people out of the caste system or untouchables called Dalits. These castes are classified into the constitution of India and now addressed as Scheduled Caste (SC), Scheduled Tribes (ST), and Other backward Classes (OBCs). The caste system is more pronounced in rural areas (Gang et al., 2017) but its ramenents show up at times in the urban areas also particularly in the form of subtle discrimination (Jodhka, 2008).

Indians know from their childhood how to behave with seniors and juniors in the family. mAtR devo bhava, pitR devo bhava, AcArya devo bhava, atithi deve bhava.[2] These value statements create hierarchy based on sraddha (respect and devotion). The pragmatic Indian is willing to collude with a stronger power. They must also cajole, appease, and ingratiate the powerful and superiors in order to get what they want (Sinha, 1990). There are different types of superiors. Saints and sAdhus are revered for who they are, but other superiors are venerated only if they have helped one in a significant way. Otherwise, it is simply respecting the position. When the person is not in that position, there is no veneration for him or her. However, if the person did help in a significant way, then the veneration continues for life.

Roland (1998, p. 4) opines similarly in the following words:

> ...deep respect and veneration are only given to those who are indeed superior persons, no matter where they might be in the formal hierarchy.

Paternalism is the cornerstone of Indian social and cultural organizations. Kings were supposed to treat their subjects, prajA, like children, and it is no surprise that the word prajA also means children. Similarly, gurus are supposed to treat their students as their own children. Paternalism extends in some form or other in Indian (work) organizations

---

[1] Regulations to stop untouchability, harassment, assault, discrimination and for the protection of the rights and liberty of the scheduled classes, upto 50% of reservation for them in the government own institutions of higher education and government jobs, and so forth.

[2] Meaning of these statements: Mother, father, and teachers are as revered as God.

too. In work organizations too, Indians look for a father figure (symbolically speaking) maai-baap for empowering, protection, grooming, and development. Tied to paternalism are such traits as familiarity, sense of security, respect for seniority, importance of the personality of the leader, forms of authoritarianism, obedience to authority, and patronage (Virmani & Guptan, 1991). An ideal superior is one who is altruistic towards his subordinates by being self-sacrificing and keeping subordinates' interest above his own and provides subordinates with patronage, guidance, and direction to subordinates. The superior feels concerned for the well-being of their subordinates and promote them in both formal and informal relationships. The suitability of Nurturant Task Leadership in organizations in India is because of these aspects of Indian mindset. The concept of nurturant task leadership is explained in Chapter 8 of this handbook on effective organizational leadership in the Indian context (Panda, 2020).

Socialization in family and schools plays very important roles in shaping the mindset of the individuals. At home there is Pati Alamban (dependence over husband) and Patni Alamban (dependence over wife). Each depends on the other comfortably on different aspects of life. Similarly, Pitra Alamban (dependence over parents) is acceptable upto the mid-twenties or even later in Indian families. *Pitra Alamban* replaces the *Acharya Alamban* (dependence over teacher) in schools and even colleges and *Varishtha Alamban* (dependence over elders) at the workplace. Though Indian culture does emphasize Swablamban (swa meaning self and alamban meaning dependence), it deeply values interdependence. That is why Rin or debt is such an important construct. The notion of Rin is described in Chapter 2 of this book by Pandey (2020). Societal values of personalized relationships based on sneh-shraddha results in Indian child to learn the values of obedience, conformity, humility, and dependency over independence, self-help, assertion, and autonomy. As a result, in the adult stage, superior's affection for Indian subordinates and a subordinate's deference to the superior encourage them to maintain amicable relationships in personal and professional lives (Budhwar & Boyne, 2004; Sinha, 1990). Employees feel left out if the superior remains impersonal or distant (Pandey, 1981; Sinha, 1990).

Pandey (1981) identified eight ways of ingratiation that Indian superiors and subordinates employ in order to either influence each other or prevent the relationship from drifting into a confrontational mode—other enhancement, instrumental dependency, self-enhancement, support, name dropping, yielding, conformity, and self-presentation. In order to gain a continuous pat on their back or a shoulder to lean on, Indian subordinates tend to appease their superiors, strive for their proximity and affinity and feel energized whenever they receive praise or are called for any errands that instil the superior's confidence in them (Sinha, 1990, 2014).

This has its enabling and disabling effects. Indians find it extremely uncomfortable to say no to their seniors, and it is equally true that seniors do not appreciate hearing in negation for requests made (Sinha & Kumar, 2004). Indians seem only too eager to agree with their superior and flatter him when an opportunity presents itself. Agreeing with a superior and flattering him were approved if not prescribed ways of getting on, and every patron attracts one or more flatterers (Srinivas 1988/1997, p. 266). However, when situations are contrary, there exists some evidence that Indian subordinates sabotage favourite projects of their disliked bosses, change allegiance from old to new bosses and locate more powerful contacts to put reverse-pressure on their bosses (Sinha, 1995). Personal loyalty and need to seek adulation of people in authority (Agarwal & Rai, 2019; Kakar, 1971; Sinha, 1990) also tends to foster high degree of conformity often encouraging silence, irrespective of wrongdoings (Agarwala, 2003; Bhatnagar et al., 2010; Budhwar et al., 2006; Som, 2008). This trend is relevant in Indian corporates, public and private sectors even today (Agarwal et al., 2016).

In reciprocation, employees rely on their supervisors to "take care of them" (Patel et al., 2012; Varma & Budhwar, 2012), enhancing their "dependence proneness". Excessive dependency has been identified as one of the core Indian characteristics from country's mud huts to company boardrooms in three independent studies by investigators in the 1970s (Barkow et al., 1975; Chattopadhyay, 1975; Pareek, 1968; Sinha, 1970). Pareek considered it as one of the three most dominant motivations, and Sinha saw its overwhelming presence in the young as well in adults in various walks of life. Perceiving as equals in the social comparison process causes uncertainty about one's position in the hierarchy and confusion about how to behave. In organizations, a vertical team headed by a superior is better than the one where all members are treated as equal for participating and making decisions. Indians find it easier to work in superior-subordinate relationship than as equals (Kothari, 1970). It is a well-acknowledged aspect that Indians avoid taking decisions and responsibility for anything and have a tendency to push decisions to the seniors or immediate supervisor (Philip & Ganguly, 2014) not only to avoid blame if things go wrong but also as a strategic mechanism to maintain and regulate their relationship with the supervisor (Jain, 2015). As noted, Indian subordinates depend on their superiors and want to receive their affection and affiliation and look to them as father figures. So, it may also be argued that employee silence can be used as a tool for avoiding confrontation or assertion with supervisor or for earning affection and affiliation as a mark of obedience and conformity in the Indian work context (Jain, 2015).

High-power distance, paternalism, and relationship orientation have been sound to have bearing on HR processes too, such as PMS (Budhwar et al., 2006). The inequality in the distribution of power is both approved and un-resented. People of the lower social status are attuned to unfairness committed by authority figures because they perceive these actions as part of their role-defined privilege (Agarwal et al., 2016). Kakar (1982) observed that as the power difference in the families are reducing with time the younger generation is growing up with more comfortable with authorities and power difference reducing in the Indian society.

Collectivist Mindset

India is high on collectivism (Hofstede, 1980). Collectivism is distinguished between horizontal and vertical collectivism. Horizontal collectivism displays a sense of oneness with members of in-group and vertical collectivism recognizing the difference among the members of in group. Vertical collectivism is common in high power difference cultures as is the case in India. Collectivism "pertains to societies in which people from birth onwards are integrated into strong, cohesive in-groups, which throughout people's lifetime continue to protect them in exchange for unquestioning loyalty" (Hofstede, 1980). Collectivists cultivate highly personalized and complicated networks of familial, blood, caste, and other forms of relationships with heightened mutual expectations and obligations. Relational orientation is a virtue (Hofstede, 1991) where preserving social relationships is considered as the paramount goal (Li & Cropanzano, 2009, p. 2) and is regarded as an end in itself (Kirkman et al., 2006; Shao et al., 2013; Triandis, 1994).

Collectivism constitutes a core of the Indian mindset and Indians experienced self is structured more around we, ours, and us than around I, mine or me. Pober et al. (1986) contended: "Every individual in India is always linked to the rest of the social body by a network of incredibly diversified ties, with the result that no one in this gigantic country of 700 and 50 million [now above 1 billion] inhabitants could ever be completely abandoned" (p. 56). This embeddedness has led Indians to emphasize protection and caring [of those below in hierarchy] in their social (and political) relations (Kakar, 1982; Triandis, 1995).

Although the extent of need may vary, Indian employees have an intrinsic need to connect at an emotional level. They enjoy social support and have a greater sense of well-being. Studies have found that individuals having social support are more optimistic, cheerful, playful, and have less vulnerable to the stresses and strains of life, lesser feelings of frustrations, anxiety, and loneliness (Sinha & Verma, 1994). Indians tend to seek other's attention, emotional support, guidance, direction, help, and inspiration even in situations in which they can make up their own mind and act on their own. Given the imminent position of the supervisor, a study by Budhwar and Boyne (2004) found that Indian firms in the public and private sectors tend to communicate with employees mainly through immediate superior rather than through any other formal channel. Agarwal et al. (2012) study found the critical role of supportive organizational practices as well as supervisors in shaping employee-organization relationship and fostering positive work attitude. Given cultural orientations of collectivism and high power distance, Agarwal and Bhargava (2014) found important role of immediate leader in shaping employees psychological contracts from their organizations.

Other studies have argued for the role of friends at work to dampen the intensity of stress at work (Rai & Agarwal, 2018) is significantly impacts well-being and in turn organizational productivity.

Apane-Paraye: The Special Feature of Collectivist Mind of India

There are two structural dimensions of how persons are interrelated in the Indian society: affinity and hierarchy. Affinity represents the dimension of apane (in-group)—paraye (out-group). Family members, friends, and relatives are generally apane; others are paraye. The second dimension—hierarchy—signifies vertical relationship—a person having better qualities, greater power, more money, or superior position than another person. Greater power and influence are exerted, resisted, sought after, or utilized in case of apane log (our people). With apane (in-group), they tend to establish long-term trusting relationships with heightened affective reciprocity and do not calculate what they give and get in such a relationship. Power flows freely among apane log, who trust each other, cater to each other's needs and expectations, give and receive resources, and enhance harmony. Power relationships with the out-group members, on the contrary, follow the principle of exchange with vigorous attempts to increase the power distance, usurp resources, control, and exploit others.

Trust and Keeping Promise in Indian Mindset

In India relationships include a strong normative component and are built on the edifice of trust and are not based on quid pro quo (Doney et al., 1998). There is implicit trust that a partner would not do anything to harm the relationship. Breach of promises runs counter to the foundations of collectivism (Hofstede, 1991) and interactions between employees and their organizations are based on customs and informal relationships (Aycan et al., 1999; Shah, 2000; Sinha, 1990). Mythology and religious texts narrate accounts of revered figures such as Lord Rama or his ancestors who made personal sacrifices to fulfil promises. The fulfilment of promises is a defining characteristic of dignity and upbringing Pran jaye par vachan na jaye (I can let go of my life but not my promise).

Employment relationships are open-ended, flexible, and unrestricted by socio-political and legal systems (Aryee et al., 2002; Shah, 2000; Sinha & Sinha, 1990). Agarwal and Bhargava (2014) found that employees interpret breach of promises (explicit and implicit promises) as a natural lapse that will be rectified and believe that promise fulfilment was delayed rather than abandoned as long as they had trust.

Collectivist Mindset and HRM Practices

It is not only power and influence, but also a whole range of behaviour that is shaped by the degrees of affinity and the levels of hierarchy which has impact on both enabling and disabling potential. Group dynamics of the family and friends have a determining role in decisions that are pertinent to the individuals. Research suggests that this social stratification plays an important role, explicit and implicit, in recruitment, selection, and other HRM policies and practices (Budhwar, 2003; Budhwar & Sparrow, 2002). Family and group affiliations take precedence over performance (Kanungo & Mendonca, 1994; Khatri et al., 2001). In many Indian organizations HRM practices, including appraisals and promotions, continue to be ad hoc and are easily manipulated by employers (Lawler et al., 1995; Saini & Budhwar, 2004; Sparrow & Budhwar, 1997). In private sector organizations in India, decisions related to promotions, transfers and benefits are influenced by social contacts and personalized relationships (Dutta, 1997) affects pay and promotion decisions (Gopalan & Rivera, 1997). Varma et al. (2005) compared American and Indian appraisers and found that Indian appraisers inflated ratings of low performers more based on their affect for appraisee.

High degree of collectivism has its limitations in social relationships. Studies suggests that individually, because of their largely collectivist culture, Indians tend to remain embedded in various in-groups and collectives, tied up with ecology and continuously engaged with others, this results in delayed in decision making. Indians are brilliant and are likely to be very successful in favourable situations but may turn out to be counterproductive collectively since they are so oriented to others, they are also highly receptive to their expectations, sensitive to situational cues and alert to opportunities (Sinha, 2014). The Indian model of man places strong emphasis on realization of the self, although one is also asked to transcend it in the interest of the larger society. In Indian society, individualism and collectivism act like figure and ground. Depending on the situations, one rises to form the figure while the other recedes into the background (Tripathi, 1988, pp. 324–325).

Adaptability (Response According to Desh, Kaal, and Paatra)

In the globalized world, people from different places, demographic backgrounds and mindset meet, interact, work, or live together. They have to converge enough in their thought and behaviour in order to relate and deal with others. This requires stretching of their own beliefs, values, and norms, which, however, tend to resist deviations beyond a point. Indians have an edge over many other nationalities in the world that is globalizing fast. Indian cultural receptivity to new experiences has its origin in the oldest of the scriptures and philosophical texts, RigVeda, that prescribed, "Let noble thoughts come to us from all directions" (1.89.9). The new does not replace the old, nor does it cause an inevitable dissonance or discomfort in the minds of Indians (Bharati, 1985). Indians, according to Carl Jung, "do not mind seemingly intolerable contradictions" (quoted by Sinha and Tripathi [1994, p. 125]). "When Indians learn, quite expertly, modern science, business, or technology, they 'compartmentalize' these interests… the new ways of thought and behaviour do not replace but live along with the old 'religious' ways" (Ramanujan, 1989).

Indians are "capable of living simultaneously and effortlessly on two mutually opposed planes" and "can make quantum leap from one epoch to another without showing any strain". They do a fine act of balancing one extreme thought or behaviour by its opposite that may be equally extreme (Sinha & Kanungo, 1997). It is often conceded that, "there is not a thought that is being thought in the West or East that is not active in some Indian mind" (Thompson cited by Tharoor [1997, p. 9]). In fact, they are active in most Indians' mind. The great adaptive capabilities and coping of Indians result in advantage over other nationalities in accommodating and settling down in off-shore projects, adjustment with multi-cultural teams lower acculturalization cost. In a study by Sinha (2004), it was found that Japanese managers in a joint Indo-Japanese venture in India worked very efficiently so long as the systems and procedures that they had meticulously formulated were functioning normally. But they were rather lost in situations that turned unexpectedly adverse. Indian managers, who were ordinarily less efficient than the Japanese, turned out to be better tuned to firefighting. There are reports, for example, that Indian managers in a Korean organization behaved like Koreans (Sinha, 2004). They stayed at work overtime, even stood before their offices in the morning, exercised and shouted company slogans like Koreans. On the contrary, Indian managers in a Swedish company left the office right on time, walked to their subordinates' desk if needed, and behaved in many other egalitarian ways like their Swedish expatriates. In an American company, Indian managers were informal like their counterparts, calling their superiors by their first name and being participative in team deliberations. Not that they genuinely liked or believed in all that they were doing but felt it necessary to comply with organizational systems and norms and to work amicably with expatriates. The same Indians simultaneously behaved in typical Indian ways with their compatriots (Sinha, 2004). Indians are able to adapt easily to life in different countries and integrate with the local culture, which is essential when it comes to business leadership. Adaptability of Indians explains their holding top jobs in Corporate and academic world—Satya Nadella of Microsoft, Sundar Pichai of Google, Shantanu Narayen of Adobe, Rajeev Suri, Nokia, Sandeep Mathrani of WeWorks, and Francisco D'Souza of Cognizant. Recent years have also witnessed several Indian Americans have taken the helm of US business schools: Nitin Nohria at Harvard, Dipak Jain at Northwestern, Sunil Kumar of Johns Hopkins University, Rangarajan Sundaram at NYU and Paul Almeida at

Georgetown. A growing number of Indians are heading—Nitin Nohra of Harvard Business School, Dr Kinshuk, University of North Texas.

There is evidence that Indians are very good at making elaborate plans and setting up laudable goals that can hardly be questioned but poor in implementing what they decide (Sinha & Kumar, 2004). Unlike people in the West who apply abstract principles and generalized norms to decide how to behave in different situations, Indians organize their thoughts, feelings, and behaviour in order to meet specific contextual demands (Sinha & Kanungo, 1997).

Spirituality and Materialism

Ideal mental makeup of Indians is not rational and socially autonomous person but rather that of a person centred in a spiritual consciousness and being (Roland, 1988; Sinha, 2014). Most Indian bilinguals translate spirituality as adhyAtma and spiritual as Ad-hyAtmika or dhArmika in common parlance. adhyAtmika is also contrasted with sAMsArika, which refers to a person who is chasing material goods and success, and so saMsArika may be considered the antonym of adhyAtmika (Bhawuk, 2019). Spiritual consciousness of Indians emanates from Sanātana Dharma which is the overarching term originally used for so many religious and spiritual paths practised in Hindu society in ancient India. Sanātana Dharma is translated as "eternal tradition". It is not limited to the single scripture, historical figure, church, community, or particular historical end.

Despite the spread of the industrial society in the past few decades, spiritual and religious practices continue in life of Indians. The Indian approach to spirituality and materialism is inclusive. Tatva—the matter; jivaatma—essence of living beings including human beings; and Brahman—the ultimate being are distinct but expression of the same constant integrated consciousness. The existential reality of the material world is accepted, but it does not preclude the possibility that human beings are capable of simultaneously experiencing spirituality. Even mundane activities are made into spiritual and Indian emphasis on spirituality in all domains of life. As a result there is never a gap between spiritual and secular in Sanatan Dharma (Bhawuk, 2019). One of the most important questions for the Indian mindset is to how to attain spirituality while living in a material life. The doctrine of karma and sanskar is very important aspects of the Indian mindset. The doctrine of Karma is based on the notion of cosmic system where good or bad consequences of all actions naturally follow. The essence of human self or Jivaatman carries the traces of accumulated good and bad conducts across past lives.

Good conducts like kindness, nonviolence, non-stealing, non-hoarding are first step and defining characteristics of spirituality. Daivi sampadas like abhyam (courage), purity (satva), giving selflessly (daan), control of senses (Daman) and so on are mentioned as desirable characteristics in human being in Bhagwad Gita. Yam, social ethics like Ahimsa (nonviolence), Satya (truthfulness), non-stealing (Asteya) and Niyam, self-development and transformation processes like swadhyaya (self-study), Santosh (contentment), shauch (inner and outer cleansing) are the first two steps of Yoga process. adhyAtma is not only a construct but also a practice; it encompasses both the state, the presence of brahman in human body, and the method that leads to realizing brahman, thus emphasizing the role of spirituality in the pursuit of mokSa or liberation (Bhawuk, 2019).

Spirituality involves the search for the divine within oneself, which remains unchanged through the entire passage of life. The notion of Sādhanā is very important in this regard in the Indian mindset. Sādhanā means the practices that aid the aspirant to realize the sense of the unity of all life in Brahman and being free from ignorance about one's divine nature. Hindu traditional wisdom recognizes the infinite ways to self-realization and self-transformation. These pathways are chiefly classified into paths oriented to intellectual discernment (Jnan Marg), devotion (Bhakti Marg), service (Karm), and Samādhi (Ashtanga Yoga) and each offers practices to mitigate suffering and aims at total personal transformation or attaining higher levels of consciousness.

Spirituality and religiosity are perhaps the most unique yet elusive aspects of Indian mindset. In society we see that religiosity is evoked by religious leaders as well as political parties in pursuance of their objectives. Many times it is difficult to figure out whether they are evoking the religious sentiments for religious purpose or for exercising their personal influence. Very few business organizations explicitly mention about spiritual enrichment of the employees or society as their goal. Religiosity is acknowledged and expressed in many organizations in the form of having place of worship in the factories, celebrating festivals, payment of yearly bonus around the festival of Diwali, worshiping machines (or Vishwakarma), and so forth.

Indian workforce is young. About half of the total workforce is of less than forty years. Indian educated youth employed in IT industry look for meaning and purpose at work which is the expression of spirituality. A combination of spirituality with religiosity is visible in the collective celebrations of the festivals in the workplace. Spirituality is entering workplace through the wellness programs and interventions based on mindfulness and Yoga. Since these programs are aimed at holistic life the aspect of spirituality invariably comes in along with physical and mental well-being (Garg, 2017).

There are empirical studies suggesting the positive impact of spirituality in the workplace in the form of customers' service (Pandey et al., 2009), learning and innovative behaviour in teams (Pandey et al., 2019; Pandey et al., 2019), employees engagement (Mishra, 1994; Gupta et al., 2014) and organization citizenship behaviour (Belwalkar & Vohra, 2016).

Indian Culture and Mindset: Enabling and Disabaling Potentials

Situations vary in their enabling and disabling potentials. Enabling situations generally raise the expectancy among citizens to select from the positive parts of the paradoxes. So, the person feels motivated, engaged, and committed to creative solutions having positive implications for self and others. On the contrary, adverse or disabling situations make people disillusioned, emotionally exhausted, disengaged, often increasing cynicism and counterproductive behaviours.

Indian culture has its shades of both enabling and disabling features inducing people to think, feel and behave in consistent as well as inconsistent ways by drawing on paradoxical ideas, which significantly impact employee performance and productivity as well ease of doing business in India. The section below examines the enabling and disabling aspects of Indian culture.

Decision Making

Personal criteria and relationships as a basis for decision making and action (Whitely & England, 1977) are characteristic of collectivist societies (Farh et al., 2007; Kirkman et al., 2009). Pluralist mindset, relationship orientation, need to maintain harmony, and need to appease the superiors have resulted in dependence proneness. However, such dependence proneness is considered a strong deterrent to the country's development, since it has implication on the speed of decision making (Sinha, 1970; Sinha & Pandey, 2007). Moreover, the characteristic feature of maintaining harmony and managing (read reconciling) expectations results in compromising meritocracy. The need to respect people in power and maintain harmony and the sentiment of Log kyaa kahenge (what people will say) and dependence proneness is a deterrent in taking appropriate decisions. If the decision cannot wait, they hesitate and reluctantly go through the process, but feel unsure and uncomfortable unless and until they get a positive feedback from seniors or those in power. They are even willing to have second thoughts and backtrack when challenged or criticized. In context of work, this may not necessarily result in positive outcomes, especially in terms of organization structure. In a vertical team the leader listens to all but takes and owns the decision and its outcome. It spares the team members from the stress of making decisions as well as the risk of getting wrong.

As globalization process has begun to penetrate, the salience of in-groups in terms of family, relatives, and close friends is becoming a constraint Indians would need to re-define apane and paraye in broader terms keeping in view their own future prospects as well as the prospects of the network of organizations through which they are seeking their own prospect. The criteria for whom to take on the bandwagon for marching ahead are going to be totally different. Fortunately, composite cultural heritages equip Indians to make this transition by encompassing with the new equity-driven situational demands within the cultural ethos to ensure individuals' and collectives' effectiveness as well as social capital (Fukuyama, 1995).

Innovation

Innovation in Indian organizations seems paradoxical. On the one hand, Indians are know for jugaad (improvisation) and frugal innovation (Prabhu & Jain, 2015), ever increasing number of start-up companies in last decades in the sectors ranging from agro products to IT/ITES (Information Technology and Information Technology Enabled Service) to medical devises and has attracted many MNCs to establish R$D centres (e.g. GE, Intel, Adobe and Cisco) and on other hand in many organizations mostly legacy of colonial times and government owned, Indians are so deferential to the superior that they do not feel like expressing their thoughts, feelings and ideas to them, generally traditional in their thought and behaviour, conformists to social norms, obedient to authority and superiors and passive and apathetic in their reactions. High degree of dependence proneness acts as a roadblock in efforts to try new or innovative ways of doing anything in the organizations of the second category.

Indians today are heading some of the most popular global companies; thought leaders are occupying top universities in the West and Indian diaspora is visibly entrepreneurial and affluent. Indian innovators have made their mark in the Silicon Valley. They lead the list of the USA top 50 venture companies that are funding even American start-ups. Indians' talent and entrepreneurial energy is enabling the Bay Area's research institutions and technology companies to unleash powerful business and create wealth (Randolph & Erich, 2009). They are creative and innovative in situations. But if situations are contrary, and they sense other's intentions and the demands in contrast to their point of view, even when pertinent, they pull out their ideas and silence their contributions.

Bhawuk (2003) postulated that culture, Zeitgeist, i.e. spirit of the time, and genius have reciprocal relationships in shaping creative behaviours. Since spirituality is valued in the Indian culture, he argued that creative geniuses are readily channelled in this field of human endeavour in Indian culture. Through the historical analysis, he showed that Indian culture continues to produce eminent spiritual gurus. The innovations made by the spiritual gurus offered thoughts or techniques that were unheard of in human civilizations hitherto, either in India or elsewhere. He also points out that how some of the current culture theories are unable to explain this process.

Corruption

Indians in a favourable milieu are generally prosocial, helpful, generous and trusting. Many among them demonstrate humane qualities, help people in distress and contribute significantly to common causes. There are also instances of very bright and highly educated young men and women who leave or refuse to join the corporate world and get deeply involved in education of deprived children, primary health care of poor, or development in very backward areas. There are observations that groups of Indians under highly adverse situations generally show remarkable resilience to survive, though by resorting to dubious ways. Those who are entrusted with government programmes or funds from international agencies to facilitate development schemes distribute relief to victims of a disaster or to train rural youth in basic life skills or to provide employment to daily wage earners siphon off part of the money. In other words, Indians who look so manipulative and corrupt in starkly adverse situation prove to be competent, motivated, high achieving and even morally guided when opportunities beckon them. Corruption is deep-rooted in India. According to Corruption Perceptions Index (CPI) for 2018 released by Transparency International (TI), the global civil society organization India is currently the 78th most corrupt country in the world among a total of 180 countries. Arrogance of power, lack of accountability and transparency, absence of checks and balances, and a culture of silence are seen to form the harmful concoction for corrupt and unethical practices to thrive in public/government institutions. There is an unholy nexus of those inside the institutions with those outside. Many times, corruption is not evident because the corrupt displays a farcical face of honesty. The powerless may have very less chance of indulging in corruption, but they are often made scapegoats by the corrupt ones in power. Those who dare to question the corrupt face the risk of harassment in different ways and in the worst-case scenario—retaliation by trapping them in false cases. Resultantly, Whistle Blowing in Indian organizations is a rarity.

Agarwal (2014) found that about 85% of the Indian managers perceived high levels of politics in their organizations and this impact their work attitudes and behaviours. He found that Indians no longer accept power and politics as 'given' and are not affected by its prevalence (D'Cruz & Bharat, 2001). Like managers in the west, perception of suppressive behaviour has detrimental effects on Indians managers' engagement, innovativeness, and intention to leave the organization. Work environment with unfair decisions, nepotism, and favouritism impedes engagement, innovative work behaviour and manager retention. It is critical for top management to focus on reducing perceptions of organizational politics and provide clear feedback regarding desirable behaviours (Rosen et al., 2006). This is a joint function of the exposure to the West and new assertiveness.

They also don't accept regressive behaviours from their seniors to maintain harmony. However, recent study by Agarwal and Rai (2019) contradicts these assumptions. They show that, like in the West, workplace bullying has strong detrimental effects on Indian managers' outcomes. These are interesting findings as they challenge the commonly held assumption that employees' workplace behaviours and attitudes are less contingent upon supervisory treatment if they endorsed power distance (Mellahi et al., 2010). There are two plausible explanations; this could be because Indian values are changing due partly to the increasing influence of Western management practices such as empowerment of subordinates. Another plausible explanation for these findings may be derived from the studies that have shown that resource loss in response to negative workplace experiences may be less susceptible to cultural influence because it seems universal to lose resource in response to negative workplace experiences and to engage in resource conservation to deal with a negative experience (Deng et al., 2017).

Violence and Nonviolence

Nonviolence (*ahimsa*) is the core of spirituality and the highly espoused value in Indian culture. It is equally valued in Sanatan Dharma where it is identified as a Daivi Sampad (devine quality), tradition of Ashtanga Yoga (eight limbs of Yoga) where it one of the five Yamas (acts to be avoided), Buddhism where it is integral part of general and spiritual practices and Jainism where it is perhaps the most important value and practice.

One of the drivers of collectivism is availability of limited infrastructure. Historically, Indians suffer from inadequate infrastructure and impoverished living conditions, as a result of which they depend on each other's help and support (Sinha, 2014). The divisiveness of apne and paraye affects distribution of resources too. When tolerance crosses the threshold, Indians seem to be prone to explode into both collective and inter-personal and intra-personal level violence. Though the grossly less powerful yields and surrenders, not because it is of his or her liking, but because it is expedient and imperative. The latter, however, does nurse resentment, waits for an opportunity to strike back and settle the scores. Restricted autonomy, the absence of egalitarianism and lack of connectedness could precipitate a sense of alienation, unfairness and even exploitation, leading to covert or overt aggression (Sinha & Sinha, 1990). Inter-personal and intergroup conflict are the natural outcomes (Sinha & Sinha, 1990; Varma et al., 2005). Thus, despite that nonviolence (ahimsa) is the core of spirituality and the highly espoused values, the Indian milieu is smeared with conflicts and violence as there are frequent occurrence of all kinds of violence and conflict—religious, communal, political, regional, transnational, economic, and above all inter-personal. In addition, there are instances of inter-castes, inter-groups, and inter-states conflicts and violence. There are increasing instances of domestic violence, street violence as well as violence directed to the self in terms of suicides by farmers and young boys and girls.

Changing Values

The socio-economic landscape of the country has changed drastically since the 1990s, and the changes are accelerating much faster than before. People face many challenges and are called upon to respond to many more new opportunities arising from globalization, technological revolution, and shortening distances in the flat world. The class and caste arrangement worked clearly in traditional Indian culture. For example, Brahmins were mostly engaged in educational, religious, and spiritual activities, Kshatriyas were warriors and sudras were engaged mostly in craft and maintenance-related work in society. The vertical and horizontal mobility of people was not totally prohibited but much restricted. However, one's skills, expertise, and experiences can take a person to any height now and caste, gender, and age are no longer so important in professional life.

There is indeed evidence of how Indians are competing and excelling other nationalities internationally and how traditional hierarchies are changing in India. A sense of hierarchy still persists, but it has begun to share space with equity. The mindset of collectivist is gradually undergoing change (Mishra, 1994). Younger, urbanized, and better educated persons are relatively more individualists than older, rural, and less educated Indians. Similarly, the GLOBE study (House et al., 2004) also reported that Indian managers are becoming individualists because they are now younger and face tough competition every day at work where they are pressed more to perform than to build relationships. This may be the result of context sensitive nature of Indian as well as society is more vocal, sensitive for values like democracy, competitiveness, individuality, and materialistic criterions of performance are valued more.

The changing values and priorities have significant impact on work values of employees. Studies (Agarwal & Bhargava, 2014; Agarwal & Rai, 2019) suggest that although employees in India ascribe great importance to people in authority (Sinha & Sinha, 1990), they are equally vulnerable to incidences to organizational mistreatment impacting work outcomes. Although it is believed that the hierarchical nature of the society and the need to maintain social harmony may infer that Indians would accept power and politics as 'given' and not be affected by its prevalence (D Cruz & Bharat, 2001). These new genres of employees, though collectivist, possess strands of thoughts, feelings, and actions that reflect underlying individualism; they nourish Western values of achievement and advancement, but also demand fairness and equity.

Conclusion

The most crucial Indian cultural factors are the pluralistic worldview welcoming ideas from different sources and the habit of not replacing the old by the new ideas, but adding to them to the old resulting into an amalgam of consistent as well as diverse, discrepant, and even contradictory beliefs, preferences, and practices. The external ideas and influences emanate from waves of invasions, migrations, and deepening exposure to the western cultures. As a result, Indian mindset consists of paradoxes. For example, Arth (material gains) has been the most basic goal, and Indians were expected to mind the mundane first, but while being immersed in them, they were required to get detached and rise, step by step, on spirituality. Arth is equally important pursuit of human life than Dharm (righteousness and harmony within self and surroundings), Kama (sensual pleasure), and Moksha (self-realization of liberation), particularly for the householders.

Indians have both collectivistic and individualistic orientations from the ancient time. Now part of population is getting more individualistic under western influences. But they still use collective means to serve individual's interests and vice versa. Findings of Gupta and Panda suggest that the qualified technocrats in India are guided by both collectivistic and individualistic value orientations, the latter is the dominant one in organizational settings. This conceptualization is also consistent with Sinha's and Sinha et al.'s observations on individualistic tendencies of the Indians and Parikh's attempt to explain the co-existence of individualism and collectivism. In nutshell these findings suggest that Indians show more individualist orientation at workplace particularly in MNCs whereas more collectivist orientation in family situation.

Hierarchy has been endemic to Indian thought. Almost everything and every relationship are organized hierarchically, but merit was valued strongly. Dependence proneness has been pervasive, but highly dependence prone persons show amazing extent of entrepreneurship if a situation becomes favourable or require the application of creativity and innovations. The success of many Indian companies and Indian entrepreneurs in IT/ITES is an example of how the supportive policies and business environment can enable Indians to reach to the high levels of excellence.

Practical Implications

In this section, we primarily dwell into the question that with such a mindset, how do Indians prioritize their thoughts and actions. That is, how do they select ideas and organize them into a new set in order to make decisions and act accordingly so that they can maximize their gains and/or minimize their costs.

Based on his research and general body of knowledge available on mindset, Kanungo et al. (2020) say that Indians go by the salient demands of a situation as they have high context sensitivity and a tendency to balance the discrepant and contradictory ideas. They consider desh, kaal, and paatra to decide what is most appropriate or effective way to act in a situation. People in all cultures tend to match their acts with specific situational demands. Those in a bi-cultural setting change the cultural frame drawing from the source or host cultures. Indians mix all old and new diverse, discrepant, and contradictory ideas to form a unique response set. They are much more dynamic in their choice, because they can mix from various sets—some old and others new. They examine whether and which of the desh, kaal, and paatra are enabling or disabling, should they move to a survival mode, a waiting stance to let the situation throw up its demands more clearly, or proactive one, sacrificing or selfish, short-term quick gain or long-term patience, and so on.

With such a flexible and dynamic mindset, Indians have the potentials to be highly innovative and proactive through jugaru (improvisers, fire fighters, expedient; Prabhu & Jain, 2015) to extremely opportunists and short sighted. They are more capable to see the big picture and design long-term strategies. They can also manipulate the system to any extent. They are capable of abstract thinking and quite prone to change the track for new reality. The rise of many expatriates to the CEO's position in enabling multinationals testifies. Increasing number of multinationals investing profusely in R&D in India is another indication. They are also vulnerable to unethical practices. There are numerous examples of business angels having clay feet. The solution is to create enabling persons, work settings and demands, and their stability over time.

Research Implications

Mindset affects almost all the aspects of life at individual and collective level. Enabling and disabling conditions arising out of Indian mindset presented in this chapter provide the glimpse of its pervasive impact. The research implications in the field of mindset can be drawn from this acknowledgement. The research implications of Indian mindset are the indicative of three streams. The potential areas of research suggested elaborated in this section are just the indicative of those streams which are; first, on expression of the different aspects of mindset in the different context, second, reflection of mindset on various organizational and individual processes, third, macro-level and policy-related impacts of the Indian mindset.

The first stream of the research in the field of the Indian mindsets is the expression of those in different contexts or different kinds of organizations. It has been shown that Indians draw from different cultural influences for a specific mindset appropriate or effective in a situation. But the process of drawing ideas and forming a mindset is still unspecified. We have to discover the principle that guide in selecting mindset, the factors that moderate the process, and those that interfere with it. We still do not know beyond hypothesis making what are enabling and disabling factors for desh (place), Kaal (time), and paatra (person), how are they triggered, how are they prioritized, which ones among the three play more critical role and so forth. Context sensitivity is still an unexplored landscape. All we know is that East Asians including

Indians are more context sensitive than western people. But our knowledge about it is nested in the circular reasoning. That is, behaviour is explained by context sensitivity which is assessed by how differently we behave. Mapping of the different contexts, developing their taxonomy, and identifying their relative weights in the combination to determine the decision and choice of actions, etc. constitute a key research agenda.

The second stream of research in our view is that Indian mindset research can inform the nuances of various individual, group and organizational process. With the exception of the research related to Nurturant Task Leadership, this area of research is largely unexplored. A nurturant leader "cares for his subordinates, shows affection, takes personal interest in their well-being, and above all is committed to their growth". Relationship of understanding, lent, paternal symbol, warmth, and interdependence, leading to higher productivity and better growth of both subordinate and the leader, are the hallmarks of nurturant task leader and subordinate relationship. Sinha shows that appropriateness of nurturant task leadership is drawn from the Indian mindset of respect for hierarchy, sneh-shradha-based relationship between the superior and subordinate and dependence proneness. Bhawuk opined that Nurturant task leaders derive the moral superiority from the principle of Lokasaṃgraha. 'Loka' means a society (people) and a larger cosmic system (nature) and 'Saṃgraha' means to gather, protect, nourish, regulate, etc. When individual develops the sense of interconnectedness and interdependence between self and nature, performs actions with the purpose of contributing to larger social and natural environment, it is referred as 'Lokasaṃgraha'. Bhawuk (2019) presents the Lokasaṃgraha as the Indian model of leadership. This is a fruitful area of examining the Indian model of leadership and its interplay with the mindset of leaders and followers.

Spirituality is one of the foremost features of Indian mindset. Religion is the way of expressing and living spirituality. Spiritual and religious organizations, like Art of Living, Chinmaya Mission, Gayatri Pariwar, ISKON, Patanjali Yoga Foundation, Yogoda Satsanga Society, Sathya Sai Sewa Organization, Ramkrishna Mission, Yogoda Society, have active membership of millions of followers. There are a large number of the active members of numerous living traditions of different branches of spirituality embraced in Hindu religion or Sanatan Dharma which emphasize on different expressions of spirituality like based on love for different forms of divine called Bhakti Marg, based on knowledge and insight about life and divinity known as Jnan Marg, based on service to the needy and poors in society called Sewa marg of based on the path of Yoga and meditations. These organizations carry out the activities related to spiritual growth and social service. These organizations can be the sites of studying many unique aspects of organizing, organization design and culture, leadership organization and society interface, and so on. We propose this as the third stream of plausible research on Indian mindsets.

The fourth stream of the potential research in the field of Indian mindset can be conceptualized at the societal level and its expression in policy formulation and implementation, social development and financial and economic system. Social work research dwells on the issues of welfare of child, women, youth, aged, downtrodden caste groups, poverty alleviation, physical and mental disabilities, juvenile delinquency, crime and correction, management of social welfare department and organization disaster management, industrial social work, and so on. Social mobilization, community involvement, social leadership at grass-roots level, societal communication, social influence, and behavioural change are few of the very important aspects of social work. The concepts and practices in the field of social work also can be informed by understanding the Indian mindset.

The impact of national and societal culture on the nature of financial system (e.g. Kwok & Tadesse, 2006) and economic ideologies and their implementation is the fifth useful area of research. Chapter 9 of this volume initiates the conversation in this field by delineating the unique features of Indian economic and financial system. This line of research can be enriched by examining the role of Indian mindset on the features of Indian economic and financial systems like management of family business, leadership effectiveness in organizations on the face of different kinds of challenges (e.g. need for enhancing efficiency, need for transformation, and so on), innovation in Indian organizations, management, and leadership in Indian multinational corporations, success of joint ventures of Indian organizations.

References

Agarwal, U. A. (2014). *Linking justice, trust and innovative work behaviour to work engagement*. Personnel Review.

Agarwal, U. A., & Bhargava, S. (2014). The role of social exchange on work outcomes: A study of Indian managers. *The International Journal of Human Resource Management, 25*(10), 1484–1504.

Agarwal, U. A., Datta, S., Blake-Beard, S., & Bhargava, S. (2012). *Linking LMX, innovative work behaviour and turnover intentions: The mediating role of work engagement*. Career development international.

Aryee, S., Budhwar, P. S., & Chen, Z. X. (2002). Trust as a mediator of the relationship between organizational justice and work outcomes: Test of a social exchange model. *Journal of Organizational Behavior: The International Journal of Industrial, Occupational and Organizational Psychology and Behavior, 23*(3), 267–285.

Agarwal, U. A., & Rai, A. (2019). Exploring bullying among Indian managers: A grounded theory approach. *Journal of Asia Business Studies, 13*(4), 588–611.

Agarwal, U. A., Stokes, P., & Smith, S. (2016). Examining perceived organizational politics among Indian managers: Engagement as mediator and locus of control as moderator. *International Journal of Organizational Analysis, 24*(3). Available at http://www.emeraldinsight.com/doi/abs/10.1108/IJOA-07-2014-0786. Accessed 15 October 2016.

Agarwala, T. (2003). Innovative human resource practices and organizational commitment: An empirical investigation. *International Journal of Human Resource Management, 14*(2), 175–197.

Amba-Rao, S. C., Petrick, J. A., Gupta, J. N., & Embse, T. J. V. D. (2000). Comparative performance appraisal practices and management values among foreign and domestic firms in India. *International Journal of Human Resource Management, 11*(1), 60–89.

Aycan, Z., Kanungo, R. N., & Sinha, J. B. (1999). Organizational culture and human resource management practices: The model of culture fit. *Journal of Cross-Cultural Psychology, 30*(4), 501–526.

Barkow, J. H., Akiwowo, A. A., Barua, T. K., Chance, M. R. A., Chapple, E. D., Chattopadhyay, G. P., Freedman, D. G., et al. (1975). Prestige and culture: A biosocial interpretation [and comments and replies]. *Current Anthropology, 16*(4), 553–572.

Belwalkar, S., & Vohra, V. (2016). Workplace spirituality, job satisfaction and organizational citizenship behaviors: A theoretical model. *International Journal of Business and Management, 11*(8), 256–262.

Bharati, A. (1985). The self in Hindu thought and action, In A. J. Marsella, G. DeVos, & F. L. K. Hsu (Eds.), *Culture and self: Asian and Western perspectives* (pp. 185–230). Tavistock Publications.

Bhawuk, D. P. (2019). *AdhyAtma* or spirituality: Construct definition and elaboration using multiple methods. In S. Mishra, & A. Varma (Eds.), *Spirituality in management*. Palgrave Studies in Indian Management. Palgrave Macmillan.

Bhawuk, D. P. (2003). Culture's influence on creativity: The case of Indian spirituality. *International Journal of Intercultural Relations, 27*(1), 1–22.

Bhatnagar, J., Budhwar, P., Srivastava, P., & Saini, D. S. (2010). Organizational change and development in India: A case of strategic organizational change and transformation. *Journal of Organizational Change Management, 23*(5), 485–499.

Budhwar, P. S. (2003). Employment relations in India. *Employee Relations, 25*(2), 132–148.

Budhwar, P. S., & Sparrow, P. R. (2002). An integrative framework for understanding cross-national human resource management practices. *Human Resource Management Review, 12*(3), 377–403.

Budhwar, P. S., & Boyne, G. (2004). Human resource management in the Indian public and private sectors: An empirical comparison. *The International Journal of Human Resource Management, 15*(2), 346–370.

Budhwar, P. S., Varma, A., Singh, V., & Dhar, R. (2006). HRM systems of Indian call centres: An exploratory study. *The International Journal of Human Resource Management, 17*(5), 881–897.

Chattopadhyay, G. P. (1975). Dependence in Indian culture: From mud huts to company board rooms. *Economic and Political Weekly, Review of Management*, M30–M39.

Cortina, L. M., & Wasti, S. A. (2005). Profiles in coping: Responses to sexual harassment across persons, organizations, and cultures. *Journal of Applied Psychology, 90*(1), 182.

D'Cruz, P., & Bharat, S. (2001). Beyond joint and nuclear: The Indian family revisited. *Journal of Comparative Family Studies, 32*(2), 167–194.

Deng, H., Coyle-Shapiro, J., & Yang, Q. (2017). *Beyond reciprocity: A conservation of resources view on the effects of psychological contract violation on third parties.*

Doney, P. M., Cannon, J. P., & Mullen, M. R. (1998). Understanding the influence of national culture on the development of trust. *Academy of Management Review, 23*(3), 601–620.

Dutta, S. (1997). *Family business in India*. Sage.

Erdogan, B., & Liden, R. C. (2006). Collectivism as a moderator of responses to organizational justice: Implications for leader-member exchange and ingratiation. *Journal of Organizational Behavior, 27*(1), 1–17.

Farh, J.-L., Hackett, R. D., & Liang, J. (2007). Individual-level cultural values as moderators of perceived organizational support–employee outcome relationships in China: Comparing the effects of power distance and traditionality. *Academy of Management Journal, 50*(3), 715–729.

Fukuyama, F. (1995). Social capital and the global economy. *Foreign Affairs, 74*, 89.

Garg, N. (2017). Workplace spirituality and employee well-being: An empirical exploration. *Journal of Human Values, 23*(2), 129–147.

Gang, I. N., Sen, K., & Yun, M. S. (2017). Is caste destiny? Occupational diversification among Dalits in rural India. *The European Journal of Development Research, 29*(2), 476–492.

Gopalan, S., & Rivera, J. B. (1997). Gaining a perspective on Indian value orientations: Implications for expatriate managers. *The International Journal of Organizational Analysis, 5*(2), 156–179.

Gupta, M., Kumar, V., & Singh, M. (2014). Creating satisfied employees through workplace spirituality: A study of the private insurance sector in Punjab (India). *Journal of Business Ethics, 122*(1), 79–88.

Hofstede, G. (1980). Culture and organizations. *International Studies of Management & Organization, 10*(4), 15–41.

Hofstede, G. (1991). *Organizations and cultures: Software of the mind*. McGrawHill.

House, R. J., Hanges, P. J., Javidan, M., Dorfman, P. W., & Gupta, V. (2004). *Leadership, culture, and organizations: The GLOBE study of 62 Societies*. Sage.

Jain, A. K. (2015). An interpersonal perspective to study silence in Indian organizations: Investigation of dimensionality and development of measures. *Personnel Review, 44*(6), 1010–1036.

Jodhka, S. S. (2008). Caste & the corporate sector. *Indian Journal of Industrial Relations*, 185–193.

Kakar, S. (1971). Authority patterns and subordinate behavior in Indian organizations. *Administrative Science Quarterly, 16*(3), 298–307.

Kakar, S. (1978). *The inner world: A psycho-analytic study of childhood and society in India*. Oxford University Press Delhi.

Kakar, S. (1982). Reflections on psychoanalysis, Indian culture and mysticism. *Journal of Indian Philosophy, 10*(3), 289–297.

Kanungo, R. N., & Mendonca, M. (1994). *Work motivation: Models for developing countries* (Vol. 1). Sage.

Kanungo, R. N., Aycan, Z., & Sinha, J. B. (2020). Socio-cultural environment, work culture, and managerial practices: The model of culture Fit. In *Latest contributions to cross-cultural psychology* (pp. 269–285). Routledge.

Khatri, N., Fern, C. T., & Budhwar, P. (2001). Explaining employee turnover in an Asian context. *Human Resource Management Journal, 11*(1), 54–74.

Kirkman, B. L., Chen, G., Farh, J.-L., Chen, Z. X., & Lowe, K. B. (2009). Individual power distance orientation and follower reactions to transformational leaders: A cross-level, cross-cultural examination. *Academy of Management Journal, 52*(4), 744–764.

Kirkman, B. L., Lowe, K. B., & Gibson, C. B. (2006). A quarter century of culture's consequences: A review of empirical research incorporating Hofstede's cultural values framework. *Journal of International Business Studies, 37*(3), 285–320.

Kothari, R. (1970). *Politics in India* Orient Blackswan.

Kwok, C. C., & Tadesse, S. (2006). The MNC as an agent of change for host-country institutions: FDI and corruption. *Journal of International Business Studies, 37*(6), 767–785.

Lawler, J. J., Jain, H. C., Venkata Ratnam, C. S., & Atmiyanandana, V. (1995). Human resource management in developing economies: A comparison of India and Thailand. *International Journal of Human Resource Management, 6*(2), 319–346.

Li, A., & Cropanzano, R. (2009). Fairness at the group level: Justice climate and intraunit justice climate. *Journal of Management, 35*(3), 564–599.

Markus, H. R., & Kitayama, S. (1991). Cultural variation in the self-concept. In *The self: Interdisciplinary approaches* (pp. 18–48). Springer.

Mellahi, K., Budhwar, P. S., & Li, B. (2010). A study of the relationship between exit, voice, loyalty and neglect and commitment in India. *Human Relations, 63*(3), 349–369.

Mishra, R. C. (1994). *Individualist and collectivist orientations across generations.*

Pandey, J. (1981). Ingratiation tactics in India. *The Journal of Social Psychology, 113*(1), 147–148.

Pandey, A., Gupta, R. K., & Arora, A. P. (2009). Spiritual climate of business organizations and its impact on customers' experience. *Journal of Business Ethics, 88*(2), 313–332.

Pandey, A., Gupta, V., & Gupta, R. K. (2019). Spirituality and innovative behavior in teams: Examining the mediating role of team learning. *IIMB Management Review, 31*, 116–126.

Pareek, U. (1968). Motivational patterns and planned social change. *International Social Science Journal, 20*(3), 464–473.

Patel, C., Budhwar, P., & Varma, A. (2012). Overall justice, work group identification and work outcomes: Test of moderated mediation process. *Journal of World Business, 47*(2), 213–222.

Philip, L., & Ganguly, D. (2014). Argumentative & too emotional: Are Indians tough to work with. *The Economic Times*, 26.

Pio, E. (2007). HRM and Indian epistemologies: A review and avenues for future research. *Human Resource Management Review, 17*(3), 319–335.

Pober, J. S., Gimbrone, M. A., Lapierre, L. A., Mendrick, D. L., Fiers, W., Rothlein, R., & Springer, T. A. (1986). Overlapping patterns of activation of human endothelial cells by interleukin 1, tumor necrosis factor, and immune interferon. *The Journal of Immunology, 137*(6), 1893–1896.

Porter, L. W., Allen, R. W., & Angle, H. L. (2003). The politics of upward influence in organizations. *Organizational Influence Processes, 2*, 431–445.

Prabhu, J., & Jain, S. (2015). Innovation and entrepreneurship in India: Understanding jugaad. *Asia Pacific Journal of Management, 32*(4), 843–868.

Radhakrishnan, S. (1948/2009). *The Bhagavadgita*. HarperCollins Publishers.

Rai, A., & Agarwal, U. A. (2018). Workplace bullying and employee silence: A moderated mediation model of psychological contract violation and workplace friendship. *Personnel Review, 47*(1), 226–256.

Ramanujan, A. K. (1989). Is there an Indian way of thinking? An informal essay. *Contributions to Indian Sociology, 23*(1), 41–58.

Randolph, R. S., & Erich, N. (2009). *Global reach: Emerging ties between the San Francisco Bay Area and India.* Bay Area Council Economic Institute.

Roland, A. (1988). In search of self in India and Japan: Toward a cross-cultural. Free Association Books. *International Journal of Psycho-Analysis, 45*, 558–566.

Rosen, B., Furst, S., & Blackburn, R. (2006). Training for virtual teams: An investigation of current practices and future needs. *Human Resource Management, 45*(2), 229–247.

Saini, D. & Budhwar, P. (2004). Managing human resources in Asia-Pacific. HRM in India. In A. B. Shah, & C. R. M. Rao (1965), Tradition and Modernity in India, Manaktalas.

Shah, S. (2000). Caste, commitments, and change. In *Psychological contracts in employment: Cross-national perspectives* (p. 104). Sage.

Shao, R., Rupp, D. E., Skarlicki, D. P., & Jones, K. S. (2013). Employee justice across cultures a meta-analytic review. *Journal of Management, 39*(1), 263–301.

Sinha, D., & Tripathi, R. C. (1994). Individualism in a collectivist culture: A case of coexistence of opposites.

Sinha, J. B. P. (1970). *Development through Behaviour Modification* (Vol. 5). Allied Publishers.

Sinha, J. B. P. (1990). *Work culture in the Indian context*. Sage. Available at http://www.getcited.org/pub/102868052. Accessed 13 April 2013.

Sinha, J. B. P. (1995). Factors facilitating and impeding growth of psychology in South Asia with special reference to India. *International Journal of Psychology, 30*(6), 741–753.

Sinha, J. B. P. (2004). *Multinationals in India: Managing the interface of cultures.* Sage.

Sinha, J. B. P. (2014). *Psycho-social analysis of the Indian mindset*. Springer.

Sinha, J. B. P., & Kanungo, R. N. (1997). Context sensitivity and balancing in Indian organizational behaviour. *International Journal of Psychology, 32*(2), 93–106.

Sinha, J. B. P., & Kumar, R. (2004). Methodology for understanding Indian culture. *The Copenhagen Journal of Asian Studies, 19*, 89–104.

Sinha, J. B. P., & Pandey, A. (2007). Indians' mindsets and the conditions that evoke them. *Psychological Studies-University of Calicut, 52*(1), 1.

Sinha, J. B. P., & Sinha, D. (1990). Role of social values in Indian organizations. *International Journal of Psychology, 25*(3–6), 705–714.

Sinha, J. B. P., & Verma, J. (1994). Collectivism and socio-economic and psychological well-being. In *Individualism and collectivism: Theory, method, and applications* (pp. 267–275).

Sinha, J. B., Singh, S., Gupta, P., Srivastava, K. B., Sinha, R. B. N., Srivastava, S., & Pandey, A. (2010). An exploration of the Indian mindset. *Psychological Studies, 55*(1), 3–17.

Som, A. (2008). *Organization redesign and innovative HRM*. Oxford University Press.

Sparrow, P. R., & Budhwar, P. S. (1997). Competition and change: Mapping the Indian HRM recipe against world-wide patterns. *Journal of World Business, 32*(3), 224–242.

Srinivas, M. N. (1988/1997). *The remembered village* (4th ed.). Oxford University Press.

Triandis, H. C. (1994). *Culture and social behaviour*. Mcgraw-Hill Book Company. Available at http://psycnet.apa.org/psycinfo/1993-99058-000. Accessed 9 May 2016.

Triandis, H. C. (1995). *Individualism & collectivism*. Westview Press. Available at http://psycnet.apa.org/psycinfo/1995-97791-000. Accessed 23 January 2017.

Tripathi, R. C. (1988). *Aligning development to values in India*. Sage.

Varma, A., & Budhwar, P. (2012). International human resource management in the Indian context. *Journal of World Business, 2*(47), 157–158.

Varma, A., Pichler, S., & Srinivas, E. S. (2005). The role of interpersonal affect in performance appraisal: Evidence from two samples–the US and India. *The International Journal of Human Resource Management, 16*(11), 2029–2044.

Virmani, B. R., & Guptan, S. U. (1991). *Indian management*. Vision Books.

Vivekananda, S. (1896). *Practical vedanta*. http://www.vivekananda.net/PDFBooks/PracticalVedanta.pdf. As on 9 October 2017.

Whitely, W., & England, G. W. (1977). Managerial values as a reflection of culture and the process of industrialization. *Academy of Management Journal, 20*(3), 439–453.

8

Effective Organizational Leadership in Indian Context

Abinash Panda

Trend in Leadership Studies in India

Leadership studies, during initial decades of post-independence India, were dominated by studies of business families and the patriarchs heading these families, primarily by business historians and sociologists. These studies were descriptive in nature, describing the entrepreneurial journey undertaken by these families. Subsequently, during the sixties and the seventies, academic scholars from the USA got inquisitive about if participative/democratic leadership style (vis-à-vis authoritarian style) would be as effective in the Indian context as in the US context. This research agenda was driven by the academic scholars from the USA supported by scholars in India who were deeply influenced by the western thoughts and academic traditions.

A. Panda (✉)
Management Development Institute, Gurgaon, India
e-mail: abinash.panda@mdi.ac.in

© The Author(s), under exclusive license to Springer Nature Switzerland AG 2022
A. Pandey et al. (eds.), *Indigenous Indian Management*, Palgrave Studies in Indian Management,
https://doi.org/10.1007/978-3-030-87906-8_8

Findings of these leadership studies were mostly inconsistent, and hence, confusing. Such results encouraged scholars to take up indigenous-emic studies to develop native understanding of leadership in India and also to identify effective leadership style for the Indian context. All these efforts led to conceptualization of leadership concepts such as Nurturant Task Leadership (NTL) by Sinha (1980, 1995), paternalistic leadership (Guptan, 1988), consultative managerial leadership (CSML) (Kalra, 2004), *Sannyasin* and *Karmayogin* leaders (Bhawuk, 2008, 2011), *lokasamgraha* (doing good for the society at large) as a leadership approach (Bhawuk, 2019) besides many others, and are claimed to be effective in Indian context.

This chapter presents a detailed review and synthesis of leadership studies in India and sets agenda for future academic research. It also delves into alternate profiles of effective leaders in the Indian context; why leadership development efforts have not been as effective as it should be in grooming leaders in spite of having access to rich academic research insights; how leaders in India learn to lead; what organizations need to do to groom effective leaders and finally presents themes for future leadership research in the Indian context.

Themes of Leadership Studies in India

The focus of leadership studies in India has evolved over time in response to the way corporate India has evolved. As indicated above, initially, when business families dominated corporate India, the focus of leadership studies were primarily on business and industrial houses and the patriarchs of these houses. Most of the studies were descriptive, presenting the evolutionary account of these entrepreneurial leaders and business houses.

Subsequently, when these business families welcomed management scholars/professionals from the USA to professionalize their businesses, during the Sixties and the Seventies, the leadership studies were primarily guided by the inquisitiveness to examine the efficacy of participative/democratic leadership in the Indian context vis-à-vis authoritarian one (e.g. Meade, 1967; Meyers, 1960). Participative style was then found to be effective in US context and Western scholars assumed that given the authoritarian nature of Indian society, authoritarian leadership style rather than participative one would be effective in Indian work context (e.g. Meyers, 1960) These studies were driven by academic scholars from the USA with the active support of scholars from India, who were positively influenced by the Western thought process and ideas.

The third group of leadership studies was influenced by the desire by a few Indian scholars to have a native understanding of effective leadership in the Indian context. These indigenous leadership studies conducted during and after 1980s were triggered by two things. First, there were inconsistencies in the findings of various leadership studies conducted in 1960s and 1970s. Secondly, academic community acknowledged the influence of cultural contexts (amongst others) on the effectiveness of leadership. Hence, many academic scholars started working on leadership style that is effective in the Indian cultural context. Scholars conceptualized culturally appropriate leadership approaches which they claim to be more effective in the Indian set-up as compared to pure participative or authoritarian leadership, as presented by the scholars from the west.

Thematically speaking, leadership studies in India can be clustered into three groups. The first group of descriptive studies is about the evolutionary account of business families. The second group of studies focused on examining the efficacy of participative/democratic leadership for the Indian context. Third group of studies includes indigenous leadership studies.

Descriptive and Evolutionary Account of Business Families

The industrial activities in 1947 were limited primarily to textiles, open field coal mining and an Iron and Steel factory (Sinha, 2001, p.429). Much of these business activities were in the hands of a few business families, operating in multiple industries. The Tatas were into electric power and heavy industry, especially steel and locomotives, whereas the Birlas were in cotton textiles and jute, manufacturing of textile machinery, bicycles and cars. The Walchands though initially confined their operations to construction works and shipping, subsequently they moved into engineering and sugar industries. Other leading business families like the Dalmias, the Jalans, Singhanias, the Goenkas (Sir Badridas), the Thomases and the Thapars likewise ran a miscellany of enterprises. There were a few other business communities of lesser industrial significance, such as the Punjabis, Sindhis, Muslims and Bengalis. Some of the new breed of entrepreneurs who emerged post-independence were members of trading and money-lending castes such as the Chettiars of South India (Lamb, 1956).

In the post-independence era, for instance in 1951, 12 business houses dominated corporate India: Tatas, Birlas, Dalmia-Sahu Jain, Kirloskar, Shriram, Lalbhai, Walchands, Thapar, Mafatlal, Mahindra, Bangur and Singhanias. Their companies were listed amongst the top 100 companies in 1997.

Sinha (2004) analysed exhaustively the organizational characteristics prior to liberalization. He found two types of organizations: family managed businesses and public sector organizations dominating corporate India at that time. There were few professionally trained managers working for these business families, who often complained about limited autonomy or prospect for advancement. The final authority and ultimate decision-making power was the preserve of relatives of the family head or of the family's close community associates.

Studies conducted during pre-independence period and after independence, indicated that Brahmins dominated the administrative and supervisory occupations (e.g. Gadgil's Poona survey, 1951; Ghurye, 1961; Kassenbanm & Sagar, 1974; Sovani et al., 1954). Kalra's (1976) study on Caste system and achievement values indicated that the Brahmins had higher level of aspirations than other castes. Kalra attributed it to (a) high aspirations of Brahmins contributing to their high need for achievement, (b) importance attached to education, as teaching and learning were supposed to be major duties of the Brahmins and (c) lack of inhibition amongst the Brahmins because of their superior status in caste hierarchy, which helped them to develop positive outlook and confidence.

Many business historians documented and presented evolutionary account of the growth and decline of business families much later (e.g. Gadgil, 1951; Hazari, 1966; Levi, 2016; Piramal, 1998, 2011, 2015; Piramal & Herdeck, 1986; Ray, 1992; Subramanian, 2016; Timberg, 1978; Tripathi, 1981, 1984, 1987, 2004; Tripathi & Mehta, 1990). Many of these accounts were hagiographic in nature and undertaken by journalists (e.g. Karkaria, 2003). Brief delineation of the contributions of Tripathi, Piramal and Lala is worth mentioning here to understand the family business in India, which still is a dominant segment in corporate India.

Contributions of Thomas Timberg to Understand the Marwaris

Thomas Timberg (1978, 2015) has studied in depth the way the *Marwaris* conduct their business. In *The Marwaris: From Jagat Seth to the Birlas,* he had taken a deep dive into how the Marwaris have expanded their businesses with a strong sense of business ethics. Timberg presents their evolution as a business community from the 1600s, when they moved to smaller kingdoms across India as traders, merchants, lenders and bankers. Subsequently, during the British Raj their roles changed, when they formed the 'great firms', became "Banians" or guaranteed brokers to British firms. The author shows how the Marwaris as a community adapted to changing realities and gainfully leveraged their extended family network to thrive and prosper.

Contributions of Dwijendra Tripathi to Understand Business Communities

Tripathi and his co-researchers have through several intellectual contributions over decades have enriched understanding of entrepreneurial history of Indian business communities, especially of Gujaratis and other business communities from the Western part of India. *Business Houses in Western India: A Study of Entrepreneurial Response* (Tripathi & Mehta, 1990) unravels the entrepreneurial journey of Gujarat and Gujarati, besides other business communities in the Western part of India. *The Dynamics of a Tradition: Kasturbhai Lalbhai and His Entrepreneurship* (Tripathi, 1981) narrates the business endeavours of Kasturbhai Lalbhai, founder of Ahmedabad based textile manufacturing industrial house, Ahmedabad. Tripathi (1984) has studied the business communities in India and presented the findings in the tile *Business Communities in India.* Tripathi (1991) has presented a historical account of business and politics in India from an evolutionary perspective in the title *Business and Politics in India from a historical perspective. The Oxford History of Indian Businesses* (Tripathi, 2004) offers an authentic understanding of the genesis of modern business practices in India. The author begins with a discussion of the backdrop in 1700: the period that shaped the strategies and structures that characterize the contours of Indian business today. He goes on the detail the aftermath of the imperial crisis; the onslaught of the industrial revolution and its impact in India; the rise of the managing agency system; and the beginning of industrial capitalism. *The Concise Oxford History of Indian Business* (Tripathi & Jumani, 2006) presents the story of the evolution of Indian business from merchants to service providers, focusing on the entrepreneur whose exploits made the transition possible. The authors narrate a historical and evolutionary account of the business methods and families that makes Indian business what it is today in a highly engaging manner. *The Oxford History of Contemporary Indian Business* (Tripathi & Jumani, 2013) provides a comprehensive analysis of the making of modern business and the modern business class, covering the period from 1947 to the first decade of twenty-first century. The book covers a vast canvas-from industrial licensing and planned economy, to the experiments in cooperative undertakings, and the opening up of the Indian economy and liberalization.

Contributions of Gita Piramal to Understand Business Leaders

While Dwijendra Tripathi focused his attention on business communities in India, Gita Piramal focused her attention on business leaders. Piramal

(2015) has studied life histories of business leaders such as Kamalnayan Bajaj, the founding architect of the Bajaj Group. In *Kamalnayan Bajaj-architect of the Bajaj Group,* she has narrated how Kamalnayan set up the Bajaj group against the backdrop of turmoil due to partition, famine and other resource constraints, including license-raj in the thirties and fourties. In *Business Maharaja,* Piramal (2011) has unravelled and narrated the success stories of eight business leaders in a very authentic and honest manner. In another contribution, Piramal (1998) in *Business Legends* has profiled four business legends of pre-independence era namely G.D. Birla, Walchand Hirachand, Kasturbhai Lalbhai and J.R.D. Tata. She has also presented authentic accounts of lives and times of these leaders in a highly engaging and sensitive manner. *Smart Leadership: Insights for CEOs* (Piramal, 2005) is about twelve CEOs who have set new benchmarks for growth and performance in their respective industry in the process and how they succeeded in a ferociously competitive, rapidly changing and fluid business environment. Gita Piramal and her co-author Jennifer Netarwala have drawn insights from the lives of these leaders and narrated what others can learn from their struggles in some of the core aspects of leadership: decision making, building teams, nurturing talent, managing change and an unwavering focus on growth. It offers practical tips on transforming business.

Contributions of R.M. Lala in Understanding Tata Group/Leaders

R. M Lala's contributions towards the understanding of the Tata Group are profound. *Beyond the last blue mountain: A life of J.R.D. Tata* (Lala, 1993), for instance is the biography of J.R.D. Tata, that narrates how J R D Tata pioneered aviation in India, and presided over the development of the country's steel, cement, truck and vegetable oils industry. *The Creation of Wealth: The Tatas from the 19th to 21st Century* (Lala, 1981), on the other hand, offers an inside and authentic account of how the Tatas have been taking the lead as industrialists and entrepreneurs to have made significant contributions in areas like factory reforms, labour and social welfare, medical research, higher education, culture and arts and rural development. It also presents how Ratan Tata had to deal with the leadership challenges post-1992 era of economic reforms.

The Heartbeat of the Trust (Lala, 1999) narrates how Sir Dorabji Tata Trust evolved over time to make significant contributions to society at large. Lala recounts the struggle for finances, of survival under control regime, the evolution of humane labour practices and so on. *For the love of India: The life and times of Jamsetji Tata* (Lala, 2003) is a biographical account of the life and significant contributions of Jamsetji Tata that includes ideating about institutions such as Indian Institute of Science in Bangalore, Tata Steel plant, Jamshedpur, the Taj Mahal hotel in Mumbai and so on.

Frank Harris (2014), in *Jamsetji Nusserwanji Tata: A Chronicle of His Life* narrates the life of Jamsetji Nusserwanji Tata in an objective and detached, yet in a fascinating manner. A recent contribution on the Tata Group has been made by Shah in his magnum opus The Tata Group: From Torchbearers to Trailblazers (2018) was published on the occasion of the conglomerate's 150th anniversary. While Lala's work focused on the Tatas up to the early 1990s, this book captures the learnings during the two decades thereafter, when the group became India's most globalized conglomerate with a presence in 150 countries. The book elaborates the leadership of JRD and Ratan and also explains how the Tata Group combined international best practices with Indian values, and blended the capitalist spirit with socialist primacies in leading Tata companies like TCS, Tata Steel, Tata Motors, Titan, Tata Chemicals, Tata Power, Voltas, Tata Global Beverages, JLR, Tetley and many more.

Contributions of H. McDonald to Understand the Ambanis

McDonald (1998) in his book titled *The Polyester Prince: The Rise of Dhirubhai Ambani* presents a fascinating account of Indian textile tycoon Dhirubhai Ambani—the story of a rising capitalist group in post-independence India. *Ambani & sons* (McDonald, 2010), on the other hand, is an account of Reliance group since 2002, when Mukesh Ambani and Anil Ambani led the group in 2002 after the death of Dhirubhai Ambani including the family feud between both.

Synthesizing the Studies on Family Business in India

Family businesses in India are owned and managed by founders' family. Most of the successful family businesses in India today have their origin in pre-independence India, which has evolved over time adapting to the changing and ever evolving business environments. There have not been many systematic academic studies on the management and organization of family businesses. Understanding of family businesses are based on anecdotal accounts, personal experiences or biographies of leaders and studies on business communities mostly by D. Tripathi and his co-researchers. Patriarchs of family businesses in India have forged, nurtured and leveraged their relationships with government and politicians, which have helped them to tide over crises from time to time. However, it has also brought disrepute to the way businesses are conducted in family-owned and managed entities and are labelled as 'crony capitalism'.

Leadership Studies Shaped by Western Thoughts and Led by Western Scholars

In the sixties, business families in India needed professionally qualified managers and were recruited by many for their managerial talents irrespective of one's community. They also approached scholars from the west for guidance. Western scholars became interested to understand organizations and leadership. They wanted to investigate whether management concepts developed in their parts of the world would be applicable in Indian context. The dominant thought process was as Indian society was traditional, the culture would primarily be authoritarian in nature (Lewis, 1962). Western scholars assumed that participative leadership would be effective in every cultural context. Hence, they conducted series of studies on the effectiveness of participative leadership in Indian context.

Meyers (1960, p. 166) noted, "many Indian top managements are relatively authoritarian in their relationships with lower management and with labour". Ganguli (1964) found the superior-subordinate relationship predominantly to be midway between the bureaucratic and the autocratic. Many leadership studies conducted during this phase (e.g. Meade, 1967; Cascio, 1974; Ganguli, 1964; Meyers, 1960; Thiagrajan & Deep, 1970; Punekar & Savur, 1969) supported the notion that Indian culture is authoritarian; therefore, a task-oriented authoritarian leader was argued to be more effective in Indian context. Most of these studies conducted during this phase, given the intent, were replicative in nature (Sahay et al., 1994) and were guided by western concepts, theories, models and tools (Sinha, D., 1972). They focused their investigations to validate participative and democratic leadership styles.

Cascio (1974) in his comparative study of seven cultures found that most of Indian managers satisfied in such decision making process where the subordinates were uninvolved and passive. Only one-third of the Indian subordinates preferred participative approach to decision making with their superiors. Organizational scholars in India, in the absence of indigenous perspective, subscribed the western perspective on organizational leadership.

The argument that Indians prefer and perform better under authoritarian leadership was challenged by a group of scholars (Kalra, 1988; Sinha, 1980; Sinha & Sinha, 1974). Sinha (1980) disputed the view that Indian culture is truly authoritarian in character. Kakar (1971a, 1971b, 1972) worked extensively to understand the nature of authority relationship in Indian work context. Studies conducted by J.B.P. Sinha and his co-researchers on Indian mindset and effective leadership in Indian context are significant.

J.B.P. Sinha's Contributions on Indian Mindset and Effective Leadership

Sinha's work on unravelling the complexity of Indian mindset is worth understanding as it influences the effectiveness of any leadership style. Equipped with both Hindu-agrarian and Anglo-Saxon worldviews, Indians tend to display duplicity in their behavioural disposition. Indians also manifest high discrepancy in their beliefs, preferences, action orientations and high sensitivity to contextual cues (Sinha et al., 2010) as they rarely demonstrate a purely individualist pattern of behaviour and intention. Their behavioural response depends on the situational characteristics (Sinha et al., 2002). Sinha's (2014) *Psychosocial Analysis of Indian Mindset* offers insights into the complexity of the Indian psyche. Chapter twelve on psycho-social analysis of Indian Mindset by Agrawal and Pandey extensively presents the findings of J.B.P. Sinha on Indian mindset.

Sinha (1974) found that participative management was of limited effectiveness and may be effective when organizations went through change in Indian organizations. When organization stabilizes and reaches an equilibrium phase, there was a reversal and one of the possible reasons for the reversal could be attributed to the surrounding 'authoritarian' societal culture. In a dependency prone, high power distance hierarchical societies such as India, a manager with participative style may be viewed as incompetent and weak. In some cases, participative leadership were viewed by the followers as abdication of responsibilities, which is considered a sign of weakness. In some other cases (Kalra, 1988; Sinha, 1976), both job satisfaction and employees' morale were found to be positively related to authoritarian style of leadership.

Sinha (1995) has reported that in the Indian context, participative leadership is not viewed positively by subordinates. They perceive such as leadership style as abdication of authority and responsibility on the part of the leader and a sign of weakness. Hence, in many cases such a style contributes confusion, anxiety and tension amongst the subordinates. Sinha (1980, 1995) instead conceptualized a culturally contingent leadership style, the nurturant task (NT) leadership model, which has been found to be effective. High NT Leaders create synergistic organizational culture, whereas weak NT Leaders create a soft organizational culture that is less productive as it is prone to external manipulations by government, union and other stakeholders, and thereby, deviating from organizational goals.

Sinha and his co-researchers (Sinha et al., 2010) revealed that Indians working under an "enabling" reporting manager, tend to be motivated to perform, come up with innovative ideas and share the same with the team, transparent and open with respect to sharing feelings and views with the reporting manager and colleagues. An enabling manager believes in empowerment, and hence, involves subordinates by making them participate in discussing ideas, encouraging team members to contribute and nurtures them by offering help and guidance, supporting ideas. Indians, when led by such enabling leaders, tend to be sensitive to the needs of peer group without losing focus on the goals. They try to balance both by working diligently, availing of challenging opportunities and remaining optimistic even in adverse situations. On the other hand, employees working under disabling reporting managers tend to carefully evaluate how they can serve their self-interests. They may say what persons in the position of authority (powerful, in that sense) want to hear. "Disabling" reporting manager tends to be "autocratic, expecting personal loyalty, sycophancy and compliance from the subordinates. Such manager is driven by the need for power".

Kakar's Contributions on Authority Relationship in the Indian Work Organization

Kakar's (1971a) study on authority in social relations in India revealed that the main source of the authority which conditions its acceptance is traditional-moral rather than the rational-legal, person and individual competence. Kakar also found that arousal of guilt and emotional rewards as the two chief means of exacting obedience to the superior's wishes. Indian culture is more of a *guilt* culture (Kakar et al., 2002, pp. 137–140).

It was also found that the ideal superior behaviour which made the subordinate anticipate the superior's wishes or accept them without conscious questioning was a benevolent one. This kind of superior enforced compliance to his wishes by the provision of emotional rewards or by the arousal of guilt. Though both the autocratic and the benevolent superior models exist in other areas of social relations in India, it is the benevolent superior who is held to be the most effective one.

Kakar (1971b) has mentioned that the dominance of the parental ideology in Indian organizations, especially in the form of assertive superior behaviour which is high on task control and low on emotional affiliation. The authority relationship in work organization context is characterized by a high degree of control of subordinate task performance by the superior (Kakar, 1972), which means '"nurturant" superiors would likely to exact greater obedience than "assertive" ones, since the former are more likely to regulate behaviour by emotional rewards and later by punitive means' (Kakar et al., 2002, p. 138). Kakar defined 'nurturant' as 'active submission, without a high degree of conflict in the subordinates'. Kakar (1978, p. 125) also observed that what an Indian is 'sensitive to (or concerned with) are not the goals or work and productivity that are external to the relationship, but the unfolding of emotional affinity'.

Dayal's Contribution on Effective Leadership and Organization Design

Dayal's (1999) study revealed that effective leaders were found to have common characteristics that included acquiring knowledge from variety of sources, using this knowledge in their work and life, and seeking feedback. Leaders, through action, convey (a) credibility that is practicing what they profess; (b) courage in dealing with problems; and (c) confidence and a strong sense of personal responsibility. They are easily accessible, have a strong urge to succeed and they involve people in accomplishing the task. Dayal, on the basis of this study, identified three emergent leadership styles namely: the entrepreneurial, the professional-bureaucratic and the people oriented. Entrepreneurial leader focuses on assets creation and aggressive organizational growth, whereas professional/bureaucratic leader emphasizes on setting high-performance goals and process. Finally, people-oriented leader emphasizes on the development of people through empowerment and consultative processes. Employees are groomed to develop necessary organizational systems and processes.

Dayal (2000) found that the entrepreneurial and the bureaucratic leader styles strengthen the feelings of dependence amongst the subordinates, who get used to doing what they are told. These styles may also inhibit team working and hence ineffective in Indian context. Dayal (2000) has argued that people-oriented leaders would be most effective in Indian context.

Satish K. Kalra Contributions to Leadership Research

Kalra (1988) made a distinction between subordinates accepting authoritarian leadership style of their leaders 'with liking' and 'without liking'. Findings of his study showed that comparatively bigger number of Indian executives were inclined to accept authoritarian behaviour from superiors in the sense of 'acceptance without liking' than reported in comparable studies of American executives. However, professionally qualified executives were found not to be comfortable with authoritarian leadership.

Kalra and Gupta (1999) have found that effective leaders in Indian context tend to be high on supportive, patronising and paternalistic; moderate on prescriptive and low on task obsession. Effective leaders in Indian context are neither highly task obsessive nor authoritarian. Patronizing in the Indian context is associated with taking care of subordinates and hence is viewed positively.

Consultative Style Managerial Leadership (CSML), as conceptualized by Kalra (2004), is characterized by the managers' ability to make decisions by involving the subordinates in getting their suggestions/ideas with or without any discussion on them and with the manager having the sole discretion of either accepting or rejecting any idea with or without giving any reason or logic thereof and thus making the final decision by himself and by giving the subordinates a feeling of being heard. Consultative style leadership is based on underlying assumption that individual has the potential to think, offer relevant and useful suggestions and ideas. The role of the leader is to motivate and encourage them to do so. Kalra argues that CSML fits with the average Indian's psyche, which is dependency prone, feels comfortable in hierarchical structures, looks for support/ approval from superiors and even being heard by the boss gives him a feeling of acceptance.

Other Conceptualizations of Leadership in Indian Context

Guptan (1988) has conceptualized the idea of paternalistic leadership that he argues to be effective in the Indian context. Guptan's conceptualization of paternalism refers to the relationship between a father figure and a large joint family where the father figure goes beyond merely professional relationships and is concerned about all aspects of an individual's life. Chakraborty (1987) drew on traditional Indian wisdom to argue that in Indian context, a leader, instead of being analytical and technical should be synthetic and spiritual by inculcating a sense of duty and sacrifice in his followers. Khandwalla (1988) conceptualized pioneering-innovative (PI) model of leadership, which is characterized by commitment to pioneering novel and sophisticated technologies, products and services, high risk taking and emphasis on creativity and adaptability. He argued that such an approach to management and leadership is a modern outgrowth of an entrepreneurial tradition of India.

Study of Effective Indian CEO (Spencer et al., 2007)

Leadership study jointly conducted by Public Enterprise Selection Board, Bharat Petroleum Corporate Limited and Hay Group by Spencer et al. (2007) identified four broad areas of competencies amongst the best CEOs in India. They are: (a) socially responsible business excellence; (b) energizing team; (c) managing the environment; and (d) inner strength.

Socially responsible business excellence category of competencies is related to underlying traits that help the leader make effective business decisions in order to determine when to invest and in what, what risks to take, and which innovations to adopt. Energizing team category of competencies is about one's ability to engage the energy and thoughts of all the employees to work together towards the common goal. Managing the environment is about how the leader is responsible for managing the boundaries between the enterprise and the surrounding environment. Indian leaders, compared to the leaders from many other western countries, tend to spend more time and energy in managing relationship with governmental agencies and the media. Indian executives tend to be bolder in seeking out information using personal contacts and network. Finally, inner strength category of competencies provides moral compass for both the leader and the organization. These competencies, that include executive maturity and transcending self, guide both the leader and organization to take difficult decisions. This study also revealed four unique competencies of Indian leaders namely: (a) single minded focus on growth; (b) adapting ideas and technology to Indian conditions; (c) entrepreneurship; and (d) working to make India great.

Leadership Study by Cappelli et al.

Cappelli and co-researchers (2010) studied successful organizations in India to find how Indian leaders are unique compared to the leaders from the West. Effective Indian leaders invest in people and take a long-term, internally focused view; make aggressive investment in employee development, despite tight labour market and widespread job hopping; strive for a high level of employee engagement and openness and create a sense of social mission that is served when business succeeds.

These leaders view themselves as architect of organizational strategy and as custodians and keepers of organizational culture. They guide and mentor and act as role models for their subordinates. They motivate and inspire their employees by creating a sense of mission; engaging through transparency and accountability; empowering through communication; and investing in training.

GLOBE (Global Leadership and Organizational Behavioural Effectiveness) Study

The GLOBE research programme examined the interrelationships between societal culture, societal effectiveness and organizational leadership has defined leadership as the ability of an individual to influence, motivate and enable others to contribute towards the effectiveness and success of the organizations of which they are members. The findings of GLOBE study (Chhokar, 1998) have revealed that characteristics such as action-orientation and charisma are salient to be effective as a leader in Indian context. Moreover, relationship orientation is found to be a more important characteristic of effective leaders in India than performance or task orientation. The most effective leadership style in India would thus combine integrity, being organized, an action orientation, being a self-starter, charisma and a collective orientation; with being a problem solver, a visionary, entrepreneurial and inspirational, in that order. The study also offered pointers on why it could tough to be an effective leader in Indian context. It is due to the co-existence of two sets of seemingly contradictory sets of values—vertical collectivism and individualism (Sinha, 1997, p. 60). India has been placed in South Asian country cluster in GLOBE study, where effective leaders are found to be visionary and inspirational, who are decisive, performance oriented and possess high level of integrity and are willing to make personal sacrifices (Gupta et al., 2002). In addition, leaders who are team builders, collaborative and diplomatic are highly respected. These attributes are congruent with the cluster's high power distance and family-centric societal culture. Leaders are expected to act as patriarchs who guide and help subordinates. Leaders must act and decide in such a manner, which help and develop and sustain the team and family orientations in their organizations. Leaders who are modest and caring and delegate responsibilities to others are also effective to an extent. Authoritarian leaders occupying any position or role are expected to be benevolent and paternalistic and allow for inputs from others.

Indigenous Leadership Studies

As mentioned above, few indigenous leadership concepts have been proposed by scholars. The idea of Nurturant Task Leadership has been conceived by J.B.P. Sinha (1980, 1995) based on his cultural experiences. The idea of *lokasamgraha* as a leadership approach has been proposed by D.P.S. Bhawuk (2019). Bhawuk (2008, 2011) has also identified two unique leadership styles namely *sannyasin* and *karmayogin* leaders found in India, inspired primarily by Indian spirituality.

Araam Culture, Poverty Syndrome and Nurturant Task Leadership

Sinha (2010) has acknowledged that the idea of dependency proneness emanated from his personal experience of Indian culture, which got crystallized over a series of collaborative studies, which helped him define and operationalize the construct and measure its antecedents and consequences thus developing a theory about it.

Sinha (1980) developed the concept of Nurturant Task Leadership (NTL), which he found was more relevant and effective in Indian context that is characterized by dependency proneness, *Aram* culture (proneness not to work too hard) and poverty syndrome. His observations were: (a) individuals who are prone to high degree of dependency took greater risk if supervisor expected them to do so and helping them to address their needs; (b) the idea of *nitizloka* that parents should shower love on their children up to the age five, discipline them for the next ten years and treat them as friends when they turn sixteen; and (c) cultural pattern of *Aram*.

The NT leader cares for his (or her) subordinates, shows affection, takes personal interest in their well-being, and committed to their growth. The idea of NTL is guided by superior's affection (*Sneh*) for subordinates and subordinates' deference (*Shraddha*) to superior/leader. It is based on the cultural assumption that unconditional nurturance/support turn subordinates into unproductive sycophants. NTL has been found to be 'more congruent with Indian cultural values and behaviour dispositions. The style is essentially paternalistic, drawing heavily on patterns of interaction typifying family dynamics in India' (Sinha, D., 1999) where subordinates are generally dependence prone, status conscious and not too work oriented.

NTL derives the moral superiority from acting for lokasamgraha, and not merely maximizing his or her personal gain. The idea of *lokasamgraha,* Bhawuk (2019) argues, forms the implicit foundation of Nurturant Task Leaders (NTL). NTL leaders focus on the general good of the organization and the society.

Bhawuk's Conceptualization of Lokasamgraha as an Indigenous Leadership Approach

Bhawuk's conceptualization of *lokasamgraha* as an indigenous Indian leadership approach captures the essence of "doing good for the society". Bhawuk argues that in Indian context, effective leadership is about focusing on serving others; leadership is about *lokasamgraha*, or, acting to hold people together in harmony. This conceptualization resonates well with Chakraborty's (1987) idea that a leader should act in the service of others in such a manner that his or her individual self expands to encompass the subordinates creating a larger collective self. Leaders and subordinates sacrifice for each other unconditionally, and such interactions transform the leader, the subordinates and the organization (Bhawuk et al., 2009).

Leaders are expected to guide people on the right path to achieve what is envisioned, and in that sense lokasamgraha is about leadership. Unlike traditional leadership, which focuses on the leader as a person, lokasamgraha shifts the focus to the well-being of the society. The idea of *lokasamgraha* as a leadership approach is based on the premise that not only leaders but also their followers should act so that all their actions are directed towards the greater public good. In other words, leadership is about serving others.

Four Types of Leaders: Sannyasin, Karmayogin, Pragmatic and Legitimate Non-Leader

Bhawuk (2008, 2011) conceptualized and proposed two types of leaders that are unique and indigenous to India, *sannyasin* and *karmayogin* leaders, who are inspired by spirituality. These kinds of leaders are found in spiritual and religious organizations. Indian spiritual and religious organizations are effectively guided and led by active *sannyasin* leaders, who have created various religious and spiritual institutions such as Swami Vivekananda (Ramakrishna Mission), Swami Chinmayananda (Chinmaya Mission) and so on.

A karmayogin leader focuses on work without paying attention to the fruits of the work, which is a concept derived from the Bhagavad Gita. A karmayogin leader pursues *lokasamgraha* or social good in all his or her actions. Gandhi, Vinoba Bhave, Gopala Krisna Gokhale and Bala Gangadhara Tilak are exemplars of karmayogin leaders who followed the principles of *lokasamgraha.* Bhawuk argues that such leaders are also found in business organizations. There should be conscious effort to explore if such leaders are effective in business organizations. One needs to identify key behavioural attributes of such business leaders.

Pragmatic organizational leaders, who believe in doing social good and follow the principles of *lokasamgraha,* invest their efforts and energy to direct organizational efforts towards social good.

Bhawuk has also pointed out the presence of legitimate non-leaders holding leadership positions in organizations. Legitimate non-leaders are individuals without leadership capabilities who are thrust in the position of leadership by organization. Technically, they are leaders with legitimate authority but lack leadership quality or fail to exercise leadership.

Drawing Inferences for Organizations: Synthesizing the Findings of Leadership Studies

A leader would be effective if one meets the expectations, psychological and otherwise, expectations of the subordinates/followers. More importantly, the expectations of followers from their leaders are conditioned by the cultural context. When leaders meet the psychological expectations of their followers, they are more likely to be effective in that cultural context. The expectations of followers in Indian cultural context and the expected nature of leader and followers' interactions are unique (Kakar et al., 2002; Panda, 2019). Indians generally long for an authoritative leader, who is strict, demanding but also caring and nurturing. Such leaders are similar to *karta,* the paternalistic head of a typical Indian (joint) family. Sinha (1980) calls such leaders the NT Leaders. The cultural preference for the NT leader is related to a strong desire for power and dependency needs. The followers want to remain in close proximity to their leaders both physically and psychologically (Nandy & Kakar, 1980; Sinha, D., 1972). Hence, followers tend to display ingratiating behaviour towards their leaders (Pandey, 1981). Leaders, on the other hand, have a tendency to seek higher status through power. Followers are comfortable with powerful leaders. Followers/subordinates tend to idealize their leaders and look on them as repository of virtues, deserving faith and respect. Leaders are expected to be role models with many facets—high integrity, system builder and humane father figure. The leaders are expected to act as benevolent guides to their subordinates and taking personal interest in their well-being and growth. Followers expect a personalized mode of relationship with their leaders (Garg & Parikh, 1995).

Effective Leader: A Karta in Organizational Setting

A review of indigenous leadership concepts reveals that an effective leader in Indian context should be like the karta in an Indian joint family. The karta is a father figure who is nurturant, caring, dependable, sacrificing and yet demanding, authoritative and strict disciplinarian. He evokes feelings of security, trust and dependability in creating a familial culture. He empowers grooms, guides and protects. He also mediates if there are any family disputes and generally his decisions are accepted and respected. In Indian cultural context, effective leadership style is primarily shaped and influenced by the karta psyche through the transference of father-son relationship to the boss-subordinate relationship in work situation. Kalra (2004) argued that the concept of 'karta' indigenous, and hence relevant to Indian cultural context. It influences the psyche of Indian managers/leaders through the process of 'kartarisation', which is a process characterized by 'the internalization and transference of many of the ritualistic and symbolic behaviours and associated beliefs, values and attitudes of 'karta' of the Indian joint family to various organizational and non-organizational roles outside the family, such as managers, colleagues and subordinates etc.'. He further added, 'the development of 'karta' psyche in Indian managers takes place through the process of 'kartarisation' and it strongly influences their managerial behaviour'.

Kalra, using the concept of karta, proposed consultative style managerial leadership (CSML), which he argued to be effective in Indian context besides Nurturant Task Leadership conceptualized by Sinha (1980).

Singh and Bhandarkar's (1990) conceptualization of transformational leadership was based on the idea of *karta*—head of Indian family. Such leaders empower followers, take risk, are visionary; have clarity in what they do. They, similar to NT leadership style, groom, guide, mentor and protect followers. Followers view their leaders as their father figure. Virmani and Guptan (1991) have found that effective leaders in formal organizations also play the role of karta, besides the role of a professional leader. Sinha (1995) argues that the leader has to be like family head. There is no demarcation between home and work domains, between work relations and personal relations with the subordinates.

Nurturant Task Leadership (NTL): The Effective Leadership Style

NTL is found to be most effective in Indian context as it is congruent with Indian cultural values and behavioural dispositions. This style is essentially paternalistic, drawing heavily on the patterns of interactions typifying family dynamics in India. It is in congruent with the findings of Kalra and Gupta's studies (1999) that indicated that effective managers were high on nurturance, moderate on prescription and low on task obsession.

On the whole, an effective leader in Indian context should nurture and mentor subordinates; be mildly prescriptive, and task oriented; patronise subordinates; shows his interest in subordinates' growth and well-being; and involves subordinates in organizational activities.

There are two criticisms of NTL. First, Kalra and Gupta (1999) have questioned the 'task' orientation aspect of Sinha's NTL. Kalra (2004) has argued that NTL may not be effective amongst the professionally qualified, autonomy-seeking executives as they want to be more empowered.

Kalra and Gupta (1999) found that effective managers, as perceived by colleagues in the organization, were those who exhibit patronizing behaviour along with being supportive, normative and problem solving oriented. 'Indian subordinates do not see patronizing as ineffective managerial style provided it is not clubbed with prescriptive, task-obsessive, bohemian, aggressive and avoidant managerial style or behaviour. If the boss is supportive and patronizing along with other functional ego styles, he is seen as effective by the subordinates' (Kalra & Gupta, 1999, p. 295).

Kalra (2004) made a case for consultative style leadership, as an alternative to Nurturant Task Leadership (Sinha, 1980), given the average Indian psyche, which is dependence prone, feels comfortable in hierarchical structures, looks for support/approval from superiors and even being heard by the boss gives him a feeling of acceptance. His argument is that professionally qualified executives may seek more autonomy and empowerment. They may wish for more participation, which counters the fundamental assumptions underlying NT leadership. NT leadership assumes that subordinates need to be initiated, guided and directed to work hard and maintain desired level of productivity. Once subordinates prove their capability and achieve desired goals, the leader may become more participative and less directive in his approach of leading.

Being Effective in Leadership Role: What Leaders Need to Do in India?

Organizational leaders need to do create a family-like work environment; demonstrate leadership that nurtures subordinates; ensure performance without being task obsessive; and engage with subordinates beyond work boundaries to create a truly familial organization in spirit.

In a family-like work environment, the leader is like the head of the family (*karta*). If the leader-subordinate relationship is marked by relationship of *sneh* (affection) and *shradha* (deference), subordinates would go to any extent for her or his paternal superior to get the work done. Indian employees generally feel anxious and insecure if their superiors maintain contractual/professional relationship. Such relationship may demotivate and alienate employees.

By implication, organizational leaders may effectively elicit productive behaviour from Indian employees, by judiciously lubricating task relationship with emotional reciprocity and compassion. The work culture needs to be based on 'emotional reciprocity' and 'trust', nee a typical Indian family. If organizational leaders can recreate family-like environment, employees may exhibit a sense of belongingness and emotional connect with the organization. If employees can develop a sense of belongingness, they would be productive.

Secondly, organizational leaders should nurture subordinates through appreciation, guidance, recognition and develop them through empowerment. First, organizational leaders need to address the deep urge for appreciation and recognition of Indian employees. They desire that people who matter should recognize the tasks they have been doing. Indian employees tend to be more productive and effective under a leader, who empowers them and includes them in the organizational decision making.

Organizational leaders should also ensure that subordinates' self-efficacy is enhanced through job performance by ensuring that bureaucratic and other organizational constraints do not become roadblocks for task performance and they develop necessary capabilities, required to execute the job effectively, through appropriate learning and developmental interventions.

Effective leaders in India, as perceived by their subordinates, tend to be patronising along with being supportive, normative and problem solving oriented. They also tend to be innovative, confronting/assertive and respectful. Hence, patronizing as leadership style is not considered ineffective in Indian context if it is blended with problem solving approach. The leaders must focus on achievement of performance. Nurturance should be made conditional, contingent upon task performance. Task obsessive approach may not be effective in Indian context.

The work culture must be meritocratic with unambiguous articulation of performance norms and expectations and merit-centric organizational systems and processes. Along with stringent performance criteria, organizational leaders should express confidence in the ability of subordinates.

The leaders may use punitive measures such as disciplinary actions to ensure performance and curb undesirable work behaviour, as mentioned above.

Finally, organizational leaders should participate in non-work practices (NWPs) (Awasthy & Gupta, 2011), that include three kinds of activities including individual celebrations such as birthday celebration, family function of employees, religious celebrations with employee family members; activities facilitated through organization such as picnics to understand and connect with employees at personal level and activities where the superior is personally involved with juniors, such as superiors' participation with junior in recreational activities, or visiting subordinates during family celebrations such as marriage etc.

When possible, organizational leaders should voluntarily participate in such NWPs and personal involvement of the leaders may enhance employees' commitment. It is consistent with the principles of participative management, and the idea that employees prefer work environments where they can contribute to work they find meaningful.

Participating in religious festivities and family celebration of employees may also encourage employees to accept organizational leaders as one of the family members. The employees may feel personally obliged to the leader(s). Involvement of leaders in NWPs is significant in Indian context as it fosters the spirit of 'truly familial organisation' (Gupta, 1999).

Corporate India has changed significantly over the last two decades with many entrepreneurial ventures; professionally managed entities in IT, ITeS, tech-enabled entities. Indians in current generations seem to be different from Indians of yester-years in terms of their aspirations, mindsets and behavioural dispositions. Given that there is a need to explore the cultural anchors and examine the efficacy of above mentioned recommendations for effective leadership.

Addressing Leadership Deficit in Indian Organizations

Despite the access to significant insights (knowledge) and understanding on leadership and leadership development in the world of scholarships and availability of resources for grooming leaders, organizations in India still experience the brunt of leadership deficit (Hou, 2010; Panda, 2017; Shyamsunder et al., 2011).

Organizations are generally obsessed with tangible outcomes and efficiency at the expense of employee development. The design of organization is guided by rationality and desire to control, which is conducive for imbibing managerial mindset amongst organizational members. In such organizations, one finds efficiency and control-driven managerial culture. Organizations with managerial culture tend to groom employees through socialization. Such an approach ignores development through self-mastery, which is key to leadership development.

Hence, many of the leadership development programs tend to be informational and knowledge-based. In reality, there is a huge disconnect between 'knowing', 'being' and 'doing'. Knowing does not automatically lead to requisite changes in the being and doing of an individual (Reddy & Srinivasan, 2015, p. 46). Enhanced cognitive understanding at the individual level does not automatically translate into internalization and change in behaviour in the real-world context.

Kalra (1997) has proposed the concept of human potential management (HPM) to argue that treating human beings as a resource to be used, utilized or manipulated like any other resource is demeaning. With the increasing number of highly skilled knowledge workers, resentment of the word "resource" is likely to increase, since knowledge workers are likely to prefer the organization to enable them to fulfil their true potential and, in so doing, help the organization to achieve its objectives. The learning leaders in organizations need to take note of this and strategize the learning and development strategies for their organizations.

Panda (2019) in his study on why leadership development has not been as effective in Indian context has argued that individuals with potential can only become effective leaders, if they are psychologically ready and have developed an emotional connect with the organizations. Secondly, individuals' psychological readiness is influenced by the way they are socialized in their families. Hence, in-family socialization contributes to one's psychological preparedness. Though, developmental experiences and meaningful relationships, besides class-room interventions provide opportunities to individuals to learn how to lead, yet individuals with psychological readiness have greater probability learning from developmental opportunities with the support of their mentors.

Primary socialization in typical Indian family tends to imbibe values, behaviours and attitudes which, are argued to be not helpful in developing leadership mindset. It imbibes a deep need for dependency, personalized and familial relationship with emotional reciprocity (Dayal, 1999, p. 79), many a times at the expense of independence and self-identity (Garg & Parikh, 1995).

Developing Effective Leaders for the Indian Context

First, development of people is not a mechanical exercise. Rather, it is an organic process which needs to be seamlessly integrated and aligned with other people processes. The organization has to initiate management and supervisory practices that could generate amongst employees a desire for self-development (Dayal, 2000).

Secondly, organizational leaders should stop viewing human beings as a resource to be used, utilized or manipulated like any other resource, which is demeaning (Kalra, 1997). Everyone has hidden potential that needs to be identified, nurtured and leveraged. The learning and development process has a significant role to play. Dayal's (1999) study has identified three critical processes in leader development, which included developing three qualities amongst potential leaders (i) the urge to achieve, to succeed, (ii) the process of maturing and (iii) the process of becoming oneself.

Dayal (1999, 2007) has pointed out that achievement orientation can be inculcated amongst the executives through systematic external interventions such as by (a) institutionalizing a culture of achievement and learning; (b) instilling a sense of belongingness amongst the employees;

and (c) fostering a feeling of being accepted by the peer groups and work communities. Challenging experiences provide requisite opportunities to develop an urge to achieve.

Moreover, the organization practices which contribute to the process of maturing are: (a) challenging assignments and performance review by superiors; (b) openness to ask questions without adverse effect on a person's career; and (c) giving feedback to authorities on a variety of issues which give the individual a feeling of belonging and acceptance in the organization. The process of becoming "oneself" is aided by gaining new ideas, experiences and insights and using them in the work situation.

Lessons of Experience (LOE) study conducted jointly by Tata Management Training Centre (TMTC) and the Centre for Creative Leadership (CCL) revealed interesting findings on how leaders in India learn to lead. Organizational leaders mentioned of 24 distinct developmental experiences (excluding coursework and training), which facilitated development and honing of 29 unique leadership competencies (lessons) (Panda, 2017). The 24 developmental experiences (excluding coursework and training) are clustered in four distinct categories that include (a) Challenging assignment (work context); (b) Mistakes, Crises and Hardship; (c) Other people including role models, mentors and coaches; and finally (d) Other developmental experiences including personal experiences, early life/job experiences.

Challenging assignments and role modelling were found to be the most powerful learning experiences as they together constituted around fifty per cent of the total instances of developmental experiences and facilitated the learning of more than 65% of the leadership lessons. Firstly, challenging assignments are found to be more effective than job rotations for leader development. Secondly, as reporting managers and other significant superiors are acknowledged as role models, they should mentor and coach their junior colleagues. Thirdly, Indian leaders were found to learn leadership from their personal experiences. Hence, the interaction between the mentor/coach and the protégé may provide a psychologically safe platform to build on personal experiences to make the protégé aware of self and gain confidence. Wilson (2010) presented the findings of Lessons of Experience study in the title *Developing Tomorrow's Leaders Today.* She has categorized all leadership lessons into eleven clusters and mapped those lessons to seven key experiences that matter in Indian context namely: boss and superiors, turnaround, new initiative, horizontal move, cultural crossing, increased job scope and first professional job. Business executives in India are expected to understand and appreciate the saliency of leadership lessons that matter in Indian context and more importantly they can identify the experiences from which these lessons can be acquired or developed. The right blend of developmental opportunities in Indian context, going by the findings of Lessons of Experience India (LOEI) study (Panda, 2017), would be challenging assignments such as fix it/turnaround situations; enriching and enlarging the jobs; Greenfield projects; cross-functional moves and rural stints; besides targeted role modelling and mentoring, which offers learning opportunities to executives. They should also be exposed to educational and training programs as 'deliberate practices' (Day, 2010) with specific learning outcomes.

Executives are encouraged to experiment and explore new ideas on the job. As an approach, learners work and reflect synchronously on real-time problems occurring in their own work setting (Raelin & Coghlan, 2006). In the process the executives reflect their own assumptions, mental maps and thinking pattern and change, if needed to be more effective. Action learning is guided by Schön's (1983) "reflection-in-action" principle as the executive as learner reframes unanticipated problem situations in order to see experience differently.

Individuals learn and grow when the ecosystem offers the following four learning conditions: first, individuals generally learn from experience, if they find the experience 'meaningful' and the relationships 'developmental'. Such experience and relationship trigger appraisal and recognition of self-worth and make individual confident. Organizations need to create a psychologically safe environment, which is conducive of experimentation and exploration of new ideas followed by critical reflection of one's actions. Individuals are encouraged to try out new ideas/insights gained from various training and learning inputs and reflect on those experiences to gain newer insights. It depends on an individual's absorptive capacity (Cohen & Levinthal, 1990), which primarily depends on the knowledge source and prior knowledge (Todorova & Durisin, 2007).

Dayal (2007) proposes that organizations must create an ecosystem where (a) employees feel as part of work community and are accepted without evaluation by peers and superiors; and (b) the norms of work community should be similar to what employees are socialized to in family and society at large and are comfortable with. Besides, individuals should also be psychologically ready to take advantage of the learning opportunities. Thirdly, they need to reflect on their experiences to discover new insights. Many a time, executives need to be guided on how to reflect with a purpose. Hence, organizational leaders as reporting managers, coaches and mentors have critical roles to play in guiding executives to reflect on experiences and draw meaningful insights.

Leadership development process begins with the identification of developmental needs of executives. TV Rao has emphasized the importance of 360 degree and multi-rater assessment tools for identifying developmental needs for executives. *The Power of 360° Feedback: The India Way for Leadership Effectiveness*, authored by Rao and Rao (2014), presents in-depth details about the process of developing managers into leaders and outlines methodologies for designing and using a 360 Degree Programme for managers at all levels. Once the developmental needs are identified, executives go through preparation, exposure, action and reflection phases, which has been captured by an integrated leadership development framework titled "PEAR" framework developed by Panda (2019). First, the executive in target (with leadership potential) needs to be psychologically ready and must demonstrate requisite maturity to leverage developmental opportunities for personal growth. Once, the executive is psychologically ready she/he is exposed to relevant developmental experiences that provide opportunities to experiment and explore. Executives are encouraged to reflect and learn on-the job under the guidance and support of mentors and coaches.

Challenges of Developing Leaders in India

Gupta and Panda (2003, p. 377) observed that development of effective leaders in India is a daunting challenge. They identified three core challenges that need to be addressed in developing effective leadership in

Indian cultural context. Narrow base of social identity due to the peculiarities of primary socialization, suppression of religious urge through British model of education system, peculiar emotional dynamics of the Indians and lack of leadership mindset due to dependence syndrome come in the way of grooming effective leaders in Indian cultural and organizational context. Indian mindset makes Indians better subordinate than a leader because of their proneness for dependency. Since the leader would be acceptable to the followers only if he understands and responds to their culturally specific psychological needs. Since Indian followers expect parental caring from their leaders, the leaders will have to learn to be both 'fatherly' and 'motherly'. Hence, leadership development requires that potential leaders learn through experiential learning methods to be purposeful and emotionally sensitive simultaneously (Gupta & Panda, 2003, pp. 377–378).

Due to their dependency proneness, Indians tend to give more salience to their subordinate role than to their role as a leader of people. Consequently, there tends to be a paucity of the necessary leadership behaviour at middle levels. This necessitates specially designed training and development interventions in which they are able to play the dual roles of superior and subordinate without creating cultural disharmony (Gupta & Panda, 2003, p. 378).

Future Research Agenda

Though leadership as a theme is researched extensively over time, there are a few aspects of leadership that should be taken up to have a comprehensive and holistic understanding of effective leadership in Indian context. First, not many studies have been undertaken to examine this aspect of family business in India We need to identify, understand and appreciate the uniqueness and peculiarities of family businesses in India. Moreover, business families from different communities conduct their businesses in their own ways. The Marwaris' way of doing business could be different from the way Parsis or Gujaratis do business. Gupta and Panda (2009) have urged scholars to understand the uniqueness of the way different business communities or conglomerates do their businesses. There could possibly be multiple business systems in India, based on region, community or family lineage to understand the way family-owned and managed organizations are led.

Secondly, though there is a general acknowledgement amongst scholars about the effectiveness of NTL in Indian context, we need to examine if NTL is still the effective leadership style, given the changing and evolving demographics. Is this leadership style effective in organizations where employees are mostly professionally qualified with a need for autonomy and less dependence prone? Leadership scholars need to empirically examine the efficacy of alternate leadership styles such as CSML and patronizing styles proposed by Kalra (2004) and Kalra and Gupta (1999), respectively. There is a need to examine the effectiveness of these leadership styles in new forms of organizations in IT, ITeS enabled entrepreneurial startups.

Thirdly, Khandelwal as the Chairman and Managing Director (CMD) of Bank of Baroda transformed the bank leveraging his "tough love" (Panda, 2020). Khandelwal believes that compassion, fairness and showing dignity to subordinates are key leadership attributes in Indian context (Panda, 2020). Leadership studies in India have not examined the efficacy of these three leadership attributes in Indian context, which should be examined from the perspective of positive organizational scholarship.

Fourthly, leadership development is rarely distinguished from leader development, though they are different. Leader development is about equipping an individual with desirable leadership behaviours, whereas leadership is about the process of achieving goal(s) by mobilizing resources including one's followers. Not much research has been conducted on how leaders exercise leadership. Without adequate understanding of the process of exercising leadership, leadership development programmes may not be effective. Academic scholars in collaboration with learning leaders from organizations needs to understand why leaders fail to exercise leadership, in spite of having requisite capabilities.

Fifthly, a sincere effort is called for to examine the efficacy of *sannyasin* and *karmayogin* leadership approach, which are found to be effective in religious and spiritual organizations, in formal business organizations. Sixthly, given the changes in corporate India, where many new forms of organizations co-existing with traditional entities, it is worthwhile to refine and redefine leadership scales suitable for Indian context or different forms of Indian organizations (IT-enabled startups, traditional family-owned and managed entities or Indian multinational corporations with global presence).

Finally, one should also understand why and when leaders fail to exercise leadership or get derailed? This could possibly third important theme of leadership research. Insights gained from such studies may help organizations arrest derailment of competent leaders through appropriate developmental interventions. Further, such insights would help organizations to tweaking leadership development interventions to proactively helping leaders to grow without getting derailed or plateaued.

References

Awasthy, R., & Gupta, R. (2011). Do non-work Practices in MNCs operating in India impact organizational commitment? *Organizations and Markets in Emerging Economies, 2*(4), 28–52.

Bhawuk, D. P. S. (2008). Toward an Indian Organizational psychology. In K. R. Rao, A. C. Paranjpe, & A. K. Dalal (Eds.), *Handbook of Indian psychology* (pp. 471–491). Cambridge University Press.

Bhawuk, D. P. S. (2011). *Spirituality and Indian psychology: Lessons from the Bhagavad-Gita*. Springer.

Bhawuk, D. P. S. (2019). *lokasaMgraha*: An indigenous construct of leadership and its measure. In S. Dhiman & A. D. Amar (Eds.), *Managing by the Bhagavad Gita: Timeless lessons for today's managers* (pp. 273-297). Springer.

Bhawuk, D. P. S., Mrazek, S., & Munusamy, V. P. (2009). From social engineering to Community transformation: Amul, Grameen Bank, and Mondragon as exemplar Organization. *Peace & Policy: Ethical Transformations for a Sustainable Future, 14*, 36–63.

Cappelli, P., Singh, H., Singh, Jitendra V., & Useem, M. (2010) *The India way: How India's top business leaders are revolutionizing management.* Harvard Business Press.

Cascio, W. O. (1974). Functional specialisation, culture and preference for participative management. *Personnel Psychology, 27*(4), 593–603.

Chakraborty, S. K. (1987). *Managerial effectiveness and quality of work life: Indian insights*. McGraw Hill.
Chhokar, J. (1998). Leadership and culture in India: The GLOBE Research Project. Accessed through https://pdfs.semanticscholar.org/a4b2/20d558 62c4e58692c71211692929a0ecb5ca.pdf?_ga=2.67368017.1179847869. 1593266091-1891295235.1581481378
Cohen, M. W., & Levinthal, D. A. (1990). Absorptive capacity: A new perspective on learning and innovation. *Administrative Science Quarterly, 38*, 128–152.
Day, D. V. (2010). The difficulties of learning form experience and need for deliberate practice. *Industrial and Organizational Psychology, 3*(1), 41–44.
Dayal, I. (1999). *Can organizations develop leaders: A study of effective leaders*. Mittal Publications.
Dayal, I. (2000). Leadership styles: Some implications for organizations in India. *Global Business Review, 1*(1), 67–74.
Dayal, I. (2007). Indianising Indian management: A framework. *Indian Journal of Industrial Relations, 43*(1), 87–99.
Gadgil, D. R. (1951, April). (with Staff of Gokhale Institute of Politics and Economics, Poona, India). Notes on the rise of the business communities in India. Mimeograph, International Secretariat, Institute of Pacific Relations, New York, NY.
Ganguli, H. C. (1964). *Structure and process of organisation*. Asia Publishing House.
Garg, P. K., & Parikh, I. J. (1995). *Young Managers at the cross roads: The Trishanku complex*. Sage.
Ghurye, G. S. (1961). *Caste, class and occupation,* popular book depot: Bombay.
Gupta, R. K. (1999). The truly familial organisation: Extending the organizational boundary to include employees' families. In H. S. R. Kao, D. Sinha, & Sek-Hong Ng (Eds.), *Management and cultural values* (pp 102–120). Sage.
Gupta, R. K., & Panda, A. (2003). Cultural imperatives in developing leaders, teams and organizations in Indian context. In A. K. Singh & D. Chauhan (Eds.), *Developing leaders* (pp. 371–388). Excel Books.
Gupta, R. K., & Panda, A. (2009). Culture, institutions and organization in India. In G. Misra (Ed.), *ICSSR survey of advances in research: Psychology in India, Volume II (Social and organizational processes)* (pp. 215–355). Pearson Education. ICSSR.
Gupta, V., Surie, G., Javidan, M., & Chhokar, J. (2002). South Asian cluster: Where the old meet the new. *Journal of World Business, 37*, 16–27.

Guptan, S. U. (1988). Paternalism in Indian organizations. *ASCI Journal of Management, 18*(1), 77–86.

Harris, F. (2014). *Jamsetji Nusserwanji Tata: A Chronicle of his life.* Rupa Publications.

Hazari, R. K. (1966). *The structure of the corporate private sector: A study of concentration, ownership and control*. Asia Publishing House.

Hou, W. C. (2010). Developing Asia's corporate leadership: Challenges and moving forward. In D. Ulrich (Ed.), *Leadership in Asia* (pp.40–52). McGraw Hill.

Kakar, S. (1971a). The theme of authority in social relations in India. *The Journal of Social Psychology, 84*(1), 93–101.

Kakar, S. (1971b). Authority patterns and subordinates behaviour in Indian organizations. *Administrative Science Quarterly, 16*, 298–307.

Kakar, S. (1972). Authority relations in Indian organizations. *Management International Review, 12*(1), 51–56.

Kakar, S. (1978). *The inner world: A psychoanalytic study of childhood and society in India.* Oxford University Press.

Kakar, S., Kets de Vries, M. F. R., Kakar, S., & Vrignaud, P. (2002). Leadership in Indian organizations from a comparative perspective. *International Journal of Cross Cultural Management, 2*(2), 239–250.

Karkaria, B. J. (2003). *Dare to dream: The life of M S Oberoi.* Portfolio Books.

Kalra, S. K. (1976). Caste and achievement values. *Indian Journal of Social Work, XXXVII*(1), 25–29.

Kalra, S. K. (1997). Human potential management: Time to move beyond the concept of human resource management? *Journal of European Industrial Training, 21*(5), 176–180.

Kalra, S. K. (1988). Reaction to authoritarian leadership: A projective study. *Indian Journal of Social Work, 39*(1), 27–43.

Kalra, S. K. (2004). Consultative managerial leadership style in India: A viable alternative. In C. Sengupta & P. N. Mukherji (Eds.), *Indigeneity and universality in social science: A South Asian response* (pp. 407–428). Sage.

Kalra, S. K., & Gupta, R. K. (1999). Some behavioural dimensions of effective managerial style in the Indian context. In H. S. R. Kao, D. Sinha, & B. Wilpert (Eds.), *Management and cultural values: The indigenization of organizations in Asia* (pp. 287–296). Sage.

Kassebanm, G., & Vidya Sagar, N. E. C. (1974). A survey of occupational mobility in small city in India. *Man in India, 54*(4), 253–270.

Khandwalla, P. N. (1988). Organizational effectiveness. In J. Pandey (Ed.), *Psychology in India: The state of art* (Vol. 3, pp. 97–216). Sage.

Lala, R. M. (1981). *The creation of wealth: The tatas from the 19th 5o 21st Century,* Penguin India
Lala, R. M. (1993). *Beyond the last blue mountain: A life of J R D Tata.* Penguin.
Lala, R. M. (1999). *The heart beat of a trust.* McGraw Hill.
Lala, R. M. (2003). *For the love of India: The life and times of Jamsetji Tata.* Penguin.
Lamb, H. B. (1956). Business organization and leadership in India Today. In *Economic development program India.* Centre for International Studies, MIT, Massachusetts.
Levi, S. C. (2016). *Caravans: Punjabi Khatri merchants on the Silk Road.* Portfolio Books.
Lewis, O. (1962). *Village life in Northern India.* Vintage Publishers.
McDonald, H. (1998). *The polyester prince: The rise of Dhirubhai Ambani.* HarperCollins.
McDonald, H. (2010). *Ambani and sons.* Roli Books
Meade, R. D. (1967). An experimental study of leadership in India. *Journal of Social Psychology, 72*, 35–43.
Meyers, C. A. (1960). *Industrial relations in India.* Asia Publishing House.
Nandy, A., & Kakar, S. (1980). Çulture and Personality. In U. Pareek (Ed.), *A survey of research in psychology- 1971–1976* (Part I, pp. 136–167). Popular Prakashan.
Panda, A. (2017). Experience-centric leadership development process: Challenges and way forward for organizations in India. *International Journal of Indian Culture and Business Management, 16*(1), 99–116.
Panda, A. (2019). Why do leadership development efforts fail in organisations in India and what can be done about it? *International Journal Indian Culture and Business Management, 18*(2), 184–217.
Panda, A. (2020). Interview with Dr Anil K. Khandelwal: Leading transformation of a public sector bank through people processes and building intangibles. *South Asian Journal of Human Resource Management, 7*(1), 135–143.
Pandey, J. (1981). Ingratiation as social behaviour. In J. Pandey (Ed.), *Perspectives on experimental psychology* (pp. 157–187). Concept.
Piramal, G. (1998). *Business legends.* Viking Penguin India.
Piramal, G. (2011). *Business Maharajas.* Portfolio Books.
Piramal, G. (2015). *Kamalnayan Bajaj: Architect of the Bajaj Group.* Kamalnayan Bajaj Charitable Trust Book, Pune.
Piramal, G., & Herdeck, M. L. (1986). *India's industrialists.* Lynne Rienner Publishers.

Piramal, G. (with Jennifer Netarwala). (2005). *Smart leadership: Insights for CEOs*. Portfolio.

Punekar, S. D., & Savur, M. G. (1969). *Management White Collar relations*. Popular Prakashan.

Raelin, J. A., & Coghlan, D. (2006). Developing managers as learners and researchers: Using action learning and action research. *Journal of Management Education, 30*(5), 670–689.

Ray, R. K. (1992). Entrepreneurship and industry in India: 1800–1947. Oxford University Press.

Rao, T. V., & Rao, R. (2014). *The power of 360° feedback: The India way for leadership effectiveness*. Sage.

Reddy, C. M., & Srinivasan, V. (2015). Dialogue on leadership development. *IIMB Management Review, 27*(1), 44–55.

Sahay, A., Kalra, S. K., & Gupta, R. K. (1994). A bibliography of managerial leadership in the Indian context: From 1985 to early 1992. *Indian Journal of Training and Development, 24*(2), 162–176.

Schön, D. (1983). *The reflective practitioner: How professionals think in action*. Basic Books.

Shah, S. (2018). *The Tata Group: From Torchbearers to Trailblazers*. Penguin Random House India Pvt. Ltd.

Shyamsunder, A., Anand, S., Punj, A., & Shatdal, A. (2011). Leadership development in organizations in India: The why and how of it (Part I and II). *Vikalpa, 36*(3–4): 61–132.

Singh, P., & Bhandarkar, A. (1990). *Corporate success and transformational leadership*. Wiley Eastern Limited.

Sinha, D. (1972). Industrial psychology. In S. K. Mitra (Ed.), *A survey of research in psychology* (pp. 175–237). Popular Prakashan.

Sinha, J. B. P. (1974). A case of reversal in participative management. *Indian Journal of Industrial Relations, 10*(2), 179–187.

Sinha, J. B. P. (1976). The authoritative leadership: A style of effective management. *Indian Journal of Industrial Relations., 11*, 381–389.

Sinha, J. B. P. (1980). *The nurturant task leader: A model of effective executive*. Concept.

Sinha, J. B. P. (1995). *The cultural context of leadership and power*. Sage.

Sinha, J. B. P. (1997). A cultural perspective on organizational behavior in India. In C. P. Earley & M. Erez (Eds.), *New perspectives on international industrial/organizational psychology* (pp. 53–74). New Lexington Press.

Sinha, D. (1999). Approaches to indigenous management. In H. S. R. Kao, D. Sinha, & B. Wilpert (Eds.), *Management and cultural values: The indigenization of organizations in Asia* (pp. 43–52). Sage.

Sinha, J. B. P. (2001). Evolving perspectives on Indian organizations and leadership. *Indian Journal of Industrial Relations, 36*(4), 428–443.

Sinha, J. B. P. (2004). *Multinationals in India.* Sage.

Sinha, J. B. P. (2010). Living and doing psychology. *Psychology and developing societies, 22*(1), 95–1F20.

Sinha, J. B. P. (2014). *Psychosocial analysis of Indian mindset*. Springer.

Sinha, J. B. P., & Sinha, M. (1974). Middle class values in organizational perspective. *Journal of Social and Economic Studies, 1*, 95–114.

Sinha, J. B. P. Singh., S., Gupta, P., Srivastava, K. B. L., Sinha, R. B. N., Srivastava, S., Ghosh, A., Siddiqui, R. N., Tripathi, N., Gupta, M., Srivastava, S., Mulla, Z., Vijayalaksmi, C., & Pandey, A. (2010). An exploration of Indian mindset. *Psychological Studiers, 55*, 3–17.

Sinha, J. B. P., Vohra, N., Singhal, S., Sinha, R. B. N., & Ushashree, S. (2002). Normative predictions of collectivist- individualist intentions and behaviour of Indians. *International Journal of Psychology,* 37(5), 309–319.

Sovani, N. V., Apte, D. P., Pendse, R. G., & Gadgil, D. R. Poona: A Re-survey: The changing pattern of employment and earnings. Gokhale Institute of Politics and Economics.

Spencer, S., Rajah, T., Narayan, S. A., Mohan, S., & Lahiri, G. (2007). *Indian CEO: A portrait of excellence*. Response Books.

Subramanian, L. (2016). *Three merchants of Bombay: Business pioneers of the nineteenth century*. Portfolio Books.

Thiagarajan, K. M., & Deep, S. D. (1970). A study of supervisor-subordinate influence and satisfaction in four cultures. *Journal of Social Psychology, 82*, 173–180.

Timberg, T. A. (1978). *The Marwaris*. Vikas.

Timberg, T. A. (2015). *The Marwaris: From Jagat Seth to the Birlas*. Penguin Books.

Todorova, G., & Durisin, B. (2007). Note: Absorptive capacity: Valuing a reconceptualization. *Academy of Management Review, 32*(3), 774–786.

Tripathi, D. (1981). *The dynamics of tradition: Kasturbhai Lalbhai and his entrepreneurship*. Manohar.

Tripathi, D. (1984). *Business communities of India: A historical perspective*. Manohar.

Tripathi, D. (1987). *State and business in India: A historical perspective*. Manohar.

Tripathi, D. (1991). *Business and politics in India: A Historical Perspective*. Manohar.
Tripathi, D. (2004). *The Oxford History of Indian businesses*. Oxford University Press.
Tripathi, D., & Jumani, J. (2006). *The concise Oxford history of Indian business*. Oxford University Press.
Tripathi, D., & Jumani, J. (2013). *The Oxford history of contemporary Indian business*. Oxford University Press.
Tripathi, D., & Mehta, M. (1990). *Business houses of Western India: A study of entrepreneurial response, 1850–1956*. Manohar.
Virmani, B. R., & Guptan, S. V. (1991). *Indian management*. Vision.
Wilson, M. S. (2010). *Developing tomorrow's leaders today: Insights from Corporate India* (Times Group Book). Wiley India.

9

Unique Features of Indian Economic and Business System

Juili Ballal and Varadraj Bapat

Introduction

India is a nation with a long history of cultural, social, business and economic development. Till 1700, it was a major contributor to the world GDP. Share of the India's contribution to the world GDP declined along with colonization in nineteenth and twentieth centuries (Maddison, 2003). Gradually, after independence in 1947, the Indian economy gathered itself and now has been growing at for more than a quarter century, which makes it one of the fastest growing economies in the world (Singh & Pathak, 2019). Reserve Bank of India notes that the

J. Ballal · V. Bapat (✉)
Indian Institute of Technology Bombay, Mumbai, India
e-mail: varadraj@som.iitb.ac.in

J. Ballal
e-mail: Juili.ballal@som.iitb.ac.in

© The Author(s), under exclusive license to Springer Nature Switzerland AG 2022
A. Pandey et al. (eds.), *Indigenous Indian Management*, Palgrave Studies in Indian Management,
https://doi.org/10.1007/978-3-030-87906-8_9

Indian economy rebounded strongly in 2010–2011 from the moderation induced by the global economic crisis. A report of the Asian Development Bank (2018) predicts that India will continue to be the world's fastest growing major economy.[1] Indian businesses have also gained worldwide recognition, an evidence of which is, out of the 100 local companies identified by the Boston Consulting Group as the new global challengers from 20 rapidly developing economies, there were 16 Indian companies ("Engines of emerging markets", 2016).[2] Amid the COVID-19 induced global crisis, India is expected to successfully come out of the economic distress caused by the pandemic, as it has a high percentage of working population and middle-class households.

This chapter is written with the objective to describe Indian economic thoughts and their impact on business. The chapter comprises of six sections. In the following section, we elicit a brief historical account of Indian economy. In section three, we discuss the unique features of Indian business and economic system arising out of socio-cultural characteristics of India. In section four, we summarize the ancient Indian economic thoughts and posit the core economic ideas of some of the most influential leaders of modern India. In section five, we discuss the findings, and in the last section, we conclude the chapter and present the scope of future research.

Indian Economy and Business: Historical Perspective

Historical records show that India was a strong economy since ancient times. Travelogues by several foreign visitors have documented ancient and medieval India as prosperous nation. For instance, Ctesias, a Greek physician (400 BC); Megasthenes, an ambassador of Seleucus I Nicator of the Seleucid dynasty to Chandragupta Maurya in Pataliputra (302

---

[1] PTI (2018) 'Ahead of China, India to Remain Fastest Growing Economy in FY19 and FY20: ADB' *TheEconomic Times*: https://economictimes.indiatimes.com/news/economy/finance/india-fastest-growing-economy-in-asia-on-track-to-meet-fy18-target-adb/articleshow/65049353.cms.

[2] The Boston Consulting Group, 'Global Leaders, Challengers, and Champions: The Engines of Emerging Markets', BCG Report, The Boston Consulting Group Inc., June 2016.

BCE–298 BCE); Faxian, a Buddhist monk who travelled from China to India from 399 to 412 AD; and Marco Polo, who was one of the earliest European travellers to India in medieval times have all described India as the most prosperous among the countries in the world that they had seen.

There was considerable trading and manufacturing activity in goods like cotton and silk clothes, spices and artwork. The trades were regulated by the chiefs or syndics of municipal and industrial organization of the cities. The industrial centres were connected by roads which facilitated traffic. Early in India the external and internal commerce had assumed high importance and found mention in the Buddha Jataka a league of caravan leaders. Buddhist literature testifies that the ancient systems of simple barter as well as of reckoning value of cows or rice measures had for the most part been replaced by the use of metal currency, was well understood and generally accepted exchange value. Basic banking was available. There was no taboo on loaning of money and according to Gautama interest was sought in six different ways. Indian goods were exported by both land and sea route to different countries (Ambedkar, 1915b). India had a strong maritime trade tradition. Apart from the trade and business, the ancient India is known to be the pioneer of introducing the 'corporate form' or organization known as srenis from around 800 B.C. well before the earliest Roman proto-corporations. Also, the historical development of the sreni indicates that the factors leading to its growth are consistent with those put forward for the growth of organizational entities in Europe (Vikramaditya, 2013). Awasthi gives a detailed account of historical development of businesses and business organization in India in the chapter thirteen of this book.

India was the dominant economic force until 1760 (Kennedy, 1989). India alone was contributing almost one-third of the Global GDP in 0CE. The vital sector that contributed to the growth of Indian economy was agriculture while industry, education and science were the other critical sectors. China and India combined used to produce nearly half of the world's economic output in 1820 compared to just 1.8% for the USA (Milken, 2006). In addition, India had a 25% share of the global trade in textiles in the early eighteenth century and it had a higher GDP per capita than Europe in 1750 (Bairoch, 1995).

Table 9.1 Share of world GDP from year 0 to 1998

Year	0	1000	1500	1600	1700	1820	1870	1913	1950	1973	1998
W. Eur	10.8	8.7	17.9	19.9	22.5	23.6	33.6	33.5	26.3	25.7	20.6
USA	0	0	0.3	0.2	0.1	1.8	8.9	19.1	27.3	22.0	21.9
China	26.2	22.7	25.0	29.2	22.3	32.9	17.2	8.9	4.5	4.6	11.5
India	**32.9**	**28.9**	**24.5**	**22.6**	**24.4**	**16.0**	**12.2**	**7.6**	**4.2**	**3.1**	**5.0**
World	100	100	100	100	100	100	100	100	100	100	100

Source Table-B-20 Appendix B; pp263; The world economy: A millennial Perspective—Angus Maddison OECD Development Centre Studies—2007

Sunderland (1932) had underlined the prosperity of India at the time of the arrival of the British in the following words: 'This wealth was created by the Hindus' vast and varied industries...India was a far greater industrial and manufacturing nation than any in Europe or than any other in Asia...Such was the India which the British found when they came'. The share of GDP of different countries and regions of the world is shown in Table 9.1. From the table, it can be observed that India's contribution to GDP saw a steep decline after the arrival of the British. By 1765, the company's influence had grown to such an extent that the British were effectively controlling most parts of the country (Bayly & Bayly, 1987). Theory of Drain of Wealth (Naoroji, 1867) unravelled the extraction of wealth from the Indian soil by the British. This collapse of Indian industry during the colonial period drove people back to the farms (Gurumurthy, 2013). Naoroji (1901) proved that internal factors were not the reasons of poverty in India but it was caused by the colonial rule (Raychaudhuri, 1966).

Unique Features of Indian Economic and Business System

Although the forces of globalization and technological changes have impacted economic and business systems, the Indian economy and business continue to exhibit some unique features which have been listed and elaborated in this section.

Family System

India has had a strong family-based culture since time immemorial (Merchant et al., 2017). The Indian society is family based and it is the families that drive the economy of India (Kanagasabapathi, 2013). The Indian family is considered strong, stable, close, resilient and enduring (Mullatti, 1995; Shangle, 1995). Indians are collectivist and people tend to prioritize their family interests over individual interests (Chadda & Deb, 2013). The joint family system or an extended family has been one of the important features of Indian culture and an institution by itself (Naidu, 2014). One of the main advantages of a family system is the strong bonding among siblings and other members, providing a sense of security to all. The bonding and bonhomie one finds in close-knit joint families have a positive impact on the emotional quotient of children (Naidu, 2014). Families have their share of conflict situations, quarrels and misunderstandings. Nonetheless, family values play an important role in shaping the outlook of people. For example, respect and care for elders and nurturance of the younger are among the central principles in Indian family system. Festivals play an important role in preserving and promoting these values.[3]

Arthashastra, an ancient Indian Sanskrit treatise on statecraft, economic policy and military strategy written by Kautilya, notes that the Dharma (duty) of the head of the family is to sacrifice his own pleasures for the sake of the family members. According to Kautilya, 'Every man has an obligation to maintain his wife, children, parents, minor brothers and dependent (unmarried or widowed) sisters. No man shall renounce the life of a householder in order to become an ascetic without providing for the maintenance of his wife and children (2.1)' (Rangarajan, 1992). It is the general norm in the Indian families that parents make sacrifice for children and later, when the children grow up, they take care of their elders (Kanagasabapathi, 2013). For instance, in India, most parents fund their child's education and 89% of the Indian parents are willing to 'make sacrifices' for their children's education (HSBC, 2017).

[3] http://www.businessworld.in/article/Indian-festivals-promote-family-values-Vice-President-/03-08-2020-304530/.

One of the biggest financial commitments of parents is paying for their child's education. Indian parents prioritize their children needs over their own needs. Many times they sacrifice their current pleasures and also post-retirement security in the process. In addition to this, almost 32% of the parents work extra hours in their existing job and over 27% contribute less to their own long-term savings or investments or have done so in the past. 59% Indians fund their child's education from day-to-day incomes, 48% get the money from general savings, investments or insurance, and almost 30% get the money through a specific education savings or investment plan.

The family members tend to restrain their consumption and save money for the future of the family. This could be one of the reasons for high personal savings rate in India. Families take care of children, elders, unemployed, sick and disabled. This reduces burden on society and the government. The social security burden in India on government is much lower as compared to that in developed countries.

Family Business

The joint family system has been the backbone of family businesses which provide the required resources and capital for the cohesion and growth of the firms (Basuthakur, 2020). Family business is the leading and the most prevalent type of entity in the world (Sharma et al., 2012). Family firms contribute to two-thirds of all businesses across the globe, generate around 70–90% of annual global GDP and create 50–80% of jobs in the majority of countries worldwide (Family Firm Institute, 2017). In India, more than 85% of businesses being recognized as family enterprises (Ramchandran & Bhatnagar, 2012). Family businesses contribute to two-third of India's GDP, 79% of organized private sector employment and 27% of overall employment (KPMG, 2013). A culture of family business can thrive typically when the families are close knit and the family members share a strong bond with each other. When it comes to the next gen, 73% of family businesses in India (compared to 65% globally) have them working in the business and 60% (compared to 57% globally) plan to pass on management and/or ownership to the next gen (PwC, 2019).

India has one of the highest numbers of family-owned businesses in the world. The country, with its emphasis on relationships and family bonds, enjoys obvious benefits. If there's any culture that is as rich in tradition as Indian business, families are blessed to have a culture that is effective at promoting family coherence.[4]

In a family business, family members working in the business are likely to share the same set of values, beliefs and ethos, and develop common values (Carlock & Ward, 2010). A family member working in his/her family business is more likely to put in extra hours of work, compared to other organization showing a strong commitment to the organization. Family members are likely to be willing to wear different hats and to take on the work outside of their formal job description in order to ensure the success of the company presenting flexibility in job classification (Birol, 2013). Since family members work to build the business for future generations, they support long-term thinking for growth and success. The founder typically tends to be a leader for a long term and provides stability unless a life event such as illness, retirement or death results in change. There is usually longevity in leadership, which results in overall stability within the organization. Passing of contacts and technology may be smooth in family business. Family members may be more willing to make financial sacrifices for the sake of the business decreasing the cost of operation. For example, they may accept lower pay than they would get elsewhere to help the business in the longer term, or deferring wages during a cash flow crisis. The potential successors are exposed to in-house training which enables them to join the family business with ease as they have already received the required training from the incumbents (Duh, 2014).

[4] https://littleindia.com/indian-business-families-blessed-culture-promotes-coherence-mitzi-perdue/.

Community Orientation and Social Capital

It is the families and communities that constitute the society in India. It is the family set-up that provides the foundation for what the economists now call as 'social capital'. The social capital provides a strong base to the economic development, apart from maintaining peace and order in the society. In addition to the families and communities, the role of varna or caste system is very important in the Indian economic and business system. India's varna system is based on profession. The four main varnas are brahmins, the class of people traditionally engaged in knowledge generation and dissemination; kshatriya, the class of the people traditionally engaged in armed forces, police and political leaders; vaishyasa, the people engaged in agriculture and entrepreneurial activities; and shudras are the people engaged in working with tools for the production activities.

Some of the modern experts believe that the varna or caste-based community system in India helped in the development of the economic and business systems (Merchant et al., 2017). The jati or community or caste plays a major role in entrepreneurship and also facilitates the upward mobility of the whole caste rather than individual. Thousands of caste-based economic clusters are spread across India, providing millions of jobs and creating wealth. Traditional business communities like Marwaris, Sindhis, Patels, Bohras and Kutchis have been extremely successful in forming global business networks. Importantly, such economic clusters are usually self-financed. They maintain a fine balance between cooperation and competition (Vaidyanathan, 2012). In addition, caste familiarity generates trust, and the caste itself turns into an open-air business school of self-learning for entrepreneurs, teaching them to build businesses (Gurumurthy, 2013).

In the nineteenth century, British colonialists used to blame the caste system for everything wrong in India (Das, 2002). It is better to understand the impact of varna on competitiveness rather than morally judging it. Being endowed with commercial skills is a source of advantage in the global economy. For instance, Bania traders possess financial resources and financial acumen and more importantly know how to accumulate and manage capital.

Due to historical reasons, different castes were and even today to a large extent are concentrated in different regions and places. People belonging to different castes share certain social relationships with each other. These social relationships, however small they may be, result in trust and create social capital which is a very important asset for an economy (Kanagasabapathi, 2013). Additionally, the community orientation creates trust among the members of the society (Durkheim, 1893). Trust has some economic value, and Fukuyama (1995) noted that the ability to associate depends on the degree to which communities share norms and values and are able to subordinate individual interests to those of larger groups.

Social capital refers to the quality of human relations within some well-defined social group that enables members of the group to act in cooperation with one another for achieving mutual benefits (Krishna, 2004). Caste is viewed as a form of social capital, and the use of caste-based networks is supported for attaining positive outcomes in entrepreneurship (Alha, 2018). Caste plays a positive role in building social capital in the society (Vaidyanathan, 2012).

Self-Employment and Entrepreneurial Orientation

Self-employment and entrepreneurial orientation is another feature of Indian economic and financial system. The concept of self-employment is popular in India, which is evident from the statistics provided by the International Labour Organization (ILO) in 2018. In Fig. 9.1, the self-employment rate as a percentage of total employment is given for the top 10 economies (in terms of GDP) of the world.

India scores the highest in terms of self-employment as a percentage of total employment in comparison with comparable economies (see Fig. 9.1). The self-employment rate in India as of 2018 is 78.3%. Next to India is China with a self-employment rate of 46.9%. In other words, Indian economy can be called as proprietorship economy (Vaidyanathan, 2012).

In India, entrepreneurial activities take place even in low socio-economic neighbourhood. For instance, there is an area named Dharavi

Fig. 9.1 Self-employment rate as a percentage of total employment in world, 2018 (*Source* International Labour Organization, ILOSTAT database. Data retrieved in September 2019)

in Mumbai. Dharavi is known to the outside world as the largest slum in India (Iyer et al., 2009). The locality is dominated by a population of ex- 'untouchables', conventionally stigmatized by poverty and low status (Saglio-Yatzimirsky, 2013). Despite being populated by poor people, it is not just a locality of labourers, it is a locality of small entrepreneurs. It presents a fascinating paradox: the convergence of stereotypes associated with the slum—poverty and misery—and an effervescent economic vitality, impelled by globalization and international capital flows. The annual turnover from Dharavi's myriad enterprises is anywhere between Rs 1500 crore and Rs. 3500 crore (around $2 billion–$5 billion). According to official sources, there are 4902 industrial units in Dharavi, of which textiles form 1,036, pottery 932, leather 567, plastic processing 478 and Jari stitching 498 (Menon, 2004).

The non-corporate sector has the largest share in India's national income, manufacturing activities, services, savings, investments, both direct and indirect taxes, credit market, employment and foreign exchange earnings (Vaidyanathan, 2004). Thus, the widespread dominance of non-corporate sector cannot be ignored. It is interesting to note that the entities in the non-corporate sector are not listed in any of the stock exchanges; they are not even companies. They are mostly proprietorship and partnership firms. But it is they who dominate the fastest growing activities of the Indian economy.

They are organized or unorganized, depending upon regulations/reporting, etc. They may have a regular labour force or an informal type (of workforce), depending on the size. This non-corporate segment accounts for around 40% of national income (Vaidyanathan, 2014). Indian value system encourages one to be self-employed and supports decentralized economy consisting of small businesses. Small businesses empower people and avoid concentration of wealth in few hands (Gandhi, 1909; Schumacher, 1974).

Pre-eminence of Informal Sources of Financing

Though there are different formal sources of financing operational in India, informal financing continues to be a major source. Informal sources of finance refer to seeking financial help from family, friends, community, moneylenders, and rotating savings and credit associations (Shankar, 2019).

Out of the total financing that is available to MSMEs (micro, small and medium enterprises), only 22% comes through formal sources of finance like banks and other financial institutions, with the balance coming from self-finance or informal finance (Shankar, 2019). Caste/community plays a major role in promoting, organizing, financing, marketing and financing of business organizations (Vaidyanathan, 2012).

There are many community organizations which provide financing to the entrepreneurs especially budding youngsters from the community. Members of the community pool resources to finance businesses from the community. For instance, JITO (Jain International Trade Organization), a unique multi-stakeholder community of Jain industrialists, businessmen and professionals, provides a stable platform to young entrepreneurs by facilitating them with right business contacts and capital, as and when required. JITO is a worldwide organization of businessmen, industrialists, knowledge workers and professionals reflecting the glory of ethical business practices. It is a global organization present across 11 countries and has around 14,000 members. Its vision and mission mainly focus on economic empowerment (Aarthik Sudradhata), knowledge (Shiksha) and service (Seva) and the community and the society at large. JITO is registered as a company under section 25 of the Companies Act, 1956 (now under section 8 of the Companies Act, 2013).[5]

Chit funds are indigenous financial institutions in India that combines credit and savings in a single scheme. In a chit fund scheme, a group of individuals come together for a predetermined time period and contribute to a common pool at regular intervals (Kapoor et al., 2011). There are chits that involve savings of Rs. 100 every month to Rs. 1,00,000 and more. In certain areas where chit funds are popular, when people need funds to promote a venture, they mobilize their relatives and friends and organize a chit so that it would help them with the funds (Kanagasabapathi, 2013). Chit fund is a popular financing mechanism in Indian states like Tamil Nadu, Kerala, Andhra Pradesh and Karnataka. Community funding and chit fund mechanism are not only indigenous but also relationship-based and state-independent. In all these cases, it is the society that comes out with initiatives like these, based on their conveniences and needs (Kanagasabapathi, 2013).

Cooperative credit society is another financing source for small sector. A cooperative credit society is defined as a cooperative society, 'the primary objective of which is to provide financial accommodation to its members and includes a cooperative land mortgage bank' (RBI, 1999). A cooperative is an autonomous association of persons united voluntarily to meet their common economic, social and cultural needs and aspirations through a jointly-owned and democratically-controlled enterprise. Ranging from small-scale to multi-million dollar businesses across the globe, cooperatives employ more than 100 million women and men and have more than 800 million individual members. Self-help, self-responsibility, democracy, equality, equity and solidarity are core espoused values of any cooperatives. Cooperatives are often floated

[5] https://jito.org/.

by communities or social groups for helping each other and are popular in India.

Microfinance is another source of informal financing. It is an economic development tool whose objective is to assist the poor to work their way out of poverty. It covers a range of services such as savings, insurance, money transfers and counselling in addition to the provision of credit.[6] Microfinance is being seen as a practical instrument to achieve the holy-trinity of outreach, impact and sustainability (Fischer & Sriram, 2002). Since 1970s, microfinance, that is, extension of small amounts of collateral-free institutional loans to jointly liable poor group members for their self-employment and income-generation, has become a major tool of promoting inclusive growth and sustainable development (Yunus, 1998). To support the microfinancing activity, in 2015, Indian government introduced MUDRA (Micro Units Development and Refinance Agency) bank that offered loans at low rate to microfinance institutions which then provided credit to MSMEs. MUDRA bank is an innovation meant for 'funding the unfunded' and 'banking the un-banked'. Provision of institutional finance to such micro and small business units and enterprises will not only help in improving the quality of life of these entrepreneurs, but also turn them into strong instruments of growth and employment generation (Kaur, 2016). The idea of cooperative economic activity to achieve beneficial social goals is valued in societal culture of India. Hindu teaching is also realistic about the need for interest rates to compensate for business risks and transaction costs, and emphasizes the importance of the repayment of debts. It is therefore no surprise that the Indian microcredit sector has grown rapidly in recent years (Ashta & Hannam, 2014).

National Bank for Agriculture and Rural Development (NABARD) introduced the idea of mobilizing small, cohesive and participatory groups, known as self-help groups (SHGs) (Fernandez, 2007), a channel of microfinance. A self-help group is a financial intermediary committee usually composed of 10–20 local women or men. Most of the SHGs are formed for the purpose of better financial security among its members. SHGs can exist with or without registration. SHGs in India often work

[6] The definition of Microfinance is given by the Reserve Bank of India.

in association with banks (SHG—Bank Linkage Programme). SHGs strive to integrate the microfinance services into broader strategy to decrease poverty (Fisher & Sriram, 2002) and contribute to an increased income of poor through collective performance. What started as a pilot to link around 500 SHGs of poor to the formal financial institutions during the year 1992–1993 has now become the largest microfinance programme in the world, in terms of the client base and outreach. The SHGs, which follow 'Panchsutras', i.e. five key points, conduct of regular group meetings, regular savings within the group, internal lending based on the demand of members, timely repayment of loan and maintenance of proper books of accounts, are considered to be of good quality and over years have proved themselves to be good customers of banks.

The Non-Government Sector (NGO) has played a prominent role of working as a Self Help Group Promoting Institution (SHPI) by organizing, nurturing and enabling credit linkage of SHGs with banks. NABARD later co-opted many others as SHPIs including the rural financial institutions (RRBs, DCCBs, PACS), Farmers' Clubs (FCs), SHG Federations, Individual Rural Volunteers (IRVs), etc. These stakeholders were encouraged to take up promotion of SHGs by way of promotional grant assistance from NABARD. This savings led microfinance model has now become the largest coordinated financial inclusion programme in the world covering almost 100 million households in the country. With more than 84% of the groups being exclusively women groups, the programme has provided the much needed push to empowerment of women in the country.[7]

The SHG-bank linkage programme has proved to be cost-effective for banks as group loans lower the operational costs and delinquency rates. This programme has been considered to be the world's largest and fastest growing microfinance programme that goes beyond mere financial services provision to encompass wider goals of securing livelihoods, reviving local economies and empowering women through trainings, confidence building and leadership development (Fischer & Sriram, 2002; Seibel, 2005). As on March 2018, there were 8.74 million SHGs, of which 58% were credit-linked and 90% were all women groups

[7] https://www.nabard.org/contentsearch.aspx?AID=225&Key=shg+bank+linkage+programme.

(NABARD, 2018). Around 100 million people are involved in SHGs in India that have an aggregate bank balance of Rs. 65 billion. An extensive use of various informal community-driven financing is very much in tune with Indian ethos.

High Savings Society

The Indian society avoids unnecessary consumption and is savings oriented. It is a part of Indian culture and a way of life, for both rich and poor. The father saves for the family and many a times the mother saves without the other family members even knowing about it, in small sums. Spending more than what is necessary is considered a sin in the traditional Indian system.

Indian citizens tend to save more, primarily due to their family orientation. The saving in India is sometimes called as dynastic savings as people save not only for themselves but also for the next generations.[8]

Indian culture teaches avoidance of indulgence and control over desires and impulses. As per survey by Hofstede Insights, India receives a low score of 26 in indulgence, meaning that it is a culture of Restraint.[9] Indian thinkers right from Vedic times have advocated simple living and avoidance of excessive consumption. Gandhi recommended a frugal lifestyle to be followed by poor and rich (Gandhi, 1909).

Juxtaposing the gross domestic savings as a percentage of GDP of India, Brazil, Pakistan and USA between the period 1990 and 2020 (refer Fig. 9.2), it can be observed that the savings rate in India has been consistently higher than the aforementioned countries over the 30-year time span. It is worth noting that high saving rate in India is despite a very low per capita income. The data of USA is just used as a proxy representing the Western part of the world, Brazil as a proxy for an emerging economy and Pakistan as a proxy for an South Asian country. It is worth noting that high savings rate is maintained despite low per capita income in India.

[8] CEIC data; www.ceicdata.com.

[9] https://www.hofstede-insights.com/country/india/.

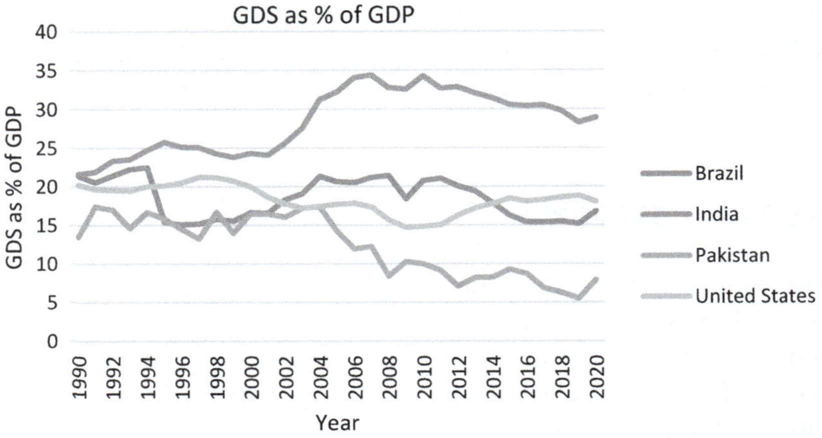

Fig. 9.2 Gross Domestic savings as a percentage of GDP of India, Brazil, Pakistan and USA (1990–2020) (*Source* World Bank)

Passion for Gold

Considering the high savings and strong family structure, the Indian economy is indeed feminine in its soul (Gurumurthy, 2015). India is one of the largest buyers of gold in the world. Gold is considered not just an investment in India; it is also treated as insurance and a social security for the large majority of people (Kanagasabapathi, 2013). The investment is done in gold mainly for cultural reasons. Table 9.2 shows the trend of gold consumption for India, China and USA. These three countries are compared since they are among the top global economies as well as the highest gold consumers in the world.

Table 9.2 Consumption of Gold in metric tons (2005–2020)

Country	2005	2008	2011	2014	2017	2020
India	722	713	933	843	650	850
China	293	432	811	813	1089	910
USA	377	267	195	179	170	190

Source World Gold Council, Bullion By Post

Gold demand in India is principally met through imports. The import of gold was a major cause for the country's trade deficit. To curb imports, the government changed India's gold import policy. This was done by introducing a higher import duty and allowing import only via nominated agencies which were notified by the Reserve Bank of India and the Directorate General of Foreign Trade. With respect to long-term investment in gold, majority of the times it has given stable return. Unlike investment in properties, even small amounts can be invested in gold making it a preferred choice in rural India.

It is also known that gold is considered to be a part of social security for most Indians and is close to their heart culturally. Most of the people in the country aspire to keep a certain part of their savings in gold. It is an essential part of most religious ceremonies and weddings in the family. As gifting gold is the core of marriage rituals, weddings are estimated to generate nearly 50% demand for the precious metal.

Remittances from Abroad

Another distinguishing factor of Indian economy is the remittances. Remittances are money transfers from people employed outside the country to family, friends or relatives residing in their own country.

One of the reasons for high remittances coming to India from Indian diaspora is the prevalence of strong family ties and family bond. Peter (2010) observed that migrants remit primarily to promote familial belonging. The migrants express their family membership through remittances that are considered to be disposable social goods. As a result, their socio-cultural values proliferate as the attached social, cognitive and affective meanings to the recipients of the remittances increase (MacKinnon & Langford, 1994) (Table 9.3).

India is the world's leading receiver of remittances, claiming more than 12% of the world's remittances in 2015.[10] Remittances to India stood at US$ 68.97 billion in 2017 and remittances from India to other countries accounted for US$ 5.71 billion, for a net inflow of US$ 63.26 billion in

[10] https://www.worldbank.org/en/news/press-release/2015/12/18/international-migrants-and-remittances-continue-to-grow-as-people-search-for-better-opportunities-new-report-finds.

Table 9.3 Top five recipient countries of foreign remittances (in billions of US dollars)

Country	2008	2011	2014	2017	2020
India	50	64	71	69	83
China	23	40	61	64	60
Philippines	26	24	28	31	35
Mexico	19	23	25	33	43
Nigeria	19	21	21	22	17

Source Migration and Development Brief 29
Data source https://www.migrationdataportal.org/themes/remittances and https://www.vanguardngr.com/2021/05/nigeriasdiaspora-remittances-fall-27-7-in-2020-world-bank/

2017.[11] As per the Ministry of Overseas Indian Affairs (MOIA), remittance is received from approximately 35 million members of the Indian diaspora far ahead of the China (23 billion $) placed second in the list.

Ancient and Contemporary Indian Economic Thoughts

The ancient Indian writings capture the economic thoughts and wisdom. The genesis of Indian ancient economic thoughts is since the Vedic age, which dates back to at least 8000 BCE (Kak, 1987). Upanishads, which are the earliest philosophical texts of human civilization extracted from Vedas (Gewali, 2013), also discuss economics.

Ancient Indian economic theory is different from modern economic theory in the sense that modern economic theory focuses on pursuit of material progress alone whereas ancient economic theory is based on fourfold life objectives—Dharma, Artha, Kama and Moksha. These aspects are explained by Pandey in Chapter 2 of this book.

[11] https://www.pewresearch.org/global/interactives/remittance-flows-by-country/.

Indian Economic Thoughts and Practices

The importance of money in Hindu Dharma is reinforced by the place assigned to Lakshmi, the Goddess of Wealth. Hindu Dharma also recognizes the mercurial nature of money and the need for Lakshmi to move: she should therefore not be hoarded but passed on (Ashta & Hannam, 2014). Hindu economic philosophy is characterized by the principles of hard and honest work to create wealth (Nadkarni, 2012), respect for wealth and wealth creators (*Lakshmi pooja*), earning wealth through ethical means (*shubhlabh*) (Garg & Saluja, 2017), restrained consumption, giving back to society. The first verse of Ishopnishad captures these ideals in the following words: (तेनत्यक्तेनभुञ्जीथामागृधःकस्यस्विद्धनम् *tenatyaktenabhunjitha; ma gridhahkasyasviddhanam).* Meaning, wealth, may be enjoyed after making sacrifice, and one should not steal others' wealth. The Hindu business philosophy values the satisfaction from the work and not from the rewards of work (*karma yoga*). Well-being for all (*sarvebhavantusukhinah)* is essence of most of the Vedic prayers.

Rig Veda, which has 1028 hymns, 10,600 verses, in 10 books, is the world's oldest religious text in continuous use till date (Klostermaier, 2006). There are many hymns which relate to matters on material prosperity, prices, bargaining and taxes. Hymn 112 of Book IX of the Rig Veda explains how one can follow his/her desires. It says, 'We all have diverse hopes and plans. We strive for wealth in different ways' (Griffiths, 1886).

Panchatantra by Vishnu Sharma written at around 200 BCE also drives home importance of money motive through his stories of the wise conduct. According to Kautilya, acquisition of material wealth is supreme, for the other things are dependent on it. In Kurals, wealth in the hands of great wise men is compared to the lake filled with good drinking water (Thiruvalluvar, 1990). According to Valluvar, wealth leads us to the joys of this world. Valluvar has devoted a complete chapter with ten couplets on wealth which suggests that wealth makes people important and wealth acquired with proper means will yield virtues and happiness. Kalidas, a Sanskrit playwright in fifth century CE, commented about the taxation system in one of the Sanskrit plays,

Raghuvansham (Rao, 2010), in Chapter 1.18: 'The state collects tax for the greater welfare of its citizens in the same way as the sun evaporates water, only to return it manifold in the form of rain'.

Basham and Rizvi (1956) noted that the ancient Indian business functioned on higher ideals. Even when making money was one of the most important objectives in the ancient India, the Indian society emphasized on higher principles in business and creating wealth. Indian writers have always integrated ethics with economics. Earning through unethical means is shunned. It emphasizes that one must not appropriate others' wealth (Bokare, 2009).

Access to borrowed funds is an important component of market facilitation. In the Indian tradition, debt (Rna) as well as its repayment has often been mentioned in Rig Veda but whether or not interest was charged is not clear (Keith & MacDonnell, 1912). However, circa 700 BCE, Panini, the grammarian, had laid down rules and symbols for expressing interest in percent terms (Datta, 1927). In fact, even the daily and compound interest was thought through. A grammarian would only systematize what is in vogue in society. Hence, expressing interest as a percent of debt must have been known to Indians prior to 700 BCE. This notion of expressing interest as a 'percent' originated in India and the Dharmashastras written after Panini's grammar confirm that money lending and charging interest was a legitimate occupation (Jain, 1929).

In the Vedic Civilization, there are evidences of financial system of states as well as borrowing and lending activities (Chugh, 2005). It is in the Rigveda that moneylenders lent money on interest. He who did not return debt had to serve moneylender for prescribed period of time (Mann, 2002). Belief goes that transition from money lending to banking occurred even before Manu, the shlokas or hymns of Manusmriti proves that in ancient India, banking and lending activities were not only performed but also there were specific rules regarding return of money, pledging and other related activities (Müller, 1886).

Regarding Pledge, the Manusmriti recommends that the pledgee should not use the pledger's goods. 'If pledgee uses them, then pledgee should not charge interest or should pay back the price of the goods to the pledger; otherwise, pledgee will be called thief of pledge and will be prosecuted as thief'. Rules regarding guarantee say that the person who guarantee to lender or court for physically presentation of borrower, but when borrower is not coming then it is the duty of guarantor to pay the whole debt of borrower. A lending contract with drunkard, lunatic, very sick/old persons, mentally depressed persons, minor is treated as void (Kumar, 1995). Manusmriti also speaks of judicial proceedings in which credit investments were called for, interest of loans on bankers, usurers and even of the renewal of commercial papers. Even with regard to safety of deposits, Manu has made suggestions. The bankers in this period performed many functions that a modern banker performs these days.

Further, in Indian scriptures, *daan* or donation or charity has very important place in individual and social economic life. The importance of daan has been repeatedly emphasized in *Ved*, *Upanishad*, *Puran*, *Smriti*, as also other scriptures including Buddha, Jain and Sikh traditions (Agarwal, 2010). *Matsya Puran* devotes a chapter in praise of *daanas* (Ved Vyas, 2004). Generous *daan* can help a person win both the worlds—there is no one who is beyond the influence of *daan*. A generous donor is praised by all. Even persons who do not accept *daan* themselves start acting favourably towards a generous donor. Daan made in one place has the capacity to influence people in other places as well. According to Bhartrihari (fifth century CE), the hands of the worthy look better when adorned by *daan*, and not just by gold bracelets (Gopinath, 2002). According to Bhagwad Maha Purana, a man should divide his income into five parts: (1) dharma-oriented deeds, (2) contingency situations, (3) flourishment of business, (4) livelihood and (5) well-being of his family and relatives (Garg & Saluja, 2017). *Ramcharitmanas* compares *daan* with an axe in the battle of life. As you slay enemies with a battle axe, so you slay sins and hardships with *daan* (Sharan, 2001).

Important forms of dana included godāna (donation of a cow), bhudāna(भूदान) (donation of land) and vidyādāna or jñānadāna (विद्यादान, ज्ञानदान): sharing knowledge and teaching skills; aushadhādāna (औषधदान): charity of care for the sick and diseased; abhayadāna (अभयदान): giving freedom from fear (asylum, protection to someone facing imminent injury); and anna dāna (अन्नादान): giving food to the poor, needy and all visitors (Dubois, 2007).

Tradition of *Daan* or charity had significant social benefits and helps in building social infrastructure like schools, hospitals, *Dharmashalas* (place for stay in the areas of pilgrimage) and community halls. Mandirs acted as great centres for education and social service. Education and health facilities were made available to everyone in society.

Indian Economic Thinkers

Economic thoughts were usually integrated with other social thoughts in the ancient times. We discuss in brief the economic thoughts of a few significant economic thinkers in India.

Chanakya (371 BC–283 BC)

Kautilya popularly known as Vishnugupta or Chanakya was an ancient Indian teacher, philosopher, economist, jurist and royal advisor. *Arthashastra* was the culmination of the thoughts that had appeared in sacred and secular texts over the millennia. Kautilya informs that his ideas of political economy were based on the synthesis and improvement of the accumulated knowledge received from ancient seers (1.1.1). The objective of the text was to have a manual for a centralized administrative system with economic and political stability. Sometimes Kautilya is compared with the Italian writer Machiavelli. However, one needs to remember that Machiavelli wrote *The Prince* almost a millennium after Kautilya and focused his attention solely on advice to the ruler for smooth continuance of his authority. Kautilya, on the other hand, devoted his attention to state administration, advice for smooth continuity of the ruler, as well as economic matters (Deodhar, 2018). Kautilya's treatise was more academic and universal in nature and did not make any specific reference to the historical situation of that period (Kangle, 1965). Spengler, while comparing Kautilya with Greek writers, opined: 'It is in the *Arthashastra* literature that economic discussion was most highly developed, much more fully than one finds it in classical

Greek economics' (Spengler, 1971). Kautilya's Arthashastra is a distinguished economic thought that stresses on the importance of economic growth and welfare of all. According to him, poverty is like a living death. He concentrated on devising economic policies to achieve salvation from poverty but without compromising with ethical values unless survival of the state was threatened (Sihag, 2005). Kautilya clearly mentions in (2.1.26) that the helpless among children, aged persons and those in distress must be looked after by the state. Thus, Kautilya makes the idea of welfare state and identification of public goods very ancient (Deodhar, 2018).

Remarkably, two millennia prior to Smith, it was Kautilya who proposed the real-world applications of political economy in his treatise Arthashastra (Kangle, 1965). Kautilya seems to be aware of the broader context of sciences within which he had written the treatise. He had identified four sciences, which in his opinion covered all branches of learning known at that time (1.2.1). The first was Anwikshiki or the philosophical sciences, both theistic and atheistic, which deal with logic, reason and the inquiry of the soul (Barnett, 1923); the second was Trayi or the first three Vedas which invoke the spiritual good (1.3.1); third was Vaarta or the economic livelihood which includes agriculture, animal husbandry, and trade and commerce (1.4.1); and the fourth was Dandaniti or political administration (1.4.3) (Deodhar, 2018).

According to Chanakya, in the absence of dharma (righteousness), there is no society. He opined that ethical values help the people to pave the way to the both: spiritual development and material. He understood both the intrinsic and instrumental value of ethics (Elster, 1989). Unlike the Greek thinkers, he believed that ethical values and prosperity were interdependent (Sihag, 2005). He also developed a mechanism to deal with conflict of interest arising from the growth and power of business. Integration of ethics and economics was the major contribution of Chanakya. He also explained the way of living in Chanakaya Neeti.

Kautilya gave significant importance to public finance. He opines that revenue generation by the state should be considered as compensation to the ruler for bringing order, well-being and security (1.13.5–7, 9) (Deodhar, 2018). Kautilya's theory of public finance was both comprehensive and probably one of the world's most ancient (Saletore, 1963).

Kautilya knew that it is not excessive taxes but market facilitation and increase in output that would result in increased material well-being as well as increased treasury. For example, he asserts that promoting prosperous activities, improved agriculture and control on crime would ensure increase in treasury (2.8.3). To him, upholding property rights was important to promote livelihood (8.3.28–29). Kautilya gave detailed account of weights and measures, specifications for coin content, and the strict punishments for their violations are indicative of his understanding of market failure due to asymmetric information. Kautilya's detailed documentation of prices, cost, domestic markets and foreign trade was exemplary for his times. Spengler (1971) acknowledges the recognition of the role of price and market in Kautiya's writings than in those of Aristotle, viewed by some as the founder of economics.

Kautilya suggested fixation of interest rates by regulatory authority. Kautilya's Arthashastra considers that the interest shall be 1.25% per month (15% per year) for the normal transaction. Further, the interest rates were linked to risk and uncertainty, and other situations characterizing the loans (3.11.1). Moreover, the interest rate has to be determined at the time of making a loan. Once interest rate is fixed for a loan, it cannot be changed. The Arthashastra also details the rules permitting a person to sue for recovery of debt. These rules indicate that debts might be passed on to the next generation. The obligation to repay shall devolve upon sons, grandsons and kinsmen who inherit the debtor's property (Rangarajan, 1992). Kautilya has suggested minimum wage for unskilled and skilled labour in different sectors and also recommends incentive plans for improving productivity. Kautilya prohibits slavery and provides for labourer's rights and occupational safety (Deodhar, 2018).

Mahatma Gandhi (1869–1948)

Mohandas Karamchand Gandhi was an Indian lawyer, anti-colonial nationalist and political ethicist, who employed non-violent resistance to lead the campaign for India's independence from British rule and in turn inspired movements for civil rights and freedom across the world. Gandhian economic thinking is based on simplicity, decentralization, self-sufficiency, cooperation, equality, non-violence, human values, self-sufficient units, Swadeshi (indigenous) and the theory of trusteeship. Gandhian economics is largely characterized by rejection of the concept of the human being as a rational actor always seeking to maximize material self-interest that underlies classical economic thinking (Kumarappa, 1946).

Mahatma Gandhi's vision of a future India seeks a distinctive path for India, by rejecting the materialism of socialism and capitalism alike, by rejecting the individualism of modern society in favour of a holistic, varnadharma-based community, insisting upon an infusion of religious and moral values in politics, and seeking a culturally authentic mode of modernization that preserves Hindu values (Nanda, 2003). Where Western economic systems were (and are) based on what he called the multiplication of wants, Gandhi felt that this was both unsustainable and devastating to the human spirit. His model, by contrast, aimed at the fulfilment of needs—including the need for meaning and community.

Gandhi also espoused the notion of 'trusteeship' (Gandhi, 1927). Trusteeship is a socio-economic philosophy that provides a means by which the wealthy people consider themselves as the trustees of the wealth and looked after the welfare of the people in general. Gandhi believed that the wealthy people could be persuaded to part with their wealth to help the poor. Putting it in Gandhiji's words, 'Supposing I have come by a fair amount of wealth – either by way of legacy, or by means of trade and industry – I must know that all that wealth does not belong to me; what belongs to me is the right to an honourable livelihood by millions of others. The rest of my wealth belongs to the community and must be used for the welfare of the community'.

Gandhi's economic thought lays special emphasis on 'simple living' which helps in cutting down wants and being self-reliant (Mishra, 1999). He advocated for the distinction to be made between 'Standard of Living' and 'Standard of Life', where the former merely states the material and physical standard of food, cloth and housing. A higher standard of life, on the other hand, could be attained only if, along with material advancement, there was a sincere attempt to imbibe cultural and spiritual values and qualities.

Decentralization is another distinguishing feature of economic thoughts of Mahatma Gandhi. According to him, centralization, that is power in the hands of the state, harms the humankind and destroys individual diversity. Therefore, if India has to evolve, it has to follow the path of decentralization (Dalton, 2012). Gandhi advocated Swadeshi, which is a philosophy of political, economic, administrative and technological decentralization and diversity. It requires, among other things, the development and use of the simple, soft labour-intensive, non-violent human-faced, small scaled, decentralized, indigenous and local technologies (Bhole, 2000).

Bhimrao Ambedkar (1891–1956)

Dr. Bhimrao Ramji Ambedkar, popularly known as Babasaheb Ambedkar, was an Indian jurist, economist, politician and social reformer, with a doctorate in economics from both Columbia University and London School of Economics.

In his first thesis on Ancient Indian Commerce, Ambedkar (1915) described the well-developed economy, commerce and trade in ancient India. In his article, 'Commercial Relations of India in the Middle Ages', he has described about the business relationship in Europe, India and Arabia. He has analysed complex relationships between trades and political movements, rise of Muslim, wars and invasions in Europe and Asia characterized by geographical barriers in setting trade routes.

Dr. Ambedkar wrote three scholarly books on economics, namely Administration and Finance of the East India Company in 1915, The Problem of the Rupee: Its Origin and Its Solution in 1923 and The Evolution of Provincial Finance in British India—A Study in the Provincial Decentralization of Imperial Finance in 1925. Apart from the three books that he wrote, he presented his deep insights into India's economic problems by way of various memoranda and statements to the government under British rule as well as independent India. The Reserve Bank of India (RBI) was formed on the basis of his presentation to the Hilton Young Commission. Dr. Ambedkar's speeches are replete with stimulating economic thoughts. Ambedkar presented a perceptive critique of

Marxism in his essay, 'Buddha or Karl Marx' (Ambedkar, 1956; Omvedt, 2017). According to Ambedkar, humanity needs economic prosperity with spiritual values. Communist Dictatorship has paid no attention to spiritual values and does not seem to intend to. Marxist Philosophy is wrong for the aim of their philosophy seems to be fattening pigs as though men are no better than pigs. Man must grow materially as well as spiritually (Ambedkar, 1956).

Deendayal Upadhyaya (1916–1968)

Pandit Deendayal Upadhyaya was an Indian politician and thinker. He presented the concept of integral humanism that advocates the simultaneous and integrated program of the body, mind, intellect and soul of each human being. He stated that as an independent nation, India cannot and need not be dependent on Western concepts like individualism, democracy, socialism, communism and capitalism. He believed that Indian intellect was getting suffocated by the Western theories and ideologies, and consequently, there was a big roadblock on the growth and expansion of original Bharatiya thought (Upadhyaya, 1965).

'Integral humanism' is a critique of both communism and capitalism and put for the holistic perspective as an alternative for political action and statecraft. Upadhyaya pointed out that Western thought have looked at individual, family, society, and humanity as separate and non-interacting entities. When dealing with the individual, they lost sight of other organs of the society. The same applies to their thinking on family, society and humanity. Against this, Indian arrangement, which is not new but ancient, is an ever-expanding spiral. It begins with the individual but goes on enlarging to family, family to society, society to nation, nation to humanity and ultimately to the universe or Srishti without ever de-linking with the centre, i.e., the individual (Upadhyaya, 1965). Upadhyaya was of the opinion that integral humanism followed the tradition of advaita developed by Adi Sankara, which represented the unifying principle of every object in the universe, and of which humankind was a part (Bhatt, 2020).

Indian philosophy admits that human being is an economic being and needs food, sleep, fear and sex (aahaar, nidra, bhaya and maithunam). But this was not enough. Human being was something more than economic being. Human being is a physical, psychological, political, social and spiritual being too. Integral humanism attempts to develop all aspects in integral manner. Dharma is understood as dynamic principle of ethics and moral is considered as the governing principle in the integral humanism for the production, distribution and consumption of wealth. Society and nation are not just a conglomeration of individuals having living entity by itself. Like individual, human collectivity of society and nation also needs to discover their true purpose of existence. The purpose of existence at all the levels should be such that facilitates the well-being for all. He suggested a system based on Bharatiya values which advocates decentralized development and avoiding exploitation of nature. The philosophy of integral humanism, like Gandhian approach, opposes unbridled consumerism, putting restraints on one's desires and advocates contentment rather than ruthless pursuit of material wealth for realizing its purpose (Malik & Singh, 1995). Deendayal Upadhyaya recommended decentralization and self-reliance in the economy in terms of thinking, social arrangements, methods, ways of production, technology and so forth. Integral humanism aims at economic democracy through 'Antyodaya' which means the 'rise of the last person' and 'Sarvodaya' the development of all.

Conclusion

India was a recognized economic power for several centuries, the longest number of years for any nation recorded in the history. An accomplishment of such a high level of continual economic dominance would have been impossible without a strong economic thinking and business approach. Despite significant impact of colonization and globalization, Indian economy and business exhibit some unique features. Family system, family business, community orientation, entrepreneurial bend, community financing, high savings, gold, foreign remittances and sustainable business practices, among many, are the distinct features that set apart India from its global counterparts. Family and community systems play a pivotal role in the financial and economic decision-making process. It is a decentralized economy where small business plays a major role in providing employment and contributing to GDP. These features stand on the strong foundation of Indian culture nourished by ancient Indian philosophy. The ancient Indian philosophy is characterized by the principles of hard and honest work to create wealth, respect for wealth and wealth creators, earning wealth through ethical means, restrained consumption, giving back to society, decentralization, sustainable thinking and higher purpose. In addition, the ancient Indian philosophy also entails business objectives of maximizing wellness for everyone, seeking satisfaction from the effort (and not from its rewards), recognizing the immense potential of human resources, giving importance to human resources and developing family-like relationship with all stakeholders.

Scope of Future Research

There is plenty of scope to undertake future research in this field. The researchers are encouraged to undertake studies related to Indian economic and business history. Further, thematic research on public finance, taxation, welfare policies, use of currency/coins, banking, lending, financing, role of donations, business structure, trade, services, accounting, business education and skill training can be considered.

In this chapter, the unique features of Indian economic and financial system that sets the country apart from its global counterparts are discussed. Some of the future research agenda includes: (a) studying the detailed impact of each unique feature like family system, family business, community orientation, entrepreneurial bend, community financing, high savings, gold, foreign remittances and sustainable business practices, role of women; (b) comparing the pre-independence India with post-independence India with special focus on the unique features stated in the chapter; (c) studying the impact of globalization, modern education and technology on Indian economic and business system; (d) analysing the economic ideas proposed in various ancient scriptures, Vedas, Upanishads, Samhitas, Brahmanas, Vedang, Upaveda, Ramayana, Mahabharata, Jatak Kathas, Jain Agamas, as well as the economic thoughts of other Indian economists and thinkers, apart from the ones mentioned in this chapter; and (e) drawing relevance of the ancient texts in current times.

References

Agarwal, S. (2010). *Daan and other giving traditions in India: The forgotten pot of gold*. AccountAid India.

Alha, A. (2018). The other side of caste as social capital. *Social Change, 48*(4), 575–588.

Ambedkar, B. R. (1915a). Administration and finance of the East India Company. *Submitted in partial fulfillment of requirements of the degree of Master of Arts.*

Ambedkar, B. R. (1915b). *Ancient Indian commerce.* Retrieved from http://www.ambedkar.org/ambcd/46.%20Ancient%20Indian%20Commerce.htm

Ambedkar, B. R. (1956). *Buddha or Karl Marx. MD Panchbhai, Nagpur.* (Annual Report 2010–11, p. 1). Reserve Bank of India.

Ashta, A., & Hannam, M. (2014). Hinduism and microcredit. *Journal of Management Development, 33*(8/9), 891–904.

Bairoch, P. (1995). *Economics and world history: Myths and paradoxes.* University of Chicago Press.

Barnett, L. D. (1923). Indica-24. A manual of higher Sanskrit grammar and composition. By Upendranath Vidyabhushana. Pts. I, II. 7¼ × 5¼. Calcutta: 1919, 1921. *Journal of the Royal Asiatic Society, 55*(3), 436.

Basham, A. L., & Rizvi, S. A. A. (1956). *The wonder that was India* (p. 300). London: Sidgwick and Jackson.

Basuthakur, Y. (2020). *The magnificent history of Indian family businesses.* Family Business United.

Bayly, C. A., & Bayly, C. A. (1987). *Indian society and the making of the British Empire* (Vol. 2). Cambridge University Press.

Bhatt, C. (2020). *Hindu nationalism: Origins, ideologies and modern myths.* Routledge.

Bhole, L. M. (2000). *Essays on Gandhian socio-economic thought*. Shipra.

Birol, A. (2013, November). *4 ways you can succeed with a staff that 'wears multiple hats'*. Retrieved from https://www.bizjournals.com/bizjournals/how-to/growth-strategies/2013/11/working-here-means-wearing-multiple.html

Bokare, M. (2009). *Hindu economics* (2nd ed.). Dr. M.G. Bokare Memorial Foundation.

Müller, F. M. (Ed.). (1886). *The laws of Manu* (Vol. 25). Clarendon Press.

Carlock, R. S., & Ward, J. L. (2010). Family values and business culture. In *When family businesses are best* (pp. 53–82). Palgrave Macmillan.

Chadda, R. K., & Deb, K. S. (2013). Indian family systems, collectivistic society and psychotherapy. *Indian Journal of Psychiatry, 55*(2), 299–309.

Chugh, P. K. (2005). *Indian banking today: Impact of reforms*. Kanishka Publishers.

Dalton, D. (2012). *Mahatma Gandhi: Nonviolent power in action*. Columbia University Press.

Das, G. (2002). *India unbound*. Anchor.

Datta, B. (1927). Early history of the arithmetic of zero and infinity in India. *Bulletin of the Calcutta Mathematical Society, 18*, 165–176.

Deodhar, S. Y. (2018). *Indian antecedents to modern economic thought*. Indian Institute of Management.

Dubois, A. J. (2007). *Hindu manners, customs and ceremonies*. Cosimo, Inc.

Duh, M. (2014). Family business succession as knowledge creation process. *Kybernetes*.

Durkheim, E. (1893). *The division of labor in society* (G. Simpson, Trans.). Macmillan. [you did not utilize it much except for citing it.].

Elster, J. (1989). Social norms and economic theory. *Journal of Economic Perspectives, 3*(4), 99–117.

Family Firm Institute. (2017). *Global data points*. http://www.ffi.org/page/globaldatapoints

Fernandez, A. (2007). *History and spread of the self-help affinity group movement in India*. International Fund for Agricultural Development (IFAD). Accessed on 5 May 2009.

Fischer, T., & Sriram, M. S. (2002). *Beyond micro credit, putting development back into micro-finance*. Vistaar Publications.

Fukuyama, F. (1995). *Trust: The social virtues and the creation of prosperity* (Vol. 99). Free press.

Gandhi, M. (1909). *Hind Swaraj*.

Gandhi, M. K. (1927). *My experiments with truth*. Navjivan Publishing House.

Garg, R., & Saluja, D. (2017). A business paradigm for corporate ShubhLabh: An inquest study. *Jindal Journal of Business Research, 6*(2), 146–154.
Gewali, B. R. (2013). Isha-Upanishad and economics consideration: An elucidation. *Economic Literature, 11*, 35–39.
Gopinath, P. (2002). *Bhartrihari's Shataktrayam* (N. S. Singh, Ed.). Rashtriya Sanskrit Sansthan.
Griffiths, R. (1886). *Hymns of the Rigveda*, Internet sacred text achieve, Book 9, Hymn 112; and, Book IV, Hymn 24. Accessed from http://www.sacred-texts.com/hin/rigveda/, on 22 October 2020
Gurumurthy, S. (2013, November 15). *Communities as open-air business schools*. The Hindu Business Line.
Gurumurthy, S. (2015, September 20). *How gold schemes work for Indians and India*. The New Indian Express.
HSBC. (2017). *The value of education: Higher and higher*. Retrieved from https://www.hsbc.com/-/files/hsbc/media/media-release/2017/170628-the-value-of-education-higher-and-higher-global-report.pdf
Iyer, L., Macomber, J. D., & Arora, N. (2009). Dharavi: Developing Asia's largest slum. *HBS Case*, (710–004).
Jain, L. C. (1929). *Indigenous banking in India*. Macmillan and Co, Limited.
Kak, S. C. (1987). On the chronology of ancient India. *Indian Journal of History of Science, 22*, 222–234.
Kanagasabapathi, P. (2013). *Indian models of economy, business and management*. PHI Learning Pvt. Ltd.
Kangle, R. P. (1965). *The Kautilya Arthashastra, Part I, II and III*.
Kapoor, M., Schoar, A., Rao, P., & Buteau, S. (2011). Chit funds as an innovative access to finance for low-income households. *Review of Market Integration, 3*(3), 287–333.
Kaur, H. V. (2016). Can MUDRA bank be a game changer for India? *Asian Journal of Management, 7*(4), 247–250.
Keith, A. B., & Macdonell, A. A. (1912). *Vedic index of names and subjects, by Arthur Anthony Macdonell and Arthur Berriedale Keith*. Motilal Banarsidass.
Kennedy, P. (1989). The costs and benefits of British imperialism 1846–1914. *Past & Present*, (125), 186–192.
Klostermaier, K. K. (2006). *Mythologies and philosophies of salvation in the theistic traditions of India* (Vol. 5). Wilfrid Laurier University Press.
KPMG. (2013). *Family business survey 2013: Performers, resilient, adaptable, sustainable*. Family Business Australia.

Krishna, A. (2004). Understanding, measuring and utilizing social capital: Clarifying concepts and presenting a field application from India. *Agricultural Systems, 82*(3), 291–305.

Kumar, S. (1995). *The Manusmriti.* Arya Sahitya Prachar Trust.

Kumarappa, J. C. (1946). *The economy of permanence.* CP, All India Village Industries Association.

MacKinnon, N. J., & Langford, T. (1994). The meaning of occupational prestige scores: A social psychological analysis and interpretation. *The Sociological Quarterly, 35*(2), 215–245.

Maddison, A. (2003). *Development centre studies the world economy historical statistics: Historical statistics.* OECD Publishing.

Malik, Y. K., & Singh, V. B. (1995). *Hindu nationalists in India: The rise of the Bharatiya Janata Party*. Vistaar Publication

Mann, M. S. (2002). *History of ancient India.* Raj Publisher.

Menon, M. (2004). *Dharavi residents wary of new project*. The Hindu.

Merchant, P., Kumar, A., & Mallik, D. (2017). The role of quality of relations in succession planning of family businesses in India. *Journal of Asian Finance, Economics and Business, 4*(3), 45–56.

Milken, M. (2006, September 19). Seventh decade. *The Wall Street Journal.* https://www.wsj.com/articles/SB115862648061466997

Mishra, A. D. (Ed.). (1999). *Gandhism after Gandhi.* Mittal Publications.

Mullatti, L. (1995). Religious and ideological orientations and characteristics. *Journal of Comparative Family Studies, Special Issue: Families in Asia: Beliefs and Realities*, 11–25.

NABARD. (2018). *Status of microfinance in India, 2017–18.* Annual Report Published by NABARD.

Nadkarni, M. (2012). Hindu economic philosophy. In *The Oxford handbook of Hindu economics and business* (H. Vinod, Ed.). Oxford University Press

Naidu, V. (2014, May 14). *Why the Indian family is a great institution.* Business Line.

Nanda, M. (2003). *Prophets facing backward: Postmodern critiques of science and Hindu nationalism in India.* Rutgers University Press.

Naoroji, D. (1867). Observations on Mr. John Crawfurd's paper on the European and Asiatic Races. *Transactions of the Ethnological Society of London, 5,* 127–149.

Naoroji, D. (1901). Poverty and Un-British rule in India. *Dadabhai Naoroji, 12,* 1.

Omvedt, G. (2017). *Ambedkar: Towards an enlightened India.* Penguin UK.

Peter, K. B. (2010). Transnational family ties, remittance motives, and social death among Congolese migrants: A socio-anthropological analysis. *Journal of Comparative Family Studies, 41*(2), 225–243.

PTI. (2018, July 19). Ahead of China, India to remain fastest growing economy in FY19 and FY20: ADB. *The Economic Times*. https://economictimes.indiatimes.com/news/economy/finance/india-fastest-growing-economy-inasia-on-track-to-meet-fy18-target-adb/articleshow/65049353.cms

PwC. (2019). *PwC India family business survey 2019 powerhouses of opportunity*. Retrieved from https://www.pwc.in/assets/pdfs/research-insights/fbs/2019/pwc-india-family-business-survey-2019.pdf

Ramchandran, K., & Bhatnagar, N. (2012). *Challenges faced by family businesses in India [White Paper]*. Retrieved August 13, 2018 from https://www.isb.edu/sites/default/files/challengesfacedbyindian_1.pdf

Rangarajan, L. N. (Ed.). (1992). *The Arthashastra*. Penguin Books India.

Rao, D. (2010). *Raghuvamsham by Kalidas* (English translation). Accessed from Giirvaani at http://sanskritdocuments.org/sites/giirvaani/giirvaani/rv/sargas/01_rv.htm on 11 July 2017

Raychaudhuri, G. S. (1966). On some estimates of national income: Indian economy 1858–1947. *Economic and Political Weekly*, 673–679.

Reserve Bank of India. (1999). *Conversion of cooperative credit societies into urban cooperative banks*. https://www.rbi.org.in/Scripts/PublicationReportDetails.aspx?UrlPage=&ID=136

Saglio-Yatzimirsky, M. C. (2013). *Dharavi: From mega-slum to urban paradigm*.

Saletore, B. A. (1963). *Ancient Indian political thoughts and institutions*. Asia Publishing House.

Schumacher, E. F. (1974). *Small is Beautiful: A study of economics as if people mattered*. Blond and Briggs.

Seibel, H. D. (2005). *SHG banking in India: The evolution of a rural financial innovation* (No. 2005, 9). Working Paper.

Shangle, S. C. (1995). A view into the family and social life in India. *Family Perspective, 29*, 423–446.

Shankar, S. (2019). *The role of credit rating agencies in addressing gaps in micro and small enterprise financing: The case of India* (pp. 72–87). Routledge.

Sharan, A. (Ed.). (2001). *Manas Peeyush*. Gita Press.

Sharma, P., Chrisman, J. J., & Gersick, K. E. (2012). 25 years of family business review: Reflections on the past and perspectives for the future. *Family Business Review, 25*(1), 5–15.

Sihag, B. S. (2005). Kautilya on ethics and economics. *Humanomics, 21*(3), 1–28.

Singh, R. P. P., & Pathak, D. M. (2019). Complementarity of qualitative higher education and skill India mission: An evaluation in the light of opportunities and challenges. *Jamshedpur Research Review*, 14.

Spengler, J. (1971). *Indian economic thought*. Duke University Press.

Sunderland, J. T. (1932). *India in bondage*. Lewis Copeland Company.

The Boston Consulting Group. (2016). *Global leaders, challengers, and champions*. https://www.bcg.com/publications/2016/growth-global-leaders-challengers-champions

Thiruvalluvar. (1990). *Kural* (P. Sundaram, Trans.). Penguin.

Upadhyaya, D. (1965). *Integral humanism*. Bharatiya Janta Party.

Vaidyanathan, R. (2004). *Understanding the unorganised sector*. The Hindu Business Line.

Vaidyanathan, R. (2012). *India growth: The untold story caste as social capital*. Oxford University Press.

Vaidyanathan, R. (2014). *Explaining India unincorporated*. Live Mint.

Ved Vyas. (2004). *MatsyaPuran*. Gita Press.

Vikramaditya, S. K. (2013). The economic history of the corporate form in ancient India (PDF). *Archived from the original (PDF) on*, 10–19.

Yunus, M. (1998). *Banker to the poor: The autobiography of Muhammad Yunus*. Aurum Press.

10

Understanding Organizations and Business Ecosystems in India Using Business Systems Framework

Abinash Panda and Rajen K. Gupta

Setting the Context

The chapter has twin purposes. First, it presents business system framework as a unit of organizational analysis. Business system is a holistic perspective which attempts to understand and analyse organizations in a context from a cross-disciplinary and evolutionary perspective. Business system is a specific pattern of aggregate economic organization, conceptualized initially by sociologist Richard Whitley (1992a, 1992b), which has been further detailed by Gordon Redding (2002). Second, it presents Indian business system (IBS) for understanding Indian business

A. Panda (✉)
Management Development Institute, Gurgaon, India
e-mail: abinash.panda@mdi.ac.in

R. K. Gupta
Indian Institute of Management, Sirmaur, India

© The Author(s), under exclusive license to Springer Nature Switzerland AG 2022
A. Pandey et al. (eds.), *Indigenous Indian Management*, Palgrave Studies in Indian Management,
https://doi.org/10.1007/978-3-030-87906-8_10

ecosystem and analysing organizations in India within it. The chapter presents the IBS as of today as a starting point for further research. The authors have not dealt with how the current business system has evolved over time, which has been discussed in great detail in Gupta and Panda's (2009) review of culture, institutions and organizations in India. Their review of studies in the domain of organization and management in India indicate that the domains and scope of studies have remained *limited primarily to individuals and groups in the organizational context*. They also discovered that not many studies in India have dealt with the influence of institutions on organizational patterns and management systems in India. Even in international comparative studies which have included India, researchers have adopted a cultural frame of reference, ignoring institutional differences across societies and nations. This chapter has attempted to bridge these knowledge gaps.

Why Indian Business System (IBS)

India is a multi-lingual, multi-ethnic country. Different ethnic groups tend to exhibit different cultural traits and patterns of behaviour in various domains including work domains. India is a unique nation with diversity and inherent contradictions. A brief overview of India's place in various country clusters in various cross-national comparative studies reveals that Indian cultural profile is too complex to be easily pigeonholed. Researchers have placed India in Anglo, Latin American, Far Eastern, South Asian and even as an unclassifiable culture! This makes understanding India and Indians equally challenging for expatriates and academic scholars. India also presents a unique challenge, given that the state institutions have not evolved organically from traditional social institutions. State institutions, which were imposed during colonial period (and that thinking has persisted in the post-independence period), are guided by Anglo-Saxon rationality. On the other hand, socio-cultural institutions, which have evolved over time, are guided by traditional rationality. There seems to be a significant disconnect between socio-cultural institutions and state institutions, which poses a huge challenge for business organizations operating in India, especially the multinationals from abroad.

Virmani and his colleagues (Virmani, 2000; Virmani & Guptan, 1991) have found distinct hiatus between the professed policies and the actual practices followed in Indian organizations, which they have attributed to having alien Western systems thrust on resident Indian practices and expectations. The traditional familial ethos, to which Indians are socialized to, are rooted in traditional agrarian familial ethos emphasizing on personalized relationship, whereas formal behaviours mandated by formal organizations are based on Western industrial ethos, which is rooted in Anglo-Saxon rationale. This encourages employees to demonstrate transactional relationship with colleagues and be guided by self-interest, independence and individual autonomy. Panda and Gupta (2004) have suggested the need for context-specific emic explanation for the paradoxes and duality in management of organizations in India. An understanding of the business ecosystem from a holistic perspective is then a must for managing and leading organizations effectively in the Indian context. Business system framework offers the requisite template to develop a holistic understanding of Indian business ecosystem. Moreover, corporate India is also dominated by family owned and managed conglomerates, besides public enterprises and Indian subsidiaries of European and American multinationals. There has not been any systematic effort to understand the Indian business system, which has evolved over time. The chapter provides an updated version of IBS initially developed in 2009 (Gupta & Panda, 2009) by incorporating changes in Indian cultural and institutional context during last one decade (2008–2018).

Organization of the Chapter

The chapter is organized into five broad sections. The first section titled 'Business System Framework: An holistic perspective for Organizational Analysis' discusses how business system perspective is more comprehensive and holistic for organizational analysis vis-à-vis other perspectives. The second section describes Indian Business System along with its three key sub-systems. The third section discusses the takeaways for organizational leaders and academic researchers. The authors have identified potential areas of academic research. The concluding section presents the summary and concludes the chapter by reiterating the core arguments of the chapter.

Business System Framework: A Holistic Perspective for Organizational Analysis

Organization theorists from various academic disciplines have attempted to explore and understand the form, characteristics and economic behaviour of organizations from different perspectives. Universalists base their arguments on the premises of economic rationality and neo-classical theory of economics. Economic rationalists believe in market determinism and are dismissive of social institutions. Neo-classical economists centre their arguments around market equilibrium: price mechanism through voluntary exchange. These perspectives are neither bound to specific spatio-temporal coordinates nor history-bound (e.g. Schumpeter, 1949) and concentrate on the universal conditions that guide organizations' economic behaviour (Foss, 1999). Institutionalism, in contrast, argues that organizations adapt to environmental changes and questions the basic tenant of universalism to take into account the social and political realities, besides economic rationale, from a long-term perspective.

Sociologists such as Granovetter (1992) and Polanyi (1944) argue that pure economic analysis excluding the social context in which organizations are situated, may not be helpful to understand organizations and societies. Their rationality for organizing and the evolution of various forms of organizations are context specific.

In late 1970s and early 1980s, critics of non-cultural approaches (economic rationalism and market determinism) became concerned with the deterministic orientation and the underestimation of the role of culture in explaining organizational phenomena. Child (1981) studied the role of culture by comparing organizational research across cultures and noted that macro-level variables such as structure and technology of the organizations themselves become more and more similar while micro-level variables, i.e. behaviour of people continue to retain their identity. Organizations are inherently culture bound.

Within the relativistic school of thought, two strands of arguments are put forward. Culturists argue for cultural determinism, whereas institutionalists argue for institutional determinism. Institutionalists tend to argue that the differences among organizations located in various countries are not found in their institutions. Culturists regard differences in social conventions, rationalities and moral codes to be so strong across societies that they generate highly distinctive forms of successful business organization and practices which are specific to their context. Institutionalists tend to ignore or put less emphasis on socio-cultural norms in their analysis and overemphasize the saliency of institutions. They argue that market efficiency is 'institutionally constructed' and hence '.... different institutional environments generate different kinds of technically efficient business systems (Whitley, 1992a: 8)'.

As independent/separate approaches, Lowe (1998) argues, both culturist and institutionalist explanations are partial. In his attempt to provide a holistic picture, he suggested a theoretical framework that synthesizes both culturist and institutional approaches. The relationship between structure (institutional system/framework) and culture is conceptualized to be dialectical, which is to say, the two are seen to mutually affect each other (Jain, 2001: 30). The nature of institutions and institutional arrangement in a nation do differ. To understand these differences, one needs to have an understanding of historical evolution of the society and for that one needs to appreciate emic cultural assumptions—the underlying rationale. The causality between institutions and culture is circular: they cannot be separated (Hofstede, 1996). Berger and Luckmann (1966) view cultural features of a society as institutions. Cultural systems as institutions, help to shape and reproduce predictable behaviour guided by societal norms. 'Culture is the mother; institutions are the children (Etounga-Manguelle, 2000, p. 75)'.

Integration of Cultural and Institutional Perspectives

Business system perspective, as an approach, integrates both cultural and institutional perspectives and in the process provides a holistic framework for organizational analysis from a path-dependent and evolutionary perspectives.

The idea of a business system offers a holistic unit of analysis for academic scholars to understand and analyse business system as a whole. The 'whole' in business system framework is the business system itself, which includes cultural system, institutional system and business system. Such a framework offers emic, holistic and cross-disciplinary understanding of organizations from an evolutionary perspective. The institutional embeddedness is an important cause of the diversity of business systems. The interaction between the business system and the institutional context of its national host is a co-evolutionary process that is strongly path-dependent. Moreover, even abstracting from this co-evolutionary process, business systems are strongly path-dependent. Essentially, this is because of '... the mutually reinforcing nature of many business systems' (Whitley, 1994: 154).

Business systems in different societies are characterized by features such as (a) Ways of organizing and coordinating transactions are different across different business systems and are the mix of hierarchical and market-organized transactions; (b) Different types and levels of specialization (preference for particular kinds of activities and skills) across business systems; (c) The degree of separation between ownership and control, that is, the mode of corporate governance differs; and (d) Organizing principles that influence firm routines and capabilities through their influence on authority relations, organizational structures, relations between the professions etc. across business systems.

National Business System (NBS)

Whitley's conceptualization of NBS provided a new way of organizational analysis distinctly different from other perspectives because firstly, NBS acknowledges that organizations are deeply embedded in institutional contexts, that 'efficiency' must always be defined relative to this context, and, therefore, that there cannot be any universal models of what is the 'best' type of economic organization and secondly, there could be different-forms of viable business systems, such as the business systems of Japan, South Korea, Taiwan and Hong Kong, all are effective though not similar to Western model of business system. Business systems are embedded in an institutional context that is specific to a nation or regions because of its institutional arrangements and rationale underlying its cultural system.

Whitley further makes a distinction between 'background institutions' (trust, norms, etc.) and 'proximate institutions' (particularly the state), where the former is meant to encapsulate primary socialization while the latter refer to more explicit, formal institutions. Redding's business system framework (2002), which is an improvement upon Whitley's framework, is a more elaborate and detailed. Redding has explicitly assumed culture to be the shaper of institutions, which was implicitly assumed in Whitley's framework. Secondly, in addition to authority and trust (which Redding has named authority and identity); Redding has incorporated 'rationale' as the third background or cultural variable. By incorporating 'rationality' as background variable, Redding enriches the framework through explicit acknowledgement of the notion of rationality as a variable across societies. The third improvement Redding has made over Whitley's framework is by placing the role of government between culture and the institutions, as the key mediating force which integrates the two.

Redding (2001) has identified six distinct forms of business systems, namely (a) Anglo-Saxon individualist form, dominant in North America and the UK that includes firms whose purpose is primarily to provide maximize shareholders' value and return; (b) The European large scale form, which is more communitarian in nature, includes firms with a more complex set of purposes with explicit commitment to societal duties and obligations; (c) The European industrial district form of networked enterprises found in parts of Italy and Scandinavian countries, which is based on family ownership and managed by skilled and committed employees; (d) The Japanese form represented by *Keiretsu*, an integrated and complex group of organizations with attendant connections and networks; (e) The Korean form represented by *Chaebol*, similar to *Keiretsu,* which are in existence to primarily fulfil their allocated plan for national economic development; and (f) The Chinese capitalist form, based on family ownership with a primary objective to enhance owner-family's wealth.

Witt et al. (2018) have found nine main types of business systems: Highly Coordinated, Coordinated Market, Liberal Market, European Peripheral, Advanced Emerging, Advanced City, Arab Oil Based, Emerging and Socialist Economies. India is included in Emerging Economies business system cluster, which is characterized by weak past and current education, short-term job tenures, private skills acquisition, suppressed unions, bank-led finance allocated on the basis of relationships and state guidance, top-down decision-making inside firms with low delegation and promotion based on relationships, family and state ownership of firms with often poor investor protection, low rule of law, predatory state policies with developmental admixtures in some cases, top-down state decision-making with generally low levels of voice and accountability and poor state effectiveness.

Witt et al. (2018) have placed India among the other emerging nations. Their analysis, though insightful, yet insufficient to capture unique characteristics and peculiarities of each nation, including India. Hence, there is a need to take a deep dive into each the business system of each nation. This chapter has carried out a detailed analysis and presented Indian business system from an emic perspective.

Indian Business System

Indian business system, which is presented in this chapter, is based on Redding's business system framework. There are three key sub-systems of a business system: the cultural system, the institutional fabric of the society and the business system. Three aspects of the culture of a society are (a) the rationale, which underlies general behaviour; (b) identity, which captures a society's ideals and norms governing its system of horizontal order; and (c) authority, which captures the values and norms governing vertical order. The institutional sub-system continuously evolves in constant interaction with its culture, influenced by external ideational and material influences and guided and regulated by the Government. The institutional fabric includes the nature of (a) financial capital, (b) human capital and (c) social capital. The first one deals with the source of finance for business organization, whereas the second one is about sources of human capital and institutional arrangements that create quality human capital, and the final one is about the sources of radii of social capital. The third sub-system, the business system that includes (a) ownership pattern that deals with ownership pattern in business entities (b) networks, which is about formal and informal networks operating in the corporate world and (c) managing, which is about authority relationship, leadership and motivation in the organizational context. The business system dynamics evolve over time, in response to cultural, institutional systems and external influences, which could be material or ideational. The role of government, civil societies (including non-governmental organizations) and elite groups in shaping the nature of business system in a country is immense. The role of government is important in framing the institutional framework. The Fig. 10.1 presents the various elements of a business system.

Corporate India: An Overview

Corporate India boasts of two kinds of capitalism—state-organized capitalism, which is prevalent in public sector enterprises and other one is family capitalism, which is found in family managed private enterprises. They have evolved over time in response to the institutional fabric in which these organizations are embedded in. The character and form of institutional environment, over years, have undergone changes in a disconnected fashion, since pre-colonial (European/Moguls) period, then colonial, then post-Independence controlled regime and finally current partially liberalized regime, though the traditional social institutions have evolved relatively in a connected fashion in interactions with external influences: material and ideational. Institutional fabric is underpinned by Western business model based on Anglo-Saxon rationale. Over time, the indigenous cultural values and societal norms/ideals have been suppressed or marginalized. For instance, the rationale which underlies

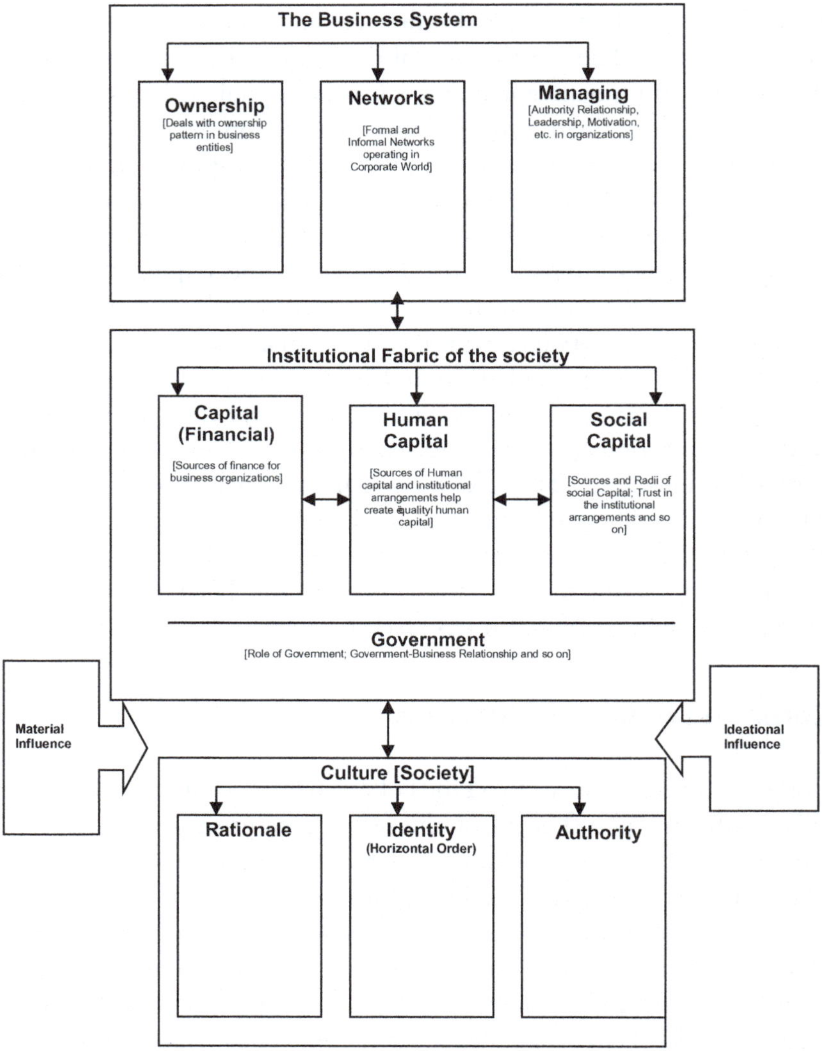

Fig. 10.1 Elements of a business system

family capitalism, specifically the family as basis for identity and loyalty and trust, is unlikely to change. Similarly, the emphasis on bureaucratic order and coordination found in public sector enterprises, which is the core of Anglo-Saxon rationale may remain salient irrespective of context.

Sub-Systems of IBS

Business systems, according to Business System Framework, are shaped by the institutional context. A society's institutional framework continuously evolves as it constantly interacts with its culture. The following section discusses the elements of Indian business system.

Cultural Sub-System

Within the base set of cultural influences lie the value and norms of the society, the ground rules used to achieve social order, and based in social traditions and ideals. There are three cultural aspects: underlying rationale, authority relations and identity.

Underlying Rationale: The development of successful societies is commonly attributed to their having incorporated rationality in their formulae for a civilized existence. Weber (1930) had seen rationality to be context sensitive and subjective. Redding defines rationality as 'the application of reasoning, i.e. defensible logic, weighing evidence, in some forms- the use of calculation, to the achievement of specified ends' (Redding, 2002: 227). He distinguishes rationality from rationale, which he defines as 'the purposes which underlie behaviour, i.e. the set of reasons for doing things, but on the basis that a broad set of understanding about how the society sees reality are implicit in it' (Redding, 2002: 228).

According to Redding (2002: 228), formal rationality is 'the objective, scientific, value-neutral calculation of the best means to achieve something, whereas substantive rationality deals with 'the purposes of the economic system, and more specifically these usually finish up with the question of how the system's benefits are to be allocated....this lies at the heart of a culture's system of power' (Redding, 2002: 228).

Further, as Redding puts it, substantive rationality is 'rationality being put in use in practice and manifest in its application. It is rationality given substance, as opposed to rationality lying available for use in abstract logics or mathematical formulae' (Redding, 2002: 229). In Indian context, the indigenous or traditional ordering devices, as identified by many scholars, are: (a) Hindu belief system, (b) Caste system and (c) Agricultural mode of production. The three sources of external influences on Indian society have been (a) European, (b) Mughal's Rule and (c) Colonial (British). The rationale underlying both traditional Indian and modern European ordering devices were different, yet they interacted with each other 'in the minds of the actors and in everyday social practice' (Saberwal, 2001: 35). Indian way of thinking seems to have been primarily influenced by Hindu *Brahminical* world view, where the doctrines of karma (law of cause and effect), *dharma* (guidelines about proper personal conduct) and *moksha* (Salvation) become critical. The effect of *karma* can be transgressed. There is a powerful influence of mysticism in Indian way of thinking, which puts forth the belief that all perceptual phenomena are illusory (*maya*). Supremacy is accorded to non-rational thinking, as it is believed that reason is unable to discover truth, in spite of the fact that formal logic was well developed in India. Indian society has also been influenced by Anglo-Saxon world view, besides the influence of Mughals. The interplay between primary Hindu world view and secondary Anglo-Saxon world view contributed to the development of its dualistic value orientations.

Substantive rationality has two components: value rationality and instrumental rationality. These two components of substantive rationality are based in formal rationality; they interact with each other to give shape to substantive rationality. Value rationality is concerned with ends, whereas instrumental rationality is concerned with means. 'It is the interplay between these two, bringing into use as needed the tools of formal rationality, which connects the purposes into behaviours and structures of the society' (Redding, 2002: 229). Its value rationality may be seen along the following seven dimensions, which seem to constitute the guiding principles of action. Though the list is selective, these values are salient in terms of its relevance to general pattern of behaviour in Indian organizations. They are: *(a) collectivist orientation; (b) societal order interdependence; (c) hierarchy (respect for status and power); (d) personalized relationship; (e) desire to be embedded in preferred in-group; (f) family orientation; and (g) religious-spiritualistic orientation.* These seven core values seem to constitute an integrated total reflecting the Indian traditional value base. All these are the outcome of (a) caste-based occupational differentiation; (b) order in and interdependence between various caste groups; (c) agricultural mode of production where interdependence and reciprocity are valued and most importantly; and (d) Hindu *Brahminical* world view. These cultural traits tend to influence the Indians' understanding of ends or desired conditions of life. Indians, in general, attach high saliency to these values. This set of cultural values tends to play a significant role in shaping the institutional structure/fabric of Indian society.

The 'primary' modes of instrumental rationality that have evolved in Indian society includes (a) *Jajmani* system; (b) occupational differentiation along caste lines; (c) family (private) businesses; (d) community-based identity, and hence, (e) inter-firm relationship based on selective trust; (f) kingship to control the society and religious institutions; and finally (g) secrecy and distrust, which perpetuated caste-based order. The 'secondary' mode of instrumental rationality, in case of India, has not truly flowed from the primary mode of rationality. Rather, these were all imposed by external rulers through occupation, some of which fitted well in Indian society and many did not gel. *Jagir* system introduced during the Mughal phase, gained acceptance partially as Hindu kingdoms used to rely on secrecy and distrust to control the ruled. *Jagir* system, in a way, was the forerunner of 'licensing raj' that was adopted later. Post-independence, India, guided by socialistic pattern of thinking adopted mixed economy, which gave birth to government-owned enterprises. European traders and British rulers introduced professional way of managing things through impersonal institutions based on bureaucracy and open-ended social relationship. Judiciary system was put in place which took care of societal order based on legal codes (rule of law). Trade and commerce was conducted through cooperation with partners and bankers. Company was introduced as an impersonal instrument of ownership. Communication system helped dissemination of information and knowledge across the country. The Fig. 10.2 presents the rationale underlying the institutional framework of Indian society.

Authority Relation: The caste system has contributed to the acceptance of some dominant value orientations related status, power, and relationships with other people. People are status conscious, finding it easier to work in superior-subordinate relationships that are personalised rather than with equals on contractual terms (Sinha, 1988). They are comfortable in a hierarchical set up- seemingly a manifestation of traditional caste system and caste-based identity. The primary moral basis for

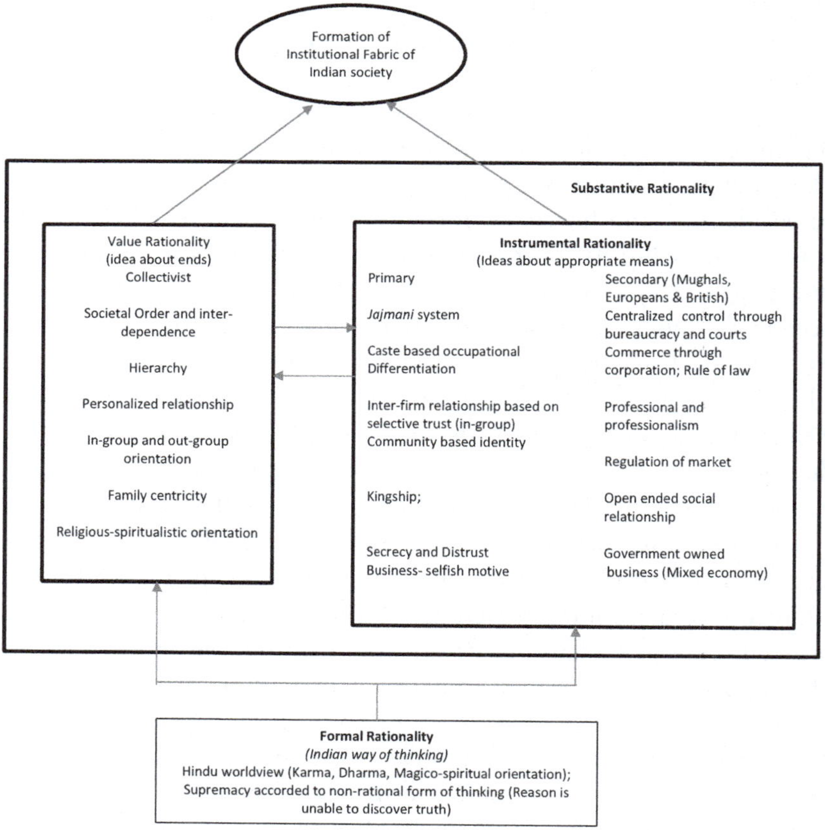

Fig. 10.2 Rationale underlying institutional fabric of Indian society

authority is paternalism. The superior subordinate relationship is a relationship of dependency. Indian society gives primacy to one's roles. Garg and Parikh (1995) have discussed the role bounded (p. 101) nature of Indian society. Indian society has been historically feudalistic in nature. Identity: Indians are found to possess three kinds of selves- collectivistic familial, individualistic-private and spiritual (Sinha, 2005). Paranjape (1988) mentions spiritual pursuits are always individualistic in nature. According to Spratt (1966), the modal Hindu personality of Indians is characterized by narcissism and mother fixation. Roland (1988) views Indian self to be primarily familial self, which is characterized by interdependence through personalized relationship. Indians tend to embed themselves in their native groups- either family or community they belong to, and thus reflecting ethics of particularistic trustworthiness. They trust members belonging to their in-group and tend to distrust members of out-groups. Indian society is a vertical collectivist society, with respect for hierarchy and attaching saliency to collectivism. Under the influence of modern and/or western world views, the collectivist familial self seems to be getting individualised (Gupta & Panda, 2003), with educated elite Indians striving to serve their self-interests and to achieve individual distinctions (Sinha et al., 2001, 2002).

The Institutional Sub-Systems

For Redding, the institutional fabric in which the business system is embedded is constituted of three main elements, 'each of them being a set of institutions which act to amplify or suppress access by economic actors to the most critical resources needed for use in economic exchange' (Redding, 2002: 226). These represent the repertoire of institutions with a capacity to transform the society (Eisenstadt, 1968). Redding identifies three such institutions in his framework: (a) capital (i.e. finance) as accessed through a banking or stock market system together with legal and professional support structures which make that happen; (b) human capital, or the skills and abilities of people as shaped by the education and employment systems of a society; and (c) social capital, or the amount of trust available in the society to facilitate exchange and reduce transaction cost.

Financial Capital: The system of capital (finance) is both credit and equity-market based. Capital market is gradually replacing banking sector as the main source of capital for corporate India. The capital market is becoming more and more robust with Security Exchange Board of India (SEBI) insisting on disclosure norms to be strictly followed and regulating the market for eliminating any inefficiency. Shareholders, who used to be passive, are becoming more and more active with SEBI guarding their interests. Venture Capitalists such as Soft Bank Vision Fund, Sequoia Capital, Helion Capital, Accel Partners, Intel Capital India and Blume Venture have become alternate sources of Capital for entrepreneurs in India. Softbank, for instance has also taken lead in investing in startups in India. Funding is not a problem for startups in India and more over Indian economy is more seamlessly integrated with other economies, compared to the past.

Human Capital: The professional education and training system in India is considered at par with global standards with management and technical institutes of global standard in place. Head hunting and placement firms act as a broker for the organizations in accessing skilled and experienced manpower, which is available in plenty. In recent years, the government has opened a number of institutes focusing on grooming technical and managerial skills. As of today, there are 20 Indian Institutes of Management and 23 Indian Institutes of Technology. In addition, in order to enhance the quality of education, the Ministry of Human Resource Development, Government of India has introduced a scheme to select 20 Institutions of Eminence—10 public institutions and 10 private—that will enjoy complete academic and administrative autonomy. The 10 government ones would also receive special funding. Institutes with the status of eminence will get greater autonomy to start new courses, admit foreign students, hire foreign faculty and collaborate with foreign educational institutions without the need for government approval.

The National Skill Development Corporation India (NSDC) was setup as a one of its kind, Public-Private Partnership Company with the primary mandate of catalyzing the skills landscape in India. The Ministry of Skill Development and Entrepreneurship[1] has created the National Council for Vocational Education and Training (NCVET) to regulate the functioning of entities engaged in vocational education and training. The mandate is to revamp 2,500 Industrial Training Institutes (ITIs) to impart improved training to make youth job ready; create mechanisms to boost apprenticeship; set quality standards and monitor skill-related schemes.

The aim is to make India skill capital of the world by developing relevant skills among 40 crore Indian youths by 2022 through flagship schemes such as Pradhan Mantri Rojgar Prohatsan Yojana (PMRPY), Deen Dayal Upadhyaya Grameen Kaushalya Yojana and the National Apprenticeship Promotion Scheme. Along with all these, the GoI intends to come up with National Policy[2] to reskill and upskill the workforce capable of handling emerging trends such as artificial intelligence (AI) and internet of things (IoT). The GoI has identified select sectors such as Banking, Financial Services and Insurance (BFSI), Information Technology Enabled Services (ITeS), Manufacturing, E-commerce, Retail, Logistics, Healthcare and Telecommunications to focus on.

Organizations have been investing resources to develop their leadership capability. Consequently, leadership Development and Coaching Institutions such as The Centre for Creative Leadership (CCL) and Development Dimension International (DDI) have established themselves as go to organizations for leadership coaching and development. Simultaneously, compared to earlier times, the frequency of labour unrest due to unionism has gone down significantly. The growth of employment in service sector seems to have contributed to the reduction in the number of instances of labour unrest.

Social Capital: A high level of social capital exists in a society when people can do business comfortably with strangers. When this happens, it is because trust is at a high level, not just in terms of shared ideals, but also in terms of open information, reliable legal systems for protection and supporting institutions such as professions, understood procedures

[1] 'Getting Regulator Started, ITI Revamp Top Skilling Agenda', *The Economic Times*, New Delhi Edition, 21 May, 2019, p. 13.

[2] 'Skill India may be expanded to Include AI and IoT', *The Economic Times*, New Delhi Edition, 27 May, 2019, p. 13.

and monitoring devices. India is weak in this area, and the level of social capital is low. Exchange is restricted to those who are known personally or belong to same caste and community. Morris (2002), on the basis of social capital and poverty in India, has found out that different states/regions have different level of social capital. Widespread corruption in bureaucracy has contributed to the low level of institutional trust. Indian institutional context seems to be highly litigated infested with large numbers of Public Interest Litigations (PILs). Judiciary seems to be acting as the mediator and arbitrator in most of the cases. India has, however, improved its ranking on a global corruption index in 2018 by three points to 78 in the list of 180 countries in the world.

Role of Government

The role of government, in Redding's framework, is seen as mediating between the culture and the institutional fabric, which integrates the two. The role of government is critical in the sense that the rationale behind a set of institutions functioning in a society is legitimized by it. As Redding mentions, 'government is seen as a principle interpreter of the cultural values and ideals of the society, in that it plays a very significant part (although not with monopoly) in the shaping of the institutional fabric' (2002: 239). The legitimacy of the government depends on its capability to shape and/ or interpret the society's values. Such influences are transparent in democratic country like India, where debating arena is present in public domain. In case of totalitarian state, societal values, norms or ideology may get buried under value systems imposed by the establishment. The role of government in regulating market forces has started to diminish since the liberalization process started in 1991 in right earnest. Corporate India is becoming more and more globalized with cross-national mergers and acquisitions. The regulatory role of the government seems to be waning. Information technology industry, which started dominating corporate India after 1991 when the government initiated liberalization process, has been operating in relatively less-constrained business environment compared to traditional sectors. Currently, the Business Process Outsourcing industry is booming in India. Further, there are instances of public-private participation in developmental activities particularly related to infrastructural industry.

The nature of relationship between the Government and business/economic organizations in India is primarily regulatory and to a lesser extent facilitative. As a regulator, the Government of India has introduced legislations such as Securitisation and Reconstruction of Financial Assets and Enforcement of Security Interest Act, 2002 (SARFAESI Act, 2002), The Insolvency and Bankruptcy Code (IBC), 2016, Goods and Services Tax (GST) Act, 2016, The Real Estate (Regulation and Development) (RERA) Act, 2016 and so on. Along with being the key regulator, in recent past, the government of India has been trying to act as more as a facilitator rather than a regulator. That has been reflected in India's high rank in World Bank's Ease of Doing Business Report, 2019. India has leapfrogged to the 77th rank in the World Bank's latest Ease of Doing Business rankings, jumping 23 notches from 2018. The report also recognizes India as one of the top 10 improvers in this year's assessment.

Developmental changes such as Goods and Services Tax (GST), digitization drive, institutional reforms, Foreign Direct Investments (FDIs) infrastructure, technology readiness and others have contributed to a facilitative Business Ecosystem. Further, the Department of Promotion of Industry and Internal Trade (DPIIT)[3] has plans to set up an India Startup Fund with initial amount of INR 1000 crore. The Government also proposes to offer seed funds for high-tech, cutting-edge startups. It proposes to provide seed funds to 5000 startups in priority areas, which is in addition to Funds for Startups (FFS) set up in 2016 by Small Industries Development Bank of India (SIDBI). The DPIIT and the Revenue department of Government of India (GoI) have proposed to offer tax and other benefits[4] to both categories of Alternate Investment Funds (AIF). Category I AIFs are meant for economically and socially relevant startups and SMEs. Category II is proposed to include PE or

[3] 'Govt Plans Rs. 1000- Crore Funds for Startups in Priority Areas', *The Economic Times*, New Delhi, 23 May 2019, p. 11.

[4] 'Govt plans fresh set of tax sops for startups in budget', *The Times of India*, New Delhi Edition, 17 June 2019, p. 17.

debt funds. Government is also planning to simplify the tax norms on Employee Stock Option Scheme, which is used by organizations as a talent retention mechanism.

The Government has proposal to encourage in-house researchers through sabbaticals and risk funding to take up entrepreneurship. There is a proposal to revamp the Special Economic Zones (SEZ) framework[5] to house wider range of companies, allow flexible long-term leases and make exits easy to invite investment. India, as of today has 232 SEZs of which 25 are multi-product ones and the rest are sector-specific ones. The government plans to relax procedures to introduce uniformity and consistency; set up integrated portal to process proposals for investment in SEZ. Planning commission has been replaced with NITI Ayog that works on policy guidelines and processes to ease the challenges of doing business in India. The Government of India has been aiming for economic stability through various mechanisms and initiatives towards anti-corruption and tax compliance. It has implemented the Insolvency and Bankruptcy Code (IBC) to tackle willful defaulters of loans; introduced Goods and Services Tax, which has effectively eliminated cascading effects of taxes, thereby increasing the profitability for businesses. It has implemented single-window clearance system in Delhi and the online building permit approval system in Mumbai. India has also streamlined and centralized its construction permitting process. India has also decreased border and documentary compliance time for both exports and imports. The Real Estate sector that has traditionally been plagued by regulatory opaqueness got a shot in the arm with the Real Estate Regulatory Act (RERA), leading to transparent auction. Investors, hitherto sceptical, have become eager to invest money in this sector. On the 'distance to frontier metric', a measure to gauge how far an economy's policies are from global best practices, India's score improved to 67.23 from 60.76 last year. NGOs are quite active in India taking up issues with corporate India as well as government if anything is found to be against public interests.

[5] 'New SEZ Policy Bats for Easy Exits and Flexibility in Leases', *The Economic Times*, 27 May 2019.

External Influences

External influences, both material logic of price and technology and ideational logic of external values and ideas, are accepted to be affecting the evolution of business system. The ideational logics of values and ideas are also seen to be conditioning the influence of indigenous culture. In Weber's conceptualization, these two streams of influence contribute to the shaping up of the institutional fabric of the society. With respect to material influence, for instance, price structures and mechanisms of world industry determine the price responses of any national industry. Organizations in a particular industry, also guided by market logics, reorganize themselves in a nation. This is evident most in the oil industry, which is sensitive to global oil prices. Further, externally derived technology, as mentioned by Redding (2002: 242), has also had a large effect, not just in terms of production machinery, but also managerial technology, information technology and organizational system technology. Joint ventures between domestic company and Multi National Corporation (MNC) facilitate these inflows. Technology transfer takes place through joint ventures or technical collaboration.

As far as ideational influences are concerned, ideas like modernization, globalization and notions of progress and growth, pluralism, participation and democracy influence the norms and behaviour or corporate world in a nation. Modernization, for instance, which is about the emergence of new ideas, can counter traditionalism. This is a major challenge for India, whose traditional Hindu world view has long been considered and seen as a handicap to its development. Understanding of culture requires an understanding of the ideational aspect of culture, the underlying processes of sense making, the cognitive constructions or cultural knowledge that exist in a particular setting and that are used to attribute meaning to observable behaviours. Indian mythologies may also turn out to be more apt sources of insights on Indian culture and values. There is a need to leverage narratives methods to dig out meanings embedded within Indian mythologies.

The system which is presented here is open. It is affected by the inflow of both material and ideational influences. Some of these are so forceful, like an international price, or customer requirement, or a new technology, that they cannot be denied their full effect. Others, such as popular culture, may meet resistance as they arrive and may have limited influence.

Material Influences: Subsequent to the liberalization of Indian economy, Indian organizations have started spreading their arms beyond the national boundary. Cross-national acquisitions and joint ventures are on rise, as well as foreign direct investment (FDI). Three logics namely technologies, capital and economic seem to be influencing corporate India. A significant instrument facilitating such inflows of influence has been joint venture, through transfer of best practices.

The Indian economy began to liberalize and globalize in earnest beginning in 1991, which led to a creation of a far more competitive and turbulent but also opportunity-rich market environment. Liberalization and globalization of India economy played important roles in shaping economic behaviour of corporate India (Khandwalla, 1996). They intensified competition due to the ease of entry barriers. It opened up opportunities for growth through expansion and diversification; becoming competitive through the import of advance technology. They enabled organizations to become more globalized and competitive with the help of management professionals. Economic liberalization in 1991 and subsequent reforms, and globalization encouraged organizations in India to professionalize their approach to management and introduce employee-friendly people practices (Khandwalla, 2006).

Organizations develop strategy in response to the environmental contingencies faced by a firm. Khandwalla (1976) found that managers who perceive their environment as complex and dynamic (therefore, uncertain) tend to employ more comprehensive strategies. Further, Khandwalla (2002), based on prior Western and Indian research has suggested a model to cope with such a market environment. The model argues that the greater use of policy frameworks representing entrepreneurial, organic, professional and participatory styles of management, and mechanisms of uncertainty reduction, differentiation and integration tend to enhance corporate performance in such an environment.

Besides, the advancement in the field of Information and Communication Technology (ICT) that has triggered Fourth Industrial Revolution

(4IR) has impacted the economic behaviour of traditional organizations and led to the creation of 'gig economy'. The technology has provided the required platform, which has enabled new-gen organizations (IT-enabled startups) to adopt new business model, which is asset-light and free-flowing. Indian startups such as Flipkart, Ola, Lenskart, Oyo and Milk basket have leveraged technology to venture into new businesses and succeeded. Advancement in ICT has also impacted the way organizations organize themselves and inter-organizational relationships. This aspect is discussed under business sub-system later in this chapter.

Ideational influences: India's participation in multinational for a like WTO has facilitated inflow of ideas from developed countries. Ideas like globalization, material progress through wealth creation, sustainable development (like Greenpeace movement) and civil society seem to have influenced corporate India to a great extent. Besides, innovation in business models, especially in start-up ecosystem has been triggered by global trend, ideas from Silicon Valley and globalization with unrestricted access to ideas available anywhere in the globe. There are venture capitalists willing to back these ideas, irrespective of geography and context.

Business Sub-System

The business subsystem has three key aspects, namely ownership, networks and managing. Ownership is about the patterns of ownership in business enterprises. Networks are about formal and informal networks that are active in corporate world. Managing includes nature of authority relationship and how leader motivate and lead employees in organizational context.

Ownership: Direct owner control is typical of corporate India. In public sector organization, the ownership and management rest with the government. The private sector is dominated by family owned business. The owner-family usually has the management control over the organization. The shareholders do not have major say in the management of the organization. As per 'Credit Suisse Family 1000 in 2018' study conducted by Credit Suisse, India ranks third globally in terms of number of family owned businesses with 111 companies having a total market capitalization of $839 Billion.[6] The report also found that family owned businesses had been outperforming their peers irrespective of where they were operating, industry sector and size of the organization. They were found to rely less on external funding, while investing more on research and development.

Some of the family managed organizations have initiated professionalizing the management of the organization, which is, however, still rare. As shareholders are passive and relatively less strict norms of disclosure compared to western world, the owners tend to pursue their whims and self-interests. Family managed businesses no longer dominate corporate India. Even government has begun shedding its equities from many governments owned entities through disinvestment via initial public offers (IPOs).

Network: Formal corporate networks like Confederation of Indian Industries (CII), Federation of Indian Chamber of Commerce and Industry (FICCI), The Associated Chambers of Commerce and Industry of India (ASSOCHAM), The National Association of Software and Services Companies (NASSCOM) take up policy-related issues with the government and lobby for various industries. Forums such as Entrepreneurs Council of India (ECI), Startup India (SuI) provide much-needed platform to budding entrepreneurs to fine-tune their business ideas for commercial success.

Startup incubators such as Angel Prime, Khosla Labs, Science and Technology Entrepreneurship Park (STEP), Seedfarm, Seedfund and many others have been helping and guiding startup entrepreneurs by nurturing their ideas to commercial success. Y Combinator, for instance, has picked 15 startups from India, which is a record number, for its summer batch of 2019.[7] Till 2019, Y Combinator has nurtured 40 startups from India.

Managing: The form of coordination of economic behaviour is at the core of how managers pull together the various resources into efficient system of coordinated action. Sinha (1990) has identified two dominant

[6] Accessed from https://timesofindia.indiatimes.com/business/india-business/india-ranks-3rd-on-family-owned-business-list/articleshow/65817744.cms, on 4 June 2019.

[7] 'Y Combinator selects record 15 desi startups', *The Times of India*, New Delhi Edition, page 25, 30 May 2019.

work cultures prevalent in Indian organizations, namely 'soft' and 'synergistic' work culture. The soft work culture, where 'profit and productivity yield to familial ethic and in-group considerations' (Sinha & Kanungo, 1997, p. 102), whereas the synergistic work culture, where 'the organisations have been able to set up the objective of self-reliance, developed strong work-related norms, unequivocal performance standards and a generous reward system-all supported by people-oriented management' (Sinha & Kanungo, 1997, p. 102).

Khandwalla (1995) has identified ten archetypal styles of top management, namely conservative, entrepreneurial, professional, bureaucratic, organic, authoritarian, participative, intuitive, familial and altruistic. The most effective top management styles were found to be participative, professional and altruistic management styles, which contributed significantly to organizational effectiveness and excellence.

The chief source of authority has been traditional-moral (Kakar et al., 2002). In most situations, the subordinate act either to anticipate and carry out superior's wishes or accept the superior's orders without conscious questioning. Nurturant superiors tend to exact greater obedience than assertive ones, since the former are more likely to regulate behaviour by emotional rewards and latter by punitive means (Kakar et al., 2002). Indians have a strong need for power (McClelland, 1975), which is primarily expressed through 'giving'. Chattopadhyay (1986) mentioned that giving power to others in India is assumed to be an abdication of responsibilities. Hence, empowerment is low in most aspects of organizational life.

On the whole, the management in Indian organizations is typically of paternalistic or patronage type. The high centralization of power in the organization is typical of Indian organizations. Supervisors/managers have high control over the subordinates. Subordinates are comfortable in a dependent relationship with the superiors. The communication pattern within organizations tends to be top down through designated chains of command with little voluntary feedback from below. While formal processes are bureaucratic and regulative, the informal aspects tend to display efficiency and flexibility in terms of particularism and are sometimes characterized by ingratiating relationship between subordinates and superiors. The leader must balance performance orientation and patronizing and nurturance. Too much nurturance without performance focus or too much task obsession without patronizing approach may not be effective in Indian context. Moreover, she/he should be compassionate and caring towards subordinates.

The work behaviour of the employees in organizations in India is shaped by how employees generally respond to the conflict between the social values they are socialized to and the rationale and values imposed on them through formal organizations. Indians who are socialized to attach saliency to 'personalised relationship' and suppress one's own feelings, are expected to demonstrate behaviour, formally espoused by the organization.

The general pattern of work behaviour reflects context sensitivity, and a tendency to balance by integrating, pluralistic considerations (Sinha & Kanungo, 1997, p. 100). Indians prefer authoritative and hierarchical forms of management. They respond favourably to close supervision (Roland, 1980) and prefer clear and direct orders from superiors. They value personalised relationship they have with their reporting managers, while demonstrating reverence and respect towards them. Leaders, in return, offer protection and support to and express concern for subordinates (Sinha & Kanungo, 1977). Nurturant task leadership has been found to be effective in Indian work organizations as it is congruent with Indian cultural values and behaviour dispositions (Sinha, D., 1999). The following Fig. 10.3 presents Indian Business System Framework.

Advancement in Information and Communication Technology (ICT) has impacted the business subsystem in a significant manner. The ongoing Covid pandemic has triggered the process of digitization of business model leading to organizations moving towards hybrid model (online and brick and mortar co-existing) or pure online business model. This has impacted the nature of peer-to-peer relationships within the organization and inter-organizational relationships. Superior-subordinate relationships are affected; the subordinates feel more empowered. Organizational boundaries have become more porous and permeable. Geographical distance does not matter too much. Information is available and accessible on the go. Virtual network has reinforced the physical

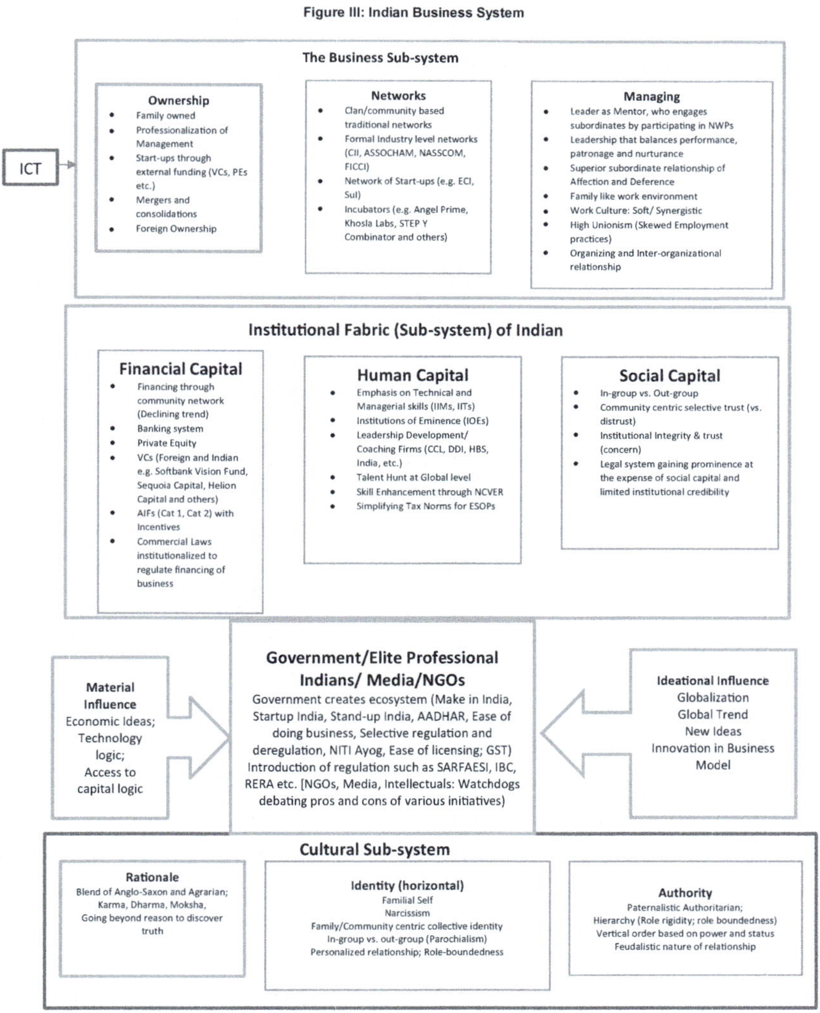

Fig. 10.3 Indian business system

face-to-face network leading to e-enabled inter-organizational relationships. Crowd-funding has become another option to raise funds for a common cause.

What It Means for Organizational Leaders and Academic Scholars?

Given the duality and paradoxes of India's socio-cultural and institutional contexts, academicians and organization theorists in India find it tough to understand Indian organizations with Western conceptual frameworks (Gupta, 1994). It offers significant guidance to organizational leaders on how to be effective in Indian cultural context. Moreover, this chapter also opens up new avenues for academic research.

Takeaways for organizational leaders: Organizational leaders in corporate India, to be effective, should create a family like work environment; nurture and mentor subordinates; involve subordinates in organizational activities; ensure performance without being task obsessive. He should be mildly prescriptive; and engage subordinates beyond work boundaries and shows his interest in subordinates' growth and well-being to create a truly familial organization in spirit. Unlike in Western world, the leaders in India should participate in non-work practices (Awasthy & Gupta, 2011). Organizational leaders may like to leverage these socio-cultural cues to develop strategies to be effective in their business contexts. This approach may be effective in organizations that are family owned and managed; may be less effective in professionally managed organizations.

Newer avenues for Academic Research: Business system framework as an analytic tool has gained significant attention from academic scholars to understand business ecosystem of various regions. Carney and Gedajlovic (2001) have compared three kinds of capitalisms—managerial, alliance and personal from corporate governance and firm capabilities perspectives. They have proposed that governance reform in East Asian economies should try at cultivating alternative governance institutions alongside existing relational institutions, rather than imitating 'Anglo-American' model. Estevez-Abe et al. (2001) have argued that social protection rescues the market from itself by preventing market failures. They contend that social protection aids the market by helping economic actors overcome market failures in skill formation. Hancke (2001) has analysed the coordination mechanism in the French Business System. Whitley and Czaban (1998) examined the economic behaviour of Hungarian firms, and their practices against the backdrop of

Hungarian state capitalism in 1990s. They found no significant change in firms' behaviour as the institutional ecosystems did not change immediately subsequent to the change in ownership pattern in state-owned firms. Lane and Bachmann (1996) have shown that trust-based relations between buyer and supplier firms rarely evolve spontaneously on the level of individual interaction but are highly dependent on the existence of stable legal, political and social institutions. Windolf and Beyer (1996) have examined the capital network (ownership) and the network of interlocking directorates among the 623 largest business firms in Germany and the 520 largest in Britain.

Academic scholars have attempted to understand and explain various organizational phenomena and practices using business system framework. Ahmad and Ercek (2019) have explained the link between national business system (NBS) and innovation decisions at the firm level in Pakistan business context by offering sequentially ordered sense-making mechanisms that enable the formation of firm-specific knowledge repositories and knowledge-processing capabilities. Haak-Saheem and Festing (2020) have examined HRM practices in Dubai from a national business systems perspective, by exploring the institutional factors that influence work, employment and HRM in the business system context of Dubai and thus identifying the underlying mechanisms of the interplay between institutional factors, work, employment relations and HRM. Sahasranamam and Ball (2018) have employed National Business System perspective to examine how institutional contexts impact the nature of social entrepreneurship from a comparative perspective. The have compared the design and behaviour of social entrepreneurship in institutional contexts of India and Scotland. Rana and Allen (2018), with the help of business system theory have explained entrepreneurship and entrepreneurial behaviour. They have presented how BST can help to explain entrepreneurial decision-making, motivation, venture and industry creation, social entrepreneurship, diaspora entrepreneurship, and, above all, institutional entrepreneurship in national and comparative institutional contexts. Fainshmidt et al. (2018) have proposed varieties of institutional systems to capture the diverse and unique institutional context of understudied economies in Africa, Middle East, East Europe, Latin America and Asia.

Moreover, business system framework is a useful tool to understand why a particular industry becomes successful in a particular country context. For instance, Bhatnagar (2006), while analysing the success of Indian software industry though did not explicitly rely on Business System perspective, yet his approach has all the elements of this perspective. By implication, business system perspective is not only useful in understanding business ecosystem at the country/region level; it is also useful in understanding relative success or failure of an Industry. Bhatnagar (2006) analysed the global success of Indian Software Industry. He identified critical factors such as (a) facilitating role of the Government of India such as creating and expanding computer department in existing engineering colleges; monitoring the quality of computer education through All India Council of Technical Education (AICTE) and Computer Society of India (CSI); encouraging private sector to open computer training institutes such as National Institute of Information Technology (NIIT) etc.; (b) huge investment in Technical (Computer) Education; (c) constructive role of Industry Organization such as NASSCOM in helping organizations in software industry to access American and European markets then; (d) setting up of STPs (Software Technology Parks) by the Government to provide dedicated infrastructure to export software; (e) positive role of Indian Diaspora (in the US) in many ways to market Indian software organizations in the US. The success of Indian Software Industry can be holistically understood and explained using Business System Framework (BSF) from an evolutionary perspective. The institutional arrangement, which is one of the core sub-systems of BSF, helped Indian Software industry to achieve initial success at Global level. The following figure depicts the same (For details, please refer to Bhatnagar, 2006). The following Fig. 10.4) explains the success of Indian software industry with the help of business system framework.

The emic and evolutionary nature of this framework helps scholars to develop a proper historical understanding of any business ecosystem. Such an understanding of Indian business ecosystem is important and urgent. In India, however, studies in business history are few and far between with the exception of the work of Tripathi (e.g. Tripathi, 1981, 1984, 1987, 2004). As mentioned above, historically, India has been

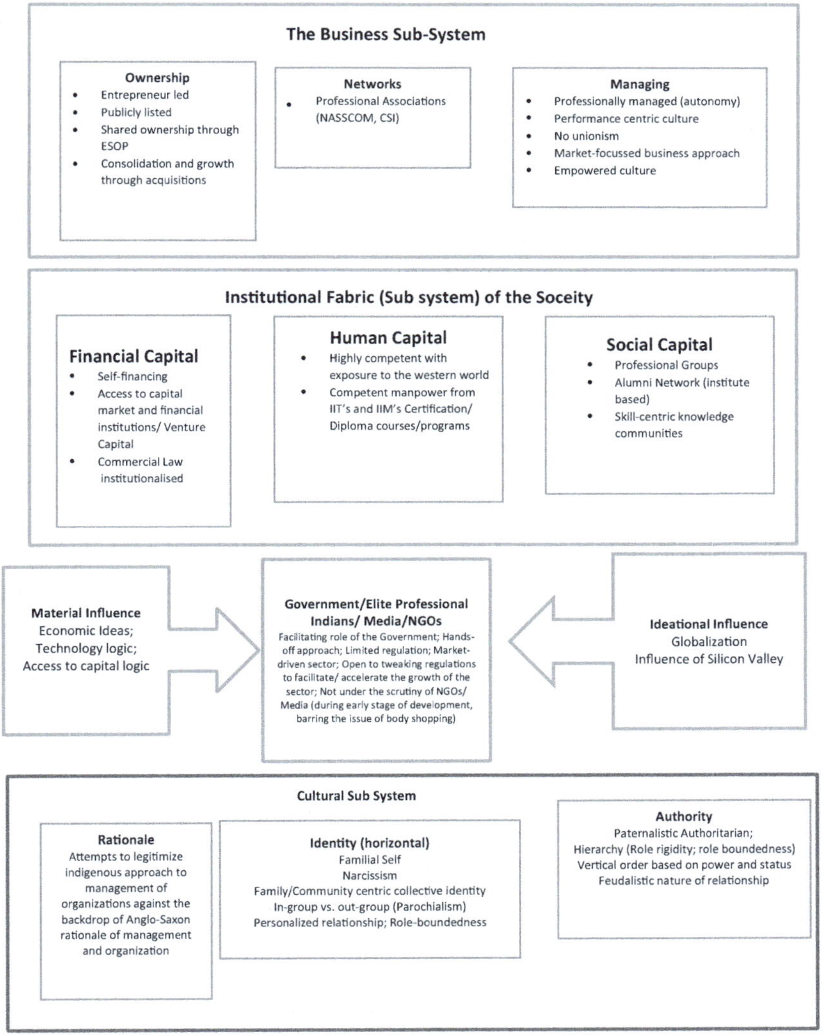

Fig. 10.4 Explaining the success of Indian software industry

governed/ ruled by various rulers (like Moghul Period, British Period and Post-Colonial Independent India with controlled regime, and current liberalization era), with varied ideological underpinnings and rationality, which needs to be understood for their implications on the evolution of both traditional and modern work organizations.

Given the hiatus between cultural sub-systems (informal background institutions) and institutional sub-system (formal institutional framework), management of organizations in India seems to be impacted by duality and paradoxical. The behaviour of Indians seems to be highly sensitive to context (context sensitive behaviour). There is a need to understand how organizations in India are actually managed; what is the nature of interactions between formal institutions and informal cultural institutions. It is important because formal institutions, which establish patterned ways of solving problems have not evolved organically from informal cultural institutions. Rather they have been imposed upon them creating a fault-line between both. Hence, it becomes a necessity to understand the indigenous nature of managing and organizing in the Indian context.

The contribution of the framework potentially is to contextualize findings, and to enrich understanding of the inner working of a business system. It would also provide much-needed fillip to the movement for indigenous management. Business system, as an analytic framework, has addressed the unit of analysis dilemma to a significant extent. Scholars have found variable-based quantitative approach that uses large amount of data to draw inferences, quite shallow lacking depth, whereas case-based qualitative approach may be good at offering in-depth understanding with rich insight is weak with respect to generalizability.

With this framework, organizational behaviour can be understood by analysing the interflow of connections and influences between parts of the framework such as the cultural and institutional characteristics of the context, the role of the government. The focus is to understand the unique economic behaviour within one society or state. This is because the role of state is powerful in shaping the system and so tends to make the boundary follow its sphere of influence. This business framework as presented in this chapter should be the starting point for academic scholars in India to conduct relevant research that would enhance one's understanding of business ecosystem of India. There would be a few genuine dilemmas for academic scholars. First, given the diversity in the way people (including corporate executives) think and behave in different parts of India, raises doubt if there is any one way of managing and organizing in Indian context? There is a possibility of multiple ways of managing and organizing organizations located in different parts of India. Researchers have taken ethnicity as the boundary cutting across states, as with Chinese Family Capitalism. Industry sector could also be set as the boundary of analysis. The idea is that in a country like India, 'one state can contain several identifiable business systems within it' (Redding, 2002, p. 223).

As a way forward, one may like to segregate India into different logical units (state, community, region, linguistic group and so on) and look for variation in cultural characteristics and explore their impacts on the management and organizing process. This is a challenge the researcher has to face when he/she takes up such a study in Indian context. The focus should be within-boundary homogeneity and across-boundary heterogeneity. It could be community, sector, region or any other relevant one given the scope of the study. Such studies would provide empirical evidence on the cultural diversity within India and its influences on management practices. Such a comparative approach would help us understand why organizations in some sector are doing better than others or why business practices are different in different sector. It would also provide fillip to movement for indigenization through 'native' or 'indigenous' understanding of the organizational practices.

A select few research themes could possibly be: (a) what is unique about the way organizations in India are managed and led? Are there different ways of managing and leading, depending on the community/region the promoter(s) belong(s) to? (b) Identifying cultural anchors of successful native Indian organizations that primarily rely on indigenous management practices. Family owned/managed Indian organizations fall within this cluster. (c) Identifying aspects which should form the core of the institutional framework of Indian Business System. These core aspects should be aligned with the socio-cultural realities of India. (d) Why some industry is globally more competitive compared to others? For instance, the IT sector is globally competitive, whereas the manufacturing sector has been struggling? Some specific questions that need to be examined given that India aspires to become global hub for manufacturing include (a) How to make manufacturing sector globally competitive? (b) What should be the institutional framework? and (c) What could be various policy and process interventions? (d) Does India's business system framework conducive for India to become competitive in any sector? If so, which one?

Moreover, one needs to examine where lies India's competitiveness given its business system. Haake (2002) has argued that industry-specific competitiveness is an outcome of a fit between patterns of national business systems and patterns of industrial task environment. Porter (1980) has contended that national competitive advantage is industry-specific. For instance, the United States, which has individualistic business systems appears to be strong in two groups of industries—high technology industries (Information Technology and Life Sciences) and service industries ranging from Consulting and Financial Services to motion pictures. Japan, which has communitarian business systems on the other hand is strong in the complex assembly manufacturing of miniaturized products, such as consumer electronics, cameras, photocopiers, machines tools and cars, but weak in financial services, consulting, software and biotechnology. The performance of companies can be related to the national conditions within which these companies operate. Communitarian business system is a business system in which actors share tight interfaces that turn these parties into interconnected communities. Tight interface essentially means an interface that is based on an intimate relationship between idiosyncratic set of parties, typically of an obligational nature. On the other hand, in individualistic business system, actors safeguard their individual autonomy through loose interface. Loose interface is defined as a short-term, circumscribed interface between a changeable set of parties, typically of a non-obligatory in nature. A few specific research questions that need to be examined are: (a) is Indian business system communitarian, individualistic or hybrid? (b) What is the nature of interface between actors/players?

Summary and Conclusions

This chapter has presented Indian business system using Redding's business system framework, which the authors believe will help practitioners, organizational leaders and academic researchers to develop an emic and holistic understanding of business ecosystem in India. The authors have argued that business system framework as a unit of analysis is comprehensive and holistic to gain insight on organizations and industry. Further, as an approach, it integrates both cultural and institutional perspectives to offer a holistic perspective. Economic behaviour of organizations is better understood in conjunction with socio-cultural and institutional contexts.

The authors have briefly presented how business system framework is conceived in order to address inadequacies found in cultural and institutional perspectives by integrating both perspectives. Subsequently, a section has been devoted to present key take aways for organizational leaders and academic scholars. The authors have suggested a few pointers that might help practitioners to be effective in organizational leadership roles in Indian context. They have also proposed a few research themes for academic scholars to pursue in their future research endeavour using business system framework.

References

Ahmad, B., & Erçek, M. (2019). Linking national business system and firm level innovation: A serial mediation analysis with intellectual capital and absorptive capacity. *European Journal of Innovation Management, 23*(5), 765–788. https://doi.org/10.1108/EJIM-01-2019-0016

Awasthy, R., & Gupta, R. (2011). Do non-work practices in MNCs operating in India impact organizational commitment? *Organizations and Markets in Emerging Economies, 2*(4), 28–52.

Berger, P. L., & Luckmann, T. (1966). *The social construction of reality: A treatise in the sociology of knowledge*. Harmondsworth, Middlesex: Penguin.

Bhatnagar, S. (2006). India's software industry. In V. Chandra (Ed.), *Technology, adaptation and exports: How some developing countries got it right* (pp. 95–124). World Bank.

Carney, M., & Gedajlovic, E. (2001). Corporate governance and firm capabilities: A comparison of managerial, alliance and personal capitalisms. *Asia Pacific Journal of Management, 18*(3), 335–354.

Chattopadhyay, G. P. (1986). Insights into Indian organizations: Motivation and leadership styles. In G. P. Chattopadhyay, Z. H. Gangjee, M. Linda Hunt, & W. Gordon Lawrence (Eds.), *When the Twain Meet: Western theory and eastern insights in exploring Indian organizations*. Wheelers and Co. Private Limited

Child, J. (1981). Culture, contingency and capitalism in the cross-national study of organization. In L. L. Cummings & B. M. Staw (Eds.), *Research in organizational behaviour* (Vol. 3, 303–356). JAI Press.

Eisenstadt, S. N. (1968). The protestant ethic thesis in an analytical and comparative framework. In S. N. Eisenstadt (Ed.), *The protestant ethic and modernization: A comparative view* (pp. 3-45). New York: Basic Books.

Eounga-Manguelle, D. (2000). Does Africa need a cultural adjustment program? L. E. Harrison & S. P. Huntington (Eds.), *Culture matters* (pp. 65–77). Basic Books.

Estevez-Abe, M., Iversen, T., & Soskice, D. (2001). Social protection and the formation of skills: A reinterpretation of the welfare state. In P. A. Hall & D. Soskice (Eds.), *Varieties of capitalism: The institutional foundations of comparative advantage* (pp. 145–183). Oxford University Press.

Fainshmidt, S., Judge, W. Q., Aguilera, R. V., & Smith, A. (2018). Varieties of institutional systems: A contextual taxonomy of understudied countries. *Journal of World Business, 53*(3), 307–322.

Foss, N. J. (1999). The challenge of business systems and challenge to business systems. *International Studies of Management and Organization, 29*(2), 9–24.

Garg, P. K., & Parikh, I. J. (1995). *Crossroads of culture: A study in the culture of transience.* Sage.

Granovetter, M. (1992). The nature of economic relations. In S. Ortiz & S. Lees (Eds.), *Understanding economic process* (pp. 21–37). University Press of America (for Society for Economic Anthropology),

Gupta, R. (1994). Challenges in developing indigenous theories of organization and management: An Indian perspective. *Indian Journal of Social Work, 55*(2), 220–248.

Gupta, R. K., & Panda, A. (2003). Individualised familial self: The evolving self of qualified technocrats in India. *Psychology and Developing Societies, 15*(1), 1–29.

Gupta, R. K., & Panda, A. (2009). Culture, institutions and organization in India. In G. Misra (Ed.), *ICSSR survey of advances in research: Psychology in*

India (Vol. 2, pp. 215–355) (Social and Organizational Processes), Pearson Education. ICSSR.

Haake, S. (2002). National business systems and industry-specific competitiveness. *Organization Studies, 23*(5), 711–736.

Haak-Saheem, W., & Festing, M. (2020). Human resource management—A national business system perspective. *The International Journal of Human Resource Management, 31*(14), 1863–1890.

Hancke, B. (2001). Revisiting the French model: Coordination and restructuring in French industry, Chapter 9. In P. A. Hall & D. Soskice (Eds.), *Varieties of capitalism: The institutional foundations of competitive advantage* (pp. 305–334). Oxford University Press.

Hofstede, G. (1996). An American in Paris: The influence of nationality on organization theories. *Organization Studies, 17*(3), 525–537.

Jain, S. (2001). Structure and culture: The debate. In S. Visvanathan (Ed.), *Structure and transformation theory and society in India.* Oxford University Press.

Kakar S., Kets de Vries, M. F. R., Kakar S., & Vrignaud, P. (2002). Leadership in Indian organizations from a comparative perspective. *International Journal of Cross Cultural Management, 2*(2), 239–250.

Khandwalla, P. (1976). The techno economic ecology of corporate strategy. *Journal of Management Studies, 13*(1), 62–75.

Khandwalla, P. (1995). *Effective management styles: An Indian study* (IIMA Working Papers WP1995-03-01_01317). Indian Institute of Management Ahmedabad, Research and Publication Department.

Khandwalla, P. (2002). Effective organizational response by corporates to India's liberalisation and globalisation. *Asia Pacific Journal of Management, 19*, 423–448.

Khandwalla, P. (2006). Tools for enhancing innovativeness in enterprises. *Vikalpa, 31*(1), 1–16.

Khandwalla, P. N. (1996). *Management styles.* Tata McGraw Hill, New Delhi.

Lane, C., & Bachmann, R. (1996). The social constitution of trust: Supplier relations in Britain and Germany. *Organization Studies, 17*, 365–395.

Lowe, S. (1998, March). Culture and network institutions in Hong Kong: A hierarchy of perspectives. A response to Wilkinson's 'culture, institutions and business in East Asia',—Response to Barry Wilkinson. *Organization Studies* (Vol. 17). https://doi.org/10.1177%2F017084069801900208

McClelland, D. C. (1975). *Power: The inner experience.* New York: Free Press.

Morris, M. (2002). *Social capital and poverty in India* (IDS Working Paper 61). UK Department of International Development.

Panda, A., & Gupta, R. K. (2004). Mapping cultural diversity within India: A meta-analysis of some recent studies. *Global Business Review, 5*(1), 27–49.

Paranjape, A. C. (1988). A personality theory according to Vedanta. In A. C. Paranjape, D. X. E. Ho, & R. W. Ribber (Eds.), *Asian contribution to psychology*. Praeger.

Polanyi, K. (1944). The great transformation. Beacon Press.

Porter, M. (1980). *The competitive advantage of nations.* McMillan.

Rana, M. B., & Allen M. M. C. (2018). Business systems perspective on entrepreneurship. In R. Turcan & N. Fraser (Eds.), *The Palgrave handbook of multidisciplinary perspectives on entrepreneurship* (pp. 271–291). Palgrave Macmillan. https://doi.org/10.1007/978-3-319-91611-8_13

Redding, G. (2001). The evolution of business systems (INSEAD Working Paper Series, Euro Asia Centre [EAC] 2003/47/ABA/ EAC 3).

Redding, G. (2002). The capitalist business system of China and its rationale. *Asia Pacific Journal of Management, 19*(2–3), 221–249.

Roland, A. (1980). *Towards a psychoanalytic psychology of hierarchical relationships in Hindu India.* Paper presented to the Indian Psychoanalytic Society.

Roland, A. (1988). In *search of self in India and Japan: Towards a cross-cultural psychology*. New Jersey: Princeton University Press.

Saberwal, S. (2001). Framework in change: Colonial India Society. In S. Visvanathan (Ed.), *Structure and transformation theory and society in India* (pp. 33–57). Oxford University Press.

Sahasranamam, S., & Ball, C. (2018). National business context matters: Influence of national business system on social enterprises in Scotland and India. In L. J. Spence, J. G. Frynas, J. N. Mathuri, & J. Navare (Eds.), *Research handbook on small business social responsibility* (pp. 23–46). https://doi.org/10.4337/9781784711825.00009. Edward Elgar Publishing Limited.

Schumpeter, J. A. (1949). The Communist manifesto in sociology and economics. *Journal of Political Economy, 57*, 199–212.

Sinha, D. (1988). Basic Indian values and behaviour disposition in the context of national development. In D. Sinha & H. S. R. Kao (Eds.), *Social values and development: Asian perspectives* (pp. 31–55). New Delhi: Sage.

Sinha, D. (1999). Approaches to indigenous management. In H. S. R. Kao, D. Sinha, & Sek-Hong Ng (Eds.), *Management and cultural values* (pp. 43–52).

Sinha, J. B. P. (1990). *Work culture in the Indian context*. Sage.

Sinha, J. B. P. (2005, April 14–16). *Indians' shifting cultural frame for managing people in organizations.* Paper presented during the workshop on Indian Culture and Management at COSMODE Management Research Center.

Sinha, J. B. P., & Kanungo, R. N. (1997). Context sensitivity and balancing in organizational behaviour. *International Journal of Psychology, 32*, 93–105.
Sinha, J. B. P., Gupta, P., Singh, S., Srinivas, E. S., & Vijaykumar, V. S. R. (2001). Societal beliefs, organizational climate and managers' self-perceptions. *Vikalpa, 26*(1), 33–47.
Sinha, J. B. P., Vohra, N., Singhal, S., Sinha, R. B. N., & Ushashree, S. (2002). Normative predictions of collectivist- individualist intentions and behaviour of Indians'. *International Journal of Psychology, 37*, 309–319.
Spratt, P. (1966). *Hindu culture and personality.* Manaktalas.
Tripathi, D. (1981). *The dynamics of tradition: Kasturbhai Lalbhai and his entrepreneurship.* Manohar.
Tripathi, D. (1984). *Business communities of India: A historical perspective.* Manohar.
Tripathi, D. (1987). *State and business in India: A historical perspective.* Manohar.
Tripathi, D. (2004). *The Oxford history of Indian businesses.* Oxford University Press.
Virmani, B. R. (2000). *Managing people in organizations: The challenges of change, response books.* Sage.
Virmani, B. R., & Guptan, S. (1991). *Indian management.* Vision Books.
Weber, M. (1930). *The protestant ethic and the spirit of capitalism.* London: Urwin.
Whitley, R. (1992a). *Business systems in East Asia.* Sage.
Whitley, R. (1992b). *European business systems.* Sage.
Whitley, R. (1994). *European business systems, firms and markets in their national context.* Sage.
Whitley, R., & Czaban, L. (1998). Institutional change and enterprise transformation in an emergent capitalist economy: The case of Hungary. *Organization Studies, 18*, 259–280.
Windolf, P., & Beyer, J. (1996). Co-operative capitalism: Corporate networks in Germany and Britain. *British Journal of Sociology, 47*, 205–231.
Witt, M. A., Ricardo de Castro, L., Amaeshi, K., Mahroum, S., Bohle, D., & Saez, L. (2018). Mapping the business systems of 61 major economies: A taxonomy and implications for varieties of capitalism and business system research. *Socio-Economic Review, 18*(1), 5–38.

11

Social Entrepreneurship in India

Nisha Pandey and Arunaditya Sahay

Introduction

Social Entrepreneurship (SE) is a way to bring about positive change in the society by adopting a mission to create and sustain social value and not just private value (Zahra et al., 2009). It is a composition of several sub-concepts like social value creation, the social entrepreneur, the social entrepreneurship organization, market orientation and social innovation (Choi & Mujumdar, 2014). SE involves recognizing and pursuing new opportunities to serve that mission of creating social value, engaging in a process of continuous innovation, adaptation and learning, acting boldly

N. Pandey (✉)
VES Business School, Mumbai, India
e-mail: nisha.pandey@ves.ac.in

A. Sahay
Birla Institute of Management Technology, Greater Noida, India

© The Author(s), under exclusive license to Springer Nature Switzerland AG 2022
A. Pandey et al. (eds.), *Indigenous Indian Management*, Palgrave Studies in Indian Management,
https://doi.org/10.1007/978-3-030-87906-8_11

without being limited by readily available resources, and exhibiting a heightened sense of accountability to the constituencies served and for the outcomes created (Dees, 1998). It is a response to failure of market, state or both in meeting needs of society at bottom of pyramid (Wallace, 1999). SE is increasingly recognized as a strong force to bridge the gap between the demand and supply for fulfilment of socio-economic and environmental needs (Gupta et al., 2017).

SE focus on working while considering the societal values and move forward in the directions that can pave the way for the development at the bottom of the pyramid. Therefore, SE results in new forms of organizations that move away from the solely following a market logic to the organization which incorporate the institutional logic of society and community along logic of the market (Di Domenico et al., 2010). Social enterprise is a hybrid organization that tries to achieve both market orientation and social value creation for a double bottom-line. The phenomenon is strongly influenced by contextual, structural and institutional forces, thereby leading to regional perspectives (Kerlin, 2010; Sengupta & Sahay, 2017). Figure 11.1 summarizes how social entrepreneurs emerges and life cycle of social enterprise.

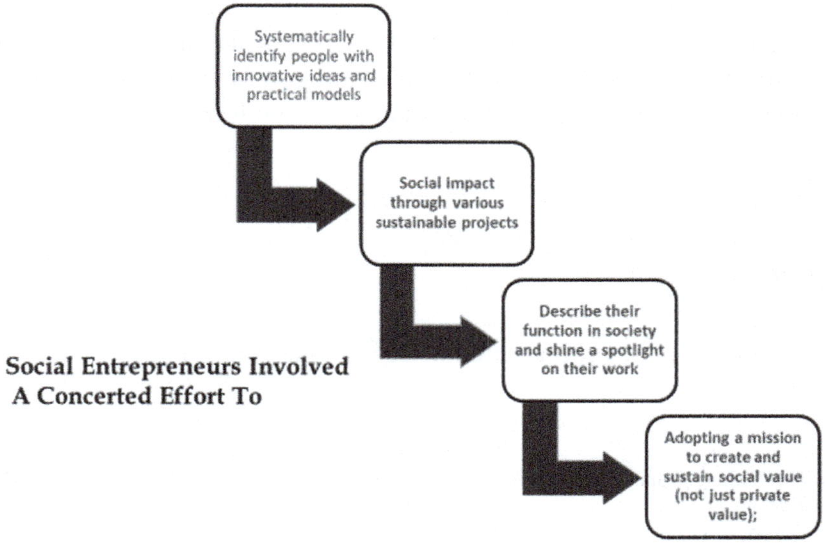

Fig. 11.1 Emergence of social enterprises (Author creation)

This chapter is written with the twin objectives of explicating the emergence, cultural foundation and nuances of social entrepreneurship in India and to develop a research agenda for the field. This chapter is structured in nine section. In the second section, we present a historical account of SE in India based on few remarkable case examples. Remaining sections elaborate on how social entrepreneurship works, why social entrepreneurship is important for India, social entrepreneurship and cultural values of India, taxonomy of entrepreneurs, theoretical foundations of social entrepreneurship add implications for research before drawing conclusion.

Social Entrepreneurship in India: A Historical Perspective

The term 'social entrepreneurship' was formally introduced in India when Ashoka Foundation set up operations in 1981 which formed a community of change makers who sought to design, launch and scale high-impact ideas in low-income markets. The founder of Ashoka Foundation gained the practical exposure to the Gandhian approach in the Sarvodaya movement under the mentorship of Vinoba Bhave in 1960s. Gandhian thought goes into the basic tenets of Ashoka Foundation.[1] However, there are many social movements and organizations in India emerged in last seventy years which have formed and shaped the basic approach of SE in India and many other parts of the world.

In this section, we describe the Bhoodan (Land Gift) Movement, Gujrat Milk Marketing Federation (GMMF), Self Employed Women's Association (SEWA), Mysore Resettlement and Development Agency (MYRADA) which set the precedent for India's future social enterprises. These four examples symbolize the four very different types of organizational designs employed to address the social issues and to address the needs of society not addressed by the market or state. We also describe the newer SEs like Solar Electric Light Company (SELCO), Bhartiya Samruddhi Investments and Consulting Services Ltd., promoted by

[1] https://www.ashoka.org/en-in/story/bill-drayton-half-population-out-game.

Professional Assistance for Development Action (PRADAN). That owns the brand name BASIX (BASIX is the brand name of a group of companies belonging to Bhartiya Samruddhi Investments and Consulting Services Ltd.), to present the evolutionary trajectory and the unique features of SEs in India. We also provide a note on National Bank for Agriculture and Rural Development (NABARD) which has played a very crucial role in nurturing SE in India.

Bhoodaan Movement in India: Tale of Imagination and Inspiration Meeting Core Indian Values

Mahatama Gandhi had worked on translating the model of Gramswaraj (rural independence) into practice. The followers of Gandhiji consolidate this idea of Gramswaraj and formulate a new structure for rural reconstruction. Known as spiritual heir of Mahatama Gandhi, Vinoba Bhave, can probably be called the India's first social entrepreneur who founded and led the Land Gift Movement.

Acharya Vinova Bhave, born (September 2, 1896) in a village in Maharashtra, gave the provision of Land by gift for the common benefit of the landless and marginalized. This proposition of donating land to landless farmers was the foundation of the Bhoodan movement. Bhoodan means land gift. 'Bhoo' in Sanskrit is Land and Dan is gift. Daan in Hindu religion and tradition is considered very pious. Bhoodan for land gift had great appeal among the people. Bhoodan (land gift) began in 1951 and soon became a movement in whole of India, about 4 million acres of land was received as daan (gift) till 1970.

Nanekar and Khandewale (1973) studied the Bhoodan experiment in early seventies and divided the Movement into two phases; first is from 1951 to 1957 and the second is from 1958 to 1969. The first phase was divided (1951–1957) into four distinct phases by intensity of the Movement. First, palliative; i.e. phase of removal of local grievances; second, calling attention, i.e. a phase of creating a wider understanding of the movement and calling attention of the nation; third, fortification of faith, i.e. a phase of building confidence among the workers about the possibility of the giant mission, and fourth phase was the extensive land gift phase.

Land distribution took place as soon as the declaration was made by the donor. Grantee was given a kachha patta, and only after the gift was verified and approved as legal, a pucca patta was given to the lessee. It entered the record of rights of village revenue record.

Although, Bhoodan was not an official programme but the then Prime Minister of India, Jawaharlal Nehru, constituted and supported it by legal provisions for legalizing the transfers of land. State governments developed legal arrangements for accepting the gift and for redistribution. Procedures were laid down for transfer of land by a person owning a transferable interest in land to the Bhoodan Mandal. A declaration had to be made by any person desiring to transfer the land to the Revenue officer. It was examined and when found legal and without any problem relating to title etc., the gift was registered under Indian Registration Act of 1908. To provide it legislature support, a model Gramdan Bill was prepared by Dr. Ram Krishna Patil a prominent Sarvodaya worker and the member of Planning Commission. A number of states like Bihar, Orissa, Assam, Madhya Pradesh, Maharashtra, Gujarat and Tamilnadu formulated such laws.

The Bhoodaan movement gradually culminated into Gramdan, where the land of the entire village was donated to the community and treated as community property. There were three stages under Gramdan. In the first stage, village would agree to donate all its land. In the second stage, after the gift papers were received by Sarvoday Mandal, the village would be declared as Gramdan village. In the third stage, the village would be registered as a Gramdani village in government records. Gramdan was the voluntary approach by the land owners to relinquish the right of land in favour of the village community. It was conducted with democratic procedure where decisions were taken by the Gramsabha as a whole of which each adult resident was a member. The movement was very well planned and stepped in a systematic ways in the mind of villagers. By removal of local grievance first they made them comfortable with each other and then created wider understanding of the movement. The entire movement became possible by building faith and creating confidence among workers. Evaluating the movement in terms of getting land as achievement is not a right criterion, it should be considered as one of the remarkable experiments to provide a peaceful solution of the grassroots problem of labours and farmers which was not properly solved by the government and market forces but it was solved through voluntary action involving the masses. It was original in its conception, novel in methods, and yet revolutionary to bring equality in society.

Kaira District Co-operative Milk Producers' Union, Gujrat Milk Marketing Federation and Amul India

Over seven decades ago, farmers in Kaira, Gujrat were living in adverse conditions. Their income was derived from seasonal crops. Many poor farmers faced starvation during off-seasons. Their income from milk was unreliable. The milk marketing system was controlled by contractors and middlemen. As milk is perishable, farmers were compelled to sell their milk for unreasonable prices. They were in general illiterate. But they could see that the system under which contractors could buy their produce at a low price and arrange to sell it at huge profits.

As a result of the farmers' poor conditions, who were also receiving low prices of milk products and unreasonable behaviour by the middlemen, Kaira District Milk Union Limited was created in 1946 (later Renamed as Amul) by Tribhuvandas Patel under the guidance of Sardar Vallabhbhai Patel. Tribhuvandas was the founding chairman of the Kaira District Co-operative Milk and led it until his retirement in 70s. He was a freedom fighter, a Gandhian, a fearless leader, a social worker, a tireless advocate, a cooperative philosopher who worked selflessly for the benefit of millions of people in India.

Under the chairmanship of Tribhuvandas, Dr. Kurien was initially the general manager and helped in the technical and marketing efforts of Amul. Dr. Kurien was elected as the chairman of Amul after Tribhuvandas Patel died in 1994. The cooperative was further developed and managed by Dr. Verghese Kurien with H.M. Dalaya. Dalaya's innovation of making skim milk powder from buffalo milk (for the first time in the world), and a little later, with Kurien's help, making it on a commercial scale, led to the first modern dairy of the cooperative at Anand.

The trio's (T. K. Patel, Kurien and Dalaya's) success at the cooperative's dairy soon spread to Anand's neighbourhood in Gujarat. Within a short span, five unions in other districts—Mehsana, Banaskantha, Baroda, Sabarkantha and Surat were set up, following the approach sometimes described as the Anand pattern. There are, in all, 18 District Co-operative Milk Producers' Unions federated to Gujarat Co-operative Milk Marketing Federation Limited (GMMF), Anand which markets milk and milk products under the brand of Amul & Sagar.[2] Amul is one of the most reputed and well-known brand created and owned by GMMF. This was probably the first business model where low-income dairy farmers formed a professionally managed and privately owned supply chain in Gujrat. They took ownership of distribution and lifted themselves out of poverty.

Self Employed Women Association (SEWA)

SEWA is a trade union registered in 1972. It is the oldest union of self-employed workers. Ela R. Bhatt is the 'founder' of SEWA. She hails from family of the freedom fighters and the ardent followers of Gandhiji. She describes herself as a product of the later years of the freedom movement, the independence movement of India.

It is an organization of poor and self-employed women workers. These are women who earn a living through their own efforts or small businesses. They do not obtain regular salaried employment with welfare benefits like workers in the organized sector. They are the unprotected labour force of our country. The SEWA movement is enhanced by its being a *sangam* or confluence of the labour movement, cooperative Movement and women's Movement. The main goal of SEWA is to organize women workers for full employment. Full employment means employment whereby workers obtain work security, income security, food security and social security (at least health care, child care and shelter).

[2] http://www.amuldairy.com/index.php/the-organization/an-overview.

Practically, the strategy is carried out through the joint action of union and cooperatives. Gandhian thinking is the guiding force for SEWA and follows the principles of SWAV—satya (truth), ahimsa (non-violence), sarvadharma (integrating all faiths, all people) and khadi (propagation of local employment and self-reliance). Microcredit is a very important element of the co-trade union cum operative model of SEWA. More than 100 cooperatives helped women to improve the marketing, quality, and design of the handicraft and woven items to ensure consistency, timely delivery and saleability. Cooperatives also promote new agricultural products and techniques that add value to traditional products. Other cooperatives include a rural marketing organization and a Trade Facilitation Centre. SEWA was successful by mass transformation of behaviour, public participation from village, partnership from government and local bodies, financed by World Bank and supported by government. SEWA attained the status of Union Federation in 2011 and has members in their Union exceeding 100 trades. SEWA has a membership of over 700,000 with 535,000 from the State of Gujarat alone, the membership is growing at a rate of 25–35% per annum.

One of the notable achievement of SEWA has been to promote unique types of institution dealing with different themes such as banking, Mahila Udyog, Insurance, education of women, schools, apex federation of women etc. SEWA has given various aspects of women's movement in the informal sectors. It is an achievement because a concept of SEWA is a union of unorganized women labour is itself an innovation and therefore to sustain, the SEWA has introduced nearly 20 organization. In addition, SEWA has setup organizations of social security and also introduced international network in South Asian region. Further, services of regarding child welfare, housing, etc., are also addressed by SEWA. Cooperatives complement SEWA's union efforts against employers by giving informal workers an alternative income source drawing from group-based support. In addition to its cooperative, in 2003, SEWA launched the Trade Facilitation Center (TFC), which is registered as a non-profit company with worker shareholders.[3] What is noteworthy

[3] Rina Agarwala Redefining Exploitation: Self-Employed Workers' Movements in India's Garments and Trash Collection Industries International Labor and Working-Class History No. 89, Spring 2016, pp. 107–130.

about all this development is that SEWA has been able to bring out nearly 50 publications on various aspects which suggest that the promoters and management have included the concept and practices of knowledge management—production and distribution.[4]

Mysore Resettlement and Development Agency (MYRADA) and Other Examples

MYRADA is a non-government organization started in 1968 working in backward and drought-prone areas. It has worked with more than a million families in 18 districts of Karnataka, Andhra Pradesh and Tamil Nadu, for strengthening community based organizations (CBOs), promoting livelihood activities, improving health and education status of the community to raise and manage resources independently. Its focus right through has been on building local people's institutions. The pioneering work done in forming and establishing self-help groups of poor rural women is what has put MYRADA on the national and international map and remained a grassroots organization.

'Influencing policy' has been overarching feature of their work—in favour of the poor, MYRADA has constantly advocated for policy changes at every level—from the district to the state to the national level. They have influenced state policy in many sectors—from livelihoods, to natural resource management to skill training and health. In particular, MYRADA has achieved important success in two focused areas; savings and credit management through self-help affinity groups and participatory watershed management. Both of which have been built on and mainstreamed in Indian State policies for poverty alleviation, women's empowerment and natural resources management. The Community Managed Resource Centers (CMRC) concept was started by MYRADA and is gaining traction with governments beginning to consider it as a viable option.

Harish Hande, a social entrepreneur, had set up a Sustainable Business Model in 1995—Solar Electric Light Company (SELCO), which provided low-cost products, servicing and financing through rural banks

[4] http://www.sewa.org/Sewa_Services.asp.

and cooperative societies. SELCO Solar has installed over 450,000 solar solutions for the poor which have been paid for by the poor using various financing methods designed by SELCO and its financial partners that match their cash flows.

In 1996, realizing the need to attract mainstream financial resources, Vijay Mahajan (the President of Microfinance Institutions Network of India) conceptualized BASIX, an institution devoted to promoting livelihoods for the poor on a sustainable basis. At a time when limited financial and non-financial support was available to social entrepreneurs, SELCO and BASIX developed sustainable business models for bringing rural services to poor households.

In 1997, Grassroots Innovations Augmentation Network (GIAN) became India's first non-profit socially minded venture capital fund (VCF), and in 2001 Aavishkaar became the country's first for-profit counterpart. It marked the beginning of what is now an extensive network of social enterprise enablers. India saw its first impact investment in 2001 when Acumen Fund invested in Aravind Eye Hospital. Unique model of Arvind Eye hospital is described in Chapter 9 of this handbook. The presence of the Acumen Fund and Aavishkaar in India spurred the demand for early stage investments in for-profit organizations with a social impact.

In India, social entrepreneurs adopt social innovation at various level, they build applicable and sustainable solutions, work as bridge between capitalism and socialism and create both economic and social values with market-oriented approach to sustain in the market. Most observed and identified drivers to motivate these change makers are their market-oriented capabilities, business modelling and their leadership style.

National Bank for Agriculture and Rural Development (NABARD)

The importance of institutional credit in boosting rural economy has been clear to the Government of India right from its early stages of planning. Therefore, the Reserve Bank of India (RBI) at the insistence of the

Government of India, constituted a Committee to Review the Arrangements for Institutional Credit for Agriculture and Rural Development (CRAFICARD) to look into these very critical aspects. National Bank for Agriculture and Rural Development (NABARD) was approved by the Parliament through Act 61 of 1981. NABARD was set up in July 1982.

The mission of NABARD is to promote sustainable and equitable agriculture and rural development through effective credit support, related services, institution building and other innovative initiatives. In pursuing this mission, NABARD focuses its activities on: Credit functions, involving preparation of potential-linked credit plans annually for all districts of the country for identification of credit potential, monitoring the flow of ground level rural credit, issuing policy and operational guidelines to rural financing institutions and providing credit facilities to eligible institutions. It also provides facilities for training, dissemination of information and promotion of research in the field of rural banking, agriculture and rural development. NABARD functions on overall rural development by ways of capacity building and income generating interventions. The organization is also aimed at supplementing the credit functions as well as making credit more productive, supervisory functions, ensuring the proper functioning of cooperative banks and regional rural banks.

The contributions of NABARD in directly or indirectly creating a base for promoting SE in India is by setting up Alternate Investment Funds, financing and supporting Producer Organizations (PO) like Producers Cooperatives, registered Farmer Federations, MACS (Mutually Aided Cooperative society) and Industrial Cooperative Societies. NABARD has many off the form initiatives to its credit to promote social enterprises like Rural Innovation Fund (RIF), Rural Entrepreneurship Development Programmes (REDPs) and Skill Development Programmes (SDPs) for facilitating generation of self-employment and wage employment opportunities in rural areas. NABARD has been implementing the Cluster Development Programme under the National Programme on Rural Industrialisation (NPRI) since 1999–2000. NABARD has cumulatively approved a total of 119 clusters in 110 districts across 22 States. Focus was given on development of clusters in north eastern region (NER) with as many as 23 clusters in the NER and backward regions. Prominent clusters supported under the programme were Handloom (57), Handicrafts (43) and Food processing and rural tourism (7 each). NABARD, through its' Micro Credit Innovations Department, has continued its role as the facilitator and mentor of microfinance initiatives in the country. It has been continuously focusing on bringing in various stakeholders on a common platform and building their capacities to take the initiatives forward. This has resulted in tremendous growth of microfinance sector in India through different approaches like Self Help Group–Bank Linkage Programme (SHG-BLP).

How Social Entrepreneurship Works?

SEs address the social and unaddressed problems in a systematic ways. First of all, social entrepreneurs identify stable but unjust equilibrium in prevailing society, for instance health problem in unauthorized housing slums. The families living in these slums are stable but having numerous health issues which are not taken care by state or local government. These problems create unrest and also create meaning for these change makers. This is the first stage when social entrepreneurs start thinking to solve the problems and create change. In second phase, they start to develop solution, scaling, testing, refining their own actions and plans and deploy a social value proposition to challenge the status quo of the society which is suffering from various problems. For example, founder of Mann Desi Bank, first collected information from all the villages and women suffering from their husbands and troubled by the social trauma. The founder then proposed a new bank for the rural women in Maharashtra who can save their own earned money. She proposed a new social value proposition to challenge stable equilibrium and created new equilibrium in the village by starting women driven bank in the village (Bhushan, 2018).

While the other types of entrepreneurship engage in value creation and appropriation, social enterprises engage only in value creation. In this case, the value is to be appropriated by the primary and secondary stakeholders. In the second phase, they prepare a background and strategies to implement their solutions made to address the unaddressed social problems.

In the third stage, they create new and stable equilibrium by implementing innovative social value proposition proposed in second phase. In new equilibrium, the solution of unaddressed problem start working. New solutions start to deliver results and satisfaction and also give directions to face new challenges. This proposition becomes the new stable model. For example, Ms Chetna Gala Sinha who proposed the bank for women, now this bank ('Mann Desi') has started to work for women, by the women to support them for saving day to day earning (Bhushan, 2018; Shukla, 2019). Starting new bank in the village with the help of Government and with her passion, Ms. Chetna has created new and stable equilibrium. Figure 11.2 represents the way SE works in any society.

Sengupta and Sahay (2017) proposed a comprehensive framework based on their findings on social entrepreneurship in the context of the emerging economies. As per their findings, there are five constructs that are identified as sub-concepts coming together under the concept of social entrepreneurship, they are: Social Welfare (creating significant social values), Social Capital (creating a rich human resources

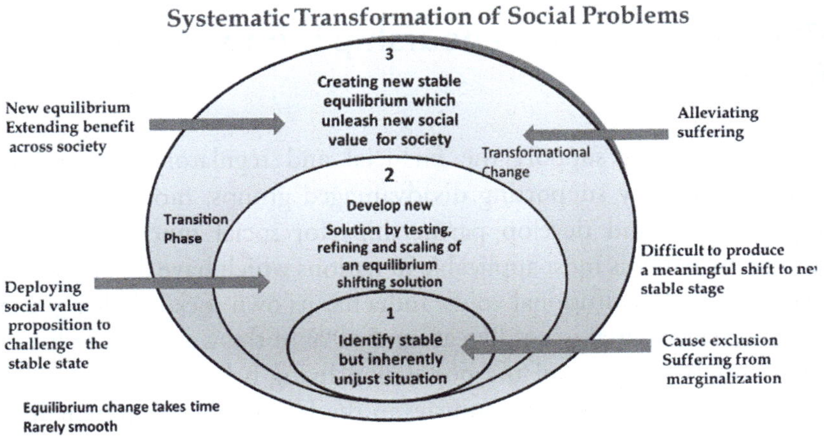

Fig. 11.2 Ways the SE works in a society (Author creation)

through community participation), Economic Values (for financial sustainability), Collective Endurance (efforts to battle challenges at regulatory and institutional level) and Social Entrepreneurs (who takes all initiatives).

Social entrepreneurs focus their efforts on identifying the positives which can be leveraged, build capacities to develop more empowered participants from local communities to address social and market dynamics. They aim at re-crafting the value chains which connect players and locations. They need the collaboration among diverse stakeholders like participation from Government, community, NGOs, and technology and experts from various domains. Continuous learning, innovation and self-correction are the inherent aspects of the success of social entrepreneurship. The social problems are complex, multi-faceted and multi-layered like malnutrition among village children, conditions of landless farmers and gender discrimination; hence, the solutions to social problems are also not simple and linear. The impact of social interventions is not immediately visible. The time required to get the positive impact on these challenges is prolonged due to these complexities. Hence, social entrepreneurs require long-term engagement and creating solutions for the marginalized segments and changing the socio-economic equilibrium which is self-sustainable (Shukla, 2019).

Why Social Entrepreneurship is Important for India?

Social enterprises support the financial and regulatory sustainability of civil society by supporting disadvantaged groups, mobilize community resources and develop partnerships for social innovation. Social entrepreneurship is most applicable in nations which have developmental challenges and institutional voids. India has its own social challenges and social developmental issues like around 40% of the world's poor lives in India and 30 per cent of the population living below the poverty line. It ranks 131th among 188 countries in the Human Development Index (UNDP, 2020). The country is facing various socio-economic challenges like illiteracy, malnutrition, and poor healthcare, gender issues, poor housing and poor infrastructure in rural India. Institutional voids are referred to as situations where formal institutions supporting market such as property rights, governance structures, etc., are either absent or are too weak to perform (Mair & Marti, 2009). The institutional voids hinder market activities aimed at alleviating poverty which in turn help in addressing various challenges of socio-economic development (McKague et al., 2015). SE helps in filling the institutional voids (Stephan et al., 2016).

The government alone cannot address these challenges at the grass-roots level and remove the inequalities prevailing in society. These factors and driving forces underscores the emergence of social entrepreneurs in India who work as public welfare bodies, developmental aid provider, some time they work with close engagement with key stakeholders, individual training provider, crises management and poverty alleviation. This leads to a transformation of the production process and the ways in activities are undertaken; the providers and users work jointly in the creation of demand and supply and also the management of activities and services (Defourny & Nyssens, 2013). Challenges related to socio-economic development and institutional voids are addressed by SE in India by enhancing social cohesion, values-based development and addressing social inequalities.

Social Cohesion

Social cohesion is one of the main objectives and focus areas of activities of SEs. In this sense, their ultimate objective is to remove the roadblocks to social cohesion such as a lack of social and healthcare services, the lack of education, skills or employment, welfare benefits, societal and cultural norms that moves people away from social inclusion.

Value-Based Development

Value-based development is creating employment and enhancing employability in various forms of business by changing or substantially redrafting the traditional way of doing business. Companies like Essence

Fibres and Champs Eco Sign Unit operating in Maharashtra are the examples in this regard. They make yarn from banana fibres for Saree making by employing rural women from the lower socio-economic strata of the locality. The example of making fibres from Banana Stems is redrafting the traditional way of saree making and use of banana stem. The business has created employment as well as enhanced employability of rural poor women. Similarly, the Help Us Green enterprise, initiated by two young students from Kanpur for creating values from used and waste flowers from religious places offered by devotees. They created new proposition and convert the waste material into a new for-profit social business. Social enterprises like Essence Fibres and Help Us Green provide employment to those who belongs to bottom of the pyramid. The enterprise created employment and employability for these unskilled women.

Addressing Social Inequalities

Addressing social inequality is the driving force of taking initiative by social entrepreneurs. In this case, the change makers observe that there are inequalities in society in the form of economic status, social structure, gender disparity, availability of nutritional food or human rights. Inequality makes them restless and provokes them to work for some sustainable solution to remove or decrease the inequalities appearing in various forms in the society. For example, founder of Microfinance—Yunus started giving a small loan of only $27 to those poor people who were suffering because of a traditional money lender and exploited by them.

Another example of addressing social inequality is Jayshree Industries in Coimbatore who are providing dignity to women by making sanitary towels affordable and provide them with an income at the same time. The founder of Jayshree Industries—Arunachalam Muruganathamis changed the life of poor women who were using dirty clothes during their menstrual period. He created the world's first low-cost machine to produce sanitary towels.

Social Entrepreneurship and Cultural Values of India

Indian culture suggests that human life be organized on the basis of four 'Purusharthas: Dhrama (nature, acquisition of knowledge, right path, duties and intrinsic code of conduct), Artha (wealth and resources), Kama (satisfy needs, mainly something that gives happiness through matter or material) and Moksha (attain salvation, or free oneself from the circle of birth and death). Indian culture promotes a holistic approach to life, and this has been captured aptly by Sharma (2007) in Basket of Needs, where he discusses six needs—biological, economic, sociological, psychological, power and spiritual that exist in tandem. Interesting aspect here is that, as per the Bharatiya (Indian) philosophy, materialism and spirituality can go hand in hand. Dharm is the essential feature of the Indian cultural value that is defined as thing that ensures both Abhyuday (materialistic development) and Nishreyas (spiritual development).[5]

Indian culture embraces the notion of *Shubh-Labh* where in labh, i.e. gains of profit preceded by *shubh*, i.e. auspicious demarcate that profit is not bad, but it should not be just profit after tax, it should be '*shubh*' that takes care of self, family, society, nation and environment in all aspects. *Loksangrah*, *Nishkam Karma* and *Karma Yoga* are the examples of other Indian constructs explained in detail in the Chapter 3 on Karma yoga which symbolize the idea that material wealth has to be earned with *Dharmik* means and in conjunction with spiritual goals. The notion of Ṛṇa or pious obligations is also an integral to the Indian value system which is explained in Chapter 1 that signifies the ways of day to day action in life can attain spiritual significance. The notion of Rnas or 'pious obligations' still remains a popular notion in Hinduism that suggests that all human beings must discharge certain obligations towards parents, masters and teachers, fellow human beings, other creatures and general natural environment.

---

[5] यतोऽभ्युदयनिःश्रेयससिद्धिः स धर्मः । १,१.२। yato'bhyudayaniḥśreyasasiddhiḥ sa dharmaḥ | 1.1.2 |
Ref: Maharshi Kanada, Vaisheshika Sutras.
Meaning: That which leads to the attainment of Abhyudaya (prosperity in this world) and Nihshreyasa (total cessation of pain and attainment of eternal bliss hereafter) is Dharma.

In the folk literature, such as the Panchtantra, the Hitopadesa, the Kathasaritsagara and the Buddhist Jatakas, one finds the description of two types of merchants in the society of those days; the ordinary shop-keeper and the travelling sales-man of goods called setthis moving from one ward of the city to another and making far from substantial profit. Further, Indian society has had an ethos of giving, Daanam (in Sanskrit) or Daan (in Hindi) altruistic giving is recognized as an important value in the Vedic tradition and core of the Indian culture (Narayanan, 2020). Once Daan is given, the donor is not supposed to have 'any attachment or relationship with the recipient Bornstein (2004)'.[6] This idea of non-reciprocity is deeply ingrained in the Hindu ethos. 'Sarva loka hitam' or 'well-being of all' is the ideal of human life and signifies the greatness in the Vedic literatures. Buddhism and Jainism in ancient India flourished with remarkable support of mercantile class in general and by setthi in particular (Gokhale, 1977). Mercantile class provided perhaps the most substantial support to their monastic and other needs. That the traditional businessmen invested in temples, orphanages, community drinking water points (*pyaus*) and low-cost hotels (*sarais*) is evident from our literary references. This thought was in the name of charity and philanthropy rather than corporate sustainability.

Sundar (2000) identified four phases of social engagement and responsibility of business in India in the modern times. During the early years of industrialization (1850–1914), social responsibility of business corporations in India was predominantly related to business philanthropy, as rich business families set up trusts and institutions such as schools, colleges and hospitals. During the years of the Indian freedom struggle and independence (1914–1960), Indian businesses supported the freedom movement and various social and cultural causes associated with the nationalist movement. During the next phase—1960–1980, the general climate of mistrust towards corporations in socialist India corresponded with a decline in business philanthropy and an increase in state-led development. Finally, after economic liberalization in the 1990s, a combination of extreme social need, limited public finance, improved

[6] Eck (2013) quotes Bornstein, E. (2004). *The spirit of development: Protestant NGOs, morality and economics in Zimbabwe*. Routledge.

returns to industry, a pro-business environment and the emergence of a strong civil society called for increased initiatives in social work by the business community (Mohan, 2001; Sundar, 2000). The influence of Gandhian thoughts on the business and its social engagement is a very important aspect to understand the emergence of social entrepreneurship in India and across the world. It is important to note that Ashoka Foundation has played very important role in supporting and developing social entrepreneurship in the world. The founder of Ashoka Foundation gained the practical exposure to the Gandhian approach in the Sarvodaya movement under the mentorship of Vinoba Bhave in 1960s. Gandhian thought goes into the basic tenets of Ashoka Foundation.[7] The following sub section elaborates social entrepreneurship from the Gandhian perspective.

Gandhian Perspective and Social Entrepreneurship

Mahatma Gandhi is the most influential thinker of twentieth century. As a social reformer, political thinker and activist, spiritual seeker and interpreter and a prolific author and communicator who has great sensitivity towards natural environment, Gandhi has inspired and guided almost every vocation and profession in India and the world. We would like to quote his statement about the business enterprises. In 1908, in his book Hind Swarajya, Gandhiji initiated a concept of Sarvoday Society. Sarvodaya is a Gujarati term that roughly translates into 'well-being for all', 'progress for all' or 'universal uplift'. He believed in living in harmony with nature and a simple life. The crux of it being to 'generate more, from less, for more people'. In 1928, he wrote that 'God forbid that India should ever take to industrialism after the manner of the West. If an entire nation of 300 million took to similar economic exploitation, it would strip of the world bare like locusts'. During India's struggle for freedom, Mahatma Gandhi's influence and his coinage of the term 'applied trusteeship' was behind the engagement of several industrialists in social activities. Even before India got freedom, Gandhiji propagated

[7] https://www.ashoka.org/en-in/story/bill-drayton-half-population-out-game.

the thought that corporate responsibility extended to public welfare instead of being restricted to their owners, employees and customers, or state and legal requisites.

Gandhi held that the individual happiness lies in the happiness of society. The essence of Gandhian philosophy is that the human values and not the market should govern life. Ghosh (2007) brings out the basic objectives of the Gandhian scheme of holistic development:

Human development for capability expansion.
Balanced Development (development of body, mind and soul).
Development with social justice, rights and freedom.
Accomplishment of self-sufficiency and self-reliance by rural development.

The commonality of the objectives and espoused goals of SE and Gandhian perspective of societal development is quite evident here. Many of these ideal have inspired the earliest development of SE in India during the freedom struggle and after attaining freedom which we explain in the next session.

Taxonomy of Entrepreneurs

In an analysis of many case studies of social entrepreneurs, it is found that all of them had given different and innovative solution to solve a given problem. Although, they are similar in common features like mission orientation, addressing social problem, use of entrepreneurial strategy, innovative and cost effective and sustainable solutions, they differ in their style of addressing social problems.

Shukla (2019) gave the typology of SEs suitable for the Indian context based on his extensive field work. According to him, social entrepreneurs can be categorized as Local change maker, Public goods providers, Constructive opportunist, Social transformers and Ecosystem builder. Each of these categories, their name in hindi according to our understanding are explained in the next sub section with suitable examples.

Local Change Makers (*Sthaniya Parivartankari Udhyami*)

Local change makers see local problem to meet the need of local community. They are more sensitive about solving local problem and leverage the highly contextual and local knowledge to identify critical social problems, mobilize local resources and develop a solution which is relevant and viable in the local context. The issues addressed by these social entrepreneurs are unique, and both the problems and their solutions are relevant to a locally unique condition. Their impact in terms of size of the population or regions covered is limited to that particular location. Their impact is limited to local context, but at times these projects are scalable and replicable.

Aarti Naik, a slum-based young girl is an example of 'Local changemaker'. She has been building basic educational capacities for other girls living in slums to create quality learning spaces for girl in the slums of Mumbai, India (Matofska & Sheinwald, 2019). Aarti is working to teach life skills to the girls and allows them to learn with confidence. Initially, these slum girls were struggling to read and write but the continuous effort of Aarti enable slum girls to build basic literacy and numeracy skills within their community.

Public Goods Provider (*Jan Sansadhan Pradayi and Vistarak Udyami*)

Providing social goods and services was mostly considered as an act of philanthropy rather than entrepreneurship in traditional system (Martin & Osberg, 2007). Over the period, it was realized that only philanthropy will not provide sustainable and long-term solution to solve unaddressed problems of society.

Many social entrepreneurs create models of delivering public goods, services and goods which are different than the conventional ways of doing like affordable housing, roads, electricity and health. These solutions are innovative, sustainable and create visible impact. Some of the social entrepreneurs work towards generating more employment, earning nominal profit to sustain with the objective of social mission. The public goods providers work for building stronger community for promoting equity and social justice.

The Council for Advancement of People's Action and Rural Technology (CAPART) is an example of Public Goods Provider. It was setup in September 1986 by the amalgamation of the People's Action for Development India (PADI) and Council for Advancement of Rural Technology (CART) to encourage, promote and assist voluntary action in the implementation of projects for the enhancement of rural prosperity. The objective of CAPART is to strength and to promote the voluntary efforts in rural development with the focus on injecting new technological inputs. It aims to act as the national nodal point for coordination, as a catalyst for development of technology appropriate for the rural areas and funding research and development efforts. CAPART works to enable participatory decentralized planning by communities, peoples' networks and state institutions and the advocacy of the policies and programmes for the well-being of rural people, particularly of the vulnerable, excluded and marginalized communities. CAPART also works for supporting to enhance inner capacity and skills for innovation and entrepreneurship in rural India (Shah, 2007).

The Social Goods providers adopt specific strategies for making stronger community like first they identify opportunity in the neglected problems of society. They identify a gap in the nature of services provided by the government and other agencies. After analysis of prevailing conditions, they craft innovative solutions to leverage the opportunity they have identified and focus on scale and sustainability of proposed solution.

Constructive Opportunists (*Rachnatmak Avasargrahi Udyami*)

Constructive Opportunists are sensitive to and actively seek opportunities in the unattended markets and then leverage them to create ventures to address a social problem on an ongoing basis. Mostly these ventures are for-profit in nature, or at least have an earned-income strategy.

However, their focus remains on their social goals and aim at remaining profitable rather than on profit maximization.

Saral Design Solutions is a for-profit social enterprise focused on designing products to provide access to affordable and quality menstrual hygiene in India. It was an opportunity for those who want to solve social problems with for-profit approach. Due to poor infrastructure, either distribution costs make the products 60% more expensive in products like pads and diapers, or the existing brands not catering to remote locations. The Founder, Suhani Mohan, created change by recognizing the opportunity about the immense potential of local production which not just reduces distribution costs but making sanitary pads becomes affordable. This local production of low caste napkins created local livelihood opportunities for women also (Mohan & Bagayatkar, 2019). Using decentralized automatic machine technology for last mile menstrual health delivery.

Social Transformers (*Samaj Sudharak Udyami*)

Many social problems are so deeply rooted in society that they cannot be solved within the existing social institutions, cultural practices and regulatory systems like child labour, caste-based discrimination, gender violence, and exploitation of poor and marginalized.

The reasons for the continuance of such problems can be varied. The only way in which such social issues can be addressed is by changing the very nature of institutions and systems. It seems that the institutions and regulations to manage these issues are inadequate or do not have proper instruments or resources to solve these problems.

The change makers who address this type of problems create change in existing bureaucratic institutions, regulations and social practices. They are ideologically inclined social activists and advocates for causes. The story of Right to Information (RTI) movement, which finally resulted in the RTI Act (Bakshi, 2000; Roy, 2018) is the best example to understand how Social Transformers operate by working with the support of community, and create permanent solution and that's how social transformations happen.

Ecosystem Builders (*Paritantra Nirmankarta Udyami*)

The success or failure of the ventures also depends on the support systems and services provided by other stakeholders (e.g. funding, domain expertise and advisories, pipeline of talent and policy guidelines). The support system and other service providers are essential for the growth of both the mainstream ventures and the sector or industry for providing sustainable and creative solutions for grassroots problems.

Asha Impact is an impact investment and policy advocacy platform for business leaders is an example of Ecosystem builder. Asha Impact is a venture capital firm specialized in early stage investments. The firm co-invests and engaged at the board level and prefers to invests in basic infrastructure and services which includes affordable housing, access to energy, water & sanitation and waste management, vocational training, education technology and livelihoods.

Another example of this category is Bamboo Finance (BF). BF is a commercial private equity firm investing in business models that benefit low-income communities in emerging markets. BF uses a market-oriented approach to deliver social and environmental value with a goal to demonstrate that private capital can be profitably deployed as a tool for effective change. BF invest in three sectors—finance, energy and healthcare—where BF found mass-market opportunities for high growth and social impact.

SE Education in India

Social entrepreneurship as a course, stream and discipline is at its very early stage in most higher education institutes in India. SE in India has moved beyond a few management schools to university programmes beyond business management to social work, law, innovation, design, engineering, sustainability studies and other institutional homes. There are also courses, both online and full or part time, outside formal academic institutions—like the Centre for Social Innovation and Management (CSIM) or Deshpande Foundation, in some cases for over a decade—that have not been included in this collection.

Prof Trilochan Sastry first introduced social entrepreneurship at the Indian Institute of Management Bangalore (IIMB) in 2004. Ashoka foundation's roadshow in Indian campuses celebrated its 25th year in 2005 and helped a few institutes like XLRI (Xavier Labour Relations Institute), XIMB (Xavier Institute of Management) and IIFM (Indian Institute of Forest Management) start their own courses in 2006 for the first time. Villgro with IIT-Madras's Centre for Social Innovation and Entrepreneurship (CSIE) instituted awards for academic contribution to the field in 2012 and 2013. The Tata Institute of Social Sciences (TISS) took the big leap and became the first academic institution to create a specialized Masters programme on social entrepreneurship in 2007. A landscape document by Ashoka indicates four kinds of engagement by academic institutions that included an SE module in current courses (e.g. Indian Social and Political Environment at IIMA (Indian Institute of Management Ahmedabad)); SE classroom courses at IIMB, XLRI, XIMB and IRMA (Institute of Rural Management); SE lab courses (e.g. Shodh Yatra in IIMA). The university structure provides for greater opportunities to enhance learning over a semester as in the case of TISS, Azim Premji University or Jindal University whereas the term-based business school structure can be constricting. IRMA has a compressed 0.5 credit core but XLRI has chosen to run the course over two terms. There is clearly no one size fits all which needs to be welcomed given India's diversity as well as the institutional contexts of individual programmes. As SE teaching deepens its roots in academia, academia needs to play an active role as part of the larger (social) entrepreneurial ecosystem both within India and elsewhere. It is hoped that a long standing need of cases and material by Indian academia that would better reflect field level realities and complexities of running social enterprises or being a social entrepreneur would be part of future course curriculum.

Theoretical Foundations of SE

The field of SE is shoring up its theoretical foundations as it is maturing. A robust theory of SE will help to clarify what is and is not known and guide the answers to questions like is social change driven by SE, by movements, teams or networks, or through regulation and their interconnection; why do some SE ventures grow well and others do not; role of socio-cultural factors in success of SE, identifying the sites for the natural experiments, ways of measurement of the performance of SE and so on.

Mair and Marti (2006) suggest the structuration theory wherein agency and the structure are considered as the constantly interacting and influencing entities for the study of SE. The examples of the Aravind Eye Hospital of Dr. Venkataswamy in Tamilnadu and 'Society for Education, Action and Research in Community Health' (SEARCH) of Dr. Abhay and Rani Bang are the relevant examples in India. Their actions altered the socio-economic context. The SE of the category of social transformer in the above shared typology by Shukla (2019) can be studied using structuration theory.

Institutional logics approach can also be a very relevant theoretical lens to study SE. Institutional logics are the guiding principles on 'how to interpret organisational reality, what constitutes appropriate behaviour, and how to succeed' (Friedland & Alford, 1991). Institutional logics are societal logics based on the logics of institutions in society at large such as state, market, religion, family, corporation profession and community. SE generally combines two or more logics in their functioning. Institutional theory can be use lens to study SE in India. Alexander et al. (2019) proposed the cultural-religious-spiritual logic as an important form of the institutional logics in India. With examples of Art of Living Foundation and Patanjali Yoga Peeth they proposed that religious-spiritual logic is visible in the success of many SE ventures. This aspect of institutional logic can be further examined in Indian context.

In terms of Positive theory of SE, Santos (2012) argues that what distinguishes social entrepreneurship from commercial entrepreneurship is a predominant focus on value creation as opposed to value capture. Here, value creation is a concept measured at the societal or system level, while value capture is measured at the organizational or unit level. The traditional notion of profit is no more than an estimate of the value captured by an organization. SE addresses the opportunities for value creation in a distributed way and drive the economy closer to an efficient outcome by systematically identifying unmet social problems. Santos

(2012) distinguishes that the capitalist system is based on ideas of self-interested individual behaviours resulting into benevolent invisible hand that in turn results into socially optimal outcomes whereas SE is based on other rather than self-interest. Individuals who are inclined to work on others-interest incline to associate together in the context of value creation to maximize the benefits for the society, in contrast with the persons who inclined to work for value appropriation or value capture.

Many of the Indian notions and constructs can be very relevant to understand SE in Indian context. We mention four examples here; Dharma, Paropkar, Daan, Sewa and Loksangrah. The universe is a large social system and human beings are its integral part. Dharma is the common thread which entwines the components of this larger system with 'self'. Dharma means that which one lays hold of and which holds things together, the law, the norm, the rule of nature, action and life (Aurobindo, 1922). The actionable definition given in the Vaisheshiks Darshan of Indian tradition says that *yato bhyudayanihshreyasasiddhih sa dharmah*; i.e. Dharma is that which brings about the worldly progress (bhyuday) of every living being and causing progress in the spiritual realm (nihshreya). Paropkar (beneficence or benevolence) and Daan (giving or generosity) are the two of the most prominent values in the worldly interactions. Widely referred couplets in Indian society say that in all the eighteen Puranas (scritures), only two messages of Maharshi Vyas (the author of all Puranans) hold prominence: Doing favour to others is the 'Punya' and giving troubles to others is the 'Paap'. Similarly, another very popular couplet says that दानेन तुल्यो विधिरास्ति i.e. there is no vidhi (ritual) which is as noble as donation. SEWA is representing selfless service through community action as goodwill towards fellow members. In scripture, the theology, and hermeneutics a service is which is performed without any expectation of result or award for performing it for needy (Hīnasevā), parents (Pitraseva), teachers (Guruseva) and so forth. Such services can be performed to benefit other human beings or society. 'Loka' means a society (people) and a larger cosmic system (nature). 'Saṃgraha' means to gather, protect, nourish, regulate, etc., and bring collective prosperity. Radhakrishnan (1948), one of the most reputed scholar in the Indian philosophy and wisdom literature, defined Lokasaṃgraha as 'working for world maintenance' (Chapter on Karm

Yoga explains this in detail). An urge for taking the responsibility to make a positive difference to the world (dharma), values of selfless service (SEWA), giving (Daan), benevolence to others (Paropkar) and performing work for the world maintenance (Loksangrah) are the recurring themes of the motivation and functioning of social entrepreneurs. These constructs can be micro foundations for SE research in Indian context.

Implications for Research

Intended beneficiaries of SEs generally are the uneducated and poor with limited communication skills and language barriers and there are severe challenges of managing stakeholder (Arvind Eye care, JaipurFoot, Jaipur rugs, Goonj and Pratham) relations. Local institutions are often inefficient or corrupt or both which create conflict between them and the SEs. There are risks from the entrenched bureaucracies at the block, district and state levels in India. There is also an absence of an institutional mechanism which will monitor at the local level the interactions between SEs and various stakeholders. These situations warrant the need for field studies, case studies using grounded theory approach for developing fresh propositions in the field of SE which have novel theoretical insights and strong policy implications.

Social enterprises are the hybrid organizations that combine institutional logics of society, community and market (Battilana & Dorado, 2010). Generally, they are market-based hybrids that combine the principles of market such as efficiency and profitability to solve complex social problems (Di Domenico et al., 2010). Stephan et al. (2016) point out that research in social entrepreneurship is predominantly centred on social entrepreneurs and rarely examines the SE organization in relation to their context. Organization design, supply chain, networking of the different social groups and actors in SE ventures are some of the promising areas of research in the field of SE in India. In this chapter, we presented the case examples of Bhoodan movement, SEWA, MYRADA and GMMF. All these organizations are exemplar social enterprises but employ very different organizational designs.

In spite of the divergence on the specific objectives and constituency of theses, SEs there seems to be common features and principles behind the success of these SE. These may be arising out of the unique cultural and social situations and level the maturity of different institutions of India. Promotion of local human and social capital, enhancing and supporting village development and local economic development, empowering poor and grassroots development, insistence on social harmony and equality on the basis of cast, creed or community are some of the common core principles of the successful SEs in India.

Research in strategy, human resource management, leadership, motivation and performance management can be greatly informed after adding value creation in development agenda, and it can also be managed by the various aspects taking into consideration like inolving propomoters, donors for establishing small business at community level in the field of SE. In management education, competitive strategy is taught to the management students and the practicing manager whereas SE works in collaborative strategy for creating larger impact in society. There will be certainly a positive impact in the field of strategy for commercial enterprises if they adopt strategies form SE's perspective. The field of SE has a wide scope to study in the field training and development, reward system and means of recruitment etc. How the business strategy and value creation by social enterprise are guided by the social mission, which is not applicable in case of commercial enterprise, this could be a novel area for researchers, to look at both the perspectives (Gupta et al., 2020). SE marketing strategies, values creation and dissemination and the internationalization are another set of research field parallel to the ways these activities are carried out and research upon in the context of commercial organization.

Social enterprises emerge when institutional voids exist (Dacin et al., 2010). Strategy and management scholars argue that this situation impedes market development and economic growth (Khanna & Palepu, 1997). In developing economies, arguably it is not just the absence of formal institutions that prevent market development but also the presence of constraining informal institutions like caste, religion and gender role that prevent the poor from participating in markets (Mair & Marti,

2009). These issues are pertinent in Indian context and indicate the need for research.

Social enterprises adopt capabilities to penetrate potential markets for awareness, revenue generation and to attract additional resources for more growth opportunities (Dohrmann et al., 2015; Liu et al., 2015; Mottner & Ford, 2005). Despite current understanding that market orientation is an important ingredient for the success of SE the research is scarce on how social enterprises actually develop market orientation (Dohrmann et al., 2015; Liu et al., 2015). This is another important area for research.

In a recently issued statement, shareholder primacy as the core concern of the existence of the corporations has given away to the concern for most stakeholder i.e. customers, employees, suppliers, communities and shareholders by the Business Roundtable, a large group of top CEOs. This shift has implication on firm boundaries, the nature of value creation systems and theory regarding the destruction of stakeholder value (Harrison et al., 2020). Moreover, the COVID-19 pandemic has exposed the societal inequalities (Bapuji et al., 2020). Many of these inequalities can be attributed to the irresponsible business and economic activities and inherent imperfections of market mechanism (Bapuji et al., 2018). While organizations do contribute to increasing inequalities in society, they also have a role in reducing these inequalities. SEs brings human well-being and societal concerns to the centre of the business. SEs can be the predominant way of conducting business for sustainable development of societies and mankind. That demands a reexamination of the macro foundations about business organizations in terms of role of firm in society, organization design, business and community development and micro foundations like motivation, identity and leadership. Indian examples of SEs and Indian values can be fruitful areas for inquiry to examine and realize this possibility which seems to be the ideal scenario but essential for the sustainable future. From the above perspectives, several areas are emerging as future direction of research like social capital formation, social innovation and development, community managed enterprises, collective actions of local communities in improving socio-economic development, social learning through interactive, adaptive and encouraged learning process, ways and means of bringing changes in social and economic well-being through upskilling etc.

Indian Government initiated steps in the budget presented in 2019 towards creating an electronic fund-raising platform, a social stock exchange, under SEBI for listing social enterprises and volunteer organizations. Exchanges like these already exist in countries like United Kingdom, Canada, Singapore, South Africa and Brazil and it may be useful study the factors of success and obstacles in flow of funds from the masses and from impact investors to the social enterprises. The success of SE in an economy needs finance and business support, availability of human capital and infrastructure, social support in the form of media and publications, professional associations, social organizations that support a culture of entrepreneurship, market support, scientific and research support. The nature and extend of support required in India for developing an ecosystem of SE in India is an important area for research.

Regulatory interventions, actual or plausible, impacting SE is a very important area for research in India. Regulatory efforts to consolidate and recognize the organizational forms that compose the social enterprise sector are still not formed in India. Developing networks of social entrepreneurs and enterprises is another important area for nurturing the field. Among other things, networks can facilitate productive alliances, foster human resource development, leadership and knowledge dissemination in the field SE. These are important areas of exploration for action and research in the field of SE.

Most of the research studies in the field of SE are about the success stories of social entrepreneurs. Research about the challenges faced by social entrepreneurs and ways of developing competencies of SE is a rarely explored area of research. Research in this field will have practical implications on education and policy formulation in SE and theoretical implications on leadership, stakeholder management, community mobilizations and so on.

Generally, SEs pick up social problems such as poverty, health, education and unemployment and at times the less explored areas gender difference, gender discrimination, women and children rights, safety and women's empowerment. The study of SE in these areas may inform the regulatory policy as well as in these fields. For example, home care developed and popularized by Abhay and Rani Bang has influenced the health policy in Maharashtra and then many parts of India. SE may take shape of social movement and pave the way for policy formulation or cause cultural shifts and lead to formation of new organizations.

Conclusion

The literature on entrepreneurship has focused on the psychological and sociological aspects of personality of entrepreneurs; their sources of origin; leadership and management styles; business orientations; negotiation skills and achieving and servicing success. However, more specifically, this literature is extremely meagre in regard to these aspects of social entrepreneurship. While in generic terms reports and studies by the international institutions, government sources and consultants analyze the role of SE in an economy, they do not shed enough light on when and how SE as an organization graduates to an institution. Since by the very concept and nature SEs are individual driven, small scale and limited resource base organizations they need a longer lead time to move successfully towards the growth and later at the maturity stages of organization life cycle. SEs are the promoter driven organizations with informal internal organization management practices. Since they move further towards growth and maturity stages of organization life cycle they need to have more professional orientations, trained cadres of people, specialists as also generalists and a distinctive management style of their own.

If social enterprises replicate their experiences in creating and servicing their social value country wide, they are more likely to contribute to public welfare in an economy. Initially and individually, social enterprises may not create an apparent social value but over time as they grow and diversify they do create social value which can be measured. As in the long run, their coverage and outreach expands and their process and delivery mechanisms get institutionalized. So, a group of social actors tend to create collective welfare rather than a single actor in a society. SEs represent the core notion of inclusive growth in which all the local target stakeholders derive social value.

The notion of social entrepreneurship represents a social mission, that arises to serve social cause. Such a cause can be pursued only by those individuals or institutions that are willing and capable of confronting the existing social issues. There is a collective belief in India that the social cause is not fulfilled by either the market or the state. It can be served at best only partially; and hence, the alternate space is provided by the social entrepreneurship actions. Many social entrepreneurs are creating added social value and their work also brings about a sustained shift in the social and economic changes in context of relations of disadvantaged and marginalized groups. For example, when the state government of Rajasthan in India was running a few primary schools in some rural areas, there was no consistent effort to convince the parents of the girl child for her enrolment in the primary schools; hence, the rate of enrolment of girl child was very low but when Bharti Foundation took over and organize stakeholder dialogue gradually they were able to overcome local resistance to girls' education. In this instance, there was a need to change the mindset of the village elders and community leaders. SE naturally support the dialogue among governing bodies, local governing bodies and social leaders to work on creating social values with economic values.

References

Alexander, A. A., Jha, S., & Pandey, A. (2019). Understanding how hybrid organisations tackle social challenges: An institutional logics approach. *South Asian Journal of Business Studies.*

Anat-Beck, A. (2018). The law of social entrepreneurship—Creating shared value through the lens of Sandra Day O'Connor's iCivics. *University of Pansylvania Journal of Buiness Law, 20*, 520.

Aurobindo, S. (1922). Essays on the Gita (7th ed.). Sri Aurobindo Ashram Trust.

Bakshi, R. (2000). "Bapu Kuti." Penguin Books.

Bapuji, H., Husted, B. W., Lu, J., & Mir, R. (2018). Value creation, appropriation, and distribution: How firms contribute to societal economic inequality. *Business & Society, 57*, 983–1009.

Bapuji, H., Patel, C., Ertug, G., & Allen, D. G. (2020). Corona crisis and inequality: Why management research needs a societal turn. *Journal of Management, 46*(7), 1205–1222.

Battilana, J., & Dorado, S. (2010). Building sustainable hybrid organizations: The case of commercial microfinance organizations. *Academy of Management Journal, 53*, 1419–1440.

Bhushan, B. (2018). Stimulated innovation cycle to serve the poor: A case of Mann Deshi Mahila Group. In *Social entrepreneurship and sustainable business models* (pp. 177–205). Palgrave Macmillan.

Borzaga, C., & Galera, G. (2012). The concept and practice of social enterprise: Lessons from the Italian experience. *International Review of Social Research, 2*(2), 85–102.

Brouard, F., & Larivet, S. (2010). Essay of clarifications and definitions of the related concepts of social enterprise, social entrepreneur and social entrepreneurship. In A. Fayolle & H. Matlay (Eds.), *Handbook of research on social entrepreneurship*. Edward Elgar.

Choi, N., & Mujumdar, S. (2014). Social entrepreneurship as an essentially contested concept: Opening a new avenue for systematic future research. *Journal of Business Venture, 29*(3), 363–376. https://doi.org/10.1016/j.jbusvent.2013.05.001

Dacin, P. A., Dacin, M. A., & Matear, M. (2010). Social entrepreneurship: Why we don't need a new theory and how we move forward from here. *Academy of Management Perspectives, 24*(3), 37–57.

Dees, J. G. (1998). *The meaningof social entrepreneurship*. Stanford Business School Centre for Social Innovation.

Dees, J. G. (2001). *The Meaning of Social Entrepreneurship, 8*(1), 52–54. http://www.fuqua.duke.edu/centers/case/documents/dees_SE.pdf

Defourny, J., & Nyssens, M. (2013). Social innovation, social economy and social enterprise: What can the European debate tell us?

Di Domenico, M., Haugh, H., & Tracey, P. (2010). Social bricolage: Theorizing social value creation in social enterprises. *Entrepreneurship Theory and Practice, 34*(4), 681–703.

Dohrmann, S., Raith, M., & Siebold, N. (2015). Monetizing social value creation: A business model approach. *Entrepreneurship Research Journal, 5*(2), 127–154.

Freeman, R. E. (1984). *Strategic management: A stakeholder approach*. Pitman.

Friedman, M. (1962). *Capitalism and freedom*. University of Chicago Press.

Friedland, R., & Alford, R. R. (1991). Bringing society back in: Symbols, practices, and institutional contradictions. In W. W. Powell & P. J. DiMaggio (Eds.), *The new institutionalism in organizational analysis* (pp. 232–263).
Ghosh, B. N. (2007). *Gandhian political economy: Principles, practice and policy*. Ashgate Publishing.
Grassl, W. (2012, February). Business models of social enterprise: A design approach to hybridity ACRN. *Journal of Entrepreneurship Perspectives, 1*(1), 37–60.
Grieco, C. (2015). Conceptualizing social entrepreneurship. In *Assessing social impact of social enterprises* (pp. 5–36). Springer.
Gokhale, B. G. (1977). The merchant in ancient India. *Journal of the American Oriental Society, 97*(2), 125–130.
Gupta, A., Dey, A., & Singh, G. (2017). Connecting corporations and communities: Towards a theory of social inclusive open innovation. *Journal of Open Innovation: Technology, Market, and Complexity, 3*(3), 17.
Gupta, P., Chauhan, S., Paul, J., & Jaiswal, M. P. (2020). Social entrepreneurship research: A review and future research agenda. *Journal of Business Research, 113*, 209–229.
Harrison, J. S., Phillips, R. A., & Freeman, R. E. (2020). On the 2019 business roundtable "statement on the purpose of a corporation." *Journal of Management, 46*(7), 1223–1237.
Jiao, H. (2011). A conceptual model for social entrepreneurship directed toward social impact on society. *Social Enterprise Journal, 7*(2), 130–149.
Jones, T. M. (1995). Instrumental stakeholder theory: A synthesis of ethics & economic. *Academy of Management Review, 20*, 404–437.
Kerlin, J. A. (2010). A comparative analysis of the global emergence of social enterprise. *VOLUNTAS: International Journal of Voluntary and Nonprofit Organizations, 21*(2), 162–179.
Khanna, T., & Palepu, K. (1997). Why focused strategies. *Harvard Business Review, 75*(4), 41–51.
Krugman, P. (2008). *The return of depression economics and the crisis of 2008*. Penguin Books.
Mair, J., & Marti, I. (2006). Social entrepreneurship research: A source of explanation, prediction, and delight. *Journal of World Bus, 41*(1), 36–44.
Mair, J., & Marti, I. (2009). Entrepreneurship in and around institutional voids: A case study from Bangladesh. *Journal of Business Venturing, 24*(5), 419–435.
Martin, R. L., & Osberg, S. (2007). Social entrepreneurship: The case for definition. *Stanford Social Innovation Review, 5*(2), 28–39.

Matofska, B., & Sheinwald, S. (2019). *Generation share: The change-makers building the sharing economy*. Policy Press
McKague, K., Zietsma, C., & Oliver, C. (2015). Building the social structure of a market. *Organization Studies, 36*(8), 1063–1093.
Mohan, G. (2001). Participatory development. In V. Desai & R. B. Potter (Eds.), *The Arnold companion to development studies* (pp. 49–54). London, UK: Hodder.
Mohan, S., & Bagayatkar, S. (2019). Using decentralized automatic machine technology for last mile menstrual health delivery. *Gates Open Research, 3*.
Nanekar, K. R., & Khandewale, S. V. (1973). *Bhoodan and the Landless*. Popular Prakashan.
Narayanan, A. C. C. (2020). *The meaning of generosity: A subjective culture study in India* (Doctoral dissertation). University of Hawai'i at Manoa.
Radhakrishnan, S. (1948/2009). *The Bhagavadgita*. HarperCollins Publishers.
Reis, T. K., & Clobesy, S. J. (2001). Unleashing new resources and entrepreneurship for the common good: A philanthropic renaissance. *New Directions for Philanthropic Fundraising, 32*, 109–144.
Roy, A. (2018). *The RTI story: Power to the people*. Roli Books.
Santos, F. M. (2012). A positive theory of social entrepreneurship. *Journal of Business Ethics, 111*(3), 335–351.
Sengupta, S., & Sahay, A. (2017). Social entrepreneurship research in Asia-Pacific: Perspectives and opportunities. *Social Enterprise Journal, 13*(1), 17–37.
Shah, M. (2007). A new beginning for CAPART. *Economic and Political Weekly, 42*(8), 633–635.
Sharma, S. (2002). Corporate Rishi leadership model: An Indian model for corporate development & ethical leadership. In *Human resource development in Asia: Trends and challenges* (pp. 291–296). Oxford & IBH.
Sharma, S. (2007). *New mantras in corporate corridors: From ancient roots to global routes*. New Age International (P) Limited, Publishers.
Shukla, M. (2019). *Social entrepreneurship in India: Quarter idealism and a pound of pragmatism*. Sage Publications Pvt. Limited.
Stephan, U., Patterson, M., Kelly, C., & Mair, J. (2016). Organizations driving positive social change: A review and an integrative framework of change processes. *Journal of Management, 42*(5), 1250–1281.
Sundar, P. (2000). *Beyond business: From merchant charity to corporate citizenship: Indian business philanthropy through the ages*. Tata McGraw Hill
UNDP. (2020). United Nations Development Programme, Human Development Reports. http://hdr.undp.org/en/2020-report

Wallace, S. L. (1999). Social entrepreneurship: The role of social purpose enterprises in facilitating community economic development. *Journal of Developmental Entrepreneurship, 4*(2), 153.

Walsh, J. P. (2005). Taking stock of stakeholder management. *Academy of Management Review, 30*(2), 426–438.

Zahra, S. A., Gedajlovic, E., Neubaum, D. O., & Shulman, J. M. (2009). A typology of social entrepreneurs: Motives, search processes and ethical challenges. *Journal of Business Venturing, 24*(5), 519–532.

12

Made in India: Business Models for Affordable Healthcare

Som Sekhar Bhattacharyya and Rajesh Chandwani

Introduction

Indian civilization has had a long and rich history of giving and caring. The Hindu, Buddhist and Jain religious scriptures celebrated the notion of the wealthy and healthy taking care of the poor and the sick. Given the legacy of Indian civilization, since ancient times, Indian traders and businesses had engaged with society. Indian economy and Indian culture both have a rich and long history spanning around a few thousand years (Avari, 2007; Cohn, 2017). It is thus tautological to observe that both these intersected across a variety of points (Bose & Jalal, 2017; Gupta,

S. S. Bhattacharyya (✉)
Indian Institute of Management, Nagpur, India

R. Chandwani
Indian Institute of Management Ahmedabad, Ahmedabad, India
e-mail: rajeshc@iima.ac.in

© The Author(s), under exclusive license to Springer Nature Switzerland AG 2022
A. Pandey et al. (eds.), *Indigenous Indian Management*, Palgrave Studies in Indian Management,
https://doi.org/10.1007/978-3-030-87906-8_12

2005). In Indian culture, the notion of giving and sharing has been well weaved in the tapestry of life and living (Sharma, 2007). Taking care of the destitute and the poor has been specially advocated in Hindu scriptures and philosophies as a virtue (Dalal, 2002; Kumar, 2010). In the Bhagavad Gita, taking care of the needy and the ill has been advised as a duty of the wealthy and the healthy (Bhawuk, 2011). In India, at the family level, drawn from these traditions of both 'Dharma' and 'Karma', the health care requirements of the elderly and the sick was expected to be the responsibility of the young and the able family members (Deshpande et al., 2005). The concept of hospitals was weak and home treatment of the sick amidst the warmth and emotive care of family members was practiced (Padma et al., 2009). The manned care and logistics of such care giving services was the duty of the many family members (James, 1994; Westerhof et al., 2001). Further, at family and household level in Indian families even until the early 2000s the notion of health insurance was largely absent (Ito & Kono, 2010). This was because, for the elderly in the family (like parents and grandparents) the young family (working) members undertook the healthcare expenses (Deshpande et al., 2005). This was the accepted and expected behavior, any deviation from this behavior was viewed as negative (James, 1994). In the last few decades, Indian firms have formed strategic alliances with foreign firms to educate and create a market for health insurance (Bhattacharyya & Shaik, 2009), resulting in the corporatization of the healthcare system in India. The chapter has been structured in the following manner. First an overview regarding the state of affairs of healthcare in India is provided. Second, innovations in healthcare management in India are discussed. Subsequently, the key characteristics of Indian healthcare management system are explained. In future comparative analysis of various business models could be carried out.

Healthcare in India

In ancient and medieval India, traders and business owners were expected to feed the hungry and support the insalubrious sections of society (Bhattacharyya et al., 2009; Muniapan & Dass, 2008; Muniapan,

2014). This was the expected good behavior to be followed that is 'Dharma' (Ketola et al., 2009). Further, taking care of the ill was also according to Hindu scriptures and philosophy rewarding for life later or even in after life so this was good 'Karma' (Bhattacharyya, 2011). This narrative was emphatic in Indian traditions for thousands of years and this legacy continues to the present day (Sharma, 1973). The teachings of 'Bhagavad Gita' had been a core anchor of this perspective throughout ages in India. In modern times, multiple perspectives have been derived regarding the dos and don'ts about management of firm and the behaviors of managers based upon the teachings of 'Bhagavad Gita' but one that had reverberated in multitude has been regarding the notion that business firms being expected to contribute toward society (Chinna et al., 2009; Sharma, 1999). The theme of healthcare as a sector was well aligned in such thinking (Chakravarthi, 2011). The work of Mahatma Gandhi further reinforced this thinking (Chakrabarty, 2006). Gandhi also argued that business houses should take care of the weaker sections of society specially the sick (Ketola et al., 2009; Rivett, 1959). In India, the notion of Corporate Social Responsibility (CSR) has a long and highly embedded background (Muniapan & Satpathy, 2013). One could argue that the concept of CSR had evolved into widespread practice in India long before the idea of CSR became popular in the Western developed world (Bhattacharyya et al., 2009).

In India, the provision of healthcare both in terms of Indian political philosophy and socio-cultural milieu had been a duty of rulers and states (Altekar, 2002; Thapar, 1990; Tripathi, 2004). This was based upon the notion of 'Dharma' (Chattopadhyay, 2007; Dam, 2015). Thus, healthcare infrastructure was a priority area for both the state as well as the traders during ancient and medieval India (Thapar, 2015). This tradition continued in the twentieth century when big Indian business houses like the Tata Group established hospitals to facilitate treatment (Chakravarthi, 2011). These hospitals most importantly treated patients who belonged from weak economic background in society (Shah, 2014; Srivastava et al., 2012). Thus, the thoughts and actions surrounding business participation in health care has been a continuing conversation (Chakravarthi, 2011). Given the background of the notion of CSR as mentioned earlier, Indian corporations had addressed healthcare as a part of its CSR agenda (Bhattacharyya, 2012). This was apart from the firms that were operating in the healthcare space (Rohini & Mahadevappa, 2010). However, both set of firms confronted two predominant challenges. First, the dearth of infrastructure both soft (human capabilities) as well as hard (equipment and physical infrastructure) in the Indian healthcare space (Bhandari & Dutta, 2007; Ramani & Mavalankar, 2006; Rao, 2012; Rao et al., 2011). The second being the expectation, that quality healthcare was required to be provided at affordable rates (Kumar, 2009; Modi, 2011; Pramesh et al., 2014). This should come as no surprise in India as there has been presence of substantial section of economically poor population (Thorat et al., 2017). This had been christened as Bottom of Pyramid (BoP) customers, who have been living in survival mode far removed from the wellbeing state, as they couldn't afford pricey things in life like tertiary healthcare (Lenssen et al., 2012). The BoP individuals are the ones who earn less than Indian rupees 5,000 per year or Indian rupees 70 to 150 per day, on a daily basis. Primary and secondary healthcare consisted of sub centers and Primary Health Centres (PHCs) which took care of minor and moderate ailments. Tertiary care involved medical colleges which took care of serious ailments. However, the inability to pay didn't diminish the BoP customers desire for quality products and services (Jaiswal & Gupta, 2015), like healthcare at affordable rate across various ailments. Some of the major ailments and BoP expectations were regarding receiving affordable dialysis or kidney transplantation for chronic renal failure or inexpensive chemotherapy for treatment of cancer (Chatterjee et al., 2013; Jha, 2004; Pal & Mittal, 2004). Even for pharmaceutical drugs the expectation has been that life saving and critical drugs should be affordable for BoP customers (Sawant, 2014). Such expectations were across a wide range of diseases specially regarding tertiary care (Lenssen et al., 2012).

India is a large country with wide geographic distance between the urban pockets inter spaced with rural areas. In India, there are government hospitals, private hospitals, nursing homes and private practitioners (who either operate from their own office or from a pharmacy store). Further, doctor as an entrepreneur was a unique aspect of Indian healthcare system. The aim of each one of these has been to cater to the requirements of different sections of society based upon ability to pay, types of disease as well as location. However, India has one of the lowest ratios of doctors and paramedics to the size of population and tautologically the number of patients in the world. So, the business of providing healthcare service to such a large population, which is geographically dispersed, is resource intensive and investment heavy (Alur & Schoormans, 2011). Indian hospitals could be segmented across high end to very low end. High end hospitals catered to the needs of high net worth individuals (HNI). Government hospitals in India generally are the mainstay of medical treatment of the poor. Premium hospitals in India are exclusively catering to the rich and famous. Many of the premier hospitals in India have however started earmarking certain amount toward the economically needy patients as part of social responsibility and proactive responsiveness.

In soft infrastructure like manpower such as, doctors and health paramedics have been involved (De Costa et al., 2009). Historically, Ayurveda practitioners catered to the Indian populace at large (Mishra et al., 2001). Since the advent of the British, modern practices of medication (dominantly allopathy) and its service infrastructure got developed (Banerji, 1973; Jaggi & Chattopadhyaya, 2000). This was constituted by doctors, paramedics and even pharmacists (Richards, 1985). Thus, medical colleges, nursing institutes, pharmacy colleges and such others got developed (Kumar, 1997). Post-independence the government of India through its five-year plans expanded these infrastructures so as to develop more medical professionals to dispense quality services (Pandve & Pandve, 2013). Subsequently, the participation of private players was allowed to meet the ever-soaring demand for healthcare (Shah, 2010). Shortage of doctors in India have always been a cause of concern especially in remote and rural areas (Bajpai, 2014; Deo, 2013). In India, given the large population and its geographic spread, it required distributed medical facilities manned with doctors and paramedics in these locations (Deo, 2013; Kumar et al., 2007; Patil et al., 2002).

Often, India has been viewed as a country that lacked entrepreneurship (Medhora, 1965; Patel & Chavda, 2013; Tripathi, 1971). In recent decades it has been pointed out that India displayed abundance of entrepreneurship (Dana, 2000). It has been evident in the ubiquitous street side vendors lying in plain sight of most passersby on roads. Over the years, in the healthcare space also this omnipresence of medical services entrepreneurship has been evident. In India studying medicine has been both expensive and time consuming. Medical students often aimed to provide medical service to the geographically defined community where they grew up. This was because, while growing up in these communities it became evident to the young medical profession aspirants that medical services were mostly absent or were poorly present. Becoming a doctor was not an individual goal but rather a community goal. If a student did well in medical examination and secured admission into a medical college, then the entire community felt elated as they wanted someone of their own to be a doctor. So, when these young students cleared medical examinations the entire community rejoiced. Thus, the notion of strong bonds with such a community as expected. After becoming a doctor often such individuals were interested to set up a medical clinic to serve their geography centric community. Thus, a doctor also became an entrepreneur. However, such doctors often faced challenges related to management of finance, real estate, human resource management and business strategy in their owned new medical clinics (Rhodes, 2012). This was because the doctor for starting up the medical clinic in their neighborhood competed with other entities for setting up the enterprise and often lacked business management expertise (Chatterjee, 2008). This still continues to be a challenge for the doctors' who had ventured into entrepreneurial ventures and were dependent on others for securing management expertise. Policy level focus from Indian government was then much needed (Golechha, 2015).

Health paramedics manpower in India also evolved slowly and has been becoming a very important subcomponent of the healthcare ecosystem (Motkuri et al., 2017). In the developed countries, healthcare ecosystem has been well built. In India, the offtake of the health paramedic segment had been slow (Rao et al., 2013). This was also because in India cultural (as mentioned earlier) relationships were not transactional but one of giving care. As has been already pointed out, in India the young took care of the elderly when the sick or the elderly required support. In Indian joint families, the extra pair of hands would always be extended for a worthy cause such as taking care of elderly who were sick. In the last decade, with increase in the number of nuclear families, both spouse working families and such emergent realities the need of paramedical support at home became a business reality. Even then the notion of 'Dharma' still resonated in the minds of a young family members to serve an elderly who were ill. Dedicated paramedic and assistant services have been developing over a period of time but still there remained a hiatus. Thus, to serve the Indian healthcare market, innovative thinking has been much required to develop both hard and soft infrastructure and provide it to BoP customers at affordable rates.

Innovations in Healthcare Management in India

Indian civilization had always had technology as a key element in the socio-economic landscape since ancient times (Bhardwaj, 1979). India always had relatively larger population base, thus, to serve such vast base of population with limited resources required a frugal way of thinking (Annala et al., 2018; Banerjee, 2013). The notion of 'Jugaad' has been one such aspect that transcended the Indian cultural (Prabhu & Jain, 2015). This entailed the twin perspectives of frugality and conservation emphasized, in the absence of plenitude of resources (especially technological in nature) in the Indian business realm (Kumar & Bhaduri, 2014; Prabhu & Jain, 2015). 'Jugaad' thus was a way of thinking regarding how more value could be created with less resources (Tasavori et al., 2016). Verma and Bhattacharyya (2016) noted that there was substantial scope for application of emerging technologies for serving BoP markets at low costs. Healthcare in India was a sector that required such innovative thinking not just as fragmented islands but one which was omnipresent (Bound & Thornton, 2012; Honavar, 2019). Thus, in healthcare in India, both technology as well as 'Jugaad' thinking worked in tandem to provide affordable health care. Even in Indian health insurance industry, technology has been deployed to serve the previously unserved (Nayak et al., 2019a, 2019b). Thus, technology in healthcare as a narrative has been slowly building up momentum but the essence was in arriving at a favorable benefit to cost ratio.

The various aspects surrounding healthcare in Indian context in terms of its numerous elements like hard infrastructure, capabilities, innovation and business model are presented in Table 12.1. The articles selected the analysis are based upon the search keywords of 'Indian healthcare', and 'Indian Innovation' in the title, abstract and keywords. A total of 42 articles were reported based upon the search, out of which the authors selected thirty-five articles for detailed analysis. Seven articles were not selected for detailed analysis as the authors felt that these articles made marginal contribution.

The authors also tabulated a dozen best-case examples in Indian healthcare spanning the entire spectrum of healthcare products, services, process and business model. These are presented in Table 12.2.

The authors synthesized the themes emerging from the discussion of articles reported in Table 12.1 and cases reported in Table 12.2 to identify unique aspects of Indian healthcare industry, system and management. In the next section, the authors conclude the insights drawn from the current analysis and also highlight the directions for future research.

Key Characteristics of Indian Healthcare Management

A synthesis of Tables 12.1 and 12.2 has been prepared by the authors and is tabulated and presented in Table 12.3. From Table 12.3 it can be inferred that there are four innovations that were prominent. These are 'Product', 'Service', 'Process' and 'Business model' innovations. As per the perspectives provided in Tables 12.1 and 12.2, product innovation manifested into the launch of new product offerings while service innovation leads to introduction of new service offerings. The process innovation entails new ways of doing firm activities while the business model innovation incorporated firm efforts that altered the firm sources of revenues and the way of doing business.

The two benefits that transpired from these four types of innovation are cost reduction and better-quality management. One could note that in all four innovations in the Indian health care system cost reduction occurred. Four stars (****) depicts very high-cost savings, three stars (***)

Table 12.1 Indian healthcare landscape

S.No	Author(s)	Findings	Methodology	Context
1	Ramdorai and Herstatt (2017)	In all the GE Healthcare's products introduced in the developing world (including India) the key consistent features were low complexity, high ease of use, high reliability and high serviceability. In product design environmental fit, local use cases, cost effectiveness and clinical efficacy were also ascertained. Authors identified that GE was able to overcome innovator's dilemma (Henderson, 2006) by having a dedicated process, reconfigured values (Healthymagination initiative), dedicated resources and long-term capability development. Authors had found that ambidexterity of differentiated and integrated structures as well as an overarching vision would help organizations to serving low-income market segments in health care	Exploratory case study methodology was chosen for this research	Authors explored the approach & process required to develop successful products/services for the BoP markets in healthcare
2	Bhatti et al. (2017)	Authors argued that healthcare needs should be the prime source of motivation behind product development. Identification & diffusion of frugal healthcare delivery innovations were identified as key challenges by the authors	An exploratory and non-experimental descriptive mixed methods research design was chosen to search for, assess and analyze frugal innovations in healthcare	Authors comprehensively searched for frugal innovations which could be undertaken for reverse diffusion into the healthcare system of developed economies

(continued)

Table 12.1 (continued)

S.No	Author(s)	Findings	Methodology	Context
3	Mukerjee (2012)	Author proposed that affordability (with state-of-art quality) and knowledge of target customer's critical conditions were the two most critical factors to be considered when innovating for the low-income market. Author has also proposed that firms must reconfigure the firm value chains in order to facilitate frugal innovations in emerging markets	A conceptual study was undertaken	Author recommended the approach required to develop product and service offerings that would succeed in emerging markets
4	Agarwal and Brem (2012)	Authors advocated that the success of MNCs trying to innovate for the low-income market depended upon the proximity of the entire value chain to the local market. This was identified as a critical factor. Further, firm management had to completely understand the core value needs of the targeted customers. Firms were advocated to also focus for reverse innovations because frugal products could also had potential for the developed world	Qualitative analysis & evaluation of Seimens SMART products was done	Authors focused on the strategies adopted by MNCs for establishing themselves into emerging markets like India

S.No	Author(s)	Findings	Methodology	Context
5	Kumar et al. (2011)	Authors identified several policy responses needed to transform the healthcare delivery in India. These are, first the introduction of appropriate incentive systems to ensure that the states were financially rewarded for effective use of allocated funds. Secondly, the steps needed to improve performance, efficiency & accountability of public healthcare delivery was required to be well laid out. Further, the policy and legislative changes that would be required to contain the rising medical expenditure had to be ascertained. The authors also recommended that a single payer system would prove to be advantageous in Indian context	Publicly available health financing & health expenditure data of 14 major Indian states were analyzed	Policy interventions required from the government side to achieve an inclusive healthcare ecosystem in India was suggested
6	Berman (1998)	Author highlighted that private ambulatory care providers held critical importance in India's healthcare system. Author also argued that in Indian context, it was impossible to completely substitute public system with private provision. Hence, interventions were required to be focused on improving the efficiency and coverage of both public and private healthcare services	Publicly available health-related data was studied to develop a conceptual framework	Author examined the role of private healthcare institutions in India for serving the needs of its vast heterogeneous population

(continued)

Table 12.1 (continued)

S.No	Author(s)	Findings	Methodology	Context
7	Ramdorai and Herstatt (2015)	Authors grouped the main challenges of doing business at the BoP as market challenges, distribution challenges and organization challenges. Authors argued that just introducing cheaper products would not guarantee success in the market. Instead, firms managers were required to immerse themselves in the BoP market to get a comprehensive grasp of customer needs and develop product that fit the buying power of the market. Authors depicted that disruptive innovations were critical to serve BoP markets. Also, in the context of emerging markets, authors demonstrated how successful firms interlinked frugal innovations, inclusive innovations, reverse innovations, 'Gandhian innovations' and disruptive innovations. Authors highlighted that best cases like Narayana Health (NH) and Arvind Eye Care Systems (AECS) innovated for BoP markets could as well be significantly utilized in the developed economies. Extreme need for cost-effectiveness, clinical volumes & BoP specific knowledge were the key drivers behind NH and AECS like innovations. Authors also advocated that firm managers needed to create new value networks having innovative partnerships and affiliations to cater to the needs of BoP market. Authors suggested that developed market firms scouting disruptive innovation	Exploratory case study method was followed	Authors discussed the importance of frugal innovations in serving the BoP market. Characteristics and features required for success of frugal product/service offerings were examined

S.No	Author(s)	Findings	Methodology	Context
		could either focus directly toward BoP markets or co-develop solutions with local firms serving the BoP market. Emerging economies like India were viewed as appropriate for disruptive innovations because of significant resource constraints and significant volume of unmet needs. For developed market, firm managers could innovate with lessons picked up from the highly price sensitive emerging economies which were previously not using advanced products or were using a poor substitute. In addition to price, the new value segment products should include portability, reliability and ease of use as key performance attributes for success. Authors have suggested that MNCs tying to serve BoP markets could learn the ambidexterity of differentiated and integrated structures from GE healthcare's healthymagination initiative. Authors used the case of 'Tata Swach' to advocate that senior leadership in the firm would play a significant role in success of disruptive innovation. Authors also identified that there could be static structural ambidexterity (GE Healthcare) and dynamic structural ambidexterity (Tata Swach) which could enable a firm to achieve success in BoP market. Authors suggested that in order to serve the vast unmet needs of Indian healthcare ecosystem, firms could set up local R&D units to pursue disruptive innovation		

(continued)

Table 12.1 (continued)

S.No	Author(s)	Findings	Methodology	Context
8	Prahalad (2012)	Author emphasized that firms must operate on 4A model. The 4A's being awareness, access, affordability and availability for developing products for the BoP markets. The author also suggested that the products developed should be modern, have aspirational value, adhere to global safety standards, be scalable and most importantly be affordable. The author advocated that instead of just developing a product, BoP innovations should develop an ecosystem that would enable a new business system to thrive. The author had also argued that emerging markets were critical for sustained and profitable growth of global firms. Also, the experience gained in BoP markets would enable the firms to enhance its global competitiveness	A conceptual study was undertaken	The process and approach of developing products for BoP population has been elucidated and tested using a live example
9	Tiwari et al. (2014)	Authors propounded that active search of inventive analogies in other industry domains and openness of management as well as development teams would play a critical role in successful development of frugal innovations. Authors also argued that firms could substantially reduce its development costs & time by incorporating inventive analogies (within-industry & cross-industry) toward product development	Cases of three frugal innovations from India were studied	Role of applying inventive analogies in the development process of frugal innovations was studied

S.No	Author(s)	Findings	Methodology	Context
10	Tiwari and Herstatt (2012)	In addition to the 4A's model, the product developed for emerging markets should have a specific value proposition, volume opportunities, a robust design, fault resistant mechanism and low cost of ownership. Authors advocated that an emerging market like India perfectly befit the definition of lead market. Hence, firms were required to actively participate in Indian market to identify the market needs early and develop products that could even get diffused overseas	Cases of four successful product innovation from India were studie	Factors impacting India's potential as a lead market for frugal innovations have been studied
11	Gardner et al. (2007)	Authors suggested that local R&D partnerships and policy networks led by developing countries could help in significant enhancement of global healthcare system	A conceptual study was undertaken	Authors elucidated the importance of R&D partnerships and implementation research networks in the enhancement of global healthcare system
12	Engel et al. (2012)	Authors argued that in addition to developing new tools, healthcare delivery models (inclusive to all stakeholders) must be given due importance	Meeting report of a conference themed on "TB diagnostics in India: from importation and imitation to innovation" was developed	Alternative ways of innovating new diagnostics that would fit in the local context was studied

(continued)

Table 12.1 (continued)

S.No	Author(s)	Findings	Methodology	Context
13	Brown and Wyatt (2010)	Authors advocated that by adopting design thinking (inspiration, ideation, implementation), organizations could be a better enabler in developing successful social innovations	A conceptual study was undertaken	Importance of design thinking to develop social innovations was elucidated
14	Prabhu and Jain (2015)	Authors highlighted that combination of grassroot innovations (jugaad) with formal business process would help to serve the need of emerging markets across the globe. Authors also identified frugality, flexibility and inclusivity as key characteristics of jugaad innovations	A conceptual study was undertaken	The concept of jugaad and its relevance in Indian context for innovation and entrepreneurship was studied
15	Bhowmik et al. (2013)	Authors advocated that low-cost tele-medicine model and other remote healthcare delivery solutions would significantly bridge the existing gap in Indian healthcare ecosystem	A conceptual study was undertaken	Opportunities of transforming healthcare through tele-medicine technology have been explored
16	Govindarajan and Euchner (2012)	Authors identified that the five key factors which differentiated the needs of developing market from the developed market were performance gap, infrastructure gap, sustainability gap, regulatory gap, and preferences gap. Authors have argued that reverse innovation would help global firms to gain sustained competitive advantage	Conceptual study was done consisting of eight case studies of innovations done by global firms in emerging markets	Role played by reverse innovation in tapping the emerging markets in the developing world was studied and highlighted

S.No	Author(s)	Findings	Methodology	Context
17	Esposito et al. (2012)	Authors identified the key operating principles of BoP healthcare. These are listed as- • Non-homogeneous BoP market must be clearly segmented • Firms should focus of 4As model & scalability in product/service offerings • Engaging the BoP with help firms in building trust and transparency • Firms could follow NH and AECS models of local capacity building for bridging demand supply gap of skilled resources • Experimentation of products and services would premise a successful BoP venture • A collaborative network would be required to build a sustainable BoP business venture • Firms should focus on end-to-end needs of the BoP market • Technology would prove to be a game changer in BoP product/service offerings • Firms must build a decentralized organizational structure and passionate leadership to achieve success in the BoP market In order for firms to be successful, firms were required to incorporate these elements in the BoP healthcare market	Empirical study of published case studies was done	Underlying principles of innovative business models aimed at providing affordable healthcare to BoP population was examined

(continued)

Table 12.1 (continued)

S.No	Author(s)	Findings	Methodology	Context
18	Malik et al. (2017)	Authors argued that Human Resources Management (HRM) practices would play a significant role in driving ambidexterity and flexibility in the organization. This was noted as central to building sustainable low-cost healthcare solutions	Cases of two healthcare organizations were studied	Role of HRM practices in resource-constraint innovations were examined
19	Kapoor and Goyal (2013)	Authors argued that all the three successful organizations studied had similar strategies for value offering, operations (passionate leadership & continuous cost control), finance (focus on cost control and technological integration) and customer engagement (focus on building trust and transparency). Scalability and technological focus also helped significantly in achieving success Authors recommended that BoP segment should also be viewed as a producer, employee and micro-entrepreneur hence, all stakeholders must be engaged to drive the healthcare service	Empirical study of three firms having innovative business models was done	Social business ventures serving the healthcare needs of BoP population using sustainable and innovate business model alterations were studied
20	Keown et al. (2014)	Authors argued that cultural factors would foster innovation diffusion in an organization. The seven key cultural factors identified were empowering patients, engaging healthcare professionals, adapting innovations to the local context, identifying and supporting champions, promoting learning, new ways of working, eliminating legacy practices, and promoting future transformation	Conceptual framework was developed using data of healthcare innovations from eight countries	Emphasis on attributes required for global diffusion of healthcare innovations was presented

S.No	Author(s)	Findings	Methodology	Context
21	McMahon and Thorsteins-dóttir (2013)	Authors advocated that developing country firms were not only getting well established into low-cost products but were also parallelly developing high-tech products/services to meet the vast demand of local healthcare market	Conceptual study based on Regenerative Medicine (RM) activity data of three countries	Authors discussed the occurrence & characteristics of high-tech innovations like RM in developing countries
22	Velamuri et al. (2015)	Authors highlighted that focused customer identification, proactive customer engagement, innovative revenue models, resource optimization, quality control, cost control and in-house talent developments were key features of success in balancing financial and social aspects of business. Authors also advocated that in addition to direct impact, organizations like AECS influenced national and international healthcare outcomes	Exploratory case analysis of three hospitals in India was carried out	Authors documented the contribution of business model characteristics in the ability of organizations to deliver high-quality healthcare at very low costs
23	Hansen (2008)	Author argued that new healthcare markets, innovative Information Communication Technologies (ICT) solutions and patient-centered services were outrunning and outperforming the state-run healthcare systems. Hence, government bodies were advocated to upgrade the prevalent methods of healthcare delivery	A conceptual study was undertaken	Changing trends of healthcare market across the globe was discussed

(continued)

Table 12.1 (continued)

S.No	Author(s)	Findings	Methodology	Context
24	Shet and De Costa (2011)	Authors emphasized that mobile phones could potentially transform the current resource-limited healthcare via empowered connectivity of relevant stakeholders	Empirical study on 322 HIV patients was carried out	Opportunities of utilizing mobile phone technology and infrastructure for healthcare enhancement was explored
25	Singh et al. (2011)	Authors advocated that Indian innovation ecosystem was on the path of maturity and an increase in local emphasis was identified in the product/service development cycle. Authors also suggested that India should prepare itself for an open innovation ecosystem with close collaboration to extract the best solutions	A conceptual study was undertaken	Commonalities, enablers and certain characteristics of recent affordable innovations in India were discussed
26	Davidson (2015)	Firms were advocated to innovate its pricing structure, technology integration, marketing strategy or service delivery to serve the need of emerging markets. Author suggested that establishment of micro-venture funds, support from larger corporation and participation of intellectual talent would help India in creating successful business ventures which would serve the BoP markets	Exploratory case analysis was done	Author identified the factors responsible for success & failure of an innovation in the BoP market
27	Alur and Schoormans (2011)	Authors emphasized that the BoP markets could be well served by social franchisee expansion route. Authors argued that success of social franchisee expansion would depend of qualitative factors-based selection of franchisee	Exploratory field study was done in India	The article proposed an alternative method of solving the issue of BoP markets using social franchisee model

S.No	Author(s)	Findings	Methodology	Context
28	Parthasarathy et al. (2015)	Authors identified cross subsidization, robinhood model, use of ICT-based technologies, customer engagement as major factors which determined the success of firms in serving the BoP market	Case analysis of four companies was carried out	Authors analyzed different models & characteristics of product/service development for serving low-income segment
29	Moons et al. (2019)	Authors advocated that efficiency and performance of internal supply chain would critically affect the quality & service of hospital. Authors identified the elements that determined the efficiency of supply chain inside the hospitals	A literature review study was undertaken	Business criticality of internal supply chain performance of hospitals was studied
30	Haenssgen and Ariana (2017)	Authors argued that a detailed analytical assessment of sequential healthcare behavior would help in evaluation of entire healthcare delivery aspects	Original survey data from rural India and China containing 119 unique healthcare pathways among 637 respondents was analyzed	Importance of analyzing sequence sensitive and sequence insensitive healthcare behavior was emphasized
31	Budrionis and Bellika (2016)	Authors highlighted that Learning Healthcare System (LHS) which incorporated health data & patient's perspectives into healthcare models would enable for delivering customized care at lower costs with minimized consumption of resources	Literature review on LHS was carried out	Extant research on LHS was studied to identify opportunities and gaps

(continued)

Table 12.1 (continued)

S.No	Author(s)	Findings	Methodology	Context
32	Kumar et al. (2014)	Authors argued that Health Technology Assessment (HTA) should be adapted as tool for policy and decision making. It would enable to bridge the current gap of divergent and loosely coordinated healthcare organizations	A conceptual study was undertaken	Authors identified the use cases of HTA in Indian healthcare sector
33	Rebecchi et al. (2016)	Authors undertook a meta-analysis of projects that incorporated several local ground realities for effective response to healthcare needs of population in emerging economies	Three different healthcare levels were analyzed to develop the meta-project	Authors developed a framework for local-oriented healthcare delivery ecosystem
34	Arya et al. (2015)	Authors advocated that collaboration and alliances in high technology healthcare supply chain would significantly improve the cost effectiveness and performance of healthcare supply chain	Case of dental implants has been discussed	Importance of collaboration in high technology healthcare supply chain was emphasized
35	Kumar and Kumar (2014)	Authors proposed that modeling of healthcare supply chain using system dynamics would assist in effective policy making. Hence, overall healthcare delivery would be improved significantly	A survey study was conducted in the state of Uttrakhand in India to collect data for model development	Authors identified the gaps and opportunities in rural healthcare supply chain using system dynamics modeling

Table 12.2 Key firms involved in innovations for BoP healthcare in India

S.No	Organization	Innovation	Type of innovation
1	Jaipur foot	Manufactured and fitted low-cost prosthetic leg	Product
2	Aravind Eye Care	Hospital network that performed low-cost cataract surgeries for millions of patients through strategic cost control interventions	Process
3	Narayana Hrudayalaya	Hospital that performed low-cost cardiac surgeries and had expanded to other health services as well	Process
4	EMRI	Low cost emergency services were provided	Service
5	Lupin	Lost cost drug for psoriasis was provided	Product
6	TATA	Water purifier at a fraction cost of other available purifiers in the market to reduce incidences of illness caused because of consumption of contaminated water	Product
7	General Electric	Healthymagination, a technology based healthcare initiative	Business model alteration
8	LV Prasad Eye Institute	Affordable eye care to the poor	Service
9	LifeSpring Hospitals	Low-cost maternity care hospital chain	Service
10	Narayana Hrudayalya	'Yeshasvini Insurance Scheme' provided insurance for cardiac surgeries at an annual premium of only US$1.5 per annum	Business model alteration
11	Embrace Global	Low-cost incubators for preventing neo-natal deaths	Product

(continued)

Table 12.2 (continued)

S.No	Organization	Innovation	Type of innovation
12	Teleradiology Solutions	Delivered radiology services remotely	Service

Table 12.3 General analysis of Indian healthcare

Type of innovation	Cost reduction	Quality management
Product innovation	****	**
Service innovation	***	*
Process innovation	**	*
Business model innovation	*	**

depicts high-cost savings, double stars (**) depicts moderate-cost savings while single star (*) depicts marginal-cost savings. In quality management, when both quality of healthcare management as well as quality of healthcare infrastructure improved then it was depicted by double stars (**) while when quality of healthcare management improved but the quality of healthcare infrastructure deteriorated then it was depicted by single star (*).

Low-cost medical services are much needed in India, given two thirds of the population lives on a daily income of less than Indian rupees 150. With the notion of providing affordable healthcare to the BoP customers in tertiary Indian healthcare industry also attracts patients from the developed world (Western countries included) as well (Maheshwari et al., 2012; Reddy
& Qadeer, 2010). Thus, given this context, India healthcare industry has become a world leader in affordable quality tertiary healthcare which had remained elusive to patients from other countries (see Maheshwari et al., 2012; Reddy & Qadeer, 2010).It would be important to note that India has been a leader in setting leadership position globally (Bhattacharyya, 2019). India has been the only major economy in the world where in CSR initiatives are made mandatory (Nair & Bhattacharyya, 2019). So, for the firms earning higher level of profit, sacrifice of significant amount of profit amount dedicated toward the

case of CSR spend was required (Gatti et al., 2018). This was two percentage points of the average net profits secured by the firm for previous three years (Nair & Bhattacharyya, 2019). In the healthcare industry, because of the past legacy of 'Dharma' and 'Krama' such sacrifice has rather been viewed as an investment. This investment was meant to be toward taking care of social aspects in business with society. The cause of Indian firms (as well as some foreign ones) has been aided with highly potent but relatively cheaper and low-investment technology. Healthcare thematic CSR has been pursued by firms extensively even when it hadn't necessarily been Strategic CSR initiatives (Bhattacharyya, 2010, 2012). This indicated the commitment of business firms toward the healthcare as a priority theme of intervention. Healthcare was an industry, wherein just seeking more profit (unlike any other industry) has not been seen as righteous. Indian hospitals have responded to this through taking care of economically backward patients. It would be important to note that the premier hospitals in India are industry leaders with the best possible doctors, most modern infrastructure and other facilities. These hospitals were islands of excellence in an otherwise ocean of weak healthcare landscape. The quest would be to innovate further technologically and more importantly through business model improvements so as to provide advanced healthcare facilities (like tertiary care) at affordable price points that the Indian mass population would be able to afford. Lean and 'Juggad' thinking along with application of emerging technologies would continue to be vital to cater to this worthy quest (Prabhu & Jain, 2015).

Individual Cognition and Behavior and Its Impact on Business Models and Innovation

One of the major directions that emerges from the above analysis is the need to explore the relationships between concepts embedded in traditions such as altruism and dharma and the contemporary entrepreneurship compulsions and behaviours (Tan et al., 2005). For example, how do the innovators incorporate, if at all, the concepts of dharma in the design of business models. Dharma is one of the four purusharthas discussed in the traditional Indian literature, the others being kama, arth, and mokhsa that relate to the fulfillment of desire, creation of wealth and personal liberation respectively (Rajasakran et al., 2014). While kama and arth can be linked to the design of profitable businesses that can create wealth, dharma relates to the deontic motivation toward society. The extensive work on hybrid organizations has explored how the individuals (and organizations) manage the balance between the social cause (*dharma*) and profitability (*Arth* and *Kama*) (Smith et al., 2013) while the linkages between businesses and spiritual aspects captured in moksha has been largely unexplored. Future research can explore, whether there is, if any, significant impact of spirituality in designing business models or participation in CSR activities. How does the Gandhian concept of involvement of businesses in CSR activities relate to *dharma* and materialistic aspects or both? How do innovators and entrepreneurs look at their involvement along the four dimensions of *purusharthas*?

While many of the business models, especially healthcare technology related ones, are founded by non-medical professionals, some of these initiatives such as NH, AECS and Karuna Trust have been founded by physicians. The training of physicians involves spending more than a decade in learning clinical work and the curriculum prepares them for clinical practice. What motivates these professionals to indulge in entrepreneurship and innovative ventures? Where do the doctors gain knowledge and resources for the same? Investigating these questions would also allow researchers to understand the ecosystem required for stimulating innovation among medical professionals.

India has emerged as a technology hub in the recent years. There is a rapid growth of technology based startups in India, driven by the Government's push to promote an entrepreneurial culture in the country (Subrahmanya, 2017). Several of these startups target the healthcare space and attempt to contribute to affordability and accessibility. While some of these startups may be motivated by altruistic motivation, more often than not, the founders target profitable business models. It would be interesting to know the relationship between altruism and the types of business models in terms of target markets, pricing mechanisms etc. Further, many of these initiatives, though driven by profit motive, adopt the rhetoric of developmental impact (Chandra, 2016). Future research should explore which type of startups attract funding agencies related to impact and development and which business models attract the private equity funds targeting quick profits. Further, though some businesses or innovations might be driven by profit, does the rhetoric emphasized by the founders and the funding agencies emphasize altruism and focus on dharma. Furthermore, it would be worthwhile to explore the antecedents such as motivations of these entrepreneurs to get involved in health technology. Also, the processual analysis of the innovation, from idea formulation to implementation to scaling up would illuminate what type of ecosystems are required for promoting these startups.

Organization Design and Business Models

There has been a substantial influence of Gandhian philosophy in the Indian thought processes. While the Gandhian philosophy emphasized localized solutions embedded in the context, the conversations in the innovation and entrepreneurship scholarship and practice focuses on achieving scale (Williams, 2019). Indeed the funding agencies and institutions look for scalability as the primary characteristic, which in turn is presumed to lead to future profitability. An interesting research question that needs to be explored is how do the entrepreneurs and innovators who are driven by Gandhian philosophy of caring, altruism and designing community based context-sensitive solutions marry the concept of localized solutions with scalability. The hub and spoke design of Aravind Eye Care System, for example, consists of rurally located small vision centers linked to the large hub hospital located in the urban area. The model provides for local connect and responsiveness as well as scalability. It would be interesting to understand the dilemmas faced by innovators and to comprehend how the innovators and entrepreneurs manage them. Some of the business models such as the provision of healthcare services for the elderly at home closely relate to an important aspect of dharma—taking care of the elderly. Traditionally, the Indian families had been structured as joint families where multiple generations of family stayed together and the work, including taking care of dependent children and elderly, was distributed (Dhanaraj & Mahambare, 2019). With increasing prevalence of dual earner couples, especially in the fast growing urban population, has not only affected the care of elderly and children but also interfaces with the concept of dharma. Future researchers could examine how the businesses that provide care at home relate to the concept of dharma. Also, whether such initiatives develop and promulgate the rhetoric of dharma to push their businesses? And if so how do the customers perceive the same?

In the present analysis, we have examined multiple innovative models that provide affordable, accessible and quality healthcare to underprivileged populations. However, the literature, including our research, largely focuses on the successful models. There may be multiple reasons for the absence of literature on failed models, including lack of availability of data, the structured process of publication etc. However, we posit that an in-depth study of failed models or comparative analysis between failed and successful models can provide useful insights for both academicians and practitioners interested in comprehending the critical factors that lead to success/failure of such initiatives.

Furthermore, many such success stories represent pilot projects that have achieved success at a small scale. Studying projects that have scaled to programs or models that have sustained for long duration could highlight factors critical for scaling up of such initiatives. Further research is also required to examine the politico-social ecosystem required for supporting the innovations to scale and to sustain. Both scaling up and sustainability of the innovations are important for creating long-term value and impact.

Government Policies; Systems and Stakeholders

Several government regulations directly impact the design and implementation of innovations and initiatives related to socially relevant aspects such as health. One of the major recent being mandatory CSR spending for profit making organizations (Gatti et al., 2018). Future research can explore the impact of the CSR regulation on the initiatives undertaken by organizations. There are many interesting questions that need to be examined. Is there any difference between the modes of spending in organizations operating in the healthcare domain versus those involved in other industries? Further, how has the regulation affected the CSR spending of the organizations that were already spending more than mandated 2% of their profits in CSR? How much percentage of the CSR funds goes toward provision of healthcare? Which aspect of healthcare attracts the CSR funds, primary, secondary or tertiary? Which one is the most effective and efficient way of involving organizations in CSR activities related to healthcare?

As shared above, innovation in the Indian context has been closely linked to the concept of 'Jugaad'—generating more value with scarce resources (Tasavori et al., 2016). While there have been several studies on the frugal design of products using jugaad, the same can be applied to developing relationships and using relationships as a resource for scaling up. Future researchers can explore how the entrepreneurs incorporate the concept of 'jugad' into the design of relationships among diverse stakeholders, such as managing PPPs or working with the government in a contractual relationship.

The public healthcare system in India has been designed in a three tiered system to enable access. The design envisaged a smooth interface between PHC (Primary Health centers) at the village level, CHC (Community Health Centers) at the Taluka level and District Civil Hospitals at the district headquarters. However, the public system, over the years, has not been able to deliver accessible, affordable and quality healthcare, resulting in mushrooming of the private sector (Bagchi et al., 2020). Recently, there have been several initiatives in a PPP (Public private partnership) mode where the two diverse stakeholders come together for delivering healthcare. Such initiatives have been implemented at all levels: Primary care, for example, Karuna trust and Tata Trusts have entered into agreements with respective state governments to manage primary health centers in Karnataka and Maharashtra respectively. While the Gandhian philosophy emphasized philanthropic involvement of the private sector in the healthcare sector, the management of PPP involves building exchange based relationships, preferable long-term relationships, between the diverse stakeholders (Rajasulochana & Maurya, 2020). Such initiatives, if managed properly, can enhance the sustainability of the initiatives.

Conclusion

The above analysis presents several interesting areas for future research. The potential research areas have been described at three broad levels—Individual (entrepreneur/innovator's behavioral aspects); business models (organization design) and systems and policy level (impact of government regulations and policies on design of organizations and strategies adopted and involvement of multiple stakeholders). The authors emphasize that these levels are representatives and not compartmental, and that there would be considerable overlap among these levels while conducting the research, both design and implementation aspects. Future research could explore how the Gandhian approach driven by altruism influences the management of PPPs. Further research can also explore the processual aspects of evolution of successful as well as unsuccessful PPPs so as to comprehend the dynamics of relationships involved in nurturing the partnership.

References

Agarwal, N., & Brem, A. (2012). June. Frugal and reverse innovation-Literature overview and case study insights from a German MNC in India and China. In *2012 18th International ICE Conference on Engineering, Technology and Innovation* (pp. 1–11). IEEE.

Altekar, A. S. (2002). *State and government in ancient India.* Motilal Banarsidass Publication.

Alur, S., & Schoormans, J. P. (2011). Sustainable rural healthcare and social franchisee selection–an India study. *Journal of Medical Marketing, 11*(3), 230–236.

Annala, L., Sarin, A., & Green, J. L. (2018). Co-production of frugal innovation: Case of low cost reverse osmosis water filters in India. *Journal of Cleaner Production, 171*, S110–S118.

Arya, V., Deshmukh, S. G., & Bhatnagar, N. (2015). High technology health care supply chains: Issues in collaboration. *Procedia-Social and Behavioral Sciences, 189*, 40–47.

Avari, B. (2007). *India: The ancient past: A history of the Indian sub-continent from c. 7000 bc to ad 1200*. Routledge.

Bagchi, T., Das, A., Dawad, S., & Dalal, K. (2020). Non-utilization of public healthcare facilities during sickness: A national study in India. *Journal of Public Health*, 1–9.

Bajpai, V. (2014). The challenges confronting public hospitals in India, their origins, and possible solutions. *Advances in Public Health, 2014*.

Banerjee, P. M. (2013). The "frugal" in frugal innovation. In *Evolution of Innovation Management* (pp. 290–310). Palgrave Macmillan.

Banerji, D. (1973). Social orientation of medical education in India. *Economic and Political Weekly*, 485–488.

Berman, P. A. (1998). Rethinking health care systems: Private health care provision in India. *World Development, 26*(8), 1463–1479.

Bhandari, L., & Dutta, S. (2007). Health infrastructure in rural India. *India Infrastructure Report*, 265–271. http://citeseerx.ist.psu.edu/viewdoc/download?doi=10.1.1.463.4188&rep=rep1&type=pdf. Accessed 1 October 2019.

Bhardwaj, H. C. (1979). *Aspects of ancient Indian technology*. Motilal Banarsidass Publications.

Bhattacharyya, S. S. (2010). Development of a scale on strategic corporate social responsibility constructs. *International Journal of Indian Culture and Business Management, 3*(2), 181–207.

Bhattacharyya, S. S. (2011). Reflections on reincarnation, coincidences, Organisational Karma, Soul Groups and its implication for business organisational success. *International Journal of Indian Culture and Business Management, 4*(3), 241–271.

Bhattacharyya, S. S. (2012). Observations on the realities regarding corporate social responsibility from the emerging economy of India. *International Journal of Indian Culture and Business Management, 5*(2), 162–183.

Bhattacharyya, S. S. (2019). Exploratory study of international Corporate Social Responsibility initiatives of Indian firms. *Business Strategy & Development, 2*(1), 51–62.

Bhattacharyya, S. S., Chaturvedi, A., & Chaturvedi, A. (2009). A journey through the labyrinth of the business and society concepts. *International Journal of Business Environment, 2*(3), 281–306.

Bhattacharyya, S. S., & Shaik, J. (2009). Topic–strategic alliances: Perspectives from Indian life insurance industry. *International Journal of Indian Culture and Business Management, 3*(1), 98–120.

Bhatti, Y. A., Prime, M., Harris, M., Wadge, H., McQueen, J., Patel, H., Carter, A. W., Parston, G., & Darzi, A. (2017). The search for the holy grail: Frugal innovation in healthcare from low-income or middle-income countries for reverse innovation to developed countries. *BMJ Innovations, 3*(4), 212–220.

Bhawuk, D. (2011). *Spirituality and Indian Psychology: Lessons from the Bhagavad-Gita*. Springer Science & Business Media.

Bhowmik, D., Duraivel, S., Singh, R. K., & Kumar, K. S. (2013). Telemedicine-an innovating healthcare system in India. *The Pharma Innovation, 2*(4, Part A), 1.

Bose, S., & Jalal, A. (2017). *Modern South Asia: History, culture, political economy*. Routledge.

Bound, K., & Thornton, I. W. (2012). *Our frugal future: Lessons from India's innovation system*. Nesta.

Brown, T., & Wyatt, J. (2010). Design thinking for social innovation. *Development Outreach, 12*(1), 29–43.

Budrionis, A., & Bellika, J. G. (2016). The learning healthcare system: Where are we now? A systematic review. *Journal of Biomedical Informatics, 64*, 87–92.

Chakrabarty, B. (2006). *Social and political thought of Mahatma Gandhi*. Routledge.

Chakravarthi, I. (2011). Corporate presence in healthcare sector in India. *Social Medicine, 5*(4), 192–204.

Chandra, Y. (2016). A rhetoric-orientation view of social entrepreneurship. *Social Enterprise Journal*.

Chatterjee, P. (2008). *Factors that Frustrate Growth of Private Health Sector in India*. http://medind.nic.in/haa/t08/i1/haat08i1p5.pdf. Accessed 8 October 2019.

Chatterjee, S., Levin, C., & Laxminarayan, R. (2013). Unit cost of medical services at different hospitals in India. *PLoS ONE, 8*(7), e69728. https://doi.org/10.1371/journal.pone.0069728

Chattopadhyay, S. (2007). Religion, spirituality, health and medicine: Why should Indian physicians care? *Journal of Postgraduate Medicine, 53*(4), 262.

Chinna Natesan, N., Keeffe, M. J., & Darling, J. R. (2009). Enhancement of global business practices: Lessons from the Hindu Bhagavad Gita. *European Business Review, 21*(2), 128–143.

Cohn, B. S. (2017). Notes on the history of the study of Indian society and culture. In *Structure and change in Indian society* (pp. 3–28). Routledge.

Dalal, A. K. (2002). Disability rehabilitation in a traditional Indian society. *Asia Pacific Disability Rehabilitation Journal, 15*(2). http://www.aifoeng.it/archives/disability/apdrj/2002_selected_readings_cbr.pdf#page=18. Accessed 1 October 2019.

Dam, A. (2015). *Wading through quicksand: Palliative care*. Notion Press.

Dana, L. P. (2000). Creating entrepreneurs in India. *Journal of Small Business Management, 38*(1), 86.

Davidson, L. (2015). Do frugal innovations lead to frugal outcomes? A case study of healthcare in India.

De Costa, A., Al-Muniri, A., Diwan, V. K., & Eriksson, B. (2009). Where are healthcare providers? Exploring relationships between context and human resources for health Madhya Pradesh province India. *Health Policy, 93*(1), 41–47.

Deo, M. G. (2013). Doctor population ratio for India—The reality. *The Indian Journal of Medical Research, 137*(4), 632.

Deshpande, O., Reid, M. C., & Rao, A. S. (2005). Attitudes of Asian-Indian Hindus toward end-of-life care. *Journal of the American Geriatrics Society, 53*(1), 131–135.

Dhanaraj, S., & Mahambare, V. (2019). Family structure, education and women's employment in rural India. *World Development, 115*, 17–29.

Engel, N., Kenneth, J., & Pai, M. (2012). TB diagnostics in India: Creating an ecosystem for innovation. *Expert Review of Molecular Diagnostics, 12*(1), 21–24.

Esposito, M., Kapoor, A., & Goyal, S. (2012). Enabling healthcare services for the rural and semi-urban segments in India: When shared value meets the bottom of the pyramid. *Corporate Governance: The International Journal of Business in Society, 12*(4), 514–533.

Gardner, C. A., Acharya, T., & Yach, D. (2007). Technological and social innovation: A unifying new paradigm for global health. *Health Affairs, 26*(4), 1052–1061.

Gatti, L., Vishwanath, B., Seele, P., & Cottier, B. (2018). Are we moving beyond voluntary CSR? Exploring theoretical and managerial implications of mandatory CSR resulting from the New Indian Companies Act. *Journal of Business Ethics*, 1–12.

Golechha, M. (2015). Healthcare agenda for the Indian government. *The Indian Journal of Medical Research, 141*(2), 151.

Govindarajan, V., & Euchner, J. (2012). Reverse innovation. *Research-Technology Management, 55*(6), 13–17.

Gupta, D. (2005). Whither the Indian village: culture and agriculture in'rural'India. *Economic and Political Weekly*, 751–758.

Haenssgen, M. J., & Ariana, P. (2017). Healthcare access: A sequence-sensitive approach. *SSM-Population Health, 3*, 37–47.

Hansen, F. (2008). A revolution in healthcare: Medicine meets the marketplace. *Institute of Public Affairs Review: A Quarterly Review of Politics and Public Affairs, the, 59*(4), 43.

Henderson, R. (2006). The innovator's dilemma as a problem of organizational competence. *Journal of Product Innovation Management, 23*(1), 5–11.

Honavar, S. G. (2019). "Indovation" in ophthalmology—The potential power of frugal innovations. *Indian Journal of Ophthalmology, 67*(4), 447.

Ito, S., & Kono, H. (2010). Why is the take-up of microinsurance so low? Evidence from a health insurance scheme in India. *The Developing Economies, 48*(1), 74–101.

Jaggi, O. P., & Chattopadhyaya, D. P. (2000). *Medicine in India: Modern period*. Oxford University Press.

Jaiswal, A. K., & Gupta, S. (2015). The influence of marketing on consumption behavior at the bottom of the pyramid. *Journal of Consumer Marketing, 32*(2), 113–124.

James, K. S. (1994). Indian elderly: Asset or liability. *Economic and Political Weekly*, 2335–2339.

Jha, V. (2004). End-stage renal care in developing countries: The India experience. *Renal Failure, 26*(3), 201–208.

Kapoor, A., & Goyal, S. (2013). Inclusive healthcare at base of the pyramid (BoP) in India. *International Journal of Trade and Global Markets, 6*(1), 22–39.

Keown, O. P., Parston, G., Patel, H., Rennie, F., Saoud, F., Al Kuwari, H., & Darzi, A. (2014). Lessons from eight countries on diffusing innovation in health care. *Health Affairs, 33*(9), 1516–1522.

Ketola, T., Sharma, M. K., & Agarwal, P. (2009). Hindu philosophy: bridging corporate governance and CSR. *Management of Environmental Quality: An International Journal*. https://www.emerald.com/insight/content/doi/10.1108/14777830910950694/full/html. Accessed 1 October 2019.

Kumar, A. S., Chen, L. C., Choudhury, M., Ganju, S., Mahajan, V., Sinha, A., & Sen, A. (2011). Financing health care for all: Challenges and opportunities. *The Lancet, 377*(9766), 668–679.

Kumar, D. (1997). Medical encounters in British India, 1820–1920. *Economic and Political Weekly*, 166–170.

Kumar, D., & Kumar, D. (2014). Modelling rural healthcare supply chain in India using system dynamics. *Procedia Engineering, 97*, 2204–2212.

Kumar, H., & Bhaduri, S. (2014). Jugaad to grassroot innovations: Understanding the landscape of the informal sector innovations in India. *African Journal of Science, Technology, Innovation and Development, 6*(1), 13–22.

Kumar, M., Taylor, F. C., Chokshi, M. A. U. L. I. K., Ebrahim, S. H. A. H., Gabbay, J., & Taylor, F. C. (2014). Health technology assessment in India: The potential for improved healthcare decision-making. *National Medical Journal of India, 27*(3), 159–163.

Kumar, M. (2010). Hinduism and Social Work. *Origin and Development of Social Work in India*. http://www.egyankosh.ac.in/bitstream/123456789/52005/1/Block-1.pdf#page=145. Accessed 1 October 2019.

Kumar, R., Jaiswal, V., Tripathi, S., Kumar, A., & Idris, M. Z. (2007). Inequity in health care delivery in India: The problem of rural medical practitioners. *Health Care Analysis, 15*(3), 223–233.

Kumar, S. (2009). Designing promotional strategies for medical tourism in India: A case study of an ophthalmic hospital in NCR. *Health and Population: Perspectives and Issues, 32*(2), 86–95.

Lenssen, G., Van Wassenhove, L., Pickard, S., Lenssen, J. J., Esposito, M., Kapoor, A., & Goyal, S. (2012). Enabling healthcare services for the rural and semi-urban segments in India: When shared value meets the bottom of the pyramid. *Corporate Governance: The International Journal of Business in Society*.

Maheshwari, S., Animasahun, B. A., & Njokanma, O. F. (2012). International patients with congenital heart disease: What brings them to India? *Indian Heart Journal, 64*(1), 50–53.

Malik, A., Boyle, B., & Mitchell, R. (2017). Contextual ambidexterity and innovation in healthcare in India: The role of HRM. *Personnel Review, 46*(7), 1358–1380.

McMahon, D., & Thorsteinsdóttir, H. (2013). Pursuing endogenous high-tech innovation in developing countries: A look at regenerative medicine innovation in Brazil China and India. *Research Policy, 42*(4), 965–974.

Medhora, P. B. (1965). Entrepreneurship in India. *Political Science Quarterly, 80*(4), 558–580.

Mishra, L. C., Singh, B. B., & Dagenais, S. (2001). Ayurveda: A historical perspective and principles of the traditional healthcare system in India. *Alternative Therapies in Health and Medicine, 7*(2), 36–43.

Modi, R. (2011). Offshore healthcare management: Medical tourism between Kenya, Tanzania and India. *Emma Mawdsley & Gerard McCann, India in Africa: Changing geographies of power*, 125–139.

Moons, K., Waeyenbergh, G., & Pintelon, L. (2019). Measuring the logistics performance of internal hospital supply chains—A literature study. *Omega, 82*, 205–217.

Motkuri, V., Vardhan, T. S., & Ahmad, S. (2017). *Quantity and Quality of Human Resources in Health Care: Shortage of Health Workers in India*. https://mpra.ub.uni-muenchen.de/84332/1/MPRA_paper_84332.pdf. Accessed on 8 October 2019.

Mukerjee, K. (2012). Frugal innovation: The key to penetrating emerging markets. *Ivey Business Journal, 76*(4).

Muniapan, B., & Dass, M. (2008). Corporate social responsibility: A philosophical approach from an ancient Indian perspective. *International Journal of Indian Culture and Business Management, 1*(4), 408–420.

Muniapan, B., & Satpathy, B. (2013). The 'dharma'and 'karma'of CSR from the Bhagavad-Gita. *Journal of Human Values, 19*(2), 173–187.

Muniapan, B. (2014). The roots of Indian corporate social responsibility (CSR) practice from a Vedantic perspective. In *Corporate Social Responsibility in Asia* (pp. 19–33). Springer.

Nair, A. K., & Bhattacharyya, S. S. (2019). Mandatory corporate social responsibility in India and its effect on corporate financial performance: Perspectives from institutional theory and resource-based view. *Business Strategy & Development, 2*(2), 106–116.

Nayak, B., Bhattacharyya, S. S., & Krishnamoorthy, B. (2019a). Application of digital technologies in health insurance for social good of bottom of pyramid customers in India. *International Journal of Sociology and Social Policy, 39*(9/10), 752–772. https://doi.org/10.1108/IJSSP-05-2019-0095

Nayak, B., Bhattacharyya, S. S., & Krishnamoorthy, B. (2019b). Democratizing health insurance services; accelerating social inclusion through technology policy of health insurance firms. *Business Strategy & Development, 2*(1), 242–252.

Padma, P., Rajendran, C., & Sai, L. P. (2009). A conceptual framework of service quality in healthcare: Perspectives of Indian patients and their attendants. *Benchmarking: An International Journal, 16*(2), 157–191.

Pal, S. K., & Mittal, B. (2004, April–June). Improving cancer care in India: Prospects and challenges. *Asian Pacific Journal of Cancer Prevention, 5*(2), 226–228.

Pandve, H. T., & Pandve, T. K. (2013). Primary healthcare system in India: Evolution and challenges. *International Journal of Health System and Disaster Management, 1*(3), 125.

Parthasarathy, B., Aoyama, Y., & Menon, N. (2015). Innovating for the bottom of the pyramid: Case studies in healthcare from India. In *Technologies for Development* (pp. 55–69). Springer.

Patel, B., & Chavda, K. (2013). Rural entrepreneurship in India: Challenge and problems. *International Journal of Advance Research in Computer Science and Management Studies, 1*(2).

Patil, A. V., Somasundaram, K. V., & Goyal, R. C. (2002). Current health scenario in rural India. *Australian Journal of Rural Health, 10*(2), 129–135.

Prabhu, J., & Jain, S. (2015). Innovation and entrepreneurship in India: Understanding jugaad. *Asia Pacific Journal of Management, 32*(4), 843–868.

Prahalad, C. K. (2012). Bottom of the pyramid as a source of breakthrough innovations. *Journal of Product Innovation Management, 29*(1), 6–12.

Pramesh, C. S., Badwe, R. A., Borthakur, B. B., Chandra, M., Raj, E. H., Kannan, T., & Rath, G. K. (2014). Delivery of affordable and equitable cancer care in India. *The Lancet Oncology, 15*(6), e223–e233.

Rajasakran, T., Sinnappan, S., & Raja, S. S. (2014). Purushartha: Maslow's need hierarchy revisited. *The Anthropologist, 18*(1), 199–203.

Rajasulochana, S. R., & Maurya, D. (2020). Lessons from Healthcare PPP's in India. *International Journal of Rural Management, 16*(1), 7–12.

Ramani, K. V., & Mavalankar, D. (2006). Health system in India: Opportunities and challenges for improvements. *Journal of Health Organization and Management, 20*(6), 560–572.

Ramdorai, A., & Herstatt, C. (2015). Frugal innovation in healthcare. *India Studies in Business and Economics.*

Ramdorai, A., & Herstatt, C. (2017). Lessons from low-cost healthcare innovations for the Base-of the Pyramid markets: How incumbents can systematically create disruptive innovations. In *Lead Market India* (pp. 119–144). Springer.

Rao, K. D., Sundararaman, T., Bhatnagar, A., Gupta, G., Kokho, P., & Jain, K. (2013). Which doctor for primary health care? Quality of care and non-physician clinicians in India. *Social Science & Medicine, 84*, 30–34.

Rao, M., Rao, K. D., Kumar, A. S., Chatterjee, M., & Sundararaman, T. (2011). Human resources for health in India. *The Lancet, 377*(9765), 587–598.

Rao, P. H. (2012). The private health sector in India: A framework for improving the quality of care. *ASCI Journal of Management, 41*(2), 14–39.

Rebecchi, A., Gola, M., Kulkarni, M., Lettieri, E., Paoletti, I., & Capolongo, S. (2016). Healthcare for all in emerging countries: A preliminary investigation of facilities in Kolkata India. *Annali Dell'istituto Superiore Di Sanita, 52*(1), 88–97.

Reddy, S., & Qadeer, I. (2010). Medical tourism in India: Progress or predicament? *Economic and Political Weekly*, 69–75.

Rhodes, G. (2012). The medical mandala: The public health benefits of entrepreneurship tools and skills among medical students in India. *Indian Journal of Public Health, 56*(2), 105.

Richards, T. (1985). Medical education in India—In poor health. *British Medical Journal (clinical Research Ed.), 290*(6475), 1132.

Rivett, K. (1959). The economic thought of Mahatma Gandhi. *British Journal of Sociology*, 1–15.

Rohini, R., & Mahadevappa, B. (2010). Social responsibility of hospitals: An Indian context. *Social Responsibility Journal, 6*(2), 268–285.

Sawant, P. D. (2014). Corporate social responsibility of select pharma companies in India: An exploratory study. *Global Journal of Commerce & Management Perspective, 3*(4), 205–219.

Shah, S. (2014). Corporate social responsibility: A way of life at the Tata Group. *Journal of Human Values, 20*(1), 59–74.

Shah, U. (2010). Private sector in Indian healthcare delivery: Consumer perspective and government policies to promote private sector. *Information Management and Business Review, 1*(2), 79–87.

Sharma, R. S. (2007). *Material culture & Social formations in ancient India.* Macmillan.

Sharma, S. (1999). Corporate Gita: Lessons for management, administration and leadership. *Journal of Human Values, 5*(2), 103–123.

Sharma, U. (1973). Theodicy and the Doctrine of Karma. *Man, 8*(3), 347–364.

Shet, A., & De Costa, A. (2011). India calling: Harnessing the promise of mobile phones for HIV healthcare. *Tropical Medicine & International Health, 16*(2), 214–216.

Singh, M. G., Gambhir, A. N. U. R. A. J., & Dasgupta, J. (2011). Innovation in India: Affordable innovations. In *The Global Innovation Index* (pp. 77–86).

Smith, W. K., Gonin, M., & Besharov, M. L. (2013). Managing social-business tensions: A review and research agenda for social enterprise. *Business Ethics Quarterly, 23*(3), 407–442.

Srivastava, A. K., Negi, G., Mishra, V., & Pandey, S. (2012). Corporate social responsibility: A case study of TATA group. *IOSR Journal of Business and Management, 3*(5), 17–27.

Subrahmanya, M. B. (2017). Comparing the entrepreneurial ecosystems for technology startups in Bangalore and Hyderabad, India. *Technology Innovation Management Review, 7*(7).

Tan, W. L., Williams, J., & Tan, T. M. (2005). Defining the 'social' in 'social entrepreneurship': Altruism and entrepreneurship. *The International Entrepreneurship and Management Journal, 1*(3), 353–365.

Tasavori, M., Ghauri, P. N., & Zaefarian, R. (2016). Entering the base of the pyramid market in India: A corporate social entrepreneurship perspective. *International Marketing Review, 33*(4), 555–579.

Thapar, R. (1990). *A history of India*. Penguin.

Thapar, R. (2015). *The Penguin history of early India: From the origins to AD 1300*. Penguin UK.

Thorat, A., Vanneman, R., Desai, S., & Dubey, A. (2017). Escaping and falling into poverty in India today. *World Development, 93*, 413–426.

Tiwari, R., Kalogerakis, K., & Herstatt, C. (2014). Frugal innovation and analogies: Some propositions for product development in emerging economies.

Tiwari, R., & Herstatt, C. (2012). Assessing India's lead market potential for cost-effective innovations. *Journal of Indian Business Research, 4*(2), 97–115.

Tripathi, D. (1971). Indian entrepreneurship in historical perspective: A re-interpretation. *Economic and Political Weekly, 6*(22), M59–M66.

Tripathi, D. (2004). *The Oxford history of Indian business*. Oxford University Press.

Velamuri, S. R., Anant, P., & Kumar, V. (2015). Doing well to do good: Business model innovation for social healthcare. In *Business models and modelling* (pp. 279–308). Emerald Group Publishing Limited.
Verma, S., & Bhattacharyya, S. S. (2016). Micro-foundation strategies of IOT, BDA, Cloud Computing: Do they really matter in bottom of pyramid? *Strategic Direction, 32*(8), 36–38.
Westerhof, G. J., Katzko, M. W., Dittmann-Kohli, F., & Hayslip, B., Jr. (2001). Life contexts and health-related selves in old age: Perspectives from the United States, India and Congo/Zaire. *Journal of Aging Studies, 15*(2), 105–126.
Williams, L. D. (2019). Balancing the scales: Appropriate technology and social entrepreneurship. In *Eradicating blindness* (pp. 77–109). Palgrave Macmillan.

13

Management Practices in Changing Indian Society

Richa Awasthy

Introduction

Organizations are sub-system of society and influence mutually. Emery's (1959) framework of Socio-Technical systems view of organization helps to understand interface between technical, social and managerial components. The technological system includes all equipment, infrastructure and technology in the workplace. The social system includes human aspects such as cultural diversity of groups and the social processes. Technological changes have had a substantial impact on social and management system. Current chapter presents changing landscape of India from—Vedic era to fourth Industrial Revolution while focusing on the nature of organizations and sociocultural ecosystem. Interface

R. Awasthy (✉)
School of Business, Public Policy and Social Entrepreneurship,
Dr. B. R. Ambedkar University Delhi, Delhi, India
e-mail: richa@aud.ac.in

© The Author(s), under exclusive license to Springer Nature Switzerland AG 2022

A. Pandey et al. (eds.), *Indigenous Indian Management*,
Palgrave Studies in Indian Management,
https://doi.org/10.1007/978-3-030-87906-8_13

between foreign culture, technological advancement and societal culture has uniquely evolved the organizations in India. While traversing from agriculture to technology-intensive society the interplay between societal values and management practices have considerably influenced each other. Purpose of this chapter is to decode interplay between societal culture and management practices ranging from Vedic era to twenty-first century and discuss its implications. Implication section covers summation of types and nature of organizations and response of Indian society *to those*—mutations in terms of being adaptable, mutually respectful as well as acceptance of diverse perceptive and socio-cultural diversity of society.

Changing Landscape of India from Vedic Period till Date

This section is broadly classified into six sub-sections. (1) Beginning from Vedic period (BCE); (2) Medieval period (1 CE–1100 CE); (3) Sultanate and Mughal period (1100–1700 CE); (4) EIC & British Raj (1700 CE to 1947 CE); (5) India post-independence till turn of the century (1947 CE to 2000 CE); (6) India 2001 CE onwards: Fourth Industrial Revolution.

Vedic Period (BCE)

Vedic period of India cover the period from near about 1800 BCE–500 BCE, when the Indus Valley was invaded by Indo-European group known as *Aryans*, who are considered responsible for Sanskrit language and *Vedic* religion. The term *Vedic* comes from *Vedas*, which denotes superior knowledge. It contains fundamental knowledge about underlying cause of existence and evolution of Hinduism. It is believed that *Vedas* have no beginning. They are *apaurusheya* (no man's creation) and were compiled by Rishis (those who had a direct and clear understanding and vision of the entire picture, Devi, 2018). Among the four Vedas, *Rig Veda* (near about 1500 BC-plus minus 100 years) is the earliest, which explains the knowledge of physical world; *Yajur Veda* is about rules to be followed at the time of sacrifices; third is the *Sam Veda*—called book of chants and considered origin of Indian music; and the fourth is *Atharva Veda* which contains details of rituals. The fourth Veda has two extensions: *Dhanur Veda*, which explains tricks of about arrow-bow and *Ayur Veda* gives details of medicines. *Aryans* introduced Indo-*Aryan* language, a language of conqueror representing a superior civilization/inhabitants. *Aryans* emerged as superior race and the broad two classes springing out of this were *Aryan (Arya)* and *Dasa/Dassyu (anarya, people living in outskirt)*. According to *Rig- Veda*, the *Dasa/Dassyu* is described as physically dissimilar to the *Aryan*, with reference to skin colour. Race was seen as emergence of *varnas* or class representing major racial groups (Thapar, 2003). Class is not as fixed. *VarNAzrama dharma* is based on *guNakarmavibhAgazaH* (*gItA* 4.13; *guNa vibhAgazaH,* division is based on *guNas, the qualities and karma vibhAgazaH,* the (action/work) and not the class system based on birth. It was *karma* based society and *varna-vyavastha* (social stratification) was based on the task performed for smooth functioning of society and explained importance of division of labor and establish eternal order. Four *Varnas* origin is explained in *Rig veda's 10th mandal*. Those are *Brahman* (priests, intellectuals, teachers), *Kshtriya* (nobles, warriors, administrators), *Vaishya* (commoners, farmers, traders) and *Shudra* (to render services to others, workers). During Rig Vedic era all genders were allowed to study Vedas. Rig-Veda-Samhita explained prominent role of women in that era such as *Sulabha, Maitreyi, Gargi, Lopamudra Ghosa, Sikata* (Pal, 2019). Women had freedom to select their spouse and remarriage. This era is known for the knowledge of astronomy, astronomical research and mathematics (Kak, 1995) signified by the call of Rig Veda that "let noble thoughts come to us from all directions" (189.9). Cattle were principal property of people and unit of value in large transactions and reason for restriction in geographical expansion.

Battle of ten Kings (*Dasarjana*) (middle of *Rig Veda* around 3700 BCE) with King *Sudas*, *Bharata* King, who was leading the tribe of Trtsu (located around present day Punjab). King Sudas defeated the coalition of ten Kings and many hymns depict God *Indra* and *Varun* helping *Sudas* in winning the battle (Banerjee, 2019). The purpose of war was to take control over rich fertile land. The facilitating factors for victory were combination of courage of King *Sudas* war strategy and innovation by *Rishi* (mentor, teacher) *Vashishta.* Iron was not discovered in this era and *Rishi Vashishta* invented sharp-edged stone chips to make sword and arrow ends.

Later Vedic period was synthesis of *Brahmin Granth, Aranyakas Granth,* and *Upanishads. Upanishads* (earliest Upanishad was compiled around 500 BCE and there are 108 *Upanishad*) are Hindu scriptures which primarily discuss philosophy, meditation, nature of God and raised many other issues for reflection. They are compilation of dialogue, intellectually stimulating discourse between *guru* and pupil and it was beginning of *gurukul* era or inception of academy similar to Western philosophical approaches such as Platonic tradition academy (c. 387 BC). It was era of complete freedom of enquiry, self-experience (Thakar, 1991) and emphasis was laid on developing bird's eye view by logical and analytical thinking *Upanishads* reiterate *Rig Vedas* approach that there are many paths to the truth. Spirituality, humanism and science are major focal areas in *Upanishads* and in Indian tradition religion and philosophy were similar (Raju, 1952). Pluralistic worldview of Indians has its root in Vedic tradition (Sinha, 2014).

Population increased around river Ganga and Yamuna belt so as emergence of Kingdom. This era witnessed emergence of belief in King as the supreme power who looks into the issues of war, peace and finances. As time passed (around 700–500 BC), *Dharma* was eclipsed with customs, ceremonies introduced by Brahmans/priests. Brahman started operating on their knowledge power and *yagna* and *bali pratha* (sacrificial system to express gratitude toward God) became popular and *sashtangansh* (one-sixth part) should be offered to God. Also one-sixth of *bali* and produce (it was tax in that era) was offered to King. Hence *Kshtriya* and *Brahmans* emerged as superior class. This was an era of 16 *janapadas* (well-defined boundaries of urban settlements where people lived through many generations and share common customs, dialect and rituals) democracies, *mahajanpads* (more than one urban territory) and republics. Administration had strong control on society. Pali text includes details about administration in *mahajanpad* era. Terms like *vetana/bhattavetana* (professional wages), *rasika* (revenue), *donamapaka* (minister measuring revenue with dona), *rajabali* (king's share), *sunka* (toll tax), *rajakosa* (royal treasury), *senanayak* (a general) and so on. This literature indicates well defined economic, taxation and military system (Sarao, 2013). Evolution of market comes from surplus agricultural produce and handicrafts. Surplus was also possible because of freedom to select profession as well as innovative abilities of Indian society. Markets were running mainly on barter system and it seems wooden vessels used to measure grains and four fingers was used to make assessments of measurements. However taxes and economic exchange were based on extending services and products. Such as farmer offer produce of soil, craft worker had to pay taxes in the form of free labor for King, This era saw beginning of metallic and silver coins.

Organized administration was in place around 600 BC. *Kasi* was one of the sixteen *mahajanpad*, had its capital at *Baranasi*. Baranasi was mentioned as trade and manufacturing hub for ships, clothes and sandalwood. Merchants from South Asia used to travel to *Baranasi* for trade. *Magadha* was one of the sixteen *mahajanpads* and two major religion originated from here—Jainism and Buddhism. Both Jainism and Buddhism rejected *chaturvarna* (four class) hierarchy and Brahmanical superiority. King Mahavir gave titrants (three principles) of Jainism: right faith, right knowledge and right conduct. Mahavir popularized notion of ahimsa (non-violence) and restriction on animal sacrifice (*bali*) and Brahmanical superiority. Over centuries class system converted into caste.

Further, this era is marked with the great Kings like *Chandragupta Maurya,* Bimbisara, Bindusara, and *Asoka.* Economy and trade was well flourished in this era. Awareness about monsoon wind helped to expand maritime trade from India to South Asia and Mediterranean regions (Tripati, 2011). Society was not class-rigid till Asoka era in terms of freedom to work. In terms of trade, Indian fabric like muslin was very popular in Rome and has been leading export to different part of world. *Chandragupta Maurya* (C 321–C 297 BCE) developed elaborate administration system where power was mainly concentrated in his hands. He was assisted by council of ministers and committees to undertake various social and economic activities. *Chandragupta (belonged to Shudra class, yet became King and served as Kshatriya)* is known for setting up the first pan-Indian empire and his mentor *Chankya. Chankya* had mastery over variety of fields like political science, economics, governance, accounting, foreign policy and so on. He wrote *Arthashastra* around 300 BC. He laid strong emphasis on good governance, which can be achieved by efficient systems and rules to prevent misuse of power. *Chankya* prescribed divide and rule strategy, which laid foundation of inability to create united India and resulted in political slavery.[1]

One of his greatest contributions was to highlight paramount importance of ethics and character building to avert unethical behavior. Along with strong governance and army, he advocated public welfare in terms of looking after weaker sections of society, creating avenues of livelihood, protecting animals, consumers, and extending support whenever needed (Sihag, 2009). According to *Chankya,* King's *dharma* is to be fair and protect his people. Under his mentorship, Maurya destiny had holistic view of governance by looking into foreign policy, nation security, taxation, labor management, financial management. Salient features of accounting system was to have independent periodic audits and created two separate offices—The Treasurer and Comptroller-Auditor to ensure accountability and specialization, and reduce the scope of conflict (Sihag, 2004). *Danda-Neeti* (law and order, administration) cover punishment policy and political social affairs of the state with no exemption to courtiers and the king (Gupta, 2004). In sum *Chankaya*'s contribution is phenomenal and the era is marked as the first social welfare state, as well set the foundation stone for unique Indian management system. Key feature of this era is *dharma. Dharma* is the guiding force and it was defined for everybody such as *rajdharama* (King *dharma*), *prajaa dharama* (public dharma). It acts as a moral gate and brought precision in everyone's role. The notion of *Dharma* is explained in Chapter 2. This era indicates pluralistic characteristic of Indian society as there was no single code of conduct applicable for all, hence religious and cultural differences were accepted and respected (Sur, 2017). In the later Vedic period, on one hand ritualistic, unchallenged belief about multiplicity of

[1] Based on discussion with an author of unpublished book by Vilas Ghodeswar.

God was emerging, on the other hand philosophers like *Adi Shankaraycharya* challenged (788 AD) this ideology and highlighted that all deities are different forms of one *Brahma*. Aforementioned discussion can be summed up highlighting India's long tradition of religiosity, spirituality and plurality.

Medieval Period (1 CE to 1100 CE)

From 1 to 1000 CE Indian economy was the largest in the world (Maddison, 2007). Pliny (73 AD), a Roman historian complained that every year India was draining Roman economy by exporting cotton goods and silk.[2] India shared good trade relations with neighboring and western countries. Indian economy continued to be the biggest of that time, however started to decline due to paucity and debasement of coins, gradual disappearance of guild, regionalization of socio-economic structure and trade (Goyal, 1997). Travel from sea route was abandoned due to socio-religious reasons, which caused restriction of Indian merchants traveling to other markets. Early Medieval period in Indian history comprises a large number of regional and local powers. Prominent dynasties were *Rashtrakuta, Chola, Chalukya, Pallava, Pala*. During 700–1000 AD, emperors grant land to temples, and state officials. This was beginning of feudalism and heightened the power of Brahmins (Thapar, 2003). Feudalism implies holding of land in return for services. With the result some of them shed their priest role and concentrated on management of land. It was an unequal society rather than hierarchical-with chiefs rather than nobles (Goyal, 1997). Social stratification converted into strict regular caste. Because of apathy of king, people were loaded with heavy taxes. Long distance trade also declined in this period, especially with Roman trade. It was a movement from knowledge power to coercive power. This was the beginning of dark era when religious teachings were started being blindly followed, logical discourse started diminishing and rigid stratification of class and caste started emerging. Surplus of production diminished in this period though trade of spices

[2] http://www.bangladesh.50megs.com/muslin.htm. Accessed on 30.10.2020.

like black pepper continued. Major writings come from Brahmins in this era and a great contribution is *Aryabhatt's* invention of zero. Towards the tenth century, *Chola* dynasty in today's Tamil Nadu emerged as a significant dynasty where art, literature and trade flourished. The popularity of the image of *Natraj*, the dancing Shiva in that era symbolizes the reputation of art in that society.

Sultanate and Mughal Period (1100–1750 CE)

The invasion and control of Mohammad Gauri from 1192 to 1700 led to various socio-economic changes in India. Manufacturing was in the hands of artisans. During this period organizations were mainly kingdoms, military, temples, independent artisans and traders.

Traders either went by road in *carvans* (a group of travelers or merchants) or sailed in ships to various destinations to sell goods. Merchants generally stayed in *carvan-sarai* (guest house). Once they sold their goods, they invested their capital to start money lending business to local agriculture, business and warlords. In some cases traders stayed for 15–20 years and many large Hindu–Indian settlements were established near Kabul, Kandahar and other cities, where the local Muslims protested against Hindu–Indian rituals like cremation (Levi, 2015). Modus operandi as described by Levi (2015) was complex. Investments were made by *Sahs* (firm directors), who recruited and trained *gumashtas*, then sent them to foreign market to invest in buying merchandizing, trading and lending. One of the oldest international trade routes in history is between West and Asia, particularly Asian countries, popularly known as Silk Route.[3] The Silk Route is a network of land and sea trade route across Asia that has been in use for thousands of years (approximately 2500–3000 BC), which passed through Central Asia (Khan, 2005). Merchants used to move in *caravans* for trade and carry variety of products such as silk, spices, cotton, ivory work, stone work, jewel and pearls. Merchants from Mughal empire could travel and conduct businesses as comfortably in Central Asia as within Mughal empire.

[3] The term silk route was first used by German geographer Ferdinand Von Richthofen in nineteenth century about ancient trunk road crossing central Asia (Foltz, 1999).

Buddhism was the first religious faith to get advantage of Silk Route to extend its reach far beyond native ground, northern eastern India. Silk route is an example of political, cultural integration due to inter-regional trade.

The merchants funded trade and Kings and in general operated in 'bazaar' economy (Ray, 1988). *Hiranand Sahu*, a jeweler turned money lender, laid the foundation of *Marwari* enterprises in India and was involved in banking system in seventeenth century. His son went to various cities (such as Patliputra, now Bihar, Dacca, now Dhaka) to expand his business in banking. He explored the business possibility of getting into cotton, silk and opium businesses. Another influential figure is *Manik Chand*, who was instrumental in bringing land and agrarian reforms during *Aurangzeb* era and gave financial support to Kingdom. He was bestowed with the title of *Nagar Seth* by Emperor *Farrukh Siyar*. *Manik Chand* died in 1714 and his adopted son and nephew *Fateh Chand* took over the business. *Fateh Chand* of *Murshidabad*, who was indispensable as the most important moneylender on whom the title of *Jagat Seth* (Banker to the world) was bestowed by Emperor *Mahmud Shah* in 1723. *Jagat Seth* banking and *Hundi* system network was extensive and had presence in all major cities across the subcontinent. He encouraged development of trade in bills of exchange in Bengal, where *Jagat Seth* had virtual monopoly on this trade. Due to safety issue people could not carry money, hence they carried piece of paper written in *Hindvi* characters without a seal or envelope (called *Hundi*) addressed to their agents, who had their shops across India. The document could be sold at a place other than the one where payment is promised. *Hundi* was sold for the fund it is specified, and the purchaser, obtaining a small amount from the seller, received the sum stated in it, at the promised place (Habib, 1971). *Jagat Seth* established relationship with big banking houses across India such as *Chellabys* of Surat, which helped to establish financial structure that cover all over India. Considering his popularity, East India Company (EIC) also partnered with him. However after his death in 1744, his successors increased the bank exposure, loaning increasingly large amounts to the declining Mughal empire, suffering heavy losses when Afghan invaders sacked Delhi.

There was high degree of competence among Indian merchants. Some were specialist in wholesale trade and others in retail. There was special class called *Banjaras, mainly cattle keeper,* who were specialist in carrying trade such as food grains, salt, etc. across deserts and arid terrain. This was an informal arrangement as compared to *caravans* (Thapar, 2003). Mostly villages were self-sustaining so trade was limited in local India and focused more on international trade.

Most of the organizations were managed in an efficient way in terms of clear roles and responsibilities. However there was respect for hierarchy and all important decisions were taken by senior functionaries and Emperor in an authoritarian and hierarchical way. Caste considerations, as explained earlier in the Vedic era description, were applicable on interest rates also, *Brahmins* were imposed least interest of two percent and *shudra* five percent (Thapar, 2003). Mughals made a conscious choice of socially relevant recruitment to combat rebellions in the region and appointed people from higher caste in key position in government. Offices of revenue ministry were mostly filled with *kayastha and Khatri (secretarial class).* Mughal also collected pilgrim (*Jizya*) taxes (first imposed by *Qutab ud din Aibak* and later by *Aurangzeb*) from non-Muslim farmers, traders on the basis of caste (Stein, 2011). Pilgrim tax was abolished by Akbar in 1563 (Stein, 2011). Another practice adopted during Akbar era was that the produce was divided between the peasants and the State in a fixed proportion. In order to maintain control Akbar needed strong Army and introduced the *mansabdari*[4] system (administrative role) to maintain large Army and manage local *Zamindaris*[5] to collect land revenue. *Mansabdari* was a unique practice adopted in India to gain greater integration among different segment of government spread across the country. Provisions were made to include mixed group from Rajputs, Mughal, Pathans and other non-Muslims. Akbar tried to improve administration by introducing departmentalization (i.e. revenue, military, judicial department), yet maintained tight control or centralization to take decisions (Chandra, 2004). Recruitment, promotion and dismissal were in the hands of the emperor on the

[4] *Mansab* denotes a rank of office which had its obligations, precedence and grade of pay.

[5] The owner of agricultural estate.

basis of loyalty to the throne, competency and efficiency. Dispersion of justice was speedy and mostly addressed grievances raised by individuals. Religious matters were referred to religious experts *(Pandits/Quazi)* of Hindus and Muslims. Persian was the language of the Mughal court since Akbar's era and it also became language of Muslim elite. Persian was also learnt by Hindus, particularly *Kayasthas and Khatris.* Many Hindu scripts like *Ramayan* and *Mahabharat* were translated into Persian language (Alam, 1998). Mostly early Mughal's were extremely control oriented and since Akbar's era some amount of stability came in the administration. Akbar overhauled the revenue by having permanent revenue rates per unit of areas fixed on the basis of information obtained for ten years and varied considering contextual factors such as soil fertility and nature of crop (Habib, 2012).

Interface with Indian culture : Different facets of life including gender orientation, language, attire, religion, family ties and friendships were affected. Position of women particularly worsened during Mughal's invasion as they were considered mentally inferior and treated as an object of pleasure by men. Women were mainly regulated by male figures like Father, Husband, Son, and forced into *parda* (veil system) and *sati pratha* (ritual of burning women on funeral pyre of their dead husband) (Thapar, 2003). However women from affluent background enjoyed better status (such as *Noor Jahan, Jahaan Aara, Rani Durgawati*) and exposure to education at home (Basu, 1991). In general education system taking into account both Hindu and Muslim and both *madrasa* (cater to Muslim students) and *pathshala* (cater to Hindu students) were common (Rezavi, 2007). Persian language became official language and teaching of Urdu in schools was started from the regime of Emperor Akbar (Alam, 1998). Art, paintings, culture and music were result of synthesis of elements throughout Asian land where Persian-Islamic culture was dominant. Over the decades Hindu–Muslim friendships, festival celebrations, business partnership became common, which was an evidence of mutual acceptance and respect of Mughal art and culture. Though Mughals sustained agricultural and trade based—economy of India yet the era had a divesting impact on culture, especially discrimination on the basis of caste and gender. Mughals lost control by end of 18th Century. With all these complexity, British entered India and the first Industrial Revolution was experienced from the lens of British.

East India Company (EIC) and British Raj (1700 CE to 1947 CE)

Many unique features are noticeable during this era. It was the end of Mughal era and power moved into the hands of EIC. Other features of these times are impact of first wave of Industrial Revolution (IR), role of Parsi community in India and emergence of India as an independent nation and several socio-cultural reforms.

Creation of Parsi settlements in India was an outcome of migration of Zoroastrian from Iran somewhere around tenth century. Parsis were allowed to settle in India on the condition of peaceful existence. They kept their word and as they assimilated into Indian society, pressure from Hindus compelled Parsis to accept certain socio-religious practice such as draping saree by Parsi women (Indian women attire) with little variation. So somewhere Parsis mingled well with the Indians yet retained their religious-cultural beliefs. Over a period of time Parsi business community emerged as comprador capitalist class, which avoided competition with British and other European companies doing business in India. By 1800 many Parsi firms were founded in India. By 1805 there were 18 Parsi and 15 Hindu firms in Bombay (Guha, 1970). Parsis were known to be expert ship builders since seventeenth century. One of the few famous ship owners, Hirji Jivanji Readymoney was the first Parsi to visit China in 1756 (Douglas, 1883 in Guha, 1970), Parsi entrepreneurs were among the first to construct textile mill in Bombay (now Mumbai) and cracked the opium trade (Chopra, 2012). Jamsetjee Jejeebhoy (1783–1859) was the first Parsi-Indian to receive knighthood from the British Queen in 1842 for his philanthropy and in 1857, he was granted a hereditary baronetcy, becoming first baronet. Another great Parsi Jamsetji Nusserwanji Tata (1839–1904) is well known for his contribution to business and society. Parsis were the first with whom EIC started collaborating and they were able to exist well during the British era. Parsis believe in existence of one invisible God and believe that water, earth, air and fire need to be preserved. They think there is a war between good and evil and by doing good deeds leads to win good forces. This thought has been the guiding force for Parsi community to contribute to industry and philanthropy (Patankar & Mehta, 2018).

Industrial Revolution (IR) can be traced back somewhere in the late eighteenth to early nineteenth century in Britain. IR is a complex interplay of changes in machine, technology, education, culture, which resulted in replacing human labor with mechanical work. It was also the beginning of pushing back agrarian society gradually displacing the capitalist economy. Commencement of India was among the first few colonial countries experiencing the impact of Britain's IR. On one hand IR resulted into increase in their Gross Domestic Product (GDP), on the other hand it had profound impact on social relations, structure of society, emergence of educated middle class, greater interaction with people of different countries for trade and business. India's GDP peaked in 1 CE (32% of world GDP), and dropped to 24% in 1700, and kept dropping when UK gained from the above-mentioned first IR. Indian economy was systematically destroyed, and it was not simply the efficiency of the steam powered textile industry that hurt the Indian economy. In 1869 Inland Custom Line (or the Great Hedge of India) was developed by EIC and stretched from the Indus to the Mahanadi in Odisha to prevent movement of salt from one part to another. It was built to collect salt tax by the British across India. However it caused suffering to poor in India. During EIC era peasant paid two month wages or 17% of their income for family's annual salt consumption, whereas it was 1% for English laborer (Moxham, 2001). Later salt became a symbol of Indian freedom movement with salt movement by Gandhi in 1930.

EIC was formed in London on last day of 1600 by a group of Merchants, mariners, politicians and explorers. Its mandate was to finance trading voyage to India and other South East Asia and China. EIC offered private trade option to overseas employees, which helped them to expand its territory (Robins, 2006), which later became cause of conflict with company and self-interest of their employees It was a unique organization as it was backed by Crown, which facilitated negotiations in overseas setting and empowered overseas branches. EIC had monopoly created by the State and permission was granted to impose taxes on consumer and producers which were unjustified. EIC drained India's rich and natural resources. They decided what to produce, how to produce and sell at what cost. Between 1718–1730, the East India Company (EIC) took an average of Rs. 4 Lakh credit a year from Jagat Seth firm. After 1757, when EIC took control over the governance of Bengal, British relationship with India became exploitative. Export to Britain and opium to China was financed from Bengal tax revenue (Maddison, 2007). One of the crucial episodes is the famine of 1770 in Bengal when around 10 million people died because of cruel policy of EIC by increase in taxes. Monopoly of EIC was abandoned in 1843 and it continued to work as government agency until 1857.

The Industrial Revolution in eighteenth century led British to identify India as potential market for purchasing raw material and selling goods. It was perfect timings for British to enter India as internal power struggle was going on within Mughals. Thus British adopted all possible means to get control all over the country. They invested heavily in transport and communications system to ensure convenient transfer of raw material from India and finished goods from Britain to Indian market. Their influence was evident on many industries in India such as textile, paper, glass and metal. Indian market became consumer for these and many more British products. Indian railway was set up by British rulers to ease transportation of goods and their travel of their bureaucrats.

Trade policy related to government rate of tariff, duties, trades agreement, which is instrumental in deciding price and quantities exported and imported to India did not promote the interest of Indian consumers. Overall there was preferential treatment in British government purchases. The business exchange between India and UK began with India exporting goods to UK and in exchange money flowing into India. With the greater control of EIC, there was only goods flow to UK without having a focus on appropriate remuneration coming back to India, and finally there was goods flow to UK and also money flow to UK. From 1846 British government decided 3.5% duty on cotton twist and yarn and 5% on all other goods imported from Britain. For import from all other countries, the rates were doubled. Again in 1860 import rate was increased to 5% on twist and yarn and all these raises led to increase in price for Indian consumers. Thus IR turned out to be an evil for Indian cotton and other industries.

This period saw the beginning of modern bureaucracy under the British rule. Organizations became process and rule oriented. However social norms were of adjustment and respect driven. In terms of organizational processes they replaced aristocracies by a bureaucratic-military way of management (Maddison, 1971). Industrialization led to create greater disparity between urban and rural India in terms of convenience and access to machinery, medicine and other benefits. Buchanan (1934) argued that changes introduced (under the IR 1 & 2) were mainly commercial rather than industrial. Compared to the huge size of the country and population, factory industry was still very small.

On the eve of First World War with the growing commercialization of agriculture, villages lost their earthy unique self-sufficient characteristics (Rao, 1950). The turn of nineteenth century was marked with the decline of handicrafts, which had an unrivalled position before the IR. Further with the advent of transport system and factories in India, and people, particularly young males started migrating from villages to cities for employment. According to Naoroji (1867), the drain of wealth indicates the portion of India's wealth and economy that was not available to Indians and Britain was draining India. The constant outflow of national wealth from India without any adequate economic, commercial, material compensation was the major reason for poverty in India. Colonial government was utilizing Indian revenue from agriculture, raw material for developing British industries and neglected circulation of wealth and resources among the Indian population. This led to one-fourth of country's resources going out to feed England's economy. Naoroji's summation to this state of affairs was that *swaraj* (self-government) was the only solution to stop this drain of wealth (Patel, 2015).

Indian traders during British era : Nineteenth century India witnessed globalization as traders were involved in trade, investment and migration, which led to create readiness for relocation and cross cultural transactions. Another important feature of this era was foreign traders in India were concentrated around ports and Indian traders were dominating interior towns. Indian firms relied more on family ties and trust than formal partnerships. Most of the European firms operating in India tried to maintain control by means of managing agency contract, interlocked directorships and debt transactions (Roy, 2014). However with the advent of railways boundaries started blurring and lot of movement happened across country. Merchants and bankers preferred to deal with people they knew personally. Working within the community and family was the norm. Marwari community dominated the jute trade whereas leather trade was mainly handled by Muslim and Eurasians, and Hindu Banian[6] groups were involved into the grain trade. Many Marwaris in this era were engaged as intermediaries between domestic producers and consumers and foreign exporters and importers. It is interesting to find variations in management style among Indian business groups. Such as Bansilal Abirchand of Nagpur and Tarachand Ghanshyamdas tried to have each branch operate independently and around 1880s Abirchand firms used to send semi-annual statements to proprietors. *Abirchand's* branch managers functioned as independent units and had full autonomy to take business decisions. However this lack of centralization was unusual of Marwari firms. Such as Goculdas Malpani of Sevaram Khushalchand of Jabalpur used to spend nine months on travel to keep a close check on branches (Timberg, 1973). He transferred clerks frequently and without prior notice so that they do not get time to manipulate records. Also there was a practices not to hire relatives together in same branch. The large firms such as Tara Chand Ghanshyam Das, had branches within India and abroad. All the branches were in rented premises perhaps to keep the cost low. Central feature of those structure was *Gaddi* (white cotton covered mattresses), which indicates top most hierarchy in the organization.[7] The branch was overseen by a *munim* (chief manager) with many *gomashtas* (sub-managers). Each *gomashtas* had separate kind of ledger to maintain separate account of each kind of business. The *darwans* (security guard) of the *Gaddi*

[6] Banian is a person by whom all purchases and sales of goods, merchandize and produces are made. Through whom all shipments are made on behalf of merchants or merchantile firm in whose establishment he is banian.

[7] In Indian context Gaddi also means raja-gaddi. It is the seat of power. It is interesting and informative to discuss gaddi and its various cultural meanings. As British firms began their own warehouse, role of Banian evolved into guaranteed broker.

were mainly from *Chaubes* or *Brahman Chaturvedi* (elite service class), mostly wrestler. Daily records of cash and credit details needed to be sent to head office. Godowns and sometimes kitchen were located in the backyard of the office. Beside their pay, managers in *Ghanshyam Das* firm often received a share in the profits of the firm. However it was not uniformly followed practice among great firms of those days (Timberg, 2014). *Bansilal Abirchand* of Nagpur and *Mahasingh Rai Meghraj Bahadur* did not offer share in profit to managers. *Abirchand* had helped British during the war of 1857) and was rewarded in return. *Tarachand Ghanshyam Das* became agent for selling the British firm, the petroleum giant, Burmah Oil. In fact, family business firm, especially *marwaris* responded to the opportunities which came through foreign businesses interested in Indian partners. 'Parta' indigenous system of accounting has been in use since nineteenth century among Marwari business firms which helped in monitoring and financial control. It is a system of daily cash-based accounting, which helps to keep close check on business trends. Once Aditya Birla in late 1980s observed in a conference that the Parta system helped to save Rs. 100 crore. The system emphasized on speed of reporting (Piramal, 1996). However in 2003, Kumar Mangalam Birla replaced Parta system with 'cash value added' method of reporting looked equally at profitability, asset productivity and growth. In addition, 'Parcha' system (credit note) of Marwari management is also considered an important factor for their success.

Prominent Marwaris such as G.D. Birla, Jamnalal Bajaj, R.P. Goenka and others took active part in India's freedom movement with Gandhiji. Timberg[8] in his thesis in 1960s described Marwari management system. He highlighted that Marwaris do write memoirs for posterity and they maintain family records, which was not found in other business community. Timberg (2014) offered important lessons on Marwari business style ranging from fund management to workplace culture—Funds needed to be closely monitored, also for circulating investment funds to more profitable options; based on the performance portfolios were given to executives and family members; kept a focus on growth and

[8] Thomas A Timberg doctoral thesis (1973) from Harvard Business School based on Marwaris' as a business entrepreneurs.

expansion which was boosted by an appropriate organizational culture of timely alignment with business environment; being pioneer and thinking ahead of time was one of the key features of Marwari community, thus they were able to adapt to changing scenario. In the former role they provided credit, information and initial employment to Marwari emigrants. In the later role, the great firms moved into commercial line to take forward their business fortunes. Briefly they got into trade of wool, then opium, and imported clothes, jute and cotton, and finally it helped in the general Marwari community evolution. G.D. Birla was against debt and usually set 25% of firm's startup value aside as a support fund. Marwaris controlled most of the business by First World War and turned to industry after the war and head most of the private sector by 1970. Their success can be attributed to flexible mindset, rationality, work ethics, hard work, high-risk appetite, and thrift. One of the unique traits of Indian business is balance between risk and trust/*sakh*. *Sakh* is seen as a crucial factor of merchant's standing as it means more than wealth and financial strength. The cotton trader of those days Ramvillas Poddar began as humble *dalal* (broker) in raw cotton trade but soon got acceptance in the market because of his reputation for honesty and *sakh* (Timberg, 2014). Bhawuk (2019) explained significance of *sakh* in trade and maintained along with profit orientation. It seems to be based on the deep rooted value that people act honestly. In addition due to complex political scenario with the rise of Communist party (Marxist) in Calcutta and trade union militancy in Bombay around 1960 caused many Marwari traders to move to Delhi.

In Indian context 1857 was turning point with the revolt of 1857 (first war of independence in India) and the consequences led to freedom movement against British raj, which ended with India's independence in 1947. From management perspective, revolt of 1857 was initiated by sepoy against the administrative practice of EIC and beginning of British Raj. There were grievances related to socio-religious, economic, political and military. British had abandoned the policy of non-interference in social—religious life, such as sati abolishment, remarrying of widow and entry of missionaries with the objective of proselytizing. Among the economic factors, demolition of self-sufficiency of villages, commercialization of agriculture and free trade and deindustrialization led to drain of wealth. Military had major concern related to service conditions. Sepoys were expected to be posted away from hometown without any extra *bhatta* (allowance). The Post Office Act of 1854 withdrew free postal service for sepoys. The most disturbing practice was General Service Enlistment Act 1856, sepoys could be asked to cross the seas whenever required. Further humiliating successor policy toward Mughals further aggravated anger against British.

From management perspective, this era is marked as a beginning of technological revolution, an era of innovation in technology. Innovation in the area of electricity, steel and petroleum led to development of public transport and airlines. One of the landmarks of this era was Ford's assembly line introduced in 1913 to increase efficiency and mass production. It was an era of expansion of telegraph, rail networks, gas and water supply and sewage system. This phase was mainly concentrated in few countries Britain, United States of America, and Germany, and also in France, and Italy. However India was badly hit by Britain capturing Indian market, especially textile industry. Mechanized steaming and weaving in textile manufacturing came much later. It was around 1854 India started experiencing IR with the first steam powered textile mill in Asia opened in Mumbai (then Bombay) and Ahmedabad. The first jute mill was established in 1854 and expanded mainly in and around Calcutta (now Kolkatta). The industry was largely in the hands of foreigners (mainly Scots) (Maddison, 2007). During this period jute mills in Kolkatta were established. Keshram Poddar (1883–1945), Sarupchand Hukumchand of Indore and G.D. Birla (1918–1919) were among the first few Marwari's to enter the jute industry and Indian-controlled jute mills. The jute industry in colonial India outstripped the leading Dundee industry in manufacturing and international marketing (Sethia, 1996). Tata established the India's first steel mill in Jamshedpur in 1907 by Dorabji Tata. Tatas were the first group to work for the welfare of workers, much before Corporate Social Responsibility became a norm and then regulation.

In subsequent years many MNCs showed interest such as Uniliver, Swedish Match, Singer Sewing Machine. It was not only Indian businessmen who operated in British India but also the Sassoons from

Baghdad and the Aga Khans from Persia who fled to Mumbai because of their precarious in the Persian Gulf region.

Indian firms in insurance, industry and banking gain a boom since 1905 with *swadeshi* movement, which was a nationalist boycott of British products in favor of Indian enterprise. During world war I, lack of British import and this gave an opportunity to Indian manufacturer to strengthen Indian textile and steel industry.

In 1922 Siemens (Electronic and Electrical Engineering) German multinational conglomerate company opened its first office in India and in 1957 it was incorporated as a company under Indian Companies Act.[9] Siemens entry goes back to 1867 when they handled construction of the Indo-European telegraph line between London and Calcutta (now Kolkata). However early era was marked by sales roles for Indians. Siemens is perceived to offer work family balance and good working environment. For Siemens till date India is a relevant market for business and availability of talent. Their India vision 2020 is focused on employee connect and their development. This involved change to foster learning culture involving mindset shift and better learning agility of people. This is seen as first of its kind in Siemens history, which reflect trust of parent company in Indian operation.

Another multinational company (MNC) which showed interest in Indian market was Dutch MNC, Unilever in 1931, which set up its first Indian subsidiary, Hindustan Vanaspati manufacturing Company. It was followed by Lever Brothers in 1933 and United Traders Limited in 1935. These three companies together formed Hindustan Unilever Limited in 1956. Summation to first and second cycle of IR is with the invasion of foreign control on Indian political and economic sphere led to decline of Indian socio-economic ecosystem. Players like Siemens and Hindustan Unilever were slowly growing. However, they were not game changer. India experienced deindustrialization in British era (Cypher, 2014) compared to Mughal era and had lower per capita income and lower urbanization (Eraly, 2007; Moosvi, 2015). In 1947 India was left with very little industries like few cotton and jute mills, tea gardens in north east, few manually operated coal mines and small iron and

[9] http://www.siemens.co.in/about-us/siemens-india.htm?stop_mobi=true. Accessed on 22.6.19.

steel factory. Most of these were managed by European Expatriates. There were few large organizations like railway, postal service, ordinance factories managed by the government.

Interface between British and other foreign collaboration and Indian culture : India was influenced by Colonial life style and language. An emerging lingo '*Babu*', meaning a 'quasi-westernized Indian' indicated how the language evolved with colonial influences. Entire India emerged as single entity against Colonial exploitation and sense of nationalism seeped into a new identity: India and Pakistan. As the tone was set in the first IR cycle economic development was restricted to urban India and as a result male member or in some cases families started moving to industrial states. Land reforms have been considered a major milestone in bringing socio-economic changes in India. This initiative was largely taken to undertake agrarian reform to transmute Indian Agriculture. Traditionally upper caste owned land and lower castes were engaged as tenants and agricultural laborers, which perpetuated social inequalities. British rule in India introduced *zamindari* system, a land revenue system. This system made *zamindars* owners of demarcated land and in return *zamindars* had to pay a fixed sum of land revenue to the British government. *Zamindars* had liberty to collect whatever land revenue they imposed on their tenants (Thimmaiah, 2001). In fact some *zamindars* had middle-level landlords in between *zamindars* and the tenants. The *zamindari* system turns out to be the most exploitative platform and strengthened the feudal socio-economic system. This system was criticized by Indian leaders and *zamindari* system was abolished after independence in 1947.

Interface Between Indian and British Culture : Organizations are sub system of society and they influence each other and it is true between of Indian and British cultures. Trade and business with Britain impacted many aspects of social life. For example, Indian firms opted for British names of their company, such as Victoria Mills, Empress Mills. The East India Company built a fort in Kolkata and named it after King William III and called it Fort William. British continued to differentiate by appointing upper caste in senior positions between 1860–1920.

Indian industry such as textile mills in Mumbai (around 1925) had 28% British working at managerial and supervisory positions and there were problems of race, language and caste distinction between management, supervisor and workers (Maddison, 2007). Post social unrest British introduced reservation of government jobs for lower caste.

Since 1950 Government of India took reservation policy forward. As per Article 15 of constitution discrimination is illegal in India. Reservations are maintained in jobs, admissions in colleges and fellowships to go for higher studies. Interface between Indian and British culture led to transform certain aspects of society in British era. Dress code is one area where disparity started. Indian men used to wear *dhoti/pajama kurta* at home and western attire typically coat-trouser at workplace. Similarly women attire transformed from traditional *sari* to western dresses. Women in Goa are often seen wearing western dresses, which was influence of Portuguese culture and over the years western outfit has become common workplace attire.

Another disparity which began to take shape in colonial era was language. Language can influence culture which is evident from the case of India in British era. English was introduced in schools and colleges to create a class of educated Indians well versed with English language to work under British rule. Another motive was to expose Indians to western world and create need for western goods. This proved to be in favor of British as they got cheap labor to work at clerical level and created the class of Indians loyal to British. This was the landmark of interface between organizational and societal culture. However Indian society, marred by discrimination on the basis of caste, class and gender, found inspiration from Reformation Movement and various revolutions of Europe. British education exposed the Indians to the idea of equality, freedom and liberty, which appealed to a large section of society. Following several reform movements in India the British government enacted several measures to eradicate some of the social evils like discrimination in the name of gender, caste and class.

They opened churches where many lower-class Indians were attracted and led to conversions. Similarly upper classes started choosing convent schools for the education and aping British life style, dance, attire, cutlery, language and many more. Further many Indians were influenced to go for higher education to England. Over the years English became the official language in India, which hindered the development and usage of regional languages and they are losing importance. However, friends and colleagues preferred to converse in Hindi outside the office. Some other social practices also modified, such as birthday celebration was very private affair among Indians and mainly happened in the form of visiting temples, prayers (or *hawans*) and donations. With the influence of British, birthday parties and cake-cutting ceremony became popular as well as English meal pattern (Breakfast, lunch, afternoon tea and dinner) (Caplan, 1995).

Though British era was longer and left deeper impact on business and socio political system but influence of France and Portuguese is also evident. Portuguese influence was evident in at least three parts of India Goa, Daman and Diu. French establishments left impact on Chandannagar Karaiikal, Mahe and Puducherry.

India Post-independence till Turn of the Century (1947 CE to 2000 CE)

India tasted benefit of IR after independence in 1947. First five year plan of India had major emphasis on agriculture, heavy industries, university level technical education and development of R&D centers. Government of India announced its first Industrial Policy (6th April 1948) laid emphasized on agriculture, development of industries and scale production and its equitable distribution. 'Nehru (first prime minister of India in post-independence) himself constantly reiterated that the entire program of industrial development depend on achieving adequate increase in agricultural productivity, which he called keystone of our planning' (Frankel, 1978: 118). Further efforts were made to create body of governance at village level, i.e. *panchayat*. Sectors were clearly demarcated between central and state government as well as private players. New India started shaping on lines of infrastructure development, higher education, manufacturing units and it led to the rise of big industries and industrialist like Bajaj, Tata and Birla. Such big industrialist took many philanthropist steps. Birlas are known for making temples, educational institutes, and generously contributed funds for various initiatives taken by Mahatma Gandhi. The second Industrial Policy Resolution is known as Economic Constitution of India (30th April 1956). The focus was laid on improving the living standard and working conditions, expand public sector and more active role of State in establishment of industrial undertaking & development of transport facility, undertake state trading on large scale, and develop transport facility. In addition the plan was to reduce disparity between regions. With all these small steps nation had moved on the growth trajectory. However initial thirty years of economic map of India had large government public and few private sector organizations. Monopolies and Restrictive trade Practice (MRTP) Act 1969[10] was enacted to avoid concentration of money and power among private sector. Around 1967 Vicks VapoRub (product of P & G[11]) was in demand, however due to MRTP company lawyer of HUL warned company that they might go to jail and do not exceed licensed capacity. Socialism made Indian business houses complacent and insensitive to customers in first forty years of independence (Timberg, 2014). State controlled key and basic industries like iron plant. At the time of independence, heavy investment led plants and expertise was missing, thus foreign collaborations were initiated. Efforts were made to reduce regional imbalance by opening state control plants managed by public sector enterprises. Banks were nationalized because private banks were mainly catering to affluent strata. Hence state control was prevalent in key or heavy investment industries and creates economic development available to all. However bribery, corruption and favoritism based on caste, class and family deteriorated and customer orientation was missing. Many state run companies became underperforming units and liability for government. Private sector was characterized by familialism and lack capability and willingness to play major role in

[10] http://www.mca.gov.in/Ministry/actsbills/pdf/The_Monopolies_and_Restrictive_Trade_Practices_Act_1969.pdf.

[11] In 1964, a public limited company, Richarson Hindustan Limited (RHL) is formed, which obtains an industrial license to undertake manufacturing of Menthol and Vicks range of products such as Vicks VapoRub, Vicks Inhaler and Vicks Cough Drop. RHL is now known as P & G (Procter and Gamble).

economic growth of India and varying interest in development and welfare of employees. The members of the family held key positions in that era. In post-independence era many of the family members in managerial positions did not study business management. Most of the private sector organizations were managed in familial, paternalistic way, hierarchical structure, centralized decision-making and personalized relationship took precedence over merit and professionalism. The relationship of employees with paternalistic management is marked by care, concern and nurture for the loyalist by the organization which also takes care of them at the time of any crisis. Public sector was excessively bureaucratic and Sinha (1973, 1997) called them Bureaupathic because it became pathological partly because of colonial worldview which made Indians inferior. *Chalta hai* work culture and favoritism were defining characteristics of workplaces in India. Public sector was largely incurring losses and government had to intervene to bail out them. Private sector was largely seen as a last option for employment and working conditions including wages in private sector were not considered at parity with government sector. Government jobs offered security and pension, which was a major differentiation. Hence government jobs were seen as status symbol and family pride. People working in banks (nationalized era, 1969[12]) were seen as respectable jobs. Some of the private firms took initiative to take care of employees in times of crisis, such as Tatas.

Gore (1965) pointed out strain in extended family was an outcome of various factors: industrial economy, urbanization blurred the bond between occupation and kinship system, different economic quest within family and liberalizing effect of education. Dube (1958) observed rapid decline in kinship orientation and increase in interest orientation among individuals. Role and status of women started getting prominence with abolishment of restriction of women in School. Women took part in Independent struggle of India and that was the first liberating experience for women. Kapur (1970) pointed out that role of women changed post-independence but there was a gap between legal, political, economic

[12] As per the Banking Companies (Acquisition and transfer pf Undertakings) Ordinance, ownership of 14 banks being transferred to the state and these banks controlled 70% of the country's deposits. Imperial Bank had been nationalized in 1955, which was called the State Bank of India.

rights and actual rights and privileges she enjoyed. British Missionaries also entered India, which resulted in conversions of Hindus to Christianity (Fernandes, 2011). Social reformist like Devendrnath was active in revitalizing Hinduism, largely in response to missionary activity.

It was marked by use of technology and shift toward automation. This revolution witnessed the rise of electronics, telecommunication and computers. The key factor that differentiates third IR from its predecessors is the notion of boundary-less world. Concepts that time has shrunk and customer centricity has increased many folds. Thus many economies shift toward expansion across globe. From independence till 1991 Indian economy was operating on largely socialist model. Most of the services such as banks, telephone, transport, electricity were run by national institutions with the motive of serving common people of India. These organizations were managed in a bureaucratic way. Economy was highly regulated and inward oriented toward domestic and trade policy (Kaplinsky., 1997). Getting license for private players was very difficult. This era is also beginning of globalization and open economy.

Context of MNCs: Liberalization, Privatization and Globalization (LPG)

In early nineties the Indian Economy emerged as a 'mixed' economy as a considerable number of the industry was funded and managed by the government. In Indian context, globalization meant significant policy reforms done in 1991 to facilitate FDIs to foreign organizations to make investment in various fields, removal of trade barrier, and to support foreign investors to open joint ventures. Further there was a shift from quantitative barriers to tariffs and duties on import in order to encourage imports. Today after three decades India is becoming globally competitive market and part of a boundary-less world. Economic reforms (LPG) by Government of India helped to expedite economic integration and growth with in India and are globally competitive. Government could promote foreign investment by decentralization of administration and investor friendly procedures. Advances in information technology played the crucial role in facilitating these cross-border flow of information and data. India was the preferred place for many foreign investors because India has the second largest English speaking population after the U.S.A and offer the largest pool of trainees, scientific and technical manpower in the world. Further this manpower is very cheap compared to costs around the world including research and development costs. Last but not the least, India is a major member of the Convention on the Multinational Investment Guarantee Agency, which provides insurance to foreign investors against political risks. Technological reforms and innovations has brought many benefits to India such as variety of product offerings, financial development, expansion of job market. India experienced boom in manufacturing and service sector. All in all, this led to mushrooming of multinational companies in India. Within the first 5 years of globalization, India's economic growth was recorded 6.7% and emerged as one of the world's fastest growing economy. Along with technology and financial transfer, foreign managers located in host country (expatriates) and management practices also transferred among multinational companies (MNCs) operating in India. Expatriates role became active in knowledge transfer and cultural adaptation between parent companies and operations in another country. Management practices, especially regarding human resource seemed to be the most vulnerable to cultural relativity. This is because they are often designed by members of one culture to handle members of that culture. Such as Management by objective (MBO) is not found very effective mechanism in Indian context as it is in contrast to Indian culture. Transfer of Japanese practices in India, such as Maruti Suzuki has led to series of conflicts, strikes and unrest among workers.

As a matter of fact, since ancient times India is discussing principles of *Vasudhaiva Kutumbakam* (unification of world as one whole family) and *Sarva Bhavantu Sukhinah* (may all be prosperous and glad), thus, India developed its own model of globalization (Kirti, 2019). On one hand, Indian market is flooded with foreign products and brands. On the other hand local markets and products are sustaining in this era of multinational companies. Indian brands like Fab India, Biba, Global Desi are creating market for themselves.

Societal Culture and MNCs: Education and skill level improved and educated young boys and girls started moving to urban India. Urban population was 11.4% in 1901 and it was about 34% in 2017. So, India is still rural, though the villages have changed in their nature with multiple shops and other facilities. These changes started having an impact on Indian family system. From extended family there was a shift toward nuclear family or immediate joint family and women started working in variety of field. These migrated families feel a tussle between regional ties and adjustment to urban life. At the same time young technology savvy Indians looked toward developed nations and emerged as cyber-coolie in Silicon Valley, USA and other parts of globe. This segment was highly influenced by West and adopted language, attire and life style. However enthusiasm and faith in Indian way of doing things, such as festival celebrations, prayers, family orientation, collectivist orientation and respect for elders continued with all the assimilation of western influence. Sinha (1984) pointed out with urbanization, industrialization and socio-economic changes Indian family is in a transitional phase.

India 2001 CE Onwards: Fourth Industrial Revolution

IR 4.0 started in Germany and picked up in other countries like USA, China and Japan. Technology and globalization are playing pivotal role in shaping business models across sectors with rapid pace of change. Computers and automation is coming in a unique way, with robotics managed through computers equipped with learning algorithms and need least human intervention. Big data analytics, autonomous robots, artificial intelligence, cloud computing, cyber security and other automated systems have changed the size and nature of the organizations. Production processes in most of the sectors are shifting toward digital technology. Smart factory, smart product, smart operations and data-driven services call for unique strategy and employee skill set. Design of the organization is moving away from long queue of hierarchical boxes, huge building to small and in many cases virtual offices and teams gaining prominence. Role of employees is to help companies realize their digital transformation. Banks are moving toward extensive automation and centralization of certain services like loan processing, document verification and so on.

India became important with its IT professional population when the world needed to solve the Y2K problem. Most western countries took Indian IT people to solve the problem. It was led by opening up of call centers and out sourcing related centers to India, which makes India important in the IT industry. Many leading global companies like Microsoft, Intel, and other IT companies have opened branches in India to be competitive by attracting locally available talent at a fraction of the cost in the Europe or USA. In this era benefit of expansion in terms of availability of goods, services and jobs reach out to backward areas of the country. Such as Project Shakti of HUL (started in 2001) reached remotest areas of India where workforce was available at low cost. According to Economist Intelligence Unit (2016[13]) healthcare sector will benefit immensely with IR 4.0 as smart phones have already started collecting data related to demographic and health status. VUCA (Volatile, Uncertain, Complex, Ambiguous) are key defining characteristics of current era, which have resulted in stress and chaos at personal, family and professional level. Divorces, live-in relationships, passing affairs, office romance, competitiveness, laisioning are very common these days. Co-existence of traditional values, family systems, loyalty to spouse and concern for elders also exist in India. A sense of duality and contradiction defines current Indian scenario. Interestingly it has a deep rooted Indian culture, with variation in contour.

As anticipated in 2000 India has emerged as hub to MNCs, which resulted into expanding job market. Indian Government started incentivizing MNCs post 2000. Hence the emerging economic environment looks more competitive, dynamic, uncertain and inviting to foreign investment and technology than ever before. Over the last almost three decades foreign investments happened in the form of financial collaboration (foreign equity participation), technical collaboration and expatriates engagement in Indian operation. India has been witnessing immense development in terms of higher literacy rate, better job prospects, increased female participation in workplace, and migration from rural to urban areas making the cultural context even more complex.

---

13 https://eiuperspectives.economist.com/technology-innovation/healthcare-benefit-most-fourth-industrial-revolution-executives-predict.

Societal Culture and Management Practices in MNCs Sinha (2002) carried out 5 mixed methodology case studies based on primary data from Anglo American, Scandinavian, Korean, Japanese and Danish firm operating in India. These MNCs had manufacturing base in India. The study findings pointed out some common trends. In all MNCs parent company provided capital depending on the percentage of share of global company. Technological support was provided by parent company and knowledge transfer was limited to maintain them. A difference was noticed in the magnitude of support. Scandinavian hub allowed greater access to Indian R&D personnel visiting their set up rather than Japanese who had reservations for entering into confidential areas in R&D center. Qualitative data indicate that Indians were comfortable with this technological dependency. Similarly supply of key parts was in the control of parent company as per the stake of the parent in Indian operations. Such as Japanese joint venture in India had 90% indigenous product but crucial 10% were supplied by parent company. Most of the MNCs keep control on subsidiary by following uniform practices of reporting and audit to do cross-country comparison. There has been varying impact on performance and commitment level of employees due to inevitable impact of Indian culture. Employees were found to follow the performance norms in MNCs however their interpersonal relationships remained typical of Indian nature.

Awasthy and Gupta (2007) study of Korean MNC resonate with Sinha's findings and explained nature of organizational commitment as 'enforced involvement' to explain stringent performance standards. However it amounts to high attrition and stress among employees. Honda also had similar approach to manage Indian operations. Practices were stringently imposed on Indians. Workers had to sign movement sheet to go to toilet and stay back every day to meet targets. Such extreme kind of control caused resentment and strikes (Sen, 2011). Same holds true for Maruti Suzuki and some other manufacturing units held by MNCs in India. Such instances raise a question about employees' commitment in MNCs. Awasthy and Gupta (2004) case study of 50:50 Indo-Japanese joint venture and examined the impact of organizational practices on organizational commitment. The nature of commitment was found to be 'conditional identification' due to benefits acquired through personalized relationships, mainly with Indian partner who was responsible to managing people and local operation. Japanese counterpart was mainly looking into technological support and production. Verma et al. (2015) conducted qualitative interviews in three Indo-Japanese joint venture. They found that national and organizational cultures are important factors for alliance management capability. The study findings pointed out significant role of trust, transparency and consensus in decision making in establishing alliances. Cultural capability and understanding of differences in culture emerged as binding force in Indo-Japanese alliances.

Awasthy and Gupta (2011) examined the degree to which non-work practices are accepted by Indian employees working in four MNCs operating in India and its impact on organizational commitment. Through Factor analysis they found three factors of non-work practices: personal celebrations (birthdays and festivals); organizational involvement (get together); and superior connect (interaction between senior and juniors beyond work). These practices have been implemented but practices which did not fit well with Indian culture were not fully accepted. Particularly practices which had a flavor of low power distance, like cleaning the work station in Korean MNC; addressing seniors by their first name in western MNCs. Most of the non-work practices were transplanted from the parent company, they were perceived alien, (except one case of the Anglo-American MNC) and had no positive impact on their organizational commitment. Gupta and Bhaskar (2016) examined how MNCs can successfully do business in India. They highlighted MNCs need to understand India culturally and offer unique cultural proposition to attract talent.

Knowledge transfer has done wonders to retail industry by introducing efficient supply chain system. As table turned, Indian expatriates are working globally. The trend is changing in IT sector where Indian companies, such as Infosys, TCS and Wipro, are providing intellectual capital to MNCs. Shah and Barker (2017) studied intercultural challenge among Indian expatriates in Australia. They found challenge in terms of inability to understand unwritten sociocultural rules of communication.

As India is hub to MNCs and moreover some States have changed their character as they cater to modern organizations. Such as Bangalore is the center of IT industry; Hyderabad has popularly called Cyberabad; Pune is large engineering center; Bombay is known as Business center. Most of these MNCs have flat structure and collegial work culture is promoted in organizations like Microsoft and Google. Recruitment in MNCs and private sector is not guided by caste and religion. Only government organizations are governed by the policy of reservation based on caste. In terms of attire Indians have made selective adaptation. Such as across India mostly women wear *salwar kameez* [indigenous attire] instead of traditional *saree*.

Implications: Key Points

Variety of Organizations Co-exist:

Indian economy is a unique case of dualism with existence of both formal and informal/unorganized sector (Kesar & Bhattacharya, 2020). keeping the focus on current twenty-first century, it is observed that though LPG has played a significant role in establishing connect with global economy yet variety of organizations exist, especially a few are unique to India. There is presence of MNCs, profit making as well as not-for-profit making organization. Also socio-religious diversity is reflected in contour of organizations in India, such as community based organization. There are also many religious-spiritual organizations like *Shri Aurobindo Ashram*,[14] *BAPS Swaminarayan Sanstha*,[15] *Arya Samaj Sanstha*,[16] which are managed by large number of volunteers.

1. Unorganized sector: India still has large number of unorganized or informal sector and its contribution seems to be 50% of the Net

[14] https://www.sriaurobindoashram.org/.

[15] https://akshardham.com/about-us/organization/.

[16] https://aryasamajsanstha.com/.

Domestic Products (Majumdar, 2008), and according to International Labor Organization informal sector in India constitutes 80% of economy. This sector includes street vendors, craftsmen, carpenters, beauticians, plumbers, tiffin service, domestic help, fashion designers, flowerist, freelancers, contractual workers or professionals who are not registered. These businesses revolve around founder and many operate from their home. They largely work on verbal commitment which is key to establish relationship and business dealings. Avoidance of labor regulations is one of the reasons for flourishing unorganized sector (Kesar & Bhattacharya, 2020).

2. Private sector: This domain includes Marwari and many other business families, such as Birla, Tata, Reliance, Bajaj. Entrepreneurs including both men-women are managing large, mid and small-size enterprises. This segment also includes 'Joint Hindu Family Business', unique to India. It is a form of business organization wherein only family members can own and manage business. These organizations are involved in variety of businesses like import, export, manufacturing, hotels, gems, carpets, handicrafts that has picked up in twenty-first century. Organizations are managed in familial way and many of them are high performing organizations, which have adopted professional practices to beat the competition.
3. Government and public sector organizations: Various organizations which exist largely for welfare of society such as defense services, academic institutes, Indian space research organization, railway. However organizations offering competitive services like private players have become performance-centric to emerge as self-sustaining entity. Hence many flexible offer and competitive price range model is adopted. Such as Telephone service, Life Insurance, etc. Indian railway is operating on low-cost model for general category trains and the first-class air conditioned coaches are sometimes as expensive as airlines fares. Similarly public sector banks have transformed themselves to compete with private banks and offering variety of financial solutions for customers (Awasthy et al., 2011). Most of the government and public sector management are based on bureaucracy model yet responsiveness to change is evident among high performing organizations,[17] such as ONGC, NTPC, Power Grid Corporation.

[17] https://www.fortuneindia.com/psu?year=2019.

4. Multinational companies: Many global companies have operation in India, such as Honda motors, Maruti Suzuki, Nestle, Siemens. These MNCs are largely performance-centric and mostly managed on the basis of transplanted practices from parent organization. Some of them adopted Glocal way of management and able to retain talent. Now Indian companies (both private and public sector) have emerged as multinational companies and have operations across globe, such as Bank of Baroda, Tata, Reliance, Infosys and so on.
5. Community based organizations: There are many organizations which are community driven. One such famous organization is '*Dabbawala*'[18] six-sigma lunch box delivery organization. They hire people mainly from one community 'malva' caste for the reasons of trust.
6. Cooperatives: Cooperatives are based on the principle of joint ownership and democratically run for profit entities. Its purpose is to serve its members and society at large. Inclusivity of lower and weaker section of society is a unique feature of cooperatives. According to Das et al. (2006) India has largest network of the cooperative credit system especially in agriculture sector. Variety of cooperatives exists in India such as Amul, Shree Mahila Graha Udyog (Lijjat Papad), Indian Farmers Fertiliser Cooperative (IFFCO), Mother Dairy.

Social enterprises: Social entrepreneurs are driven by a intermingling of financial and social return, where purpose is to utilize profits for social mission (Boschee & McClurg, 2003; Zahra et al., 2008). Sengupta and Sahay (2018) offered market orientation, social value creation, quality of change maker (social entrepreneurs) as drivers for scalability and sustainability of social enterprises. However there is no legal status to social enterprises in India.

Common aspect in managing these organizations is Indians' ability to change with time yet living with Indian value system. One such example is Kumar Mangalam Birla, Chairman of the Aditya Birla Group, one of the largest business groups. He is known for his accomplishments, professionalism and spare time for singing in weekly family *satsang*. These insights indicate Indians' strong belief in religious values and the way these values motivate them to be hardworking and adapt to variety

[18] http://mumbaidabbawala.in/.

of situations. Following section elaborates the point of adaptability as a part of Indian culture.

Adaptation to Adaptable

As discussed during Vedic period, India was much developed in terms of human and social capital. Training in reflective thinking, innovation and sense of pluralism are key features of Indian culture which are deeply interwoven into Indian culture. There has been ups and downs due to invasions, however India has emerged as a glorifying case. According to Khandwalla (2017) India's journey over two centuries toward civilization can be attributed to interplay between five factors: British influence, reformist response and resurrection of her spiritual heritage; the ethics-based struggle of independence by Mahatma Gandhi, planned economic development; and globalization and digitalization along with initial tripping of a welfare state. Poor quality of governance is a major block though paradoxically government aspire to be welfare and development oriented. He discussed three pillars of Indian nation, the government, the civil society and the business sector can strengthen their collaboration to aid India to civilization greatness. Focus should be toward developing more humane, creative and excellence oriented society. Present chapter resonate with Khandwalla's perspective on India hindering factors to growth of India and exemplar of excellent functioning by these stakeholders and future lies in strengthening collaboration between these three key stakeholders. Following section decodes facets of Indian culture, which act as facilitators to growth of India.

Foregoing discussion synthesize that Indians adaptation to Mughals, British, Portuguese and many such encounters made Indians adaptable to a variety of socio-cultural context. On one hand India fought with the Mughals, and on another hand India has long history of bonds with Muslims. Hindus going to Muslim shrines (such as Ajmer Sharif) and vice versa is quite common in India. Hindu and Muslims visit *Sai Baba* temples. Muslims have shops in places of Hindu pilgrimage like

Kumbh mela.[19] *Phool Walon ki Sair* is a symbol of national integration and harmony. It is an annual festival started way back in 1812 by then Mughal Emperor Akbar Shah II where people of both Hindu and Muslim communities participate in prayers at *Dargah* (Muslim place for prayer) and *Mandir* (Hindu place for prayer).[20] However British were not very keen to continue this tradition but people of Delhi kept it alive. In fact *Chandni Chowk* (one of the oldest business market and heritage city) reflects secularism and co-existence of diversity as it is home to different religions—*sanatan dharam, sikhism, islam, Jainism, christianity* and others. These are signs of integration in Indian society. Indians have tolerance for diversity and secularism is one of the pillars of constitution of India. In addition the roots of Indian culture and values go back to the pluralistic traditions of the *Vedas* (Radhakrishnan & Moore, 1954). There seems to be an acceptance of co-existence, discrepancies, inconsistencies and contradictions. Sinha (1987, 1997, 2014) in a series of studies highlighted contextual sensitivity as a defining characteristic of Indians. Sinha and Kanungo (1997) described *contextual sensitivity* as an important cultural aspect, which reflect people's adaptability to the current situation. Contextual sensitivity manifests a cognitive aspect and balances extreme or aversive reactions. It also equips people to judge time and place, understand other's mindset, and look for situations to turn them for their advantage. Sinha and Srivastava (2015) pointed out that contextual sensitivity promotes innovative behavior at workplace. The following section will discuss Indians adaptability in the context of MNCs. Another argument in support of Indians' ability to adapt comes from multi-layered Indian culture, wherein 'Go with the flow' or *samarpan* (devotion) as the deep-rooted philosophy or basic assumption that influences Indian values and practices (Awasthy & Gupta, 2021). Awasthy and Gupta (2005, 2009), found Indians ability to adapt with MNCs from different nationality (Japan, Korea, Sweden and Anglo-American) mainly due to contextual sensitivity (Sinha et al., 2001, 2002).

[19] Major pilgrimage and festival of Hindu.

[20] http://www.phoolwaalonkisair.com/.

Awasthy and Gupta (2005) case study examined the impact of transplanted practices on Indian employees working in Anglo American MNC operating in India. It was found that production processes were handled in a technological efficient way as per the global practices of this MNC. However Human resource related issues were taken care by 'Glocal' way. It was noticed that contextual realities were taken into account while sustaining organizational values.

Summation of the forgoing discussion is that it is inappropriate to assume the world is emerging as one uniform culture. There is a need to understand and respect societal culture while adopting management practices in MNCs. Pluralistic nature of Indian culture remained a key feature of Indian society. Indian culture manifests internal integration and external adaptation, which has been a key to cultural adaptation and success of organizations in India.

Future Research Agenda

Future research needs to examine indigenous business models which have been found successful but lack in-depth research exploration such as business model of *marwaris* in this era of globalization. How does family, government and industry influence R&D investments decision in Indian business houses? What is the success mantra of Indian Business houses like Birla, Tata and Ambani? The number of startups and social enterprises has gone up, especially after 'make in India'. Studies can be done to understand their business models and how do they cope up with competition. There is also a need to examine organizational design of various religious-spiritual organizations and derive lessons for business organizations in factor which operate on voluntary engagement model. The chapter highlighted impact of changes in our social subsystem within the organizations. Hence an empirical study is needed to study an impact of non-work practices on employee engagement. Subsequent research can attempt to explore layers of Indian culture and its interplay with management practices to capture impact of societal practices on management. Studies need to examine employees' readiness with respect to quantum of change led by IR 4.0. How to improve innovativeness of the organization is another contemporary issue which is pertinent in this era where automation and speed is a key defining feature. Studies need to explore needed skills and competencies in IR 4.0.

References

Ahuja, M. L. (2011). *Women in Indian philosophy*. Rupa publications.

Alam, M. (1998). The pursuit of Persian: Language in Mughal politics. *Modern Asian Studies, 32*(2), 317–349.

Awasthy, R., & Gupta, R. K. (2004). Case study: An Indo-Japanese MNC operating in India. *South Asian Journal of Management, 11*(3), 94–114.

Awasthy, R., & Gupta, R. K. (2009). Indian executives' perceptions of expatriate managers. *International Journal of Indian Culture and Business Management, 2*(2), 164–184.

Awasthy, R., & Gupta, R. K. (2007). Indian employee's experience with foreign MNCs: A case study of a Korean company in India. *Nirma University Journal of Business and Management Studies, 1*(4), 5–26.

Awasthy, R., & Gupta, R. K. (2005). Cross-cultural management in a multinational: A case study of an Anglo-American MNC in India. *Management and Change, 9*(1), 95–118.

Awasthy, R., & Gupta, R. K. (2011). Do non-work practices in MNCs operating in India impact organizational commitment? *Organizations and Markets in Emerging Economies, 2*(2), 28–52.

Awasthy, R., & Gupta, R. K. (2021). Unravelling the layers of Indian culture and worldview: an exploratory study. *International Journal of Indian Culture and Business Management, 22*(1), 137–166.

Awasthy, R., Chandrasekaran, V., & Gupta, R. K. (2011). Top-down change in a public sector bank: Lessons from employees' lived-in experiences. *Journal of Indian Business Research, 3*(1), 43–62.

Awasthy, R., Vijayalakshmi C., & Gupta R. K. (2009). Assessment of cultural shifts in an Indian public sector bank. *International Journal of Indian Culture and Business Management, 2*(3), 307–325.

Banerjee, S. C. (2019). The *development of Aryan invasion theory in India.* Springer Nature Pvt. Ltd, Singapore.

Basu A. (1991). Women's history in India: An historiographical survey. In K. Offen, R. R. Pierson, & J. Rendall (Eds), *Writing Women's history*. Palgrave Macmillan

Bhawuk, D. P. S. (2019). *adhyAtma* or Spirituality: Indian Perspectives on Management. In P. S. Budhwar, R. Kumar, & A. Varma (Eds), *Indian Business: Understanding a rapidly emerging economy* (pp. 256–266). Routledge.

Buchanan, D. H. (1934). *The development of capitalistic enterprise in India*. Bureau of International Research of Harvard University & Radcliffe College.

Caplan, L. (1995). Creole world, purist Rhetoric: Anglo-Indian cultural debates in colonial and contemporary Madras. *The Journal of the Royal Anthropological Institute, 1*(4), 743–762. https://doi.org/10.2307/3034959

Chandra, S. (2004). *Essays on Medieval Indian history*. Oxford University Press.

Chatterjee M. (1986). The concept of Dharma. In M. C. Doeser., & J. N. Kraay (Eds), *Facts and values* (Vol 19). Martinus Nijhoff Philosophy Library. Springer, Dordrecht.

Chopra, P. (2012). Free to move, forced to flee: The formation and dissolution of suburbs in colonial Bombay, 1750–1918. *Urban History, 39*(1), 83–107.

Cypher, J. (2014). *The process of economic development* (4th ed.). Routledge.

Das, B., Palai, N. K., & Das, K. (2006). *Problems and prospects of the cooperative movement in India under the globalization regime*. XIV International Economic History Congress. http://www.helsinki.fi/iehc2006/papers2/Das72.pdf. Accessed on August 18, 2019.

Das, G. (2010). *The difficulty of being good: On the subtle art of dharma*. Oxford University Press.

Devi, P. K. (2018). *Why I became a Hindu?*. Jagannath Vallabha Vedic Research Centre.

Douglas, J. (1883). A book of Bombay. pp 546–7. In Guha, A. (1970). Parsi Seths as Enterpreneurs, 1750–1850. *Economic and Political Weekly, 5*(35), M107+M109+M111+M113-M115.

Dube, S. C. (1958). *India's changing villages*. Routledge and Kegan Paul.

Emery, F. E. (1959). *Characteristics of socio-technical systems* (Document No. 527), Tavistock Institute of Human Relations, London.

Eraly, A. (2007). *The Mughal world: Life in India's Last Golden Age*. Penguin Books.

Fernandes, L . (2011). Unsettled territories: State, civil society, and the politics of religious conversion in India. *Politics and Religion, 4*(1), 108–135.

Foltz, Richard C. (1999). *Religions of the silk road: Overland trade and cultural exchange from antiquity to the fifteenth century*. St. Martin's.

Frankel, F. R. (1978). *India's political economy, 1947–1977*. Oxford University Press.
Ghurye, G. S. (1969). *Caste and race in India*. Popular Parkashan, Bombay.
Gore, M. S. (1965). The traditional Indian family. In M. F. Nimkoff (Ed.), *Comparative family system* (pp. 209–231). Houghten-Mifflin.
Goyal, S. (1997). Rise of Medievalism in Indian history. *Annals of the Bhandarkar Oriental Research Institute, 78*(1/4), 13–40. Retrieved October 30, 2020, from http://www.jstor.org/stable/41694939
Gupta, R. (2004). Law & order administration in ancient India. *The Indian Journal of Political Science, 65*(1), 111–122.
Gupta, S., & Bhaskar, A. U. (2016). Doing business in India: Cross-cultural issues in managing human resources. *Cross Cultural & Strategic Management, 23*(1), 184–204.
Habib, I. (1971). The system of bills of exchange ("Hundis"). In *The Mughal Empire. Proceedings of the Indian History Congress, 33*, 290–303. https://www.jstor.org/stable/44145345. Accessed April 24, 2020.
Habib, I. (2012). *The Agrarian system of Mughal India 1556–1707* (3rd ed.). Oxford University Press.
Kak, S. C. (1995). The astronomy of the age of geometric altars. *Quarterly Journal of the Royal Astronomical Society, 36*, 385–396.
Kaplinsky, R. (1997). India's industrial development: An interpretative survey. *World Development, 25*(5), 681–694.
Kapur, P. (1970). *Marriage and the working women in India*. Vikas Publications.
Kesar, S., & Bhattacharya, S. (2020). Dualism and structural transformation: The informal manufacturing sector in India. *European Journal of Development Research, 32*, 560–586.
Kirti. (2019). From globalization to glocalization: An Indian perspective. In: N. Faghih (Eds), *Globalization and development: Contributions to management science*. Springer, Cham.
Levi, S. C. (2015). *Carvans: Indian merchants on the silk road*. Penguin Books limited.
Khan, N. (2005). India's connection with the Silk Route. *India Quarterly, 61*(1), 79–117. Retrieved April 29, 2020, from www.jstor.org/stable/45073383
Khandwalla, P. (2017). *Fast forward toward civilizational greatness: Agenda for India*. Ahmedabad Management Association.
Maddison, A. (1971). *The economic and social impact of colonial rule in India Chapter 3 of class structure and economic growth: India & Pakistan*

since the Moghuls. http://www.ggdc.net/maddison/articles/moghul_3.pdf. Accessed May 27, 2019.

Maddison, A. (2007). *Contours of the world economy, 1–2030 AD: Essays in macro-economic history*. Oxford University Press.

Majumdar, D. (2008). Dissecting India's unorganized sector. *Economic and Political Weekly, 43*(6), 27–33.

Marshall, P. J. (1976). *East Indian fortunes: The British in Bengal in the eighteenth century*. Clarendon Press.

Moosvi, S. (2015). *The economy of the Mughal Empire c. 1595: A statistical study*. Oxford Scholarship Online. Oxford University Press.

Moxham, R. (2001). *The great hedge of India*. Constable.

Naoroji, D. (1867). In essays speeches and writings. In C. L. Parekh (Eds), Bombay, 1887 (pp. 29–31). In Islahi, A. A. .(1995). Dadabhai Naoroji—*from economic nationalism to political nationalism*.

Pal, B. (2019). The saga of women's status in ancient Indian civilization. *Miscellanea Geographica, 23*(3), 180–184.

Palsetia, J. S. (2005). Merchant charity and public identity formation in colonial India: The case of Jamsetjee Jejeebhoy. *Journal of Asian and African Studies, 40*(3), 197–217.

Paranjpe, A. (2013). The concept of Dharma: Classical meaning, common misconceptions and implications for psychology. *Psychology and Developing Societies, 25*(1), 1–20.

Patankar, V. A., & Mehta, N. K. (2018). Indian entrepreneurial communities: The people who set-up their businesses. *IOSR Journal of Business and Management (IOSR-JBM), 20*(2), 41–49.

Piramal, G. (1996). *Business Maharajas*. Penguin Books.

Patel, D. P. (2015). *The grand old man: Dadabhai Naoroji and the evolution of the Demand for Indian self-government*. Doctoral dissertation, Harvard University, Graduate School of Arts & Sciences. http://nrs.harvard.edu/urn-3:HUL.InstRepos:17467241. Accessed on June 14, 2020.

Perry, E. (1885). Indra in the Rig-Veda. *Journal of the American Oriental Society, 11*, 117–208. https://doi.org/10.2307/592191

Radhakrishnan, S., & Moore, C. A. (1954). *A source book in Indian philosophy*. Princeton University Press.

Raju, P. (1952). The development of Indian thought. *Journal of the History of Ideas, 13*(4), 528–550. https://doi.org/10.2307/2707716

Rao, G. (1950). The impact of industrialization on Indian society. *Columbia Journal of International Affairs, 4*(2), 50–60. http://www.jstor.org/stable/243 54473.

Ray, R. K. (1988). The Bazaar: Changing structural characteristics of the indigenous section of the Indian economy before and after the great depression. *The Indian Economic and Social History Review, 25*(3), 263–318.
Rezavi, S. (2007). The organization of education in Mughal India. *Proceedings of the Indian History Congress, 68*, 389–397. http://www.jstor.org/stable/44147851
Robins, N. (2006). *The corporation that changed the world: How the East India company shaped the modern multinational*. Pluto Press.
Roy, T. (2012). *The East India company: The world's most powerful corporation.* Penguin Books.
Roy, T. (2014). Trading firms in colonial India. *The Business History Review, 88*(1), 9–42. Retrieved June 16, 2020, from www.jstor.org/stable/43299518
Ruikar, S. S. (2014). *Good economics or bad context: attaining a balanced perspective on present practices, historical development, and the legacy of outsourcing in the context of globalization* Doctoral dissertation, University of Hawaii at Manoa.
Sarao, k. T. (2013). Janapadas, Mahājanapadas, Kingdoms, and Republics. In D. K. Chakrabarti., & M. Lal (Eds.), *A history of ancient India, Volume III: The Vedic, Buddhist and Jaina Texts, and political history and administration till c.200 BC.* Vivekananda International Foundation and Aryan Books.
Schein, E. H. (1985). *Organizational culture and leadership.* Jossey-Bass Publishers.
Sen, R. (2011). Industrial relations at Maruti-Suzuki. *Indian Journal of Industrial Relations, 47*(2), 191–205.
Sethia, T. (1996). The rise of the Jute manufacturing industry in colonial India: A Global Perspective. *Journal of World History,7*(1), 71–99. Retrieved June 22, 2020, from www.jstor.org/stable/20078659
Sengupta, S., & Sahay, A. (2018). Social enterprises in the Indian context: Conceptualizing through qualitative lens. *J Glob Entrepr Res, 8*, 1.
Shah, D., & Barker, M. (2017). Cracking the cultural code: Indian IT expatriates' intercultural communication challenges in Australia. *International Journal of Cross Cultural Management, 17*(2), 215–236.
Shukla, K., Purohit, M., & Gaur, S. P. (2017). Studying 'Make in India' from the lens of labour reforms. *Management and Labour Studies, 42*(1), 1–19.
Sihag, B. S. (2004). Kautilya on the scope and methodology of accounting, organizational design and the role of ethics in ancient India. *Accounting Historians Journal, 31*(2), 125.
Sihag, B. S. (2009). Kautilya on principles of taxation. *Humanomics, 25*(1), 55–67.

Sinha, D. (1984). Some recent changes in the Indian family and their implications for socialisation. *The Indian Journal of Social Work, 45*, 271–286.
Sinha, J. B. P. (1973). *Some problems of public sector organizations*. National Pub. House.
Sinha, J. B. P. (2014). *Psycho-social analysis of the Indian mindset*. Springer.
Sinha, J. B. P., & Verma, J. (1987). Structure of collectivism. In C. Kagitcibasi (Ed.), *Growth and progress in cross-cultural psychology* (pp. 123–129). Swets & Zeitlinger.
Sinha, J. B. P., & Kanungo, R. N. (1997). Context sensitivity and balancing in organizational behaviour. *International Journal of Psychology, 32*(2), 93–105.
Sinha, J. B. P., & Pandey, A. (2007). Indians' mindsets and the conditions that evoke them. *Psychological Studies, 52*(1), 1–13.
Sinha, J. B. P., Sinha, T. N., Verma, J., & Sinha, R. B. N. (2001). Collectivisim coexisting with individualism: An Indian scenario. *Asian Journal of Social Psychology, 4*(2), 133–145.
Sinha, J. B. P., Vohra, N., Singhal, S., Sinha, R. B. N., & Ushashree, S. (2002). Normative predictions of collectivist–individualist intentions and behaviour of Indians. *Int. J. of Psychology, 37*(5), 309–319.
Sinha, N., & Srivastava, K. B. L. (2015). Intrapreneurship orientation and innovation championing in Indian organizations. *Global Business Review, 16*(5), 760–771.
Srinivasan, D. (1978). The religious significance of divine multiple body parts in the Atharva Veda. *Numen, 25*(3), 193–225. https://doi.org/10.2307/3269536
Stein, B. (2011). *A history of India* (2nd ed.). Wiley Publishing.
Sur, S. (2017). Beyond the Indus: How Hinduism offers an alternate management paradigm. *Philosophy of Management, 16*, 69–89.
Thakar, V. (1991). *Glimpse of Ishavasya*. Vimal Prakashan Trust.
Thakur, K. K. (2013). British colonial exploitations of India and Globalization. *Proceeding of the Indian History Congress, 74*, 405–415.
Thapar, R. (2003). *The penguin history of early India: From the origins to AD 1300*. Penguin Books.
Timberg, T. A. (1973). Three types of Marwari firms. *Indian Economic Social History Review, 10*(3), 3–36.
Timberg, T. A. (2014). *The Marwaris: From Jagath Seth to the Birlas*. Penguin.
Thimmaiah, G. (2001). New perspectives on land reforms in India. *Journal of Social and Economic Development, 3*(2), 181–198.
Tripathi, D. (2004). *The Oxford history of Indian business*. Oxford University Press.

Tripati, S. (2011). Ancient maritime trade of the eastern Indian littoral. *Current Science, 100*(7), 1076–1086. Retrieved October 30, 2020, from http://www.jstor.org/stable/24076528

Verma, S., Awasthy, R., Narain, K., & Rishika. (2015). Cultural determinants of alliance management capability—An analysis of Japanese MNCs in India. *Asia Pacific Business Review, 23*(3), 424–448.

Vink, M. (2007). Indian ocean studies and the 'new thalassology.' *Journal of Global History, 2*(1), 41–62. https://doi.org/10.1017/S1740022807002033

Zahra, S. A., Rawhouser, H. N., Bhawe, N., Neubaum, D. O., & Hayton, J. C. (2008). Globalization of social entrepreneurship opportunities. *Strategic Entrepreneurship Journal, 2*(2), 117–131. https://doi.org/10.1002/sej.43

Website References

Article on Hindu Muslim Harmony. http://www.newindianexpress.com/nation/2019/mar/15/heres-how-these-youngsters-are-reminding-us-of-hindu-muslim-harmony-1951450.html

Companies with Pre- Independence roots. https://www.livemint.com/Companies/IvqNiC0KHlZg9ZOXhFbe4O/70-companies-with-pre1947-roots.html

Hindustan Unilever Limited website. https://www.hul.co.in/about/who-we-are/our-history/

Industrial Revolution. New World Encyclopedia. http://www.newworldencyclopedia.org/entry/Industrial_Revolution

Marwari model of business. The Economic Times. https://economictimes.indiatimes.com/decoding-the-marwari-model-of-business-success/articleshow/45156920.cms?from=mdr

Revolt of 1857 - http://old.mu.ac.in/wp-content/uploads/2014/04/FYBA-History-Paper-I-History-of-Modern-India-Revised-Syllabus-2018-19.pdf. Accessed on 1.7.20

The Mughal Empire. Asian History: Oxford Research Encyclopedias. https://oxfordre.com/asianhistory/view/https://doi.org/10.1093/acrefore/9780190277727.001.0001/acrefore-9780190277727-e-357

Trades policy 1800–1947. https://www.encyclopedia.com/international/encyclopedias-almanacs-transcripts-and-maps/trade-policy-1800-1947. Accessed on 12.5.20

Vedas. https://www.ancient.eu/The_Vedas/. Accessed on 17.10.2020

https://www.newworldencyclopedia.org/entry/Upanishad. Accessed on 27.10.2020

14

Influence of Indian Culture on Advertising in India

Bharadhwaj Sivakumaran and R. M. Harindranath

Introduction

Culture is the "sum total of knowledge, beliefs, art, morals, customs, and other capabilities and habits acquired by humans as members of society" (Cateora & Graham, 2005, p. 94). Essentially, it is how humans are programmed mentally and possibly; there is hardly any area that the "invisible hand of culture" does not touch. For instance, culture affects the way individuals behave with others such as parents, spouses and teachers. It affects their saving (Ersin & Eti, 2017) and spending habits; it affects the way they dress (Indians dress differently from Mexicans

B. Sivakumaran (✉)
Great Lakes Institute of Management, Chennai, India
e-mail: bwaj@greatlakes.edu.in

R. M. Harindranath
MEASI Institute of Management, Chennai, India

© The Author(s), under exclusive license to Springer Nature Switzerland AG 2022
A. Pandey et al. (eds.), *Indigenous Indian Management*, Palgrave Studies in Indian Management,
https://doi.org/10.1007/978-3-030-87906-8_14

and Eastern Europeans for instance); and so on. If the effect of culture is so pervasive, it ought to then affect the way consumers are influenced by advertising. This chapter deals with the effect of culture on advertising. Further, evidence suggests that in India, the effect of culture is stronger than in other countries. For instance, Kellogg, 25 years after market entry, continues to struggle while the likes of Haldirams thrive (Chopra, 2019). In terms of market share, Kellogg dominates but other home-grown snacks have grown much faster; for instance, Kellogg sells for Rs. 1000 crore every year (US$136 million); this is only one-tenth of Unilever India's food division sales (https://www.business-standard.com/article/companies/haldiram-s-deal-on-the-cards-kellogg-eyeing-acquisitions-to-bump-up-sales-119021400503_1.html). It is not a surprise therefore that advertising in India has used tenets of Indian culture extensively. This chapter describes extant research in this area, embellishes this with real-world examples, identifies gaps and suggests avenues for future research.

Culture and Indian Advertising: Snapshot of Extant Research

Despite its importance, there is only little structured research on the effect or importance of culture in Indian advertising. At an international level, there exists considerable research on the impact of culture or its use in advertising (Lee, 2019; Taylor, 2018). For instance, collectivist appeals in advertising have a greater influence in countries like China (Zhang & Neelankavil, 1997) and Korea (Zhang & Shavitt, 2003), whereas in countries like USA (Zhang & Neelankavil, 1997; Zhang & Shavitt, 2003) individualistic appeals strike a chord. The effectiveness of comparative advertising varies across cultures. Jeon and Beatty (2002) show that direct (indirect) comparative ads work better in Korea (USA). While the use of humor in advertising is universal, its effects are also dependent on individualism and collectivism (Alden et al., 1993). While there is India-specific work in the realm of advertising (Kalro et al., 2013, 2017), it does not deal with culture, let alone specific aspects of Indian culture. In sum, therefore, there is little structured work on aspects of

Indian culture in advertising and related marketing communicational tools like sales promotion. In India, culture is extremely embedded in the consciousness of her people. This is borne out by both anecdotal and empirical evidence. Anecdotally, brands like Kellogg and McDonalds, after decades in India, are yet to set scale heights they have in the West. India continues to stick to her traditions, languages and customs. In the empirical research domain, research shows that cultural values are strongly entrenched in the psyche of the Indian people (Sinha & Kumar, 2004). Ipso facto, the dearth of research in this domain is surprising. Given the paucity of research in this area, this chapter highlights industry practices in this domain around certain themes of Indian culture and subsequently, suggests areas on which future researchers could work on in this domain.

Before we dwell on the propositions, this paper briefly encapsulates the available literature on advertising in India and aspects related to culture. Srikandath (1991) finds that Indian ads promote values like modernity and consumerism. Srivastava and Schoeebachler (2000) find that emotional appeals are used to a greater extent in the Indian context, relative to informational cues; even recently in social media advertising, the same finding has been reported (Sidharth Muralidharan et al., 2015). According to Chandra et al. (2002), US firms find segments similar to those in the USA and try and standardize their advertising in India. Singh and Kaur (2014) report that mothers view advertising targeted at children negatively. Research by Mukherji (2005), on the other hand, found that mothers had positive attitudes toward advertising, albeit her study was not exclusively for ads targeted at children. In India, movie celebrities were more popular compared to sports celebrities (Roy et al., 2013); this is possibly contrary to the Western world.

Baidya et al. (2012) show that advertising in India has both a short-term and long-term effect. This means that making advertising more effective is imperative and this can be possibly achieved through the use of cultural elements that we highlight. For instance, though in a negative way, the craze for fair skin has been taken advantage of by advertisers in India (Karan, 2008). This chapter argues that the use of cultural elements would be efficacious for Indian advertisers in a positive way.

Key Aspects of Indian Culture

Every culture has some important tenets. For instance, in America, it is the fierce independence and individualism in people that stands out. In Singapore, it is the rule of law and sense of discipline that strikes even the casual visitor. In India, there are some key aspects. The important aspects of Indian culture include respect for one's elders (Inman et al., 2007), the mother-son relationship (Rew et al., 2013), wife-husband relationship (Nimmagadda & Cowger, 1999) and celebrating key festivals (Nimmagadda & Cowger, 1999). On the Hofstede dimensions (Singh & Kaur, 2014), the scores of India on the various dimensions are power distance = 77, individualism = 48, masculinity = 56, uncertainty avoidance = 40 and long-term orientation = 51 (Hofstede, 2019). We now expand on all the above aspects of culture and give examples to substantiate wherever possible.

Respect for One's Elders

In India, like in many other Asian countries, it is common to respect one's elders (Inman et al., 2007). This respect is demonstrated by addressing one's elders not just by name, but suffixes like "ji" (a word that denotes respect in Hindi) or the equivalent. For instance, in India's most popular game cricket, young players refer to senior players as "Bhai" (e.g. meaning "elder brother"), whereas in other countries such as England and Australia, this is rarely, if at all done. Good advertising needs to resonate with consumers, and moreover, according to means-end theory (Wansink, 2003), consumers buy for ultimately for underlying values, and not superficial attributes. Hence, Indian advertisers extensively use this theme in their advertising. For instance, even a non-Indian brand like British Airways uses this theme to advertise their services that involve a personal touch (https://www.youtube.com/watch?v=ZFb01yTR9bA). In this ad, a British air hostess (a Caucasian lady) gets emotionally attached to an old Indian woman who flies British Airways and visits her in India and almost becomes part of her family. The ad does not feature any service feature; instead, it focuses on emotional warmth.

The Mother-Son Relationship

The mother-son relationship is special in the Indian ethos. This is why popular films in India like "Deewar" in Hindi where Amitabh Bachchan (a leading actor in Hindi cinema) as a son, Rajnikanth (a leading star in south India) portraying the role of a son in "Mannan" (a movie in Tamil) and "Amma Nanna O Tamila Ammayi" (a movie in Telugu), where Ravi Teja and Jeya Sudha (two cine stars in south India) have performed the mother-son role illustrate this concept. In English movies, for instance, one can rarely, if at all, see a hero swearing undying love and respect for his mother. In Indian movies, this is commonplace. In English movies, even if the setting is Asia, there are themes like the domineering mother (e.g. in the movie "Crazy Rich Asians", this is the case; the viewer can see the trailer at https://www.youtube.com/watch?v=ZQ-YX-5bAs0&feature=youtu.be).

Even now, in Indian movies, the special mother-son relationship is highlighted. For instance, in the Hindi movie "Helicopter Eela," the heroine (a famous actress named Kajol), a single mother, and her adult son both go to college together. This film (released in 2018) prominently features the special relationship this mother has with her adult son (https://www.youtube.com/watch?v=LLiUiJz5TZc&feature=youtu.be).

Likewise, in Indian advertising, the mother-son relationship figures frequently, cutting across categories. Vicks Vaporub, a brand owned by P&G (that purportedly fights cold, congestion and cough), shows a boy bonding with his mother as a result of she applying Vicks Vaporub when he has a cold.

(https://www.youtube.com/watch?v=MqKBuAymWo0). Similarly, "Complan" helps a boy grow taller and the anxious mother's fears are assuaged (https://www.youtube.com/watch?v=b6X7YggZc6Q). It is not just male children that bond with their mothers; even adult males do in India. Nokia more recently shows an adult male too busy to spend time with his mother; he is busy with his professional work. The mother is therefore upset (it is highly unlikely that this theme of mother missing her adult son would feature in a Western ad). So he gives his mother a Nokia phone so she can stay in touch (https://www.youtube.com/watch?v=IowoYY3DogQ).

Husband-Wife Relationship

This aspect of Indian culture has been handed down from the times of the Ramayana and the Mahabharata, two Indian epics. In the Ramayana, the key protagonists (a husband-wife pair), Ram and Seetha, stay together through thick and thin. In the Mahabharata, Gandhari and Dhritharashtra, another pair, do the same thing. The Manu Smriti, a classic text of Hinduism, states that "husband and wife must respect the eternal bond of matrimony". It is possibly owing to the subtle influence of these texts, handed over from generation to the next generation, for thousands of years, that the husband-wife relationship is considered so sacred in India.

The husband-wife relationship starts with a solemn wedding in India. Many advertisers use this wedding setting in their ads. In the 1980s, for example, Godrej Storwel, a brand of bureaus in India, shows a wedding with the bride taking home a Godrej Storwel (https://www.youtube.com/watch?v=lMESVqsszno). The "Pati-Pathni" (husband-wife) relationship is possibly special throughout the world; this is why a wedding is special in almost every culture. However, in India, this relationship is not just special, but even possibly sacred. India is predominantly a Hindu country, and in Hinduism, marriage is a solemn and sacred affair, where the wife and husband live together in harmony and aid each other's "spiritual progress" (https://www.hinduwebsite.com/marriage.asp). In addition, to the wife, the husband is like a deity or God. Though times are changing, vestiges of this thinking still are very much present in India. In Indian advertising, the husband-wife relationship is part of many an ad. For example, a popular Airtel (a leading telecom provider in India) ad runs thus (https://www.youtube.com/watch?v=1MBkgLDZQVI): A lady boss tells her male subordinate to complete an important portion of a project at the workplace. The male subordinate continues working past office hours. The lady boss goes home and makes a special meal for her husband. The male subordinate in the end turns out to be her husband. Thus, the ad, rightly or wrongly, showcases a pervasive part of Indian culture: a woman, though a busy career one, is expected to go home and cook for her husband. The ad showcases how she uses the smartphone to speak with him and send photos of the meal while he is at work.

In northern parts of India, women fast for the well-being of their husbands on a day called "Karva Chauth" four days after the full moon day in the months of October or November. This is unique to India. Some ads like Hero Motorcorp seamlessly integrate this in their advertising. A confident young woman, goes to office on a Hero scooter, is busy with her work but still fasts for Karva Chauth (again, very uniquely Indian); her husband organizes a special moon lit dinner for her—he surprises her (https://www.youtube.com/watch?v=fyf-MygBBQQ). ICICI Prudential too uses the festival of Karva Chauth (https://www.youtube.com/watch?v=X1emSLM9SOE). A young lady fasts for the well-being of her husband on this day. She is worried about the financial well-being of her retiring father when her husband says he would take care with the help of ICICI Prudential.

Of late though, there is a change in the mindset of many Indians, or at least, one is witnessing the beginning of the change. Havells, a popular brand of home electrical equipment, shows a woman asking her husband to make juice by himself, rather than she doing it for him, with a Havells juicer (https://www.youtube.com/watch?v=v_jAnfwxeLg). Likewise, an aging gentleman sees his daughter supremely busy and realizes that men too need to share in household chores and that he was wrong not to do this all these years. He then helps his wife do the laundry with Ariel, a popular brand of detergent owned by P&G (https://www.youtube.com/watch?v=wJukf4ifuKs).

Celebrating Key Festivals

India has a population that is predominantly Hindu; around 80% of the population is Hindu. In India, the main festivals are Diwali (around October–November every year), Pongal/Makar Sankranti (around Jan

15th every year), Ganesh Chaturthi (around September every year) (these three are celebrated by the majority Hindu community), Onam celebrated at Kerala (during September) and Ramzan (for the sizable Muslim community). During Diwali, Hindus celebrate by wearing new clothes and bursting crackers; in some areas of India, they also buy new gadgets, appliances and durables. On Makar Sankranti day (celebrated as Pongal in the south of India), people thank the Sun God and this marks the ascendancy of the sun from Capricorn to Cancer or south to north and this is of great significance. This generally marks the harvest of a new crop and depending upon the region in India, is celebrated in different ways. Advertisers take advantage of such festivals.

Diwali (also called Deepavali, which was the original name) is the most important festival for Hindus, who comprise at least 80% of the population in India. Diwali is celebrated to signify the victory of good over evil and is marked by buying and wearing new clothes, eating sweetmeats, gifting others to friends and family, and bursting crackers. Many ads in India have the above-mentioned elements. For instance, Pantaloon (a retailer in India, predominantly selling apparel) shows a young lady befriend a gentleman who happens to be her brother's friend. They bond and fall in love over Diwali and new Pantaloon apparel (https://www.youtube.com/watch?v=kp1xseNLYAM). The Diwali theme (crackers, new clothes, sweets) is an integral part of the ad. Likewise, Cadbury, in a recent ad, shows how a couple surprises their son, who is an army officer, with Cadbury chocolates in the Diwali spirit (https://www.youtube.com/watch?v=QKt7A_wsq_8). Lenovo too showcases the Diwali spirit. A taxi driver gifts a Lenovo laptop to his son, and asks him to sit at the back, and says that he needs to become a corporate executive (armed with the Lenovo, needless to say!) and economically progress in life. Thus, diverse products showcase aspects of Diwali, an integral part of Indian culture.

Around mid-January every year, India celebrates a festival that marks the harvest of the crop for the year; this is called Pongal in the southern parts of India, Lohri in some other parts and Makar Sankranti in some others. Many brands advertise around this festival. For instance, Britannia Milk Bikis, a popular brand of biscuits that is supplemented with milk, uses the Pongal theme very aptly (https://www.youtube.com/watch?v=Bt_C6E-VhMo). In the southern state of Tamil Nadu in India, on the day of the festival, people boil milk and allow it boil or spill over, outside the vessel, symbolizing happiness and prosperity overflowing. The mother gives inadequate milk and the child uses Britannia Milk Bikis instead. Amazon too shows it is possible to celebrate Pongal even in a deserted forest (they deliver stuff even there apparently!) at https://www.youtube.com/watch?v=9P54dXASc9E.

The Onam festival is celebrated in Kerala (i.e. southern state of India) during the month of September. It is a harvesting festival. There are many advertisements during this festival. The Onam "pookkalam" featured in the "Tanishq" ad shows the importance of the Onam festival (https://www.youtube.com/watch?v=jGZhKJv-ZYI).

It is also interesting to note that while some companies customize the ads for different regions and languages, others use the same ones. For example, Amazon shows a young lady gift a smartphone to her middle aged father on Diwali day (a Hindi ad, Hindi is spoken predominantly in North India) (https://www.youtube.com/watch?v=ZEUR51wlfH4). As alluded to earlier, Amazon shows a young couple celebrate the festival of Pongal in a forest resort (a Tamil ad, Tamil is spoken in the south Indian state of Tamil Nadu). (https://www.youtube.com/watch?v=9P54dXASc9E). Here, it is apparent that Amazon customizes its ads for different occasions and/or regions. Likewise, Reliance Fresh, a major Indian retailer, has different ads for different occasions/regions. In the month of Ramadan, Muslims fast (there are around 200 million Muslims in India). In one ad, Reliance Fresh shows a young child, too young to fast, helps his mother with little chores and helping his neighbors (with products bought from Reliance Fresh, of course!) (https://www.youtube.com/watch?v=2_xEv-dx3xk). On Diwali, Reliance Fresh shows an entirely different ad, with a family celebrating Diwali and buying products from Reliance Fresh (https://www.youtube.com/watch?v=R9eP-LA4RSI). In this ad, Reliance Fresh showcases the offers and discounts it has, so everyone can buy, gift products, and spread happiness and joy.

On the other hand, a company like Pantaloon shows the same ad in West Bengal (https://www.youtube.com/watch?v=Sqn9fAhP4S4) and the rest of India (https://www.youtube.com/watch?v=bUjsNGQ6e2Y). While the West Bengal ad is in Bengali shown around Durga Pooja

(Bengali is spoken in West Bengal and Durga Pooja is the most important festival there), the Hindi ad was broadcast around Diwali. A pertinent point to note is that the ad was the same, only the language was different.

Controversies Regarding Offending Indian Culture

Culture is a touchy and sensitive issue worldwide, more so in India. Brands, particularly foreign ones, need to be careful in terms of not directly or indirectly offending aspects of Indian culture or sensibilities. For instance, Brooke Bond, a brand of tea owned by the Indian arm of Unilever used the Kumbh Mela as a setting in one its recent (2019) ads. The Kumbh Mela is a religious festival that gathers the most number of people; it is held every 12 years. The Kumbh Mela attracts a crowd of 150 million, spread over a few days; it is held at a town in the North Indian state of Uttar Pradesh (https://en.wikipedia.org/wiki/Kumbh_Mela). Due to the large congregation of people, inevitably a few people get lost or separated from their families. Brooke Bond used this theme in their ad (https://www.youtube.com/watch?v=G2MOsp-3TaA). The ad showcases a son deliberately losing his aged father in the Kumbh Mela (he sees his father as a burden and wants to get rid of him and the Kumbh Mela provides the opportunity or an excuse). The ad then shows the son regretting his act of deliberately leaving his father and walking off (he feigns that it is an accident) and Brooke Bond brings them back together finally. This ad offended Hindu sensibility in India. Many Hindus immediately reacted thus: "So does Unilever think we go to the Kumbh Mela just to leave our parents behind?". Brooke Bond had to pull the ad and apologize. Likewise, a recent ad of Unilever's Surf Excel also created controversy and affected some religious sentiments (https://www.firstpost.com/india/surf-excel-ad-does-not-promote-love-jihad-but-it-is-a-damaging-script-that-misreads-indias-inherent-pluralism-6244271.html).

Thus, the key takeaway for advertisers is that they need to avoid hurting cultural sensitivities and ads should be in sync with rather than go against grains of popular culture.

Negative Aspects of Indian Culture and Advertising

While every culture no doubt has numerous positives (e.g. egalitarianism and punctuality in the West, respect for elders and the environment in the East), many cultures have a few negatives as well. India is no different. While some negative aspects such as the caste system are left alone by advertisers, some subtle negative aspects are exploited by them. A case in point is the obsession for fair (or light colored skin) in India. In India, among many parts of the country, there is widespread perception that "fair is beautiful while dark skin is not". Many brands like Fair & Lovely (owned by the Indian arm of Unilever) and Fairever (owned by Cavinkare, an Indian company) pander to this perception. In their advertising, for many years, they have reinforced this perception and have notched up huge sales volumes by exploiting this negative perception (for instance, see the old Fair and Lovely ad at https://www.youtube.com/watch?v=ex0iJHLqxt0). The ad features a dark young woman, spurned by even her parents. After using Fair and Lovely, she becomes fair of skin, and highly successful, sought after by airline companies for the job of an airhostess and also ogled at admiringly by handsome men. While pandering to such near-racist stereotypes may be morally reprehensible, brands have done so and profited by them. However, of late, possibly due to the power of social media, brands may be diluting these messages somewhat (e.g. https://www.youtube.com/watch?v=7tJE38BW6OM; this ad features how Fair and Lovely protects the skin and keeps one fresh. Thus, the ads have toned down the "fair alone is lovely" message of late). Thus, in yesteryears, it was possible to pander to such negative cultural sensitivities, but possibly no longer. It may be safer for companies to avoid such controversies.

However, advertising can also help change some of these negative cultural sensitivities. For instance, in many Indian households, women while menstruating are not allowed to enter the kitchen and especially, touch pickles. In an ad, P&G showcases a young lady having her periods and touching the pickle (https://www.youtube.com/watch?v=PhHLAHqrGvk). This ad is an endeavor to change aspects of culture that are out of sync with modernity and current times. Likewise, in some Indian states, there is a marked preference for male children. Many a time, women once they realize that they are carrying a female child (in the early stages of pregnancy) abort it; this is nothing short of female infanticide. To change such negative cultural stereotypes, the Government of India ran a campaign called "Beti Bachao, Beti Padhao" or "save the girl child" In this ad, Prime Minister Narendra Modi is seen exhorting people in an impassioned manner to treat the girl child and the boy child equally and not discriminate against the girl child (https://www.pmindia.gov.in/en/government_tr_rec/beti-bachao-beti-padhao-caring-for-the-girl-child/). The jury is still out on whether this campaign is successful but hopefully, this will at least be a good beginning. Thus, the key takeaways from this sub-section are as follows:

- Advertising used to exploit negative cultural sensitivities in the past, but this is getting harder to do so in the present day and age. Not only is this unethical, it may not even be smart.
- Advertising can instead focus its efforts on changing such negative aspects of culture in India—this will be a win–win for all concerned. Brands will increase their sales, be seen as more responsible from a societal standpoint and society too would be a better place.

Directions for Future Research

One of the goals of this chapter is to provide guidelines for future research in this area of how Indian culture affects the impact of advertising and marketing communication in India. As previously argued and laid out, research in this area is sparse; there is little structured research in this managerially important area. Hence, we offer tips to researchers on the kind of research possibilities that exist in this area, around the following themes: content analysis of impact of culture in advertising, types of products and the impact of Indian culture in advertising, products Vs. services and the impact of Indian culture in advertising,

Westernization and impact of Indian culture in advertising and public policy implications of Indian culture in advertising.

In all the above-mentioned areas, this chapter comes up with propositions.

Content Analysis of Impact of Culture in Advertising

Content analysis is common in the realm of advertising (Banerjee et al., 1995). Even in the context of advertising in India, it is quite prevalent (Fernando et al., 2014; Kalro et al., 2010; Srivastava et al., 2017). However, in the domain of the likely impact of Indian culture in advertising, there is no content analysis extant, to the best of our knowledge. The advantage of content analysis is that it offers a snapshot of the phenomenon one is studying (e.g. Kalro et al., 2010). Therefore, research can first conduct a content analysis on the following lines, using the dimensions of Hofstede (e.g. de Mooij & Hofstede, 2002), namely individualism, uncertainty avoidance, power distance, masculinity and long-term orientation:

India scores high on collectivism (Ramamoorthy et al., 2007); for example, Airtel's classic ads typically show a group of youngsters having fun (https://www.youtube.com/watch?v=gkz2rHQZYPg). These ads do not show a single person, rather they feature a group and showcase social approval. Hence:

P1: The number of ads relating to collectivism would be higher than those relating to individualism.

India also scores high on the masculinity index (Hofstede, 1998). Traditional gender roles are emphasized in Indian society even today. However, attitudes are slowly changing with gender roles becoming more fluid (Butler, 2005). Hence, we expect:

P2: The number of ads relating to traditional gender roles would be higher than those than relate to more fluid gender roles.

P3: The difference in the number of traditional gender roles and more fluid ones would be greater for products targeted at older consumers, relative to products targeted at younger ones.

Likewise, India scores high on power distance (Singh et al., 2006). Just like gender roles are becoming more fluid, attitudes toward power distance are changing with India becoming more egalitarian. A simple example would be that in the years that went by, senior management would have one set of toilets and juniors another set. Today, it is common to find one set of toilets for all—junior of senior. Hence, we expect:

P4: The number of ads relating to high power distance would be greater than those relating to low power distance.

P5: The difference in the number of ads relating to high and low power distance would be higher for products targeted at older consumers, relative to products targeted at younger ones.

Types of Products and Impact of Indian Culture in Advertising

The invisible hand of culture touches almost every aspect of consumers' lives. Hence, its effect is likely to be felt cutting across product categories. However, extant research in the non-Indian context shows that the effect of culture is not uniform across product categories and situations. For instance, Briley et al. (2000) show that when asked to explain reasons, culture matters and it exerts a greater influence on decision-making, compared to when consumers are not asked to explain reasons. Briley and Aaker (2006) demonstrate that when consumers process information in a cursory fashion, culture exerts a powerful influence on consumer decision-making.

Products can be classified into utilitarian and hedonic products (Dhar & Wertenbroch, 2000; Kalro Arti et al., 2017). A utilitarian product is merely functional in nature, a means to an end while a hedonic product results in sensory gratification; use of a hedonic product results in pleasure (e.g. a candy bar), while the consumption of a utilitarian product does not (e.g. a safety pin). Hedonic products are related to positive affect (Kahn & Lehmann, 1991). Hedonic attributes are fuzzier, subjective and abstract (e.g. the pleasure a consumer gets from a candy bar is hard to quantify and different for different consumers), while utilitarian attributes are concrete and less ambiguous (e.g. the mileage in a car). Moreover, hedonic products possibly require greater justification relative to utilitarian ones and justification activates cultural knowledge (Briley et al., 2000), Hence, we expect:

P6: The use of cultural elements in hedonic products would be higher than in utilitarian products.

Hence, based on the above, research can study the following:

Indian Culture and Hi Tech/Hi Touch Products

Products may also be classified into hi tech (e.g. cell phones) and high touch products (e.g. wine, perfume). Hi tech products are generally used by a younger target audience who are probably more Westernized than older consumers. Hi touch products are possibly used by young and old alike. Hence, we expect:

P7: The use of Indian cultural elements would be greater in hi tech products vis-à-vis hi touch products.

Rural, Urban India and Use of Indian Cultural Elements.

Rural India is a growing market (Sridhar & Mishra, 2011), and both Indian and foreign manufacturers are eager to catch a portion of this growing pie (IBEF, 2008). There is a view that rural India is more steeped in traditional Indian culture compared to urban India (Prabhath, 2011). Hence, we expect:

P8: The use of Indian cultural elements in ads targeting rural India would be higher compared to those targeting urban India.

Products Conspicuous by Their Consumption and Indian Cultural Elements

Some products are conspicuous by their consumption (e.g. a car) and others are not (e.g. a washing machine). While buying the former, consumers indulge in a greater search effort, compared to the latter (Beatty & Smith, 1987). The former obviously requires a greater level of justification. Since justification activates cultural tenets (Briley et al., 2000), we expect:

> P9: The use of Indian cultural elements would be higher in products that are conspicuous by their consumption, compared to those that are not.

Services and the Impact of Culture in Advertising

Services are inherently different from products in that they are intangible and the purchase of a service does not result in the ownership of anything. The service sector in India is growing and accounts for more than 50% of the country's GDP (IBEF, 2019). Research in other domains of marketing has focused on services vs. products; for example, Sharma et al. (2014) investigate impulse buying in the service sector. Closer home, even in the advertising literature, there are differences in advertising for services vs. products (Stafford et al., 2011; Zinkhan et al., 1992). There is some work in the area of the use of culture in services in the international context (e.g. Song, 2014). However, in India, there is little research on how culture can be used in Indian advertising for services.

Services differ along their level of tangibility—some services are highly intangible (e.g. career advice) while others are less so (e.g. fast food restaurant). Intangible services require a greater degree of hard-sell since there is nothing tangible on which marketers can base their selling pitch on. Conventionally, the text book advice is to "tangibilizing an intangible" (An, 2014, p. 566). However, there may be an alternative approach.

According to means-end theory, consumers buy mainly for deeply held values, and not for superficially perceived attributes (Wansink, 2003). The process by which these values can be uncovered is a qualitative research technique, laddering and once these values are uncovered, they can be showcased in advertising (e.g. Sadarangani, 2017). Hence, it is plausible that Indian cultural elements can be used in ads for services and this strategy could be used to a greater extent for more (vis-à-vis less) intangible services and therefore, we expect:

P10: The use of Indian cultural elements is likely to be more effective in more (vis-à-vis) less intangible services.

Services can be classified into search, experience and credence ones (Darby & Karni, 1973). Consumers can evaluate the quality of a search service merely on the basis of information regarding this service. To evaluate an experience service, on the other hand, information alone is not sufficient, and consumption is required. Finally, for a credence service, even consumption is not sufficient; even after consuming a credence service, consumers find it difficult to evaluate service quality. Examples for the above are bank account (search service), fast food (experience service) and automobile repair (credence service). Credence services are by nature, more ambiguous, compared to the other two kinds of services. Hence, because of this ambiguity (Bowen & Jones, 1986), learning can be influenced (Wirtz & Mattila Anna, 2003) and one way of influencing this learning could be by adding Indian cultural elements, and hence, we expect:

P11: The use of Indian cultural elements would be more effective in credence services compared to experience and search services.

Public Policy and Indian Culture in Advertising

In India, there are several public policy issues, like in the rest of the world. However, what makes the case of India unique is her status as a developing country and her huge population (1.2 billion plus); besides,

India is one of the leading economies in the world. Ipso facto, problems affecting India have an effect on the rest of the world as well. India has several public policy challenges. The Government of India has launched the Swach Bharat (Clean India) movement to clean up the country. This requires private citizens to participate on a large scale. Hence, to motivate their participation, advertising is needed and is done as well (e.g. https://www.youtube.com/watch?v=9biFUaff1pI).

In this ad at https://www.youtube.com/watch?v=9biFUaff1pI, cleanliness is equated with Godliness in the form of Hindu Goddess Lakshmi. Apart from Swach Bharat, there are other pressing social and public policy initiatives—save the girl child, conserve energy and water, pay your taxes and so on. In all these, there could be elements of Indian culture placed that could affect public reaction to these. There is some emerging evidence (Williams, 2019) that incorporating religious beliefs in public policy initiatives is beneficial and moreover, consumers base their decisions on values (Wansink, 2003). Hence, we expect:

P12: Compared to public policy initiatives that do not use Indian cultural elements, those that do are more effective.

Contributions and Summary

The use of culture in advertising in India is widespread and this chapter offers a snapshot of how this is done. Further, the chapter offers specific directions for future research in this domain. Hopefully, researchers in India and elsewhere will take cognizance of these ideas and put them into practice.

References

Alden, D. L., Hoyer, W. D., & Lee, C. (1993). Identifying global and culture-specific dimensions of humor in advertising: A Multinational analysis. *Journal of Marketing, 57*(2), 64–75. https://doi.org/10.1177/002224299305700205

An, D. (2014). Tangibilizing services through visual tangible cues in corporate web sites: A six-country cross-cultural analysis. *Journal of Services Marketing, 28*(7), 566–579. https://doi.org/10.1108/JSM-04-2013-0097

Baidya, M., Maity, B., & Ghose, K. (2012). Measuring dynamic effects of advertising: A case study in India. *Journal of Indian Business Research, 4*(3), 158–169. https://doi.org/10.1108/17554191211252671

Banerjee, S., Gulas, C. S., & Iyer, E. (1995). Shades of green: A multidimensional analysis of environmental advertising. *Journal of Advertising, 24*(2), 21–31.

Beatty, S. E., & Smith, S. M. (1987). External search effort: An Investigation across several product categories. *Journal of Consumer Research, 14*(1), 83–95. https://doi.org/10.1086/209095

Bowen, D. E., & Jones, G. R. (1986). Transaction cost analysis of service organization-customer exchange. *Academy of Management Review, 11*(2), 428–441. https://doi.org/10.5465/amr.1986.4283519

Briley, D. A., & Aaker, J. L. (2006). When does culture matter? Effects of personal knowledge on the correction of culture-based judgments. *Journal of Marketing Research, 43*(3), 395–408. https://doi.org/10.1509/jmkr.43.3.395

Briley, D. A., Morris, M. W., & Simonson, I. (2000). Reasons as carriers of culture: Dynamic versus dispositional models of cultural influence on decision making. *Journal of Consumer Research, 27*(2), 157–178. https://doi.org/10.1086/314318

Butler, J. (2005). Gender trouble: Feminism and the subversion of identity GT. *Political Theory, 4*, 4–24.

Cateora, P. R., & Graham, J. L. (2005). *International marketing* (12th ed.). Richard P.Irwin.

Chandra, A., Griffith, D. A., & Ryans, J. K. (2002). Advertising standardization in India: US multinational experience. *International Journal of Advertising, 21*(1), 47–66. https://doi.org/10.1080/02650487.2002.11104916

Chopra, S. (2019). *Kellogg's eyes Indian snacks giant Haldiram's to diversify beyond core breakfast cereal category, says Global Data.* Retrieved 13 June

2019, from https://www.globaldata.com/kelloggs-eyes-indian-snacks-giant-haldirams-to-diversify-beyond-core-breakfast-cereal-category-says-global data/

Darby, M. R., & Karni, E. (1973). Free competition and the optimal amount of fraud. *The Journal of Law and Economics, 16*(1), 67–88. https://doi.org/10.1086/466756

de Mooij, M., & Hofstede, G. (2002). Convergence and divergence in consumer behavior: Implications for international retailing. *Journal of Retailing, 78*(1), 61–69. https://doi.org/10.1016/S0022-4359(01)00067-7

Dhar, R., & Wertenbroch, K. (2000). Consumer choice between hedonic and utilitarian goods. *Journal of Marketing Research, 37*(1), 60–71. https://doi.org/10.1509/jmkr.37.1.60.18718

Ersin, İ., & Eti, S. (2017). Measuring the waste-conscious and saving habits of the youth in Turkey: The sample of Istanbul Medipol university. *International Journal of Islamic Economics and Finance Studies, 3*(3).

Fernando, A. G., Sivakumaran, B., & Suganthi, L. (2014). Nature of green advertisements in India: Are they greenwashed? *Asian Journal of Communication, 24*(3), 222–241. https://doi.org/10.1080/01292986.2014.885537

Hofstede, G. (1998). *Masculinity and femininity: The taboo dimension of national cultures* (Vol. 3). Sage Publications.

Hofstede, G. (2019). *Hofstede insights*. Retrieved 14 June 2019, from https://www.hofstede-insights.com/country-comparison/india/

IBEF. (2008). *Rural market*. Retrieved 24 June 2019, from https://www.ibef.org/pages/20071

IBEF. (2019). *Services sector in India*. Retrieved 23 June 2019, from https://www.ibef.org/industry/services.aspx

Inman, A. G., Howard, E. E., Beaumont, R. L., & Walker, J. A. (2007). Cultural transmission: Influence of contextual factors in asian indian immigrant parents' experiences. *Journal of Counseling Psychology, 54*(1), 93–100. https://doi.org/10.1037/0022-0167.54.1.93

Jeon, J. O., & Beatty, S. E. (2002). Comparative advertising effectiveness in different national cultures. *Journal of Business Research, 55*(11), 907–913. https://doi.org/10.1016/S0148-2963(01)00210-7

Kahn, B. E., & Lehmann, D. R. (1991). Modeling choice among assortments. *Journal of Retailing, 67*(3), 274–299.

Kalro, A. D., Sivakumaran, B., & Marathe, R. R. (2010). Comparative advertising in India: A content analysis of English print advertisements. *Journal of International Consumer Marketing, 22*(4), 377–394.

Kalro, A. D., Sivakumaran, B., & Marathe, R. R. (2013). Direct or indirect comparative ads: The moderating role of information processing modes. *Journal of Consumer Behaviour, 12*(2), 133–147. https://doi.org/10.1002/cb.1421

Kalro, A. D., Sivakumaran, B., & Marathe, R. R. (2017). The ad format-strategy effect on comparative advertising effectiveness. *European Journal of Marketing, 51*(1), 99–122. https://doi.org/10.1108/EJM-11-2015-0764

Kalro Arti, D., Sivakumaran, B., & Marathe Rahul, R. (2017). The ad format-strategy effect on comparative advertising effectiveness. *European Journal of Marketing, 51*(1), 99–122. https://doi.org/10.1108/EJM-11-2015-0764

Karan, K. (2008). Obsessions with fair skin: Color discourses in Indian advertising. *Advertising & society review, 9*(2).

Lee, W.-N. (2019). Exploring the role of culture in advertising: Resolving persistent issues and responding to changes. *Journal of Advertising, 48*(1), 115–125. https://doi.org/10.1080/00913367.2019.1579686

Mukherji, J. (2005). Maternal communication patterns, advertising attitudes and mediation behaviours in Urban India. *Journal of Marketing Communications, 11*(4), 247–262. https://doi.org/10.1080/13527260500167223

Nimmagadda, J., & Cowger, C. D. (1999). Cross-cultural practice: Social worker ingenuity in the indigenization of practice knowledge. *International Social Work, 42*(3), 261–276. https://doi.org/10.1177/002087289904200302

Prabhath, S. V. (2011). *Role of Education and Culture in Rural Development*. https://www.mkgandhi.org/articles/role_edu.htm. Accessed January 2019.

Ramamoorthy, N., Kulkarni, S. P., Gupta, A., & Flood, P. C. (2007). Individualism–collectivism orientation and employee attitudes: A comparison of employees from the high-technology sector in India and Ireland. *Journal of International Management, 13*(2), 187–203. https://doi.org/10.1016/j.intman.2006.11.002

Rew, M., Gangoli, G., & Gill, A. K. (2013). Violence between female in-laws in India. *Journal of International Women's Studies, 14*(1), 147–160.

Roy, S., Jain, V., & Rana, P. (2013). The moderating role of consumer personality and source credibility in celebrity endorsements. *Asia-Pacific Journal of Business Administration, 5*(1), 72–88. https://doi.org/10.1108/17574321311304549

Sadarangani, P. H., Krishnamurthy, A., Bagozzi, R. P. (2017). Shared consumer needs across India and China: A path to global advertising of services? *Management International Review, 57*(3), 473-500. https://doi.org/10.1007/s11575-016-0299-2

Sharma, P., Sivakumaran, B., & Marshall, R. (2014). Exploring impulse buying in services: Toward an integrative framework. *Journal of the Academy of Marketing Science, 42*(2), 154–170. https://doi.org/10.1007/s11747-013-0346-5

Muralidharan, S., La Ferle, C., & Sung, Y. (2015). How culture influences the "social" in social media: Socializing and advertising on smartphones in India and the United States. *Cyberpsychology, Behavior, and Social Networking, 18*(6), 356–360. https://doi.org/10.1089/cyber.2015.0008

Singh, N., Fassott, G., Zhao, H., & Boughton, P. D. (2006). A cross-cultural analysis of German, Chinese and Indian consumers' perception of web site adaptation. *Journal of Consumer Behaviour, 5*(1), 56–68. https://doi.org/10.1002/cb.43

Singh, R., & Kaur, P. (2014). Maternal attitude towards TV advertising in India. *Management and Labour Studies, 39*(2), 160–173. https://doi.org/10.1177/0258042x14558182

Sinha, J. B. P., & Kumar, R. (2004). Methodology for understanding Indian culture. *The Copenhagen Journal of Asian Studies, 19*, 89–104.

Song, M. (2014). Challenging a culture of racial equivalence. *The British Journal of Sociology, 65*(1), 107–129. https://doi.org/10.1111/1468-4446.12054

Sridhar, G., & Mishra, D. (2011). Executives social representation of rurality and product adaptation: A case of rural markets in India. *Asia Pacific Journal of Marketing and Logistics, 23*(3), 285–303. https://doi.org/10.1108/13555851111143222

Srikandath, S. (1991). Cultural values depicted in Indian television advertising. *Gazette (leiden, Netherlands), 48*(3), 165–176. https://doi.org/10.1177/001654929104800302

Srivastava, E., Maheswarappa, S. S., & Sivakumaran, B. (2017). Nostalgic advertising in India: A content analysis of Indian TV advertisements. *Asia Pacific Journal of Marketing and Logistics, 29*(1), 47–69. https://doi.org/10.1108/APJML-10-2015-0152

Srivastava, T., & Schoeebachler, D. D. (2000). An examination of the information and thematic content of consumer print advertising in India. *Journal of International Consumer Marketing, 12*(2), 63–85. https://doi.org/10.1300/J046v12n02_05

Stafford, M. B. R., Reilly, T., Grove, S. J., Carlson, L., Bhandari, R., & Copeland, J. (2011). The evolution of services advertising in a services-driven national economy. *An Analysis of Progress and Missed Opportunities,*

51(150th Anniversary Supplement), 136–152. https://doi.org/10.2501/jar-51-1-136-152

Taylor, C. R. (2018). Global consumer culture and advertising research. *International Journal of Advertising, 37*(4), 505–507. https://doi.org/10.1080/02650487.2018.1474021

Wansink, B. (2003). Using laddering to understand and leverage a brand's equity. *Qualitative Market Research: An International Journal, 6*(2), 111–118. https://doi.org/10.1108/13522750310470118

Williams, J. T. B. (2019). Measles, mumps, and communion: A Vision for vaccine policy. *Health Affairs, 38*(11), 1944–1947. https://doi.org/10.1377/hlthaff.2019.00446

Wirtz, J., & Mattila Anna, S. (2003). The effects of consumer expertise on evoked set size and service loyalty. *Journal of Services Marketing, 17*(7), 649–665. https://doi.org/10.1108/08876040310501223

Zhang, J., & Shavitt, S. (2003). Cultural values in advertisements to the Chinese X-generation–promoting modernity and individualism. *Journal of Advertising, 32*(1), 23–33. https://doi.org/10.1080/00913367.2003.10639047

Zhang, Y., & Neelankavil, J. P. (1997). The influence of culture on advertising effectiveness in China and the USA: A cross-cultural study. *European Journal of Marketing, 31*(2), 134–149. https://doi.org/10.1108/03090569710157106

Zinkhan, G. M., Johnson, M., & Christian Zinkhan, F. (1992). Differences between product and services television commercials. *Journal of Services Marketing, 6*(3), 59–66. https://doi.org/10.1108/08876049210035944

15

Innovative Practices in Management Education in India

Sushant Kumar Mishra, Gopal Prasad Mahapatra, and Chirag Dagar

Introduction

Management as an educational field gained significance during the years marked by the industrial revolution, mercantilism, and market reforms. It gained momentum with a promise to contribute to business management. Borrowing from different disciplines, such as psychology,

S. K. Mishra · G. P. Mahapatra
Indian Institute of Management Bangalore, Bengaluru, Karnataka, India
e-mail: sushantam@iimb.ac.in

G. P. Mahapatra
e-mail: gopal.mahapatra@iimb.ac.in

C. Dagar (✉)
Shailesh J. Mehta School of Management, Indian Institute of Technology Bombay, Mumbai, India
e-mail: chirag.dagar@som.iitb.ac.in

© The Author(s), under exclusive license to Springer Nature Switzerland AG 2022
A. Pandey et al. (eds.), *Indigenous Indian Management*, Palgrave Studies in Indian Management,
https://doi.org/10.1007/978-3-030-87906-8_15

sociology, accounting, economics, and law, the scholarship of management expanded. Subsequently, the management literature contributed to managers' training, future managers' development through education, and the expansion of research in management scholarship. The evolution and expansion of markets popularized management education among the youth.

In modern times, the Emlyon Business School in Lyon, France, was probably the first business school established by the Lyon Chamber of Commerce and Industry in 1872. In 1881, the Wharton School of Business at the University of Pennsylvania, USA, was established by Joseph Wharton, an American entrepreneur and industrialist. The other business schools that were established during this time were Booth School of Business in 1898 (Chicago University), Harvard Business School in 1908 (Harvard University), and Kellogg School of Management in 1908 (North-western University). Many other universities in different continents joined the bandwagon of management education by starting their business schools. For instance, the London Business School (Federal University of London) was established in 1964, and the NUS Business School of Business (National University of Singapore) was established in 1965 (Jha & Kumar, 2012). Some stand-alone business schools like INSEAD (France) were established in 1957.

In India, the first management school offering management education, i.e., the Indian Institute of Social Welfare and Business Management started in 1954. It was followed by four universities: Andhra, Bombay, Delhi, and Madras, offering similar management programs (Philip, 1992). Since then, management education in India has come a long way. With the setting up of Indian Institutes of Management (IIMs) and to respond to the rising demand for managers, many universities started offering management courses thereafter. Post-liberalization of the economy in 1991, the private sector, including some of the corporate houses, entered the management education space. Consequently, private B-schools in the country offering Post-Graduate Diploma in Management have flourished (Jha & Kumar, 2012).

The relevance of management education is reflected in its ever-growing popularity globally. Management education, specifically the MBA, is a popular discourse and business qualification in the world.

It is recognized as a form of qualification for a career in management nearly by all the countries in the world. There are 800 business schools in the USA and Europe alone, and over 100,000 MBA graduates each year (Clegg & Ross-Smith, 2003). A similar trend is visible in India as well. Management education has been the most coveted and desired professional qualification among the youth pursuing higher education in India. The IIMs are known to attract some of the brightest students of the country. As a result, management education has stood the test of time and attained significance in the institutional scenario of higher education in the country and beyond. The rising number of management institutes offering a variety of programs reflects the demand that management education generates. Put differently, in India, management education represents an assured path to realize one's personal aspirations, professional success, and societal recognition (Babu & Thakur, 2017).

Despite the popularity and relevance, management education has been criticized on various grounds, including fragmentation of subject matters (Porter & McKibbin, 1988), overemphasis on analysis at the cost of skill development related to managing and leading, the relevance of MBA knowledge to professional application (Pfeffer & Fong, 2004), and broader considerations (Ghoshal, 2005) to name a few. As a consequence, a call for holistic learning integrating experiential pedagogies in the management education domain has been made. In response, various approaches and practices such as role-plays, large group exercises, simulations, case studies, and reflection have been incorporated in management courses (Kisfalvi & Oliver, 2015; Waddock & Lozano, 2013). The experiential learning approach considers "transformation of experience" (Kolb, 1984, p. 38) as the basis of learning wherein the learner is actively involved in the learning process. Business schools in India have also endeavored to develop and update the curriculum enabling the students to effectively apply management knowledge absorbed in the classroom. By designing courses and incorporating specific initiatives and practices in the curriculum, some of the business schools in India have tried to implement experiential learning, thereby keeping pace with the changing business environment, industry needs, and contributing towards achieving bigger objectives.

This chapter presents an overview of the innovative pedagogies adopted by a few leading management schools in India, which touch upon the 'Being' and 'Doing' aspects in management education. First, it briefly discusses the evolution of management education in India, specialized management education, and private sector participation in management education. Second, it delineates the new approach to management education, emphasizing experiential learning and the aspects of knowing, doing, and being. Third, the chapter elaborates on the specific pedagogical initiatives employed by Indian business schools classified under four levels (individual, department, institute, and collective).

Management Education in India

In India, management education evolved from the discipline of Commerce. The first School of Commerce, the Commercial School of Pachaiyappas' Charities, was established in Chennai (then Madras) in 1886. In 1903, the British Government began Commerce classes focusing on accounting, secretarial practices, and business communication at the Presidency College (Calcutta). Other notable colleges set up before India's independence were the Sydenham College (Mumbai) in 1913 and the Commercial College, later renamed as Shri Ram College of Commerce (New Delhi) in 1920. These colleges introduced business education in modern India (Gupta et al., 2003).

Post-independence, the Government of India attempted to enhance vocational skills and management education's social status (Gupta et al., 2003). The Indian Institute of Social Welfare & Business Management was established in 1953 and is officially regarded as India's first Management Institute. Subsequently, four universities, namely the Andhra, Bombay, Madras, and Delhi University, formed departments for management studies (Saha, 2012). During the same time, the individuals in the Indian industry also initiated activities toward management education. Sir Jahangir Ghandy of TISCO (Tata Iron and Steel Co.) formed the Board of Management Studies in 1955. The task of the Board was "evolving courses of study in management, advising All India Technical Council on the selection of suitable institutions to offer courses in management, laying down standards of the conduct of examinations leading to the award of National Diplomas and Certificates in management, and generally promoting coordinated development of management education in the country" (Philip, 1992, p. 20).

In the early 1960s, two prominent institutions were established by the Government of India. Indian Institutes of Management (IIM) at Calcutta in 1961 (West Bengal) and IIM Ahmedabad in 1961 (Gujarat). These institutes were established with the grant obtained from the Ford Foundation. IIM Calcutta was established in collaboration with the MIT Sloan School of Management and IIM Ahmedabad in collaboration with Harvard Business School (Philip, 1992). The Administrative Staff College of India (ASCI) at Hyderabad was established in 1958 on the Administrative Staff College lines at Henley-on-Thames, UK (Kumar, 2019). ASCI provided training to mid-career managers. The third Indian Institute of Management was established in Bangalore (Karnataka) in 1973. The institute was founded with a public sector orientation (Shukla, 2013). During the early globalization period (2001–2010), IIM Bangalore shifted its focus and began general management courses. Subsequently, the fourth IIM was established at Lucknow in 1984, followed by IIM Kozhikode and IIM Indore in 1996.

In the 1970s, the technical institutions started offering management programs. A majority of these institutions entered the field of management education by setting up departments. Some notable departments are the Industrial and Management Engineering at the Indian Institute of Technology (IIT) Kanpur (in 1974). In 1976, IIT Delhi established the School of System and Management Studies (Mahajan, 2015). Other notable institutions are the Vinod Gupta School of Management (IIT Kharagpur: 1993), the Shailesh J. Mehta School of Management, IIT Bombay (established in 1995, renamed in 2000), and the Department of Management Studies at IIT Roorkee, IIT Madras (in 2001), which were set up.

Specialized Management Education

While the establishment of IIMs and other management departments at various universities gave a boom to management education in India, there was a cleavage between the management graduation and the needs of particular sectors (Sriram, 2007). In an attempt to address the sectoral problems, several institutes were established. In 1928, the Indian Institute of Banking and Finance, modeled after the London Institute of Banking and Finance, was established. The Dorabji Tata Graduate School of Social Work (later renamed as Tata Institute of Social Sciences) was established for professional training in social work in 1936. Similarly, for the rural sector, the Institute of Rural Management [IRMA] was set up in 1979 under the leadership of Dr. Verghese Kurien, the then Chairman of the National Dairy Development Board (Sriram, 2007). National Institute of Industrial Engineering was created by the Government of India in 1963 to offer programs in management exclusively for engineers (Mahajan, 2015). The Indian Institute of Foreign Trade was set up in 1963 by India's Government as an autonomous organization to professionalize foreign trade. The National Institute of Bank Management, Pune, was established in 1968 to serve the banking industry (Ganesh, 1980). The Indian Institute of Forest Management was set up in 1982 in Bhopal (Madhya Pradesh) to provide specialized management education for India's entire forestry system.

Private Institutions of Management Education

While post-independence, the Government of India established institutions to impart management education in India, several private institutions were also established in the country to provide more opportunities for the same. Jesuits (the Society of Jesus) contributed to management education by establishing the Xavier Labour Relations Institute in 1949 in Jamshedpur, Jharkhand, India. Many other prominent Jesuit institutes that offered management education include Loyola, Xavier Institute of Management Bhubaneswar, and Goa Institute of Management. The

Management Development Institute (MDI), a private business school, was also established in 1973 by the Industrial Finance Corporation of India in Gurgaon. In 1981, the International Management Institute was established, the first corporate-sponsored business school by the RP Goenka Group (RPG). With the opening of the economy and the liberalization of the education system, since 2000, many private institutes have flourished in India. In 2001, the Indian School of Business was established in Hyderabad in collaboration with the Wharton School, Kellogg, and the London Business School. Many prominent institutions such as the Symbiosis Institute of Business Management Pune, the Narsee Monjee Institute of Management Studies, Institute of Management Technology Ghaziabad, S. P. Jain Institute of Management and Research, and the ICFAI Business School expanded management education in India. During this time, the 14 new IIMs were established by the Government of India. By the year 2016, there were more than 5,500 business schools in India.[1] According to a report by ASSOCHAM, only 20 percent of students get the job offer.[2] While lower-ranking schools lack quality, the high-ranking schools are striving to enhance their quality and global rankings. One aspect is the content delivery in management education.

New Approach to Management Education

The objective of educationists and educational administrators for centuries is to make education holistic and orient it towards the overall development of the participants. While management education started with scientific management, increasing efforts are noticed in making it stakeholder centric and effective. With the increasing popularity of management education in various continents, the attention to make it more impactful has grown too. In this regard, scholars have highlighted the problems associated with the MBA programs. In a critical study,

[1] Accessed from https://www.assocham.org/newsdetail.php?id=5651.%20 on August 18, 2020.

[2] Accessed from https://www.assocham.org/newsdetail.php?id=6637 on October 15, 2020.

Boyatzis et al. (2002, p. 150) emphasized that "a major challenge to MBA education is to develop the ability to use management knowledge."

Further, they argued that "cognitive and emotional intelligence competencies can be developed in MBA students, but not with a typical MBA curriculum." The other concerns about the MBA programs are the dearth of practical experiences (Salas et al., 2009), skills (Bennis & O'Toole, 2005), values, and practices (Ghoshal, 2005). MBA programs are referred to as "silos" that lacks sufficient integrative elements (Navarro, 2008), raising doubts on the legitimacy of business schools (Alajoutsijärvi et al., 2015). For example, we found that the curricula followed in the top 10 business schools in India are the 'silo' approach to management education (separate areas such as finance, marketing, and human resource), with emphasis on the knowing aspect of education.

While some scholars have provided critics of management education (Vaara & Fay, 2011), others have attempted to find out ways to improve the learning of the participants in the MBA program. For example, the use of technology, simulation-based learning (Salas et al., 2009), problem-based learning (Ungaretti et al., 2015), and integrative live cases (Venkat et al., 2019) are some of the initiatives used in academia. Besides, to make an impact, management education scholars have explored the practical aspects of management education. For example, scholars from Chicago Booth (Davis & Hogarth, 2013)[3] proposed three essential determinants of effective management education: conceptual knowledge, domain knowledge, and action skills. Similarly, scholars from Harvard Business School (Datar et al., 2010) identified three aspects of management education, namely the knowing, being, and doing.

'Knowing' refers to the cognitive aspects of management (i.e., what does one know or need to know about management and particularly business management like marketing, finance, operations management, and so on and the situations in which managers have to work which are covered in the courses like business environment, economics, etc.). 'Being' is the next aspect of management education, which is based on the premise that it is who you are affecting your ability to manage. The

[3] https://research.chicagobooth.edu/harrydavis/about-the-davis-center/about-harry-davis, accessed on November 4, 2019.

underlying values, assumptions, and beliefs about the world and the way of its functioning can shape our approach to management. Martin and Mirraboopa (2003) posited that individual's ways of being is context-dependent. According to them "We are part of the world as much as it is part of us, existing within a network of indigenous people ways of being mean relations amongst Entities that are reciprocal and occur in certain contexts. This determines and defines for us rights to be earned and bestowed as we carry out rites to country, self and others — our Ways of Being" (Martin & Mirraboopa, 2003, p. 209).

The 'Doing' aspect is about how management is practiced, applying the functional and integrative knowledge, using technology, building relationships, and networking. With an increasing focus on experiential learning and holistic education, scholars have focused on reflective learning. For example, Kolb's four learning styles, namely the opportunity for concrete experience, reflective observations, abstract conceptualization, and active experimentation, are used in the Multidisciplinary Action Projects at the Ross School of Business (see Datar et al., 2010). Peltier et al. (2006) presented "a global model of reflective learning" to engage the participants in higher levels of learning. In a similar tone, Berdrow and Evers (2010) highlighted the importance of developing "reflective practitioners" in modern organizations. Also, in a comprehensive study, Boyatzis and Saatcioglu (2008, p. 105) stressed that a "more holistic approach (i.e., developing knowledge, competencies, and values) could help dramatically improve our impact and the relevance of an MBA to their future work organizations." In this chapter, we have provided an overview on the innovative practices the management schools in India are incorporating to facilitate experiential learning in their curricula.

Management education in general, and specifically in India, over the decades appears to have been more focused on 'knowing' aspects. Knowing aspect has been criticized as it does not prepare the participants "to 'do' innovative thinking in the workplace" (Datar et al., 2010, p. 8). However, there are many institutions (at the individual level, area/department level, and institution level) trying to bring the 'being' aspect to the curriculum. In the following sections, we describe interesting practices followed by the educators in the management institutions to nurture 'being' aspects in regular management programs or executive programs in management. While scholars have focused on the concept of experiential learning (Kolb & Kolb, 2005), many institutions are practicing experiential learning (being and doing).

Innovative Pedagogies in Indian Business Schools: Classification and Description

We have classified the innovative pedagogies into four levels, namely individual faculty level (Level 1), department/Area level (Level 2), institution level (Level 3), and collective level, i.e., more than one institution (Level 4). In the following section, we elaborate on the pedagogy followed in Indian business schools. In addition to published papers, we collected information from websites of selected business schools, talking to officials of concerned institutions, reports, and newspapers. For this analysis, we interviewed faculty who have designed the respective courses, faculty coordinators, program directors, and student participants to obtain insights about the details of the courses, the conduct and components, assessments involved, and overall experience in offering and participating in the courses.

Level 1: Individual Faculty Level

Sociology of Bazzar[4] at Amrut Mody School of Management (AMSM), Ahmedabad

The Amrut Mody School of Management (AMSM) is located in Ahmedabad, in the Gujarat state of India. Ahmedabad is blessed with many business communities such as the Jains, Marwaris, Sindhis, Cheliyas,

[4] The authors are grateful to Prof. Abrar Ali Saiyed for providing the inputs. Prof. Abrar has designed and the course is in demand for several years now. Prof. Abrar is a faculty in the Entrepreneurship and Family Business Area at Ahmedabad University, Gujarat.

Bohras, Khojas, Parsis, Purohits, and Memons. This course helps the participants to study the ancient markets from the point of social, entrepreneurial, and significance of the communities. The course on entrepreneurship is a blend of both theory and practice. The first-year participants study the city's markets such as the old market, Sunday market, and flower market to understand the art and science of doing business. Field visits are common in other streams such as sociology and anthropology. In management education, students in many business schools do their internship, in which they work in an organization for about two months to understand the nuances of business. This practice is followed for two reasons. One, exposure to the functioning of real organizations. Two, possibility of converting the internship into a regular job offer. However, field visit in an informal setting as part of the course is unusual in Indian setting. The participants reach out to these trading communities to get tips on doing business in a better way. According to the professor who designed the course, "the idea is to expose participants to different aspects of entrepreneurship through experiential learning." The course provides the exposure and helps the participants understand the challenges encountered by the entrepreneurs. The participants shared their learning from different business communities. The interaction with the entrepreneurs and the observation of their business help the participants learn better in the classroom.

In the context of experiential learning, scholars have also argued in favor of bringing experiences inside the classroom. For instance, it is argued that "the experiential classroom becomes a space that can allow intense situations involving frustration, anger, and conflict as well as playfulness and discovery to arise but also to be contained" (Kisfalvi & Oliver, 2015, p. 722). In the following section, we describe one such practice followed at Indian Institute of Management Bangalore.

Management Principles of Bhagavad Gita (MPBG)

In this course, the participants were taught the management principles based on the Bhagavat Gita. The concerned faculty based on his individual expertise of Sanskrit language and Indic Wisdom of *Bhagavad*

Gita (*Gita* is a part of the Epic *Mahabharata*) prepared the course to bring the experience of *Mahabharata* to the classroom. This course is an elective for the second year MBA participants where they are taught to reflect and explore implications in business leadership and personal life. Specific linkage of strategies to action (*Karma yoga*), devotion (*Bhakti yoga*), knowledge (*Gnana yoga*) and Wisdom, and linkage with various outcomes in the materialistic/business world as well as its implications for leadership and daily life with exploration, practice, and reflection are attempted in the course. Starting as a weekend self-development/study and contemplation session over the years, it has evolved into a full-fledge management/leadership development elective. The participants remember the learning from the course years after their graduation.

The courses discussed above are driven by the expertise and interest of individual faculty members. Though the course is well received by the students, it is entirely the effort of these individual faculty members. The continuation of faculty-led courses depends on the availability of the faculty members, their interest, and the support of the institute/area. There are many such instances (e.g., the creativity course at IIMA), where courses could not continue due to faculty mobility or retirement.

Self-Awareness and Interpersonal Skills Course

This is a core course offered in the MBA program at Shailesh J. Mehta School of Management, IIT Bombay. Having a dual-component design, the first part of the course (self-awareness) focuses on the intra-personal dimension comprising of self-inquiry, while the second part builds on the interpersonal dimension *vis a vis* enhancing communication skills. The underlying idea behind the design of the course is that the human self is composed of physical, mental, emotional, social, and vital aspects; hence, the pedagogy of the course shall also be integrative in nature, touching upon all these facets.

The course integrates the traditional pedagogical methodologies (lectures, presentations, and discussions) with what is known as contemplative pedagogy (Zajonc, 2013). Therein, the course content comprising of self-regulation, emotional awareness, strengths, and personal vision is discussed by employing a mix of tools and frameworks such as time structuring matrix, *pancha-kosha* framework, energy audit, and so on. Also, the practice of reflection is emphasized by the instructor to examine the course content in light of the day-to-day experiences and events via photo-voices, group reflections, and mind mapping.

Further, a key element of the course pertains to offering Yoga (YBPs) and mindfulness-based Practices. As part of two stages, in the introductory session of 2 hours, training is offered in the externally expressed practices of Yoga like *Yamas* and *Niyamas*, *Asanas,* and *Pranayamas* based on the Common Yoga Protocol (CYP) recommended by the Ministry of AYUSH, Government of India.[5] Subsequently, a shorter version of the practices drawn from the CYP is conducted during the classes twice a week. The practices include five categories: (1) unfreezing through reverberation and body-tapping; (2) *Asanas* like *Vrikshasana, Hasthpadasana,* and *Tikonasana;* (3) *Pranayama* includes deep breathing (*Dirgha Pranayama*), high-frequency yoga breathing (HFYB; *KapalBhati*), alternate nostril breathing (*AnulomVilom*), and breathing with humming (*Bhramari*); and (4) Meditation (includes "Body Scan" and "Sitting Meditation").

Embodied and mind-body practices such as Yoga and mindfulness entail a holistic view of self and multi-dimensional well-being. The constituting elements of Yoga and mindfulness-based practices can have potential implications on time and energy management, effective learning, ethical orientation, and harmonious behavior among the students.

Research studies conducted by the instructor and his team support the efficacy of the interventions practiced in the course. They found that YBPs and mindfulness help in retaining attention to one task or a lesser number of tasks at any moment, which prevents the dissipation of energy and increases emotional and mental engagement in the medium term (Kudesia et al., 2020). Another study further demonstrates that Yoga and mindfulness-based interventions help in developing the level of

[5] https://dipp.gov.in/sites/default/files/Internatioanl_Yoga_Day_2016.pdf.

moral reasoning (a precursor of ethical behavior) by increasing compassion and decreasing ego-centric bias in a few weeks of practice (Pandey et al., 2018).

AIM2Flourish

At the Weatherhead School of Management, Case Western Reserve University, the Fowler Center for Business as an Agent of World Benefit (BAWB) created the AIM2Flourish program.[6] Considering the generally held negative belief about businesses (the instances of unethical practices, pollution, hostile takeover), the program aims at bringing a shift toward 'Business for Good' perspective by discovering stories of entrepreneurs and business leaders engaged in creating innovations for positive change.

AIM2Flourish is an experiential learning assignment, which starts in the classroom to learn about the strengths-based Appreciative Inquiry (AI) approach and the United Nations Sustainable Development Goals (SDGs). It moves out of the classroom wherein students identify, conduct in-person interview (AI), and write stories of businesses or entrepreneurs meeting one or more of the SDGs yet doing well financially. The stories are published on AIM2Flourish.com to further motivate the larger community (students, investors, and businesses).

Based on the data available on AIM2Flourish website, instructors (faculty members) from a number of Indian institutes have adopted the program in their course curriculum as means of imparting experiential learning. For reference, some of the institutes include Narsee Monjee Institute of Management Studies, Presidency University, Osmania University, Goa Institute of Management, Indian School Business, Shailesh J. Mehta School of Management (IIT Bombay), Xavier Labour Relations Institute, and Institute of Management Technology, Ghaziabad.[7]

The website also shares the stories of the respective businesses and their innovations identified by the students in India[8] which range

[6] Accessed from https://aim2flourish.com/about-us.

[7] Accessed from https://aim2flourish.com/schools/p2?location=IN.

[8] Accessed from https://aim2flourish.com/innovations/p2?schoolLocation=IN.

from providing sustainable energy solutions, waste management, natural disposables, clean energy, hydroponics, sustainable supermarkets, eco-friendly architecture, tree-free paper, sustainable and eco-fashion, and many more.

Level 2: Department Level

Explorations in Role & Identity (ERI) at IIM Ahmedabad

IIM Ahmedabad (IIMA) was set up in 1961. It is declared as an Institute of National Importance (INI) by the Government of India. INI is a status conferred on the selected public higher education institutions in India that serve pivotal players in developing highly skilled personnel in India. The INI status is passed by the Act of Parliament in India. The Motto of the IIMA in Sanskrit language is "Vidhya Viniyogat Vikashaha," i.e., in English language it reads as "Progress through the Application of Knowledge." Explorations in Role & Identity (ERI) as a course was started about three decades back by two professors from Organisational Behaviour (OB) Area. Though the concerned faculty members have retired from their work at IIMA, the course is continuing. ERI is an experience-based learning course; hence, it is designed on the assumption that an individual requires space (*sthan*), time (*kala*), and someone (*patra*) with whom he or she can reflect on the journey of their life. The focus of this course is on relating to the self and others. It enables the participants to answer a few critical "being" and "becoming" related questions. For example, the participants make an inward exploration to explain who they are, the meaning and purpose of their individual life. In addition, they explore how they shape their own life and what they offer to the world.

The methodology followed in the course is highly participative and exploratory. No solutions or specific answers are given. Each participant is invited to share whatever aspects of the journey of life and relationships which he/she wishes to share. There are no compulsions for specificities of sharing. There is only an invitation, which an individual gives himself/herself for sharing and reflection. The participants are required to maintain their individual logbook of reflection for each day of the program. They are encouraged to do a reflective book review. Finally, the participants are taken to a remote place for about a week to reflect on themselves, and they are expected to write an autobiography relating to the learning, concepts, and experience reflected in the ERI.

Indian Philosophy for Leadership Excellence[9]

The Indian Philosophy for Leadership Excellence is a course in the Organizational Behavior area offered at XLRI, Jamshedpur, Jharkhand.

Leadership holds a special significance for organizations, given its criticality for their success and growth (Sarros et al., 2008). The Indian Philosophy for Leadership Excellence course is designed with a focus on the Indian perspective concerning effective (outstanding) leadership. Considering that Indian view is shaped by its diverse cultures and traditions, the course invites the participants to explore the philosophical heritage of India to study leadership from an approach that is novel and different from the Western view.

The course aims to build an appreciation of the Indian conception of leadership by discussing the need for an Indian perspective on leadership and integrating the concepts of *Purushartha* (*dharma*, *artha*, *kaama*, and *moksha*), *lokasamgraha*, *svabhava* and *svadharma*, and *rajaniti*. In light of the above deliberation, the course discusses the elements and personal attributes of outstanding leadership, how outstanding leaders create meaning for their followers, how they promote collaboration, nurture motivation, and manage conflicts. Further, the course dwells on the issues and challenges that may arise while following the Indian philosophy of business.

On the part of students, the 3-credit elective course encompasses reading material (cases, research papers) covering the ideas of workplace spirituality, consciousness, transformational leadership, and mindfulness in leadership. It also discusses the management issues based on scriptures: decision-making (*Mahabharata*) and holistic business management

---

[9] The authors are grateful to Prof. Alok Kumar for his inputs. Prof. Alok is an Assistant Professor (Organization Behavior) at XLRI.

(*Bhagavad Gita*), and emphasizes an openness for Indian ideas to discover one's leadership potential and a willingness to think and reflect. A key component of the course includes writing a reflection paper. The reflection paper offers the students an opportunity to examine and reflect upon their own lives in light of Indian philosophy. It involves a student to consider a pressing issue in her/his life, which might pertain to the personal or interpersonal domain and may be aspirational or problematic in nature. Subsequently, the student explains in detail the key philosophical principles employed for analyzing the issue and one's learnings, and the course of action ascertained to manage the issue.

NGO Block Fieldwork[10]: Rural Practicum for MA—HRM&LR Students: TISS, Mumbai

The Tata Institute of Social Sciences (TISS) was established in 1936 with the name of a renowned industrialist in India Sir Dorabji Tata. The institute was named as the "Sir Dorabji Tata Graduate School of Social Work" in Mumbai. In the year 1944, it was renamed as the 'Tata Institute of Social Sciences.' In line with the vision of the institute, the MA (HRM&LR) program aims "to develop students into professionally competent and socially sensitive management graduates" and "to sensitize students to the social, political, economic, and ecological environments of the society.[11]" One of how the above objectives are achieved is through the classroom lectures covered in the foundation courses in the first year. Another means of exposing and sensitizing our students to social realities is the "NGO Block Fieldwork" in the fourth semester.

In the last few years, almost all leading management institutes have recognized the need for exposing their students to the economic and social realities of rural India in the course of their management education. Within TISS also, many courses, e.g., social entrepreneurship, disaster studies, social work, and habitat studies, have a rural practicum

[10] The Authors are grateful to the valuable support by Prof. S. Palo, Dean (HRM& OD), TISS, Mumbai.

[11] Accessed from https://admissions.tiss.edu/view/10/admissions/ma-admissions/ma-in-human-resource-management-labour-relations/ on July 25, 2020.

program. The students of the batch of 2014–2016 participated in a ten-day field trip to Meerut, Lucknow, and Varanasi to help the Uttar Pradesh Skill Development Mission (UPSDM) in developing skills in the traditional sectors such as sports goods, chikankari, and silk handlooms. These students till date report that this experience was their most memorable and impactful learning experience during their two years at TISS.

The practices mentioned above are the illustrations of innovative methods used at the department level. Being the colleague of the same department/area, the other faculty members learned the experiences, values, and practices of the instructors and continued to offer the course even after the initial faculty members have superannuated from the institute. The course has moved from the individual level to the area level (e.g., the ERI course offered by the OB Area at IIMA). It minimizes the dependence on the individual faculty member, facilitates in getting the support from the institute, and has, in many ways, been institutionalized as an inherent part of the MBA curriculum.

Level 3: Institution Level

Rural Engagement Program (REP)[12] at IIM Indore

IIM Indore is an IIM set up by Government of India in 1996. Rural Engagement Program (REP) at IIM Indore is a decade-old program as a part of the mandatory curriculum for the first-year MBA participants at IIM Indore. The objective of the program is to sensitize future managers and entrepreneurs regarding various schemes executed by the government for the upliftment and enhancement of rural areas, to study the operational challenges, and to analyze their effectiveness. Every year, a theme is decided in collaboration with the state government and UNICEF, an international organization. Based on the selected themes, projects are allotted to more than a hundred teams, each of which consists of five to six participants. For each team, the

---

[12] The authors are thankful to Dr. Himanshu Rai, Director, IIM Indore for sharing the information with us.

schedule is pre-decided for a week-long stay, which includes visits to rural schools, households, local offices, and other public places. Participants have an opportunity to communicate with the officials of *Gram Panchayat* (village council) and *Zila Parishad* (district council), who execute the policies, and villagers who are the beneficiaries of the same. The participant teams obtain the required information regarding the implementation of various government schemes, understand execution challenges faced by the officials, and identify operational gaps on the part of the government. At the same time, the participants research to understand the expectations of the villagers from the government to solve their problems. The reports, including observations and suggestions provided by these teams, are then shared with the Government of Madhya Pradesh. In addition to getting sensitized to social issues, these future managers also tend to acknowledge gratitude toward the privileges of urban life, which until then go unnoticed. The experience of some of the participants is provided below.

According to a female participant, "REP was one of the most memorable experiences at IIM Indore, and it sensitized me towards the way of life through unique interactions with villagers." Some participants changed their behaviors after experiencing rural India. For example, according to a participant, "after encountering a lack of the basic facilities in the village, I stopped wasting water and electricity of the hostel rooms which were earlier taken for granted and consumed with entitlement." The program is a step forward to help the participants to become a socially responsible leader.

Rural Retreat[13]: XISS, Ranchi Rural Retreat for PM & IR Students

Xavier Institute of Social Service (XISS) is located in Ranchi, the capital of the state of Jharkhand in India. It was established by Fr. M. A. Windey with the objective of training young minds on Rural Development, Personnel Management, and Industrial Relations. Rural Camp

[13] The authors are grateful to Prof. R. K. Agrawal, HOD, PM&IR, XISS, Ranchi for his valuable support.

has been an integral part of the Personnel Management and Industrial Relations (PMIR) program since its inception at XISS. The department organizes a retreat in association with some reputed NGOs like Society for Rural Industrialization (SRI) at Bariatu, Ranchi, Animation Rural Outreach Services (AROUSE) at Gumla, Jharkhand, and others. The retreat provides the students the opportunity to visit the remote areas (actual Bharat) and to discuss the societal problems and major issues with eminent social workers and activists. Bharat is the name of India in *Hindi* language. About 47% of Indian population are in agriculture, and about 22% live below the poverty line.[14] These people live in rural India and relatively less educated, poor. This world is called the Bharat. On the other hand, many people stay in urban areas, enjoy a great lifestyle, and speak foreign language. Their world is called India. There is a clear division in rural (Bharat) versus urban (India) areas. The purpose of Rural Retreat is to develop student's self-confidence and provide an opportunity to stay in the rural areas, learn from them, connect with nature, connect with natural resource management, connect with a crisis situation, and compare life between Bharat and India. During their stay in a rural camp, they also interact with villagers, village leaders, and Self-Help Groups or empowered women in different villages.

The retreat is an eye-opener for HR students for thinking out of the box, and they enjoy various sessions as a single family. Though the faculty members are supervising them, it is their program, and they are taking all the initiatives to make the program successful and meaningful.

Leadership Experiential Action Program (LEAP): Karma-Yoga

Great Lakes Institute of Management is located at Manamai village near Mahabalipuram, a UNESCO Heritage Site 50 km south of Chennai, Tamil Nadu. The Leadership Experiential Action Program (LEAP), known as Karma-Yoga, is an integral part of the two management programs that Great Lakes offer: first-year Post-Graduate Program

[14] Accessed from https://www.cia.gov/library/publications/the-world-factbook/geos/in.html on October 15, 2020.

in Management (PGPM) and second-year Post-Graduate Diploma in Management (PGDM). Karma-Yoga Project is accredited to Principles of Responsible Management Education (PRME), imparting responsible management education whereby it nurtures students to create sustainable value for business and society.

Realizing the challenge of effective leadership, the course is founded on the objective 'to connect students with ground realities and experientially learn transformational leadership.' Great Lakes has adopted 28 surrounding villages for the LEAP, wherein, as a part of the program, students visit the Karma-Yoga villages every week. Extended over two terms, the engagement in the first term is compulsory, while participation in the second term is voluntary.

The distinguishing aspect of the Karma-Yoga Program lies in its mission. Rather than having a short-term ad hoc orientation to the problems in the villages, the aim is to empower them on a continuous basis and make them self-efficacious to lead a better quality of life.[15] The students endeavor to build rapport with the designated villages via constant interactions and discussions to understand the status quo, and motivate people toward betterment through constructive suggestions and strategies, and over the years leading to lasting ties and concrete value addition.[16]

The key projects that have been implemented through the Karma-Yoga Program focus on sustainable development goals (SDGs) comprising of education, health, agriculture, and small business. For instance, with respect to the goal of poverty, students have carried out livelihood training and establishing kitchen gardens; for promoting good health and well-being, students have conducted medical camps, health and hygiene awareness; concerning the goal of quality education, students have organized spoken English and computer education classes.

[15] Accessed from https://www.greatlakes.edu.in/chennai/pgpm/karmayoga.

[16] The authors are thankful to Dr. Arulsamy, Faculty Coordinator for the Karma-Yoga Project, for his inputs and student participants for sharing their experiences. Dr. Arulsamy credits the support of Dr. Bala V. Balachandran (Chairman and Dean Emeritus), and Dr. Suresh Ramanathan (Dean and Principal) for the successful functioning of the program.

Students share their experience describing that "Karma-Yoga Program offers an opportunity to learn management and leadership in a setting that is quite distinct from an organization or classroom. Although challenging at times, it is surely big learning." Further, "Karma-Yoga Program acts as a platform to firstly get to know the people, the demography of the village and subsequently try to identify and address some of the key problems that they are facing. Coming from a privileged background, it gives an opportunity to delve into and address the real-life problems faced by people."

Non-classroom Learning: Development of Corporate Citizenship (DOCC)[17]

The Non-Classroom Learning (NCL) initiatives at S. P. Jain Institute of Management and Research (SPJIMR), Mumbai, Maharashtra, build on the ideas of living a life of authenticity, meaning, and inner satisfaction. It offers three levels of learning: self-awareness (understanding oneself), self-management (impact of self-awareness on intra- and interpersonal behavior), and societal awareness (understanding societal needs and the idea of Bharat). The five NCL initiatives comprise of *Abhyudaya* (mentorship program for underprivileged children), ADMAP (roles in committees supporting institute's administration), DOCC, PG-Lab (course on personal leadership and team-building via experiential exercises), and Science of Spirituality (integrating insights from Eastern Wisdom traditions and the field of mindfulness for inner fulfillment and build leadership capabilities).[18]

Emerging from the call for enhancing the value addition of the academic curriculum, development of the institute, and contribution to the greater society, DOCC was envisioned and is currently a 25-years-old course at SPJIMR. The course aims to expose the students to the Indian ethos and culture by working on projects in the social sector

[17] The authors are grateful to Prof. Chandrika Parmar for her support and the inputs. Prof. Parmar is an Associate Professor (Social Sector) at SPJIMR and the Program Director of DOCC.

[18] Accessed from https://www.spjimr.org/overviewnonclassroom.

encompassing health, education, aging, livelihood, women empowerment, climate change, and sustainability, to name a few, by way of a social internship. It is an institute level, 3-credit course conducted at the completion of first year requiring a full-time commitment of 4 weeks. Based on the requirement of the organizations, i.e., the 250+ partners and tie-ups across 26 states of the country, the students are randomly allocated to travel and stay with their respective organizations.

The social internship constitutes a complete on-site immersion at real locations of the partnering organizations, thereby providing a window to witness the ground reality and the unexplored side of India, i.e., rural India. It facilitates students to apply their in-class learnings in an unstructured environment to arrive at viable solutions for the prevailing problems. Over the years, students have come up with varied solutions such as branding (*dhaga* brand), business proposals, digital marketing inputs, supply chain streamlining, and so on. It seeks to establish a symbiotic and enduring relationship between the visiting students and the community. This is evident from the fact that some of the tie-ups with the partnering organizations have been decade long with some new ones coming up, even internationally (Nepal and Bangladesh).

As part of the evaluation process, the students present their work and submit their report to both the partnering organization and the designated panel comprising of faculty, alumni, representatives from the social sector, and the corporates. The criteria for evaluation include (a) students' ability to pause and reflect, i.e., their first impressions on arrival, engagement with the community, experiences, and stories on the field; (b) students' social sensitivity, i.e., their ability to identify the pressing issues, understanding them and providing potential solutions; (c) project report submitted. The social internship underlying DOCC denotes an affirmative step in cultivating broader considerations and responsible management among business school students.

Rural Living and Learning Experience[19]: School of Rural Management, XUB

Xavier University (XUB) is located in Bhubaneswar, Odisha, India. The University has many schools, including the School of Rural Management. The School offers MBA program in Rural Management (RM). Rural Living and Learning Experience (RLLE) is a unique component of MBA (RM) Core course. During RLLE, two students (in exceptional case one or three) are assigned one village to stay for forty-five nights. The idea behind RLLE is that students get a first-hand experience of the village life. RLLE is founded on the efficacy of experiential learning and the importance of learning from the very people and communities they are expected to work with. RLLE is expected to lead students to cultivate the process of un-learning and examining their own biases and prejudices about contexts and providing opportunities to re-learn. This would enable the students to develop fresh perspectives and broaden their perspectives necessary for rural management professionals. The student needs to understand the challenges faced by the poor, deprived, and marginalized, in a rapidly changing social environment. The assignments, exercises, and documentation to be done during RLLE help the student to learn the pertinent and practical application of the classroom learnings and also enrich classroom discussion. Developing an understanding of social realities leads to a definitive commitment to the welfare of people.

The scheduling and execution of the programs are facilitated by the institutions. A dedicated team of members led by a faculty member takes charge of the program. Such programs at the institution level reduce the uncertainty related to the faculty interest, availability, resource constraint, and dealing with external stakeholders. In addition, it provides legitimacy to the program.

[19] The Authors are grateful to Dr. S. S. Singh, School of HRM Xavier University, Bhubaneswar, for his valuable support.

Level 4: Collective Level

The Himalayan Outbound Program (HOP) at IIM Indore

The program is a combination of trekking in the Himalayas along with challenging team activities. The students are forced to go beyond their comfort and overcome challenges as a team, which usually results in learning from their own experiences. Students are divided into groups and given limited resources to complete the problem at hand. The teams compete against each other in a real-life setting through a series of activities and games that focus on teamwork, cooperation, and overall individual capacity building. Participants get an understanding of what leadership implies. They learn that teamwork in such settings requires a high order of cooperative skills. They learn to recognize and utilize the talents of everyone in the team. Through the physicality of the trek, they discover that most personal limitations that they have are largely imagined. The learning in this program is deep, often lifelong. The popularity of HOP practiced at IIM Indore has generated interest in other institutions. The HOP is being adopted by other institutions.

Discussion and Conclusion

Individual experiences contribute to their professional development (Lynham, 2000). As a result, experience has long been regarded as necessary in honing the necessary skills. For example, interventions such as 360° feedback (Alimo-Metcalfe, 1998), assessment development centers (Church et al., 2017), and outbound training programs (Rhodes & Martin, 2014) have long been used to develop important competencies. Surprisingly, learning through individual experiences as a pedagogical approach is in a nascent stage. In this chapter, we build on the importance of experiential learning in MBA education. Experiential learning offers a unique opportunity to narrow the knowing-doing gap. It provides a uniquely different dimension to business education by giving students to see the problem in a holistic manner, think innovatively, appreciate the challenges due to resource constraint, reflect on the theory in use, and experience the emotions of managing the task, thus helping the participants grow (Datar et al., 2010). Further, we explored how the management institutions are using this experiential learning in their course curricula. While discussing the approaches used, we highlighted the practice at four levels: individual faculty level, department/area level, institution level, and the collective level.

Experiential learning requires a significant commitment of faculty time (Datar et al., 2010). The increasing popularity of experiential learning in management education raises several new opportunities and challenges for instructors (Kisfalvi & Oliver, 2015). Some of the concerns are the current practice of discipline-based training to the faculty members may not be well-suited to develop and deliver multidisciplinary projects. Shifting instructor roles from the traditional way of providing lecture to helping participants learn through their emotions is another challenge. Some initiatives, such as adjunct faculty members, are increasingly practiced in many institutions, to facilitate integrative, experiential learning. Institutions in India have also started using simulations, role-plays to facilitate experiential knowledge of the participants. Institutions need to find out ways to facilitate experiential learning of their participants.

In this chapter, we have captured a number of powerful illustrations of experiential learning modules that are adopted and practiced successfully over the years in many business schools in India. Some of these illustrations highlight the innovative approaches at the individual faculty level, department level, institution level, and beyond the level of the institutions. These illustrations highlight two broad aspects: one, the acceptance of 'being' and 'doing' is increasing in Indian business schools. Two, the acceptance of the innovative practices is not confined to one level; they are moving from the individual level to beyond the institutional level, indicating that the practices are gaining legitimacy both within and beyond the institutions. While the above illustrations indicate the effort by few institutions/centers or even select professors, it appears to be at the threshold of further growth.

We further believe that for the success of the experiential learning approach, the active involvement of various critical stakeholders such as the faculty members, participants, and deans/directors of the institutions plays a crucial role. The leadership at these institutions needs to facilitate ownership of the faculty members, so that other modes of learning make more considerable inroads to management education.

References

Alajoutsijärvi, K., Juusola, K., & Siltaoja, M. (2015). The legitimacy paradox of business schools: Losing by gaining? *Academy of Management Learning & Education, 14*, 277–291.

Alimo-Metcalfe, B. (1998). 360 degree feedback and leadership development. *International Journal of Selection and Assessment, 6*(1), 35–44.

Babu, R. R., & Thakur, M. (2017). The state of management education in India: Trajectories and pathways. In *Management education in India* (pp. 1–20). Springer.

Bennis, W. G., & O'Toole, J. (2005). How business schools lost their way. *Harvard Business Review*, 83/5, 96–104.

Berdrow, I., & Evers, E. T. (2010). Bases of competence: A framework for facilitating reflective learner-centered educational environments. *Journal of Management Education, 35*(3), 406–427.

Boyatzis, R. E., & Saatcioglu, A. (2008). A 20-year view of trying to develop emotional, social and cognitive intelligence competencies in graduate management education. *Journal of Management Development, 27*(1), 92–108.

Boyatzis, R. E., Stubbs, E. C., & Taylor, S. N. (2002). Learning cognitive and emotional intelligence competencies through graduate management education. *Academy of Management Learning & Education, 1*, 150–163.

Church, A. H., Giudice, M. D., & Margulies, A. (2017). All that glitters is not gold: Maximizing the impact of executive assessment and development efforts. *Leadership & Organization Development Journal, 38*(6), 765–779.

Clegg, S. R., & Ross-Smith, A. (2003). Revising the boundaries: Management education and learning in a postpositivist world. *Academy of Management Learning & Education, 2*(1), 85–98.

Datar, S. M., Garvin, D. A., & Cullen, P. G. (2010). *Rethinking the MBA: Business education at a crossroads*. Harvard Business School Publishing.

Ganesh, S. R. (1980). Performance of management education institutions: An Indian sampler. *Higher Education, 9*(3), 239–253.
Ghoshal, S. (2005). Bad management theories are destroying good management practices. *Academy of Management Learning and Education, 4*(1), 75–91.
Gupta, V., Gollakota, K., & Ancheri, S. (2003). Quality in business education: A study of the Indian context. Paper presented at the *Conferences on Business Education and Emerging Market Economies: Trends and Prospects*, USA, pp. 1–30.
Jha, S., & Kumar, M. (2012). Management education in India: Issues & challenges. Available at SSRN 2140807.
Kisfalvi, V., & Oliver, D. (2015). Creating and maintaining a safe space in experiential learning. *Journal of Management Education, 39*(6), 713–740.
Kolb, D. A. (1984). *Experiential learning: Experience as the source of learning and development* (Vol. 1). Prentice Hall.
Kolb, A. Y., & Kolb, D. A. (2005). Learning styles and learning spaces: Enhancing experiential learning in higher education. *Academy of Management Learning and Education, 4*(2), 193–212.
Kudesia, R. S., Pandey, A., & Reina, C. S. (2020). Doing more with less: Interactive effects of cognitive resources and mindfulness training in coping with mental fatigue from multitasking. *Journal of Management*. https://doi.org/10.1177/0149206320964570
Kumar, A. (2019). From Henley to Harvard at Hyderabad? (Post and Neo-) colonialism in management education in India. *Enterprise & Society, 20*(2), 366–400.
Lynham, S. A. (2000). Leadership development: A review of the theory and literature. In P. Kuchinke (Ed.), *Proceedings of the 2000 academy of human resource development annual meeting.* Baton Rouge, LA.
Mahajan, R. (2015). *India's management education growth story: A retrospect.* https://apps.aima.in/ejournal_new/articlesPDF/2%20Ritika%20Mahajan.pdf
Martin, K., & Mirraboopa, B. (2003). Ways of knowing, being and doing: A theoretical framework and methods for indigenous and indigenist research. *Journal of Australian Studies, 27*(76), 203–214.
Navarro, P. (2008). The MBA core curricula of top-ranked U.S. business schools: A study in failure? *Academy of Management Learning & Education,* 7(1), 108–123.

Pandey, A., Chandwani, R., & Navare, A. (2018). How can mindfulness enhance moral reasoning? An examination using business school students. *Business Ethics: A European Review, 27*(1), 56–71.

Pfeffer, J., & Fong, C. T. (2004). The business school 'business': Some lessons from the US experience. *Journal of Management Studies, 41*(8), 1501–1520.

Peltier, J. W., Hay, A., & Drago, W. (2006). Reflecting on reflection: Scale extension and a comparison of undergraduate business students in the United States and the United Kingdom. *Journal of Marketing Education, 28*(1), 5–16.

Philip, J. (1992). Management education in India: Past, present, and future. *Vikalpa, 17*(4), 19–24.

Porter, L. W., & McKibbin, L. E. (1988). *Management education and development: Drift or thrust into the 21st century?* McGraw-Hill.

Rhodes, H. M., & Martin, A. J. (2014). Behavior change after adventure education courses: Do work colleagues notice? *Journal of Experiential Education, 37*(3), 265–284.

Saha, G. G. (2012). Management education in India: Issues & concerns. *Journal of Information, Knowledge and Research in Business and Administration,* 35–36.

Salas, E., Wildman, J. L., & Piccolo, R. F. (2009). Using simulation-based training to enhance management education. *Academy of Management Learning & Education, 8*(4), 559–573.

Sarros, J. C., Cooper, B. K., & Santora, J. C. (2008). Building a climate for innovation through transformational leadership and organizational culture. *Journal of Leadership & Organizational Studies, 15*(2), 145–158.

Shukla, S. S. (2013). Management education in India issues and concerns. *International Journal of Education and Learning, 2*(2), 15–26.

Sriram, M. S. (2007). *Rural management education in India: A retrospect*. http://vslir.iima.ac.in:8080/jspui/handle/11718/232

Ungaretti, T., Thompson, K. R., Miller, A., & Peterson, T. O. (2015). Problem-based learning: Lessons from medical education and challenges for management education. *Academy of Management Learning & Education, 14*(2), 173–186.

Vaara, E., & Fay, E. (2011). How can a Bourdieusian perspective aid analysis of MBA education? *Academy of Management Learning and Education, 10*(1), 27–39.

Venkat, G., Garg, S., & Thapliyal, S. (2019). Integrative live case: A contemporary business ethics pedagogy. *Journal of Business Ethics, 155*(4), 1009–1032.

Waddock, S., & Lozano, J. M. (2013). Developing more holistic management education: Lessons learned from two programs. *Academy of Management Learning & Education, 12*(2), 265–284.

Zajonc, A. (2013). Contemplative pedagogy: A quiet revolution in higher education. *New Directions for Teaching and Learning, 134*, 83–94.

16

Emergence of Indian Management: Cultural Ideals, Uniqueness, and Behavioural Manifestations

Ashish Pandey, Dharm P. S. Bhawuk, and Pawan Budhwar

In this book, we began with a promise to examine the field of management from an Indian perspective. We reflected on many questions. Is there a knowledge system that can be called Indian management? How is it distinct from the so-called mainstream or transnational management in theory and practice? How does Indian philosophy shape Indian management? How does Indian social setting affect Indian management? How

A. Pandey (✉)
Shailesh J. Mehta School of Management,
Indian Institute of Technology Bombay, Mumbai, India
e-mail: ashish.pandey@iitb.ac.in

D. P. S. Bhawuk
Shidler College of Business, University of Hawai'i at Mānoa, Honolulu, HI, USA

P. Budhwar
Aston University, Birmingham, UK

© The Author(s), under exclusive license to Springer Nature Switzerland AG 2022
A. Pandey et al. (eds.), *Indigenous Indian Management*, Palgrave Studies in Indian Management,
https://doi.org/10.1007/978-3-030-87906-8_16

do MNCc operating in India manage? Do Indian organizations practice what could be called Indian management? How has historical evolution of the business organization and business systems in India shaped Indian management? The chapters in the volume provided some answers. The authors have also raised new questions. In this last chapter, we present the major themes, patterns, and insights emerging from the volume, present some thoughts on where Indian management could head in the future, and reflect on challenges and opportunities in this endeavour.

Our general observation, based on the empirical research grounded in Indian context is that Indian culture, history, and current socio-economic milieu do influence and shape the strategic choices, technological choices, management practices and individual and collective human experience in the organizations India. Indian management can be understood in view of the open system of creation and dissemination of management knowledge. The world is fast turning into a global village with the power of technology and trade. Indian management has to be understood to be the resultant of the past and present experience of cultural interactions within and outside India. Indian management inevitably emerges from the tensions created by the interactions of experiences of the ancient Indian values, systems, and practices with the socio-economic processes of colonizing, modernization, and developments in India. Binary perspectives of Indian versus Western management can obstruct the understanding of Indian management, which emerges from such multifaceted interactions. We propose that Indian management can be viewed as the interaction of **(i) core cultural ideals, (ii) institutional uniqueness and hybridity, and (iii) behavioural manifestations,** which in their own form and their interaction can spin new theories and practices of management in India that have distinctive characteristics. Figure 1 represents these aspects. The porous boundries of the different factors represents their constant interaction and influence on each other.

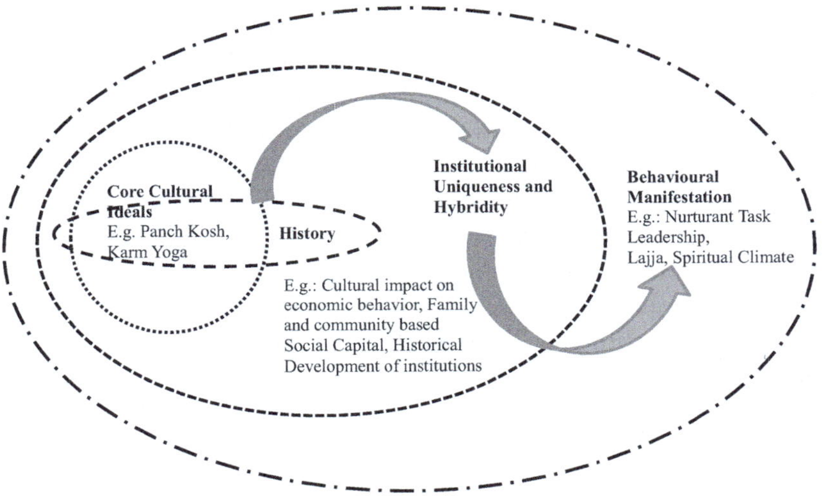

Fig. 16. 1 Various Aspects of Indigenous Indian Management

Core Cultural Ideals

To understand Indian management one needs to understand the dialectical relationship first between core cultural ideas and institutional system and then between institutions and individual level behaviours in organizations. Unique Indian perspectives derived from core cultural ideals are the first hallmark of Indian management. Interconnected worldview, responsibility of human being towards social and natural environment, spiritual realm being substratum of existence, multiple pathways (*sadhana*) for the purification of mind to realize and live this truth in day to day life are the basic tenets of Indian wisdom and hence Indian management. Chapters 2–6 pointed out aspects of the core cultural ideals from systems like Sankhya, Vedanta, and Ayurveda, which are holistic systems. Authors of these chapters explained how these systems can be the source of different theories and practices of management.

There is a rich literature in Indian philosophy that should be tapped into by management researchers. Dalmiya (2016) found resonances of care ethics in an alternative reading of some sections of the *mahAbhArata*, which can provide a rich foundation for research on business ethics in the Indian context. She challenged the fundamental western notion that knowing and caring are exclusive since knowing is prescribed in the west to be non-affective, dispassionate, and impartial. The lessons from the *mahAbhArata* allowed her to present the construct of relational humility that bridges virtuous knowing and ethical care. She also synthesized the voice of the *mahAbhArata* with feminist epistemology of care and feminist virtue epistemology of care, and examined the creative tensions amongst caring, virtue, and epistemology in the cultural context presented by the *mahAbhArata*. She has enriched the process of theorizing by bringing the *mahAbhArata* into dialogue with feminist epistemology and shown that some of the core ideas of the *mahAbhArata* can help the current feminist theorizing. Dalmiya's effort presented a new paradigm and theory of knowledge that invites us to move away from reason and reasoning process that is founded on abstraction, universalism, and impartiality, which are not only the hallmarks of reason but also science. Theories like these can enrich Indian management (IM) in the most fundamental way and allow IM to veer away from the parochial constraints of western management.

Timalsina (2020) presented a template for starting global interfaith dialogues by drawing lessons from the core cultural ideals of Indian tradition and texts. He drew on dialogues from the Vedas and the Upanishads, and also on the rich tradition of dialogues between the various Indian traditions. He identified ten conditions or characteristics of dialogue. Some of these characteristics of dialogue are quite provocative. For example, he posited that dialogue is a set of concurrent monologues, that dialogue sustains differences, and that dialogue is the essence of human existence. He also noted that sometimes the outcome of dialogue is a space for interpretation and further dialogue, i.e. dialogue is just for the sake of dialogue. In other words, dialogue can be what Kant called, a categorical imperative. He also demonstrated that opposite ideas can emerge from dialogues. His work is an exemplar of how theoretical frameworks can be derived from core cultural ideals of Indian tradition and texts. He presented a framework that can serve as the foundation for intercultural dialogues across nations and communities that is necessary for the fractured global society that we live in today.

It is found that often many commentaries on Indian texts exist, which capture debates that have gone on for centuries. Timalsina (2020) argued that Indian texts contain parallel and contradictory ideas, which are examples of the tradition of dialogue, and thoughts that capture not only the history at a given point in time but also a projection in time yet to come, time that is unfolding. Researchers working on core cultural ideals of India will find his work (Timalsina, 2008, 2014, 2015) helpful in developing theories and models of Indian management.

Institutional Uniqueness and Hybridity

Second aspect of Indian management is arising from the uniqueness and hybridity of various institutions in India. Chapters 7–15 elaborated on the uniqueness and hybridity of various aspects of social and business institutions of India. Family is perhaps the most prominent institution in India. Communities play an important role in all walks of life. Extended family and community generate unique nature of social capital in India. To understand Indian management one needs to understand the dialectical relationship between institutional system and culture. Successful MNCs in India embrace this reality and build trusting relationship between social influencers, local governments and project themselves as the responsible members of the community. Sinha (2004) found that employees in MNCs follow the performance norms of MNCs, however, their interpersonal relationships remained typical of Indian culture marked by patronizing style and recognition of familial self with *sneh-shraddha* (Sinha, 2010) being the guiding values. MNCs embracing these enjoy stronger employer branding and deeper employee commitment.

There are numerous examples of Indian managers rising to the global ranks in MNCs as more than 30 per cent of Fortune 500 companies today have Indians as their CEOs.[1] Market and state failure has resulted in vibrancy of social entrepreneurship in India. Healthcare sector is an

[1] https://www.indiaglobalbusiness.com/analyses/snap-analysis/the-indian-ceo-from-values-to-value-creation as on June 6, 2021.

example of the field, which has evolved at the interface of frugal innovation, societal challenges, and resource scarcity. Indian business sector has bloomed in many fields like IT/ITES, pharmaceutical manufacturing, diamond cutting without much support from the government. Historically, the government machinery in India is non-trusting and least facilitative of businesses. Similarly, judiciary suffers from procedural complexity and higher trial duration (Chemin, 2009), which is less friendly to businesses (Nayyar, 2019). Success of business in India lies in ingenuity of cost-effective ideas and ability to avoid interaction as much as possible with local administration and judiciary. Recent focus on ease of business in India, initiatives like Start Up India, lateral entry of experienced business leaders and professionals at senior positions in the government, credit support to small and medium size businesses through Micro Units Development & Refinance Agency Ltd. (MUDRA) by Government of India are the examples of changing pattern of interaction of the business and government towards more congenial and facilitative mode.

Behavioural Manifestations

As shown in Fig. 1, Core Cultural Ideals do influence both institutions and managerial behaviours. Many predominant dispositions amongst the Indian are the expressions of unique Indian perspective to life and the world and the result of various institutions and their temporal and interactive nature of reality. Individualized familial self, nurturant task leadership, dependence proneness, saving habits, respect for authority are the kind of values attributed to strength of family as an institution in India. Worldview of interconnectedness gives rise to lokasaMgraha as an approach to leadership. Recognition of interconnected nature of life perhaps results into context sensitivity and possibility of multiple pathways to attain the truth results into creative and frugal innovation. Tenets of the 'self' being responsible for everything leads to an entrepreneurial attitude amongst Indians. Nonetheless it is quite paradoxical that there is widespread poverty in India despite people being entrepreneurial. Many behavioural manifestations at individual or collective levels are also the result of uniqueness and hybridity of the various institutions in India. For example many administrative processes in several government organizations were laid down by the British in the nineteenth and twentieth centuries. These processes were primarily aimed at syphoning off resources from India to the United Kingdom. Many of these processes continued even after India got independence. For example, working to satisfy the superiors in the department and less concern for public who are the real beneficiaries of the department is remanence of colonization. Similarly, separation of applied and conceptual knowledge in the education sector is the legacy of education system established by the colonizers (Wilson, 2016).

Indian Management Research: The Way Forward

In this section, we share some general observations about research, practice, and concepts of Indian management and propose the way forward for future research. First, Indian culture, traditions, philosophy, and languages can be a great source for developing new concepts, constructs, and perspective relevant to management. Second, most of the Indian management research is carried out at the micro-level; either in the form of the constructs derived from wisdom tradition or the constructs derived through grounded research. The development of the macro-level concepts and constructs derived from the broader socio-economic and political environment needs attention. Third, spirituality is the recurring theme in most of the streams of research in Indian management. Fourth, there is a need to synthesize Indian and western constructs. Fifth, there is a need to adopt novel and creative research methods like historiography, case-based research, phenomenology, grounded research, and configurational research. Sixth, close collaboration between practising managers and management scholars is needed. Seventh, as indigenous epistemology, ontology, and axiology are embraced in management research in India, it is going to shape management education requiring management institutions in India to accommodate and nurture teaching of Indian management.

Development of New Constructs and Ideas from Core Cultural Ideals

Indian philosophical literature and other texts are not only valuable for Indian psychology and management, but also provide rich content on governance (e.g. Kautilya's Arthshastra), practical wisdom for day to day behaviour (e.g. Bhatrihari's Niti Shatakam), health and well-being (e.g. Ashtang Hridayam), epistemology and ontology (Nyaya), and so forth. Table 16.1 presents a partial list of historical text that can be employed for developing constructs, models, and theories. Many of these texts are widely referred to in other specialized fields. For example, Ashtang Hridayam is one of the most important texts in Ayurveda and Natya Shashtra in classical dance and drama.

Bhawuk (2020) explained how new construct can be developed by examining dictionary meanings, synonyms, and antonyms of the construct of interest in samskRtam and another Indian language. They can be further examined in multiple texts and in daily communication by examining proverbs. Bhawuk (2010) explained four ways of discovering or mining models from texts with suitable examples. First, some constructs can be readily picked up by analyzing the text of all the verses that refer to it to decipher its meaning. Second, researchers can wade through an entire text doing a content analysis of the verses and combine various verses to create a complex model. Third, recognition of what works in indigenous cultures can lead to the discovery of new constructs. And finally, new constructs can also be developed by questioning western concepts that do not work in the Indian context. Bhawuk (2011) presented many examples of models and constructs derived from the Bhagavad-Gita. Researchers can also employ autoethnography to tease out a processual understanding of a construct, which could provide indigenous insights (see Bhawuk, 2019 for a discussion of lajjA).

One of the methodological advantages of employing cultural texts for developing indigenous constructs is that it is likely to have been unaffected by distortions coming from colonization. Since texts are semantic units that are not random clauses strung together, they have a unity of meaning (Lemke, 1991) and texture (Halliday & Hasan, 1976). Verses of texts like the bhagavadgItA present the reader simultaneous experiences

Table 16.1 A partial list of the texts of ancient Indian wisdom

Time period	Title	Author	Topics covered
Fifth to third century BCE	Bhagwad-Gita	Vedavyas	Integrating day to action and spirituality
321 BCE–301 BCE	Arthaśāstra	Chanakya	– Issues on social welfare – Ethics that hold society together – Includes advice to the king about how to make changes in times of epidemic, war, and famine
Second century BCE to second century CE	Dhanurveda (Dhanusha Chandrodaya and Dhanusha Pradip)		– Methods, techniques, strategies, and ethics of war
Sixth century CE	Sushruta Samhita	Susruta	– On medicine and surgery – 186 chapters – Describes 1,120 illnesses – Describes 700 medicinal plants – Describes 64 preparations from mineral sources – Describes 57 preparations based on animal sources

(continued)

Table 16.1 (continued)

Time period	Title	Author	Topics covered
Second century BCE	Kātyāyana Sulbasutra	Kātyāyana	– Knowledge of mathematics – Includes statements on the Pythagorean theorem – Talks about geometric shapes – Gave an estimation of the square root of 2
500 BCE and 400 CE	Patanjal Yog Sutram	Patanjali	– Purpose of yoga – Ashtanga yoga—8 components of yoga
Eighth century	Nyayavinishchaya vivarana	Akalanka Deva	– On logic and reasoning – Perception of senses – Making inferences – Discourse
500 CE (or earlier)	Tirukkuṟaḷ	Thiruvalluvar	– Known as the Tamil Veda – Includes teachings on wisdom, wealth and love – Explains how different territories maximize their wealth

Time period	Title	Author	Topics covered
1250 BCE and 1000 BCE	Manusmriti	Manu & Bhrigu	– Legal text – Personal choices – Moral behaviour – Rights of women – Rules of war
Second half of seventeenth century CE	Tarka-Sangraha	Annambhatta	– Logic and reasoning – Includes basic principles of justice – Ontology of justice – Epistemology of justice
Twelfth and thirteenth century	Rasendra Chudamani	Aacharya Somadeva	– On chemistry – Using mercury for making medicine
Sixth century CE	Devichandraguptam	Vishakhadatta	– Political drama about Chandragupta II who was the emperor of Gupta Empire how he was able to defeat his enemies
500 BCE and 500 CE	Nāṭya Śāstra	Bharata Muni	– On performance arts – Details on emotions – Integrates aesthetics with mythology – Drama, poetry, dance, and music
4000 and 2000 B.C	Vastu Shastra	Mamuni Mayan	– On architecture – Describes designing, layout, measurement, and space arrangement – Integrates nature with architecture

(continued)

Table 16.1 (continued)

Time period	Title	Author	Topics covered
AD 550–600	Ashtanga Hridayam	Vagbhata	– Summary of teachings of Ayurveda – Describes 8 sections of Ayurveda
500 AD–1900 AD	Vriksha Ayurveda	Surapala	– Science of plant life – Nourishment of plants – Plant diseases and remedies
Fourth to third century	Nitisara	Kamandaka	– On politics and warfare – Use of force is the last resort – Describes the military qualities of the ruler
505 CE–587 CE	Brihat Samhita	Varāhamihira	– On agriculture – Rainfall – Seasons – Growth of crops – Cloud formation
3000–2500 BCE	Vyasa Samhita	Vyasa	– Merit of self-control – Virtue of charity
100 BCE and 400 CE	Narada Samhita	Narada	– Deals with judicature and laws – Recovery of debt – Evidence – Dispute amongst partners – Wages – Purchase, sales and delivery

Time period	Title	Author	Topics covered
700 BCE and 1000 CE	Vishnu Smrti		– Weights and measures – Criminal and civil law – Law of debt – Witnesses – Self-restraint
Third to fifth century	Yajnavalkya Smrti	Rshi Yajnavalkya	– Dana – Raja Dharma – Rna (loan and interest) – Witness – Land disputes (boundary) – Agriculture – Wages – Business in partnership, etc.
Fifth century to ninth century	Mayamatam	Maya Muni	– Architecture and engineering – Types of land – Testing of soil – Town planning
Fourth century	Manasara		– Architecture and engineering – System of measurement – Site selection – Soil examination etc.
Eleventh century	Samarangana Sutradhara	Bhojadeva	– Architecture and engineering – Land selection/evenness – Residential architecture – Temple architecture

captured in words, feelings, and spiritual depth, and provide guidance for action or therapeutic practice. For example, Jijina et al. (2020) employed the methodology recommended by Bhawuk (2010, 2020), and derived the construct of *samatva* (equanimity or even-mindedness) by analyzing 41 verses of the Bhagavad-Gita that capture the construct. They identified six themes that provide an indigenous thick-description (Bhawuk, 2020) of the construct. These themes included rising above dualities and transcendence of the three guNas (for a discussion see Jijina et al., 2020). They recommended the cultivation of samatva not only for holistic well-being but also for leadership and management. Similarly, Alok (2017) explained the notion of Sattvik leadership based on Indian wisdom and showed its practical and theoretical relevance of this concept in modern management relevance.

Advice of White (2002) may be useful in connection with the research in local terms wherein he says that researchers need to be cognizant of the conceptually equivalent phenomena whilst studying the local constructs to avoid being blind to the other contexts, and in this way perpetuating the stereotypes of individuals and organizations in the region with which such terms are linked. Similarly, the advice of Jing and Dong (2017) to examine underlying cultural assumptions, values, and logic rather than the literal meanings whilst applying indigenous cultural knowledge can be useful in research of this nature. Scholars need to understand the historical evolution, etymology, the placement of the construct in the nomological network of the other related constructs, and its relevance in the present organizational context to study the constructs drawn from the Indian scriptures, wisdom traditions, and local languages. Without contextual understanding, scholars may run the risk of interpreting indigenous concepts and values through the lens of their own perspectives.

Macro-level Research in Indian Management

Societal culture influences business systems and management practices. Business practices followed in different communities like Marwaris, Gujaratis, and others, tend to be different (Kanagasabapathi, 2013;

Vaidyanathan, 2014). Diversity in caste, language, religion, geographic location, or size of firms (small, medium, and large) has shaped organizational systems and processes of Indian management at the macro-level (organizational and social). Some have raised doubts that a capitalist industrial system cannot be developed in India due to the rigid caste system (Weber, 1962). In most of the socio-economic research, the caste system is projected as a historical legacy of rigid social hierarchical stratification across the Indian subcontinent, which causes social disharmony and prevents upward movement of the weaker sections of the society. Contrary to these notions, Srinivas (1962) argued that caste mainly existed and worked as a regional system, and Dirks (2002) pointed out that the label of 'caste' was oversimplified expression for organizing, and 'systematizing' India's diverse forms of social identity, community, and organization.

There is a little mention of varNa or jAti in the non-Sanskrit texts created in different courts in North and South India, or in the several traveller and visitor accounts in the precolonial India. Instead, Chakravorty (2019) points out there are numerous instances of 'slaves' and 'Shudras' and 'Vaishyas' who became kings; merchants and soldiers and nomads who were caste-less; large numbers of farmers who were also soldiers; and Brahmans who were farmers, soldiers, traders, or even kings. He concluded that a more dynamic system of social roles and identities became more rigid caste system after the census of 1891, 1901 and, 1911. Damodaran (2018) called this the 'Field to Factory' movement, signifying the expansion of the social base of Indian business 'beyond the Bania'; the cast traditionally connected to the field of business. The 2005 Economic Census indicated that the rise of backward classes in businesses is now becoming a massive entrepreneurial movement in which the state has had minimal direct role.

It is particularly important for management research to recognize that caste and community ties play very crucial role as the informal support system for the small and middle size businesses in India. For example, Marwaris from Rajasthan in several businesses across India, and even outside (Timberg, 2015), and the Jain community of Palanpur in diamond cutting industry in Surat (Henn, 2012) show that caste also needs to be looked at as a source of social capital. Munshi (2007) described how the Kathiawaris, community in Gujarat entered trade late but formed a new community based business network. They moved over from agriculture to international business—the diamond industry dominated by the Vaishyas, Palanpuri Jains, and Parsis—over just a single generation. Similarly, the role of Gounder community so-called backward caste is remarkable for making Tirupur as world leader in the knitted garments industry.

Tiruchengode is another example of regional or geographical identity and social capital built on that. In the 1960s, a severe water crisis forced Tiruchengode's farmers to jointly buy a rig to dig deep bore-wells. But seeing the demand for such wells, they successfully turned this into a business that soon spread over to Karnataka, Andhra Pradesh, Maharashtra, Madhya Pradesh, Rajasthan, and Odisha. Turn to the Sankagiri transport cluster in western Tamil Nadu, the second largest centre for lorry traffic in the country. Some 90% of the Sankagiri truck owners were agriculturists and a fifth were cattle grazers. They now own the largest population of Taurus vehicles in the country (Tastevin, 2017).

There are hundreds of castes and community based economic clusters spread across India that are providing millions of jobs, exporting products worth billion dollars to the global markets and creating wealth. These clusters carry out their work through medium and small size enterprises (MSMEs), which contribute around 29% of India's GDP and 49% of its exports. The MSME sector is called the backbone of the Indian economy as it provides employment to over 111 million people and produces over 8,000 products, ranging from traditional to high-tech precision items. Yet this sector has never demanded any kind of security (financial, social, medical, or pension) from the government. Even small support from the state can be valuable to this sector is evident from the Kite making industrial cluster in Gujarat (Kanagasabapathi, 2014). In 2003, the size of this activity was estimated to be 30–35 crores INR (approximately 4.5 million US dollar).

A committee lead by Kanagasabapathi (2003) based on their field survey found that a simple support to the Kite making industry can help it flourish. Government pitched in constructing the warehouse for their output, included the kite making under the cluster development scheme for cottage and rural industries, took up providing training to people engaged in the trade, besides helping the industry to make innovations. As a result of these initiatives, the kite industry grew from 35 crore in 2003–2004 to 800 crore (more than 1 billion US dollar) with simple intervention. In most of the clusters in India, the needed capital is raised within the community and family networks and social ties are the source of transmitting information and enforcing contracts. Thus, contrary to Max Weber's view, caste has actually made occupational mobility possible. When caste identity and shared values are directed towards economic goals, it often results into greater social empowerment.

The startup ecosystem in India offers a perspective on how such a diversity shapes Indian management. India had around 50,000 startups in 2018 of which about 9,000 were technology-led. In 2019 alone, 1,300 new tech startups were born. The pace of growth in the startup ecosystem increased to 15% in 2018, whilst the growth of the number of incubators and accelerators was 11%. According to the note by Ministry of Commerce & Industry released in June 2021, the recognized startups have contributed significantly to job creation, with more than half million jobs reported by 48,093 startups with an average number of 11 employees per startup. About 1.7 lakh jobs were created by recognized startups in the 2020–2021 period alone. The leadership teams of 45% of the startups have women entrepreneurs.[2]

Bangalore has been listed in the world's 20 leading startup cities in the 2019 Startup Genome Project ranking. The success of the startups depends on the startup ecosystem comprising of the leadership of the founder(s), cooperation amongst cofounders, employee relations, the role of business supporters, education system, the role of the investors, and the regulatory environment. Due to a unique socio-cultural basis, place in the trajectory of economic development, push by the government towards entrepreneurship, a peculiar system of education and the regulatory environment supporting startup system then presents a unique opportunity for the study. Studies in the Indian startup ecosystem can unravel insights about the field ranging from leadership (e.g. shared leadership), interpersonal dynamics (e.g. conflict resolution), strategic management (e.g. success factors of growth strategies of startup firms

[2] https://pib.gov.in/PressReleasePage.aspx?PRID=1724043.

across industries), financial management (e.g. early stage non institutional funding system due to being capital deficient economy), late stage financing of the family business, and so forth.

This discussion suggests that knowledge of the social and community fabric helps in understanding the economic and business system of India. Therefore, Indian management research should recognize the role of social dynamics of the communities in economic development. Granularity of the socio-economic system and its implication for management will be grossly missed out if social realities like caste are only viewed as clear-cut stratification or social hierarchy and its direct correlation with other socio-economic indicators is overlooked. Colonial interpretation of social structure and the behaviour of the various social groups need to be examined carefully to unravel the hybridity and uniqueness in the socio-economic aspects of management in India.

Management Research in View of Hybridity in Institutional Structure

We need to recognize that many of the modern Indian institutions have not evolved organically. Many modern institution like infrastructure (railways, irrigation), legal framework, and educational systems were started or overtaken by the East India Company and later by the British Empire. In fact, the political outlook of Indians towards business and business organizations has also seen major transitions during and after the freedom struggle. Moreover, unlike China and Vietnam, where traditional social relations were erased as a result of the communist revolution (Haque, 1997), the Indian republic is engaged in institutional change in a democratic manner. As a result, approach and practices of Indian management are affected by different institutions of varying maturity that are on different evolutionary trajectories. We briefly explain the hybridity and uniqueness in education system, administrative system, and political system and its implications for management.

India was more than 95% literate in the beginning of nineteenth century. Pathshalas or socially sustaining small schools were the main source of providing primary education in almost every village. Skill development used to be taken care of within the communities. British administrators influenced the primary education by specifying their standards about the paraphernalia a school should have. Pathshalas were not meeting those criteria and gradually the whole traditional system of village education was delegitimized and demolished (Dharmpal, 1983, cited in Gupta, 1994). Traditional knowledge systems were totally discarded and were not considered for development or propagation. The new education infrastructure aimed to prepare citizens who were 'a class of persons, Indian in blood and colour, but English in taste, in opinions, in morals, and in intellect'.[3]

Independent India worked on achieving universal primary education through schools, higher education of good quality in colleges and universities, and cutting edge research in various research organizations and institutions. In spite of significant progress on these objectives, it is an unfinished project. Education system is marked by class difference of its own kind. There is a marked difference in learning outcomes amongst the students in public and private schools. Levels of learning amongst the students coming out of a fraction of schools are comparable to international standard, and learning outcomes attainment in rest of the institutions is far below it (Gouda et. al., 2013; Singh & Sarkar, 2012). New education policy (2020)[4] of India articulates the aspirations of providing flexibility to the learners to choose programmes and learning trajectories. It promotes multidisciplinary and a holistic education. It allows respect for diversity and respect for the local context in all curriculum, pedagogy, and policy. Naturally, management education in India also needs to embrace these objectives and develop pedagogy and research to achieve the same.

Administrative and legal system was implemented by the British Empire without understanding Indian philosophy, diverse nature of society and negotiation with its subjects. British system was by nature an extractive system wherein revenue collection and protecting the British power were the primary goals of administrative, revenue, and legal

---

[3] Lord Macaulay's Minute on Education is available on the internet at the following site: http://www.columbia.edu/itc/mealac/pritchett/00generallinks/macaulay/txt_minute_education_1835.html.

[4] https://www.pib.gov.in/PressReleasePage.aspx?PRID=1654058.

systems (Wilson, 2016). Railways, posts and telegraph, highways, canals, ports, banking and insurance, capital cities were set up but these were subordinate to the chief motivation of the empire to rule the country and its people. After independence in 1947 though India aimed to be a public welfare state, it was bound to use the institutional framework established by the British Empire. As a result, the traction between espoused goals of welfare socialist state and extractive and non-trusting (towards citizens) nature of the system and institution has been evident all through these decades after independence. Here we briefly describe this traction visible in the political and administrative system and its impact on management.

India adopted democratic constitution upon its independence. Free periodic elections to the national Parliament and the State legislatures, and local bodies at district, village, and block level are the bedrock of democratic processes. Fundamental rights to the individuals, rights and protection of the political parties, minorities, and other organizations are guaranteed by the Constitution. Independent judiciary is there to protect and interpret the law and constitution. Electoral system in India is unparalleled in the world in terms of scale and inclusivity (Verma, 2005). However, lack of a notion of accountability and responsiveness on the part of legislators is a major obstacle in the formation of a responsible government. Public space is full of political rhetoric and polemics. Any reform in any aspects of governance whether it is land reform, agricultural reforms, privatization, labour reform, and so forth are opposed by some group or the other through agitations and dharnas (sit-down strike). Nonetheless, economic growth is on the agenda of all the political parties (Asher & Novosad, 2017). They adopt different approaches and administrative mechanisms to strive this objective. Post COVID-19 pandemic public discourse is likely to shift towards health and well-being.

In January 1991, India adopted policies supporting globalization and market economy, to stimulate competitiveness. The reforms consisted of two sets of economic policies: (a) a macro-economic stabilization programme under the influence of International Monetary Fund, and (b) a comprehensive programme for the structural change of the economy, in the fields of trade, industry, foreign investments within the public sector and the financial sector, which was inspired by the World Bank

(Jain & Bongartz, 1994). Economic reforms have shown encouraging trend in the field of infrastructure development, online and direct retail, pharmaceutical manufacturing and IT/ITES. Certain areas of reform are inherently more challenging like agriculture, land, labour, education either in terms of complexity, expertise, or diversity of interests. The reforms which involve reconstituting laws, regulations, or governance institutions are inherently more challenging than liberalization. Financial sector reforms have been mixed in pace and character. Spread of bank accounts amongst Indian population, online payment system, modernization and growth of the stock market are a few examples of reforms in the financial sector. Nature and pace of reforms are also linked to the connection between business and government. The relations between government and business organizations have shifted from nationalization of banks in 1960s to development of private sector banks in the 1990s. This process is continuing and there is a proposal for the privatization of two public sector banks in the budget of 2021. Political narrative has markedly shifted from socialist overtone where business organizations, particularly large business organizations, were looked upon with suspicion to recognition of their contribution in nation building.[5]

India has been seriously striving to reform its administrative structure for better governance and for achieving development goals. In the decade of the 1990s, along with economic reforms, Administrative Reform and the New Public administration paradigms became major focus for the subsequent governments. The conversation about New Public administration (NPA) is concurrent to economic reforms in India. Narrative of NPA revolves around caring government that is transparent, focused on the people, and characterized by commitment, accountability, responsiveness, and inclusiveness (Jain, 2013). We see many pockets of administrative excellence (e.g. Delhi Metro,[6] Swacchata Abhiyan,[7]

---

[5] Segment of the speech of Prime Minister in parliament: https://www.youtube.com/watch?v=RwIB58vIkY0.

[6] https://www.globalmasstransit.net/archive.php?id=26471.

[7] https://timesofindia.indiatimes.com/blogs/toi-edit-page/celebrating-swachh-bharat-mission-of-all-modis-projects-it-will-have-the-greatest-long-term-impact-on-peoples-lives/.

and vaccination for Children[8]) though in general public institutions are marred with acute shortage of talent, legal ambiguity, coordination between government agencies and vertical coordination between levels (or tiers) of governance and lack of accountability (Kapur et al., 2018).

In spite of these goals and values, Indian systems and institutions have a long way to go in fully realizing a transformation. Here we take three international indices to understand the institutional and systemic maturity of India; Human Development Index (HDI), World-wide Governance Index (WGI), and Ease of Doing Business Index (EDBI). HDI dimensions include health, education, and standard of living. India's ranks 131 on the Human Development Index amongst the list of 189 nations.[9] Worldwide Governance Index[10] measures voice and accountability, political stability and absence of violence, government effectiveness, regulatory quality, rule of law, control of corruption. India is in the 20th percentile on political stability and absence of violence, 60th on voice and accountability and government effectiveness, 50th on regulatory quality, and 55th on the rule of law and control of corruption. Ease of doing business Index[11] is the benchmark study about regulations related to starting and conducting business in an economy. This index takes into account ten factors such as starting a business, protecting investors, enforcing contracts, and so forth. India was placed at the sixty third position in (2019) out of 190 countries. India for the third

[8] https://www.businesstoday.in/opinion/columns/immunization-at-scale-an-indian-success-story/story/315042.html.

[9] HDI dimensions include health, education, and standard of living. Health dimension is assessed by life expectancy at birth. Education dimension is measured using average years of schooling for adults and expected years of schooling for children. Standard of living dimension is measured through gross national income per capita.

[10] The Worldwide Governance Indicators (WGI) are a research dataset summarizing the views on the quality of governance provided by a large number of enterprise, citizen, and expert survey respondents in industrial and developing countries. These data are gathered from a number of survey institutes, think tanks, non-governmental organizations, international organizations, and private sector firms. The WGI do not reflect the official views of the World Bank, its Executive Directors, or the countries they represent. The WGI are not used by the World Bank Group to allocate resources. https://info.worldbank.org/governance/wgi/Home/Reports.

[11] The report measures the performance of countries across 10 different parameters namely Starting a Business, Dealing with Construction permits, Electricity availability, Property registration, Credit availability, Protecting minority Investors, Paying Taxes, Trading across borders, Contracts enforcement, and Resolving Insolvency.

consecutive year was present in the list of 10 economies where the business climate has improved the most. A historical analysis of the growth of Indian and British institutions may provide some insight into why starting from the British ideals institutions in these two nations have become so different in ranking on global indicators, and how they shape management practices in these nations. Comparative studies like these can provide insights into the hybridity found in Indian institutions and management practices.

Uniqueness and hybridity of India and Indian management need to be understood in the light of the interaction between legacy of the institutions and current aspiration of its citizens. Panda and Gupta have described these issues in Chapter 10 of this volume. Indian management research and practices need to be informed about the challenges and contradictions of future oriented espoused goals and institutional reality shaped by history. Research on Indian management has immense scope to contribute to capability building in various institutions, enhancing coordination amongst various institutions, entrepreneurial and responsible governance, efficient management of administrative and developmental projects, and participatory management amongst public and private organizations.

Enhancing the Methodological Repertoire

Most of the research studies of management in India published in the peer-reviewed journals are hypothetico-deductive in nature. By nature, the study of this kind is more suitable for theory testing rather than theory building. New propositions, concepts, and constructs arise from the qualitative and grounded approach of research hence they are more fruitful for indigenous research in the present stage. Methodological repertoire of Indian scholars is expanding and many are employing case study based research, grounded theory approach, and mixed methods based research, which is helping in the development of new constructs. Employment of such methodologies should continue and expand further in the future. Gupta and Panda (2016) have pointed out the potential of historical analysis, natural experiments in organisational contexts, action research, and mixed methods to strengthen indigenous management research. Future research should follow the example of work of Piramal and her colleagues (2002, 2010) on business houses and families, Kumar and colleagues (Kumar, 2009; Kumar & Puranam, 2012) on emerging power and strategies of Indian business, Capelli (2009) on Indian management, Govindarajan and colleagues (Govindarajan & Ramamurti, 2011; Govindarajan, 2012) on reverse innovation. Effort should be made to draw theoretical and practical insights by synthesizing the findings with the core cultural ideal of India. Indian management research can be enriched by focusing on both deductive theory development and testing and inductive, thick descriptive approaches. Management research in general and Indian management research in particular are naturally focused on application. This suggestion is made at several places in this volume, which is in line with the Indian worldview that has a strong element of pragmatism or orientation for solving the day to day problems and challenges of life.

Chilisa (2011) noted the importance of culturally responsive methodologies to carry out indigenous research that acknowledges local histories, traditions, and knowledge systems. She emphasized the role of indigenous languages, oral literature, songs, proverbs, and storytelling for post-colonial indigenous research. She posited that proverbs may be used as conceptual frameworks or can be explored as community constructed ideologies. She also questioned whether the language of the colonizer is indeed the most appropriate medium for indigenous voice. These suggestions can be helpful in taking forward the indigenous research in Indian management.

Use of Configurational Approach and Methods of Research

Human conditions, dispositions, interactions, and collection are the foundations of a large number of research questions in management. However, most of the management research are aimed at capturing the association of atomistic variables and is subject to methodological individualism. Subjective individual dispositions are considered foundational and rather ultimate constituents of any social phenomena. Aggregation of the individual responses are equated with the representation of social reality. Research in Indian management is not an exception to that. The critics of the methodological individualism question this approach and insist on the need for understanding the social dynamics and collective expression of reality that is above and beyond the aggregated individual responses (Sarker & Valacich, 2010). There is a need for macro-level studies that consider the larger Indian context. Management knowledge is often a product of cultural logic. Indian culture tends to be family-oriented, integral, and context-sensitive, which may shape the theories and concepts in Indian management (e.g., Nurturant task leadership, Giving model of motivation, jugaad). An integral, holistic, and context-sensitive approach can help us to better understand complexity in social life for which methodological individualism may pose severe limitations to understand Indian management.

The configurational approach addresses the limitations of methodological individualism and can help understand the complex reality of Indian management. The notion of configuration is developed from a systemic perspective in which a constellation of interconnected elements is studied. The configurational approach was developed in the field of sociology and political science. It is employed by management scholars who consider organizations as clusters of interconnected structures and practices embedded in a larger socio-cultural context. The 'configurational approach' in management is frequently associated with research on organizational design, typologies, strategic groups, and archetypes of effectiveness (Misangyi et al., 2017). Qualitative Comparative Analysis (QCA) is a methodological pillar of the configurational approach and a middle way between the case-oriented (or 'qualitative') and the variable-oriented (or 'quantitative') approaches (Ragin, 1987, p. 84). Configurational research can be useful to develop the ideas at the macro level which can be further developed into robust concepts and theoretical insights.

Spirituality: The Recurring Theme of Indian Management

Adhyatma or spirituality plays an important role in Indian society. This is reflected in the four pursuits of life (puruṣārtha)—dharma, artha, kāma, and mokṣha—widely subscribed in the Hindu view of life and referred to in multiples chapters in this volume. More than in any other culture, spirituality has been emphasized for almost 3,000 years of recorded history in India (Kroeber, 1944, Simonton, 1996) and continues to grow even today like a banyan tree (Bhawuk, 2003). Comparing Western and Indian knowledge, Rolland (1960, p. 91) described Western knowledge as the 'science of facts' and spirituality as 'the science of the soul, a peculiarly Indian science'. A significant difference between philosophy and spirituality, or religion and spirituality, is that spirituality, as practised in India, has an action bias over and above cognitive (thinking or thoughts) or value (considering something important) concerns. Spirituality has both epistemic and ontological implications for Indian management. In contemporary literature, spirituality has been defined in different ways: as intelligence, developmental line, attitude, and inner experience (Pandey & Gupta, 2008).

Bhawuk (2010, 2019) defined Adhyatma by deriving the construct from the Bhagwad-Gita. Adhyatma is about centring the mind on the Self or Atman. It is the pious knowledge (jJAna or vidyA) of self and considered superior to all types of knowledge. It is to act without agency or as the servant of God in pursuit of moksha or liberation. It is the inward-looking process that leads to finding pleasure, contentment, and satisfaction in Atman such that the person interacts energetically with the outside world without neglecting it or getting ensnared in it. The notion of the four purushartha and five yajnas (explained by Pandey in the Chapter 2 of this book suggests that Adhyatma or spirituality permeates everyday living in India.

Responsible and ethical behaviour, well-being, decision making, learning, and creativity are some of the most important challenges of organizations and institutions in current times. Spirituality-based values, attitudes, and practices are found to have a major impact on all these aspects of organizational life. Indian management can continue to make important contributions in these fields. The impact of spirituality-based interventions like Yoga and mindfulness (e.g. Dagar et al., 2020; Kudesia et al., 2020) and the association of spirituality with various behavioural and attitudinal dimensions (e.g. Mishra & Varma, 2019) are important contributions of Indian management and should be examined further in the future.

Adhyatma or spirituality is expressed at the collective level as well in the organizations. Organizational spirituality can unleash the human power of introspection and reflexivity that may result in enhanced learning, development, and creativity (Freshman, 1999; Wakhlu, 2000). Organizations that are aware of spirituality are often the questioning organizations that constantly ask the question of why they exist and show the courage to stand out. Spirituality at the organizational level reflects in the ability of institutions to transcend their business boundaries and to create meaningful relationships with the larger society based on a caring attitude (Pandey & Gupta, 2008; see also the work of Dalmiya on care ethics noted above). Macro-level studies about spirituality at the workplace are fruitful areas of inquiry in Indian management, which are mostly unaddressed at present. India is also home to a large number of spirituality-based organizations.

Scholars define religion as a visible expression of a faith and belief system, via a formal or ceremonial activity whereas spirituality is defined as a broader concept related to the quest for meaning, purpose, morality, transcendence, well-being, and profound relationships with ourselves, others, and the ultimate reality (Pargament, 1999). However, the distinction between the two blurs in many large-scale developmental projects in India completed by so-called religious or faith-based organizations. Water project and super specialty hospitals in southern India set up by Sathya Sai Sewa Organization, social forestry and plantation project by Isha Foundation (also in southern India), Ayurveda and Yoga based study of Patanjali Yogapeeth in northern India are few examples of such projects. Unlike large charitable organizations funded by a few rich and philanthropic business leaders or business houses, many religious organizations in India have undertaken the projects of social development and environmental protection with the financial and voluntary support of a large number of common citizens. In a way, it is crowd funded developmental work generally under the influence of a spiritual master and religious leader. The notion of dAna (altruistic donation), sevA (selfless service), lokasaMgraha (working for common good) is combined with AdhyAtmika (spirituality-based) leadership and practice of dharm and pursuit of moksha by the common populace. Many of these organizations represent a unique combination of modern practices of professional organizations with religious values. These examples are unique to India. Interesting and useful insights can come about the collective level phenomenon like organizing, networking, the role of spirituality in development work and meso- and micro-level areas of research like motivation, leadership, psychological contract, spirituality-based leadership, and so forth through the systematic studies of these organizations.

Spirituality in management can be developed with the support of Indian Psychology. Integrally bound with Vedantic and Sankhya Darshanas, Indian Psychology (IP) has evolved not as a moralistic but as a cultural discourse on world views and epistemologies, which offers an alternative to the logico-positivistic enterprise of Western psychology (Dalal & Misra, 2010). The core concern of IP has been to free human beings from bondage and suffering, wherever they are located and whatever their sources are. This discourse has grown around the essential nature of one's being and the various paths through which one comes to know about it. IP is a much-developed field with a clear articulation of the human self, relationship, emotions, cognition from the perspective of Indian philosophy, and wisdom tradition (e.g. Cornelissen et al., 2013; Rao & Paranjpe, 2016; Rao et al., 2008). The development of most of the fields of Indian management and more so the field of spirituality in management is inexorably linked with Indian psychology, and future research should take advantage of the extant literature on IP.

Need for Engaged Indigenous Scholarship

Indigenous Indian management research is necessary to help develop theories and models that can not only serve the goals of economic growth but also answer questions related to what Indian employees, managers, leaders, and policy makers could do to achieve their goals. Indigenous research by its very nature surface and codify indigenous knowledge that addresses local problems (see the model presented by Bhawuk, 2008). It is a participative form of research that incorporates the views of various actors in a setting to unravel the complexity of the problem in its particular context. Indigenous knowledge developed with a participative or engaged research approach (for a discussion of how to create a project through participation of the community see Bhawuk et al., 2009) is likely to be more insightful and applicable in comparison to the knowledge created through an etic perspective using western frameworks and theories.

Engaged scholarship focuses on original research and advocates for an expanded view of scholarship (Van de Van et al., 2018). It encompasses the scholarly discovery of a solution to the problems of the real world, sometimes with abductive reasoning. It integrates knowledge across disciplinary boundaries. Most of the chapters in this volume are showing the features of engaged scholarship covering different aspects of Indian management. Engaged indigenous research can be worthwhile also for teaching Indian management to practitioners. Collaboration between practising managers and academicians can be very useful in this regard.

Teaching with innovative pedagogy is also a form of engaged scholarship. Management classroom are not only meant for the knowledge dissemination and can also be the site for knowledge creation. The perspective of 'classroom as an organization' (Arbaugh et al., 2009) can be useful to generate knowledge about many aspects relevant for organizations. For example, the work of Kudesia et al. (2020) on multitasking and mindfulness, Burke and Sadler-Smith (2006) on decision making, and Pandey and colleagues (2018, 2020) on Yoga and Positive Psychology came from testing some practices in the classroom over the duration of a course. Viewing classrooms as the 'sites for knowledge creation' can help in enhancing and strengthening the dialogue between management practitioners and educators.

The need for integration of emic and etic perspective becomes clear in the wake of engaged scholarship. Though each culture should be studied on its own terms and one needs to be cautious about accepting the claims about generalizability, we need to recognize that both etic and emic approaches yield important information that cannot be accounted for by either paradigm alone. The integration of these two perspectives would help advance the research on global management. The workplaces are increasingly becoming multinational and multicultural in their constitution. It is crucial to explain the strategy and policies in the plan that is expressed in the dual language of emic and etic with all of the stakeholders involved in a policy that responds to cultural differences (Morris et al., 1999).

Conclusion

We discussed four types of research studies about management in India in Chapter 1. The four types with their focus on atomistic or holistic variables examined in emic and etic ways give us an overview of research on Indian management. There is then a vast unrealized potential of research about indigenous research in management at micro atomistic constructs as well as contextual and holistic concepts and constructs. The scope for theoretical development in indigenous or emic research is perhaps the most remarkable in this field. New knowledge creation and dissemination in Indian management need to be mindful of the variety of organizations functioning in India. India has more than 300,000 micro and small enterprises that contribute towards more than half of India's GDP. More than 80% of the total number of business organizations in India are family owned. There are more than six thousand publicly listed companies in India, and more than three thousand MNCs are operating in India. India has a thriving ecosystems of startup as well. All these settings provide uniqueness to different aspects of management and hence provide a fruitful area for research and teaching in Indian management that will help in the improvement of the management practices in India. The creation of an academic body like the Indian Academy of Management (https://www.indam.in/) Indian Psychology Institute (https://www.ipi.org.in/), and Strategic Management Forum, to name a few, provides scholars with opportunities to exchange ideas about management issues, problems in India and suitable methods and theoretical lenses to examine them.

In this chapter, we summarized some of the core issues and identified the potential of indigenous management research in India. Well-being for all (sarve bhvantu sukhinaH[12]) is the supreme objective of all human endeavours in the Indian ethos. Openness for expanding the methodological repertoire, integration of etic and emic perspective in research, synthesizing the Indian ethos arising out of the tradition and culture with a transnational ethos of increasing globalizing world can be tried in the light of this ideal. There is no reason to doubt that research in Indian management conducted with this ideal will result in a theoretical and practical contribution to the global knowledge as well. We can also expect that conceptual, cultural, and practical tensions will arise in research on Indian management, which will hopefully lead to decolonization of management knowledge in India. There are about 9,100 academic institutions that teach business and management in India, of which 78% are private, 15% are public or government, and 7% are public or private, and more than 2,046 institutions awarded PhDs in management in 2018–2019. Indian management research has potential to grow given the large number of institutions. Though not discussed in this volume in detail, we acknowledge that realization of these ideals requires systemic changes which entail capability and commitment, leadership, institutional support, and so forth. We hope that this volume will be able to strengthen the scholarship and practices in Indian Management and lead to further work that can also address the limitations of this volume in its future editions.

References

Alok, K. (2017). Sāttvika leadership: An Indian model of positive leadership. *Journal of Business Ethics, 142*(1), 117–138.

[12] sarve bhavantu sukhinaH, sarve santu nirAmayAH; sarve bhadrANi pazyantu, mA kazcid duHkha bhAgbhavet (may all be happy, may all be free from illness; may all see what is auspicious, may no one suffer).

Arbaugh, J. B., Godfrey, M. R., Johnson, M., Pollack, B. L., Niendorf, B., & Wresch, W. (2009). Research in online and blended learning in the business disciplines: Key findings and possible future directions. *The Internet and Higher Education, 12*(2), 71–87.

Ardichvili, A., Jondle, D., Kowske, B., Cornachione, E., Li, J., & Thakadipuram, T. (2012). Ethical cultures in large business organizations in Brazil, Russia, India, and China. *Journal of Business Ethics, 105*(4), 415–428.

Asher, S., & Novosad, P. (2017). Politics and local economic growth: Evidence from India. *American Economic Journal: Applied Economics, 9*(1), 229–273.

Bertalanffy, V. (1968). *Organismic psychology and systems theory*. Clark University Press.

Bhagavatula, S., Elfring, T., Van Tilburg, A., & Van De Bunt, G. G. (2010). How social and human capital influence opportunity recognition and resource mobilization in India's handloom industry. *Journal of Business Venturing, 25*(3), 245–260.

Bhawuk, D. (2011). *Spirituality and Indian psychology: Lessons from the Bhagavad-Gita*. Springer. https://doi.org/10.1007/978-1-4419-8110-3

Bhawuk, D. P. (2003). Culture's influence on creativity: The case of Indian spirituality. *International Journal of Intercultural Relations, 27*(1), 1–22.

Bhawuk, D. P. S. (2008). Globalization and indigenous cultures: Homogenization or differentiation? *International Journal of Intercultural Relations, 32*(4), 305–317.

Bhawuk, D. P. S. (2010). Methodology for building psychological models from scriptures: Contributions of Indian psychology to indigenous and universal psychologies. *Psychology and Developing Societies, 22*(1), 49–93.

Bhawuk, D. P. S. (2019). adhyAtma or spirituality: Indian perspectives on management. In P. S Budhwar, R. Kumar, & A. Varma (Eds.), *Indian business: Understanding a rapidly emerging economy* (pp. 256–266). Routledge.

Bhawuk, D. P. S. (2020). Research on Śāstras in contemporary times: Methodological strategies for indigenous research. *Journal of Psychosocial Research, 15*(2), 325–338. https://doi.org/10.32381/JPR.2020.15.02.30

Bhawuk, D. P. S., Mrazek, S., & Munusamy, V. P. (2009). From social engineering to community transformation: Amul, Grameen Bank, and Mondragon as exemplar organizations. *Peace & Policy : Ethical Transformations for a Sustainable Future, 14*, 36–63.

Biswas, S., Varma, A., & Ramaswami, A. (2013). Linking distributive and procedural justice to employee engagement through social exchange: A field study in India. *The International Journal of Human Resource Management, 24*(8), 1570–1587.

Bruton, G. D., & Lau, C. M. (2008). Asian management research: Status today and future outlook. *Journal of Management Studies, 45*(3), 636–659.
Burke, L. A., & Sadler-Smith, E. (2006). Instructor intuition in the educational setting. *Academy of Management Learning & Education, 5*(2), 169–181.
Capelli, P., Singh, H., Singh, J. V., & Useem, M. (2009). The DNA of Indian Business Leadership. *NHRD Network Journal, 2*(5), 66–71.
Capelli, P., Singh, H., Singh, J., & Useem, M. (2010). *The India way*. Harvard Business Press.
Cappelli, P., Singh, H., Singh, J., & Useem, M. (2015). Indian business leadership: Broad mission and creative value. *The Leadership Quarterly, 26*(1), 7–12.
Chakraborty, S. (1991). *Management by values*. Oxford University Press.
Chakravorty, S. (2019, June 19). How the British reshaped India's caste system. BBC News.
Chari, M. D., & David, P. (2012). Sustaining superior performance in an emerging economy: An empirical test in the Indian context. *Strategic Management Journal, 33*(2), 217–229.
Chemin, M. (2009). Do judiciaries matter for development? Evidence from India. *Journal of Comparative Economics, 37*(2), 230–250.
Chen, G., Chittoor, R., & Vissa, B. (2015). Modernizing without Westernizing: Social structure and economic action in the Indian financial sector. *Academy of Management Journal, 58*(2), 511–537.
Child, J. (2000). Theorizing about organization cross-nationally. *Advances in International Comparative Management, 13*, 27–76.
Chilisa, B. (2011). *Indigenous research methodologies*. Sage.
Cornelissen, M., Misra, G., & Varma, S. V. S. S. (2013). *Foundations and applications of Indian psychology* (2nd ed.). Pearson Education India.
Dagar, C., Pandey, A., & Navare, A. (2020). How yoga-based practices build altruistic behavior? Examining the role of subjective vitality, self-transcendence, and psychological capital. *Journal of Business Ethics* 1–16.
Dalal, A. K., & Misra, G. (2010). The core and context of Indian psychology. *Psychology and Developing Societies, 22*(1), 121–155.
Dalmiya, V. (2016). *Caring to know: Comparative care ethics, feminist epistemology, and the Mahabharata*. Oxford University Press.
Damodaran, H. (2018). *India's new capitalists: caste, business, and industry in a modern nation*. Hachette India.
Dirks, N. B. (2002). *Castes of mind: Colonialism and the making of modern India*. Princeton University Press.

Dhanania, K., & Gopakumaran, S. (2005). Marwari business discourse: An analysis. *Journal of Asian Pacific Communication, 15*(2), 287–312.
Dharampal. (1983). The beautiful tree: Indigenous Indian education in the eighteenth century. Biblia Impex.
Epstein, B. (2015). *The ant trap: Rebuilding the foundations of the social sciences.* Oxford University Press.
Evered, R., & Louis, M. R. (1981). Alternative perspectives in the organizational sciences: "inquiry from the inside" and "inquiry from the outside." *Academy of Management Review, 6*(3), 385–395.
Fang, T. (2010). Asian management research needs more self-confidence: Reflection on Hofstede (2007) and beyond. *Asia Pacific Journal of Management, 27*(1), 155–170.
Freshman, B. (1999). An exploratory analysis of definitions and applications of spirituality in the workplace. *Journal of Organizational Change Management.*
Ghoshal, S., Piramal, G., & Bartlett, C. A. (2002). *Managing radical change: What Indian companies must do to become world-class.* Penguin Books.
Govindarajan, V. (2012). A reverse-innovation playbook. *Harvard Business Review, 90*, 120–124.
Govindarajan, V., & Ramamurti, R. (2011). Reverse innovation, emerging markets, and global strategy. *Global Strategy Journal, 1*(3–4), 191–205.
Gouda, J., Das, K. C., Goli, S., & Pou, L. M. A. (2013). Government versus private primary schools in India: An assessment of physical infrastructure, schooling costs and performance. *International Journal of Sociology and Social Policy, 33* (11/12), pp. 708–772.
Gupta, R. K. (1994). Challenges in developing indigenous theories of organization and management: an Indian perspective. *The Indian Journal of Social Work, LV*(2), 220–236.
Halliday, M. A. K., & Hasan, R. (1976). *Cohesion in English* (No. 9). Routledge.
Haque, M. S. (1996). The contextless nature of public administration in Third World countries. *International Review of Administrative Sciences, 62*(3), 315–329.
Haque, M. S. (1997). Incongruity between bureaucracy and society in developing nations: A critique. *Peace & Change, 22*(4), 432–462.
Harriss-White, B. (2003). *India working: Essays on society and economy* (No. 8). Cambridge University Press.
Henn, S. (2012). Transnational entrepreneurs, global pipelines and shifting production patterns: The example of the Palanpuris in the diamond sector.

In R. Grynberg & L. Mbayi (Eds.), *The global diamond industry* (pp. 87–115). Palgrave Macmillan.

Hofstede, G. (1980). *Culture's consequences: International differences in work related values*. Sage.

Jain, R. B. (2013). The quest for better governance: A case study of India. In I. Jamil, S. Askvik, & T. N. Dhakal (Eds.) *In search of better governance in South Asia and beyond* (pp. 89–106). Springer.

Jain, R. B., & Bongartz, H. (Eds.). (1994). *Structural adjustment, public policy and bureaucracy in developing societies*. Har-Anand Publications.

Jing, R., & Dong, M. 2017. Management scholars' learning from history: Direct vs. indirect approach. *Management and Organization Review, 13*(4), 905–911.

Ericsson, K. A. (Ed.). (1996). *The road to excellence: The acquisition of expert performance in the arts and sciences, sports and games*. Erlbaum.

Jijina, P., Vasa, V., & Biswas, U. N. (2020). Construct description of Samatva from the Bhagavad Gita: Implications for Holistic well-being. *PURUSHARTHA—A Journal of Management, Ethics and Spirituality, 12*(2), 1–20.

Kalra, S. K. (1997). Human potential management: Time to move beyond the concept of human resource management? *Journal of European Industrial Training, 21*(5), 176–180. https://doi.org/10.1108/03090599710171431

Kanagasabapathi, P. (2013). *Indian models of economy, business and management*. PHI Learning Pvt. Ltd.

Kanagasabapathi, P. (2014, May 4). *Success of Kite Industry and the Gujarat Model, Swarajya*. https://swarajyamag.com/commentary/success-of-kite-industry-and-the-gujarat-model

Kapur, D., Mehta, P. B., & Vaishnav, M. (Eds.). (2018). *Rethinking public institutions in India*. Oxford University Press.

Khatri, N., Ojha, A. K., Budhwar, P., Srinivasan, V., & Varma, A. (2012). Management research in India: Current state and future directions. *IIMB Management Review, 24*(2), 104–115.

Kroeber, A. L. (1944). *Configurations of culture growth*. University of California Press.

Kudesia, R. S., Pandey, A., & Reina, C. S. (2020). Doing more with less: Interactive effects of cognitive resources and mindfulness training in coping with mental fatigue from multitasking. *Journal of Management*, 0149206320964570.

Kumar, N., & Puranam, P. (2012). *India Inside: The emerging innovation challenge to the West*. Harvard Business Press.

Kumar, R., Kumar, N., with Mohapatra, P. K., & Chandrashekhar, S. (2009). *India's global powerhouses: How they are taking on the world*. Harvard Business Press.

Lemke, J. L. (1991, April 3–7). Science, semantics, and social change. Paper presented at the Annual Meeting of the American Educational Research Association, Chicago, IL. https://files.eric.ed.gov/fulltext/ED334828.pdf

Misangyi, V. F., Greckhamer, T., Furnari, S., Fiss, P. C., Crilly, D., & Aguilera, R. (2017). Embracing causal complexity: The emergence of a neo-configurational perspective. *Journal of Management, 43*(1), 255–282.

Mishra, S. K., & Varma, A. (Eds.). (2019). *Spirituality in management: Insights from India*. Springer.

Morris, M. W., Leung, K., Ames, D., & Lickel, B. (1999). Views from inside and outside: Integrating emic and etic insights about culture and justice judgment. *Academy of Management Review, 24*(4), 781–796.

Munshi, K. (2007). *From farming to international business: The social auspices of entrepreneurship in a growing economy* (NBER Working Paper No. 13065), JEL No. L14, L22,L23,L26,O12.

Nandy, A. (1989). *Intimate enemy*. Oxford University Press.

Natarajan, S., Mahmood, I. P., & Mitchell, W. (2019). Middle management involvement in resource allocation: The evolution of automated teller machines and bank branches in India. *Strategic Management Journal, 40*(7), 1070–1096.

Nayyar, S. (2019, July 15). Efficient judicial system shall improve ease of doing business. *Financial Express*. https://www.financialexpress.com/opinion/efficient-judicial-system-shall-improve-ease-of-doing-business/1644109/

Palrecha, R., Spangler, W. D., & Yammarino, F. J. (2012). A comparative study of three leadership approaches in India. *The Leadership Quarterly, 23*(1), 146–162.

Panda, A., & Gupta, R. K. (2007). Call for developing indigenous organisational theories in India: Setting agenda for future. *International Journal of Indian Culture and Business Management, 1*(1–2), 205–243.

Panda, A., & Gupta, R. K. (2016). Methodological approaches and challenges to studying Indian culture. In *Indian Culture and Work Organisations in Transition* (pp. 200–237). Routledge India.

Pandey, A., & Gupta, R. K. (2008). Spirituality in management: A review of contemporary and traditional thoughts and agenda for research. *Global Business Review, 9*(1), 65–83. https://doi.org/10.1177/097215090700900105

Pandey, A., Chandwani, R., & Navare, A. (2018). How can mindfulness enhance moral reasoning? An examination using business school students. *Business Ethics: A European Review, 27*(1), 56–71.
Pandey, J., & Varkkey, B. (2020). Impact of religion-based caste system on the dynamics of Indian trade unions: Evidence from two state-owned organizations in North India. *Business & Society, 59*(5), 995–1034.
Pargament, K. I. (1999). The psychology of religion and spirituality? Yes and no. *The International Journal for the Psychology of Religion, 9*(1), 3–16.
Pestonjee, D. M., & Purohit, S. (2017). Udai Pareek. Eminent Indian psychologists: 100 years of psychology in India (pp. 149–).
Pike, K. L. (1954), Emic and etic standpoints for the description of behavior. In K. L. Pike (Ed.), *Language in relation to a unified theory of the structure of human behavior* (pp. 8–28). Summer Institute of Linguistics.
Piramal, G. (2010). *Business legends.* Penguin Books.
Ragin, C. C. (1987). *The comparative method: Moving beyond qualitative and quantitative strategies.* University of California Press.
Rao, K. R., & Paranjpe, A. C. (2016). *Psychology in the Indian tradition.* Springer.
Rao, K., Paranjpe, A. C., & Dalal, A. K. (2008). *Handbook of Indian psychology.* Cambridge University Press India/Foundation Books.
Rolland, R. (1960). *The life of Ramakrishna.* Advaita Ashram.
Sarker, S., & Valacich, J. S. (2010). An alternative to methodological individualism: A non-reductionist approach to studying technology adoption by groups. *MIS Quarterly, 34*(4), 779–808.
Savory, A., & Butterfield, J. (1998). *Holistic management: A new framework for decision making*. Island press.
Scott, W. R. (2007). *Institutions and organizations: Ideas and interests.* Sage.
Simonton, D. K. (1996). Creative expertise: A life-span developmental perspective. In K. A. Ericsson (Ed.), *The road to excellence: The acquisition of expert performance in the arts and sciences, sports and games* (pp. 227–253). Erlbaum.
Singh, M., & Sarkar, A. (2012). The relationship between psychological empowerment and innovative behavior: A dimensional analysis with job involvement as mediator. *Journal of Personnel Psychology, 11*(3), 127–137. https://doi.org/10.1027/1866-5888/a000065
Sinha, J. B. (1984). A model of effective leadership styles in India. *International Studies of Management & Organization, 14*(2–3), 86–98.
Sinha, J. B. (2004). *Multinationals in India: Managing the interface of cultures.* SAGE.

Sinha, J. B. P. (1980). *The nurturant-task leader: A model of the effective executive*. Concept.

Sinha, J. B., Singh, S., Gupta, P., Srivastava, K. B., Sinha, R. B. N., Srivastava, S., Ghosh, A., Siddiqui, R. N., Tripathi, N., Gupta, M., & Srivastava, S. (2010). An exploration of the Indian mindset. *Psychological Studies, 55*(1), 3–17.

Smith, L. T. (2013). *Decolonizing methodologies: Research and indigenous peoples*. Zed Books Ltd.

Srinivas, M. N. (1962). Caste in modern India and other essays. In *Caste in modern India and other essays.*

Srinivasan, V. (2012). Multi generations in the workforce: Building collaboration. *IIMB Management Review, 24*(1), 48–66.

Tastevin, Y. P. (2017). From Ox-Carts to borewell rigs: Maintenance, manufacture and innovation in Tiruchengode. In *Subaltern urbanisation in India* (pp. 497–525). Springer.

Timalsina, S. (2008). *Consciousness in Indian philosophy: The Advaita doctrine of 'awareness only.'* Routledge.

Timalsina, S. (2014). Indigenous epistemology and placing the cultural self in crisis: A new hermeneutic model for cultural studies. *Southeast Review of Asian Studies, 36*, 6–29.

Timalsina, S. (2015). *Tantric visual culture: A cognitive approach*. Routledge.

Timalsina, S. (2020). Dialogue and culture: Reflections on the parameters of cultural dialogue. In D. Landis & D. P. S. Bhawuk (Eds.), *The Cambridge handbook of intercultural training* (pp. 658–679). Cambridge University Press.

Timberg, T. A. (2015). *The Marwaris: From Jagat Seth to the Birlas*. Penguin UK.

Tsui, A. S. (2004). Contributing to global management knowledge: A case for high quality indigenous research. *Asia Pacific Journal of Management, 21*(4), 491–513.

Vaidyanathan, R. (2014). *India Uninc*. Westland.

Van de Ven, A. H., Meyer, A. D., & Jing, R. (2018). Opportunities and challenges of engaged indigenous scholarship. *Management and Organization Review, 14*(3), 449–462.

Verma, A. (2005). Policing elections in India. *India Review, 4*(3–4), 354–376.

Waddock, S., & Lozano, J. M. (2013). Developing more holistic management education: Lessons learned from two programs. *Academy of Management Learning & Education, 12*(2), 265–284.

Wakhlu, A. (2000). *Managing from the heart*. Response Books.

Weber, M. (1962). *Basic concepts in sociology*. Citadel Press.
White, S. (2002). Rigor and relevance in Asian management research: Where are we and where can we go? *Asia Pacific Journal of Management, 19*, 287–352. https://doi.org/10.1023/A:1016295803623
Wilson, J. (2016). *India conquered: Britain's Raj and the chaos of empire*. Simon and Schuster.

Index

© The Editor(s) (if applicable) and The Author(s), under exclusive license to Springer Nature Switzerland AG 2022
A. Pandey et al. (eds.), *Indigenous Indian Management*, Palgrave Studies in Indian Management,
https://doi.org/10.1007/978-3-030-87906-8

The manufacturer's authorised representative in the EU is Springer Nature Customer Service Centre GmbH, Europaplatz 3, 69115 Heidelberg, Germany. If you have any concerns regarding our products, please contact ProductSafety@springernature.com

Printed and bound by CPI Group (UK) Ltd, Croydon, CR0 4YY

30/09/2026

02225499-0018